Social Security Programs and Retirement around the World

NATIONAL BUREAU of ECONOMIC RESEARCH

An NBER Conference Report

NBER

NATIONAL BUREAU *of* ECONOMIC RESEARCH

Social Security Programs and Retirement around the World: Reforms and Retirement Incentives

Edited by

Axel Börsch-Supan and Courtney C. Coile

The University of Chicago Press

Chicago and London

The University of Chicago Press, Chicago 60637
The University of Chicago Press, Ltd., London

Published 2020
Printed in the United States of America

29 28 27 26 25 24 23 22 21 20 1 2 3 4 5

ISBN-13: 978-0-226- 67410-0 (cloth)
ISBN-13: 978-0-226- 67424-7 (e-book)
DOI: https://doi.org/10.7208/chicago/9780226674247.001.0001

Library of Congress Cataloging-in-Publication Data

Names: Börsch-Supan, Axel, 1954– editor. | Coile, Courtney, editor.
Title: Social security programs and retirement around the world : reforms and retirement incentives / edited by Axel Börsch-Supan and Courtney C. Coile.
Other titles: National Bureau of Economic Research conference report.
Description: Chicago : University of Chicago Press, 2020. | Series: National Bureau of Economic Research conference report | Includes bibliographical references and index.
Identifiers: LCCN 2020004253 | ISBN 9780226674100 (cloth) | ISBN 9780226674247 (ebook)
Subjects: LCSH: Social security. | Postemployment benefits.
Classification: LCC HD7091 .S6244 2020 | DDC 368.4/3—dc23
LC record available at https://lccn.loc.gov/2020004253

♾ This paper meets the requirements of ANSI/NISO Z39.48-1992 (Permanence of Paper).

Relation of the Directors to the Work and Publications of the National Bureau of Economic Research

1. The object of the NBER is to ascertain and present to the economics profession, and to the public more generally, important economic facts and their interpretation in a scientific manner without policy recommendations. The Board of Directors is charged with the responsibility of ensuring that the work of the NBER is carried on in strict conformity with this object.

2. The President shall establish an internal review process to ensure that book manuscripts proposed for publication DO NOT contain policy recommendations. This shall apply both to the proceedings of conferences and to manuscripts by a single author or by one or more co-authors but shall not apply to authors of comments at NBER conferences who are not NBER affiliates.

3. No book manuscript reporting research shall be published by the NBER until the President has sent to each member of the Board a notice that a manuscript is recommended for publication and that in the President's opinion it is suitable for publication in accordance with the above principles of the NBER. Such notification will include a table of contents and an abstract or summary of the manuscript's content, a list of contributors if applicable, and a response form for use by Directors who desire a copy of the manuscript for review. Each manuscript shall contain a summary drawing attention to the nature and treatment of the problem studied and the main conclusions reached.

4. No volume shall be published until forty-five days have elapsed from the above notification of intention to publish it. During this period a copy shall be sent to any Director requesting it, and if any Director objects to publication on the grounds that the manuscript contains policy recommendations, the objection will be presented to the author(s) or editor(s). In case of dispute, all members of the Board shall be notified, and the President shall appoint an ad hoc committee of the Board to decide the matter; thirty days additional shall be granted for this purpose.

5. The President shall present annually to the Board a report describing the internal manuscript review process, any objections made by Directors before publication or by anyone after publication, any disputes about such matters, and how they were handled.

6. Publications of the NBER issued for informational purposes concerning the work of the Bureau, or issued to inform the public of the activities at the Bureau, including but not limited to the NBER Digest and Reporter, shall be consistent with the object stated in paragraph 1. They shall contain a specific disclaimer noting that they have not passed through the review procedures required in this resolution. The Executive Committee of the Board is charged with the review of all such publications from time to time.

7. NBER working papers and manuscripts distributed on the Bureau's web site are not deemed to be publications for the purpose of this resolution, but they shall be consistent with the object stated in paragraph 1. Working papers shall contain a specific disclaimer noting that they have not passed through the review procedures required in this resolution. The NBER's web site shall contain a similar disclaimer. The President shall establish an internal review process to ensure that the working papers and the web site do not contain policy recommendations, and shall report annually to the Board on this process and any concerns raised in connection with it.

8. Unless otherwise determined by the Board or exempted by the terms of paragraphs 6 and 7, a copy of this resolution shall be printed in each NBER publication as described in paragraph 2 above.

Contents

Acknowledgments

Funding for this project was provided by the National Institute on Aging (grant numbers P01-AG005842 and P30-AG012810), by the Social Security Administration (grant 6 RRC08098400-09-01), and by the Alfred P. Sloan Foundation, grant number G-2017-9697 to the National Bureau of Economic Research. We thank two anonymous reviewers for detailed and thoughtful comments. The views expressed herein are those of the authors and do not reflect the views of the National Institute on Aging, the Social Security Administration, any agency of the federal government, or the National Bureau of Economic Research.

Introduction

Axel Börsch-Supan and Courtney C. Coile

Project Overview

Through the coordination of the work of a team of analysts in 12 countries for 20 years, the International Social Security (ISS) project has used the vast differences in social security programs across countries as a natural laboratory to study the effects of retirement program provisions on the labor force participation of older persons and other questions related to the older workforce. The project's first several phases (Gruber and Wise 1999, 2004, 2007) documented the strong relationship across countries between social security incentives and older men's labor force participation, confirmed this relationship in microeconomic analysis, and estimated the labor market and fiscal implications of social security reform. Later volumes have examined

Axel Börsch-Supan is director of the Munich Center for the Economics of Aging (MEA) at the Max Planck Institute for Social Law and Social Policy (MPISOC), a professor of the economics of aging at the Technical University of Munich, and a research associate of the National Bureau of Economic Research.

Courtney C. Coile is a professor of economics at Wellesley College and a research associate of the National Bureau of Economic Research.

This chapter is part of the National Bureau of Economic Research's International Social Security (ISS) project. The ISS project is supported by the National Institute on Aging (grants P01-AG005842 and P30-AG012810) and by the US Social Security Administration through grant #5-RRC08098400-10 as part of the SSA Retirement Research Consortium, and by the Alfred P. Sloan Foundation, grant number G-2017-9697, to the National Bureau of Economic Research as part of the SSA Retirement Research Consortium. The findings and conclusions expressed are solely those of the authors and do not represent the views of SSA, any agency of the federal government, or NBER. The authors thank the other members of the ISS project for important methodological contributions and for the country-specific analyses on which this chapter is based. We thank Johannes Rausch for assistance with the data analysis in this chapter, Nicolas Goll for assistance with the glossary, and participants in the NBER's Summer Institute Aging Workshop for helpful comments. For acknowledgments, sources of research support, and disclosure of the authors' material financial relationships, if any, please see https://www.nber.org/chapters/c14190.ack.

the relationship between disability insurance program provisions, health, and retirement (Wise 2012, 2016) and explored whether older employment affects youth unemployment (Gruber and Wise 2010) and whether older workers are healthy enough to work longer (Wise 2017).

Most recently, the project has examined recent trends in labor force participation at older ages and potential explanations for these changes in behavior, such as cohort changes in health and education (Coile, Milligan, and Wise 2019). In the current volume, we explore how the financial incentive to work at older ages has evolved from 1980 to the present. We highlight the important role of reforms in these changing incentives and examine how changing incentives may have affected retirement behavior by comparing trends in incentive measures within and across countries to trends in employment. In future work, we will conduct country-specific econometric analyses to further explore the relationship between pension reforms and the trend toward working longer.

The results of the ongoing project are the product of analyses conducted for each country by analysts in that country. Researchers who have participated in this phase of the project are listed first below; those who have participated in prior phases are listed second in italics.

Belgium	Anne-Lore Fraikin, Alain Jousten, Mathieu Lefebvre, *Arnaud Dellis, Raphaël Desmet, Sergio Perelman, Pierre Pestieau, and Jean-Philippe Stijns*
Canada	Kevin Milligan, Tammy Schirle, *Michael Baker, and Jonathan Gruber*
Denmark	Paul Bingley, Nabanita Datta Gupta, Malene Kallestrup-Lamb, Peder J. Pedersen, *and Michael Jørgensen*
France	Didier Blanchet, Antoine Bozio, Muriel Roger, Simon Rabaté, *Luc Behaghel, Thierry Debrand, Ronan Mahieu, Louis-Paul Pelé, Corinne Prost, Melika Ben Salem, and Emmanuelle Walraet*
Germany	Nicolas Goll, Johannes Rausch, Axel Börsch-Supan, *Tabea Bucher-Koenen, Irene Ferrari, Hendrik Jürges, Simone Kohnz, Giovanni Mastrobuoni, Reinhold Schnabel, Morten Schuth, and Lars Thiel*
Italy	Agar Brugiavini, Raluca Elena Buia, Giacomo Pasini, Guglielmo Weber, *and Franco Peracchi*
Japan	Akiko Sato Oishi, Takashi Oshio, Satoshi Shimizutani, *Mayu Fujii, Emiko Usui, and Naohiro Yashiro*
Netherlands	Klaas de Vos, Adriaan Kalwij, and Arie Kapteyn
Spain	Pilar García-Gómez, Sílvia Garcia-Mandicó, Sergi Jiménez-Martín, Judit Vall-Castelló, *Michele Boldrín, and Franco Peracchi*
Sweden	Lisa Laun, Mårten Palme, *Per Johansson, and Ingemar Svensson*
United Kingdom	James Banks, Carl Emmerson, *Richard Blundell, Antonio Bozio, Paul Johnson, Costas Meghir, Sarah Smith, and Gemma Tetlow*
United States	Courtney Coile, *Peter Diamond, Jonathan Gruber, Kevin Milligan, and David Wise*

The selection of these countries was guided by four main criteria. On the one hand, they should represent different pension systems that have emerged from diverse cultural-historical backgrounds. On the other hand, however, the countries should be comparable with regard to stages of the demographic transition and of economic development with its associated job composition and quality of work. Third, the countries were selected based on the availability of the high-quality data required to precisely describe the incentives exerted by their pension systems over a relatively long time horizon. Fourth, and maybe most importantly, the 12 countries have excellent research teams well experienced in this type of analysis.

An important goal of the project has been to present results that are as comparable as possible across countries. Thus the chapters for each phase are prepared according to a detailed template that we develop in close consultation with country participants. In this introduction, we summarize the collective results of the country analyses and focus on the combined analysis of the data from each of the countries. The country chapters themselves present much more detail for each country and, in addition to the common analyses performed by all countries, often present country-specific analysis relevant to each particular country.

I.1 Introduction: Old-Age Employment

While life expectancy has risen dramatically almost everywhere in the world, the average retirement age in industrialized countries declined during much of the 20th century, putting enormous pressures on public pension systems. More recently, however, working in later life has been making a comeback. In a striking reversal of the earlier trend, almost all developed countries have seen substantial increases in the employment of older workers since the mid- to late 1990s.

This is illustrated in figure I.1 for men between ages 60 and 64. We observe a distinct U shape in the employment rate of older workers that is markedly similar across countries. On average, employment rates for men aged 60 to 64 in these countries rose by 14.9 percentage points between 1995 and 2016.

This is a remarkable reversal of the long-standing trend toward ever earlier labor force exit ages, a trend that many viewed as a natural side effect of growing prosperity and that was in contrast to increases in life expectancy. It is also striking that this trend has affected all countries even though the level of old-age employment is very different across countries. France and Belgium feature relatively low employment rates in this age group, while Japan and Sweden have very high employment rates. The trend reversal is most pronounced in Germany and the Netherlands and least in Japan.

Figure I.2 shows the corresponding employment rate for women between ages 60 and 64. While the U shape is less evident due to women's initial low levels of participation, the increase since the mid-1990s is similar to if not larger than that for men, averaging 18.6 percentage points between 1995 and 2016. Again, the cross-national differences in levels of old-age employment are considerable, with Sweden and the US at the top and Belgium and Italy at the bottom. The increase in old-age employment among women—as for men—is strongest in Germany and the Netherlands.

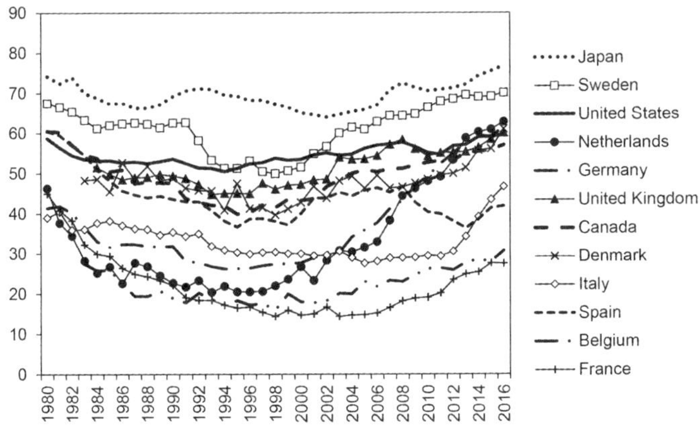

Fig. I.1 Employment rates, men aged 60 to 64, 1980–2016, percentages
Source: OECD. Data extracted on 30 Apr 2018 14:17 UTC (GMT) from OECD.Stat.

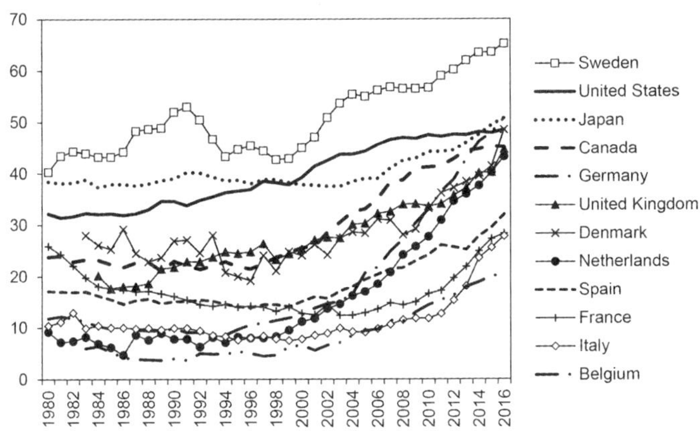

Fig. I.2 Employment rates, women aged 60 to 64, 1980–2016, percentages
Source: OECD. Data extracted on 30 Apr 2018 14:17 UTC (GMT) from OECD.Stat.

This volume is the second of three steps to explain these dramatic increases in employment at older ages. A first step has been conducted in the volume edited by Coile et al. (2019). Their research suggests that while better health, more education, and changes in labor supply behavior of married couples may have played some role in this trend reversal, these factors alone are insufficient to explain the magnitude of the employment increase and its large variation across countries. At the same time, many countries have enacted social security reforms over the past few decades that have changed eligibility ages, actuarial adjustment factors, disability benefit eligibility, and other parameters of public pension systems (Börsch-Supan 2013). Coile et al. (2019) highlight several cases where a specific reform—such as an increase in the statutory retirement age in Japan or the UK—appears to have affected employment. However, it is not yet well understood how much of the employment trend reversal in this broad set of countries can be attributed to the collective effect of the many social security reforms implemented in recent decades. This volume aims to begin to answer this question.

Past studies suggest that social security program provisions that affect the financial incentive to work at older ages can exert a powerful influence on late-career employment decisions. Gruber and Wise (1999) document that in the mid-1990s, these incentives varied dramatically across countries and were strongly related to employment at older ages. More specifically, they find that over 80 percent of the differences across countries in the share of men aged 55 to 69 who were out of the labor force could be explained by a single measure of the typical worker's incentive to work at older ages. Recent reforms are likely to have dramatically altered the financial incentives to work at older ages and thus may have affected employment.

The key research questions for this volume are therefore the following: how much has the financial incentive to work at older ages changed between 1980 and the present as a result of social security reforms, and how much of the changes in employment over this period can be explained by these changing incentives? In this volume, we will therefore first compute the incentives to work longer in each country and document how they have changed over time, paying particular attention to changes that arise from pension reforms. Next, we will compare trends in incentive measures within and across countries to trends in employment. The aim is to see whether the U-shaped development of employment visible in figures I.1 and I.2 will be matched by a similar U shape of the incentives to work longer.

The richness of our analysis comes from both the cross-country differences in social security policy across the 12 countries represented in this volume (US, Canada, Japan, and nine European countries) and the intertemporal changes in policy that have been adopted within these countries over almost four decades. The key question is whether differences in the incentive to work arising from this policy variation correspond to the large variation in levels and temporal changes that we see in old-age labor force participation among men and women in figures I.1 and I.2.

In the future, as the third and final step of our exploration of the trend of working longer and the role of pensions in that trend, we will conduct a set of formal econometric analyses for each country, similar to the microestimates in Gruber and Wise (2004) and to be published in a separate volume. These analyses will make greater use of the heterogeneity in incentives within the population and compare the role of incentives to that of other potential determinants of retirement.

This introduction starts with a brief characterization of policy changes (section I.2); introduces our key concept, the implicit tax on working longer (section I.3); and summarizes our main results (section I.4). An extended appendix describes our methodology in more detail, and a glossary defines the technical terms used in this volume.

I.2 Policy Changes

In most of the countries we study, many policy changes have occurred since 1980, and many of them are salient for changes in retirement patterns (OECD 2017; Social Security Administration 2018). A remarkable exception is the US, which has not passed a major social security reform since 1983 (although some changes mandated in the 1983 reform are still being phased in; such phase-in periods are common, though typically of shorter duration). Some countries have experienced major structural reforms (systemic changes) such as the introduction of a notional defined contribution (DC) system (e.g., Sweden and Italy) or the replacement of parts of the pay-as-you-go (PAYG) system by a fully funded system (e.g., Sweden and Germany). In some countries, changes in the private (personal and occupational) pension sector have interacted with changes in public programs or have otherwise influenced retirement behavior (e.g., UK and Netherlands). In most countries, policies followed a long-term trend (e.g., gradually increasing the retirement age, as in the US), but some countries experienced an inconsistent back and forth (e.g., raising and then lowering the statutory retirement age or increasing and then decreasing benefit generosity).

This phenomenon is visible in figure I.3, where we take Germany as an example. Germany introduced actuarial deductions for early retirement in the 1992 reform but canceled them under certain conditions in 1997 only to reintroduce them in 2000. Similarly, a gradual increase in the German statutory retirement age was legislated in 2007, but seven years later, a new pathway was created for early retirement at age 63.

As a first step of our analysis, each of the 12 country chapters starts with a description of these policy changes structured by important reform acts. These changes may include the following:

- raising or lowering the social security early or statutory eligibility ages (or years of contributions required for early claiming of social security benefits)
- introducing partial ("flexible") retirement into social security
- raising or lowering social security benefit generosity (this may include changes to the benefit formula, the number of years of earnings used in the benefit calculation, the use of wage vs. price indexation, etc.)
- strengthening or weakening the actuarial adjustment of social security benefits for early or delayed claiming
- strengthening or weakening the earnings test
- introducing a notional DC system
- strengthening or weakening other public programs that offer a pathway

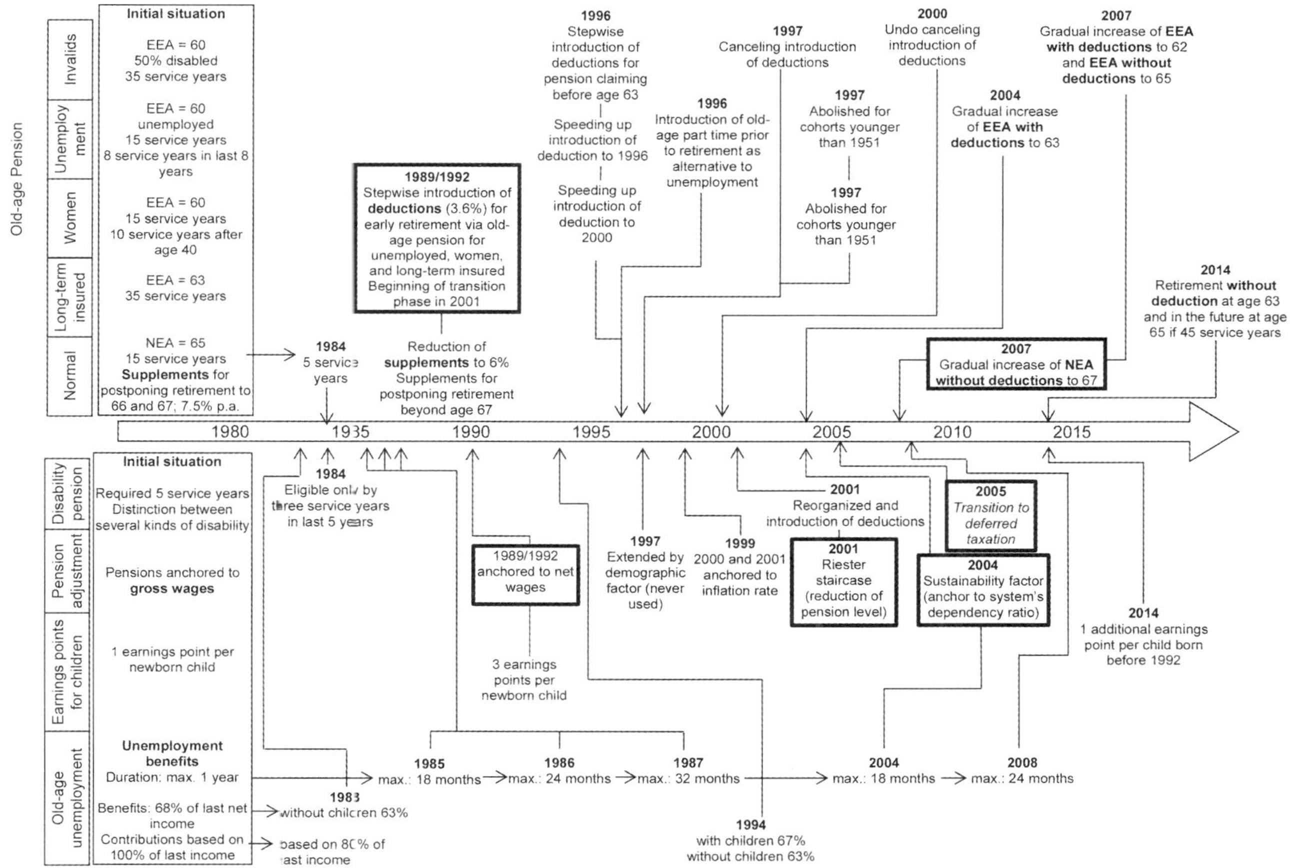

Fig. I.3 Policy changes affecting retirement age in Germany, 1980–2015

to retirement, including non–social security early retirement, disability insurance, and unemployment insurance programs

These policy changes are described verbally in a consistent manner across countries, using a common set of key words (see the glossary in the appendix). Table I.1 summarizes the key policy changes.[1]

Some distinct patterns emerge from table I.1. First, the table shows that the period since 1980 has been one of great pension reform activity. Looking down each column, it is apparent that every country has undertaken multiple types of reform—for example, making changes to social security eligibility ages and also to non–social security programs. Further, as seen in each row, for many broad types of changes, half to three-quarters of the countries have implemented a change of that type over the past 35 years.

Second, comparing across the various rows, it is clear that there have been many more reforms that strengthen the incentive to work at older ages than reforms that weaken the incentive to work. Examples of the former include reducing benefit generosity, raising eligibility ages, strengthening the actuarial adjustment, and weakening non–social security pathways to retirement. More than half of the countries have undertaken each of these reform types, far more than the number that has done the opposite.

Third, the table provides more evidence of the back-and-forth reforms described above, in that some countries have undertaken reforms of opposite types, such as weakening and strengthening the actuarial adjustments at different points in time. There are also countries that have undertaken multiple reforms of the same type, suggesting that it is often necessary to make a larger change in several smaller steps, perhaps for political reasons.

While these reforms are rather complex and not easy to quantify—pointing to the necessity of the individual country chapters in this volume, which explain the reforms in detail and show how they have affected the incentive for continued work at older ages—there are some program parameters that can be more easily quantified, such as eligibility ages.

Since 1980, changes in eligibility ages have been common. Figure I.4 shows how the social security early eligibility age (EEA) has evolved over time for men and women in our countries. The EEA is the first age at which social security benefits are available, often with an actuarial reduction relative to the benefits available at the statutory eligibility age (defined below). While one country, Canada, lowered this age from 65 to 60 for both men and women in 1987, the changes in this parameter otherwise are all in the direction of increases. In Belgium, Germany, Japan, and the UK, the EEA for women was initially lower than that for men, but it has been raised (or is

1. The years listed in the table refer to when reforms were implemented, not when a reform law was passed. A range of years indicates that the reform was phased in over time. Multiple entries in a single cell indicate that there were multiple reforms with similar effects (e.g., that reduced benefit generosity).

Table I.1 **Pension reform implementation by type and country**

Type of reform	Belgium	Canada	Denmark	France	Germany	Italy	Japan	Netherlands	Spain	Sweden	UK	US	Total # Countries
Old-age pension													
Lower early eligibility age (EEA)		1987		2003					2002				3
Raise EEA: women	1991				2012		1987–99, 2006–18				2010–		4
Raise EEA: all	2013–19		2015	2010–15	2006–12	1996–2011	2001–13	2013–	2011	1998	2018–		10
Lower statutory eligibility age (SEA)			2005–6										1
Raise SEA: women	1997–2009					2012	1987–99, 2018–2030				2010–		4
Raise SEA: all			2015	2010–15	2012–29	1994–2000, 2003–12	2013–25	2013–	2013		2018–	2003–8	9
Lower min. years for early claiming				1983									1
Raise min. years for early claiming	1997–2005, 2013–19			1993–2003, 2014		2011–							3
Introduce partial retirement					1992, 1996								
Raise benefit generosity		1980s, 2006–7, 2016			1984, 2014, 2018						2002, 2007, 2011		3
Lower benefit generosity	1997–2009	1997–99		1993	1992, 2001, 2004	1993	1986–2006	2000s	1997, 2011, 2013		1980, 1986, 1995		9
Weaken actuarial adjustment	1991, 2015			2003	1992				1997, 2007				4

(continued)

Table I.1 (continued)

Type of reform	Belgium	Canada	Denmark	France	Germany	Italy	Japan	Netherlands	Spain	Sweden	UK	US	Total # Countries
Strengthen actuarial adjustment	2007	2011–16	1999	2003, 2005	1996–2010		2005	1990s	2002, 2007			1990–2008	9
Strengthen earnings test							2002, 2005						1
Weaken earnings test	2013, 2015			2009	1992		1989, 1995, 2005		2002		1989	1990, 2000	7
Notional DC						1995–2032				1998			2
Other Pathways													
Strengthen non-SS early retirement	1984		1987, 1992, 1994, 1999	1995	2014								4
Weaken non-SS early retirement	1986–87, 1990, 1994, 2008, 2011–15		1996, 1999, 2006, 2012	1983, 1994, 2003, 2011	1996	1996–2008, 2012–		2006					6
Strengthen DI			1984		2012, 2014, 2018								2
Weaken DI			2003		1984, 2000			1985, 1990s, 1998, 2002, 2004, 2006	1985, 1997, 2004–5	1991, 1997, 2003, 2008	1995, 2008–10, 2011, 2016		6
Strengthen UI	1985, 1989, 1996			1984–2009	1984–87, 2008				1984, 1989, 2002				4
Weaken UI	2004, 2012, 2015			2012	1997, 2002, 2005			2004, 2006	2012				5

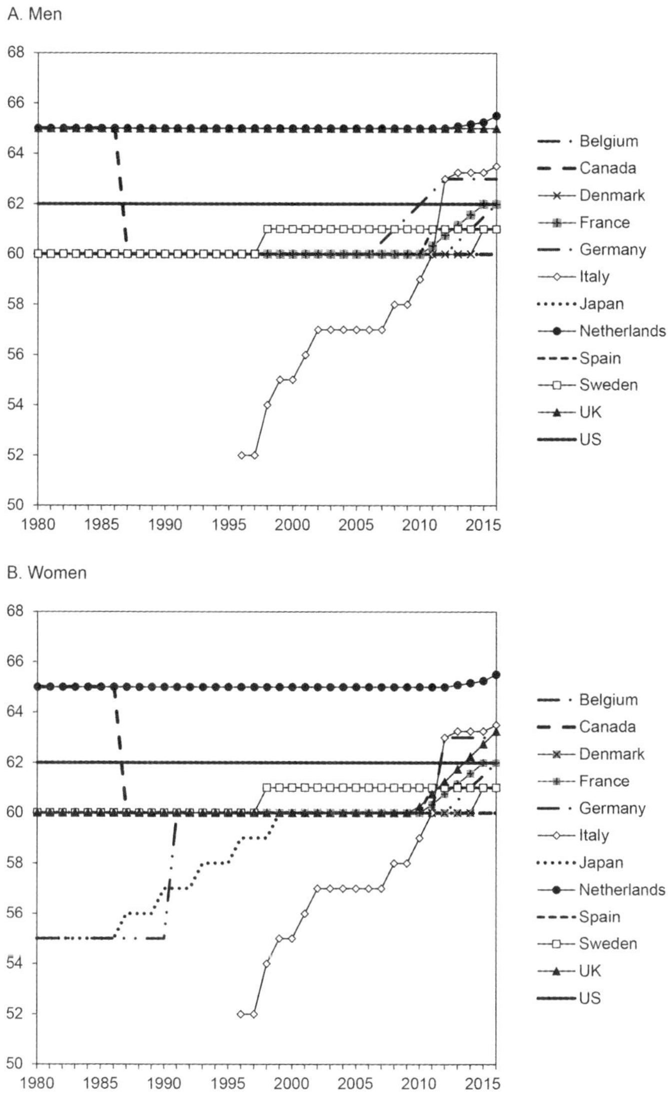

Fig. I.4 Social security early eligibility age, by sex, 1980–2016

being raised, in the case of the UK) to the same level. The US is somewhat of an outlier in not having raised the EEA during this period; only men in Japan and the UK have been similarly unaffected.

Figure I.5 shows the changes over time in the social security statutory eligibility age (SEA). This term refers to the age at which the individual is eligible for full public old-age pension benefits without reduction for early claiming (an age sometimes referred to as the full or normal retirement

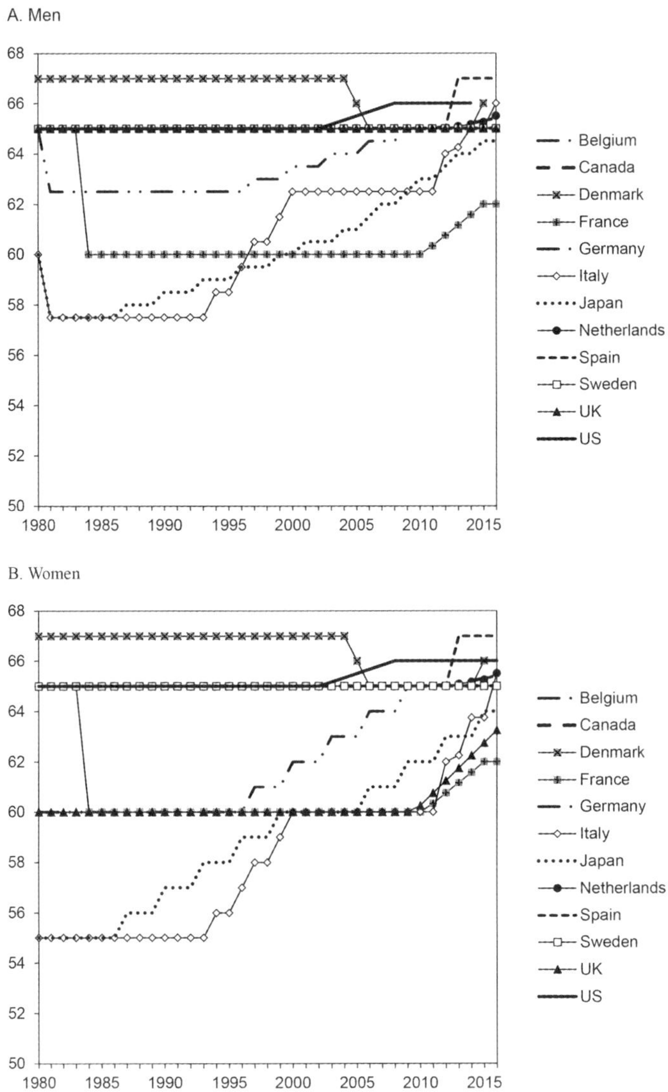

Fig. I.5 Social security statutory eligibility age, by sex, 1980–2016

age). Increases in the SEA have been near universal over this period, with all countries except Canada and Sweden raising this age. Similar to the EEA, the SEA was initially lower for women than for men in Belgium, Italy, Japan, and the UK, but these differences are being eliminated over time. An interesting difference from the EEA is that the SEA for men was cut in 6 of the 12 countries before later being increased. Variation like this in program parameters within a country over time may ultimately be used to help identify the effect of social security programs on retirement.

Actuarial adjustments define how social security benefits relate to the claiming age. They are usually defined as percentage adjustments and typically lower or raise the monthly benefit amount if the worker claims benefits before or after the SEA. Figure I.6 provides information on the actuarial reduction for early claiming, plotting the benefit available if claiming at age 62 as a share of the SEA benefit. This series is undefined for those countries that do not have early claiming prior to the SEA, such as the Netherlands. There are decreases in this series over time for several countries, corresponding to a greater actuarial penalty for early claiming. In Spain, for example, this value fell from about 80 percent in 2011 to under 60 percent in 2013. The US experienced a more modest decline, from 80 percent to 75 percent. At age 62, an actuarial neutral value would have benefits reduced by about 6.5 percent per year of claiming before the SEA (using a discount rate of 3 percent and an average life expectancy for the 12 countries). As most countries currently have an SEA of 65 or 66, a reduction to about 75 or 80 percent of the full benefit for claiming at 62 (some three to four years before the SEA) is roughly actuarially fair.

Most countries feature an earnings test at ages before the SEA. This forces individuals to stop working when they want to receive social security benefits, as benefits are taxed, often dollar for dollar, against earnings (although a small amount of earnings may be allowed without taxation). The decision to claim benefits and the decision to exit the labor force, which are independent decisions from an individual's point of view, are thus intrinsically combined in these countries; this helps explain why the word *retirement* means both decisions in these countries. An earnings test is currently in place before the SEA in Belgium, Canada, Denmark, Germany, Japan, Spain, the UK, and the US; only France eliminated its earnings test during the period we examine.

In figure I.7, we explore changes over time in the generosity of social security benefits by reporting the median earner's replacement rate. We focus on the net replacement rate, which is the average annual social security benefit net of income taxes and social contributions divided by the average annual earnings net of income taxes and social contributions. As the figure shows, replacement rates have been declining over time in a number of countries, although there are a few countries with increases. In part, declining replacement rates reflect reforms that have lowered benefit generosity—for example, increasing the number of years of earnings used in the benefit formula (which reduces the average earnings on which benefits are based by incorporating more low-earning years) or switching from wage indexation to price indexation in the benefit formula. The figure also reveals large differences across countries in the generosity of the social security program.

It is important to note the critical role that non–social security programs play in decisions to retire very early in many countries. These other programs may include disability insurance (DI), unemployment insurance (UI), and other special early retirement programs that are distinct from the social security system. As seen in table I.1, many countries have reformed these

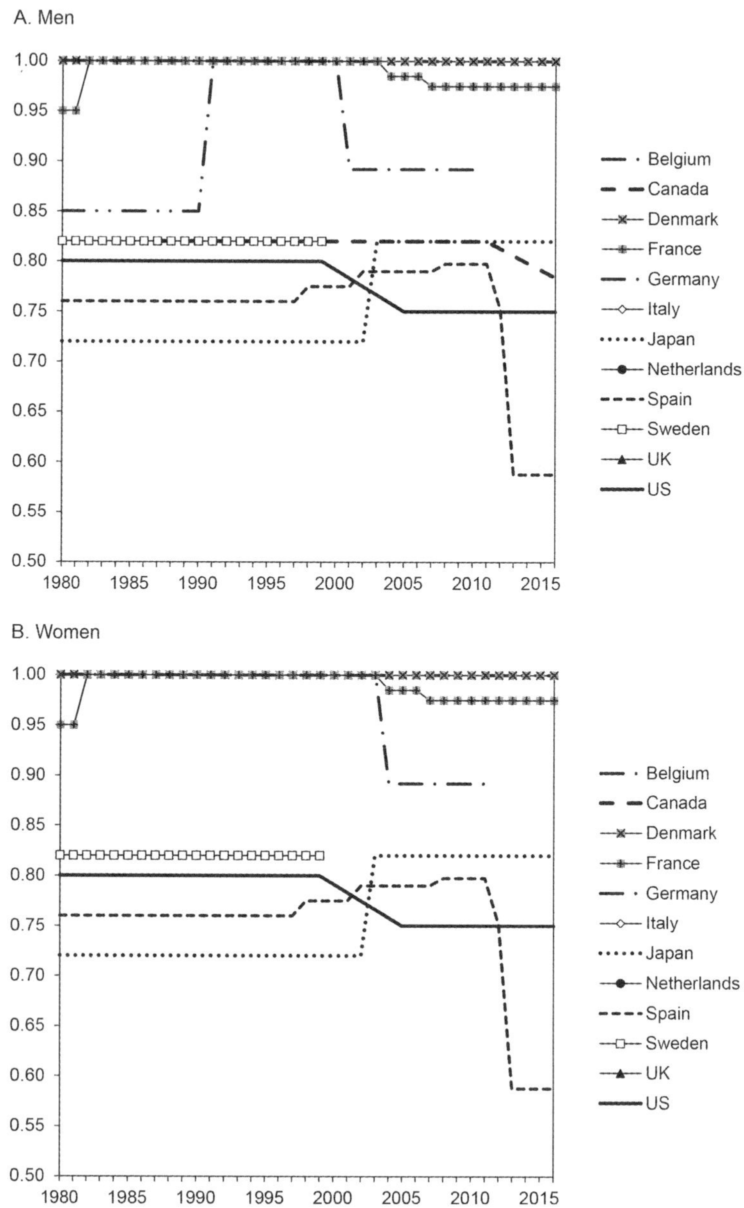

Fig. I.6 Share of SEA benefit if claiming at age 62, by sex, 1980–2016

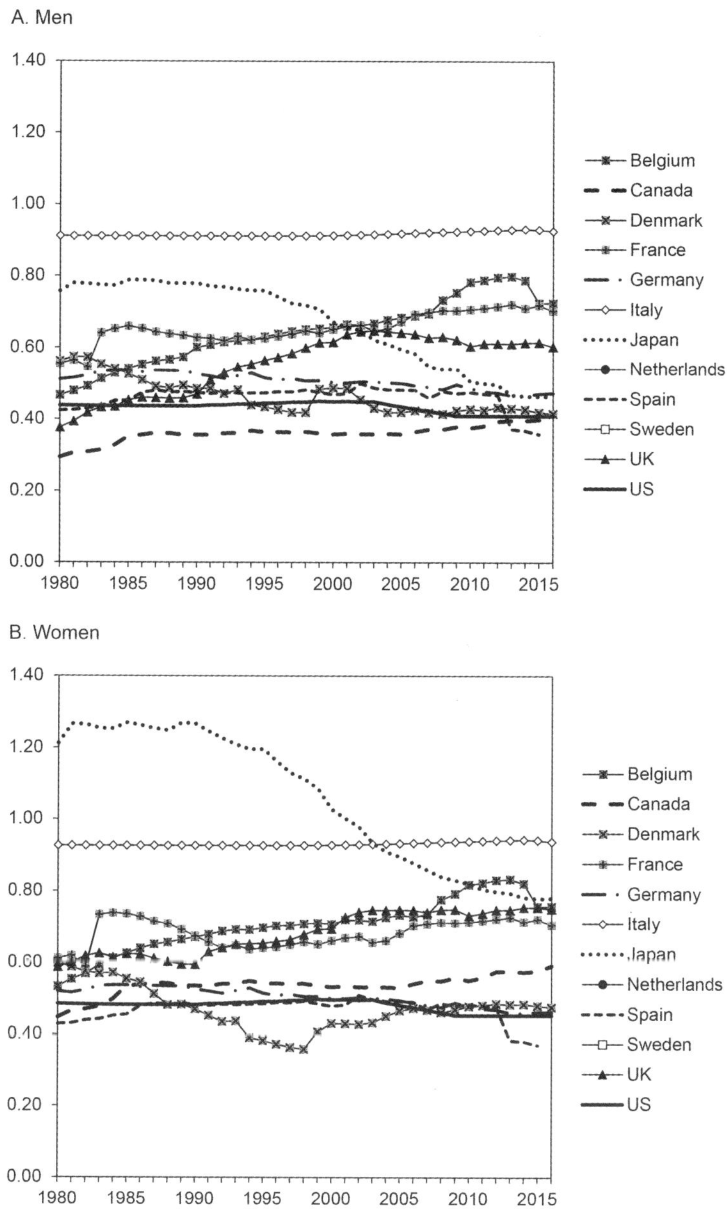

Fig. I.7 Replacement rate, by sex, 1980–2016

Note: Values calculated by authors of country chapters. The replacement rate is calculated as the average after-tax benefit at ages 62–69 relative to the average age-tax earnings at ages 55–62 for the median-earner type (described below).

other programs since 1980, often reducing benefit generosity or tightening eligibility—for example, by reducing age- or occupation-based access to DI or long-term UI benefits. In the case of DI, Wise (2012) concludes that such changes in program parameters are more important than changes in health in explaining changes in DI participation over time. More details on how these non–social security programs have changed over time are available in the country chapters.

In summary, the past three to four decades have been a period of intense pension reform activity. While the reform process sometimes includes a back-and-forth element and not all reforms push in the same direction, the general thrust over this period has been in the direction of raising eligibility ages, lowering benefit generosity, strengthening actuarial adjustments for delayed claiming, and reducing access to non–social security programs that offer alternative pathways out of the labor force. All of these changes are expected to encourage workers to retire later. Thus it is critical to try to estimate how much of the trend toward higher employment at older ages highlighted in the previous section might be driven by these substantial changes in social security and other public programs.

I.3 Pension Benefits and the Implicit Tax on Working Longer

The central piece of work in this volume is to condense the program parameters discussed in the previous section into a comprehensive, one-dimensional indicator that measures how the policy changes in table I.1 have altered the incentives to work longer. To this end, the 12 country teams have set up social security benefit calculators that compute the benefits from each salient social security program ("pathway to retirement") for a few typical benefit recipients who differ by basic socioeconomic characteristics (sex, marital status, and education). The main input for the benefit calculation is the earnings history of the individual. In the set of calculations that we focus on in this chapter, all countries use the same life-course trajectory of net earnings and the same mortality assumptions (fixed at a point in time) but use country-specific, time-varying social security rules. While this is counterfactual, it separates cross-national differences in social security policies and their changes over time from other differences across countries or over time—for example, differences in earnings histories and life expectancies. The appendix precisely defines these common assumptions. In a second set of calculations, the country chapters introduce these cross-national and time-series differences in earnings and mortality and illustrate their importance for the incentive to work at older ages.

For each typical individual, the social security benefit calculation is done for every year from 1980 to 2015, for every possible retirement age, and for every pathway to retirement (such as old-age public pension, early retirement pension, disability pensions, etc.) that is available for the individual.

For simplicity and since most countries feature earnings tests at least at ages before the SEA, we generally assume that retirement means both claiming social security benefits and stopping work, even in those countries in which no earnings tests are in effect. The variation by year captures the many changes in social security laws and regulations that occurred during this time span. The variation of social security benefits by retirement age captures whether it was advantageous for an individual of that age in a given country and year to retire or work longer, something that differs greatly across the 12 countries. Likewise, there are large differences across countries in which pathways are available for retirement, with some pathways accessible substantially earlier than the statutory eligibility age in the old-age pension in some countries.

The first product of this benefit calculation is the social security wealth, denoted by SSW. It sums up the properly discounted social security benefits from the beginning of retirement over the expected remaining life span. Postponing retirement and claiming of social security benefits by one year has several effects on social security wealth. On the one hand, the individual receives one year fewer of benefits, which decreases social security wealth. On the other hand, annual benefits increase with later claiming in most countries due to additional contributions and actuarial adjustments. Additional contributions accrue because the individual now works a year longer, and having an extra year of earnings included in the benefit computation may result in a higher benefit amount. Moreover, in almost all countries, benefits are adjusted upwardly if benefits are taken later through the actuarial adjustment. Finally, additional work results in additional payroll tax payments, the full incidence of which is assumed to fall on the worker. The balance among these mechanisms determines whether social security wealth increases or decreases with earlier or later retirement. We call the numerical increase or decrease of social security wealth the "accrual" of social security wealth. As we will see, this balance has changed between 1980 and 2015, mostly in favor of more positive accruals, favoring later retirement.

If the accrual is negative, the social security system imposes an implicit tax on working longer and claiming later. This is the key concept in this volume, abbreviated as ITAX. The implicit tax on working longer is defined as the (negative of the) accrual of social security wealth relative to the earnings of the individual. More precisely, we relate the accrual of social security wealth when postponing retirement at a given age to the earnings net of income taxes and social contributions that the individual will receive in this additional year of work. A positive value of ITAX means that there is a tax on working longer, that a negative value represents a subsidy for working longer. ITAX collapses all the various dimensions of social security policy—the discussion in the previous section features some of them—into a single dimension. This is as much an advantage as it is a disadvantage. The advantage is that the single dimension of ITAX permits us to easily display

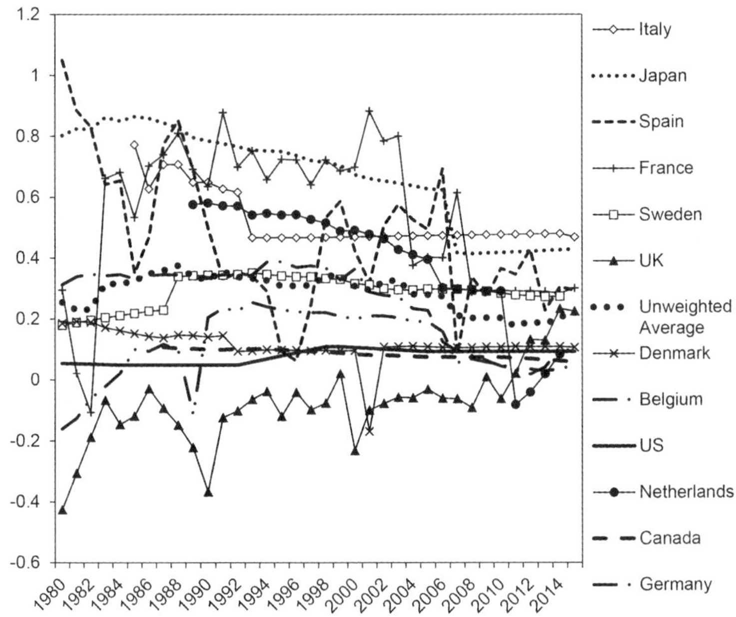

Fig. I.8 Implicit tax on working longer at age 62, men, 1980–2015

associations between policy and potential outcomes such as old-age employment or labor force participation. An obvious disadvantage is that social security policies may be more complex and may even have inconsistencies that are masked by a one-dimensional measure. In addition, different policies may have different degrees of salience for the worker, even if they have the same effect on ITAX.

The main work in this volume is for each country to compute a time series for the years 1980 to 2015 of the implicit tax rate on working longer that governs the decision to retire and claim social security benefits at age *R*, where *R* ranges in most countries from 55 to 69. Figure I.8 displays the implicit tax on working at age 62 for a typical man and its change from 1980 to 2015. We chose age 62 because it corresponds roughly to the average retirement age across the 12 countries. A "typical man" has median education and a stylized earnings history, which is common for all 12 countries. He looks forward to the median life expectancy, which again is common for all countries.

Figure I.8 shows that the 12 countries described in this volume have very different initial starting values of the implicit tax on working longer at 62 but a common declining trend. In the late 1980s and early 1990s, the implicit tax was about 35 percent on average (unweighted mean across all countries). In France and Japan, it was more than 75 percent; in Germany, 35 percent; in the UK, even negative. Despite this large heterogeneity, there was a common trend that has reduced the implicit tax substantially to only around

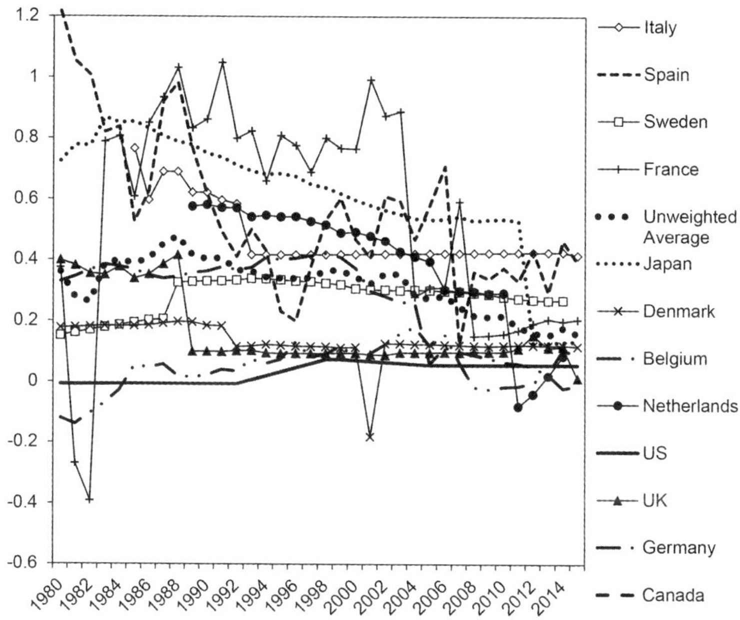

Fig. I.9 Implicit tax on working longer at age 62, women, 1980–2015

20 percent from 2007 onward on average across the 12 countries, a decline of 43 percent relative to the initial value. The decline is particularly steep for Germany, from a tax of about 40 percent in 1995 to an almost neutral value in 2013.

Figure I.9 displays the change of the implicit tax on working longer for a woman of age 62 with median education, earnings, and life expectancy. The implicit tax rates on working longer for women are similar to those for men. The decrease from 1980 to 2015 is a bit larger: the average tax rate across the 12 countries was almost 50 percent in 1988 and only 15 percent in 2015.

In figure I.10, we plot ITAX by age for each country, separately for men and women, in order to show the incentives to work across the full age range of 55 to 69 (and not just at age 62, as in the previous figures). In most cases, the implicit tax on working longer rises with age, which is consistent with declining employment at older ages; Denmark and Sweden are notable exceptions to this pattern.

As we include series for three points in time (1980, 2000, and 2014), these figures also illustrate how ITAX is changing over time. Although the patterns can be complex, in many cases the implicit tax in 2014 is lower than that in 1980. More specifically, the tax rate is more or less lower at every age in Germany, Italy, Japan, the Netherlands, Spain, and the US, falling by 40 to 60 percentage points in most of these cases. In Canada, Sweden, and the UK, the tax rate is lower at some ages and higher at others in 2014 as com-

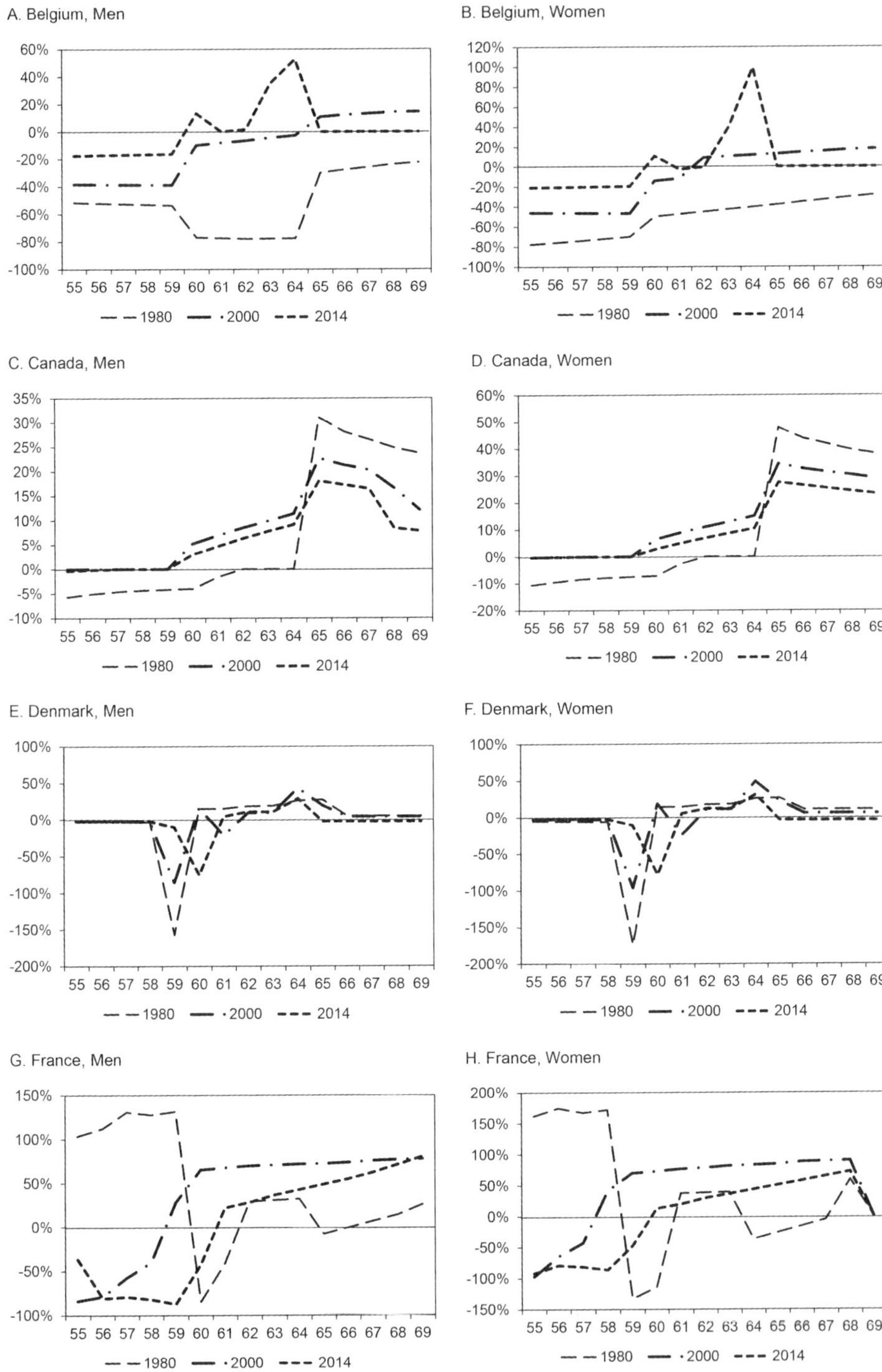

Fig. I.10 Implicit tax on claiming later by claiming age, country, and year

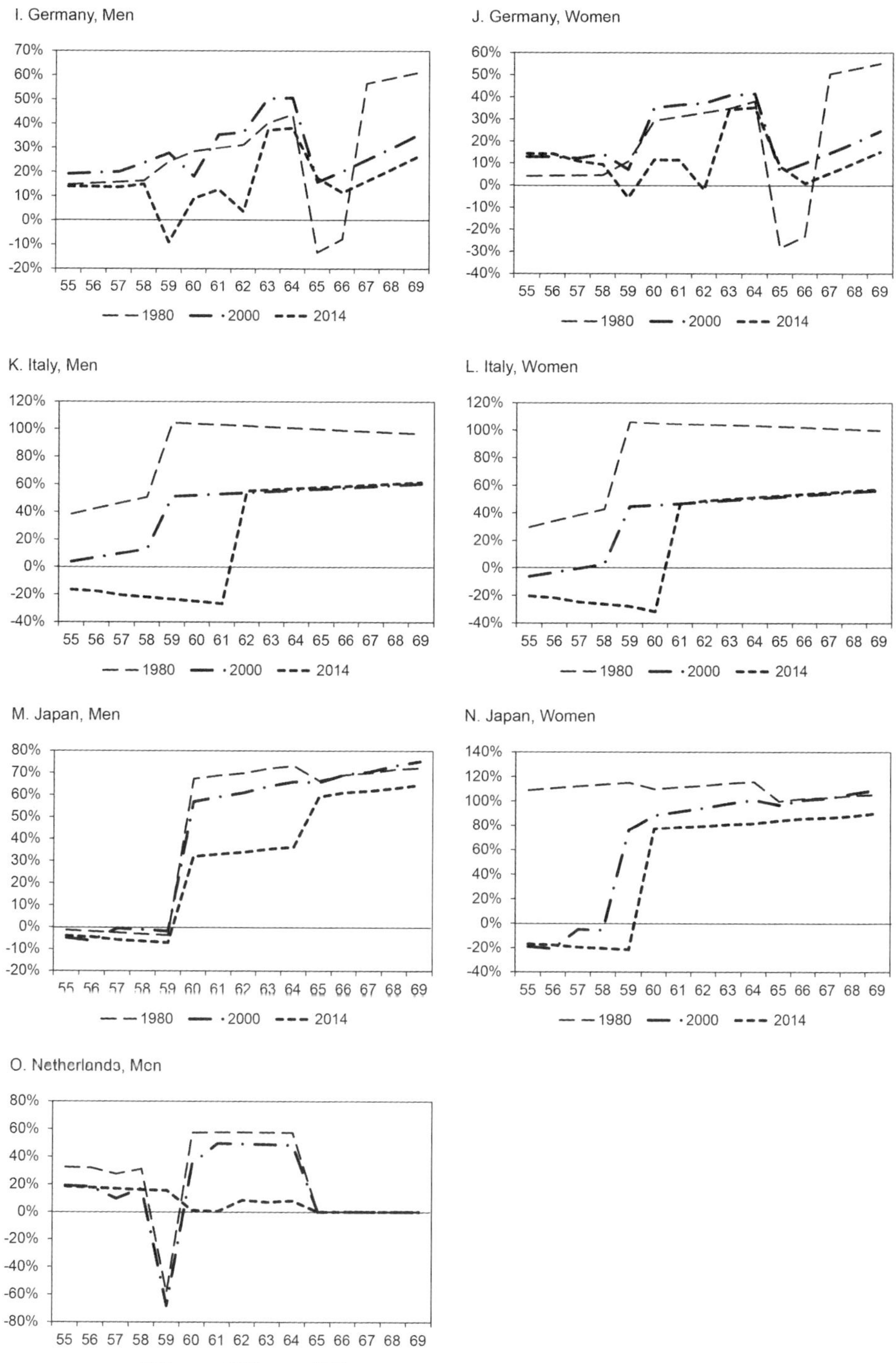
I. Germany, Men
J. Germany, Women
K. Italy, Men
L. Italy, Women
M. Japan, Men
N. Japan, Women
O. Netherlands, Men
55 56 57 58 59 60 61 62 63 64 65 66 67 68 69
1980
2000
2014

Fig. I.10 (cont.)

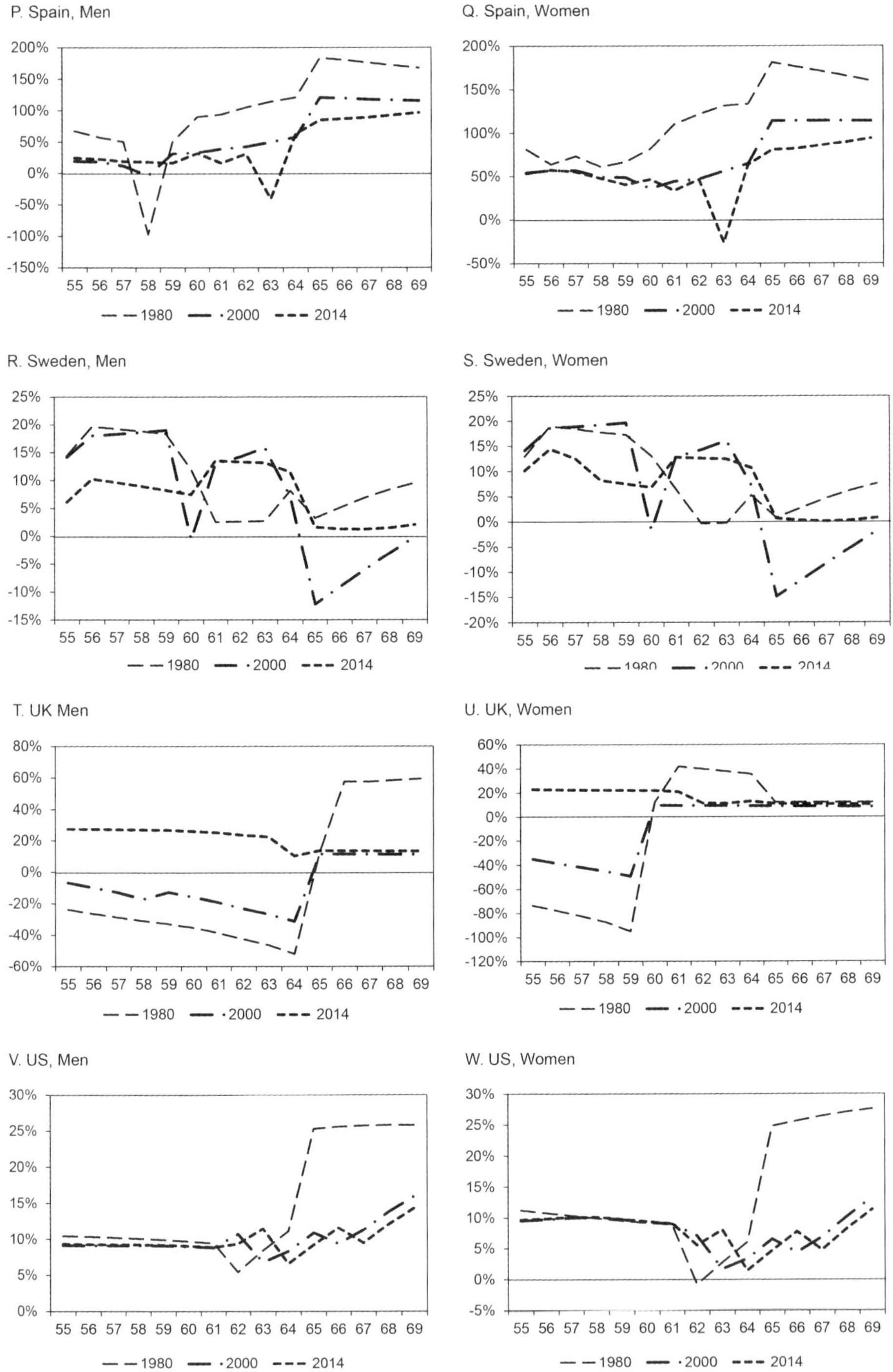
P. Spain, Men
200%
150%
100%
50%
0%
-50%
-100%
-150%
55 56 57 58 59 60 61 62 63 64 65 66 67 68 69
1980 2000 2014
Q. Spain, Women
200%
150%
100%
50%
0%
-50%
55 56 57 58 59 60 61 62 63 64 65 66 67 68 69
1980 2000 2014
R. Sweden, Men
25%
20%
15%
10%
5%
0%
-5%
-10%
-15%
55 56 57 58 59 60 61 62 63 64 65 66 67 68 69
1980 2000 2014
S. Sweden, Women
25%
20%
15%
10%
5%
0%
-5%
-10%
-15%
-20%
55 56 57 58 59 60 61 62 63 64 65 66 67 68 69
T. UK Men
80%
60%
40%
20%
0%
-20%
-40%
-60%
55 56 57 58 59 60 61 62 63 64 65 66 67 68 69
1980 2000 2014
U. UK, Women
60%
40%
20%
0%
-20%
-40%
-60%
-80%
-100%
-120%
55 56 57 58 59 60 61 62 63 64 65 66 67 68 69
1980 2000 2014
V. US, Men
30%
25%
20%
15%
10%
5%
0%
55 56 57 58 59 60 61 62 63 64 65 66 67 68 69
1980 2000 2014
W. US, Women
30%
25%
20%
15%
10%
5%
0%
-5%
55 56 57 58 59 60 61 62 63 64 65 66 67 68 69
1980 2000 2014

Fig. I.10 (cont.)

pared to 1980. The case of France is interesting because very early retirement (i.e., claiming benefits before age 60) was strongly incentivized by high implicit taxes in 1980; due to the reversal of this policy, France now has higher tax rates at older ages than it did in 1980. Belgium is the only country where the tax rate at all ages was higher in 2014 than it was in 1980.

The main policy drivers of these changes over time in ITAX are varied. Changes in the eligibility age or required minimum number of contribution years affected ITAX in Belgium, Italy, Japan, and Spain. Changes in the actuarial adjustment for delayed claiming beyond the EEA and/or SEA were important in Germany, the Netherlands, and the US. Changes in benefit generosity affected incentives in the UK, while the presence of means-tested benefits was critical in Canada. The country chapters provide much more detail on the policy changes that led to these changes in ITAX.

The country chapters show that incentives vary also with other socioeconomic characteristics—for example, education and the resulting earnings profiles. In this volume, we compute social security benefits and their implicit tax on working longer only for a small set of synthetic types of individuals that are standardized across countries, following a strict set of rules that are described in the methodological appendix of this introduction. In future work, we will apply the benefit calculators to real survey data in order to capture the full heterogeneity of life circumstances.

I.4 The Association between Employment and the Implicit Tax on Working Longer

The last step of the analyses in the 12 country chapters is to juxtapose the changes in the incentive variable ITAX with the actual change in old-age employment. Figure I.11 shows this for all participating countries, separately for men and women. Each panel has the employment rate for a specific age group on the vertical axis and the corresponding ITAX on the horizontal axis. The three age groups (55–59, 60–64, and 65–69) are drawn with different line styles; a selection of years is indicated by the size of the dots. Most countries show a negative association, most clearly in Germany and Canada and for Dutch men and Japanese and US women. This is the expected correlation: a higher implicit tax makes working longer a costly decision, since social security wealth is lost by claiming benefits later. The historical reduction of the implicit taxes by the various social security reforms in many countries, visible in figures I.8 and I.9, has made working longer more attractive again.

Not all countries exhibit such systematic associations as seen in the above examples. In the UK, there is no correlation visible, and it is positive in Sweden. There are many reasons why the negative association is weak or not observable in some countries. ITAX is one-dimensional and may not fully capture important aspects of the national social security system, such

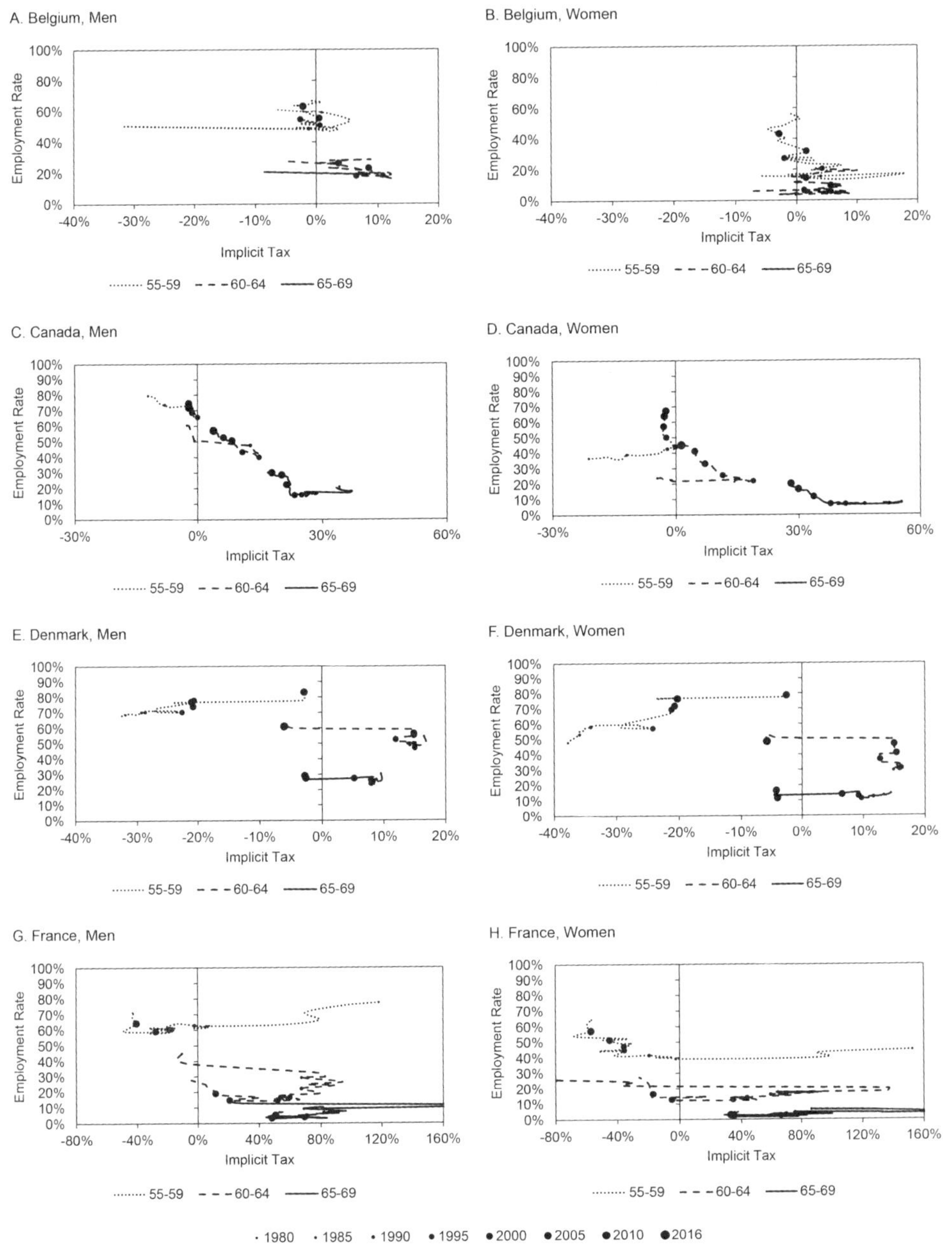

Fig. I.11 Employment rate versus implicit tax rate, 1980–2015

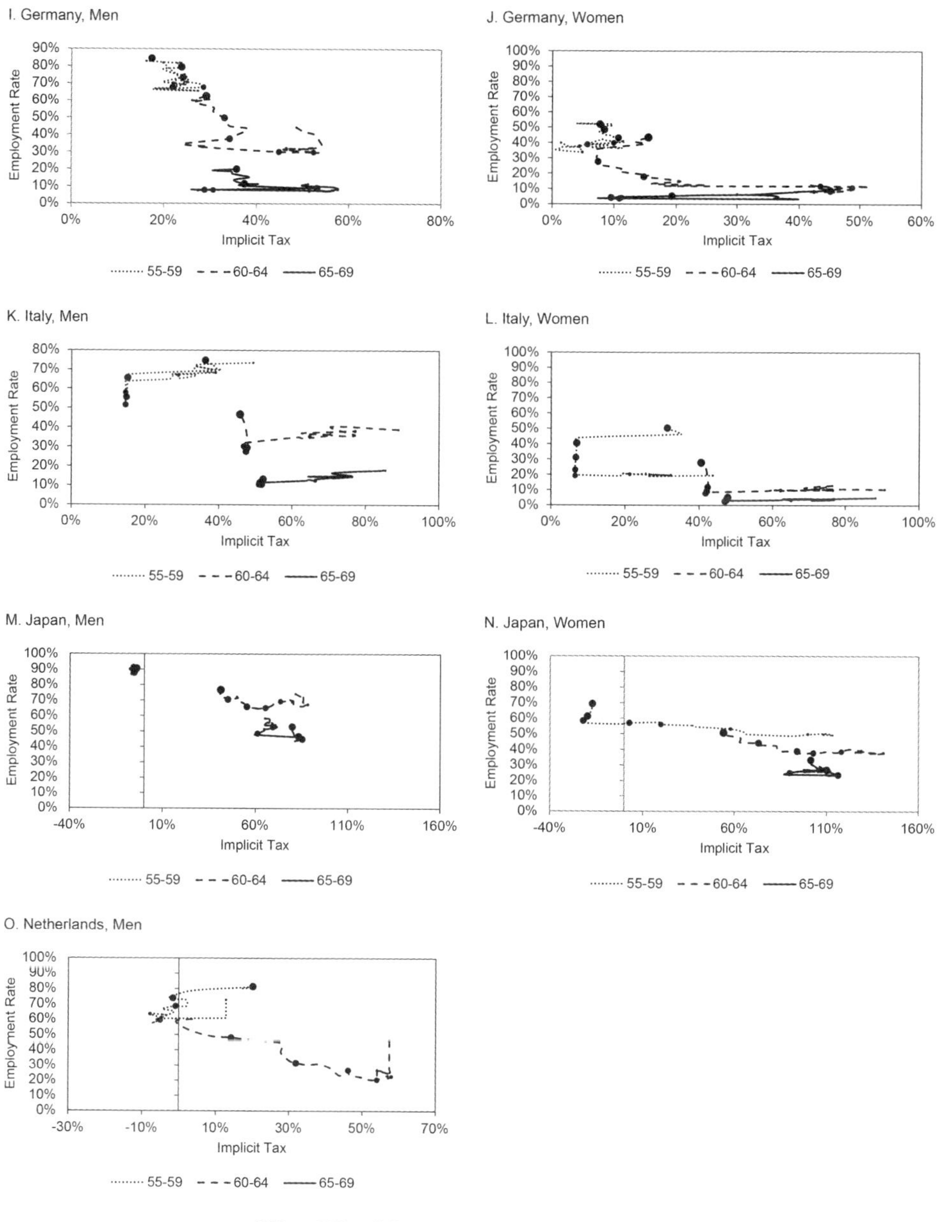
I. Germany, Men
J. Germany, Women
K. Italy, Men
L. Italy, Women
M. Japan, Men
N. Japan, Women
O. Netherlands, Men
Employment Rate
Implicit Tax
55-59
60-64
65-69
1980
1985
1990
1995
2000
2005
2010
2016

Fig. I.11 (cont.)

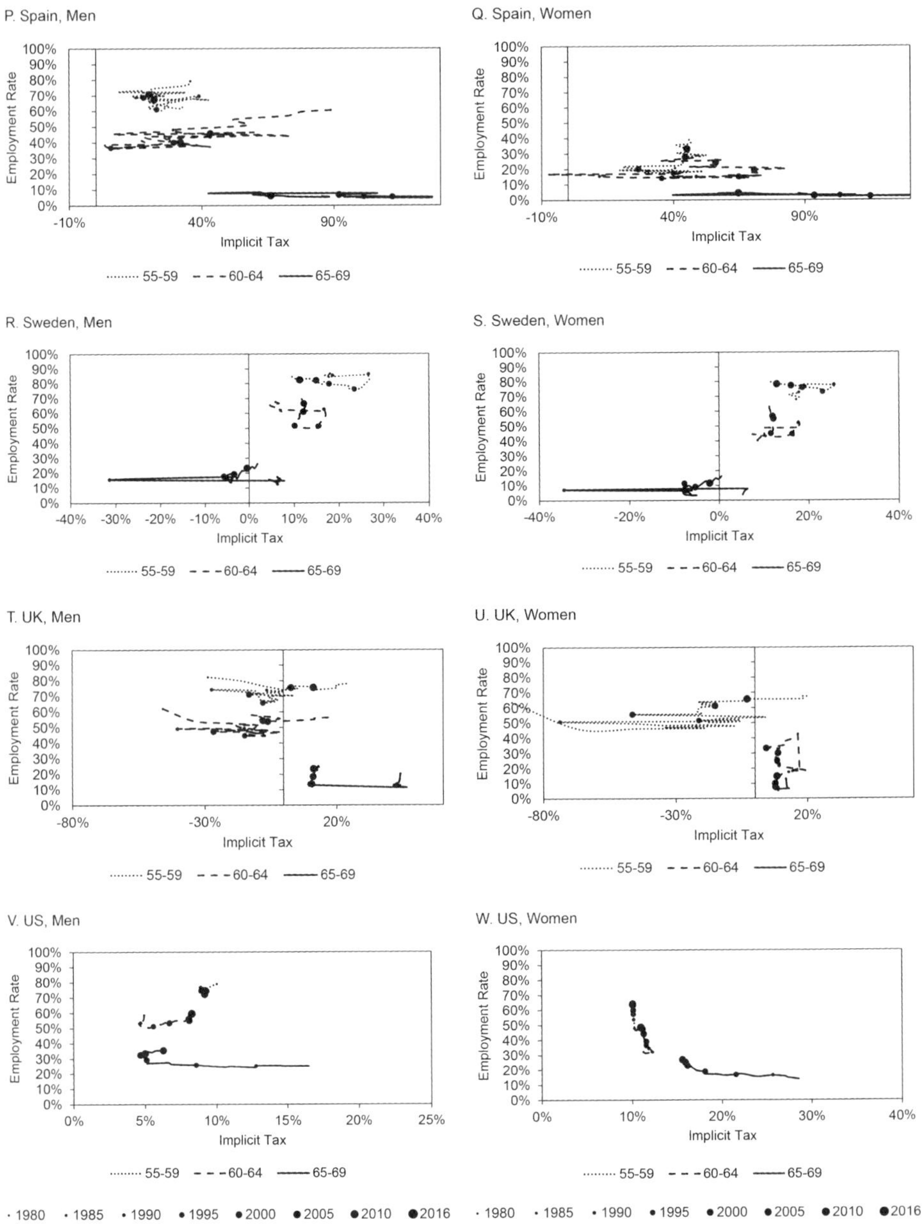

P. Spain, Men
Q. Spain, Women
R. Sweden, Men
S. Sweden, Women
T. UK, Men
U. UK, Women
V. US, Men
W. US, Women
Employment Rate
Implicit Tax
55-59
60-64
65-69
1980
1985
1990
1995
2000
2005
2010
2016

Fig. I.11 (cont.)

Table I.2 Country-specific regressions of employment rates on implicit tax rates

	Men				Women			
	Ages 60–64		Ages 65–69		Ages 60–64		Ages 65–69	
	Coeff.	*t*-stat	Coeff.	*t*-stat	Coeff.	*t*-stat	Coeff.	*t*-stat
Belgium	−0.043	−3.7	−0.016	−2.7	−0.049	−4.0	−0.001	−0.6
Canada	−1.437	−11.0	−0.435	−3.0	−1.335	−9.3	−0.397	−5.7
Denmark	−0.446	−9.0	0.076	1.9	−0.746	−9.4	−0.012	−0.6
France	−0.120	−7.5	−0.016	−1.8	−0.043	−5.3	−0.003	−1.1
Germany	−0.914	−12.2	−0.038	−0.6	−0.461	−8.4	−0.020	−0.7
Italy	0.150	2.2	0.119	4.1	0.007	0.2	0.044	4.2
Japan	−0.227	−4.1	0.000	0.0	−0.023	−0.8	0.029	1.1
Netherlands	−0.534	−5.9						
Spain	0.161	9.0	0.007	1.6	0.012	0.7	0.059	4.6
Sweden	−1.293	−7.2	0.141	3.2	−0.358	−1.9	0.109	2.2
UK	−0.045	−0.9	0.077	4.9	0.130	4.0	0.264	2.7
US	11.520	8.4	−0.359	−5.6	11.078	18.3	−0.239	−3.9

Note: The Netherlands provided only data for males in the 60–64 age range.

as changes in the earnings test. In some countries, policies have been inconsistent and/or quickly changing. Moreover, an average ITAX and an average employment rate across a heterogeneous population with different macroeconomic developments (service industry vs. manufacturing) and different regulations in some sectors (civil servants, heavy industry) may not capture the appropriate outcome and correct incentives for important subgroups of the population. Finally, employment of older workers may be driven by factors other than social security regulations—for example, employment in Spain suffered most from the financial crisis among our 12 countries.

Figure I.11 shows that there is heterogeneity across countries in how closely changes in employment over time have tracked changes in incentives, as captured by the ITAX measure. We explore this further in a set of country-specific linear regressions shown in table I.2. We conduct these analyses separately for men and women and for the main early retirement age range 60–64 and the main late-retirement age range 65–69. The dependent variable is the employment rate in a country for that age range and year, which is regressed on ITAX and social security wealth (SSW) for that age range and year, stratified by the three education categories. The unit of observation is thus an education group-year, although only the ITAX and SSW measures (and not the employment rate) vary by education. We include SSW to account for lifetime income effects. We also include dummies for the three education groups. Table I.2 only reports the 48 coefficients and their t-statistics relating to ITAX that have been obtained from the 48 country-

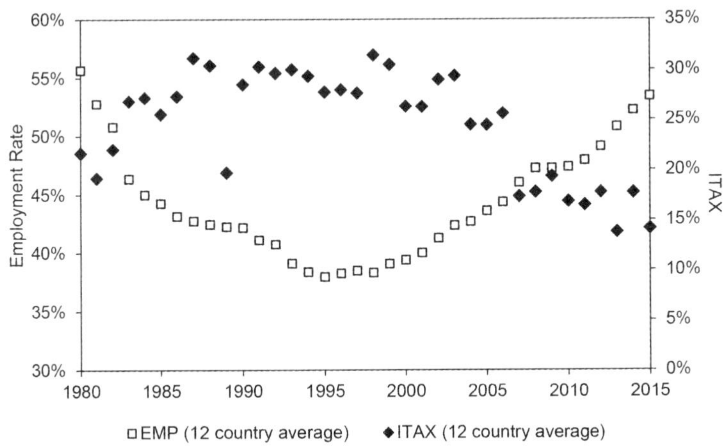

Fig. I.12 Country average employment rate and implicit tax rate over time, men ages 60–64, 1980–2015

specific regression equations. Two-thirds of the coefficients are negative, and almost half are negative and statistically significant at the conventional level ($p < 0.01$).[2] The results are much stronger for the younger age range (60–64) for both women and men. The heterogeneity across countries that was visible in figure I.11 shows up in table I.2 as large differences among the slope coefficients.

While the overall evidence from figure I.11 and table I.2 indicates a negative relationship between employment rates and implicit taxes, we now condense the evidence even further and focus solely on the time-series variation available in our data. Figure I.12 purges country heterogeneity from the data by taking (unweighted) averages across our 12 countries at each point in time. It plots the average employment rate based on data from figure I.1 against this aggregate ITAX measure, which captures the changing disincentive to work over time. The resulting figure reveals a close match between the U-shaped development of employment and the inverse U shape in the evolution of our disincentive measure.

In figure I.13, we produce a scatterplot of these data as another way of showing the association between each year's average employment rate and average ITAX. The correlation between these measures is strong, and the implied effect of ITAX on employment is large. This figure is the time-series

2. The regression results may differ from those in the country chapters. For example, in the case of the UK, the coefficient on ITAX for men is negative and statistically significant in the country chapter. The difference likely arises because that analysis uses data on ITAX and employment that varies by single year of age, education group, and year rather than the more aggregated data we use here.

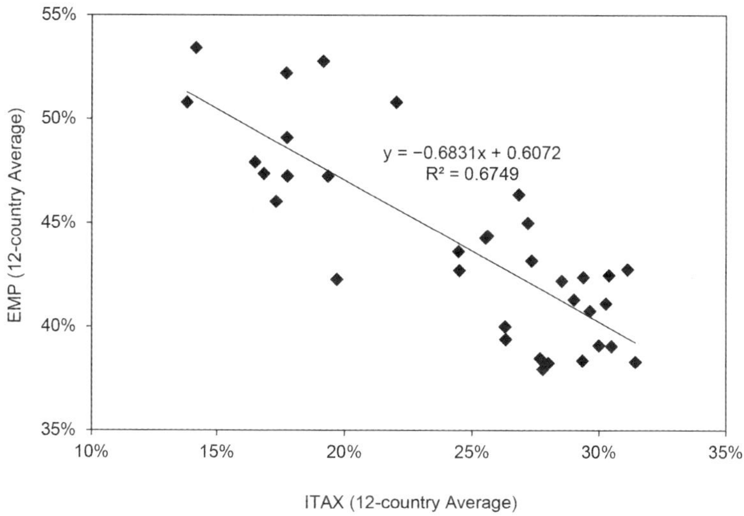

Fig. I.13 Country average employment rate versus country average implicit tax rate, men ages 60–64, 1980–2015

equivalent of the well-known cross-sectional figure in Gruber and Wise (1999) that established a strong positive association between unused capacity (nonemployment at ages 55–65) and the "tax force" to retire (essentially the sum of ITAX values from the early retirement age through age 69).

Naturally, one must exercise great caution in interpreting associations in time-series data as causal, since changes in other relevant factors that are not controlled for in the analysis may also have influenced retirement behavior. To address this concern, we combine the cross-sectional and time-series variations in a pooled regression across all countries and the entire observation period (table I.3). Similar to table I.2, the regressions are separate for men and women and the early and late retirement age range. The unit of observation is now country-year-education group. The dependent and explanatory variables are the same as in table I.2; in addition, we included country fixed effects to account for the different levels of employment in the 12 participating countries. Table I.3 now lists all coefficients and their t-statistics.

The coefficients for the ITAX variable show the statistically highly significant and economically strong relation between the incentive to work longer and the employment rate in the younger age range (60–64). Increasing the implicit tax on working longer from 0 percent to 100 percent reduces the employment of older men by 6.7 percentage points in the early retirement phase and for women by 4.6 percentage points. The effect is much smaller in the older age range (65–69; 1.8 and 0.3 percentage points for men and

Table I.3 Overall regression of employment rates on implicit tax rates

	Men				Women			
	Ages 60–64		Ages 65–69		Ages 60–64		Ages 65–69	
	Coeff.	t-stat	Coeff.	t-stat	Coeff.	t-stat	Coeff.	t-stat
ITAX	**−0.067**	**−7.0**	**−0.018**	**−2.6**	**−0.046**	**−5.8**	**−0.003**	**−0.6**
SSW	**−0.067**	**−2.0**	**0.042**	**2.2**	**0.201**	**4.3**	**0.070**	**3.6**
High earnings	−0.002	−0.3	−0.003	−1.1	−0.014	−2.9	−0.003	−1.3
Low earnings	−0.002	−0.4	0.002	0.8	0.010	2.0	0.002	1.1
Belgium	0.224	22.0	0.041	7.6	0.034	2.4	0.003	0.5
Canada	0.509	62.7	0.205	46.0	0.265	26.0	0.093	21.8
Denmark	0.541	74.9	0.267	73.0	0.363	46.1	0.133	41.3
France	0.266	20.3	0.061	7.1	0.122	8.1	0.016	2.4
Germany	0.420	49.1	0.099	19.4	0.162	19.3	0.041	11.1
Italy	0.383	33.2	0.128	17.5	0.077	5.3	0.020	3.1
Japan	0.736	84.8	0.519	87.3	0.448	39.8	0.268	46.9
Netherlands	0.381	28.4						
Spain	0.480	43.9	0.068	7.1	0.158	13.4	0.038	5.6
Sweden	0.619	91.0	0.177	50.1	0.506	74.2	0.081	27.0
UK	0.517	69.7	0.166	38.2	0.258	30.1	0.088	25.4
US	0.563	69.6	0.297	66.1	0.372	41.2	0.198	49.8
Number of obs.	1,301		1,264		1,194		1,156	
***R*-squared**	**0.981**		**0.978**		**0.957**		**0.951**	
Mean employment	0.445		0.262		0.180		0.092	
Mean ITAX	0.222		0.271		0.331		0.338	

Note: The Netherlands provided only data for males in the 60–64 age range.

women, respectively) and is insignificant for women.[3] In general, individuals with high SSW—corresponding to higher lifetime income—have a higher employment rate, although this is not true of men in the earlier age range. The country dummies reflect the level of employment, which is particularly low in Belgium and high in Japan, Sweden, and—especially for women—the US.

In conclusion, overall we find strong evidence for the expected negative association between old-age employment rates and implicit taxes on working longer. We base this conclusion on country-specific analyses that use variation within countries over time (figure I.11, table I.2), time-series analysis (figures I.12 and I.13), and panel data models that use variation across

3. We have also estimated versions of these models that include country-specific time trends. Including linear or quadratic time trends strengthens our results for men aged 60–64 in terms of both the ITAX effect magnitude and significance but slightly weakens them for women aged 60–64. The effects for the older age groups are insignificant. Including a full set of year dummies reduces the identification of the reform effects to cross-sectional variation and deviations from common reform trends. The estimated coefficient on ITAX from this specification is negative and significant for men aged 60–64, with about half of the effect magnitude compared to the specification with a country-specific quadratic time trend. It is not identified for the other groups.

countries over time (table I.3). While our results should not themselves be taken as causal, they strongly suggest that there may be a causal influence of incentives on retirement behavior, much as the cross-sectional analysis by Gruber and Wise (1999) did in launching this project.

The next step in this project is therefore to employ microdata in formal regression analyses, which will take other changes over time into account. For instance, the underlying populations are heterogeneous, and their composition may have changed; using data on individuals (rather than a small number of sample worker types, weighted to create a population average) may be important to capture the heterogeneity in incentives. Moreover, many macroeconomic changes took place over the four decades considered—for example, in health and education. These may also have affected employment at older ages and can be incorporated in a more formal analysis. These econometric analyses will be the subject of the next phase of this International Social Security project.

I.5 Summary and Conclusions

We have collected data on changes in social security laws and regulations between 1980 and 2015 in 12 countries around the globe: 9 European countries, the US and Canada, and Japan. We have computed the incentive to claim later and work longer from these laws and regulations and expressed it as the loss of social security wealth when claiming later and working longer divided by the earnings in that additional year of work. We call this the implicit tax on working longer.

While the countries differ greatly in the level of this implicit tax and its changes over time, we find a clear and common trend: the average of the implicit tax has declined substantially from the 1980s to 2015. In the late 1980s and early 1990s, the implicit tax on working longer was about 35 percent on average (unweighted mean across all countries of the tax rate at age 62) for men. In France and Japan, it was more than 75 percent; in Germany, 35 percent; and in the UK, even negative. Despite this large heterogeneity, there was a common trend that has reduced the implicit tax substantially to only around 20 percent from 2007 onward on average across the 12 countries, a decline of 43 percent. The implicit tax rates on working longer for women are similar to those for men, with an even larger decrease between 1980 and 2015: the average tax rate across the 12 countries was almost 50 percent in 1988 and only 15 percent in 2015. These declines can be linked to policy changes, such as increases in eligibility ages and in the actuarial adjustment for delayed claiming.

We then related this decline in the implicit tax on claiming later and working longer to the actual change in the employment rate. From our country-specific regressions, two-thirds of the coefficients are negative, and almost half are negative and statistically significant. Purging the data from country heterogeneity by taking country averages and focusing on the time-series variation, we find a close match between the U-shaped development of employment and the inverse U shape of our disincentive measure. The results of a pooled regression show a statistically significant and economically strong relation between the incentive to work longer and the employment rate for men and younger women. Increasing the implicit tax on working longer from 0 percent to 100 percent reduces the employment of older men by 6.7 percentage points in the early retirement phase and 1.8 percentage points in the late retirement phase. The equivalent effect for women in the early retirement phase is 4.6 percentage points. This analysis shows that those countries that have experienced larger decreases over time in the implicit tax on work have also experienced a larger increase in employment at older ages.

Overall, our findings in this volume support the hypothesis that social security reforms over the past several decades have strengthened the incentives to work at older ages and that the resulting increase in the financial incentive to work at older ages contributed to the rise in employment at older ages during this period. In future work, we will employ microdata to conduct regression analyses within and across our countries, which will allow for more accurate and causally interpretable measurements of the incentives facing individual workers and for a comparison of the relative effects of social security incentives and other factors on retirement.

Appendix

Methodology

The 12 country teams have set up social security benefit calculators (section A1) that compute the after-tax benefit stream from each salient social security program and pathway as a function of a common synthetic earnings history (section A4), common taxation assumptions (section A5), and common synthetic mortality rates (section A6). This benefit stream starts after "retirement," which may take several "pathways." This is defined more precisely in section A2. We compute the benefit stream for individuals with several stylized socioeconomic characteristics, such as sex, marital status, and education. They are defined in section A3.

I.A1 Computation of ITAX

Section A3 has described the construction of ITAX, our key indicator of retirement incentives. More formally, social security benefit calculators convert an earnings history y up to age $R-1$ into a benefit B from age R onward:

$$B_{k,t,a}(R,i) = f_{k,t,a}[y(R-1,i)], \tag{1}$$

where $B_{k,t,a}(R,i)$ is the after-tax benefit from the social security program and/or pathway k for an individual of type i and at age $a \geq R$, where R is the first year of benefit receipt occurring at calendar time t. Note that potential cohort differences are fully captured in this notation. This benefit has changed over time (index t) due to policy changes, as we know, and it may change as individuals age (index a). The benefit is dependent on the entire earnings history, as expressed by $y(R-1,i)$, which is the vector of earnings from age 15 to $R-1$ for an individual with a specific set of socioeconomic characteristics (index i). In most countries, benefit computations start at $a = 55$ and end at $a = 69$; in some countries, however, it is possible to claim pensions even earlier. Eligibility for a pathway is modeled by setting

$$B_{k,t,a}(R,i) = 0. \tag{2}$$

Summarizing and properly discounting the expected stream of social security benefits for the remaining life span yields the social security wealth, denoted by SSW. For an individual of type i starting to claim benefits from program/pathway k at age R in time t, social security wealth is the present discounted value of all future social security benefits:

$$SSW_{k,t}(R,i) = \Sigma_{a=R,T} B_{k,t,a}(R,i) s_{t,a} \beta^{a-R}. \tag{3}$$

Discounting has two components: $\sigma_{t,a}$ is the survival probability at age a in time t, and β is the usual discount factor for a discount rate of 3 percent.

Postponing claiming by one year has two effects on social security wealth. On the one hand, annual benefits $B_{k,t,a}(R,i)$ increase with later claiming in most countries due to additional contributions and actuarial adjustments. On the other hand, however, benefits are received one year fewer. The accrual of social security wealth

$$ACC_{k,t}(R,i) = SSW_{k,t+1}(R+1,i) - SSW_{k,t}(R,i) \tag{4}$$

can thus be positive, zero, or negative. If the accrual is negative, the social security system imposes an implicit tax on claiming later. This implicit tax rate is the (negative) accrual of social security wealth divided by the after-tax earnings during the additional year of work:

$$ITAX_{k,t}(R,i) = -ACC_{k,t}(R,i) / Y_{t+1,i}. \tag{5}$$

Since most countries feature earnings tests at least at ages before the statutory retirement age, this implicit tax on claiming later is also an implicit tax on working longer. ITAX is the key incentive variable that we model in this volume and associate with the change in labor force participation. A positive value of ITAX means that there is a tax on working longer; a negative value represents a subsidy for working longer. It collapses all the various dimensions of social security policy into a single dimension; this is as much an advantage as it is a disadvantage. The advantage is that the

Table I.A1 Time series of incentive variables

	55	56	. . .	68	69
1980	x(55,1980,i,k)	x(56,1980,i,k)	. . .	x(68,1980,i,k)	x(69,1980,i,k)
. . .	. . .	. . .	. . .	. . .	. . .
2015	x(55,2015,i,k)	x(56,2015,i,k)	. . .	x(68,2015,i,k)	x(69,2015,i,k)

single dimension of ITAX permits us to easily display associations between policy and potential outcomes such as old-age employment or labor force participation. The obvious disadvantage is that social security policies may be more complex and may even have inconsistencies that are masked by a one-dimensional measure.

The main work in this volume is for each country to compute a time series 1980–2016 of the implicit tax rate that governs the decision to claim social security benefits at age R, where R ranges in most countries from 55 to 69:

In this matrix, the entry $x(55,1980,i,k)$ represents the implicit tax of claiming benefits from program/pathway k one year later expressed as a percentage of the earnings in that additional year for a 55-year-old worker of type i under the pension rules that have been legislated in 1980.

I.A2 Definition of Retirement and Pathways

In many languages, there is only one word—*retirement*—for two distinct economic decisions: exiting the labor force and claiming a pension or social security benefits. For the benefit calculator, R is the combination of the age of claiming and leaving the labor force. The matrix in figure I.A1 represents the *implicit tax on working longer* only in the case when social security or other rules enforce the equality of the age of retirement from the labor force (R_L) and the age of claiming benefits (R_C). Most often, this equality is enforced by earnings tests that disallow earning more than Y_{test} and/or by clawback rules in the benefit calculation that tax earnings while receiving benefits at a high rate t in addition to earnings taxation.

In most European countries and Japan, earnings tests are still strict such that claiming benefits forces the individual to give up work for pay. In these countries, the two decisions are equivalent, and working a year longer implies postponing claiming benefits by a year. In the UK, however, earnings tests have been abolished. Hence retiring from work and claiming benefits are separate decisions in principle, although we still observe a strong habitual link between retiring from the labor force and claiming benefits.

More recently, "flexible retirement" models have been introduced by some countries, which permit part-time work and partial retirement. Where relevant, we model them as a separate pathway, using the following procedure:

- As a general rule, the yardstick of comparison (i.e., the denominator in equation 5) is the income that a nonretiring individual is projected to earn in the additional year ($Y_{t+1,i}$).
- We first compute the above matrix of the implicit tax of claiming later. This is an interesting concept per se even in the absence of earnings tests.
- In countries with a strict earnings test ($Y_{test} = 0$ and $t = 100$ percent), this is also the implicit tax on working longer.
- In countries and time periods without earnings tests, the implicit tax on working longer is zero even if the implicit tax of claiming later is not. We will therefore see a jump in the former variable when a country abolishes a strict earnings test.
- In the general case ($Y_{test} > 0$ and $t < 100$ percent), we introduce a new concept of the relative financial loss due to working one year longer and delaying claiming by one year. This financial loss has two components—namely, potential earnings lost due to the earnings test and/or partial retirement rules and the reduction of SSW. If Y_{max} is the maximum allowable net labor income while receiving benefits—that is, after respecting the earnings test, clawback rules, and wage taxation—then this financial loss due to working one year longer and delaying claiming by one year is

$$\text{(6)} \qquad \text{LOSS}_{k,t}(R,i) = -\text{ACC}_{k,t}(R,i) - [Y_{max} - Y_{t+1,i}].$$

Set relative to potential earnings, the resulting incentive variable is

$$\text{(7)} \qquad \text{RFL}_{k,t}(R,i) = \text{LOSS}_{k,t}(R,i) / Y_{t+1,i}.$$

If there is no earnings test, $Y_{max} = Y_{t+1,i}$, and a loss occurs only through a negative accrual. If there is a strict earnings test, $Y_{max} = 0$, and the loss is the negative accrual plus the entire wage that an individual could have earned in this year. In all other cases, $0 < Y_{max} < Y_{t+1,i}$.

For countries in which pathways to retirement via disability or unemployment insurance are important (e.g., Germany and Italy), we construct separate matrices for each pathway. We then compute a weighted mean over these pathways where the weights are the actual proportions in which these pathways have been selected. The country chapters show graphs of how the weights have evolved over time.

I.A3 Definition of Synthetic "Types": Socioeconomic Characteristics

We compute separate matrices for a low-skill/education worker (in countries without skill data, 50 percent of median income), a medium-skill/education worker, and a high-skill/education worker (alternatively, 200 percent of median income), separately for single women, single men, married women, and married men (index *i*), for a total of 12 matrices. For countries with split social security systems (e.g., France), we have different matrices for private- and public-sector workers (index *k*).

The index *i* distinguishes

- male single, female single, male married, female married
- low, medium, and high skill level or education (if not available, use 50 percent of median income, median income, and 200 percent of median income)

The case of couples retiring at different ages can become very complex. To keep matters simple, we focus on a male (or female) who is married to a partner 3 years younger (or older) of the same skill/education type. We assume that the spouse's retirement behavior is fixed—that is, it will not react to the worker's own retirement decision. In many countries, the case for couples is therefore identical to the unmarried case. One example of an exception is the US with their spousal benefits; other examples include survivor benefits.

I.A4 Construction of Common Earnings Histories

This volume focuses on typical workers with standardized earnings profiles over their life courses. We base the calculation on three different assumptions:

(a) *Common synthetic earnings profiles* in which the slopes are the same across all countries. We have calculated earnings profiles for the three skill/education groups from the US Current Population Survey (CPS), the German Socio-economic Panel (GSOEP), and administrative data from the Italian pension system (INPS). They are scaled such that earnings at age 50 are one. The profiles are fairly similar across the three countries, so we use the simple average of these profiles. They are smoothened to prevent artificial spikes in the implicit taxes and kept flat at higher ages when selection effects dominate the data. They are therefore synthetic profiles for the purpose of standardization. They are then scaled at age 50 to each country's median income at age 50 for the respective sex/education group. Figure I.12 depicts the average across all skill/education groups.

(b) *Country-specific earnings profiles* that are constant over time (based on 2016 or the most recent available data).

(c) *Country- and time-specific earnings profiles.*

Assumption (a) will isolate the effect of social security incentives from international differences in earnings profiles. Assumption (b) will honor the fact that earnings profiles are different across countries and exert their own incentives but isolate them from differences in earnings profiles across cohorts.

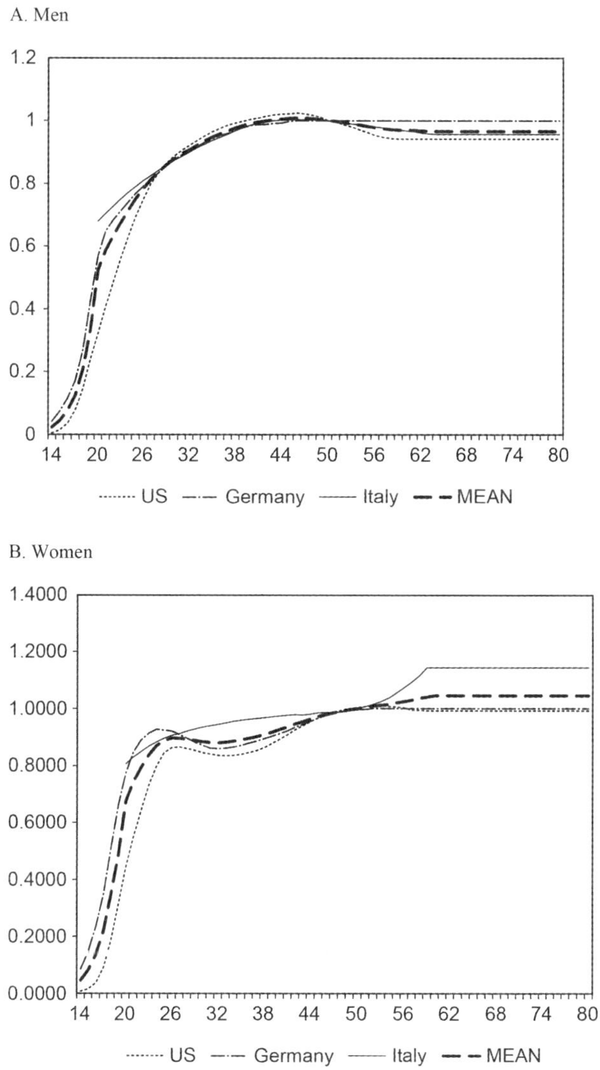

Fig. I.A1 Common earnings profiles

The country-specific earnings profiles are derived from aggregate labor force statistics available in each participating country; to account for cohort effects, these profiles are based on cohort-specific longitudinal data wherever available. With sufficient data, they are aggregated from models of the earnings process that exploit all available information on individuals' earnings histories based on regressions of the form

$$(8)\quad \Delta \ln Y_t = \alpha + X_t\delta + \beta_1 \mathrm{AGE} + \beta_2 \mathrm{AGESQ} + \beta_3 \Delta \ln Y_{t-1} + \beta_4 \Delta \ln Y_{t-2} + \beta_5 \Delta \ln Y_{t-1} * \mathrm{AGE} + \beta_6 \Delta \ln Y_{t-1} * \mathrm{AGESQ} + \beta_7 \Delta \ln Y_{t-2} * \mathrm{AGE} + \beta_8 \Delta \ln Y_{t-2} * \mathrm{AGESQ} + \mathrm{TIME}_t\lambda + \varepsilon,$$

where Y_t is the earnings of individual i in period t; X is a set of human capital control variables for individual i: education, marital status, race, tenure in the labor market, tenure at the firm, region of residence, and so on. AGE is age, AGESQ is its square; and TIME is a set of dummy variables for each year of the sample.

Earnings are deflated by a consumer price index or equivalent. The data are then differenced such that the dependent variable is the percentage change in earnings for the individual. After having run the regression on an individual basis, we aggregate the projected earnings profiles over the lower, middle, and upper tercile of the income distribution, separately for men and women.

Some countries condition the eligibility for a certain pathway (e.g., Germany) or pension benefits in general (e.g., France) to the number of years of contribution. These may include drop-out years for parents during child raising, sometimes also unemployment, further education, care for parents, and so on. In this case, we use a suitable average number of such years derived from national labor statistics.

Regarding the age of entry into the labor force, we also use common assumptions of ages 16, 20, and 25, respectively, for low, medium, and high education/skill levels. In addition, some country teams added analyses based on country-specific profiles—for example, they used the median age of labor force entry in their national data for that type of worker.

I.A5 Common Taxation

Social security benefits are computed net of applicable income taxes. The earnings in the denominator of ITAX are net of payroll taxes—that is, income taxes, mandatory social contributions, and so on.

Common approach. We used constant and flat tax rates provided by the Organisation for Economic Co-operation and Development (OECD). They are the average tax rates on gross labor income, including social security contributions from the OECD ("total tax wedge"), averaged over the years 2000, 2005, 2010, and 2015.

National approach. Some country teams used an income tax calculator (stratified by single vs. couple household) that included the preferred tax treatment of pension benefits. Other country teams used simpler alternatives—for example, applied statutory tax rates stratified by household type and income bracket.

I.A6 Common Survival Probabilities

Similar to the earnings profiles, this phase focuses on typical workers with standardized survival curves in order to isolate the effect of social security incentives from international differences in mortality (case a) plus national specifications (cases b and c):

(a) Identical age and gender-specific survival rates across all countries. We use the average survival rates provided by Eurostat, which refers to the EU-28 countries. The underlying life expectancy at age 15 is 67.8 years for women and 64.7 years for men. In addition, these rates are adjusted to generate a life expectancy that is three years higher (or lower) to reflect the difference in life expectancy across the three income categories. This adjustment is a mixture of a proportional increase (or decrease) of the survival rates and a shift of the survival curve to the right. These values are used to calculate the conditional probability that a 55-year-old will be alive at every future age (56–100) when he or she might receive benefits and so on for workers of different ages represented in the matrix.

Alternative assumptions are analogous to the respective assumptions on earnings histories:

(b) Country-specific survival rates that are constant over time.
(c) Country- and time-specific survival rates.

Assumption (b) will honor the fact that mortality rates are different across countries and exert their own incentives but isolate them from the reduction in mortality over time.

I.A7 Occupational and Private Pensions

In some countries, occupational pensions play a minor role and are simply ignored (e.g., in Italy). In other countries, they are an essential part of the old-age income provision system (e.g., in the Netherlands). If occupational pensions are included, they are treated as an "add on" to public pensions; hence public and occupational pensions are considered as a package. DC pensions are only included when they affect the eligibility for means-tested benefits (e.g., in Canada). Private pensions (e.g., IRAs in the US and Riester pensions in Germany) are not included.

Glossary

This glossary comprises the typical technical terms that are important for consistency among the country chapters. Table I.G1 lists common terms.

Table I.G1 Common terms

Term	Definition
Claiming age	The claiming age denotes the age at which an individual decides to initiate receipt of benefits from a *social security program*.
Earliest eligibility age	The earliest eligibility age is defined as the age at which *early retirement* through a *social security program* is possible, mostly with reduced benefits.
Early retirement	Early retirement is the practice of claiming benefits from a *social security program* before an individual reaches the *statutory eligibility age*. Early retirement is possible after attaining the *earliest eligibility age* and is usually dependent on fulfilling a certain number of insurance years or a specific contribution history (in some cases, more years of contributions are required than at the *statutory eligibility age*). Early retirement benefits are typically reduced relative to the benefits available at the *statutory eligibility age.*
Earnings tests	Earnings tests limit the amount of earnings that can be received by an individual who receives benefits from a *social security program*. Earning tests often apply only before the *statutory eligibility age* or are stricter before than after this age.
Implicit tax rate	The implicit tax rate is the negative of the change in social security wealth arising from an additional year of work (or the negative of the accrual) divided by the after-tax earnings. A positive value means that there is a tax on working longer; a negative value represents a subsidy for working longer.
Labor force exit age	The labor force exit age is the age at which an individual decides to stop working.
Means test	A means test is the practice of determining whether an individual qualifies for benefits from the basic social safety net, usually by comparing the individual's income and/or assets to a threshold value.
Old-age pension	Old-age pension is a government benefit where the primary eligibility requirement is attaining a certain (old) age, though a contribution history may also be required. An old-age pension is one example of a *social security program*, a broader term that encompasses other public transfer programs.
Partial ("flexible") retirement	Partial ("flexible") retirement schemes are models that permit individuals to access benefits from a *social security program* and continue working part-time in order to make a gradual transition from full-time work to full retirement possible.
Retirement age	*Retirement age* is to be avoided because it is ambiguous whether claiming age or labor force exit age is meant.
Social security program	Social security programs encompass *old-age pension* (OA), disability insurance (DI), unemployment insurance (UI), and other public transfer programs available at older ages.
Social security wealth	The social security wealth for an individual who claims benefits at a specific age and in a specific year from a *social security program* is the present discounted value of all future benefits from this social security program.
Statutory eligibility age	The statutory eligibility age is the age at which an individual is eligible for full public old-age pension benefits without reduction for early claiming. There may be a (relatively short) contribution history required, which is sometimes less than the number of years of contributions required in order to claim *early retirement* benefits.

Table I.G2 **Country-specific deviations**

Term (country-specific)	Definition	Country
Full-rate age	The full-rate age is defined as the age at which an individual is eligible for a full public old-age pension before the *statutory eligibility age* after fulfilling both a minimum contribution history and the *earliest eligibility age*.	France, Germany
Social Security	This is specific US terminology. While the term *social security* (lowercase) in Europe refers to many branches of the welfare system, including also health and unemployment insurance, the term (now capitalized) in the US refers to old age and disability benefits only.	US
State pension age	This is specific UK terminology. The state pension age is the earliest age at which an individual can start receiving the UK state pension—and the age at which the vast majority start receiving it. It varies by several eligibility criteria.	UK

Where it is impossible to harmonize the terms, there are country-specific technical terms displayed in table I.G2.

Terms in *italics* refer to other terms defined in the glossary.

References

Börsch-Supan, Axel. 2013. "Entitlement Reforms in Europe: Policy Mixes in the Current Pension Reform Process." In *Fiscal Policy after the Crisis*, edited by Alberto Alesina and Francesco Giavazzi, 405–35. Chicago: University of Chicago Press.

Coile, Courtney C., Kevin S. Milligan, and David A. Wise, eds. 2019. *Social Security Programs and Retirement around the World: Working Longer*. Chicago: University of Chicago Press.

Gruber, Jonathan, and David A. Wise, eds. 1999. *Social Security Programs and Retirement around the World*. Chicago: University of Chicago Press.

Gruber, Jonathan, and David A. Wise, eds. 2004. *Social Security Programs and Retirement around the World: Micro-estimation*. Chicago: University of Chicago Press.

Gruber, Jonathan, and David A. Wise, eds. 2007. *Social Security Programs and Retirement around the World: Fiscal Implications of Reform*. Chicago: University of Chicago Press.

Gruber, Jonathan, and David A. Wise, eds. 2010. *Social Security Programs and Retirement around the World: The Relationship to Youth Employment*. Chicago: University of Chicago Press.

OECD. 2017. "Pensions at a Glance." https://read.oecd-ilibrary.org/social-issues-migration-health/pensions-at-a-glance-2017_pension_glance-2017-en#page1.

Social Security Administration. 2018. *Social Security Programs throughout the World: Europe*. https://www.ssa.gov/policy/docs/progdesc/ssptw/2018-2019/europe/index.html.

Wise, David A., ed. 2012. *Social Security Programs and Retirement around the World: Historical Trends in Mortality and Health, Employment, and Disability Insurance Participation and Reforms*. Chicago: University of Chicago Press.

Wise, David A., ed. 2016. *Social Security Programs and Retirement around the World: Disability Insurance Programs and Retirement*. Chicago: University of Chicago Press.

Wise, David A., ed. 2017. *Social Security Programs and Retirement around the World: The Capacity to Work at Older Ages*. Chicago: University of Chicago Press.

1

Social Security Incentives in Belgium
An Analysis of Four Decades of Change

Anne-Lore Fraikin, Alain Jousten, and Mathieu Lefebvre

1.1 Introduction

Belgium has long been characterized by low employment and labor force participation rates of the elderly. In the 1990s, the country was known for having one of the lowest average effective retirement ages in the European Union—with employment of the 55–64 age group falling to 22 percent. Since then, there has been a continuous increase in these numbers, reaching 25.1 percent in 2001, 31.8 percent in 2005, and 45.4 percent in 2016.

Previous studies have pointed at the decisive role of public social security schemes in explaining the retirement patterns and low labor force participation of the elderly in Belgium (see, among others, Pestieau and Stijns 1999; Dellis et al. 2004; and Jousten and Lefebvre 2013). A common feature of these studies has been their reliance on a cross-sectional, micro-based, and supply-side approach. Relying on detailed modeling of individual retirement incentives in a given reference period, the papers document the presence of

Anne-Lore Fraikin is pursuing a PhD in innovation, economics, and governance for development at UNU-MERIT/Maastricht University and a PhD in economics and management at the University of Liège.

Alain Jousten is a professor of economics and holds the chair in public finances and economic policy at the University of Liège and is a research fellow of IZA and NETSPAR.

Mathieu Lefebvre is a professor of economics at the University of Strasbourg and an affiliated researcher at the Bureau d'Economie Théorique et Appliquée (BETA).

Fraikin acknowledges financial support through a doctoral dissertation fellowship from an FNRS/FRESH contract. The chapter was written while Jousten was on sabbatical leave with ISM (Vilnius), whose hospitality is gratefully acknowledged. Financial support was provided by FNRS and the University of Liège. This chapter uses data from the European Union Labour Force Survey (Eurostat, European Union) under contract 122/2015. Eurostat has no responsibility for the results and conclusions, which are the authors' only. For acknowledgments, sources of research support, and disclosure of the authors' material financial relationships, if any, please see https://www.nber.org/chapters/c14191.ack.

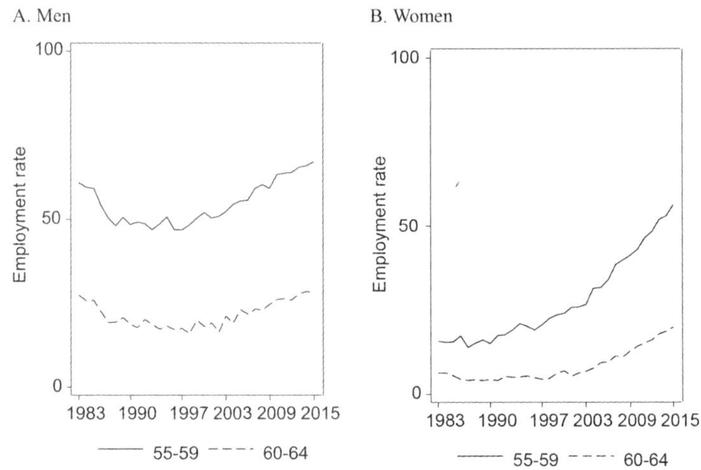

Fig. 1.1 Employment rate of older workers (aged 55–64)
Source: Eurostat *European Labour Force Survey* (2017)

strong retirement incentives and their importance in explaining observed labor supply and retirement patterns.

The cross-sectional design of the research question of these papers, however, limits their ability to explain the observed labor supply and retirement patterns in figure 1.1. Since the start of standardized collection of labor force data by the Labour Force Survey (LFS) in 1984, cohorts of older women have seen a steady upward trend in their employment rates; male employment has gone through a U-shaped pattern, with a first period of decreased employment (up to the early 1980s), followed by a period of stagnation (late 1980s to late 1990s), before finally contributing to the previously mentioned significant increase in employment rates of older cohorts since the early 2000s.

The respective importance of individual incentives and institutional changes in explaining observed labor supply and retirement patterns over the last decades remains unclear. Expressed differently, the decomposition into age and year effects remains an important and so far understudied research question in the Belgian context. Jousten and Lefebvre (2016) deliver a first step toward filling this gap in the literature. First, they provide a summary of institutional changes over the last decades—with a focus not only on pension and early retirement schemes but also on unemployment, disability, and time credit (a part-time retirement scheme). Second, they provide a detailed macroanalysis of observed employment and retirement patterns, looking not only at trends in employment and labor force participation rates but also at the changing intensity (e.g., more part-time work) and sectoral composition (e.g., a shift to service sectors) of employment in light of institutional changes.

This chapter goes further as we systematically calculate the financial incentives to exit employment for typical workers by age, year, and sex—integrating changes in both benefits and the tax system. More specifically, we construct a simulation model aimed at assessing the incentives to retire for different subgroups of the population and link these incentives with their labor outcomes. The model allows us to separate age and year effects, incidentally also permitting us to take phased reforms and grandfathering provisions into account. The model also permits the study of an array of scenarios in terms of earnings level, earnings growth, and mortality, as well as simulation of modified system parameters.

We focus our attention on the population of wage earners, leaving aside the self-employed and civil servants. We further focus our attention on single workers, hence staying clear of issues of joint or spousal retirement decisions (see Jousten and Lefebvre 2017 for a study of the role of spousal retirement incentives in the Belgian case), as well as interactions between individuals participating in different schemes. The reasons for these restrictions are linked to the overall complexity of social insurance and retirement programs in Belgium combined with a lack of structured historical information on some of them. The wage-earner scheme is by far the most important scheme in terms of enrollments and scope of coverage—encompassing all private-sector workers and also contractual workers in the public sector. Furthermore, it is the scheme with the most time-series information available on the applicable institutional setting and on the characteristics of participants. It is also the scheme that has been most extensively studied so far (see Jousten, Lefebvre, and Perelman 2012, 2016; and Jousten and Lefebvre 2016, 2017).[1]

The structure of the chapter is as follows. Section 1.2 provides a description of the pathways to retirement. After a summary of key programs and program modifications over time, the section documents the changes in observed retirement patterns in Belgium. Section 1.3 introduces the retirement incentive indicator, with a focus on singles. Section 1.4 explores the link between observed retirement patterns and incentives using a common standardized earnings profile across time and countries combined with standardized tax parameters across time. The common earnings profile and time-invariant tax parameters are chosen to allow for an easy international comparison of results. Section 1.5 deviates from this common profile by introducing specificities that are more relevant for understanding the

1. The civil servant schemes display a large heterogeneity, with only limited historical information available on both institutional details and participants. The self-employed scheme is the least well documented, as the (substantially more limited) information on participants' earnings histories has only recently been the subject of centralization efforts.

Belgian case by using different and more realistic assumptions in terms of earnings levels, career profiles, and taxation. It also discusses how benefit floors and ceilings affect incentives given these earnings histories. Section 1.6 concludes.

1.2 Pathways to Retirement

This section summarizes the main retirement pathways for the wage earners in Belgium and surveys the major changes/reforms that have been implemented since the early 1980s. There are four main components of the wage-earner social protection scheme that are of relevance when considering employment and retirement behavior: the old-age pension (OAP) system, the unemployment insurance (UI) system, the conventional early retirement (CER) system and the disability insurance (DI) system.[2]

Figure 1.2 presents the timeline of reforms implemented in each of these pathways since the early 1980s. It documents a rather sustained reform activity over the last decades.

Before proceeding, a few words of caution are in order. The figure should be seen as a stylized view on reforms of the *headline* retirement and early retirement schemes, with no claim of completeness. First, Belgium's retirement landscape is characterized by a rather extreme degree of institutional complexity—with some derogatory rules still in place for mineworkers, pilots, and so on. Second, the main legal and regulatory references are laid down in laws and in royal decrees (implementing bylaws)—and the border between the two is always clear from an economic point of view, with core policy choices relegated to royal decrees and implementation aspects in laws. Third, beyond laws and bylaws, national, sectoral, and company-wide collective bargaining agreements play a core role in the implementation and design of social protection schemes. Collective bargaining agreements are often compulsory for companies and workers in individual sectors (or even nationwide) and can sometimes substantially deviate from the headline rules laid down by the laws and bylaws. In the discussion below, we focus on the headline system only—for example, leaving aside some special early retirement conditions allowing labor force exit at ages well below the headline exit age. Fourth, employer–trade union comanagement of the social security system, the outsourcing of some operational tasks (payment of unemployment benefits by trade unions, payments of sick pay and disability insurance

2. Contrary to Jousten and Lefebvre (2017), we do not consider the time-credit system, as participation leads not to retirement at the individual level but rather to a reduction of work intensity of the worker combined with some benefit claiming—and this is irrespective of whether in aggregate the scheme leads to higher or lower employment than in its absence. We also do not consider the separate compulsory programs for workplace accident and professional disease insurance: though conceptually relevant, they remain quantitatively more limited in importance.

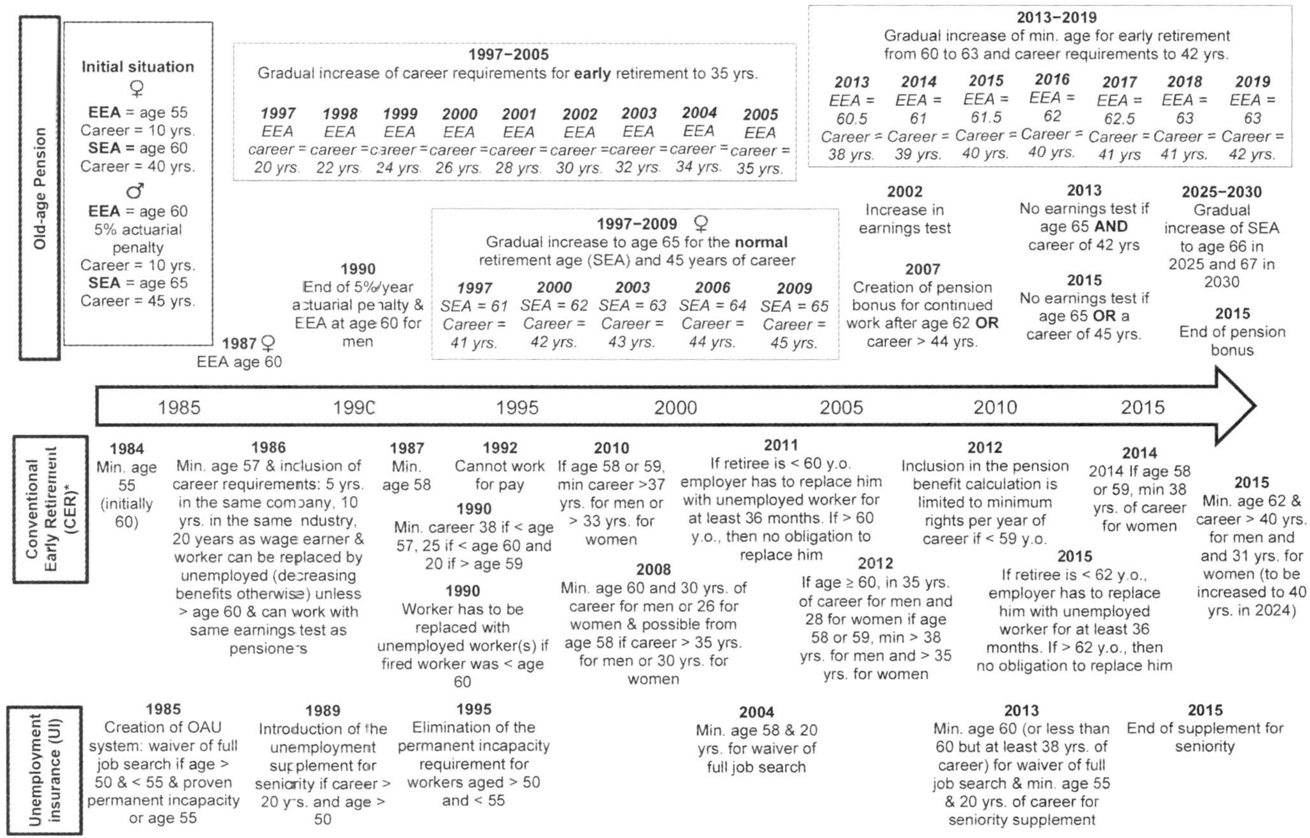

Fig. 1.2 Reforms, 1980–2016

Source: ONEM-RVA, ONP-RVP, Moniteur Belge

by health insurance funds, often having privileged links to the trade unions, etc.), and the increasing splitting of competencies across government levels (federal government, social security, regional, community, and local) further complicate the landscape. The following discussion completely leaves aside any and all changes in program implementation and management, whether country-wide or regional. Finally, as already indicated in the introduction, the present chapter focuses on single wage earners. The summary of reforms thus leaves aside any changes and reforms to the benefits of spouses and survivors, as well as those changes affecting individuals with mixed careers between different systems.

1.2.1 Old-Age Pension System

The old-age pension (OAP) system is the main public social security scheme covering the elderly. It is financed by tax-deductible employer and employee contributions but also by transfers from the federal budget. The program runs on a pay-as-you-go basis.

The statutory eligibility age (SEA) to full benefits is currently 65 and is scheduled to increase to age 66 for pensions first payable on or after February 1, 2025, and to 67 for pensions first payable on or after February 1, 2030. While an SEA of 65 has been applicable to men for several decades, the SEA for women has undergone substantial changes. Before 1997, the SEA for women was age 60. It was then increased by one-year steps every three years starting in 1997 and finishing in 2009—reaching full alignment with the male SEA in that last step.

Early retirement is possible at an early eligibility age (EEA). Since 1987, the male and female EEA have been perfectly aligned, whereas before that date, women had an EEA of 55 and men of 60. Until 2012, the EEA for men and women was 60. As of 2013, the headline EEA is on an upward path, increasing by half a year every calendar year until it reaches age 63 for pensions being first payable on or after February 1, 2018. However, the recent stepped increase in the EEA since 2013 has been accompanied by the creation of a special EEA for individuals with long careers—for example, currently still allowing early claiming at 60 for careers longer than 44 years.[3] Figures 1.3 and 1.4 present the evolution of the EEA and SEA in the OAP for men and women separately.

The EEA effectively also plays the role of a full-rate age (FRA)—that is, an age at which an individual can obtain unreduced benefits by satisfying both a minimum contribution history and the EEA. Two rules drive this equivalence between EEA and the FRA: First, the Belgian old-age pension system no longer applies actuarial adjustments in case of claiming before the SEA (beyond the effect of the shorter working history). A preexisting

3. See http://www.onprvp.fgov.be/FR/profes/benefits/retirement/age/Pages/default.aspx for details.

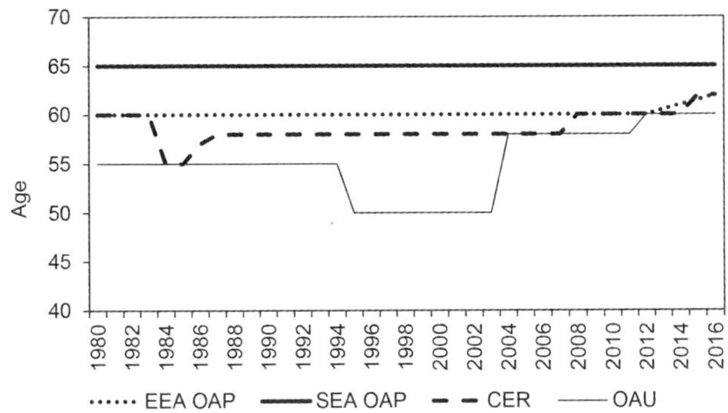

Fig. 1.3 Early and statutory retirement ages, men
Source: ONEM-RVA, ONP-RVP, Moniteur Belge

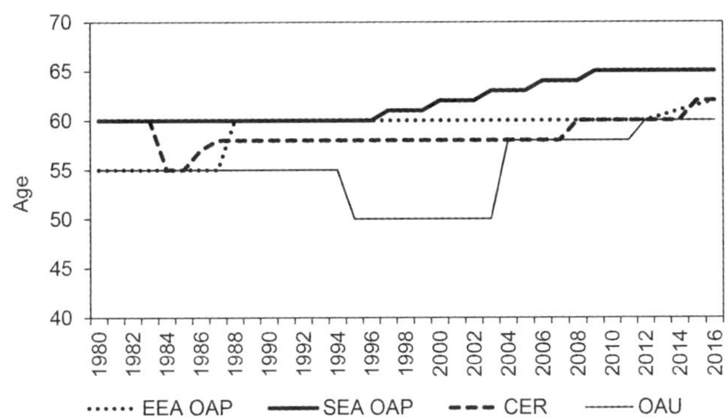

Fig. 1.4 Early and statutory retirement ages, women
Source: ONEM-RVA, ONP-RVP, Moniteur Belge

actuarial penalty mechanism of 5 percent per year of anticipation was abolished in 1990. In 2007, a lump-sum pension bonus was introduced per day of continued work after 62 or beyond a career of 44 years, but the mechanism was again abolished in 2015.[4] Second, claiming before the SEA has always been subject to career conditions. The career condition for early claiming between the EEA and the SEA has undergone substantial changes. Whereas in the early 1980s, a career of 10 years was required for men and women, between 1997 and 2005 the career condition was increased to 35 years. Since 2013, in line with the progressive increase in the EEA, career conditions for retirement have been further tightened—38 years in 2013, 39 in 2014, 40 in 2015 and 2016, 41 in 2017, and 2018 and 42 in 2019—with special early exit

4. The bonus was a flat rate until 2013, and in 2014 it was progressive as a function of the delay in claiming (but remained independent of the wage).

provisions still applying to individuals with longer careers. Though early claiming generally corresponds to reduced benefits, a worker with a full career condition (see below) upon claiming is entitled to unreduced benefits.

Combining old-age pension receipt with work is in principle possible under the old-age pension legislation but is generally subject to an earnings test.[5] The earnings test is categorical—with benefits completely suspended if surpassing a predetermined level. While the structure of the earnings test itself has not undergone major reform, it is now waived for those with careers of a minimum of 45 years or those who have reached the SRA.

Benefits depend on career earnings histories, marital status, and income. Both benefits and past earnings are indexed across time using the health index, which is essentially a slowed-down variant of the consumer price index (CPI) applicable as of 1996. Effectively, this indexing of past earnings exposes individuals to a double systematic loss: First, they are exposed to an erosion of past earnings, as the defined benefit formula does not reflect real wage growth. Second, inflation protection is not fully covered for both past earnings and benefits in payment, as the health index grows more slowly than the true cost of living summarized by the CPI.[6]

Full benefits nowadays require 45 years of earnings or assimilated periods for both males and females.[7] Assimilated periods correspond to periods of life spent on replacement income (e.g., unemployment benefits, disability benefits, career breaks) or other forms of paid or unpaid leave. Such periods fully count as years worked and at the full (last) wage in the computation of the pension benefit. Since 2012, a more restrictive policy is applicable to some types of absences from work: though the periods still count toward fulfilling the career condition, they now only enter at a minimum lump-sum amount and no longer at the full last wage.[8]

The pension benefit corresponds to 60 percent of average lifetime earnings over the best 45 years of the career.[9] There are ceilings and floors applicable to both pensionable earnings and pensions. Both pensions and ceilings are indexed to consumer prices. Pension floors are further proportionately adjusted by a ratio depending on the completeness of the career. In addition, numerous ad hoc discretionary increases of both the ceilings for pensionable earnings and the pension floors are applied—with the stated dual aim of (i)

5. Under labor legislation, it requires the explicit consent of the employer.

6. In addition to these systematic biases, more ad hoc elements apply. Until 2004, ad hoc adjustments were applied to past wages to adjust them (partially) for real wage growth. In 1984, 1985, and 1987, yearly indexing was frozen on three occasions for budgetary reasons—de facto lowering benefits on a lifetime basis.

7. The female full career condition was increased between 1997 and 2009 from 40 to 45 years in line with the increase in the SEA.

8. For details see http://www.onprvp.fgov.be/FR/profes/calculation/career/inactivity/Pages/default.aspx.

9. For married individuals, a higher household benefit rate of 75 percent is applicable (subject to a pension test of the spouse), and survivor benefits also apply.

correcting for the lack of real wage indexation and (ii) increasing minimum pensions at a faster pace than average pensions.[10] De facto, the faster growth of minimum pensions progressively makes the old-age pension system tend toward a flat-rate benefit structure.

1.2.2 Unemployment Insurance

Next to the OAP scheme, the unemployment insurance (UI) system is an important pathway to retirement. The regular UI system is available to workers of all ages under the condition of having paid contributions during at least 12 months in employment or having been in an assimilated status (sickness, etc.) in the last 18 months. The unemployment benefits are also a function of unemployment duration and household status. At the beginning of the unemployment spell, the benefits represent 60 percent of the last gross wage for unemployed persons with dependents, 55 percent for single unemployed persons, and 40 percent for individuals who are sharing their household with others (effective cohabitation). These benefits are not limited in time, with payments ending upon reemployment or reaching the SEA—in the latter case, the person is then rolled over into the OAP program. However, benefits generally decrease as a function of benefit duration, with exceptions prevailing for unemployed workers who either are aged more than 55, have worked as wage earners for at least 25 years, or can prove a disability of more than 33 percent. There are minimum and maximum unemployment benefits that also vary by household status and decreases in unemployment duration. Under the regular system, individuals have to be available for the job market and actively look for employment; the amount of benefits decreases according to the length of the unemployment status.

In 1989, a seniority supplement was introduced for those aged 50 or above and who have been employed for at least 20 years. The amount of the seniority supplement was added to the regular unemployment benefit and depended on the household status and the age. The age condition was increased to 55 in 2013, and the measure was finally abandoned in 2015.

A specific feature of the Belgian UI system is the status of old-age unemployed (OAU). Under OAU rules, the unemployed are exempted from both actively looking for a job and an availability condition for the labor market. He or she can stay unemployed until reaching the SEA of OAP with unreduced benefits. The OAU system was introduced in 1985 and was initially limited to those people aged 55 and above who were unemployed for at least two years or to those aged 50 who could prove of permanent incapacity. In 1995, the eligibility age was lowered to 50 for everyone by removing the

10. Certain increases in the pensionable earnings ceilings were more important than others, most notably in 1968, 1969, 1973, and 1981, when it increased by a real growth rate of 31.6 percent, 13.4 percent, 30.8 percent, and 15.9 percent, respectively. The two most important discretional increases in the pension floor occurred in 2001 and 2004, with a real growth rate of 3.5 percent and 3.8 percent, respectively.

permanent incapacity requirement before age 55. In 2004, the government introduced more stringent conditions to benefit from the job search and availability waiver. Only workers aged 58 and above or with long careers still benefit from a full waiver. In 2012, the eligibility age for the waiver was increased again to 60. Figures 1.3 and 1.4 show the timeline of changes in the eligibility age of OAU of men and women.

Any time spent on unemployment benefits is fully credited toward pensionable periods in the earnings history as assimilated. Until 2011, such periods were fully credited at the last real wage before entering unemployment. Since 2012, the wage crediting is limited to a lower flat-rate amount for periods of unemployment going beyond two years.

1.2.3 Conventional Early Retirement

Conventional early retirement (CER) is a parallel system of early retirement benefits created in the early 1970s. Benefits are composed of two elements. First, the early retiree is entitled to benefits from unemployment insurance that are more generous than those in the simple UI system—particularly because of the absence of degressivity with respect to benefit duration and more favorable testing on household composition. Second, these baseline UI benefits are topped up by a complementary benefit paid by the former employer—equal to half the difference between the last net wage and the UI benefit.

Up until 2015, CER beneficiaries were fully exempted from the job search and did not have to be available for the labor market. Since 2015, a new notion of "adapted availability" has been introduced in the applicable rules, essentially making numerous early retirees subject to an availability condition up until the SEA—though it remains less stringent than the regular UI.[11]

Before 2012—as for all unemployed—the time spent in the early retirement program was fully credited at the last preretirement wage. Since 2012, the last-wage crediting is limited to a lower minimum amount for individuals retiring on CER before the age of 59.

At the start of the system, the headline eligibility age was set at 60. Several collective bargaining agreements rapidly lowered the effectively applicable eligibility ages and other eligibility conditions. As a result, the Belgian reality in the area of CER has been characterized from the early days by the coexistence of regimes with different career requirements, minimum ages, and so on. Though legislation in the early 1980s tried to harmonize and apply constraints, numerous exceptions persist with respect to the general rules.

As mentioned before, we focus on the headline system as being the only economy-wide regime. Key reform steps are described as follows: Eligibil-

11. More recently in 2015, the name of the scheme has been adapted to "unemployment scheme with company supplement"—mirroring this conceptual shift.

ity has gone through several changes. While the age of 60 prevailed before 1984, it decreased to 55 in 1984, and it increased to 57 in 1986, to 58 in 1987, and to 60 in 2008 (see figures 1.3 and 1.4). Length-of-career conditions were also introduced in 1986 (see figure 1.2). Initially, the minimum length was set to 20 years. Over time, it has increased and now reaches 40 years for men and 33 years for women with a further programmed increase to 40 years for women until the year 2024.

1.2.4 Disability Insurance

The disability insurance (DI) system is the main program targeted at people withdrawing from the labor market for disability reasons—though it has become an increasingly relevant early retirement route in light of ever-tighter eligibility and benefit criteria for the CER and UI systems (see Jousten, Lefebvre, and Perelman 2012). To be eligible for the benefit, the worker has to satisfy a series of conditions. First, there is a condition in terms of the loss of earnings capacity in the usual job. In order to be eligible, the worker has to suffer from a loss of earnings capacity of 66 percent over a period of at least 12 months.[12] After the first benefit entitlement, continued eligibility is periodically validated using medical and administrative controls. Second, workers also have to satisfy minimum contributory requirements to qualify for benefits. The coverage under the system prior to the onset of the disability has to be assured for at least two quarters, combined with at least 120 days of actual or assimilated work (or 400 hours for part-time workers) before the covered event occurs.

During the first year of disability, the benefit is equal to 60 percent of reference earnings for everyone. It corresponds to the so-called period of incapacity. Afterward, the benefit level is a function of the household status of the worker and is equal to 65 percent of reference earnings if the insured has dependents, 55 percent of reference earnings if the insured lives alone, and 40 percent of reference earnings if the insured cohabits and has no dependents. Reference earnings are based on real observed earnings in the year leading up to the onset of the insured event.

As for the UI and CER systems, DI benefits are payable up to the SEA. Contrary to other social insurance replacement income programs, such as UI and CER, periods of benefit receipt continue to fully count toward the buildup of pension rights at the value of the last real wage to this date.

1.2.5 Income Taxes and Social Security Contributions

In Belgium, both earnings and benefits are subject to income taxes and mandatory social contributions. Mandatory social contributions are paid by both employees and employers. Employer social contributions amount

12. During these initial 12 months, workers are generally covered by sick pay from their employers and the sick pay insurance.

to 24.92 percent of the gross wage.[13] Personal/employee social contributions include a 13.07 percent employee contribution on wage income, a 3.5 percent contribution on DI benefits, and a 6.5 percent contribution on CER and UI benefits. A health and disability contribution of 3.5 percent on pensions becomes mandatory when the pension is above a certain threshold.[14] While social security benefits are all capped by means of program-specific ceilings, the same does not hold true on the contribution side, where no caps applicable.

The Belgian personal income tax (PIT) applies to wage, pension, and other replacement income. The PIT liability is calculated using a strongly progressive rate structure with marginal tax rates from 0 to 50 percent from 2003 onward.[15] Before 2003, the tax rates were modified substantially over the years and went as high as 70.8 percent in 1988. Nontaxable amounts vary according to marital status and to the number of dependent children of the taxpayer.

Replacement incomes (including OAP) can benefit from two types of additional tax preferences. First, there is a set of ad hoc tax deductions for the various categories of replacement income, effectively granting these types of income a preferential treatment as compared to wages and other types of income and effectively excluding a substantial share of these benefits from taxation—with the most generous rules applying to DI benefits. However, in the presence of other sources of income and depending on individual characteristics, a nonnegligible tax burden might subsist. This is where the second mechanism comes into play: a special tax deduction reduces the taxable income and hence the tax amount to zero if a person's income is exclusively composed of OAP or other replacement benefits below a given threshold. The applicable thresholds in Belgium are such that for all cases considered in sections 1.4 and 1.5, no personal income tax is due on benefits.

1.2.6 Program Participation

Figures 1.5 to 1.8 present the pathways to retirement over the period 1983 to 2015. They show for each year, and by age group, the percentage of men and women recorded as beneficiaries of each program. In each figure, we see how the structure changed over time with the implementation of reforms in some programs and the introduction of new programs as well.

13. An additional contribution is paid for annual vacation, but it concerns only blue-collar workers.

14. A "solidarity contribution" on OAP essentially taxing beneficiaries of higher pensions also exists. This contribution was introduced in 1994 and has to be paid on pension income or capital. It is calculated using a progressive rate and goes from 0 to 2 percent. It does not apply to pensions below a monthly gross amount of €2311.96. Since the maximum pension for a single earner is €2300.00, it is irrelevant for our simulation of single wage earners.

15. This excludes a local surtax on the PIT—ranging from 0 to 9 percent depending on the place of residence.

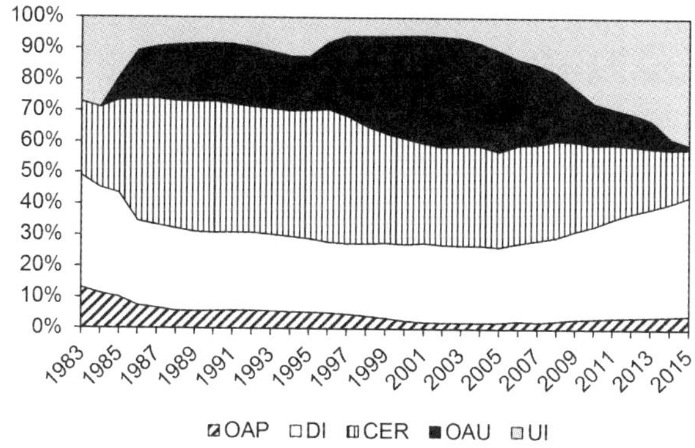

Fig. 1.5 Pathways to retirement, men aged 55–59
Source: INAMI-RIZIV, ONEM-RVA, ONP-RVP

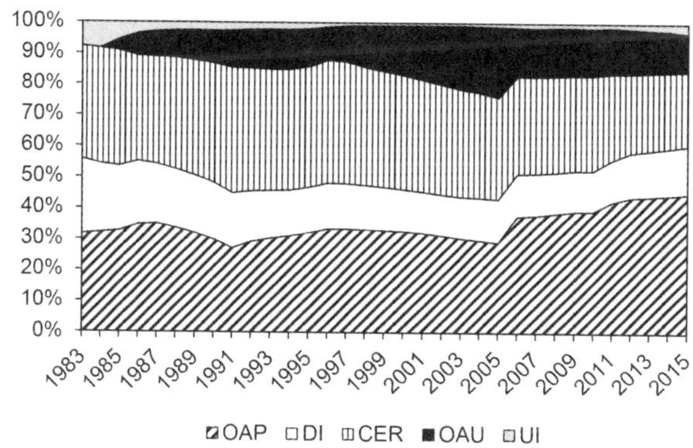

Fig. 1.6 Pathways to retirement, men aged 60–64
Source: INAMI-RIZIV, ONEM-RVA, ONP-RVP

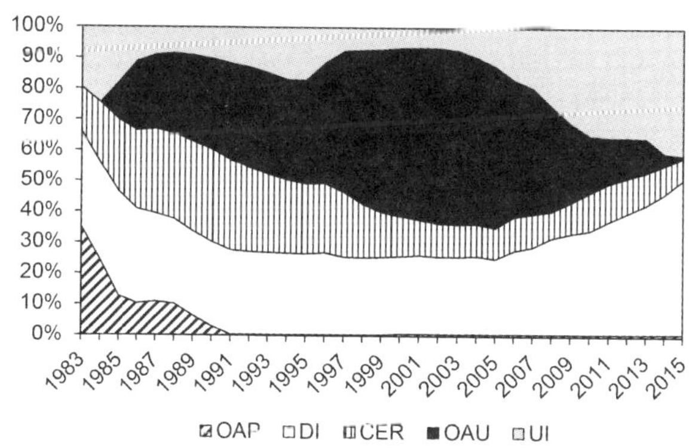

Fig. 1.7 Pathways to retirement, women aged 55–59
Source: INAMI-RIZIV, ONEM-RVA, ONP-RVP

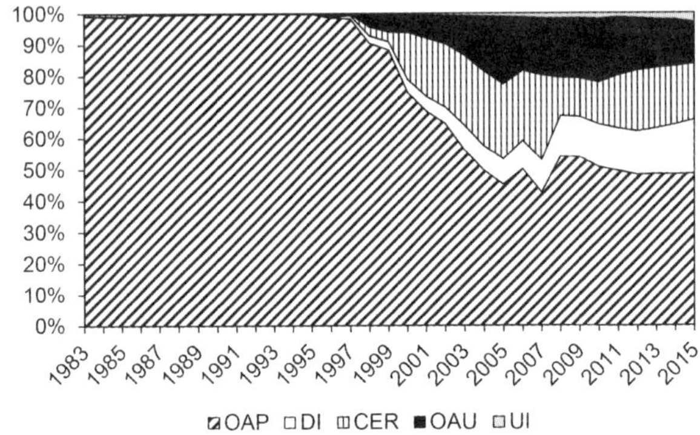

Fig. 1.8 Pathways to retirement, women aged 60–64
Source: INAMI-RIZIV, ONEM-RVA, ONP-RVP

Over the period, some pathways have gained or lost importance in the distribution of exits, reflecting the varying generosity in access conditions and benefits. These figures document the connected vessels aspect of the various social security schemes. For men aged 55–59, we observe an increase in the proportion of recipients of UI and DI benefits since 2005, at a time when CER rules have been tightened. For men aged 60–64, the proportion of pensioners has increased since 2005. For women aged 55–59, the picture is similar to that of men, but for women aged 60–64, we observe the increase of the proportion of other pathways since the end of the 1990s due to the increase of SEA in the OAP system, hence delaying the mechanical rollover of DI, UI, OAU, and CER beneficiaries into the OAP program.

1.3 Measuring Retirement Incentives

This section describes the simulation model used to quantify the work incentives created by the social security system. To observe the effect of changes and reforms over time, calculations are made for the different age cohorts in each year starting in the early 1980s.

Given the life-cycle dimension of pensions, we define a synthetic earnings history of a cohort through time and scale it to reflect differences in socioeconomic status. For each pathway and case, we calculate and aggregate the benefits the representative individual is entitled to at a given age in a given year.

1.3.1 Earning Histories

We consider two scenarios: a *common scenario* with key assumptions based on international data used for all countries in this volume and a *Belgian scenario* with assumptions based on Belgian data. We model earnings histories for two types of individuals: single males and single females. We distinguish stylized variants of low, medium, and high earners. For each year of observation, each of these six cases is associated with specific earnings level, career length, and lifetime earnings profiles. We detail the underlying calculations and assumptions below.

First, we use the median income of full-time nonmanual wage earners in 2014 as reported by Statistics Belgium to define the median worker and attribute this wage to males aged 50 in 2014. We adjust the median wage at the anchoring age of 50 to each simulation year using a fixed deflator, which is the average growth rate of the conventional wage of nonmanual wage earners between 1980 and 2016. We then define low earners as persons earning 50 percent of the median and high earners as receiving 200 percent of the median earner's income. We assume that female median earnings are 7.6 percent below the male median at age 50 for all years of study—with 7.6 percent corresponding to the average hourly wage gap between men and women in 2014 as reported by Statistics Belgium.

Second, we derive earnings histories for these six cases in the two scenarios. All earnings histories share a common assumption of no career interruptions—with any variation in effective career length simply translated into different starting dates.

In the common scenario, we assume that the low earners start working at age 16, the median earners start working at 20, and the high earners start working at 25. Once these career lengths are determined, we derive lifetime earning histories for each case. The common earnings profile uses a time-invariant common synthetic earning profile that is differentiated for men and women and for the three income levels. The profiles are calculated with data from the US, Germany, and Italy.[16] Figure 1.9 presents the patterns of the earning profiles—the same for all years concerned—each expressed as a proportion of the anchoring wage at 50.

In the Belgian scenario, we shorten the careers of men by five years in order to model more incomplete (but more realistic) careers. We further consider an average gap in career length between men and women of six years—in line with the results of a report from ONP-RVP (2005). This assumption is plausible, as compulsory schooling has gone up to age 18 for several decades already, with numerous persons studying well beyond. Also, other forms of work interruptions are not uncommon.[17] The Belgian scenario thus assumes that male (female) low earners start working at age 21 (27), male (female) median earners start working at age 25 (31), and male (female) high earners start working at age 30 (36). In a second step, the Belgium-specific earnings profile is built using the average gross monthly wage by age and is time and

16. See the US chapter in this volume for details.

17. Military service obligations for men until the late 1990s also contributed to a later start in their working lives.

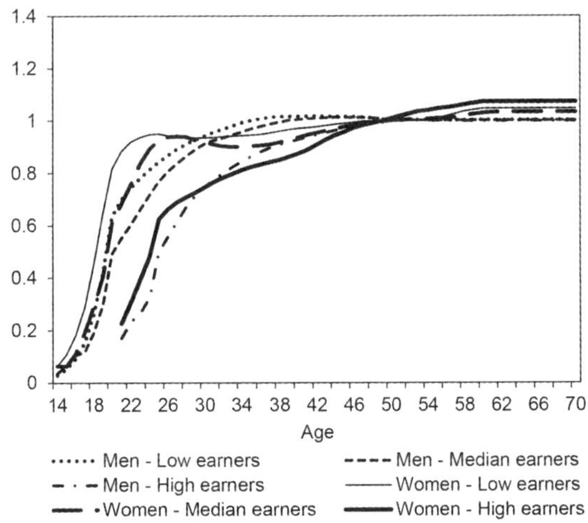

Fig. 1.9 Common earnings profiles
Source: Authors' calculations

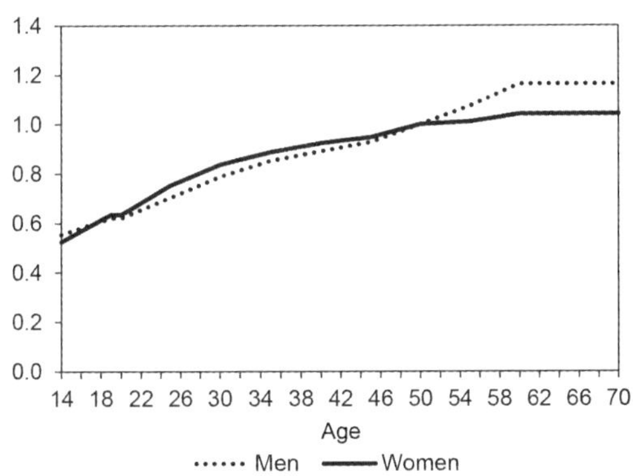

Fig. 1.10 Belgium-specific earnings profiles, average across years
Source: Authors' calculations

sex specific—but its shape does not vary by income level beyond the different starting date.[18]

Figure 1.10 presents the average of the time-specific Belgian earning profiles, again expressed as a percentage of the wage at age 50. Unlike the common profile—that assumes an important increase of the wage in the first years of the career, a decrease in the growth of wages until 50, and constancy thereafter—the Belgium-specific earnings profile displays a continuous and

18. Because of data limitations, the earnings profile is kept constant from 1980 to 1999 and from 2015 to 2016.

almost constant increase of the wage throughout the career and until age 60. Expressed differently, while the common profile captures an internationally more usual career-wage profile, the Belgium-specific pattern better fits the specificities of the Belgian wage-setting system with its automatic indexing of wages to changes in the CPI and collective wage bargaining on real wage growth across income levels.

Each scenario is accompanied by an assumption in terms of the applicable tax system. In the common scenario, we use the tax rules applicable in 2016 (in real terms) for all simulation years. The motivation for this approach is to clearly distinguish the pure effects of pension policy from those of general tax policy.[19] In the Belgian scenario, we apply the tax rules as they were applicable in all years to reflect the changes in the entire tax-benefit landscape as experienced by real-world workers.

1.3.2 Benefit Stream

From these earnings profiles, we calculate for each age-year cohort the after-tax benefit stream from each scheme presented in section 1.2. For an individual i, defined according to his or her sex and the level of career earnings, we calculate the after-tax benefit $B_{k,t,a}(R,i)$ from the program k for all ages $a \geq R$, where R is the first year of benefit receipt. Once retired, we assume benefits remain constant in real terms in future years.

We look at retirement ages ranging from 55 to 64 from 1980 to 2016. Our simulation thus takes into account any potential cohort differences and changes thereto, as well as transitory and permanent changes over time (index t) and as a function of age (index a). The lack of eligibility for pathway k at an age a at time t conditional on retirement at R is modeled by setting $B_{k,t,a}(R,i)$ equal to 0.

The simulation model allows for a rich set of scenarios in terms of individual characteristics. Also, it allows for simulations of counterfactuals and system reforms. For example, the common scenario of section 1.4 relies on a counterfactual assumption that only benefit rules have changed but that no tax changes have occurred during the entire period of analysis. The motivation for this deviation from the empirically observed institutional setting is to separate out strictly retirement-related changes from broader tax policy changes affecting the wider population. The Belgian scenario of section 1.5 explores the role of tax policy changes and also provides a counterfactual analysis of benefits indexation rules and thresholds.

1.3.3 Social Security Wealth, Accrual, and Implicit Tax

From the benefits, we calculate different indicators of social security systems' incentives. The key concept is the annual accrual of social security

19. The tax rates obtained using the 2016 rules are almost identical to those derived by the OECD tax model.

wealth (SSW). SSW is the present discounted value of all future benefit flows from a given social security program for a given individual at a given age in a given year. SSW for an individual of type i starting to claim benefits from program k at age R in time t is then given by

$$SSW_{k,t}(R,i) = B_{k,t,R} \sum_{a=R}^{T} \sigma_{i,a} \beta^{a-R},$$

where $B_{k,t,R}$ is the after-tax benefit from pathway k at age R as calculated above. The formula sums these benefits until the end of life T. Discounting is done, allowing for both time preference and mortality adjustments: $\sigma_{i,a}$ is the survival probability[20] at age a for individual i, and β is the time discount rate that we assume to be equal to 3 percent real. Since we assume a real constant benefit once in the program, the amount stays the same in the forthcoming years if the person retires on OAP. In the case of an exit through UI, CER, or DI, the benefits change according to the age, since at the SEA, the individual starts to receive OAP benefits instead of the other benefits—essentially splitting the right-hand side of the formula into two separate sums before and after the SEA.

Based on this SSW, we then compute a secondary incentive measure that represents the variation in SSW that is obtained by retiring one year later. Postponing claiming by one year has two effects on social security wealth. On the one hand, annual benefits $B_{k,t,a}(R,i)$ can vary with later claiming due to additional earnings entering the benefit formula (and possible actuarial adjustments). On the other hand, however, benefits are received one year later. The accrual of social security wealth is then given by

$$ACC_{k,t}(R,i) = SSW_{k,t+1}(R+1,i) - SSW_{k,t}(R,i).$$

The accrual can thus be positive, zero, or negative. If the accrual is negative, the social security system imposes an implicit tax on working longer (ITAX). The implicit tax rate is the (negative) accrual of social security wealth divided by the after-tax earnings during the additional year of work $Y_{t+1,i}$:

$$ITAX_{k,t(R,i)} = \frac{-ACC_{k,t}(R,i)}{Y_{t+1,i}}.$$

This last measure shows the tax on continued activity from retiring one year later. A positive value means that there is a tax on working longer; a negative value represents a subsidy for working longer.

1.4 Retirement Incentives: Common Profile

The present section presents the analysis of the incentive measures defined in the previous section for the six "common scenario" cases by sex and

20. Obtained from the average survival rates of the EU28 provided by Eurostat.

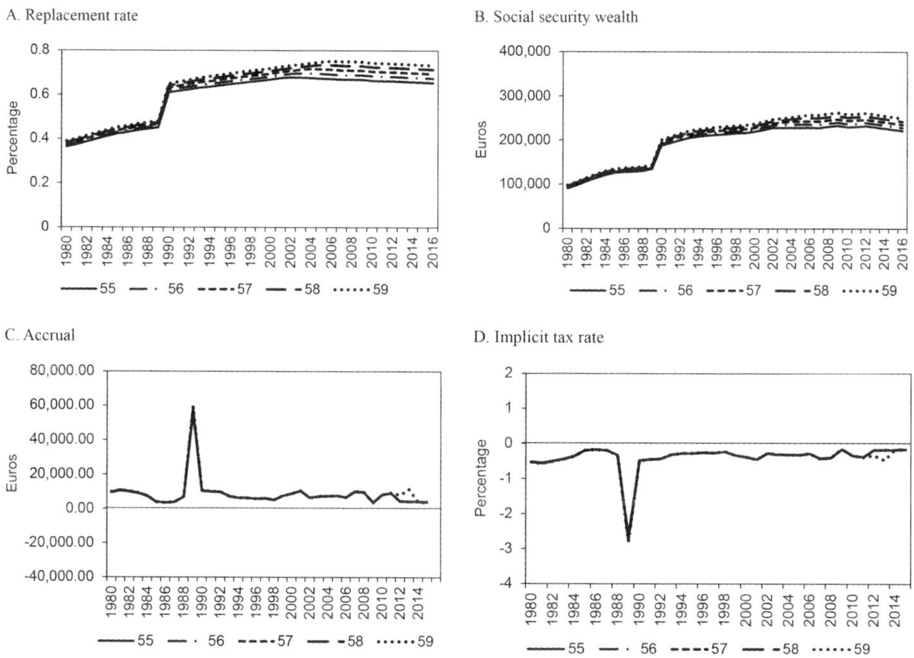

Fig. 1.11 Incentive measures, OAP, men median earners aged 55–59
Source: Authors' calculations

income level across time. To simplify the presentation, the general discussion of incentives at the level of the individual focuses on median earner profiles in the context of the OAP program. We only present ITAX measures for other benefit programs as they capture the essence of the incentive landscape. The details of the other cases can be obtained from the authors upon simple request. When discussing the impact of these individual incentive indicators for aggregate outcomes, all incentive measures are summed across programs and across earnings levels to one representative measure that is confronted with observed employment rates.

1.4.1 Incentives by Pathway

Figures 1.11 to 1.14 present the measures for the OAP scheme for median earners. Results are shown for both sexes and two age groups: 55–59 and 60–64.

For men aged 55–59, figure 1.11 displays very marked changes in SSW. The SSW of median earners displays a generally increasing trend over the years thanks to the discretionary increases of ceilings for pensionable earnings. Without such discretionary increases, SSW would be flat—reflecting the crucial role played by the floors and ceilings in the system.[21] The ensuing

21. Implicitly, the discretionary increases—imperfectly—mimic wage indexing of past earnings.

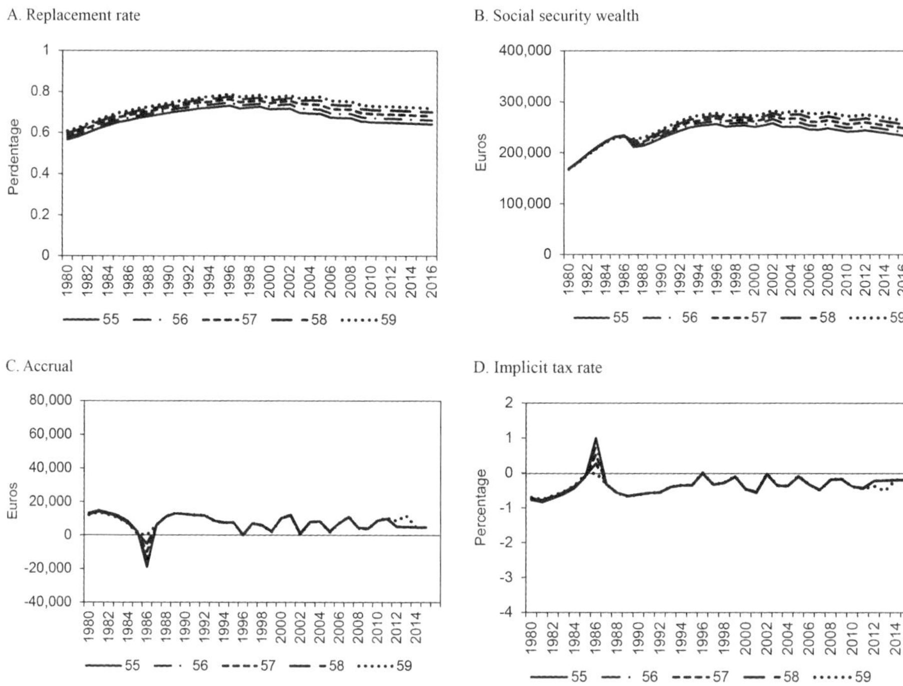

Fig. 1.12 Incentive measures, OAP, women median earners aged 55–59
Source: Authors' calculations

discrete jump of SSW curves after 1990 can be attributed to the end of the actuarial adjustment penalty of 5 percent for exits before the SEA. This translates in a large peak in the accrual and the corresponding drop in the implicit tax as a result of the discrete jump in entitlements for all individuals claiming benefits before the SEA—as is the case of individuals quitting the labor market between ages 55 and 59.

As mentioned earlier, the EEA of both men and women gradually increased from 60 to 63 between 2013 and 2018. In our simulation, we consider that if a worker exits the labor market through the OAP before the EEA, he receives a benefit of zero until he reaches the EEA. Since median earners in the common scenario do not satisfy the long-career exception, they are affected by the reform. Thus an increase in the EEA translates into a decrease in SSW because the worker starts receiving pension benefits one year later. Therefore, the downward trend in SSW as of 2013 is attributable to the increase in the EEA and the associated career requirements. Accordingly, the ITAX at age 59 increases in 2013 because there is an incentive for the worker aged 59 to exit the labor force before the EEA rises to 61 in 2014.

Figure 1.12 reports the social security incentive measures for female

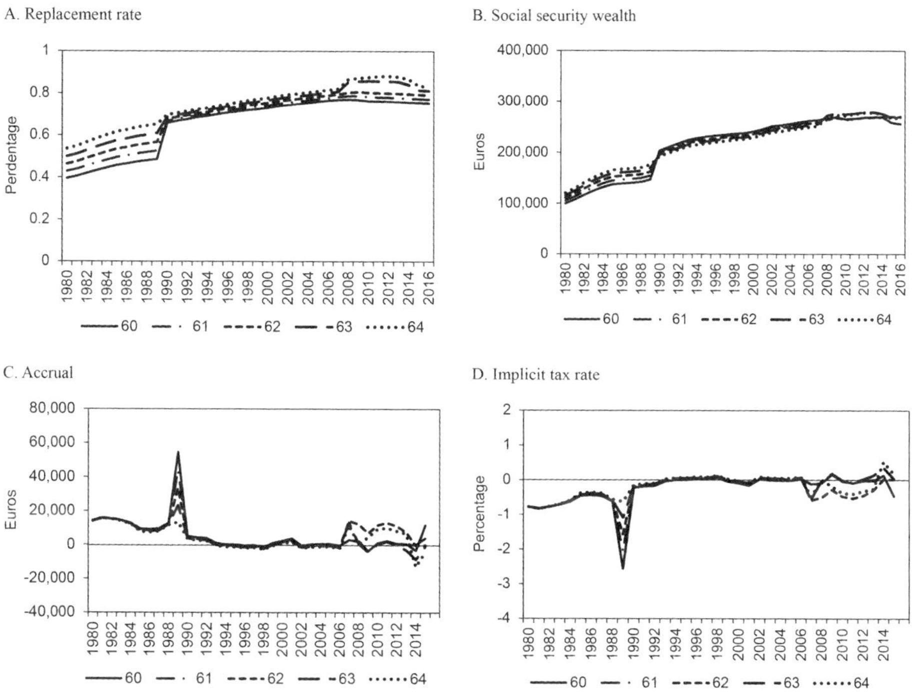

Fig. 1.13 Incentive measures, OAP, men median earners aged 60–64
Source: Authors' calculations

median earners retiring between ages 55 and 59. The results are similar to those of men except for the reform of 1987, which increases the EEA from 55 to 60, adding a sharp discontinuity by replacing every potential year of benefits before 60 by zero. Moreover, as the female SEA was already set at 60 before 1997, women were not directly impacted by the end of actuarial adjustments in 1990. In addition, other assumptions play out: as women are assumed to have the same career length as men with only slightly lower median earnings, their higher life expectancies and shorter full career conditions (until 2009 only) lead them to have a significantly higher SSW. This effect is partially canceled out between 1997 and 2009 because of the increase in full career conditions from 40 to 45 years. The resulting decrease in SSW during the latter period leads to an increased incentive to leave the labor market before each increase in career conditions and thus a positive ITAX at each step.

Figure 1.13 reports the social security incentive measures for men who retire between the ages of 60 and 64. The end of the actuarial adjustment in 1990 is still visible, but the older the person is when he retires, the less important is the jump of SSW because their pension benefits were less impacted

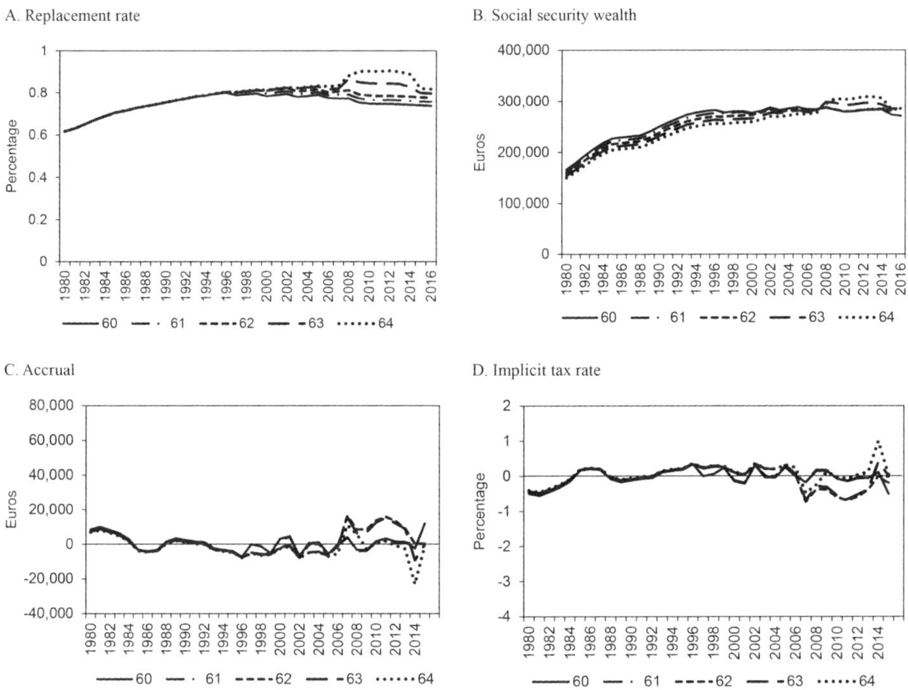

Fig. 1.14 Incentive measures, OAP, women median earners aged 60–64
Source: Authors' calculations

by the actuarial adjustment. In 2007, the flat-rate pension bonus was created for continued work after age 62 (or after 44 years of career). The program was discontinued in 2015, which translates into a fall in the accruals and an increase in the ITAX at ages 63 to 65 in 2014. In this simulation, the receipt of a pension bonus increases the pension to a level higher than the health and disability insurance contribution threshold for retirement ages of 65 in 2008 and of 64 and 65 from 2009 onward. This additional health and disability contribution limits the increase in pension benefits, and thus the increase in SSW, due to the pension bonus at ages 64 and 65. Since we assume that the median earner starts working at age 20 and works without career interruption, he is eligible for the long-career exception of the OAP scheme that allows for retirement at age 60 in 2013 and 2014 instead of 60.5 and 61, respectively. Thus, in practice, workers would only be affected by the reform if their career were insufficiently long—which is not the case for the common profile. At age 60, SSW only starts decreasing in 2015, because in 2013 and 2014, median workers still had access to an EEA of 60. In 2015, they fall out of these conditions that require 41 years of career to access OAP benefits at age 60 and now have an EEA of 61.5.

Finally, figure 1.14 depicts the social security incentive measures for

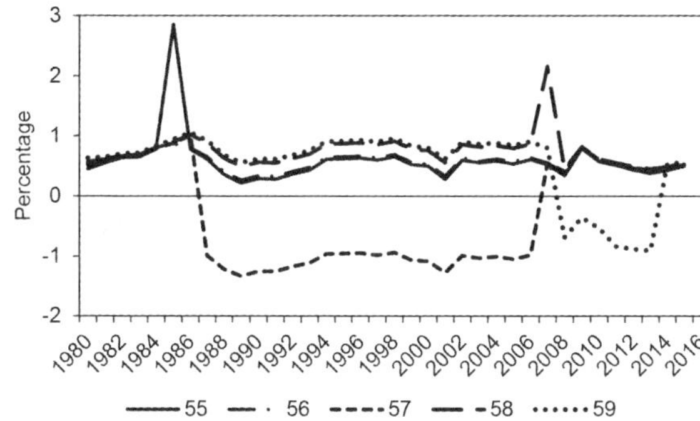

Fig. 1.15 Implicit tax CER, men median earners aged 55–59
Source: Authors' calculations

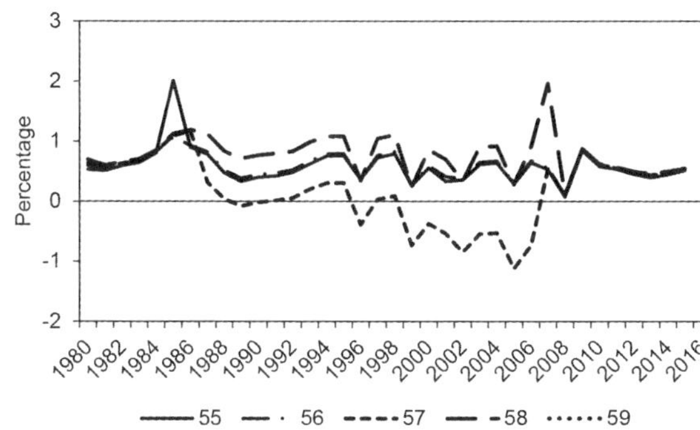

Fig. 1.16 Implicit tax CER, women median earners aged 55–59
Source: Authors' calculations

women who are median earners and retire between the ages of 60 and 64. Logically, the 1987 reform that increased the EEA of women to 60 has no impact on women who retire after 60. The effects of the increase in the full career from 1997 to 2009 and the pension bonus from 2007 to 2015 for retirement ages between 63 and 64 are also visible. Moreover, the receipt of the pension bonus at age 65 also increases the pension to a level higher than the health and disability insurance contribution threshold, which limits the increase in pension benefits due to the pension bonus at age 65.

For the other three pathways, we only present the implicit tax for each sex for reasons of brevity. Similarly, we focus on the 55–59 age group, since it is the age window where most changes in program parameters and employment have happened. Figures 1.15 and 1.16 show the evolution of the ITAX in the CER scheme for each age. Contrary to our assumption on the OAP, we consider that individuals who lose benefits in the CER program would still meet the basic conditions for UI benefits—a plausible assumption in the Belgian context. Hence benefits are not reduced to zero in the case of loss of eligibility but rather are replaced by the lower UI benefits. Figure 1.16 illustrates the evolution of the CER ITAX for men. The implicit tax for most ages is on average largely positive, meaning that there is a strong incentive to exit the labor market through the CER. The peak at age 55 in 1986 for both men and women corresponds to the increase of the eligibility age from 55 to 57. There is an incentive to quit the labor market before the reform takes place in order to be able to access the CER pathway at age 55 instead of 57. The same effect is observed at age 58 in 2008, when the eligibility age increased to 60. The ITAX at age 56 in 1986 is not impacted by the reform; the worker does not lose access to the CER exit pathway if working for one more year. In 1987, the increase in the eligibility to 58 creates a negative ITAX at 57 because the worker now has an incentive to stay on the labor market for one more year to have access to the CER program rather than exiting at 57 and remaining on lower UI benefits until the SEA. Thus from 1987 onward, the ITAX at 55 and 56 is lower than at other ages because if workers exit before 58, they receive UI benefits until the SEA. Since the UI benefits are less generous than the CER benefits, they generate a smaller incentive to leave the labor force. In 2008, the increase of the headline entitlement age for CER to 60 translates into a double effect: an increase in the ITAX at 57, resulting in an incentive to leave the labor force before the reform, and a decrease in the ITAX at 59, resulting in an incentive to stay on the labor market for one more year to receive CER rather than UI benefits until the SEA.[22] In 2015, the headline eligibility age increases to 62, and the ITAX at age 59 again increases.

From 2012 onward and for exits before age 59, longer periods on CER are no longer fully credited at the last real wage before entering CER but rather at the guaranteed minimum wage. Though the eligibility age for CER is higher than 59 in the headline regime discussed in this chapter, the CER pathway still is affected. The reason is that exits through UI as a fallback option remain possible, with UI crediting in the earnings history effectively facing the same limitations as CER after the first two years of unemployment. Therefore, workers in the headline regime are affected by the reform through the indirect channel of a decrease in the value of the UI periods in their earnings history, whereas those in special CER are directly affected—ultimately to the same effect. As a result, the reform of credited earnings in 2012 for long periods of inactivity has led to a decrease of the ITAX at every age from 2012 onward.

Figure 1.16 illustrates the evolution of the CER ITAX for women. The impact of the gradual increase of the SEA in OAP from 1997 to 2009 is particularly visible. Each stepwise increase in SEA translates into an imme-

22. Notice that the impact of the 2008 reform on the ITAX at 59 is less pronounced than the impact of the 1987 reform on the ITAX at 57 simply because the period during which CER benefits are replaced by UI benefits is longer.

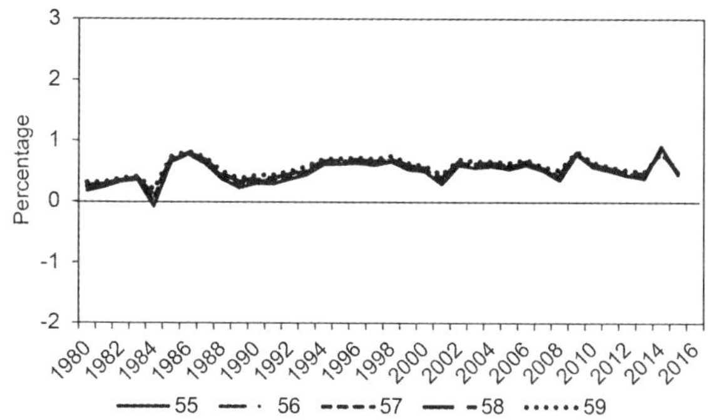

Fig. 1.17 Implicit tax UI/OAU, men median earners aged 55–59
Source: Authors' calculations

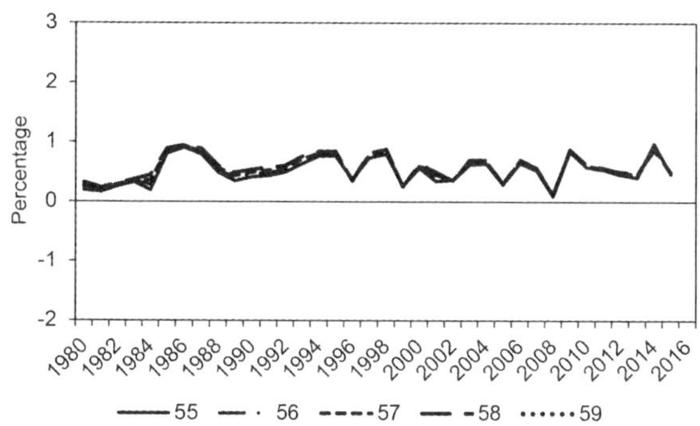

Fig. 1.18 Implicit tax UI/OAU, women median earners aged 55–59
Source: Authors' calculations

diate decrease in the ITAX because individuals receive one more year of CER benefits before they are transferred into the OAP system. Therefore, an incentive to stay at work for one more year appears at each step.

The implicit tax for UI also displays some sharp changes, as illustrated in figures 1.17 and 1.18. In 1985, the ITAX decreases sharply in a one-off fashion because of the introduction of the seniority supplement: there is an incentive to wait one more year in order to be eligible for the supplement rather than merely regular UI benefits. This effect no longer plays out with the same acuity in the following years, where only the increased generosity of the system leaves its mark through a higher implicit tax rate. In 2015, the sharp increase in the ITAX at each age is the mirror image of the one in 1985 namely, the end of the supplement for seniority. The effect of the 2012 reform that limits the valorization of UI periods in earnings histories is visible in 2011 and is translated into a gradual decrease in the ITAX. There is therefore a higher incentive to stay in the labor market because the increase

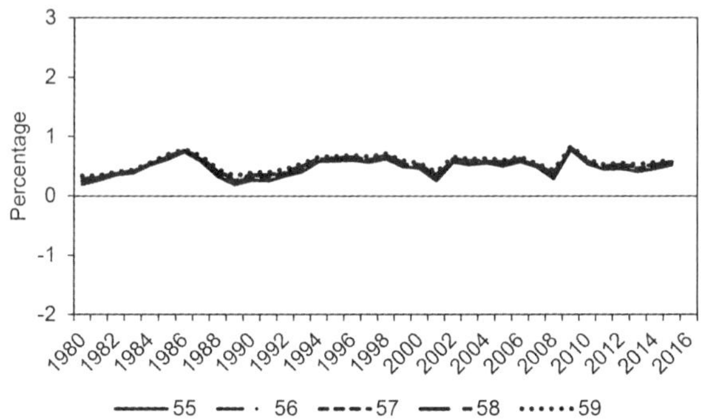

Fig. 1.19 Implicit tax DI, men median earners aged 55–59
Source: Authors' calculations

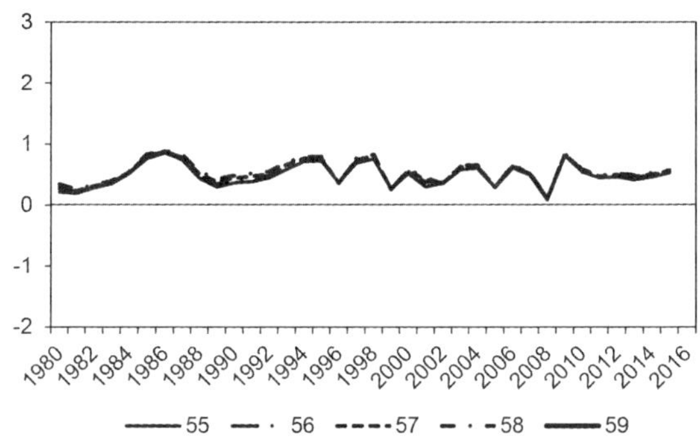

Fig. 1.20 Implicit tax DI, women median earners aged 55–59
Source: Authors' calculations

in pension benefits following the receipt of UI replacement income is now limited. For women, the increase of the OAP SEA also translates into a markedly different incentive pattern similar to the CER ITAX.

Figures 1.19 and 1.20 illustrate the evolution of the DI ITAX. Interestingly, as already noted in section 1.2, there has been little to no change in the DI program, and the statutory incentives to retire have not been impacted beyond the obvious effect of the increase in the SEA for women and the discretionary increases in ceilings for pensionable earnings.[23] As mentioned before, and short of information on implementation rules at the level of the institutions managing the DI system, these incentive measures only capture changes in the laws and leave aside changes that could have arisen because of modified implementation over time.

23. The most notable effect is the important discretionary increase in the ceiling of pensionable earnings in 1981.

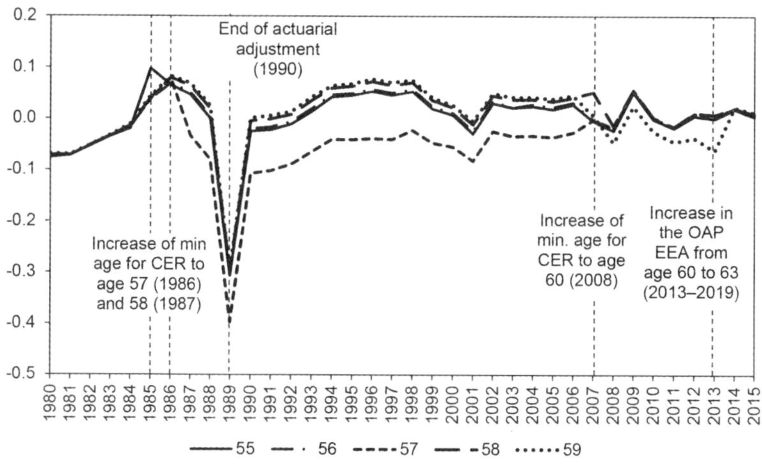

Fig. 1.21 Implicit tax for male median earners by age (55–59)
Source: Authors' calculations

1.4.2 Aggregate Incentives and Employment

To confront the stylized individual incentives with aggregate employment rates, a summary incentive indicator is derived. We rely on the administrative data of figures 1.5 to 1.8 to calculate path-specific weights corresponding to the share of the population on either UI, CER, or DI. The OAP takes the residual weight such that the sum of the weights is equal to one. These weights are obtained by year, age group (55–59 and 60–64), and gender. Finally, incentives are aggregated across income levels.

Figures 1.21 to 1.24 present the results of these aggregate incentive measures for median earners by age, year, and sex and include the major reforms that have influenced them since the 1980s. Aggregate retirement incentives are heavily influenced by the default option—namely, the OAP scheme. This is unsurprising, as this scheme represents the largest weight (see figures 1.5–1.8) and also affects the benefit that is payable for the longest period of time (from EEA or SEA until death). Because of the high participation rate of men in the CER program, it also has a nonnegligible influence on the aggregated ITAX of men for both age groups.

When aggregating across income levels and focusing on changes in retirement incentives over time, very distinct patterns can be observed. Figures 1.25 and 1.26 present the implicit tax for 4 reference years, separated by 10-year intervals each. While reforms during the first few decades have mostly focused on ages 55–59, more recently there is a clear shift toward the 60–64 age group. Results are, however, somewhat surprising: contrary to a general perception of an overall greater reward of longer working lives in recent years, our results show that incentives are actually leaning against longer working lives. Clearly, these results have to be read and interpreted with

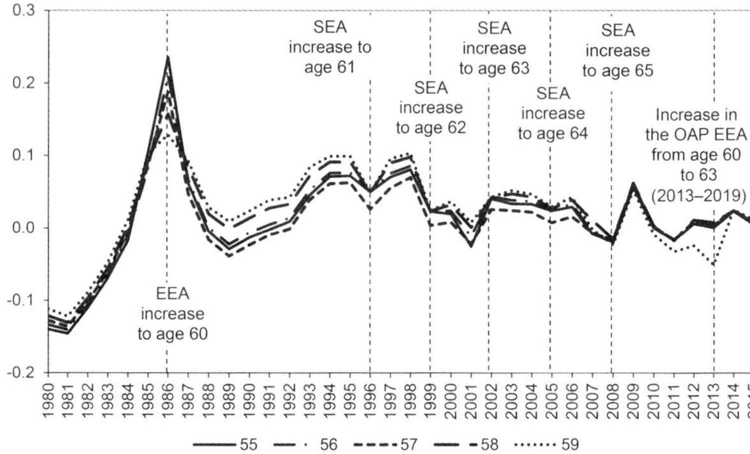

Fig. 1.22 Implicit tax for female median earners by age (55–59)
Source: Authors' calculations

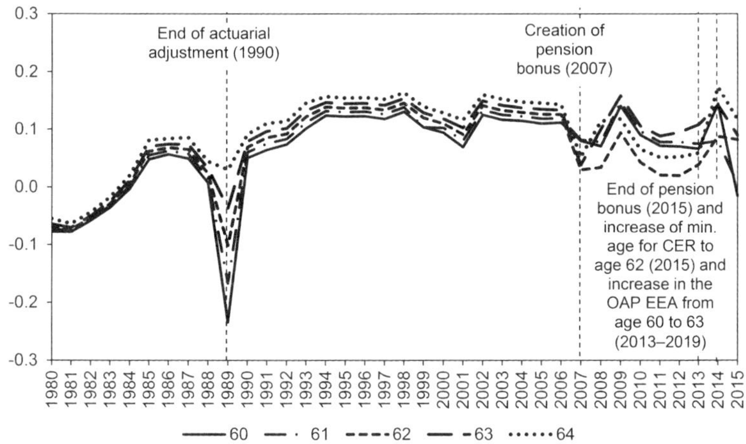

Fig. 1.23 Implicit tax for male median earners by age (60–64)
Source: Authors' calculations

some caution: for example, the numerous special early retirement regimes that existed in addition to the headline CER setup clearly affected the real-world incentives faced by individuals in ways that were sometimes quite different from the headline regime. Also, the weighting of the pathways remains somewhat contentious—with the residual weight on the OAP path likely overemphasizing its relevance.[24]

24. For example, Jousten and Lefebvre (2013) propose an alternative approach to determining the weights of the pathways.

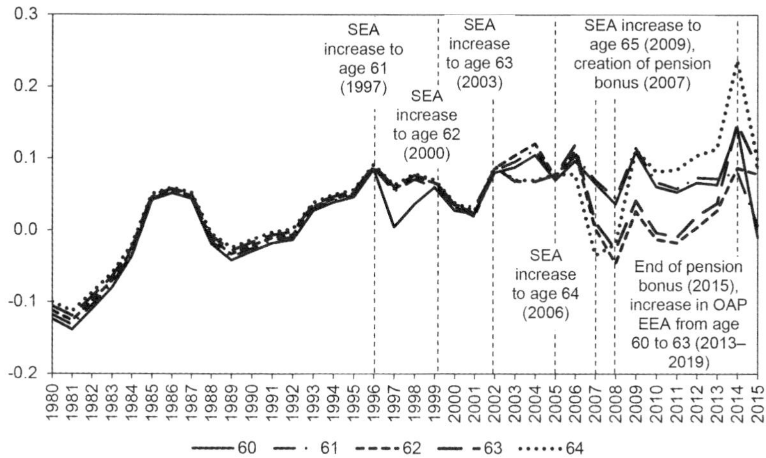

Fig. 1.24 Implicit tax for female median earners by age (60–64)
Source: Authors' calculations

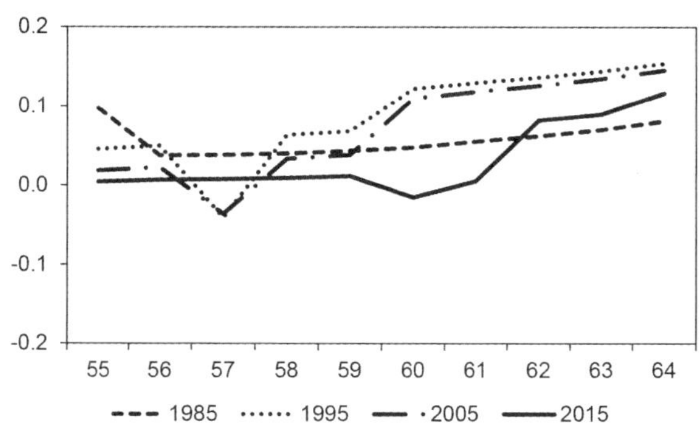

Fig. 1.25 Implicit tax for male median earners by year
Source: Authors' calculations

Similar caution should be applied when interpreting figures 1.27 to 1.30. In these, we relate the average ITAX indicator by age groups 55–59 and 60–64 in a given year to the employment rate of the same age groups in that year. Overall, a negative relationship appears between the employment rate and the ITAX, but not in a very strong manner. Clearly, the averaging across ages and the chosen weighting are likely disputable. However, we believe that even when correcting for some of these concerns (e.g., using a different weighting of exit routes that does not put the default weight on the OAP system), no stronger relation will emerge. This is likely due to the fact that individual incentives faced by real-world Belgian workers are quite substantially different from those of the typical workers we have chosen. The real world is obviously less single, less complete career, with less-stable earnings than our assumptions imply. On the other hand, it is also more

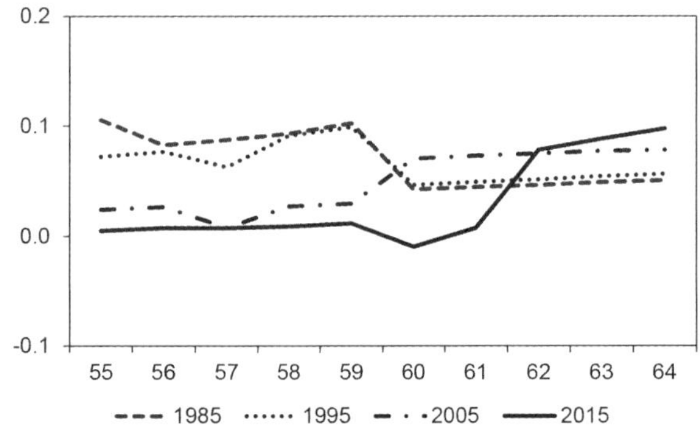

Fig. 1.26 Implicit tax for female median earners by year
Source: Authors' calculations

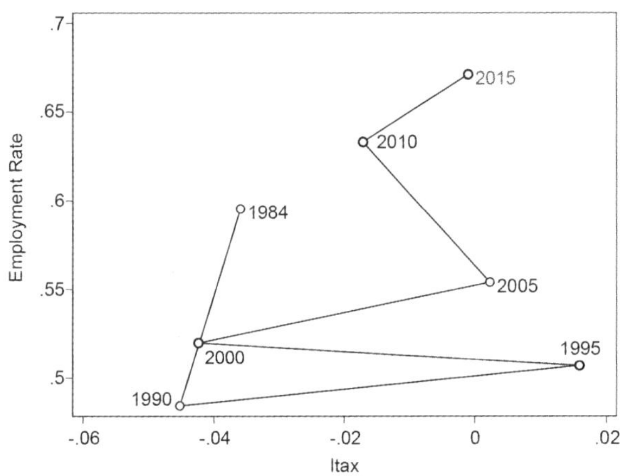

Fig. 1.27 Employment rate and ITAX, men aged 55–59
Source: Authors' calculations and Labour Force Survey

diverse, as employment as defined by the Labor Force Survey also includes civil servants and the self-employed.

1.5 Retirement Incentive: Belgium-Specific Profile

In this section, we present the incentive measures for the OAP for both sexes using the Belgium-specific scenario of earnings as described in section 1.3. In addition to the median earner case, we also report the results of low and high earners, since our assumptions on career length and earnings profiles may have important effects. For example, low income earners often qualify for the receipt of the guaranteed minimum pension, and many

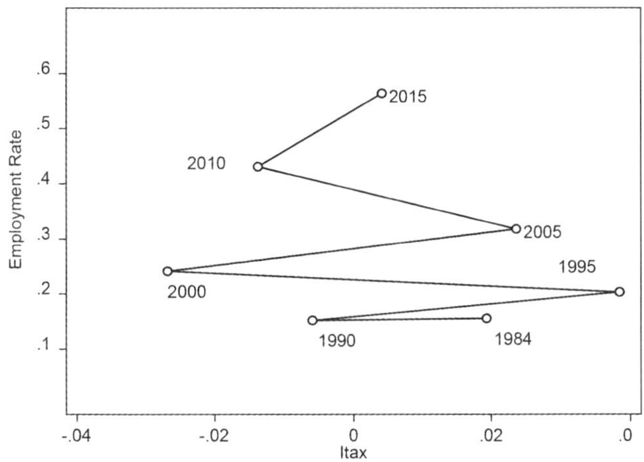

Fig. 1.28 Employment rate and ITAX, women aged 55–59
Source: Authors' calculations and Labour Force Survey

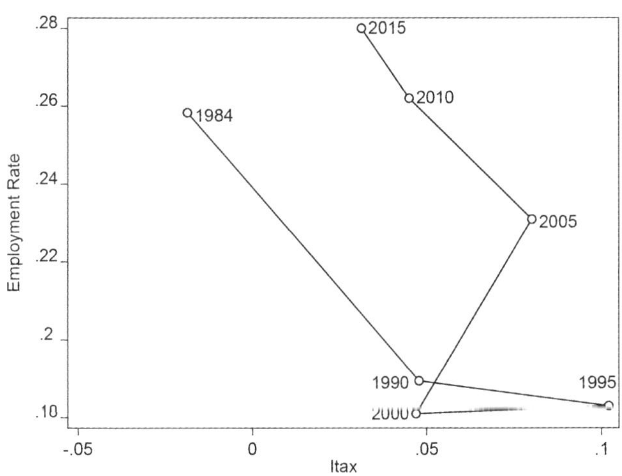

Fig. 1.29 Employment rate and ITAX, men aged 60–64
Source: Authors' calculations and Labour Force Survey

pensionable earnings of the median and high earners are replaced with the ceilings for pensionable income.

Figure 1.31 presents SSW for the OAP scheme by sex for the 60–64 age group for the three selected earnings profiles. The results are somewhat different from what we obtained with the common profile. We will emphasize three main points that explain the differences with real-world relevance in the country.

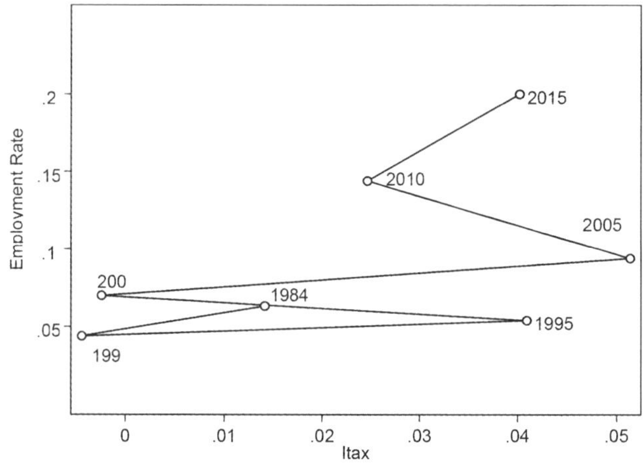

Fig. 1.30 Employment rate and ITAX, women aged 60–64
Source: Authors' calculations and Labour Force Survey

First, the Belgium-specific lifetime earnings profile assumes a continuous and almost constant increase of the wage throughout the career, while the common profile assumes an important increase of the wage in the first years of the career. Since OAP benefits are calculated on the average wage over the entire career, in the Belgium-specific scenario many more years with lower wages are included. In figure 1.31, this translates into lower SSW for all typical workers as compared to the results of the previous section. On the other hand, the use of the differently shaped Belgian earnings profile does not impact the buildup of SSW for low earners, as they are systematically benefiting from the guaranteed minimum pension under both scenarios.

Second, the Belgium-specific profile assumes shorter careers. In this scenario, each category of workers start working at a different age: low-earner men at age 21, low-earner women at age 27, median-earner men at age 25, median-earner women at age 31, high-earner men at age 30, and high-earner women at age 36. Shorter careers are translated into lower lifetime SSW for every type of worker. This is also true for the low earners, for whom the guaranteed minimum pension is adjusted for the length of a career.

Also, because we have assumed shorter careers in the Belgium-specific scenario, workers less often fulfill the career requirements for early retirement even if they reach the EEA. Most notably, the reform that increased the career conditions for early OAP claiming from 20 years in 1997 to 35 in 2005 now directly affects the SSW of low- and median-earning women as well as high earners of both sexes. This reform translates into a decrease in SSW for those who do not reach the career requirements for early retire-

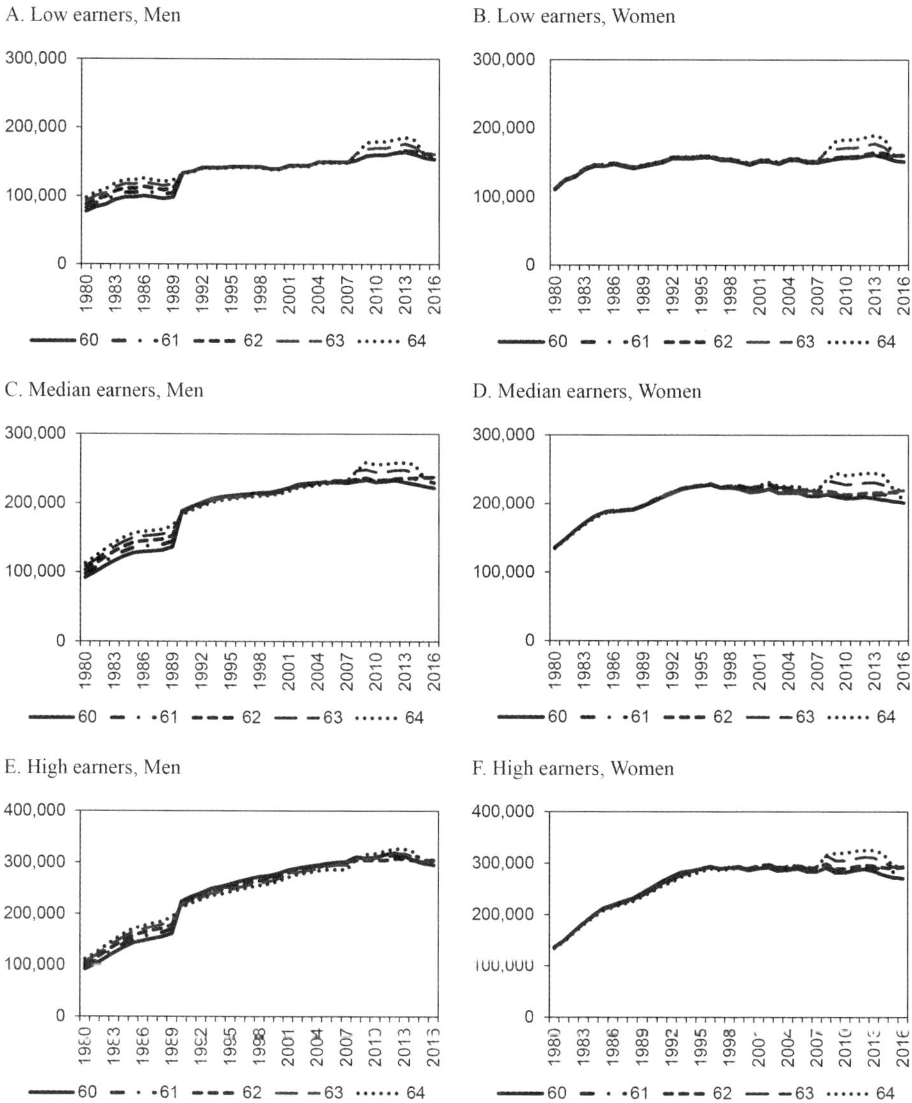

Fig. 1.31 SSW, OAP, ages 60–64
Source: Authors' calculations

ment because each year of potential benefits before the SEA is replaced by a zero.[25] Low- and median-earning men are not directly impacted by this reform, as they have sufficiently long careers to retire early. However, as a result of the general increase of the EEA and the increase in the stringency of the long-career exception, low- and median-earning men also lose access to OAP benefits at age 60 as of the year 2013. Hence their SSW at age 60 starts decreasing as of 2013 as a result of the increase in the EEA to age 60.5. Similarly, their SSW at age 61 starts decreasing in 2015 when the EEA increases to age 61.5.

Third, the impact of the 2007 reform (i.e., pension bonus) on individuals at different earnings levels can easily be identified on these graphs. The effect is comparable in absolute terms across income levels, whatever the earnings level, as the pension bonus is a lump sum amount given for any additional days worked above age 62 or after more than 44 years of career, independently of earnings levels and unaffected by pension ceilings.

Finally, the Belgium-specific scenario also allows for the taxation rules to vary over the years instead of keeping them constant using 2016 tax laws as in the common scenario. The specific impact of taxes in explaining differences in SSW between the common and the Belgium-specific scenarios is only visible for high earners above the age of 60. Given the relative brevity of assumed careers, no OAP pensioner actually has to pay the disability or solidarity contributions on pensions; high-earner OAP pensioners merely start paying a small amount of taxes at older ages from the early 1990s onward; male median-earner OAP pensioners start paying a small amount of taxes as of age 65 starting in 1996; and changes in the tax deduction for replacement income are also mostly visible for high earners only, such as the 1998 decrease of the tax deduction for CER, but remain trivial compared to the impact of eligibility reforms.

The most important change in taxation happened for taxes on personal income, which has become less progressive over the years. Smaller taxes for high earners have increased their wage, which is translated into decreasing ITAX over the years. Once again the impact of such reform is fairly limited and mostly indistinguishable next to the eligibility reforms—hence confirming the general validity of results from the common scenario analysis.

25. More specifically, at age 60, low-earner women have 33 years of career and cannot access early retirement at age 60 from 2004 onward: eligibility is age 61 in 2004 and 62 from 2005 onward. Similarly, median-earner women have a career of 29 years when they reach the age of 60 and do not meet the career requirements for early retirement from 2002 onward. High-earner men have a career of 30 years once they reach the age of 60 and hence do not meet the career requirement for early retirement from 2003 onward. Finally, high-earner women with 24 years of career at age 60 do not meet the career requirement for early retirement from 2000 onward. From 2004 onward, male high earners have to wait until age 63 to retire, and women high earners do not have any access to early retirement from 2005 onward.

1.6 Conclusion

The Belgian labor market has undergone major changes over the last decades. While the country was long characterized by low employment and labor force participation rates of the elderly male population, there was a reversal of this trend as the country witnessed a continuous increase in employment rates of older men from the early 2000s onward. In this chapter, we explore the main institutional changes that have affected the retirement pathways of older workers from the 1980s until today. We simulate the retirement incentives faced by several typical workers, differentiated by age, sex, and level of earnings, for each retirement year between 1980 and 2016, for retirement ages ranging from 55 to 64, and for the four traditional labor force exit pathways. To do so, we use the concept of social security wealth and implicit tax on continued activity, and we rely on two specific scenarios: a common one that is comparable among countries in this volume and a Belgium-specific one.

The results show that the various reforms have affected the incentive to retire through one or another pathway at the microlevel. We find that the tightening of eligibility conditions and the greater variation in the generosity of some benefits translate into important changes in our incentive measures to retire. These, in turn, appear to be correlated, although marginally, with variations in the employment rates at the macrolevel.

However, these results are far from being clear-cut, and the Belgian institutional landscape is likely to be more complex than the stylized view of the *headline* retirement and early retirement schemes we analyze in this chapter. These first results open avenues for further research better taking into account individual heterogeneity and the related social security generosity at the individual level. This would, however, require better information on eligibility of special or derogatory schemes—a nontrivial task. The results also show that there is room for microeconometric analysis exploring the large individual variation in earnings histories and incentives.

References

Dellis, A., R. Desmet, A. Jousten, and S. Perelman. 2004. "Micro-modeling of Retirement in Belgium." In *Social Security Programs and Retirement around the World: Micro-estimation*, edited by J. Gruber and D. Wise, 41–98. Chicago: University of Chicago Press.

Eurostat. 2017. *European Labour Force Survey*. Luxembourg: Eurostat.

INAMI-RIZIV. Various years. *Statistiques des indemnités*. Brussels: INAMI-RIZIV.

Jousten A., M. Lefebvre, and S. Perelman. 2012. "Disability in Belgium: There Is More Than Meets the Eye." In *Social Security Programs and Retirement around the World: Historical Trends in Mortality and Health, Employment, and Disability*

Insurance Participation and Reforms, edited by D. Wise, 251–76. Chicago: University of Chicago Press.

Jousten, A., M. Lefebvre, and S. Perelman. 2016. "Health Status, Disability, and Retirement Incentives in Belgium." In *Social Security Programs and Retirement around the World: Disability Insurance Programs and Retirement*, edited by D. Wise, 179–209. Chicago: University of Chicago Press.

Jousten A., and M. Lefebvre. 2013. "Retirement Incentives in Belgium: Estimations and Simulations Using SHARE Data." *De Economist* 161 (3): 253–76.

Jousten, A., and M. Lefebvre. 2016. "Older Men's Labor Force Participation in Belgium." e-Working Paper University of Liège.

Jousten A., and M. Lefebvre. 2017. "Spousal and Survivor Benefits in Option Value Model of Retirement: An Application to Belgium." *Journal of Pension Economics and Finance* 18 (1): 66–87.

ONEM-RVA. Various years. *Bénéficiaires de l'ONEM*. Brussels: ONEM-RVA.

ONP-RVP. 2005. *Etudes Statistiques*. Brussels: ONP-RVP.

ONP-RVP. Various years. *Statistiques annuelles des bénéficiaires de prestations*. Brussels: ONP-RVP.

Pestieau, P., and J.-P. Stijns. 1999. "Social Security and Retirement in Belgium." In *Social Security and Retirement around the World*, edited by J. Gruber and D. Wise, 37–71. Chicago: University of Chicago Press.

2

Retirement Incentives and Canada's Social Security Programs

Kevin Milligan and Tammy Schirle

2.1 Introduction

The labor force participation rates of older men and women in Canada increased after the mid-1990s, reversing decades of decline. There are several factors that may be driving these trends, including improvements in health and longevity, increasing educational attainment over time, and the greater career attachment of women at older ages (Milligan and Schirle 2018, 2019; Schirle 2008). Several studies have demonstrated the importance of public pension programs and the retirement incentives contained therein (Baker and Benjamin 1999a, 1999b; Au, Crossley, and Schellhorn 2005; Baker, Gruber, and Milligan 2003, 2007; Schirle 2010).

The purpose of this study is to document trends in employment rates over the years 1980–2016 in Canada alongside measures of retirement incentives embodied in Canada's social security system. We begin by providing some Canadian context, describing the trends in older men's and women's participation in the labor force since 1980 and key components of Canada's retirement system. We then describe how we create measures used to summarize retirement incentives. These measures are then used in simulations for three scenarios. In the first, we consider individuals described by the common synthetic environment (in terms of their age-earnings profiles, mortality, and

Kevin Milligan is a professor of economics at the Vancouver School of Economics at the University of British Columbia and a research associate of the National Bureau of Economic Research.

Tammy Schirle is a professor of economics at Wilfrid Laurier University.

This chapter is part of the National Bureau of Economic Research's International Social Security project. We thank the organizers and other country teams for their suggestions. For acknowledgments, sources of research support, and disclosure of the author's or authors' material financial relationships, if any, please see https://www.nber.org/chapters/c14192.ack.

taxation) used throughout this volume. This allows us to understand cross-national differences in public pension policy while putting aside differences in national environments. Second, we consider a scenario where Canadian age-earnings profiles and mortality rates are used but the taxation assumed in the common synthetic environment is maintained. Third, we consider a scenario with a full Canadian environment that also allows the Canadian tax system to be imposed, including changes in taxation over time.

2.2 Labor Force Participation of Older Canadians

In figure 2.1 we present the labor force participation rates for men and women at ages 55–59, 60–64, and 65–69 over the years 1980–2016. Until the mid-1990s, the participation rates of older men declined steadily. For men aged 60–64, participation rates fell 21 percentage points between 1980 and 1996. In the mid-1990s, the trend for older men reverses. For men aged 60–64, 2016 labor force participation rates have nearly reached their 1980 levels. For men aged 65–69, 2016 participation rates (at 32 percent) far exceed those seen in 1980 (at 22 percent). For women, participation rates prior to the mid-1990s follow a very different trend than for men. Among women aged 60–64, participation rates were steady around 25 percent until 1997 and then increase, reaching 49 percent in 2016.

In figure 2.2, we present the trends in participation among men and women aged 60–64 within education groups. Among those with relatively low education (having high school or less, including those with some non-certificate postsecondary education), we see lower labor force participation rates than those with higher education (postsecondary certificates or diplomas or those with a university bachelor's degree or higher). All education groups, however, show the same general trends over time.

2.3 Canada's Social Security Programs

For older Canadians, there are two major components of the social security system that we consider in this study (and are summarized in figures 2.3 and 2.4). First, there are programs designed to guarantee a minimum income for seniors. The main part of this program is Old Age Security (OAS), which provides an old-age pension to all individuals over age 65. A history of contributions is not required. However, individuals must meet residency requirements. A 15 percent clawback of OAS benefits is applied to high individual incomes.[1] The Guaranteed Income Supplement (GIS) is a means-

1. In 2016, the OAS clawback applied to income above CAD $73,756. According to the Office of the Superintendent of Financial Institutions (2017, 24), 6.9 percent of Old Age Security recipients were affected by the OAS clawback in 2016, with 2.2 percent having their benefits reduced to zero.

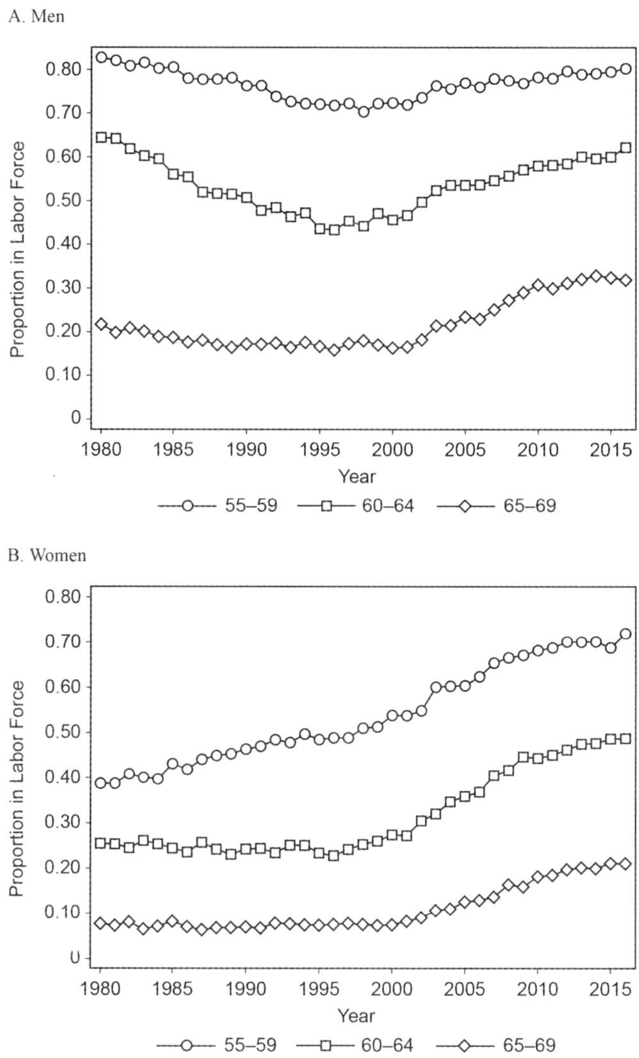

Fig. 2.1 Labor force participation rates by age and gender
Source: Authors' tabulations from the Labour Force Survey

tested benefit for those receiving OAS and is clawed back at a rate of 50 percent for taxable income earned by an individual or their spouse (see Milligan and Schirle 2008, 2014 for details). The allowance, available since 1975, provides additional means-tested benefits for married seniors aged 60–64 whose spouse is an OAS recipient. This means-tested benefit was extended to widows and widowers aged 60–64 in 1985 as a survivors' allowance. There have been few substantial changes to these programs since their introduc-

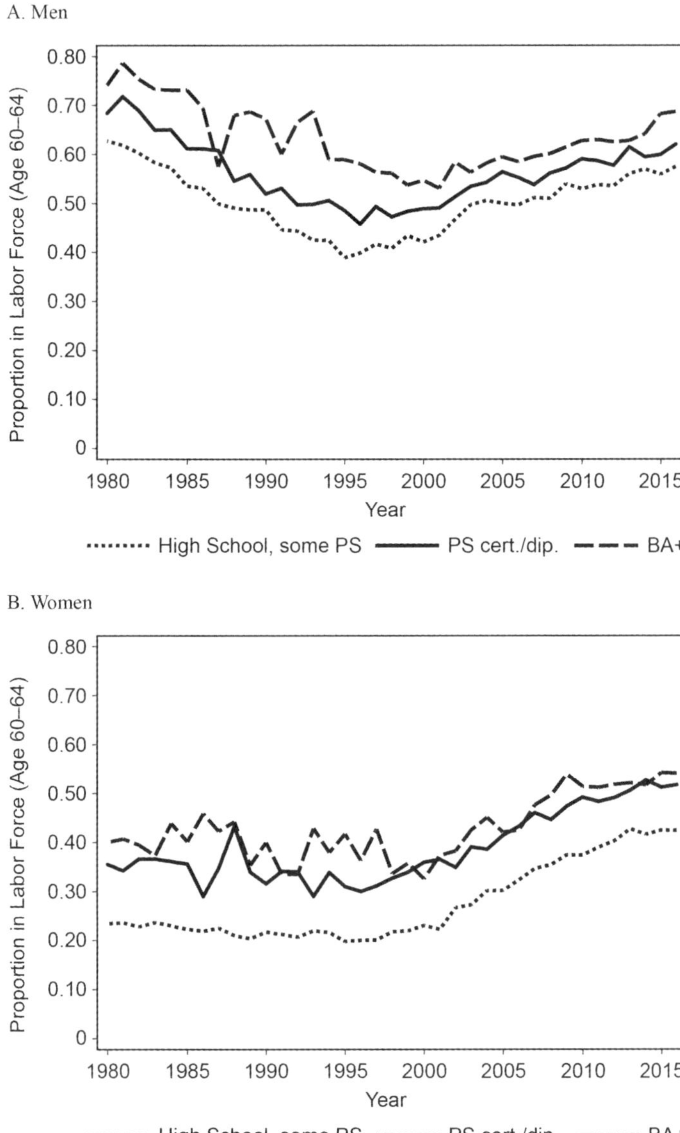

Fig. 2.2 Labor force participation rates by education and gender (ages 60–64)
Source: Authors' tabulations from the Labour Force Survey

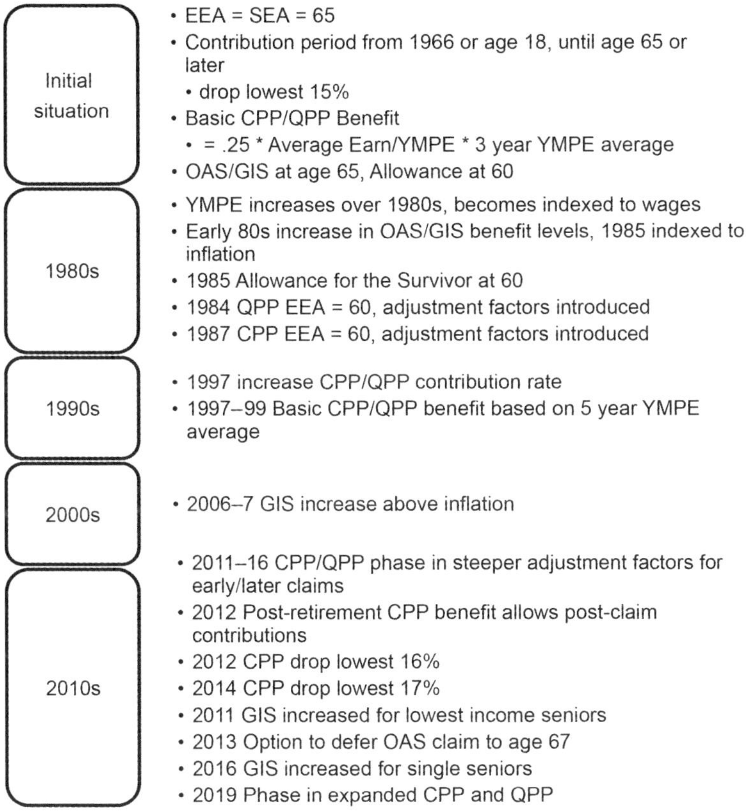

Fig. 2.3 Timeline of reforms to public pensions, 1980–2016

tion. There were slight increases in GIS benefit generosity over the 2000s and 2010s. In 2013, the option to defer OAS payments up to age 70, with an actuarial adjustment factor, was introduced. However, take-up of this option is projected to be low.[2]

The second major component is represented by the public pensions for which pension payments largely depend on an individual's earnings history and contributions: the Canada Pension Plan (CPP) and Quebec Pension Plan (QPP).[3] The CPP and QPP are funded with a payroll tax applied to earnings above a basic exemption and below the year's maximum pension-

2. See the Office of the Superintendent of Financial Institutions (2017, 45). The Chief Actuary projects a medium scenario in which 10 percent of males and 7 percent of females chose to voluntarily defer Old Age Security receipt.

3. The CPP and QPP programs are administered separately but coordinate benefits for individuals who have worked in both Quebec and other Canadian provinces. With few exceptions, the structures of CPP and QPP have been nearly identical.

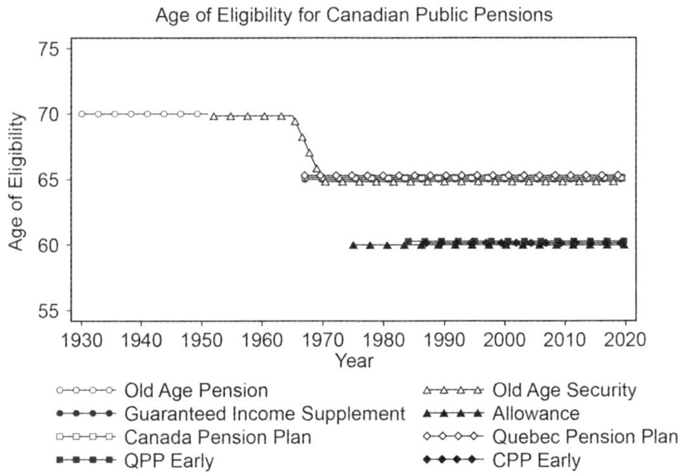

Fig. 2.4 Eligibility ages for retirement income programs
Source: Authors' tabulations

able earnings (YMPE), which was set at \$54,900 and increases with average earnings.

Until 1986, the statutory eligibility age (SEA) for the CPP was 65. In determining the relevant earnings history, earnings since 1966 (or age 18) would be considered as part of the CPP contribution period in the basic (full) annual benefit calculation. From this, individuals could drop up to 15 percent of the lowest earnings from their history before calculating their benefits. The calculation of annual CPP benefits in 1986 or earlier can be summarized as follows:

$$Benefit_t = .25 * \left(\frac{\sum_{j=1}^{N} \max[(Earn_j / YMPE_j), 1]}{N} \right) * \left(\frac{YMPE_t + YMPE_{t-1} + YMPE_{t-2}}{3} \right),$$

where j indexes earnings years included in the contribution period of N years, and the earnings history is updated using a three-year moving average of the YMPE. We highlight from this benefit formula that past and current YMPE thresholds and the length of time since 1966 or age 18 will play an important role in determining the benefits one is eligible for.

The basic benefit formula has changed very little over time. The most substantial change to the CPP occurred in 1987, at which time an early eligibility age (EEA) at age 60 was introduced. (The QPP made this change in 1984.) The basic benefit (for claiming at age 65) remained the same as above;

however, early or later claiming of CPP benefits would result in an adjusted benefit (similar to an actuarial adjustment) by 6 percent per year of delayed claiming. The earlier eligibility age also meant that the contribution period for the purposes of benefit calculation was potentially shorter. For example, if someone left the labor force at age 55 and planned to claim CPP benefits as early as possible, the contribution period would only include earnings (including zeros) until age 60. Before 1987, all zero earnings up to age 65 would have been included as part of the contribution period.

Since 1987, there have been few changes to Canada's public pensions, as summarized in figure 2.3. There have been no changes in eligibility ages for key programs (figure 2.4). In the mid-1990s, a major review of the CPP's sustainability led to an increase in employer and employee contribution rates so that the pension became partially prefunded. At this time there was a small change in the formula so that earnings would be updated using a five-year moving average of the YMPE rather than a three-year moving average.

The next modest change to the CPP benefit formula began in 2011 as new adjustment factors were introduced (see Laurin, Milligan, and Schirle 2012). When fully phased in for 2016, there is a 7.2 percent reduction in annual benefits for every year the person claims CPP benefits before age 65 and an 8.4 percent increase in annual benefits for every year the person claims CPP benefits after age 65. Other changes to social security programs do not substantially change the way benefits are determined, although there is some increase in generosity for the lowest income seniors.

In figure 2.5 we summarize the participation of men (figure 2.5a) and the average benefits received by participants from each program (figure 2.5b), with analogous figures for women as well (figures 2.5c and 2.5d). The participation rates of men in Canada's OAS and GIS programs (figure 2.5a) have always been near 100 percent, especially by age 70. Delays in claiming OAS between ages 65 and 69 reflect a need to apply for the benefit (as opposed to autoenrollment) prior to 2013. The average OAS and GIS benefits (figure 2.5b) have declined over time despite maximum benefits remaining fairly constant (or becoming more generous) over time. This will reflect reduced reliance over time on GIS benefits as the private retirement income and earnings of individuals age 65 and over increase over time. The participation of men in the CPP and the QPP increased over the 1980s and early 1990s, as did average benefits received, as individuals would have longer contribution periods since 1966. We see very few changes for men after the mid-1990s.

For women, however, we see important changes in the CPP and the QPP over time, as more women have the work histories required to qualify for benefits. The trends in CPP/QPP participation and average benefits for women in figures 2.5c and 2.5d largely reflect increases in women's labor force participation and career development at younger ages.

For most Canadians, there is but one pathway to retirement. The CPP

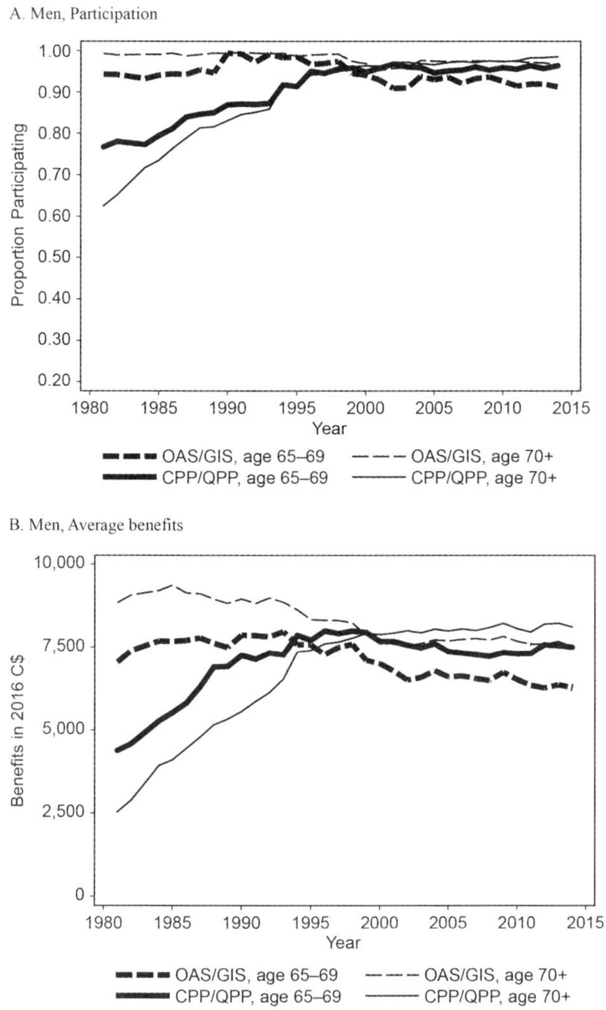

Fig. 2.5 CPP/QPP and OAS/GIS receipt and average benefits by gender

Source: Authors' tabulations from the Survey of Consumer Finances, Survey of Labour and Income Dynamics, and the Canadian Income Survey

and the QPP offer the only social security program benefits that depend on an individual's work history and offer monthly benefits for the rest of a person's life. Claiming of the CPP and the QPP does not require leaving employment permanently. There is a long-term disability benefit available (CPP-Disability) to individuals unable to work before age 65; however, at age 65 a person will lose their CPP-Disability benefit and be moved into the CPP retirement benefits. As Milligan and Schirle (2016) show, the CPP-Disability program does not create incentives distinct from the CPP retirement pro-

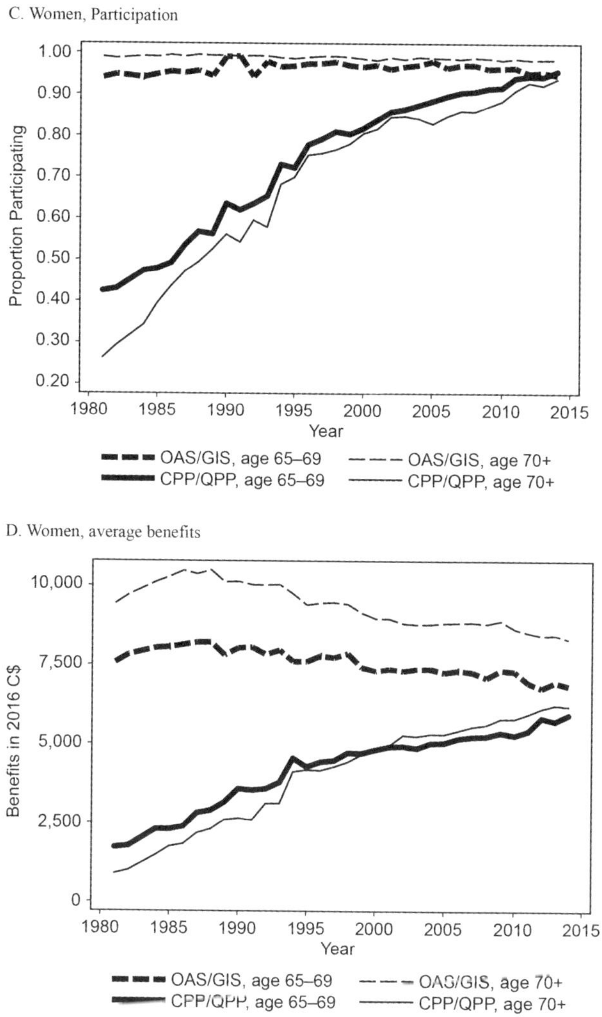

Fig. 2.5 (cont.)

gram. Other programs that supplement income tend to be short term or provide very low benefits. For example, Canada's Employment Insurance program provides income (with up to 55 percent replacement) for several months to individuals who are laid off from their jobs while they search for new employment. This would not cover someone who quit their job or was not actively searching for work. Provincial social assistance programs provide small means-tested (and often asset-tested) benefits, with benefit amounts depending on family status and the ability to work. In this context, the main path to retirement for us to consider is a full departure from the labor force, claiming CPP and QPP benefits as soon as one reaches the early eligibility age.

2.4 Measuring Incentives in the Canadian System

2.4.1 Incentives Measures

In what follows, we create several measures to summarize the evolution of Canada's social security programs for older individuals and the incentives to leave the labor force embodied therein. The measures created here are common to the literature and are structured similarly to those in Milligan and Schirle (2008). To begin, we evaluate the benefits people would expect to receive from social security programs for the rest of their lives, as those benefits depend on the policy environment in place at the time they are forming expectations, the timing of their departure from the labor force, and the time at which they initiate a claim for social security benefits.

As a first measure, we consider the extent to which income from the social security programs will replace career earnings. To do this, we create a replacement rate represented by

$$RR_{l|R} = \frac{B_{71|l,R}}{Earn_{55}},$$

where l denotes the legal situation (year) when retirement plans are being formed, R denotes the age at which the person plans to leave the labor force (and claim benefits as soon as possible), and the benefits (B) net of tax received at 71 are evaluated relative to the earnings ($Earn$) net of tax at age 55 that the individual could have earned.

To summarize the value of benefits received from the social security programs over an individual's lifetime, we construct a social security wealth (SSW) measure corresponding to the measures used in other chapters of this volume. This is given by

$$SSW_{S,l}(R) = \sum_{t=R}^{T} B_{t,k,l}(R) \cdot \sigma_{S,t} \cdot \beta^{t-S} - \sum_{t=S}^{R-1} c_{t,l} \cdot Y_t \cdot \sigma_{S,t} \cdot \beta^{t-S}.$$

Here, the individual, planning at age S and given the legal environment in year l, will consider the social security contributions they will continue to make while working between ages S and $R - 1$ (stated here as a proportion c of earnings Y). They will also consider the net benefits (B, after tax) they receive while retired from ages R to their last age T. The individual discounts future benefits using a discount rate r, where $\beta = (1/1 + r)$ and for their probability of survival to age t conditional on having lived until age S.

Postponing labor force departure (R) reduces SSW to the extent the individual gives up a year of benefits (B_t) from the CPP (and potentially the GIS) and pays contributions (c) if they continue working. Postponing labor force departure (R) may increase SSW, however, if a later R results in higher annual benefits in later years. In the Canadian system, the mechanisms affecting the impact of delayed retirement on SSW are the actuarial adjustment applied to CPP benefits when retirement is delayed (since 1987 and steepened in recent years) and an improved average earnings in the CPP benefit formula as more zero- and low-earnings periods can be removed from the earnings average. Important to keep in mind, however, is that for many low-income seniors, the boost from the CPP actuarial adjustment is dampened because any extra benefits from the CPP due to delayed claiming will reduce benefits provided by the means-tested GIS program.

To consider the incentives Canadians have to leave the labor market and claim CPP benefits, we can evaluate the extent to which SSW increases or decreases by delaying labor market departure (R) for one year—known as a one-year accrual (ACC). We define the implicit tax on continued work for one more year after age R as

$$ITAX_{l,R} = -\frac{ACC_{l,R}}{Y^{Net}},$$

where Y^{Net} represents the income that could be earned during the year of delayed labor force departure. When the implicit tax is negative, SSW can be gained with delayed labor force departure and should be viewed as a reward for continued work. A positive implicit tax, however, indicates a penalty for continued work.

2.4.2 Environments and Assumptions

2.4.2.1 General Assumptions

In mapping out the incentives and disincentives for continued work in Canada, we want to consider different types of individuals. This allows us to understand the heterogeneity of incentives across the Canadian population. Within each stylized environment described below, we consider individuals with low, medium, and high age-earnings profiles. Given the means-tested benefits available in Canada's social security programs, we will need to assume individuals either have no private retirement income (such as income from an employer-sponsored pension plan) or have some income. In the latter case, we assume private retirement income replaces 50 percent of earnings in the last year of work.

We also consider the situation of a single man, a single woman, or a couple (headed by a man or a woman). Here, men and women have different age-earnings profiles and different survival probabilities. All individuals discount the future at a rate $r = 0.03$. For couples, we assume a female spouse is three years younger than her male spouse and the spouses have the same earnings level (low, medium, or high). In this study, we do not consider couples' joint decision-making process. Rather, an individual will assess their own labor force departure and hold constant the decision of their spouse. The spouse is assumed to leave the labor force at age 65 and immediately claim benefits from social security programs.

We apply different scenarios for earnings histories and for taxes. Some of these scenarios use earnings, taxes, or mortality that are common across the countries in this volume, while others use Canada-specific earnings and taxes. These calculations reveal what aspects of retirement incentives are driven by Canada-specific rules rather than Canadian trends in earnings, taxes, or mortality.

We consider these stylized individuals in the legal environment from 1980 to 2016, as defined in the Canada Pension Plan Act and Old Age Security Act in force at the time. Planning is done from the perspective of a 55-year-old who is considering labor force departure between ages 55 and 69. Given the nature of potential retirement paths in Canada, we assume individuals will claim CPP benefits as soon as possible after leaving the labor force. We also assume individuals will apply for OAS, GIS, and other means-tested benefits as soon as they reach the first age of eligibility.

2.4.2.2 *Common Synthetic Environment*

Individuals described in this environment have earnings profiles that represent low, medium, and high skills groups based on data from the US, Germany, and Italy (as described in chapter 5 of this volume). The profiles do not change over time. For time-invariant common survival rates of men and women, an average of the EU-28 countries in Eurostat is used and adjusted to reflect differentials in life expectancy across skill groups. Canadian payroll taxes are based on the Organisation for Economic Co-operation and Development (OECD) tax database (OECD 2018) and refer to all income taxes and employee and employer social security contributions. For Canada, the income tax rates applied to low, medium, and high skill groups are 26.9 percent, 31.7 percent, and 33.3 percent, respectively, and contribution rates are 11.6 percent, 11.8 percent, and 9.7 percent, respectively. We recognize the contribution rates are higher than contribution rates for the CPP (at 9.9 percent of earnings up to the YMPE in 2016), reflecting the inclusion of employment insurance premiums in the OECD estimates.

2.4.2.3 *Canadian Environment with OECD Tax*

Individuals described in this environment have age-earnings profiles that represent low, medium, and high educated groups based on the 2014 Canadian Income Survey. *Low educated* represents individuals who have completed high school or less and includes those with some postsecondary training without a diploma or certificate. *Medium educated* represents individuals with a postsecondary diploma or certificate less than a bachelor's degree. *High educated* represents those with a bachelor's degree or more education. Age- and year-specific survival probabilities of men and women are based on data from the Human Mortality Database (2015). The survival probabilities are not adjusted to account for longevity differences across education groups. In this environment, we continue to use the OECD tax estimates from the common synthetic environment. Simulations from this environment will demonstrate how different earnings profiles and survival probabilities may affect our estimates of incentives to continue work without adding variation that comes from tax provisions.

2.4.2.4 *Canadian Environment with Canadian Taxes*

In this environment, we use the same age-earnings profiles and survival probabilities as described above for the Canadian environment. For taxes (and CPP contributions), we calculate tax liability using the Canadian Tax and Credit Simulator (CTaCS; Milligan 2016). For each year from 1980 to 2016, most aspects of the federal and provincial income tax environment are accounted for in the CTaCS program. We have assumed that the individuals in our simulations live in the province of Ontario. Notably, apart from some relatively small tax credits that change over time, the Canadian income tax system taxes income from earnings, employer-sponsored pensions, the CPP, and OAS at the same rates. Among the programs we consider, only the means-tested benefits (GIS and allowance) are not subject to income tax. Comparing results from this set of simulations to those in the Canadian environment with time-invariant OECD taxes will help demonstrate the influence of the income tax system in forming incentives to continue working.

2.5 Results

In the following sections, we present the results of the simulations used to describe the incentives to continue working in Canada. We focus our attention on a medium earner who does not have private retirement income, but we offer several other examples to demonstrate the importance of various social security program parameters.

2.5.1 Common Synthetic Environment

In figure 2.6, we present the income replacement rates for medium-education couples (with a female head) that do not have a private retirement income. Each of the lines represents the replacement rate that results when leaving the labor force at ages 55–69.

Consider first the replacement rates in figure 2.6, based on the social security programs in 1986 or early. Recall that before 1987, age 65 was the earliest age at which a person could claim CPP benefits. For those considering retirement options in 1986 or earlier, each additional year of work between ages 55 and 65 can be used to replace a zero in their earnings history with some positive earnings, thereby raising their average earnings in their benefit

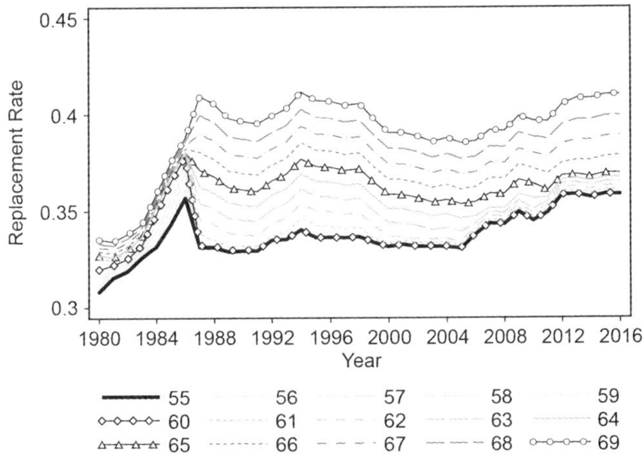

Fig. 2.6 Replacement rates in the common environment, medium-education couples

Note: Replacement rates are measured as the benefits at age 71 as a portion of earnings at age 55. Couples are assumed to have no private retirement savings.

Source: Authors' tabulations

calculation and their replacement rate. For delayed labor force departure after age 65, more low-earnings years can be removed from the contribution period when estimating average earnings, further raising the replacement rate when individuals continue working.

In 1987, the option of early claiming at age 60 is introduced, as are the adjustment factors for earlier or later CPP claims. Here, the lines representing replacement rates for each age of labor force departure between 60 and 69 fan out, illustrating the importance of adjustment factors.

After early take-up of the CPP at age 60 is introduced, those who retire between ages 55 and 59 only need be concerned with zeros in their history before claiming CPP benefits at age 60. In our example, the 55-year-old who is planning in 1987 will have a 25-year contribution window to consider (and be allowed to drop nearly 4 years from their history). Notice this drop-out provision allows for more years to be dropped with each policy year. A 55-year-old who is planning in 2016 will have a 42-year history to consider (if taking up benefits at age 60), allowing them to drop out 6.3 years of low earnings before finding average earnings. Continued work between ages 55 and 59 now has a lower (or zero) payoff in terms of this replacement rate.

There are important interactions with the GIS clawbacks that can be seen in figure 2.6. In the policy year 2016, we see very small gains in the replacement rate when labor force departure is delayed between ages 60 and 65 and much larger gains for later continued work. With delayed labor force departure, individuals may gain benefits in terms of higher average earnings and through the application of the adjustment factors. However, when the female spouse is initiating CPP benefits between ages 60 and 65, those benefits will be relatively low in magnitude, and the couple will be eligible for the GIS after age 65. For every dollar they gain in CPP payments for delayed claiming, they will lose 50 cents of their eventual GIS payment. When retiring at ages over 65, the couple's CPP income is high enough that they are no longer eligible for the GIS. As such, by delaying their benefit claim, they will enjoy the full adjustment of CPP benefits without GIS clawbacks. Note that in the mid-1990s, the couple phases out of GIS eligibility at much earlier claiming ages so that there are larger increases in replacement rates for delayed benefit claiming than in 2016.

In figure 2.7, we present similar estimates for single men (a) and single women (b). Overall, the patterns are quite similar. Though difficult to see in the graphs, the differences in replacement rates increase slightly between ages 60 and 69 due to the introduction of steeper actuarial adjustments in 2011 (which also applied to couples in figure 2.6). Replacement rates tend to be lower for single men than couples and highest for single women, which in part reflects the maximum benefits available from social security programs relative to each type's earnings while working. Over the period considered, single men and single women will qualify for GIS benefits at each age of labor force departure, with the exception of single men at age 69 in some years. In figure 2.7a, for example, for single men considering retirement in 2015, there is a jump in replacement rates between ages 68 and 69. Similar to our couples in figure 2.6, this is because the additional CPP benefits received by continuing to work one more year make the individual ineligible for GIS benefits.

Most of the differences across individuals with respect to their replacement rates will reflect differences in average earnings over one's lifetime and differences in their incomes in retirement, which determines their eligibility for the GIS. Figure 2.8 is intended to demonstrate this. We offer two further examples, with (a) a single man who had high earnings and enters retirement with a private retirement income and (b) a single man who had low earnings and no private retirement income. In the first case of the high earner, there is more to gain over age with respect to the replacement rates because this person is not eligible for the GIS at any point. The replacement rates are relatively low because their high career earnings far exceeded the upper threshold for earnings that are covered by the CPP, and OAS benefits are a fixed amount. For a lower earner (figure 2.8b), the replacement rate is much higher, but the low earner has less to gain when delaying retirement because any adjustment to CPP benefits is countered with a reduction in GIS benefits.

In figure 2.9, we present the SSW estimated in the common environment for medium-education couples (a), single men, (b) and single women (c). For a couple headed by a female (so that we are considering the choice of when the woman stops working and claims benefits), before 1987 there is

A. Men

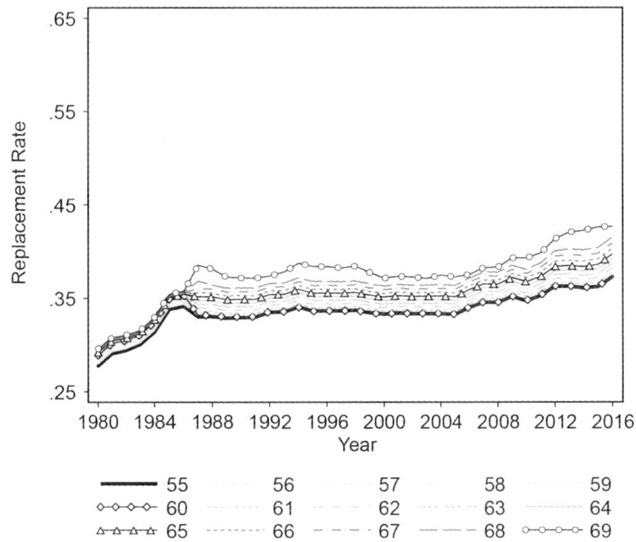

B. Women

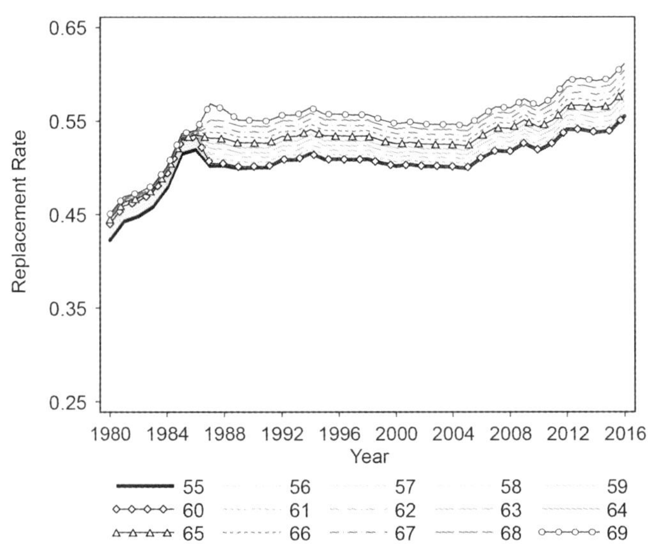

Fig. 2.7 Replacement rates in the common environment, medium-education singles

Note: Replacement rates are measured as the benefits at age 71 as a portion of earnings at age 55. Individuals are assumed to have no private retirement savings.

A. High education, with private retirement income

B. Low education, no private retirement income

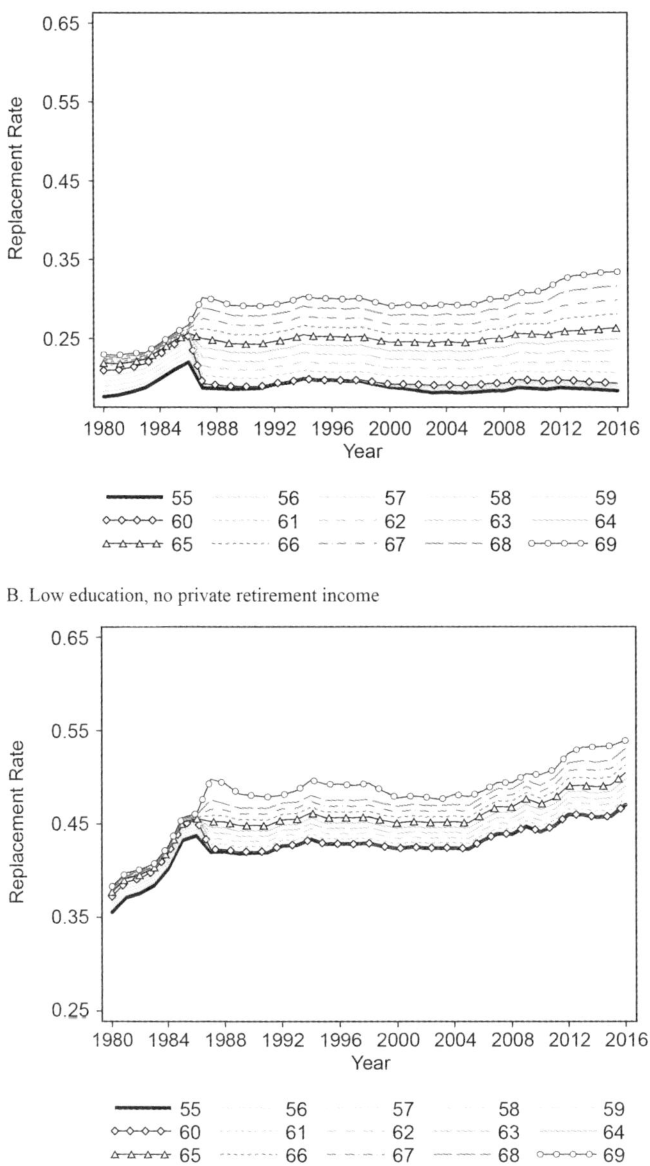

Fig. 2.8 Replacement rates in the common environment, single men
Source: Authors' tabulations

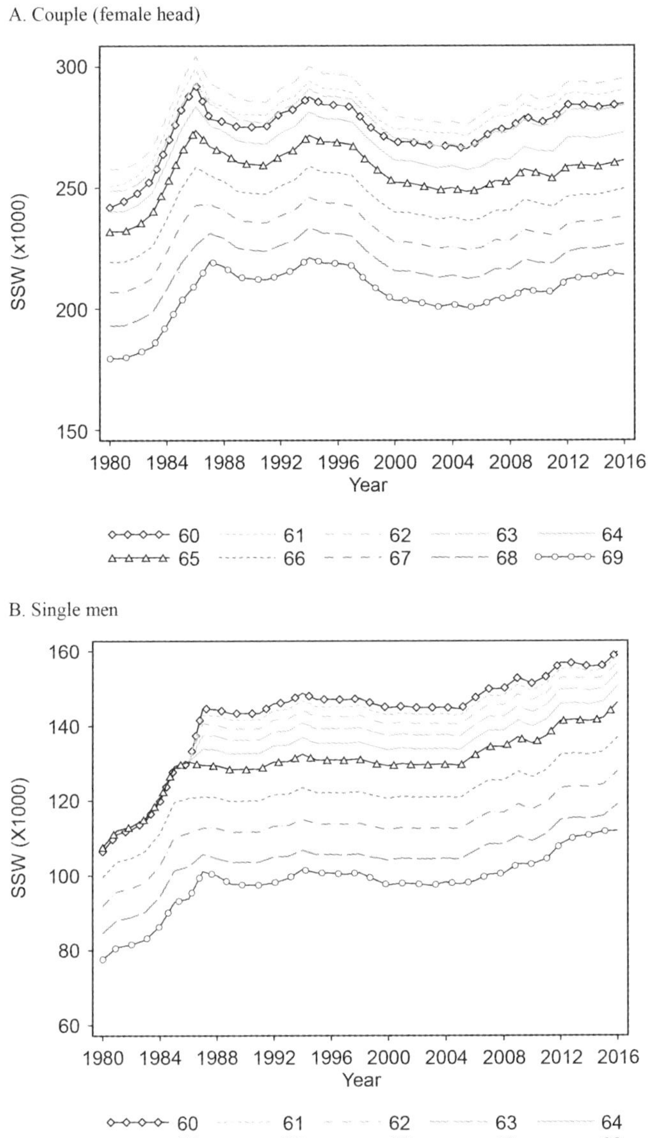

Fig. 2.9 Social security wealth in the common environment, medium education

Note: Medium education and no private retirement income are assumed.

Source: Authors' tabulations

C. Single women

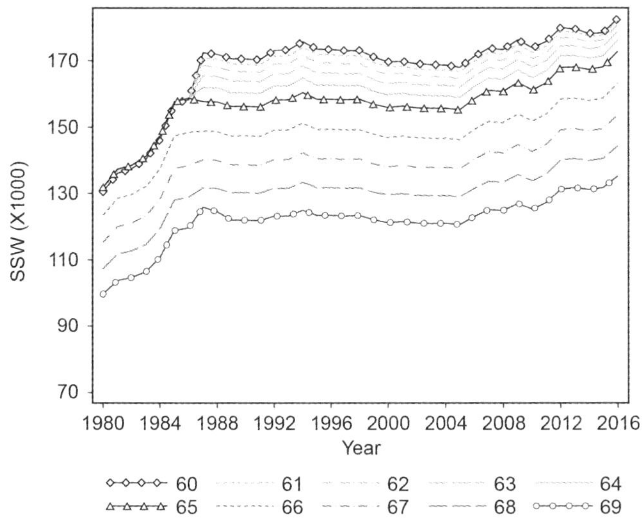

Fig. 2.9 (cont.)

no increase in SSW for continued work between the ages of 60 and 64. This is primarily because there are no actuarial adjustments or changes to the assessed contribution period when labor force departure is delayed. After age 65, the couple gives up a year of CPP benefits if they delay claiming and are not adequately rewarded in terms of a higher CPP benefit to compensate them for the year of lost benefits. As such, SSW declines after age 65.

After 1987, among couples (in figure 2.9a), there are slight increases in SSW for delayed retirement until age 62. After that, the additional benefits provided for delayed retirement are inadequate to compensate for the year of lost benefits. SSW falls with delayed retirement thereafter. We note the pattern is similar but slightly different for a couple headed by a male (not shown here). From this perspective, with different joint survival probabilities and the continuation of the younger spouse to work until age 65, SSW increases with continued work until the male head reaches age 65 and then declines for any later retirement.

For singles (figures 2.9a and 2.9b), the overall patterns are similar except that (after 1987) we can clearly see that SSW declines steadily after age 60. Note the larger declines in SSW after age 65 than before age 65. This difference results from the fact that delayed benefit claiming before age 65 requires foregoing a year of CPP benefits. Delayed benefit claiming after age 65, with continued earnings, will require foregoing a year of CPP benefits and a year of GIS benefits.

In figure 2.10, we present the one-year accrual of SSW that corresponds

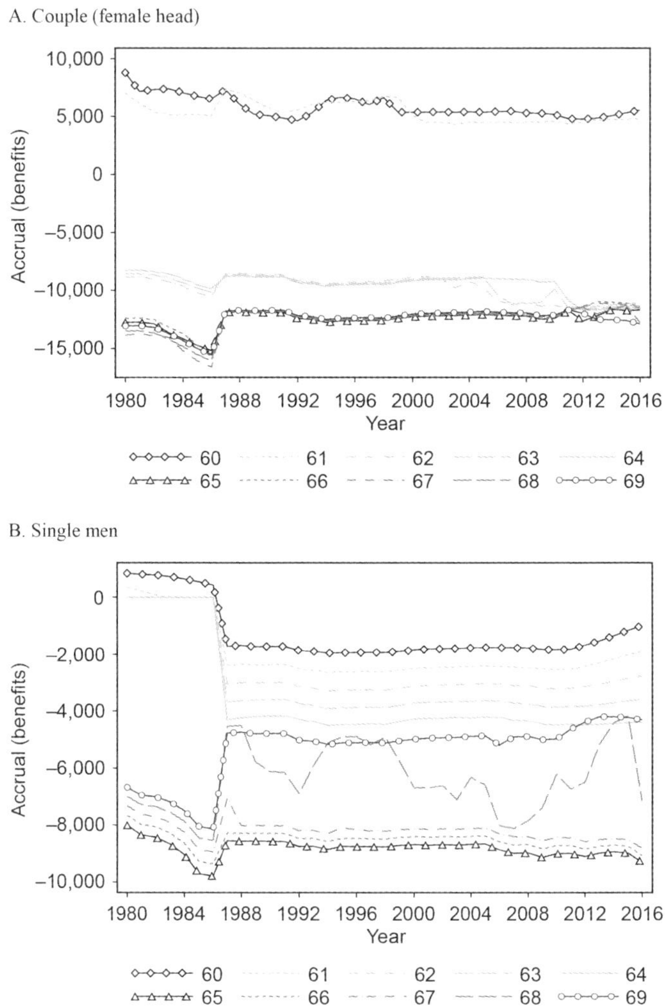

Fig. 2.10 One-year accrual in the common environment, medium education
Source: Authors' tabulations

to each of the panels in figure 2.9. Figure 2.10b, representing the accruals of single men makes the importance of GIS benefits clearer. Here, from ages 60 to 64 we see a steady negative accrual, representing the loss in CPP benefits for each year of continued work. At age 65, the negative accrual jumps downward, representing the additional loss of GIS benefits. With each year of continued work after age 65, there are smaller and smaller amounts of GIS benefits to forego, since additional CPP benefit amounts for delayed claiming will reduce the GIS benefits the man was eligible for.

C. Single women

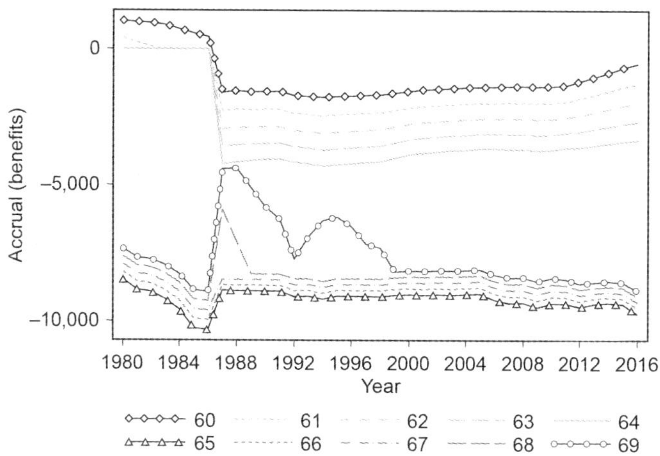

Fig. 2.10 (cont.)

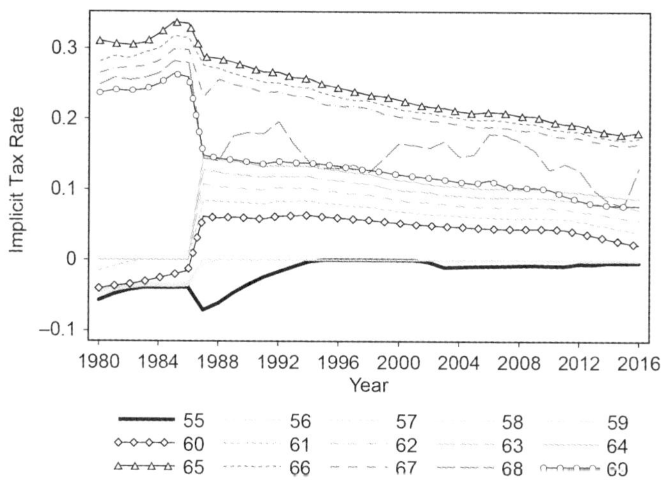

Fig. 2.11 Implicit tax rates in the common environment, medium-educated single men

Source: Authors' tabulations

In figure 2.11, we present the corresponding implicit tax rates for a single man, representing the accruals in figure 2.10b relative to the earnings a person could have if they continued to work an additional year. We repeat these in figure 2.12 for a single man by age and select years. The importance of policy parameters changing over time is made slightly clearer here. In 1980 (figure 2.12), implicit tax on continued work is negative (or zero) until

Fig. 2.12 Implicit tax rates by age, select years, medium-educated single men
Source: Authors' tabulations

age 65, when individuals are first eligible. Over these ages in 1980, only the opportunity to replace years of zero earnings in their contribution period will create incentives to continue working. After age 65, they lose years of CPP benefits with no actuarial adjustment for any years of continued work. After 1987, the loss of CPP benefits for continued work after age 60 results in a positive implicit tax on work that jumps at age 65 as individuals give up CPP and GIS benefits. The small changes in CPP policy parameters after 1987 have nudged the system toward being more neutral to continued work at older ages.

2.5.2 Canadian Environments

We repeat the simulations using the Canadian environment (with age-earnings profiles and survival rates based on Canadian data) in the case where (a) we continue to use a time-invariant approximation to the tax rate using the OECD tax database and (b) we allow taxes to change over time and reflect existing tax policy at the time planning takes place.

The resulting replacement rates are provided for single men with medium career earnings in figure 2.13. When compared to rates presented for the common environment (in figure 2.7a), the profile of replacement rates over time and across potential ages for labor force departure is nearly identical in the Canadian environment with OECD taxes (figure 2.13a). When we introduce the Canadian tax system (figure 2.13b), the general shape of the replacement rates profile remains the same. However, replacement rates generally appear higher, suggesting the OECD tax rates do not adequately reflect the progressivity of the Canadian tax system. Notably, Ontario's provincial and Canada's federal tax calculations include a substantial

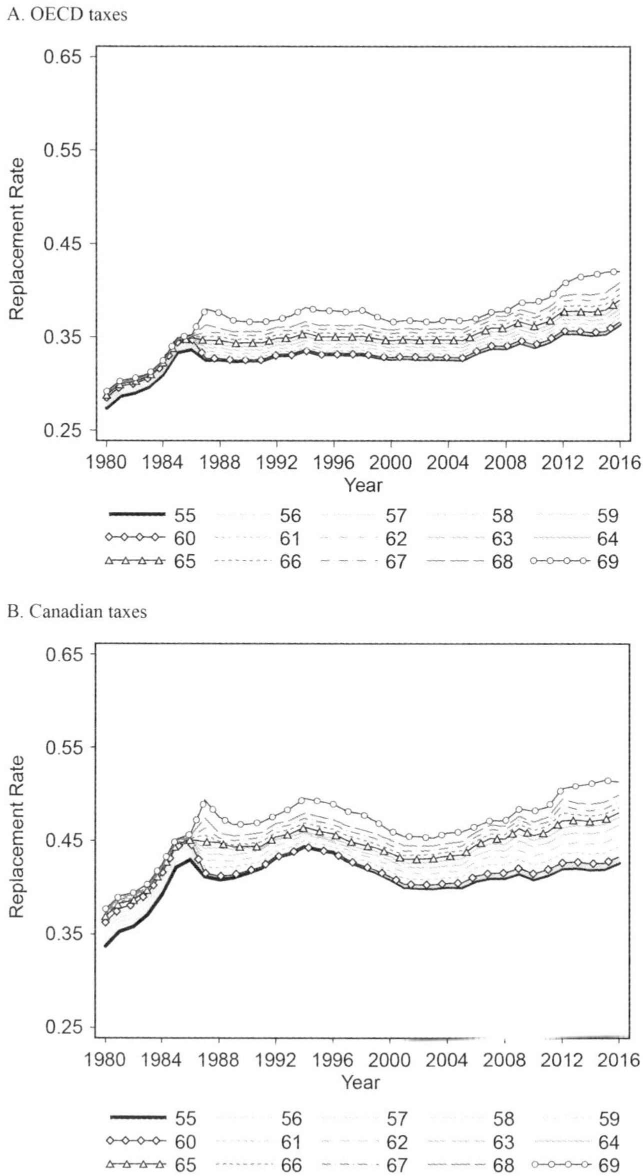

Fig. 2.13 Replacement rates in the Canadian environment, single male

Note: Medium education and no private retirement income assumed.

Source: Authors' tabulations

nonrefundable tax credit for any individuals over the age of 65, effectively exempting a large part of income at older ages from the tax system. In this example, there also appear (since 1987) slightly larger increases in replacement rates with each age of continued work between ages 60 and 64 when representing the Canadian tax system. In part, this will reflect a larger part of benefits received at older ages coming from the nontaxable GIS program rather than taxable CPP and OAS benefits. For those benefits that are taxable, additional CPP income will enter brackets in which higher (positive) tax rates are applied. As such, the increase in replacement rates for labor force departure after age 64 in this example is smaller.

The corresponding social security wealth and implicit tax rates for a single man in the Canadian environment are presented in figures 2.14 and 2.15. Both examples in figures 2.14a and 2.14b reinforce the point that the loss of a year's CPP benefits associated with continued work is not balanced by the increase in annual benefits received over future years. Differences between figures 2.14a and 2.14b illustrate the importance of accounting for taxation. We noted that as we move toward 2016, the amount of SSW lost due to a year of continued work between ages 60 and 63 falls. We align this with large expansions of the nonrefundable tax credit associated with income over age 65 so that any gains in annual benefits received over one's lifetime are made more valuable relative to the year of lost benefits for continued work at these earlier ages.

2.6 Implicit Tax Rates and Employment Rates

The broader goal of this study is to develop a better understanding of the decisions to remain employed, or not, at older ages as those decisions relate to parameters of our social security programs. In this section, we relate the implicit tax rates that result from our simulated Canadian environment with Canadian taxes to observed employment rates over the 1980–2016 period. In figure 2.16, we present this relationship between the employment rates of men (figure 2.16a) and women (figure 2.16b) by education and five-year age group and the average implicit tax rates we estimate for single men and single women within each corresponding age and education group.

For both men and women, there is a clear negative relationship between the employment rates at older ages and the implicit tax rates on continued work—when we see higher tax rates, we see lower employment rates. Much of this relationship, however, characterizes differences across education groups, reflecting differences in lifetime earnings: those with the lowest lifetime earnings generally have higher implicit tax rates. Moreover, older groups who tend to have higher implicit tax rates on continued work would generally have lower employment rates given their health and preferences for leisure. However, even within groups, there is some indication of a negative

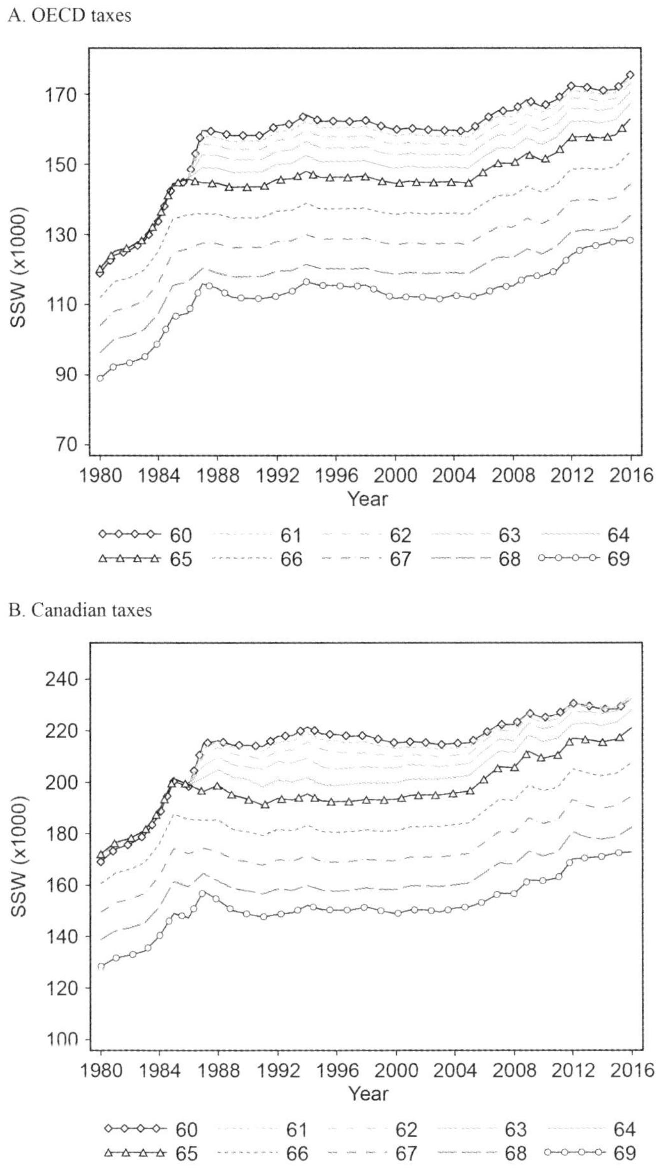

Fig. 2.14 SSW in the Canadian environment, single male

Source: Authors' tabulations

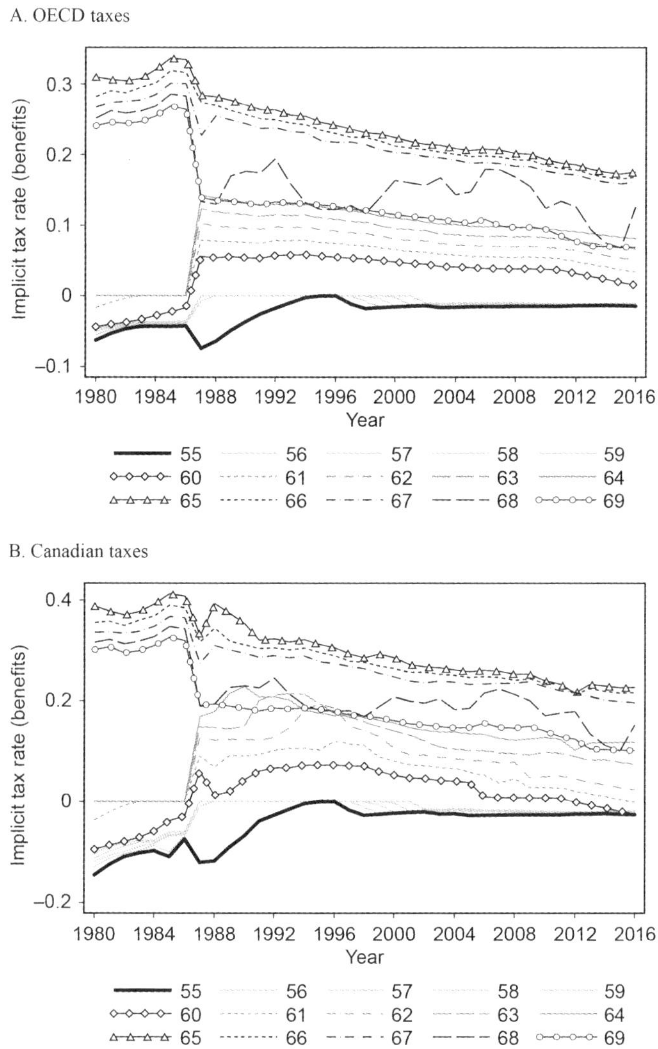

Fig. 2.15 Implicit tax rates in the Canadian environment, single men (medium educated, no pension)

Source: Authors' tabulations

relationship between the implicit tax rates and employment rates that is worthy of further investigation.

2.7 Conclusions

The employment and labor force participation rates of older Canadian men and women have increased substantially since the mid-1990s. In this

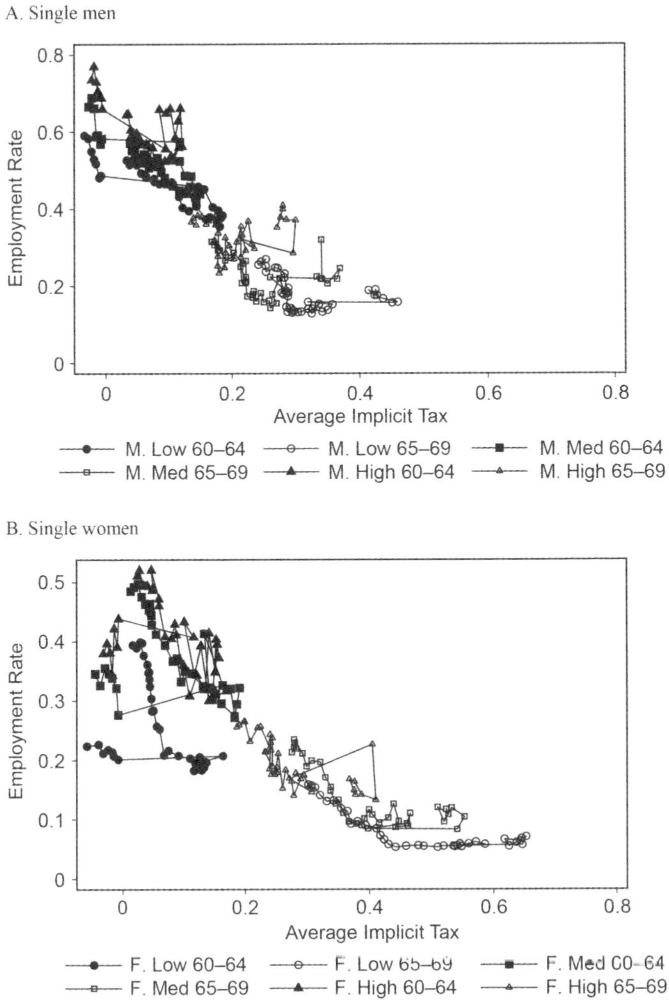

Fig. 2.16 Implicit tax and employment rates in the Canadian environment with Canadian taxes

Source: Authors' tabulations

study, we have illustrated how Canada's social security program has evolved over the 1980–2016 period alongside these trends in employment. In particular, we develop estimates of the implicit tax on continued work, representing the extent to which a person can gain or lose lifetime benefits from social security programs if they delay their departure from the labor force.

Overall, we show that the benefits a person can receive—either annually or over their lifetime—will largely depend on their earnings history. For example, high career earners are eligible to receive the highest CPP benefits and thus the highest social security wealth. However, given the modest level of maximum benefits, the replacement rates of high career earners are lower than those with low career earnings.

One of our main messages is that the means-tested benefits available to seniors play an important role in the incentives one has to continue working at older ages. For each year of delayed departure from the labor force and delayed claiming of CPP benefits, individuals will gain annual social security benefits from the actuarial adjustment applied to the CPP. However, for every dollar gained in annual CPP benefits, low-income seniors will lose 50 cents of their GIS benefits, reducing the reward for continued work. For those with low career earnings, this results in a situation where each year of continued work results in a loss of social security wealth and high implicit tax rates. The relationship we find between the implicit tax rates for continued work and observed employment rates at older ages is worthy of further investigation.

References

Au, D. W. H., T. F. Crossley, and M. Schellhorn. 2005. "The Effect of Health Changes and Long-Term Health on the Work Activity of Older Canadians." *Health Economics* 14 (10): 999–1018.

Baker, M., and D. Benjamin. 1999a. "Early Retirement Provisions and the Labor Force Behavior of Older Men: Evidence from Canada." *Journal of Labor Economics* 17 (4): 724–56.

Baker, M., and D. Benjamin. 1999b. "How Do Retirement Tests Affect the Labor Supply of Older Men?" *Journal of Public Economics* 71 (1): 27–51.

Baker, M., J. Gruber, and K. Milligan. 2003. "The Retirement Incentive Effects of Canada's Income Security Programs." *Canadian Journal of Economics/Revue canadienne d'economique* 36 (2): 261–90.

Baker, M., J. Gruber, and K. Milligan. 2007. "Simulating the Response to Reform of Canada's Income Security Program." In *Social Security and Retirement around the World: Fiscal Implications of Reform*, edited by David A. Wise and Jonathan Gruber, 83–118. Chicago: University of Chicago Press.

Human Mortality Database. 2015. *Human Mortality Database*. University of California, Berkeley (USA), and Max Planck Institute for Demographic Research (Germany). http://www.mortality.org.

Laurin, A., K. S. Milligan, and T. Schirle. 2012. "Comparing Nest Eggs: How CPP Reform Affects Retirement Choices." *C.D. Howe Institute Commentary* no. 352 (May).

Milligan, K. 2016. *Canadian Tax and Credit Simulator*. Database, software and documentation, Version 2016-2.

Milligan, K., and T. Schirle. 2019. "The Labor Force Participation of Older Men in Canada." In *Social Security Programs around the World: Working Longer*, edited by Courtney C. Coile, Kevin Milligan, and David A. Wise, 51–65. Chicago: University of Chicago Press.

Milligan, K., and T. Schirle. 2018. "Health and Capacity to Work of Older Canadians: Gender and Regional Dimensions." *Canadian Public Policy* 44 (2): 159–72.
Milligan, K., and T. Schirle. 2016. "Option Value of Disability Insurance in Canada." In *Social Security Programs and Retirement around the World: Disability Insurance Programs and Retirement*, edited by D. Wise, 137–78. Chicago: University of Chicago Press.
Milligan, K., and T. Schirle. 2014. "Simulated Replacement Rates for CPP Reform Options." *SPP Research Papers* 7 (7): 1–27.
Milligan, K., and T. Schirle. 2008. "Improving the Labor Market Incentives of Canada's Public Pensions." *Canadian Public Policy* 34 (3): 281–303.
OECD. 2018. "Table I.5 Average Personal Income Tax and Social Security Contribution Rates on Gross Labour Income." OECD Tax Database. Accessed from OECD.Stat, November 18, 2017.
Office of the Superintendent of Financial Institutions. 2017. "Actuarial Report (14th) on the Old Age Security Program." Ottawa, Ontario: Office of the Chief Actuary.
Schirle, T. 2008. "Why Have the Labor Force Participation Rates of Older Men Increased since the Mid-1990s?" *Journal of Labor Economics* 26 (4): 549–94.
Schirle, T. 2010. "Health, Pensions, and the Retirement Decision: Evidence from Canada." *Canadian Journal on Aging/La revue canadienne du vieillissement* 29 (4): 519–27.

3

Labor Force Exit in Denmark, 1980–2016
Impact from Changes in Incentives

Paul Bingley, Nabanita Datta Gupta,
Malene Kallestrup-Lamb, and Peder J. Pedersen

3.1 Introduction

Until 1980, the labor force participation rate in Denmark for men 60–64 years old was 80–90 percent, with a very modest decrease reflecting the structural shift out of agriculture. In 1979, five years after the first big oil price shock, a dramatic change occurred. With the purpose of reducing youth unemployment, an early retirement program (*efterløn*, the Post-Employment Wage, hereafter PEW) was introduced without any health or social criteria but with eligibility depending only on being 60 to 66 years old and having a required labor market tenure. The impact was a decline over the subsequent 20 years to half the initial level for labor force participation among men 60–64 years old, as illustrated in figure 3.1.

Next, from around the turn of the century, a trend reversal occurred resulting in a 20 percentage point increase in labor force participation for men and a 25 percentage point increase for women 60–64 years old (cf. figure 3.2). As is well known, this is a phenomenon observed in most Organisation for Economic Co-operation and Development (OECD) countries. Presum-

Paul Bingley is a professor at VIVE—The Danish Center for Social Science Research.

Nabanita Datta Gupta is a professor in the Department of Economics and Business Economics at Aarhus University and a research fellow of IZA.

Malene Kallestrup-Lamb is an associate professor in the Department of Economics and Business Economics at Aarhus University and a research fellow at the Center for Research in Econometric Analysis of Time Series (CREATES) at Aarhus University.

Peder J. Pedersen is an emeritus professor of the Department of Economics and Business Economics at Aarhus University, a research professor at VIVE—The Danish Centre Center for Social Science Research, and a research fellow of IZA.

For acknowledgments, sources of research support, and disclosure of the authors' material financial relationships, if any, please see https://www.nber.org/chapters/c14193.ack.

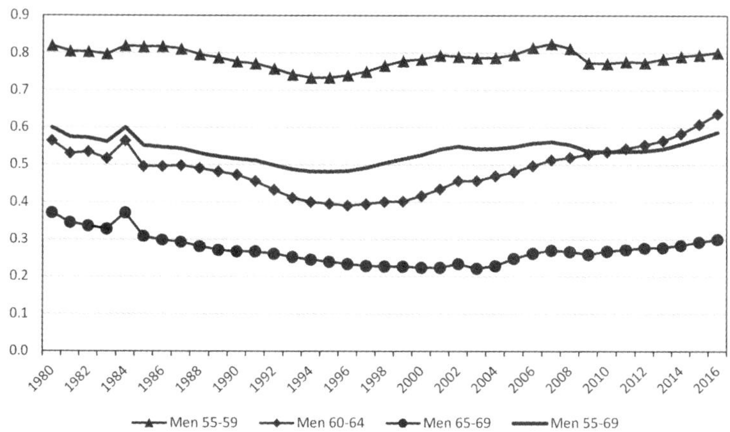

Fig. 3.1 Employment rates, men aged 55–69, 1980–2016
Source: Statistics Denmark

ably, this is the outcome of an interaction between several factors. In many countries sharing the initial decline in the average age for exit from the labor force, reforms were enacted to end or reverse this decline. At the same time, cohort-specific improvements occurred in education and health among new groups of older workers, both factors expected to lead to higher exit ages.[1] It is evident from figure 3.1 that the strongest trend reversal is found for the 60- to 64-year-old group. For the other age groups shown in figure 3.1, the initial decline in labor force participation during the first 15–20 years since 1980 is not regained fully. However, even among those 65 to 69 years old, we see an increase of about 10 percentage points since around 2000.

Figure 3.2 shows the trend reversals for different age groups among women over the same period since 1980. The most dramatic change is seen for the 55- to 59-year-old group, with an increase of about 25 percentage points from the mid-1990s to around 2008. This reflects, however, the closing of a temporary early retirement program described below. In contrast to the case for men, among women there is an ongoing cohort effect explaining part of the impressive trend reversal in the 60- to 64-year-old group from an employment rate of 20 percent to 50 percent occurring over 20 years.

The highly relevant policy question is then to sort out the separate impact from each of these interacting factors. For Denmark, Larsen and Pedersen (2013 and 2017) analyze the impact of changes in education and health on labor force participation in the 60 years and older group, also including individuals older than the normal social security labor force exit age. Bingley,

1. For instance, Datta Gupta and Bengtsson (2015) find that compulsory schooling reforms enacted in Denmark in the 1950s lowered exit via disability pension and diagnoses of chronic diseases later in life. The individuals affected by the reform were in their mid-50s in the late 1990s, around the time the reversal occurs.

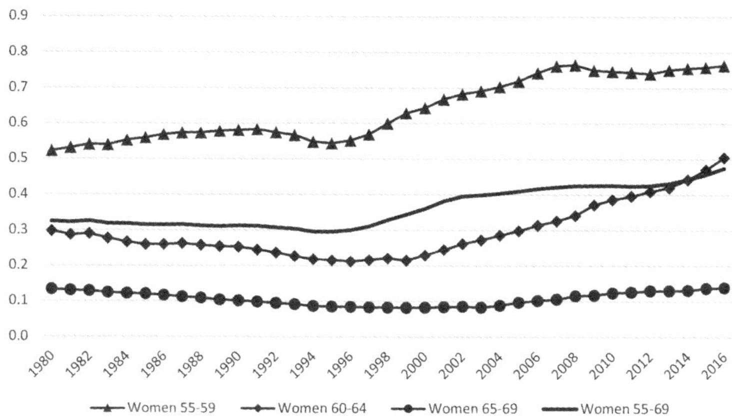

Fig. 3.2 Employment rates, women aged 55–69, 1980–2016
Source: Statistics Denmark

Fig. 3.3 Average age at exit from the labor force to early retirement in the PEW program or to old-age pension at the normal social security age, 1981–2014
Source: Own calculations based on data from Insurance and Pension Denmark (IPD), 2017

Datta Gupta, and Pedersen (2019) analyze the trend reversal with a cohort approach, including education, mortality, other health indicators, and job characteristics among the relevant explanatory factors. The focus of the present study is to determine how much of the observed trend reversal in Denmark can be explained by changes in the incentives of social security policy over the years since 1980.

The trend reversal is illustrated in an alternative way in figure 3.3, showing the average age at exit from the labor force to either PEW or old-age pension

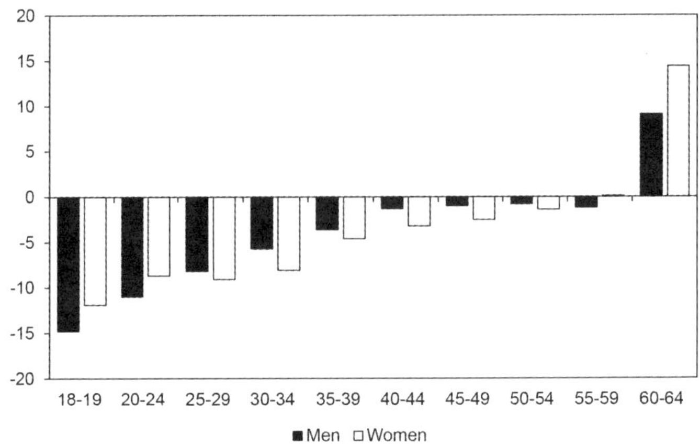

Fig. 3.4 Changes in percentage points in labor force participation by age between 2008 and 2016.

Source: Calculations based on data from Statistics Denmark

(*folkepension*, hereafter OAP) at the normal social security age of eligibility. The trend reversal we set out to explain seems even more pronounced here than in figures 3.1 and 3.2, as the average exit age ends up very close to the initial level. In fact, from a trough of 62.1 years in 1998, the rise is almost 2 full years to 63.8 years in 2014. Notice, however, that while the exit pathways included in figure 3.3 dominate, other pathways are available—that is, disability insurance (*førtidspension*, hereafter DI) and a number of smaller programs.

To provide a numerical summary, we find that for men, the percent exiting the labor market via PEW increases from 22 percent in 1980 to 50 percent in 2009. Following that, it decreases to 38 percent in 2016. For women, the percent exiting the labor market via PEW or OAP increases from 8 percent in 1980 to 58 percent in 2007 and then decreases to 46 percent. The U shape in exit ages occurs at 64.6 in 1980, at 62.1 in 1998, and at 64 in 2016.

While figures 3.1 and 3.2 collect the evidence for a 36-year period, figure 3.4 shows the surprisingly steep increase in labor force participation in the 60- to 64-year-old group after the Great Recession from 2008 to 2016. While all younger age groups experience declines in labor force participation during the financial crisis, the 60- to 64-year-old group has a quite different profile, which is about the same if we look at employment rates instead of participation.

Next, in section 3.2, we present a detailed overview of institutional changes in the retirement area since 1980, including both social security programs, occupational pensions, and the interaction between these two program groups. Section 3.2 includes information on how the reforms and policy changes in the period have resulted in specific changes in ages and other conditions for eligibility for the different pathways to exit from the labor force. Section 3.3 sets up a benefit stream for each pathway to exit from the labor force as determined by earnings history and socioeconomic background factors. In section 3.4 the benefit calculator is used to compute social security wealth accrual for specific types of individuals as a function of claiming benefits from a specific age. Section 3.5 presents the results from calculating the tax force—that is, the implicit tax on working longer—for several specific groups in the labor force. Finally, section 3.6 concludes the chapter.

3.2 Institutional Changes, 1980–2016

All major elements in the Danish pension and retirement system have undergone major changes since 1980. Based on policy reforms enacted in 2006 and 2011, further major changes will be phased in during the coming decades to reflect expected increases in life expectancy. The biggest social security program is OAP, for which everybody in 1980 was eligible, dependent on years of residence in the country. Like OAP, DI is financed from general tax revenues, with eligibility for individuals younger than the OAP age dependent on medical and/or social criteria. PEW is a program for early retirement based on specific conditions regarding labor market attachment. PEW was introduced in 1979 and is financed from general tax revenues supplemented by minor contributions from those eligible for the program. Finally, some specific groups of public-sector employees are eligible for a defined benefit (DB) program, *Tjenestemandspension*, financed from general tax revenues.

Next, mandatory defined contributions (DCs), labor market pensions introduced over the period from 1960, currently cover about 85 percent of all employees. Among funded programs, *Arbejdsmarkedets Tillægspension* (supplementary labor market pension, hereafter ATP), introduced in 1964, is a small but nearly universal program covering all employees with more than a marginal attachment to the labor force. Finally, funded programs also contain private voluntary savings for retirement purposes, mostly with a favorable tax treatment. Apart from these major programs, a few smaller, rather specific programs have been in operation for part of the time since 1980. In quantitative terms, the most important one was the transitional benefits program (*overgangsydelse*, hereafter TBP), introduced in 1992 as an early exit route for long-term unemployed in their 50s, closed to further entry in 1996, and finally phased out in 2006. The impact on the exit age is clearly visible in figures 3.1 and 3.2, especially for women.

In the following, we describe the most relevant changes in these pension programs with a focus on the incentives to leave the labor force or to continue working. For most of the period since 1980, the PEW program has been the dominant route to early retirement. The program was introduced in 1979 as a voluntary route to early retirement open for individuals 60–66 years old with membership in an unemployment insurance (UI) fund for 5 out of the most recent 10 years.[2] Initially, benefits were set at maximum UI benefits for the first 2.5 years in the program. After that, benefits were set at 82 percent of maximum UI benefits for the next two years in the program. Finally, after 4.5 years in the program, benefits were reduced further to 70 percent of maximum UI benefits. The idea behind this stepwise reduction in benefits was to make the transition to OAP at age 67 smoother. Entry to the program turned out to be much higher than expected when the law was proposed. Consequently, eligibility was gradually made dependent on still longer periods of UI fund membership. However, in all cases, the changes in rules in this area were accompanied by "grandfathering" modifications. Already in 1980, eligibility was made dependent on UI fund membership for 10 out of the most recent 15 years. A change in the opposite direction, making entry to PEW more attractive, was decided in 1987, where benefits were set at 82, and not 70 percent, of maximum UI benefits for the last 4.5 years in the program. In 1992, UI fund tenure was increased to 20 out of the most recent 25 years, again with "grandfathering." Further, a new rule was introduced stating that benefits for the whole period in the program were set at maximum UI benefits if entry was delayed to age 63 or later.

In 1992, TBP was introduced. Eligibility to this new early retirement program was conditional on being 55–59 years old, a member of a UI fund, and unemployed for at least 12 out of the last 15 months. From the beginning of 1994, the program was extended to cover 50- to 54-year-olds with the same labor market criteria as for the 55- to 59-year-olds. Benefits in the program were 82 percent of maximum UI benefits, and the duration was until the person entered PEW at the age of 60 years. Participation in the program greatly exceeded government expectations, and entry was terminated at the beginning of 1996, with the last participant leaving the program in 2006.

In 1999, a comprehensive PEW reform was undertaken. Among the main changes was a further tightening of the required UI fund membership tenure to 25 out of the most recent 30 years. Originally, a main motive behind PEW was to create an instrument to redistribute a given number of jobs from old to young workers. One rule that had originated in this way of thinking was abolished in the 1999 reform—that is, that participants in the program were not allowed to work more than 200 hours during a year. This was replaced by a more "flexible" PEW, making it financially more attractive to work while in the program—for example, working 20 percent of a year implied a reduction of annual benefits by 20 percent. The benefit profile was changed once again to 91 percent of maximum UI benefits for the duration of time in the program. Delaying entry by at least two years implied benefits at 100 percent of maximum UI benefits.

2. UI in Denmark is organized as the so-called Ghent system, implying that membership is voluntary.

Means testing relative to private pensions was made more restrictive—that is, before 1999, there was only means testing in relation to pensions directly related to earlier employment being paid out monthly. From 1999, means testing occurred during the first two years in the program, no matter whether private pensions were being paid out or still being accumulated in the pension fund. However, delaying entry by at least two years (and having worked two years after having obtained eligibility) implied means testing only against pensions paid out monthly based on an earlier employment relationship.

Further, the 1999 reform introduced a tax-exempt premium to those eligible for PEW for continuing to work from age 63 to age 65 (to the OAP age from 2004; see below). Summing up, a main element in the 1999 reform was a change from a system where benefits were reduced as a function of time spent in the program to a system where benefits depended on age at entry, with a premium for delaying entry.

As part of the 1999 reform, the age of eligibility for OAP was reduced from 67 to 65, effective from mid-2004. Superficially, this seems surprising considering the nature of the problems regarding the pension burden. However, it must be interpreted in light of, first, the widening gap at the time between the high OAP eligibility age and the declining average retirement age. Next, a major share of people 65 and 66 years old received PEW benefits, which were higher than OAP, so public expenditures were expected to decline.[3] Finally, means testing of the base amount in OAP against earnings was changed in a way to make gradual retirement more attractive. Reduction of the base amount would begin at a higher level of earnings than before, and the rate of reduction of the base amount was reduced from 60 to 30 percent, implying that the base amount would only be fully phased out at an earnings level well above the average earnings of skilled workers. Once again, this represents a change of mind among policy makers from the redistribution of a—perceived—given number of jobs to a new focus on labor supply. Finally, a new instrument was introduced, making it possible to defer take-up of OAP until 75 with an actuarial adjustment.

As part of the 1999 reform, contributions to PEW—replacing the UI fund membership condition—have to be paid for 30 years, increasing from 25 years. Contributions are required to begin no later than age 30. The changes were "grandfathered." Further, means testing against income from work was reduced for PEW participants with low hourly wages.

A final reform of PEW was enacted in 2011. The main impact of this is a reduction in the maximum number of years in the program to three—from originally seven—for individuals born after July 1, 1959. In the 2011 retirement reform, PEW benefits are means tested both against all other pensions regardless of whether or not payments have begun and against income from

3. A countering effect might come from people who have not received any income transfers but who now become eligible for OA two years earlier.

work. The impact of the 2011 reform is a decrease in the tax force for continuing to work.

Unemployment insurance (UI) has also undergone several policy changes. We summarize those of special relevance for UI as a pathway to retirement. The labor market reform in 1994 resulted in a shift from a de facto indefinite duration of benefits to a maximum duration of seven years. Shortly after, it was decided to make a stepwise reduction of the maximum duration of benefits from seven to four years over the period 1996 to 2002. Finally, the maximum duration was set at two years from 2010. For those 50 years and older, UI rules were gradually tightened. With the 1994 reform, benefit duration was extended until age 60 with entry to PEW. For those 50–54 years old, benefit duration was gradually reduced to the common level from 1999. Unemployed 58- and 59-year-olds were, however, exempt for activation programs until 2007. In 2007, the benefit duration extension for those 55–59 years old was repealed.

The main changes regarding DI were a major reform in 1984. DI could be granted on three levels depending on a loss of work capacity. Widows' pension was ended as a special program. In 2003, disability pension was reformed again with the three benefit levels consolidated to one—maximum UI benefits.

Labor market pensions were growing in importance from about 1960, with pension funds beginning for certain groups of mostly white-collar workers. From 1991, pension funds also began growing for blue-collar workers. Currently, about 85 percent of employees are covered by labor market pensions. A specific DB program, *Tjenestemandspension*, is relevant for some groups of public-sector employees. It is a very old program where currently about 15 percent of those 60 years and older receive part of their income in the form of this specific DB pension. Finally, there are tax-subsidized private pension savings. Currently about one-third of those 30–55 years old participate to some extent in funded private pension saving. From 2013, tax incentives changed along with a shift to another form of savings program, so far less popular than the earlier programs.

Those labor market and private programs interact with social security, especially OAP, and as mentioned above, also with PEW. OAP consists of a base amount and a supplementary amount that is means tested against income from the labor market pension. This is less relevant for white-collar groups where the typical income from labor market pensions and private pensions is so high that only the base amount of OAP is relevant. For many blue-collar groups, the means testing is, however, a potential challenge when the labor market pension for these groups reaches maturity. The means testing will, with current rules, imply a reduction of supplementary OAP with the same amount as the income from the labor market pension, reducing their incentive to save via labor market pension or private pension programs.

The detailed descriptions of the multitude of institutional changes since 1980 are illustrated in a compact way in figure 3.5, collecting the develop-

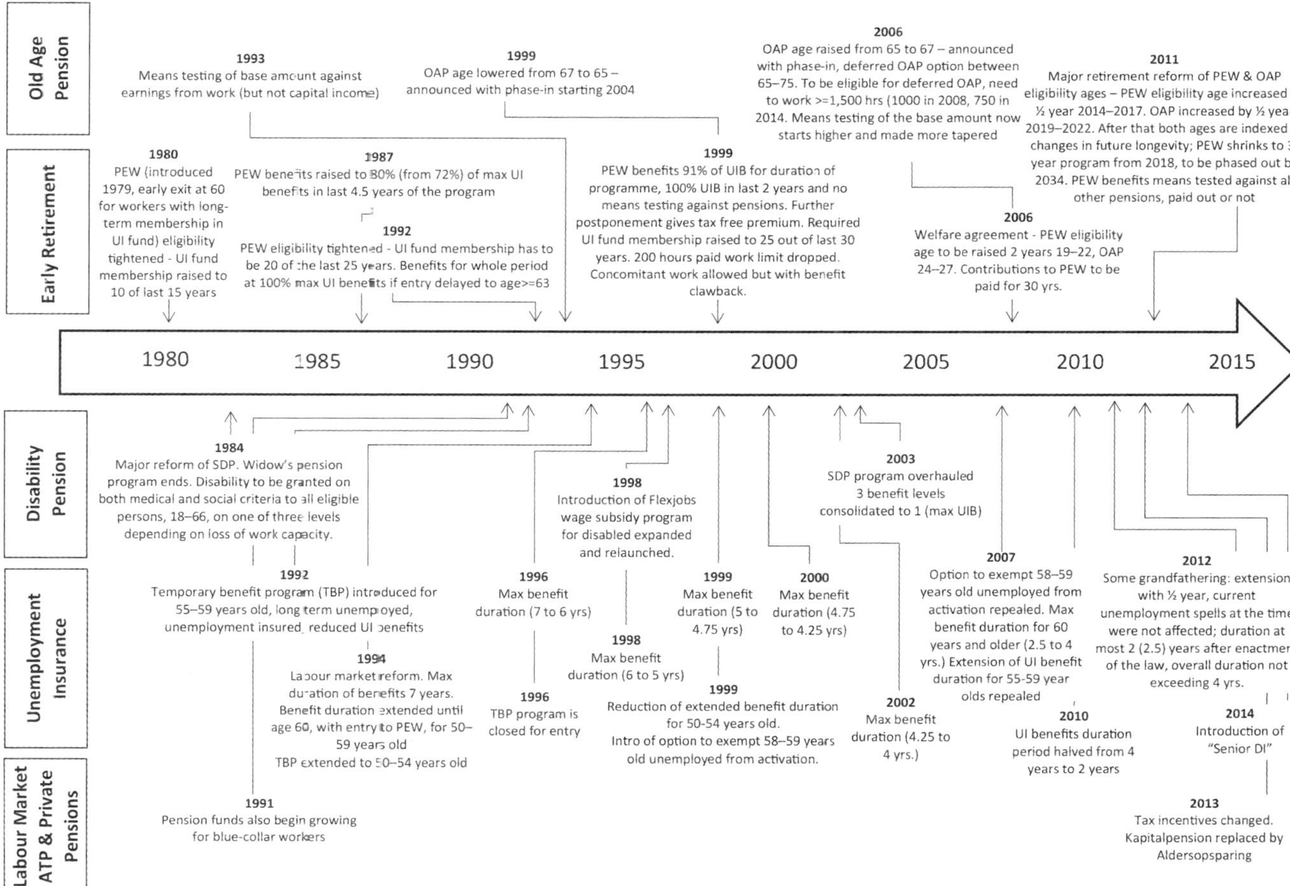

Fig. 3.5 Summary of reforms and policy changes around retirement, 1980–2015

ment in a timeline covering areas of central relevance relative to exit from the labor force—that is, old-age pension, early retirement, disability pension, interactions between unemployment insurance and exit from the labor force, and finally labor market pensions and private savings for retirement.

3.3 Benefit Calculator

We calculate pension benefits from the four largest programs supporting consumption in retirement: DI, OAP, PEW, and TBP. Pathways to DI, TBP, and OAP are weighted according to the proportion of each gender aged 50–66 joining each program. Pension benefits can only be claimed on exit from the labor market. Private and occupational pension payouts are not included in social security wealth. From 1999, a PEW clawback was introduced for those retiring at age 60 or 61 as a function of private pension wealth. We ignore this clawback.

Earnings histories are relevant for benefit calculation for the current year's earnings for PEW and for the previous two years' earnings for TBP. We use median earnings by gender at age 50 in each calendar year and assume that earnings profiles are flat. We calculate benefits separately for men and women at median earnings, 50 percent and 200 percent of median earnings, respectively. Individuals' single earnings are treated as the most important source because of the importance of separate taxation in Denmark. We assume a flat 40 percent income tax. This rate represents approximately the case for most individuals being "treated" in the benefit calculator. We take mortality from Statistics Denmark life tables by gender, age, and calendar year.

3.4 Social Security Wealth Accrual

To fix concepts, we begin with definitions of key measures. First, we define the social security wealth, SSW, of an individual of gender g and (earnings) type i at each calendar year t and labor force exit age R. This is defined as the sum from age R to the end of life T of weighted future benefits streams discounted back to current age a, where the weights denote probabilities of being observed on certain pathways (see, e.g., Gruber and Wise 2004):

$$SSW_{gt}(R,i) = \sum_{a=R}^{T} \sum_{k} \pi_{gk}.B_{at}(R,i).\sigma_{gat}.\beta^{a-R}, \; 55 \leq a \leq 69 .$$

The parameter π denotes the probability of a given pathway, σ is the survival probability, and β is the discount factor, with a discount rate of 3 percent.

We denote the change in SSW by postponing going on retirement for a year as its accrual, ACC, where

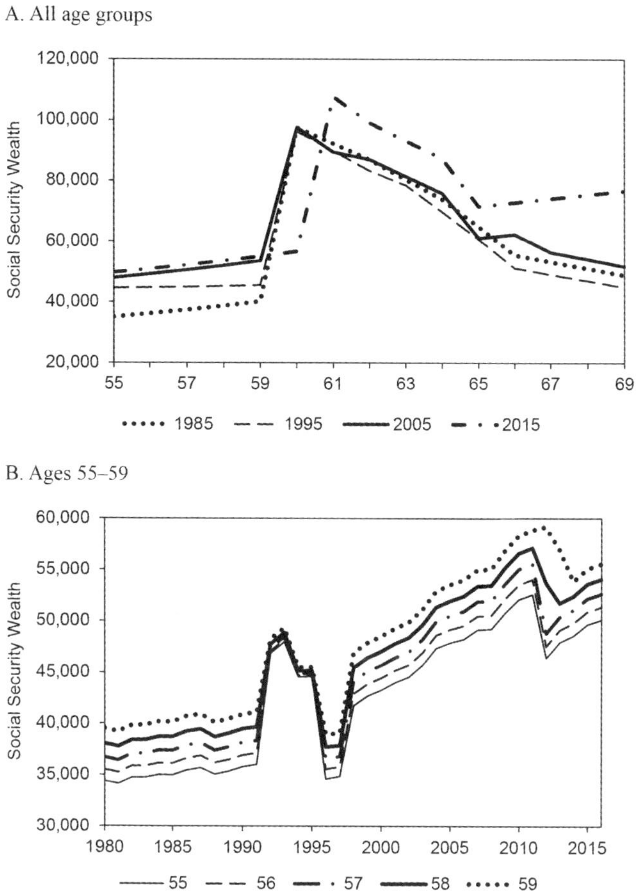

Fig. 3.6 Social security wealth, men with median earnings

$$ACC_{gt}(R,i) - SSW_{gt+1}(R+1,i) - SSW_{gt}(R,i).$$

The key summary measure of interest in this analysis is the implicit tax on working an additional year, *ITAX*, defined as

$$ITAX_{gt}(R,i) = -ACC_{gt}(R,i)/Y_{gt}(i),$$

where *Y* represents earnings from work. Thus $ITAX > 0$ (<0) when accrual is negative (positive), meaning that work is discouraged (encouraged).

To help understand the implicit tax rate figures shown below, SSW figures are shown first in figure 3.6a–d. SSW, summed across all pathways, is presented below by age and calendar year. Gender differences are due to different program weights and only have modest effects. The following SSW illustrations are for men with median earnings.

C. Ages 60–64

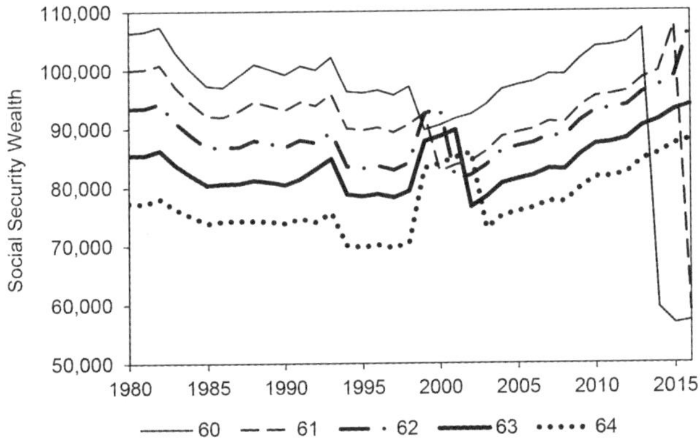

D. Ages 65–69

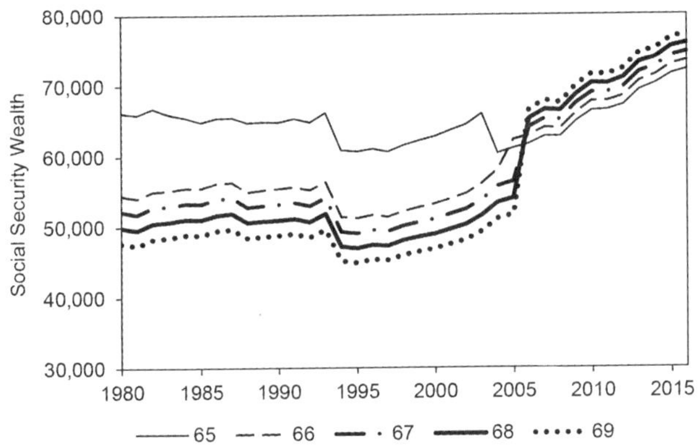

Fig. 3.6 (cont.)

First, from figure 3.6a, it can be seen from the age distribution of SSW that there is a single peak in the early 60s due to the availability of early pension benefits. However, the incentives to retire later for men have been strengthened over time as the peak in SSW has moved from 60 to 62. This change has taken place primarily in the last decade, between 2005 and 2015, suggesting the importance of the 1999 reform (that was phased in between 2004 and 2006) and the subsequent welfare and retirement reforms of 2006 and 2011. Splitting by cohort and looking at the temporal distributions in figure 3.6b, SSW is shifted up by age in the 55–59 age group, indicating retirement incentives are greater as people age. In the years 1992–95, incentives are identical for all age groups and are driven by the rules of the TBP—a program that opened and closed between these years. Again in this figure, we see the fall in retirement incentives for all age groups after 2010.

For the 60–64 age group, however, figure 3.6c shows that SSW falls with age, indicating the strong incentives for retiring early via the PEW program. However, in the late 1990s, the 62- to 64-year-olds have an incentive to retire due to the 1999 reform, whereas the 60- and 61-year-olds have an incentive to delay retirement. This pattern is due to the feature of the 1999 reform pertaining to the PEW program, whereby retirement at 62 was encouraged because of the decreased means testing if early retirement was postponed for two years. However, the effects do not last long, and incentives to retire early again begin increasing in subsequent years. At the end of the period, incentives to retire at 60 or 61 are dramatically reduced due to the 2011 reform, which essentially reduces the early retirement to a three-year program for those born after July 1, 1959.

Finally, figure 3.6d shows that SSW is relatively higher for 65-year-olds (covered by PEW) compared to the older age groups due to the relative generosity of that program compared to the OAP. From 2004 to 2006, there is an increased incentive for 65- to 67-year-olds in particular to exit the labor market due to the 1999 reform that brought the OAP age down from 67 to 65 but introduced an actuarial adjustment for delaying retirement after 65. Notice, however, that even though subsequently the decision to raise the OAP labor force exit age again from 65 to 67 was made in 2006, the actual age will not be 67 before 2022. This is because the first cohorts exposed to the change will be the 1955 birth cohort (born after July 1), who will face an OAP eligibility age of 67 again.

3.5 Tax Force, Graphical Presentations

Implicit tax rates on working longer are presented below by age and calendar year and in separate figures by gender and earnings levels (50 percent, 100 percent, and 200 percent of median).

3.5.1 Implicit Tax Rates

In figure 3.7a–f, implicit tax rates are shown for the full 55–69 age group. Females are depicted in the left panes; men in the right panes. Top panes are for 50 percent of median earnings, middle panes are for median earnings, and bottom panels are for 200 percent median earnings.

Overall, in figure 3.7a–f, when looking at the full age group, we can see that mirroring the change in SSW described above, the implicit tax is strongly negative (i.e., a subsidy encouraging working) for the age group just about to enter early retirement, but it becomes less negative between 2005 and 2015. At the same time, its peak has shifted over time by about a year. The reduction in the subsidy level is higher for median and 200 percent median earnings. Gender differences appear to be minor, except for 200 percent median earnings, where males experience a slightly lower reduction in the subsidy but the same shift. Modest taxes are seen in the age groups 63

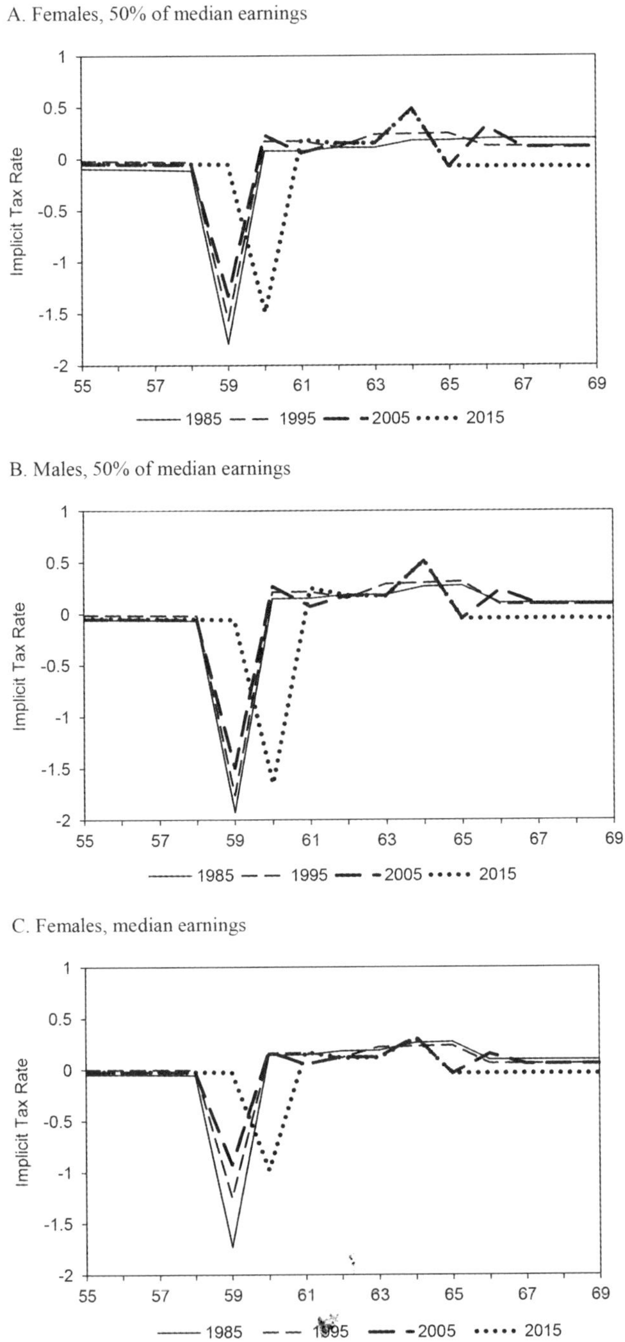

Fig. 3.7 Implicit tax rates, 55–69 age group

D. Males, median earnings

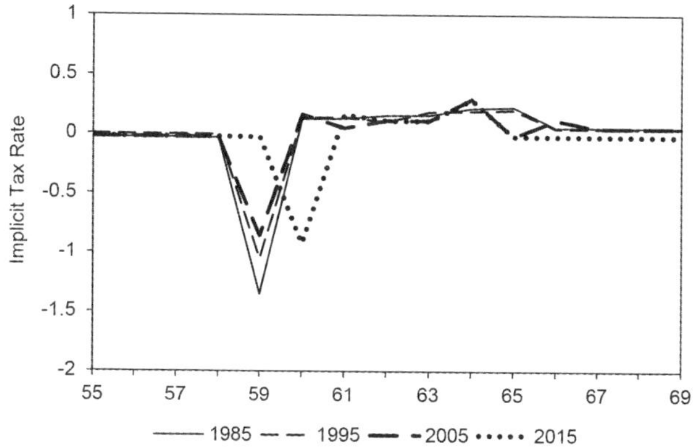

E. Females, 200% of median earnings

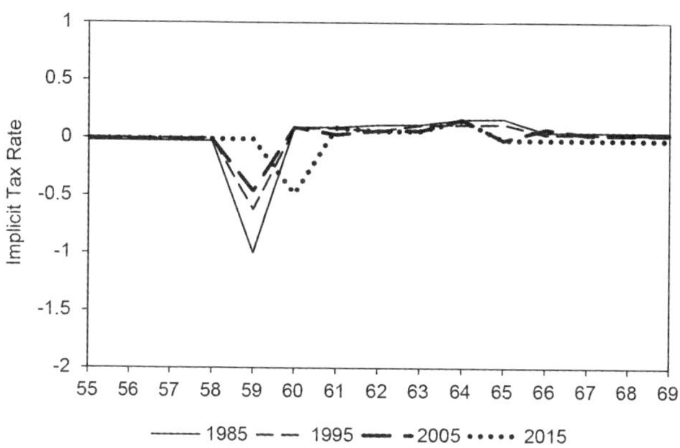

F. Males, 200% of median earnings

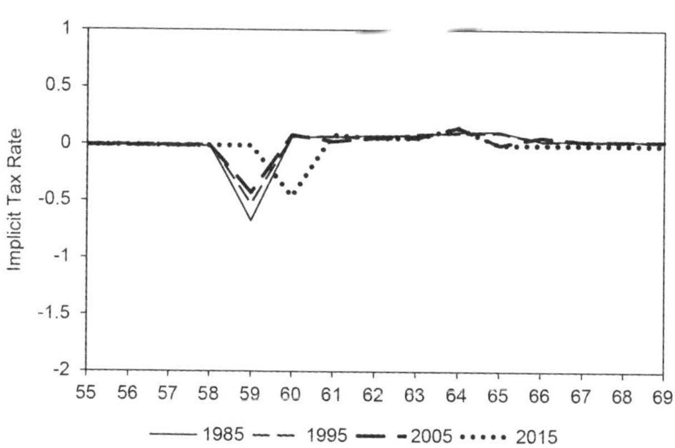

Fig. 3.7 (cont.)

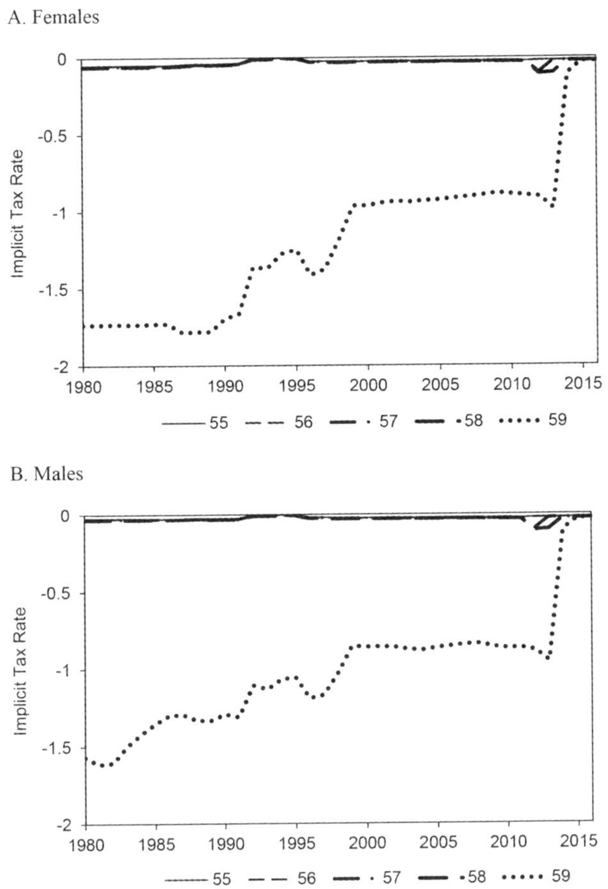

Fig. 3.8 Median earnings, 55–59 age group

and above, with a peak appearing between ages 63 and 65 in 2015, most evident at 50 percent of the median. This represents the effect of shortening the PEW to a three-year program starting at age 63 according to the 2011 reform.

Since the results shown earlier for figure 3.7 are generally similar across earnings levels, in the next set of figures, we only show the panel for median earnings in each case. In figure 3.8a–b, we show the 55–59 age group; figure 3.9a–b for the 60–64 age group; and figure 3.10a–b for the 65–69 age group. In figure 3.8a–b for the 55–59 age group, the dominating influence of the 59-year-olds is apparent.[4] They face considerably higher subsidy

4. Indeed, if the 59-year-olds are dropped from these figures, subsidies to continue working at ages 57 and 58 appear but seem to level off in the latest years. Furthermore, there is a tax to continued work at ages 55–56 in the years 1992–95, when the TBP was active (not shown).

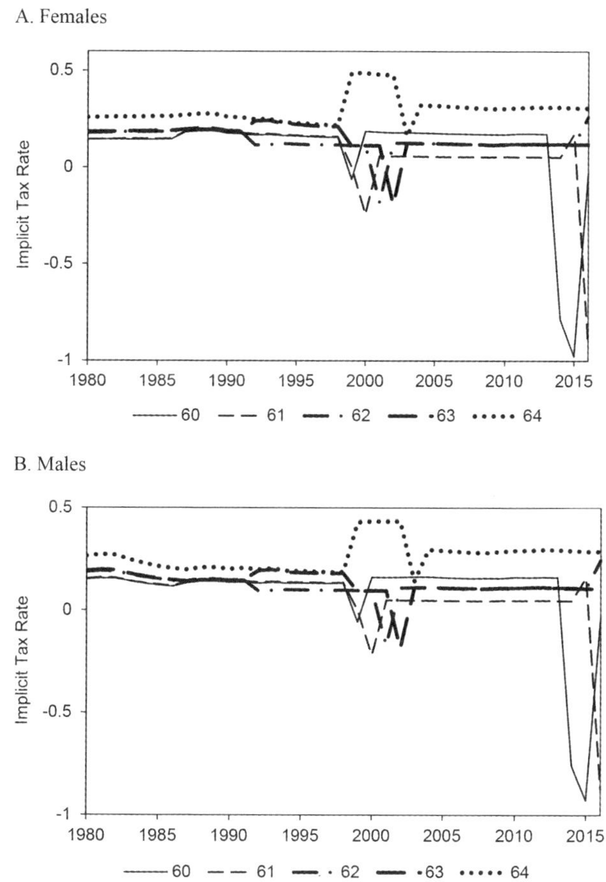

Fig. 3.9 Median earnings, 60–64 age group

rates (women more than men) than the other groups. Thus these groups face strong incentives to work up to the earliest eligibility ages. This subsidy rate, however, has been declining over time as the eligibility criteria for the PEW program are being tightened; the program is becoming less generous via means testing and gradually being reduced in duration to a three-year program. In particular, the 2011 reform brings the subsidy rate of the 59-year-olds in line with the other groups. The reason that the subsidy appears at age 59 rather than at age 60 is that the implicit tax rate is based on the forward-looking one-year accrual measure, which, relative to current earnings, encourages working at age 59 so as not to lose eligibility for early retirement at age 60.

In figure 3.9a–b, the implicit tax rates for the 60–64 age group are depicted over time. For 60 and 61-year-olds, the welfare and retirement reforms of PEW seem to have induced substantial subsidies to continue working in

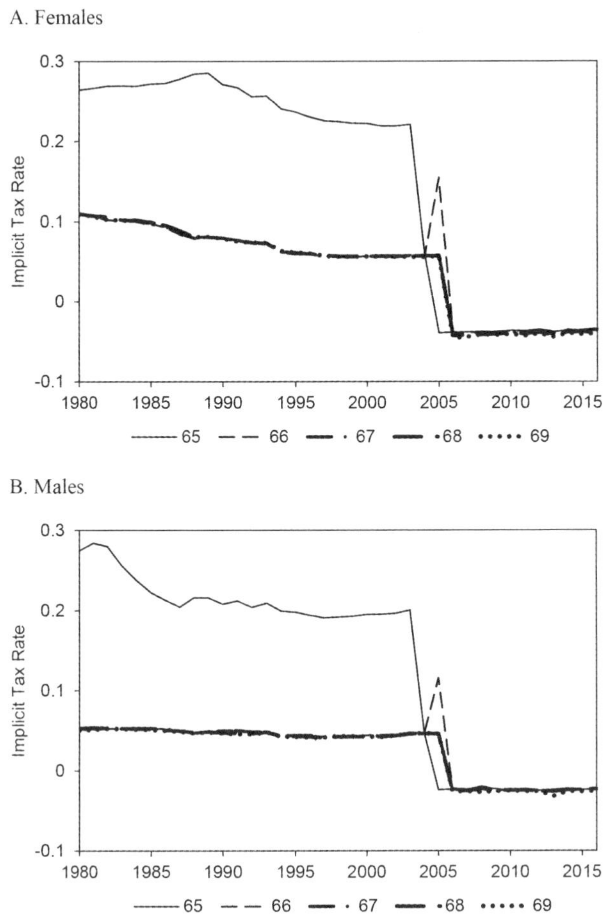

Fig. 3.10 Median earnings, 65–69 age group

2012–13. There is a tax on continued work at age 64 in the late 1990s due to the TBP, but this tax declines subsequently over time as the program closes. For the 60–63 age group, at the same time, modest subsidies to continue work appear. Both changes seem driven by the 1999 reform, which brings the OAP age forward to 65.

Finally, for the oldest age group, 65–69, it can be seen from figure 3.10a–b that there were previously taxes for continuing work at age 65, and somewhat less for 66, before 2004. For the 66-year-olds, there is a sharp spike in 2005, when the program is first introduced. However, the 1999 reform that brought retirement forward to 65 from 67 in 2004 also results in these taxes turning to subsidies after 2005 for the older age groups, 67–69. These subsidies reflect the provisions of the reform that encouraged the deferral of OAP with an actuarial adjustment.

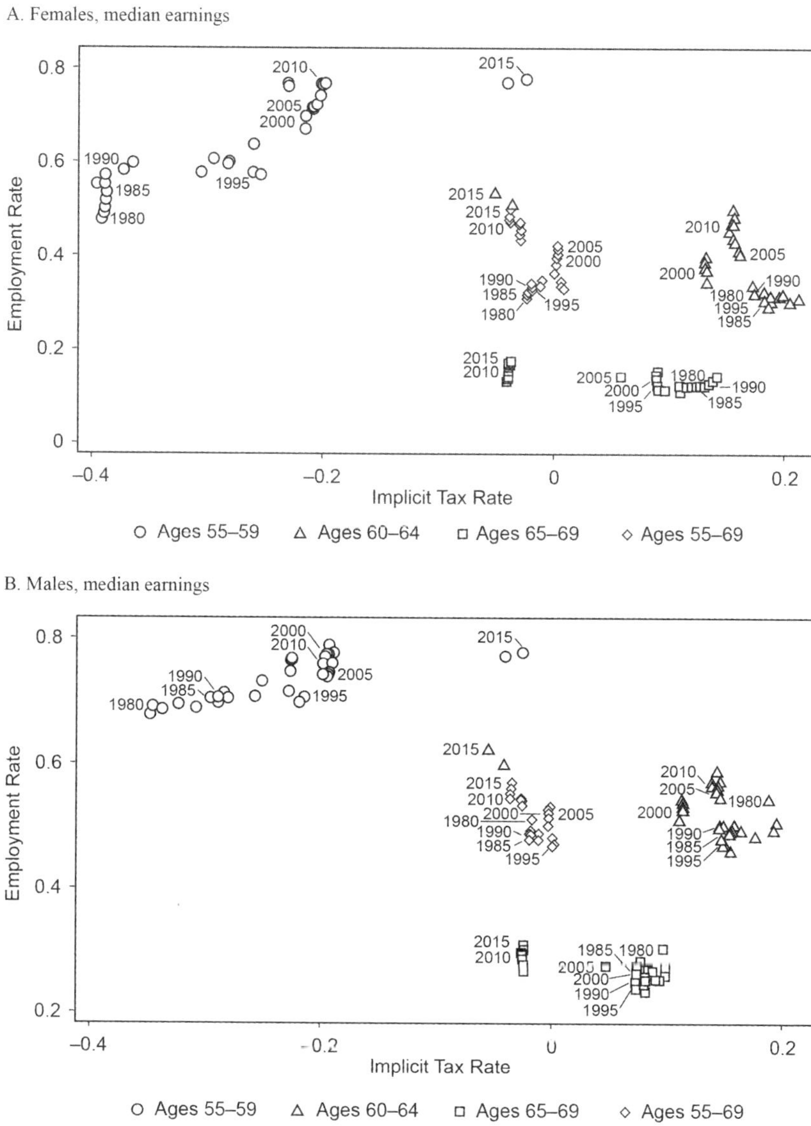

Fig. 3.11 Relationships between employment rates and implicit tax rates

3.5.2 Employment Rates–Implicit Tax Rates

The relationships between employment rates and implicit tax rates are presented below in figure 3.11a–b by age group and calendar year, again only for the median earner, as earnings differences play a minor role in the Danish context.

There is little difference in the relationships by gender. Women have lower rates of employment but face essentially the same incentives in terms of implicit tax rates as men, and the evolution over time has been similar for both groups. Implicit tax rates by employment rates show quite a discernible pattern when looking at the 55–69 age group as a whole. The direction of change over time is to move from a high-tax, low-employment regime to a low-tax, high-employment regime—that is, from southeast to northwest. For women, the pattern takes on a reversed *C* rather than a straight line; however, both men and women end with higher employment and lower taxes in 2010–15 compared to 2000–2005, and this is consistent with the changing incentives due to pension reform.

When splitting by age group, however, striking differences are seen. For the youngest age group, 55- to 59-year-olds, the employment–tax force relationship is strong and positive (i.e., high tax rate, high employment). The positive relationship is driven by the first eligibility age for PEW at 60 having a huge influence on the 55- to 59-year-old group to continue working, because retirement before age 60 disqualifies PEW eligibility. However, it seems that after 2010, the relationship has weakened, which corresponds with the retirement reform of 2011 that both shortened the duration of PEW and made it less attractive because of wider means testing. For the oldest age group, 65–69, there appears to be no relationship between the implicit tax rate and employment. This makes sense because most of this group has retired and is immune to changing incentives. Indeed, this group has the lowest employment level. For the PEW-eligible age group, 60–64, we see the highest tax rates. Females show a positive relationship over time, again indicating that even though the tax rate is increasing, this age group keeps working an additional year, say, in order to qualify for early retirement benefits because the earliest eligibility age is being shifted at the same time. Implicit tax rates are based on accrual calculations that are one year forward looking.

3.5.3 Regression Analysis

Simple OLS regressions of the effects of *ITAX* on employment rates are estimated, and results are reported in table 3.1 (males) and table 3.2 (females). For both groups, the regressions show the U shape in employment rate as the coefficient to a calendar year is negative and the coefficient to its squared term is positive. However, adding controls diminishes the significance of the basic time effect. The effect of *ITAX* is negative as expected and is highly significant for both males and females. It is also robust to adding controls for the share completing high school in the 55–64 age group, the share completing college in the 55–64 age group, and the age 60 mortality rate.

In the first three columns, the regressions are shown for the full group of, respectively, men and women. In the next three columns, we split each group according to 50 percent, 100 percent, and 200 percent median earn-

Table 3.1 **OLS regressions of employment rate on calendar time, incentives, education and mortality, 1980–2016, males**

	All	All	All	50 percent of median earnings	100 percent of median earnings	200 percent of median earnings
Year	−0.4265**	−0.3553**	0.0453	0.0738	0.0415	0.0415
Year-sq.	0.0001**	0.0001***	−0.0000	−0.0000	−0.0000	−0.0000
ITAX	—	−0.1811***	−0.1812***	−0.1438***	−0.2108***	−0.4217***
With controls	No	No	Yes	Yes	Yes	Yes
N	1,665	1,665	1,665	555	555	555
Adj. R^2	0.0207	0.1207	0.1207	0.1386	0.1262	0.1262

Standard errors in parentheses: * $p < 0.10$, ** $p < 0.05$, *** $p < 0.01$

Controls include share completing high school in 55–64 age group, share completing college in 55–64 age group, and age 60 mortality rate.

Table 3.2 **OLS regressions of employment rate on calendar time, incentives, education, and mortality, 1980-2016, females**

	All	All	All	50 percent of median earnings	100 percent of median earnings	200 percent of median earnings
Year	−0.4903**	−0.3781**	−0.4784	−0.5198	−0.4613	−0.4545
Year-sq.	0.0001**	0.0001**	0.0001	0.0001	0.0001	0.0001
ITAX	—	−0.2164***	−0.2165***	−0.1938***	−0.2074***	−0.3513***
With controls	No	No	Yes	Yes	Yes	Yes
N	1,665	1,665	1,665	555	555	555
Adj. R^2	0.0769	0.1914	0.1909	0.2135	0.1856	0.1738

Standard errors in parentheses: * $p < 0.10$, ** $p < 0.05$, *** $p < 0.01$

Controls include share completing high school in 55–64 age group, share completing college in 55–64 age group, and age 60 mortality rate.

ings. Incentives exert a similarly strong and significant effect on employment for all three groups; however, the effect is significantly higher in the case of the 200 percent of median earnings subgroup compared to the other subgroups. In each case in columns 4–6, we estimate the specification, including all controls. Finally, to shed light on the question of whether the changed incentives are responsible for the trend reversal in employment among older males and females in the Danish labor market since the mid-1990s, we see from the regressions that the U shape becomes less pronounced in column 2 in tables 3.1 and 3.2 when incentives are added. To summarize, the regression results reveal a strong and robust relationship between simulated incentives and employment in Denmark and show furthermore that incentives explain to some extent the trend reversal that has occurred.

3.6 Conclusions

A dramatic trend reversal in employment rates of 60- to 64-year-olds has occurred in many OECD countries, where a declining employment rate in the 1980s and early 1990s has been turned around since the mid-1990s and has been increasing ever since. This U shape in elderly employment is also present in Denmark. Over a 20-year period beginning in 1996, where elderly employment had reached its lowest level, men aged 60–64 have improved their employment by 20 percentage points and women by 25 percentage points. Overall, the average age at exit from the labor force via either early pension benefits or old-age pension has increased by nearly 2 years, from 62.1 years in 1996 to 63.8 years in 2016. Over the same period, pension policy reforms changing the incentives especially for going on early retirement have been enacted, concurrent with the repeated tightening of UI and DI eligibility and increasing work accommodations for the elderly with lowered working capacity via wage subsidy programs. The highly relevant question for policy purposes is, how much of the reversal of labor market trends among the elderly can be attributed to the changing incentives of the social security program?

We investigate this question by identifying key reforms of social security policy in Denmark between 1980 and 2016 and modeling these changes with a benefit calculator, which computes potential income streams in retirement according to different program pathways and retirement ages by gender and earnings level. Using our calculator, we compute social security wealth, its accrual, and the implicit tax on work separately by gender, age, and calendar year. Our computations show that the subsidies to continuing work just before the earliest eligibility age and the subsequent tax discouraging working just after the earliest eligibility age in Denmark have been reduced substantially, mainly as a result of the 1999 reform, the 2006 welfare agreement, and the 2011 retirement reform.

In addition, results of simple aggregate regression models show a significant negative and robust relationship between the implicit tax rate and the employment rate and a role for incentives in explaining the trend reversal that has occurred in the Danish labor market. Thus in the Danish case, a reduction in the tax force to retire early has contributed significantly to employment patterns among the 60–64 age group.

References

Bingley, P., N. Datta Gupta, and P. J. Pedersen. 2019. "From Early Retirement to Staying in the Job: Trend Reversal in the Danish Labor Market." In *Social Security Programs and Retirement around the World: Working Longer*, edited by Courtney C. Coile, Kevin Milligan, and David A. Wise, 67–86. Chicago: University of Chicago Press.

Datta Gupta, N., and S. Bengtsson. 2015. "The Effect of a Compulsory Schooling Reform on Disability Pensioning—Evidence from the Danish Registers." Special issue, *Annals of Economics and Statistics* 119/120:95–121.

Gruber, J., and D. Wise, eds. 2004. *Social Security Programs and Retirement around the World: Micro-estimation*. Chicago: University of Chicago Press.

Larsen, M., and P. J. Pedersen. 2013. "To Work, to Retire—or Both? Labor Market Activity after 60." *IZA Journal of European Labor Studies* 2:21.

Larsen, M., and P. J. Pedersen. 2017. "Labour Force Activity after 65: What Explain Recent Trends in Denmark, Germany and Sweden?" *Journal for Labour Market Research* 50 (1): 15–27.

4 Workers' Employment Rates and Pension Reforms in France
The Role of Implicit Labor Taxation

Didier Blanchet, Antoine Bozio, Simon Rabaté, and Muriel Roger

4.1 Introduction

France has experienced a clear reversal of older workers' labor force participation (LFP) and employment rates over the last 15 years. These two rates had continuously declined in the 1970s and the 1980s for the 60–64 age group, bringing employment rates at a low 10 percent for both genders. A similar drop took place for men in the 55–59 age group, more concentrated in time but very substantial: their employment rate lost 20 percentage points within only a few years around 1980. Women in this 55–59 age group have been the only exception to this general decline, due to the offsetting effect of increasing lifetime labor force attachment between successive cohorts. For all other groups, the trend toward earlier exits has reversed since the mid-2000s. We are now back to the levels of the 1970s for men in the 55–59 age group, and the labor force participation rate has almost doubled again for men and women in the 60–64 age group. It is now a little over 20 percent.

Both the initial decline and the subsequent U-turn have been addressed by a substantial body of literature. Blanchet and Pelé (1999) had emphasized the high level of implicit taxation of labor beyond the age of 60 that characterized the French pension system in the early 1990s. Subsequent reforms

Didier Blanchet belongs to the French National Statistical Institute (INSEE).

Antoine Bozio is the director of the Institute of Public Policy (IPP), an associate professor at the French School of Advanced Studies in the Social Sciences (EHESS), and an associate researcher at the Paris School of Economics (PSE).

Simon Rabaté is an economist at the Central Planning Office (CPB) in The Hague and a research affiliate at the Institut des Politiques Publiques (IPP) in Paris, France.

Muriel Roger is a professor of economics at CES Université Paris 1 Panthéon-Sorbonne.

For acknowledgments, sources of research support, and disclosure of the authors' material financial relationships, if any, please see https://www.nber.org/chapters/c14194.ack.

have tried to remove most of this implicit taxation, but they also modified other parameters of the retirement decision on both the supply and demand sides of the labor market: stronger requirements for reaching the pivotal age at which a "full rate" pension is obtained, lower replacement rates offered at this age, lower indexation prospects after entry into retirement, stricter control on access to early retirement routes, and reduced possibilities for firms to terminate normal labor contracts at the full-rate age. Faced with the need of evaluating the long-run impact of these reforms, several projection tools have been developed: most of them are dynamic microsimulation models, and they offer more or less sophisticated endogenizations of retirement behavior at the microlevel, either under the assumption of departures centered around the full rate or using some more structural assumptions in the spirit of Stock and Wise (1990), Mahieu and Sédillot (2000), or Mahieu and Blanchet (2004). Bachelet et al. (2011) compare messages delivered by these different ex-ante modeling approaches on reforms implemented until 2010. In parallel, with reforms beginning to produce their first observable effects, ex-post econometric evaluations start being available, generally exploiting discontinuities generated by the reforms, as in Bozio (2011) or Benallah (2011) for private-sector workers after the 2003 reform, Baraton, Beffy, and Fougère (2011) for the impact of the same reform on teachers in the public education sector, Rabaté and Rochut (2016) or Dubois and Koubi (2017) for the impact of the 2010 reform, and finally Rabaté (2017) for a more specific focus on changes that have affected mandatory retirement. To this literature can be also related empirical explorations of the so-called horizon effect by Hairault et al. (2006)—that is, the idea that changes in ages at access to retirement affect not only retirement *stricto sensu* but also general labor market behavior ahead of this retirement age.

The message that emerges from all this literature is that of a relative convergence between ex-post and ex-ante evaluations: pension reforms and associated changes in financial incentives seem to affect retirement behavior in a way that is roughly consistent with assumptions postulated by ex-ante projection models, even if some uncertainty remains about how far retirement ages can be expected to go on increasing over the next decades.

The present chapter is an addition to this literature. It essentially consists of an actualization of messages on implicit labor taxation that had been set forth by Blanchet and Pelé (1999): how did this implicit taxation change from the mid-1980s to the current period, and is this change in line with the U-shaped profile of employment rates shown in figure 4.1? The indicator is a pure financial indicator. It does not account for all other components that may affect individual decisions to retire: health, working conditions, and so on. It thus provides a partial understanding of the retirement process, a point we will emphasize in our conclusion.

The chapter will be organized as follows. Section 4.2 will detail the main changes that have affected French pension legislation since the mid-1980s.

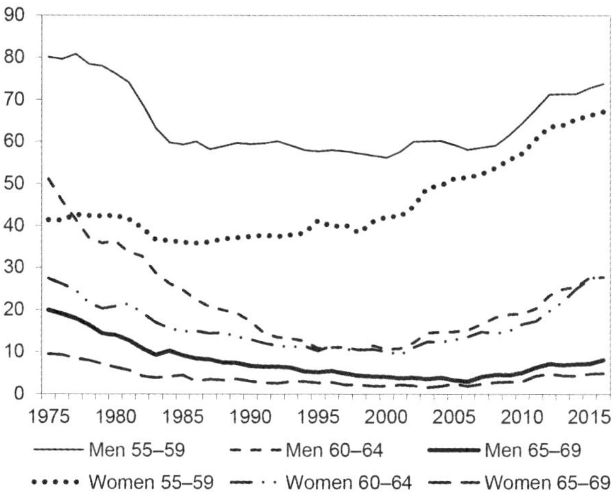

Fig. 4.1 Senior employment rates by gender and five-year age groups
Source: French Labor Force Survey

Section 4.3 will focus on the main methodological choices that have been retained for the study. Section 4.4 will present results for the case of private-sector workers: first we will focus on incentive properties of the normal pension system, and then we will examine additional incentives provided by other routes. Section 4.5 will then offer a brief examination of how incentives have changed for people working in the public sector. Section 4.6 will conclude.

4.2 The Context: A Brief Overview of the French System and Its Reforms

We document in this section the numerous reforms that have affected pension arrangements and other schemes, like early retirement or unemployment benefits, in France over the last decades.

4.2.1 Pension Reforms

Before presenting how pension rules and their reforms have shaped retirement behavior, a few words are required on the general organization of the French pension system. The core of this pension system is the *Régime général* (general regime), providing a first-pillar pension to all wage earners from the private sector. This pension scheme covers wages up to the social security ceiling, whose level is roughly equivalent to the mean wage. The principle of this general regime is to deliver a pension proportional to the number N_{rg} of years of contribution to the regime and to a reference wage W_{ref}, which is an average of wages received during the D best years of one's career, after truncation to the "social security ceiling," roughly equivalent to the average wage level.

This system entitles workers at most with a replacement rate equal to 50 percent of their reference wage. People at this level are considered to have the so-called full rate. This replacement rate thus remains rather low, and all the more so for people whose careers have ended well above the social security ceiling. Two complementary schemes provide additional pensions that raise replacement rates above this 50 percent or less ratio: respectively, the AGIRC (*Association Générale des Institutions de Retraite des Cadres*), dedicated to upper-skilled wage earners, and the ARRCO (*Association des Régimes de Retraite Complémentaires*) for all other categories of private-sector wage earners. These two schemes share a common principle: the pension they deliver is based not on the length of people's careers but on the number of points that they have accumulated over these careers through their contributions. The two basic parameters are therefore the purchasing price of these points, which determines how many points are bought a given year with contributions, and the service value of these points, which determines the amount of pension that one derives from one's accumulated account of points.

An equivalent two-pillar structure exists for self-employed people, with first-pillar pensions fully aligned on rules of the general regime and complementary pensions provided by a multiplicity of different regimes.

The last main segment of the French system is the one that applies to public-sector employees, who benefit from a single pillar-pension covering all their wages without any reference to the social security ceiling but excluding bonuses. As is the case in the general regime, the pension is proportional to the length of people's career, but the reference wage is not an average of past wages; it is equal to people's last wages or, more precisely, the wage they had over the last six months of their careers. These rules apply to the three categories of civil servants that exist in France: those employed by the central state, those employed by local authorities, and those working in the public health sector. Similar rules also apply to people who are not civil servants but work in large public or formerly public firms who have generally kept separate specific regimes (*régimes spéciaux*). A distinct feature of all these schemes is also the fact that they allow retirement much before 60—at 55 and sometimes before for some specific subcategories of workers, such as members of armed forces, the police, railway conductors, and so on.

We shall focus here on the reforms of the general regime and of the public-sector pension scheme, as their rules structure pension entitlements for a large majority of the population. The major reforms took place in 1983, 1993, 2003, 2010, and 2014 and are described in table 4.1.

Until the 1980s, all pension reforms in France aimed at increasing benefit levels and favoring early retirement. Then, starting in the 1990s, the French pension system underwent a series of new reforms going in the opposite direction, reducing benefits or increasing ages at which benefits could be claimed.

Table 4.1 **Main rules in the general regime and public-sector employees, before and after reforms**

	General regime					Public-sector employees		
	Before the 1993 reform	1993 reform	2003 reform	2010 reform	2014 reform	Before the 2003 reform	2003 reform	2010 and 2014 reforms
First age at which retirement is possible	60	No change		Increased to 62 years between cohorts 1951 and 1956	No change	55 or 60 years, depending on categories	No change	Similar to the general regime
Full-rate condition	60 or more with at least $N = 37.5$ years of contribution, or 65 without any condition on N	Duration condition raised from 37.5 years to 40 years (in 2003)	Duration condition raised to 41 (between 2008 and 2012) and to be increased to 41.75 years in 2020 and then indexed on life expectancy	No change in the duration condition. Shift to 67 or the unconditional full-rate age	Duration condition raised to 43 (for cohort 1973)	37.5 years	Duration condition raised to 41 (in 2008) and then moving as in the general regime	
Pension level at the full rate	If $N = 37.5$, 50 percent of the average of wages, truncated to the SS ceiling, over the 10 best years of one's career. If $N < 37.5$, this amount is prorated	The period over which past wages are averaged is increased from 10 to 25 years (by one year per year between cohorts 1933 and 1948)	No change			75 percent of the last wage	No change	
Penalty for retirement before the NRA	Prorating effect plus a reduction of 10 percent for each missing year	No change	Additional reduction reduced to 5 percent per missing year	No change		Only the prorating effect	Prorating effect plus a reduction of 5 percent for each missing year	
Bonification for retirement after the NRA	None	No change	3 percent for each year of postponement, increased to 5 percent in 2005	No change		None	3 percent for each year of postponement, increased to 5 percent in 2005	

The last significant reform increasing generosity occurred in 1983. This reform lowered the normal retirement age (NRA) from 65 to 60. However, it did so in a way that deserves precise explanation. Before 1983, the NRA for private-sector employees was 65. Retiring earlier was possible, as the early retirement age (ERA) was already equal to 60, but with a very strong penalty lowering the replacement rate by 5 percentage points per year of anticipation—that is, for instance, a 10 percent reduction of one's pension level if retiring at 64 rather than 65 and a replacement rate of 25 percent only if retiring at 60 instead of 65. The novelty of the 1983 reform has been to withdraw this penalty, but not in a fully unconditional way: a length-of-career condition was introduced requiring at least 37.5 years of contribution. Given that most male workers were fulfilling this condition (but not all female workers), it de facto offered to them full-rate benefits at the ERA, hence closing the practical gap between the early and normal retirement ages. Yet the two notions remained distinct, and people not reaching the 37.5 years condition remained exposed to the 10 percent penalty per year if failing to reach either this condition or the age of 65. In other words, the reform did not fully lower the NRA to 60. It did so only for one part of the population, with the side consequence of having complexified the structure of French pension rules, where three rather than two pivotal ages now coexist: the ERA, still equal to 60; an SEA (statutory eligibility age) of 65, systematically entitling one to a full-rate pension no matter the length of one's career; and the intermediate FRA (full-rate age), which is no longer an age *stricto sensu*, as it basically corresponds to a length-of-career condition.

The 1993 reform started reverting the trend toward more generous pensions. It did so for private-sector workers only, in two ways. The first instrument was the reduction of pension levels at the full rate: instead of being computed based on the 10 best years of one's career, as it used to be for people born until 1933, the average of past earnings that enters the benefit formula started being progressively computed over a longer period: up to 25 years for people born 1948 or after. This change was coupled with the application of a less generous revalorization rule for these past earnings, with reevaluation according to past wage growth being replaced by reevaluation based on past inflation only. The second instrument was a strengthening of the conditions required to get the full pension: the contribution years have been progressively increased from 37.5 to 40 years by one quarter each year from cohort 1933 to cohort 1943, with the expected effect of reincreasing the number of people unable to get a full-rate pension at the ERA, hence reopening the gap between the ERA and the FRA.

The 2003 reform extended the 1993 reform in several ways. For public-sector employees, the condition for a full-rate pension had remained at its pre-1993 value of 37.5 years of contribution, and they only incurred a small penalty for retiring before this full rate, the one automatically resulting from the proportionality between the pension level and the number of years of contribution. As a first step, the 2003 reform changed this length-of-career condition for these public-sector employees, raising it to 40 years, and it introduced a penalty of −5 percent per missing year of contribution. The penalty applying to private-sector employees was symmetrically aligned on this new value of 5 percent, as its initial level of 10 percent was much stronger than requested for actuarial neutrality. The condition for obtaining the full rate was then made more stringent for both categories of workers: starting in 2008, it has been increased from 40 to 41.5 years, and the reform introduced a mechanism linking further increases of this parameter to changes in life expectancy. Symmetrical to the move toward actuarial and homogenous penalization of early exits, the reform also introduced a new bonus for years of postponement beyond the full rate, initially equal to 3 percent and then further increased to 5 percent per year of postponement.

The 2003 reform also led to the revision of one important aspect of the French employment legislation; otherwise the implementation of bonuses for postponing beyond the full rate would have remained purely theoretical. Until the 2003 reform, the full-rate age corresponded to the normal end of the contract between the employer and the employee. A separation occurring before this age at the initiative of the employer was a layoff, with associated obligations for the employer: the need for administrative authorization, payment of dismissal indemnities, and the risk of contestation of this dismissal in professional courts. No such obligation existed once the full rate was attained: the employer could legally request the employee to claim her pension benefits without any further obligations vis-à-vis this employee. The FRA therefore corresponded to a de facto mandatory retirement age, not in the sense that it was illegal to work beyond that age, but in the sense that most wage earners in the private sector had no real choice to work later than this age. The 2003 reform suppressed this disposition of the French employment legislation, reintroducing a clear distinction between the FRA and the mandatory retirement age. The latter was first fixed to 65 and then raised to 70 in 2009.

Lastly and opposite to the general trend toward later retirement, the 2003 reform opened new derogatory possibilities for early retirement through the pension scheme itself (and not through separate early retirement schemes) under the label of *carrières longues* but was limited to a very targeted population: workers who had started working (and contributing) very early, at age 14, 15, or 16. These workers were offered the possibility to retire with the full rate as soon as 56, 57, or 58, depending on additional conditions on contribution length.

This 2003 reform had, however, still left aside some specific categories of public-sector employees: those of large public firms benefiting from "special schemes" (railways, public transportation, gas and electricity, etc.). These

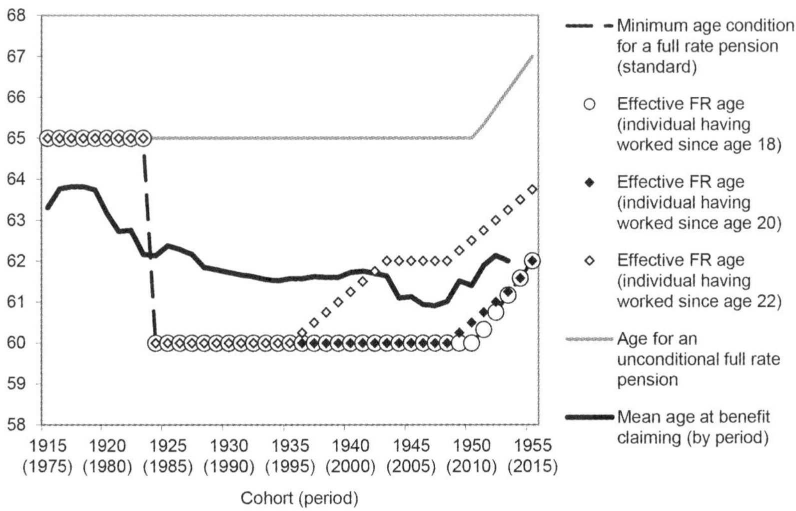

Fig. 4.2 Typical eligibility ages by cohort, private-sector employees

schemes were aligned on common rules in 2007 (contribution length, penalty for early retirement, etc.) even if pay compensation had to be offered to soothe opposition to this change.

The 2010 reform then affected all categories of workers, from both the public and private sectors. It consisted of an increase in the ERA and in the SEA. In other words, it shifted the age bracket within which people are expected to choose their retirement age, from 60–65 to 62–67. For public-sector workers who still benefited from different reference ages (i.e., the police, prison officers, or nurses), the increase was similar, with the ERA shifted from 55 to 57 and the SEA from 60 to 62.

In 2014, the last pension reform was introduced, which again strengthened the condition for full-rate benefits, increasing it from 41.5 years to 43 years. At the same time, the *carrières longues* rule was extended to include workers who started working before age 20, allowing some of them to also retire at 60, before the new ERA of 62.

Figure 4.2 tries to summarize the most salient of all these changes with time-series profiles of representative eligibility or effective retirement ages for private-sector employees. The age required for getting an "unconditional" full-rate pension has been equal to 65 over most of the period and has been increased to 67 years by the 2010 reform. Ages for accessing the full rate have had an evolution that depends on the *N* of years of contribution, here converted into a condition on age at entry into the labor force, assuming uninterrupted careers afterward, with three values for this age at entry: 18, 20, and 22. We see here the potential for an explanation of the U-shaped profile of labor force participation over time, with a drop of this age from 65 to 60 for all three cases in 1983 and then a reincrease due to the succession of reforms, initially affecting people having started working relatively late but spreading to the other cases at the end of the period, due in particular to the increase of the minimum age to 62. The last line in black on the graph shows how effective retirement behavior has resulted from a mix of these changing conditions and also of other derogatory rules not reported on the graph. For instance, before 1984, the effective age of benefit claiming was already much lower than 65, as several possibilities existed to leave with a full rate before this age. Then, over the recent period, the incentive effect of the 2003, 2010, and 2014 reforms has been dampened by the derogatory possibilities offered by the *carriers longues* system.

4.2.2 Other Schemes: Early Retirement Schemes, Unemployment, and Disability

To understand the trends in older workers' labor market participation, the description of the normal retirement pathway must be completed by a description of the possibilities offered by other exit routes. Three main pathways can be distinguished: (a) early retirement schemes (*préretraites*—i.e., state-sponsored schemes offering transitory benefits before access to normal retirement), (b) unemployment insurance, and (c) the invalidity/disability route.

Since this latter route is relatively marginal in the French case, we limit ourselves to a very brief description of its characteristics. Before the ERA, the *pension d'invalidité* is for individuals with a disability rate of over two-thirds. Workers can also be on long-term sickness leaves. After the ERA, people may be eligible for the *pension d'inaptitude* for a disability rate of over one-half. These people are treated as full-rate pensioners even if they do not fulfill conditions for the full rate. No significant reform of this system took place during the period under study.

Early retirement schemes and unemployment insurance have played a more important role during the period under review. Their main features over the last decades are given in table 4.2. This table shows that early retirement schemes were developed first, initially targeted toward the 60–64 age group and very specific sectors, under the name of *Garantie de ressources*. The first of these early retirement schemes were introduced in the early 1970s. During this first stage, early retirement was considered exceptional. However, in the face of declining labor demand and rising unemployment, the program was extended on a larger scale. The *Garantie de ressources*, initially limited to layoffs in 1972, was extended in 1977 to people having voluntarily left their job (*Garantie de Ressources Démission*, GRD). The replacement rate was 70 percent of the previous gross wage, thus higher than a full-rate pension on the general regime (not considering complementary schemes).

At the same period, the *Allocation Spécifique du Fonds National pour*

Table 4.2 **Main characteristics of anticipated retirement schemes developed since 1972**

	1972	1977	1982	1983	1985	1992	1996	1997	1999	2000	2004	2011	2017	Age groups covered
Preretirement schemes (private sector)														
Garantie de ressources licenciement (Resource guarantee—layoff)	x	x	x											60–64
Garantie de Ressources demission (Resource guarantee—resignation)		x	x											60–64
Allocation Spécifique du Fonds National pour l'Emploi (ASFNE) (Specific allowance for the national employment fund)		x	x	x	x	x	x	x	x	x	x	x		>56
Contrat de solidarité preretraite démission (Solidarity contract—resignation)			x	x										>55
Contrat de solidarité preretraite progressive (Solidarity contract—progressive retirement)			x	x										>55
Preretraites Progressives (PRP) *(Progressive preretirement)*						x	x	x	x	x	x			>55
Allocation de remplacement pour l'emploi (ARPE) (Replacement allowance for employment)							x	x	x	x				>58
Cessation anticipée de certains travailleurs salariés (CATS) (Anticipated cessation for specific categories of wage earners)										x	x	x	x	>55
Cessation anticipée d'activité des travailleurs de l'amiante (CAATA) *(Anticipated cessation for workers exposed to asbestos)*										x	x	x	x	>50
Preretirement schemes (public sector)														
Congé de fin d'activité (CFA) (End-of-career leave)									x	x	x			
Specific dispositions of unemployment insurance toward older workers														
Dispense de recherche d'emploi (DRE) (Exemption from seeking employment)					x	x	x	x	x	x	x			>57.5

Note: "x" corresponds to periods when schemes have been effective.
Source: Updated from Burricand and Roth (2000)

l'Emploi (ASFNE) was created, whose eligibility was extended in the 1980s to wage earners older than 55, together with the *Contrat de solidarité préretraite démission* (CSPRD), a scheme that offered a replacement rate of 70 percent to wage earners with more than 10 years of contributions who had resigned, hence similar to the GRD. However, this CSPRD scheme remained relatively short lived and closed in 1983; this was also the case for the associated "*Contrat de solidarité préretraite progressive*," a scheme allowing "part-time preretirement." In the meantime, the normal retirement age had been decreased to 60 in 1983, and with this decrease, early retirement schemes were planned to lose importance. Yet this took place only progressively. The *Garantie de Ressources* was gradually suppressed and the ASFNE was first restricted to wage earners older than 57 in 1994, before being definitely suppressed only in 2011.

Some new alternative schemes were created in compensation but were more specifically targeted: the *Allocation de remplacement pour l'emploi* (ARPE) and the *Congé de fin d'activité* (CFA) schemes created in the mid-1990s were targeted to wage earners older than 58 in the private and the public sectors, respectively. Employers using the ARPE had to replace early retirees with younger workers under age 26. Both were then suppressed in 2003 and replaced by two new and still more focused schemes, the *Cessation anticipée de certains travailleurs salariés* (CATS) and the *Cessation anticipée d'activité des travailleurs de l'amiante* (CAATA). The CATS was targeted to workers with especially hard work conditions (at least 15 years on an assembly line or with night work) and the CAATA scheme to workers exposed to asbestos.

The resulting expansion and contraction of numbers in preretirement for the 60–64 and 55–59 age groups can be observed in figure 4.3. The total stock of people benefiting from this *Garantie de ressources* grew rapidly between 1974 and 1983, where it amounted to about 7 percent of the 55–64 population. This growth explains the strong decline in employment rates between ages 60 and 64 shown in figure 4.1. This also explains why the introduction of retirement at age 60 in 1983 did not show up in figure 4.1 in the form of a sudden drop of employment rates in the 60–64 age bracket: to a large extent, this reform essentially consisted of a transformation of preretired people into "normal" retirees. The stock of these *Garanties de ressources* then mechanically declined during the first half of the 1980s.

This drop in the *Garantie de ressources* was initially compensated by the expansion of the ASFNE and other schemes applying to people in the 55–59 age bracket. But this expansion stopped in the mid-1990s, and these schemes have now almost disappeared, leaving room for two other routes, also represented in figure 4.3. The first one is the unemployment insurance route. This essentially took place through the creation of the *Dispense de recherche d'emploi* (DRE) that was introduced in 1984. In the 1990s, DREs became numerically more important than early retirees. The system consists

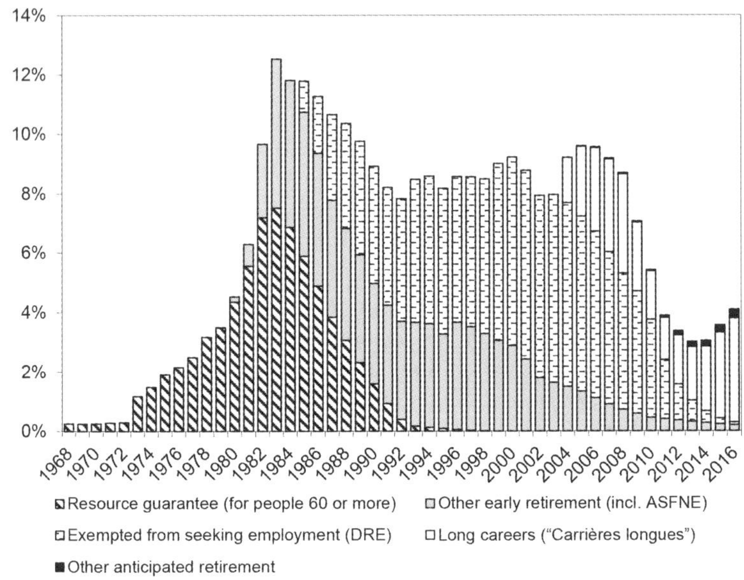

Fig. 4.3 Population in preretirement schemes (in percentage of total 55–64 population)

Source: DARES, Tableau de bord de l'activité des seniors et des politiques d'emploi (2017)

of exempting unemployed people from the active job search past a certain age: 55 at its creation. There were many changes, mostly decreases, in the eligibility age between 1984 and 2009 before a gradual increase to 60 in 2011. The DRE program was suppressed in 2012. The DRE did not give additional unemployment benefits, yet combined with the possibility to keep full unemployment benefits without any degressivity until being entitled to a full-rate pension, DRE has de facto acted as an early retirement scheme.

What ultimately took over after the suppression of the DRE has been the development of the *Carrières longues* system described earlier, which lies somewhat in between early retirement and normal retirement: it is part of the normal retirement system, but with very strong selectivity rules targeted to people having started contribution very early.

To sum up, the development of specific rules for older unemployed people in the national system of unemployment insurance and in early retirement scheme seems to explain a large part of the decline in employment rates in the 55–59 age bracket that occurred during the early 1980s. It was then followed by a period of tighter regulation of these routes, sometimes compensated by the creation of new ones but generally more focused. Until the early 2000s, the impact of all these policies has just been to maintain a relative status quo in terms of numbers of beneficiaries. This period corresponds to the bottom part of the U-shaped profile of labor force participation for men aged 55 to 59 shown in figure 4.1. The situation reversed much more significantly during the 2000s, first with the progressive extinction of early retirement schemes, of which only two very limited forms still subsist, and second with the extinction of the DREs, definitely suppressed in 2011, with a stock of beneficiaries progressively declining to zero. For some time, the resulting downward trend has been compensated by the development of the *Carrières longues* system, but this has not been enough to offset the other changes.

4.3 Key Components of the Benefit Calculator

After this first inventory of how social security rules have changed in France since the early 1980s, the rest of the chapter will be devoted to translating these rules into the common formalism of financial incentives to retire in order to allow comparison with other countries. Several measures of these incentives to retire have been proposed in the literature. We focus here on the so-called tax rate that implicitly applies to wages if one decides to postpone retirement by one year: it computes by how much discounted social security wealth (SSW) is reduced or eventually increased when choosing to work one year longer, expressed as a percentage of the current wage, with SSW being defined as the discounted sum of pension benefits over one's expected retirement period. This indicator is a pure financial indicator. It does not account for all other components that may be determinants for individuals' choices to retire: health, working conditions, and so on.

Computing these tax rates requires several conventional choices and inputs. Conventional choices are necessary to define what kind of decision is going to be modeled and for whom. Inputs will consist of data necessary to feed the pension simulator—essentially career profiles but also survival probabilities for the computation of cumulated benefits and weights to be applied to the various exit routes.

4.3.1 Basic Conventional Choices

Retirement behavior has two dimensions that ideally deserve separate modeling: one is benefit claiming and the other is exit from employment. The two decisions fully coincide for people directly moving from their last paid job into full retirement. In practice, benefit claiming can occur after or before this exit from the labor force. In France, however, despite increasing possibilities to combine paid activity with the perception of pension benefits, working after having claimed one's benefits remains a relatively marginal phenomenon that will not be addressed here. On the other hand, the end of people's paid careers very often occurs well before their access to normal retirement. In 2012, only two people out of three were still employed when claiming their pension benefits (Govillot 2013). This discrepancy generally results from temporary transitions through one of the various alternative early routes that have been described above: early retirement benefits, unemployment insurance benefits, or disability benefits.

To deal with these alternative routes, we model the fact of definitely leaving the labor force, whatever the chosen route k, rather than the fact of claiming for normal pension benefits. At a given age a and for a given route k, two cases will have to be considered.

The first one is when this route is already opened at age a. In this case, the computation is straightforward: the SSW accrual combines the negative effect of foregoing one year of benefits (a "perception duration effect") and the fact that, in case of postponement, the level of this benefit is likely to be higher (a "benefit level effect"). In the plausible case where the first effect dominates, the route under consideration will create an incentive to withdraw: in other words, this route is associated with an implicit taxation of labor.

But we also have to compute the incentive properties of routes that are not yet opened to the individual. Let's consider, for instance, an individual who has not reached the ERA associated with the normal retirement system. For this person, leaving the labor force with the plan to benefit later from this normal route is an option: the choice is between doing so at the current age a and waiting until the ERA to claim social security benefits or working one more year, generally implying higher entitlements, but for a retirement period that will also start at the ERA—that is, of exactly the same length. As a result, we expect to measure for this person a positive incentive to remain at work or, equivalently, a negative implicit taxation of labor (a subsidy). After that, if this person is still at work when reaching the ERA, we will turn again at this age to a computation that will combine the negative effect of receiving the benefit for one year less and the increment to the level of the benefit resulting from a longer career.

This convention for computing incentives before the eligibility age ignores what is certainly the strongest determinant for staying at work until the ERA for those who do not benefit from any other early retirement possibility: the loss of wage income and the fact of having to wait until the ERA without any resources. Ignoring this dimension is the consequence of focusing only on the SSW side of the problem. But this convention at least provides us with implicit tax rates at all ages for all potential routes, both those already available and those that will be available only later.

Having computed SSW for each pathway, what remains to be done is to weight these incentives. We do it conventionally using the observed shares of all these routes in global yearly exit flows, even though these probabilities are likely to be endogenous: these probabilities are equilibrium values combining the degree to which these routes are accessible to workers and their choices to make use of these routes.

The next conventional choice for simulations is to define to whom these computations will be applied. We distinguish three skill levels corresponding to low, medium, and high levels of education and consider private- and public-sector workers. Computations will be performed separately for men and women but without any distinction between single and married persons: it is only personal pensions that are simulated here. Survivor's pensions in France follow complicated rules, with some of them means tested (those delivered by the *régime général*) and others not, leading to important threshold effects according to the ratio between wages earned by both spouses. The rules did not undergo significant changes during the period under review; this relativizes the need to model them to explain behavioral changes. Of course, there could have existed a time-varying interaction between these rules and the narrowing of the wage and career gap between men and women, but these potential interactions are a priori far too complex to be usefully retraced by a limited set of typical cases.

4.3.2 Earnings Histories

Retrospective data on wages are a major component of computations. In France, microdata on wages are available either from the Labor Force Survey (LFS) or from administrative sources such as the *Declarations annuelles de données sociales*. We favor the first data source despite a smaller sample size and the lower accuracy of self-reported wage levels, as the LFS provides information on the education level, our variable of social stratification.

Based on this dataset, three variants have been tested for earnings profiles:

- *Common synthetic profiles*. These profiles use age patterns observed in three countries (Germany, Italy, and the US) normalized to 1 at age 50 for each skill and sex group and converted in national equivalents through multiplication by country and time-specific wage levels at this age of 50. Here, the role of the French LFS is only to provide the wage levels observed at each period and at age 50 to rescale these common synthetic profiles to a level corresponding to the French situation. These common synthetic profiles will be used in the baseline simulations presented in section 4.4.
- *Country-specific but time-independent profiles*. We use profiles by age estimated in 2016 using the LFS data, and then, as for common synthetic profiles, we rescale them to the observed levels at each period at age 50.
- *Country- and time-specific profiles*. The profiles are fully derived each year from successive labor force surveys, differentiated according to gender and education levels.

We produce these three sets of profiles by gender and education levels (available in Blanchet et al. 2019b). In the three cases, the method applies only from 1982, the first year for which wage data are available in the LFS. Wage levels are also required for earlier periods. For instance, people retiring at 65 in 1980 had started their careers up to 50 years before—that is, in 1930. Up to 1945, back projection is possible based on average wages provided by National Accounts. For periods that are still more remote, a conventional evolution of 2 percent per year is applied. This has limited practical incidence, as the reference wage is computed on only a short subperiod of these peoples' careers, generally located in the middle or second half of their careers.

Differences appear between the common synthetic profiles and the French profiles, mostly for high school graduates. For the synthetic profile, the increase is steep at the beginning of the period, and the wage evolution is quite flat from 30 to the end of the career. We note a small decrease at the end for men in the lower education group. As far as French profiles are concerned, the increase is smaller at younger ages, but wage profiles are rising during the whole career.

4.3.3 Survival Probabilities and Pathways

Concerning survival probabilities, as for wages, we have one "common" specification shared by all countries, used for our baseline's simulation.

For alternative pathways, we regroup them into the four main categories described in section 4.2: normal retirement, early retirement, unemployment, and invalidity. Information on access to these pathways by gender and education is provided mostly by the French LFS completed by the *Santé et Itinéraire Professionnel* survey (SIP—i.e., Health and Labor Market History) for disability.[1] Due to the small share for some exit routes for highly educated people, we compute the weights only for two education groups, considering as a whole those with high school diplomas and above. Relative weights are presented in appendix A.

For men and women aged between 55 and 59, we observe a decrease in the probability to be in either early retirement, unemployment, or disability over the period. The probability to experiment with these pathways is always lower for the higher educated. Note that for women with only primary or secondary school education, the employment rate, compared to other pathways, is quite low. We have excluded women out of the labor force for family or personal reasons and have rescaled the probabilities to 1.

Above 59, the employment rate is quite low for every group. Probabilities of unemployment or disability being very low, we observe the same pattern as in figure 4.1 for employment and the complementary pattern for retirement.

1. This second survey provides current and retrospective information on health and labor market status for 14,000 individuals aged 20 to 74 in 2010. All successive spells in labor market histories and all major health events in individuals' lives are reported. We select a subsample of spells corresponding to the states experienced by the individuals of the sample when aged 55 to 60 years old and consider the information relative to disability or sickness leave.

4.3.4 Computing Incentives, Net of Taxation, and Other Contributions

With all these elements in hand, it is possible to move to the computation of benefits. More precisely, for a given pathway k and an individual i observed at time t and age R, we compute the sequence of future benefits between ages R and T if she retires at $R, B_{k,t,a}(R,i)$ for $a = R$ to T and then sum them up with discounting and weighting by survival probabilities at each age to get the associated social security wealth $SSW_{k,t}(R,i)$, hence the accrual representing by how much this SSW increases (or decreases) in case of postponement by one year. As explained above, if R is lower than the eligibility age for the considered pathway, SSW will cumulate benefits only starting from this eligibility age. The associated accrual is

$$ACCR_{k,t}(R,i) = SSW_{k,t+1}(R + 1,i) - SSW_{k,t}(R,i).$$

Hence the tax rate is

$$ITAX_{k,t}(R,i) = -ACCR_{k,t}(R,i)/Y_{t+1,i},$$

where $Y_{t+1,i}$ is the wage that this individual will earn next year in case of postponement.

Detailed pension benefits are calculated according to successive legislation using the code embedded in the French PensIPP microsimulation model. This computation takes into account taxes or other contributions to which both wages and pensions are submitted in order to compute a net replacement rate. The general principle of taxation of public pensions in France is that social security contributions are fully deductible from income tax, but pension benefits are subject to tax when received. French income tax is based on joint taxation, whereby all incomes earned by a tax unit are added and divided by the number of parts, or the number of units composing the tax unit—that is, 1 for each adult and 0.5 for each child. In addition to the income tax, pensions can be taxed by other social security contributions, like health care contributions or general flat tax contributions like the *Contribution sociale généralisée* (CSG) and the *Contribution au remboursement de la dette sociale* (CRDS). These latter contributions have been increasing since the early 1990s and have led to a reduction in the ratio of gross pension and net pension benefits.

Given the nature of the simulations based here on average earnings at the individual level, we have abstained from precisely modeling the rules of the joint income tax and prefer to approximate the average change in the taxation of pension by simulating all the other taxes—which have changed most across time. Hence we compute health care contributions, CSG, and CRDS to obtain net pensions for our different earnings profiles. The change over time in taxation is marked, going from 0 percent in 1980 to 7.4 percent in 2015.

4.4 Wage Earners in the Private Sector

4.4.1 Incentives Provided by the Normal Retirement Route

We start the presentation of the results by focusing on incentives provided by the central route, normal retirement. Even if incentives are also formally computed for ages below the normal ERA, we focus here on the 60–64 age bracket, for which they are the most significant. Accruals and associated tax rates for men and women are presented for the three education levels. Level 1 corresponds to primary or secondary school, and individuals are assumed to have started working at 16; level 2 is for high school graduates with an entry in the labor market at 20; and level 3 corresponds to individuals having more than a high school diploma and beginning work at 25.

The first set of results is based on the common synthetic earnings profiles discussed in section 4.3.2.[2] Results are qualitatively similar for men and women and will be commented on in global terms. Indeed, we consider women with uninterrupted careers whose paths differ from those of men only in terms of wage levels, not in terms of years of contributions, and it is this latter parameter that is the main determinant of replacement rates.

Incentive profiles for men or women at level 1 read as follows. For these individuals, before the 1983 reform, the retirement route was already opened at 60, but the full-rate age was equal to 65, with a strong penalty for earlier departures of 10 percent per year of anticipation, higher than that requested by actuarial neutrality. This resulted in a strong positive accrual and, formally, a "subsidy" to working at these ages—that is, a negative tax rate. For these individuals, the 1983 reform fully reversed the pattern. Having started working early, they became entitled to a full-rate pension as soon as 60, and in the absence of any bonus for postponement beyond the full-rate age, the only impact of postponing beyond 60 was a negative perception duration effect—that is, the fact of benefiting from one's benefits one year less, hence a negative accrual of the same order of magnitude at all ages and an associated positive tax rate of about 70 percent, roughly equal by construction to the replacement level. This is the situation described in Blanchet and Pelé (1999). It remained so until the 2003 reform that introduced the bonus for postponement beyond the FRA, bringing both the accrual and the tax rate closer to zero but not entirely.

The situation of zero taxation has been fully achieved only by the 2010 reform for ages 60 and 61 but not by having brought benefits more in line with the principle of actuarial neutrality. The mechanism has been different and stems from the convention used to compute the tax incentive for people who are below the eligibility age. Let us consider the case of an individual

2. Results using the alternative profiles are available upon request but do not lead to significant changes.

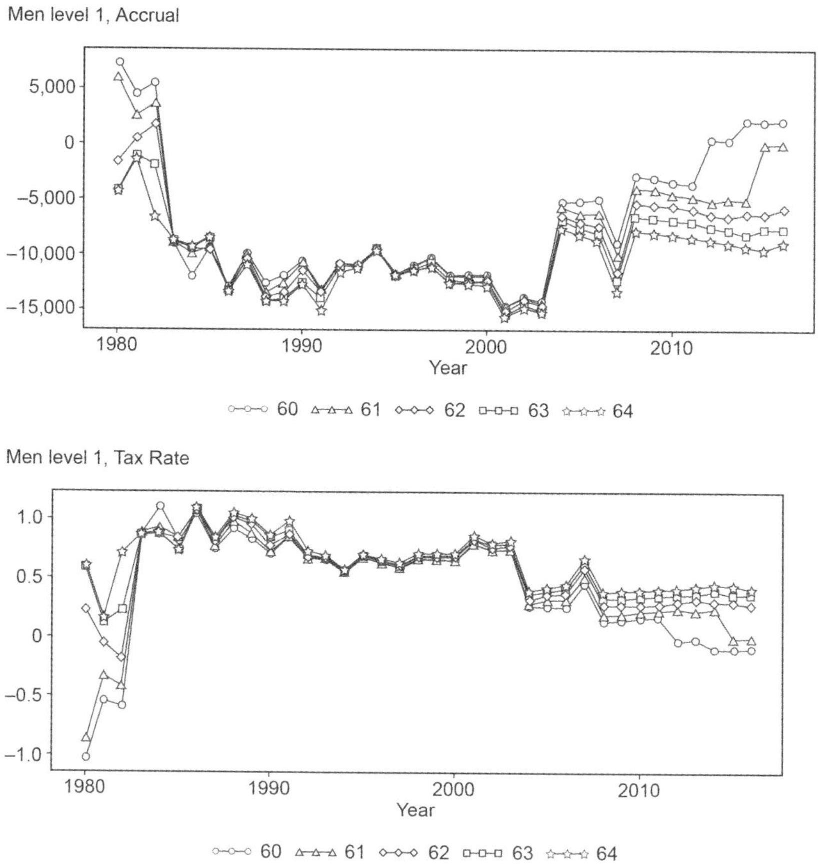

Fig. 4.4 Incentives provided by the normal pension route, 60 to 64

for whom the minimum age has been shifted to 61. For this individual, leaving the labor force at 60 and claiming for benefits at 61 generates the same stream of future benefits as leaving the labor force at 61. The perception of benefits will start at 61 in both cases. The only impact of working longer should be to accumulate higher entitlements, but this impact is marginal, as this individual will benefit anyway from the full rate at age 61, having had a sufficiently long career, and because years accumulated in excess of the full-rate condition but before 61 are not productive: only additional years of work beyond the FRA will generate additional entitlements. All this leads to the quasi neutrality of pensions rules at age 60 seen through the lenses of this tax rate indicator, as depicted by the line with circle markers. The same holds true at age 61 (line with triangle markers) for individuals retiring a few years later, for whom the minimum age has been shifted to 62.

Of course, this does not mean that the 2010 reform has led to a system

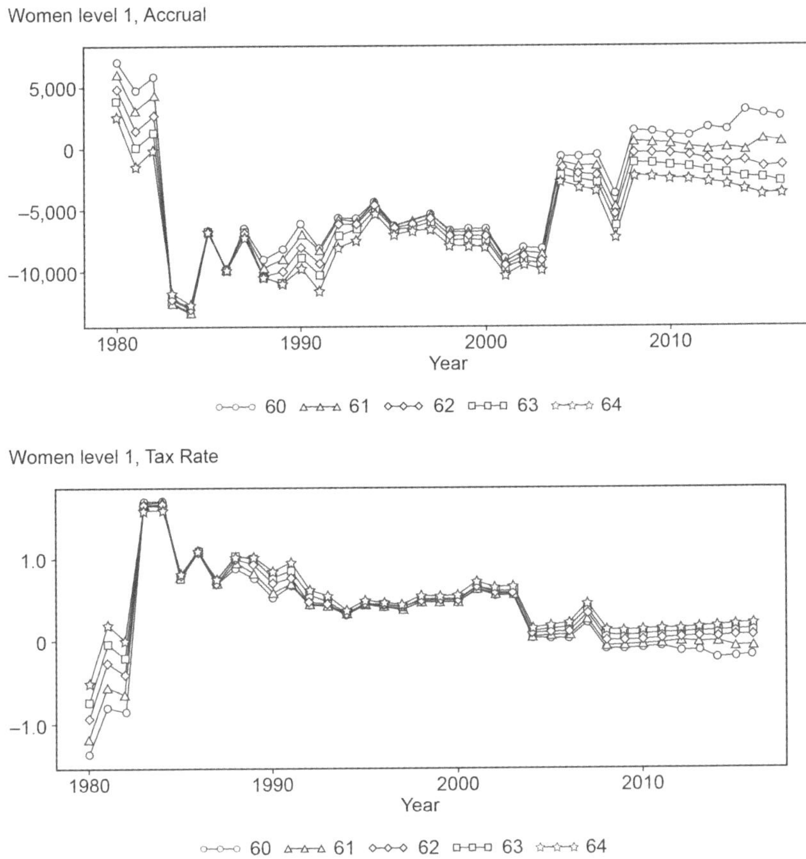

Fig. 4.4 (cont.)

that is entirely neutral for retirement behavior at ages 60 and 61—quite the contrary. We know indeed that this reform has led to substantial changes in retirement behavior in the 60–62 age group (Dubois and Koubi 2017), but this effect is not captured by the tax rate as computed here. The channel has rather been the drop to zero of the replacement rate offered at these ages.

What if we shift to the level 2 individuals having started working at age 20? The story is roughly similar, except for the absolute level of the accruals—proportional to past wages and also affected by a higher life expectancy—and also for a much stronger upward movement of the accrual at age 60 at the very end of the period due to a superposition of the effects of the 2003 and 2010 reforms. As for level 1, the effect of the 2010 reform is to suppress the duration effect of leaving employment at 61 rather than 60. But the 1993 reform adds to this a strong bonus effect, as the career length for this individual is now 41 years, no more attained at 60. For this individual, the additional year of work at 60 is therefore not lost in terms of the level of

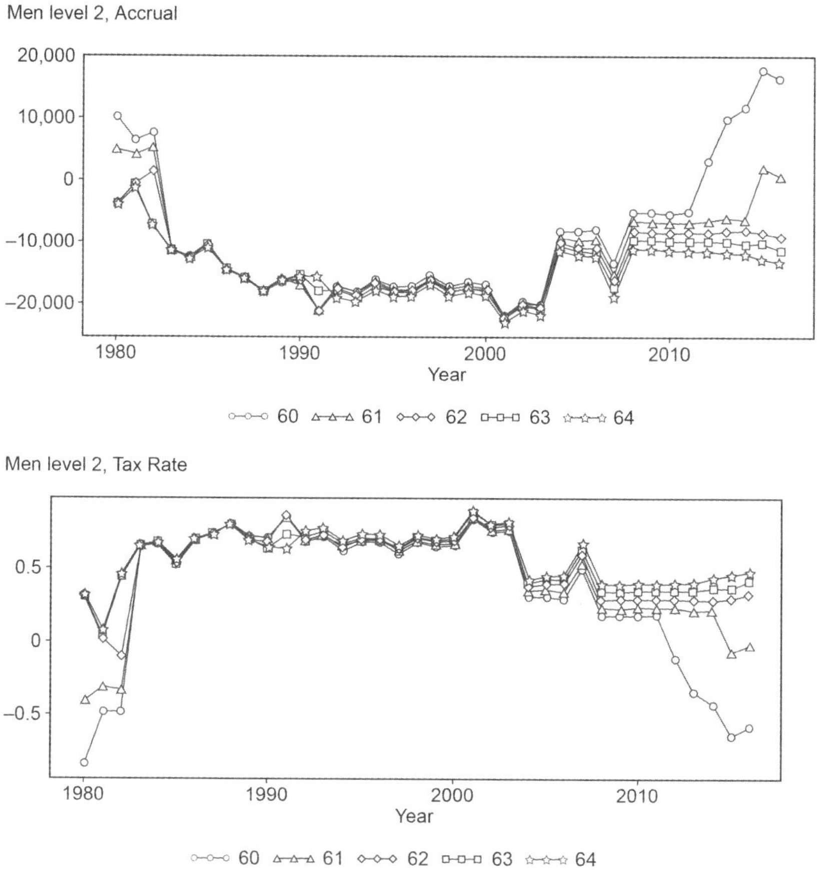

Fig. 4.4 (cont.)

benefits; it avoids a significant penalty when retiring at 61. The combination of the two elements generates a strong subsidy to working at 60—close to the one that existed before 1983.

What about the case of the type 3 individual, having started working at only 25? The interpretation of results is less straightforward. The beginning of the story is again the same as for the type 1 individual: a full-rate age equal to 65 and a strong penalty if leaving before. The absolute level of the accrual is again higher because this individual has higher earnings and is globally entitled to higher pensions with a higher life expectancy. The value of the implicit "subvention rate" is somewhat smaller, as pensions, albeit higher in absolute terms, are smaller in proportion to labor income. Yet globally, patterns are very similar between these two individuals before the 1983 reform. This reform did not strongly affect his incentive to retire at 60 or 61, since, due to his late entry into the labor market, he had to wait until 62.5 to get a full-rate pension. It is beyond this age that the initial subsidy

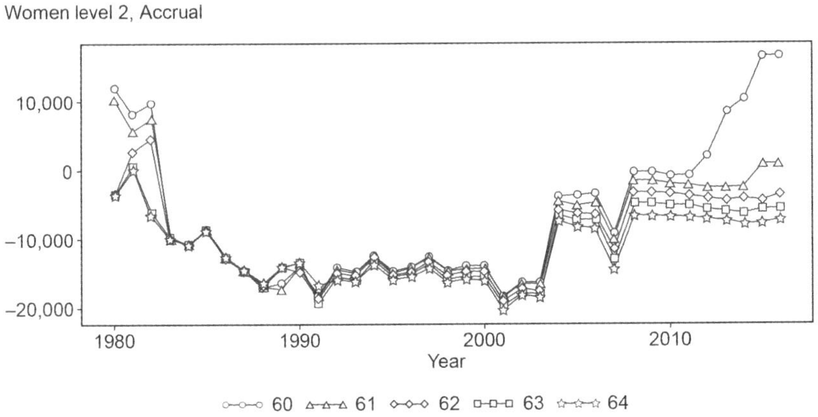

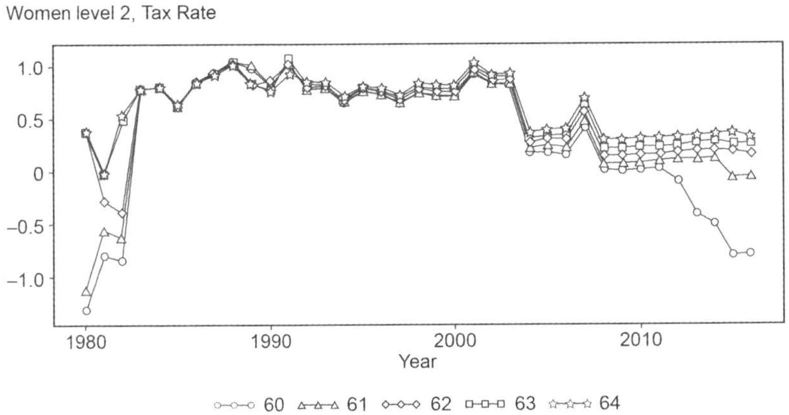

Fig. 4.4 (cont.)

is turned into taxation. But this taxation rapidly shifts to a subsidy again as a consequence of the 1993 reform that rapidly increases the age at which this individual is able to reach the full rate. This effect spreads progressively up to the higher end of the 60–64 age bracket, the move from a taxation to a subsidy being dampened somewhat by the 2003 reform that has reduced the magnitude of the penalty incurred for retiring before the full rate. For this individual, the 2010 reform also had the effect of reinforcing the subsidization of work at age 60 and then 61, but in a way that is less marked than it was for the type 1 and type 2 individuals due to the subsidization that already existed for this worker before the 2010 reform.

4.4.2 Alternative Routes

All in all, even if the tax rate does not cover all the channels through which reforms have tried to encourage later retirement, the picture is globally in line with the U-shaped employment pattern that we are expected to explain.

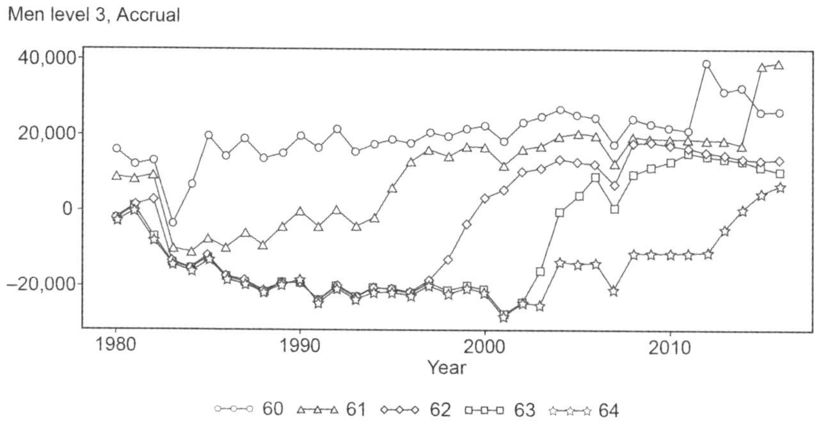

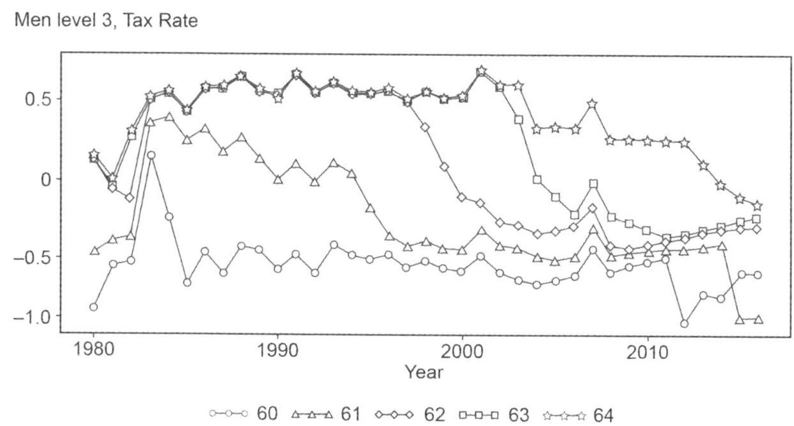

Fig. 4.4 (cont.)

Employment rates for the 60–64 age bracket have been low when the taxation of labor in this age group was high, during the second half of 1980 and 1990, and the turning point more or less coincides with a decline of these tax rates, even if the exact timing of this decline has not been uniform at all ages and for all types of workers. What if we move to the 55–59 age bracket and extend the analysis to other routes?

As mentioned above, four routes are taken into account in a stylized way. An individual aged between 55 and 59 can choose to leave employment with four options:

- either through the unemployment route or through an early retirement scheme, in these two cases with an eligibility age of 56 and a replacement rate of 60 percent;
- through disability, with an eligibility age of 55 and a replacement rate also equal to 60 percent;

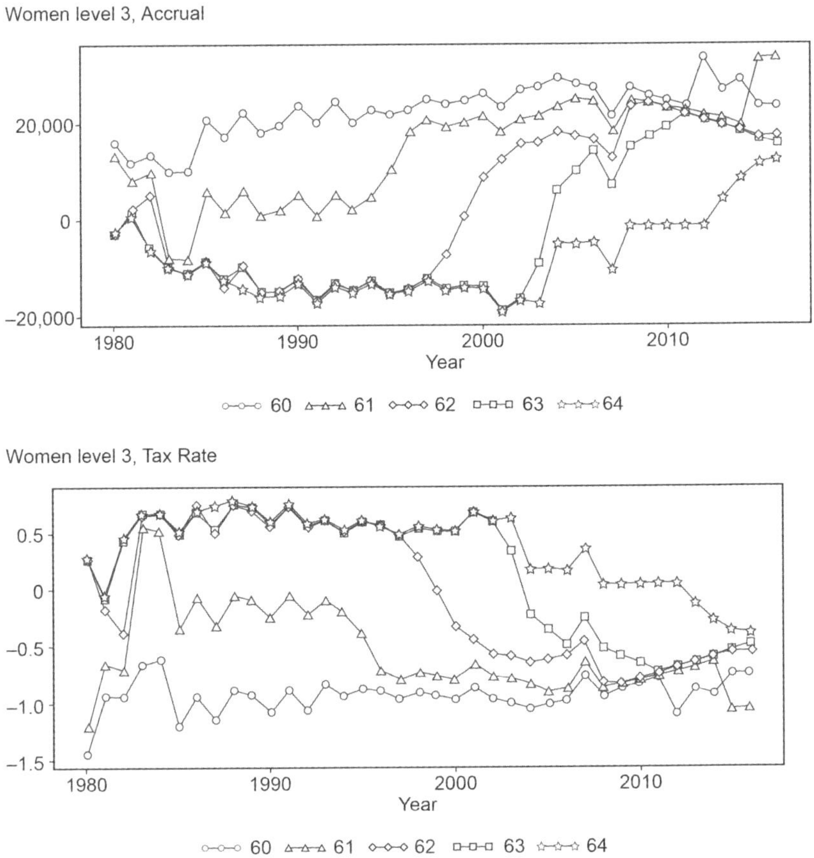

Fig. 4.4 (cont.)

- or only with the perspective of benefiting later on from a normal pension at the age of 60 before the 2010 reform, which then raised the ages to 61 and 62, with the pension offered at these respective ages but without any other forms of benefits until these ages.

Incentives associated with each of these routes are computed as for the normal route. For the first three routes, SSW is computed as the discounted sum of associated benefits until the full-rate retirement age and continued with normal pension benefits beyond this age. The problem is that these routes are not options available to everyone: benefiting from the disability route is conditional on suffering from health problems attested by special regulatory commissions; benefiting from an early retirement scheme generally results from the application to one's firm of a "social plan" negotiated between this firm and public authorities; and benefiting from unemployment insurance benefits requires having been laid off by one's employer, which here again is not a free choice made by the employee. The way to account for these limitations is to weight incentives by some probability of having access to these routes. It is ex-ante probabilities that should have been ideally used, with ex-post probabilities resulting both from these ex-ante values and from the choices made by individuals to benefit or not from these routes in response to associated expected benefits. But ex-ante probabilities are not observable, and ex-post values are used instead, despite the endogeneity problem it creates. These probabilities are those presented in figure 4.3.

Figures 4.5 and 4.6 show the results. They give the profiles of accruals from 55 to 59 for each route taken separately and their associated aggregate tax rate. Results are given for men only, as gender has little influence on results when considering people with continuous careers (results for women are given in appendix B), and they are given only for the two extreme cases of type 1 and type 3 workers.

By construction, accruals for the three routes other than normal retirement have relatively simple structures that do not significantly depend on the category of workers. For the disability route, there is a relatively flat accrual, which is about the same irrespective of age. The same applies to unemployment insurance and early retirement benefits, but only starting from 56. At 55, the accrual is close to zero, as the expected stream of benefits is the same whether one works one year more before accessing the considered route or whether one immediately stops working and has to wait one full year without resources before entering into the route under consideration. One should note incidentally that such an eventuality is not very realistic, as benefiting from an early retirement benefit or from unemployment insurance must necessarily follow a period of employment. It cannot be deferred to a later period, contrary to claiming for one's pension, which can be done at or after the minimum pension age whatever one's current status on the labor market.

The main message from figures 4.5 and 4.6 is that it is essentially incentives associated with the normal route that make the difference, however distant the perspective of a simple normal retirement can be in this 55–59 age bracket. For the type 1 individual, the general message is that of a zero accrual—no perception duration effect and no bonus effect. The reason is that at the beginning of the period, the individual has accumulated a sufficient number of years of contributions to benefit from a full-rate pension at 60, whatever his participation profile between 55 and 59. It is only at the end of the period that access to a full-rate pension at 60 starts being dependent on this participation profile, once the individual starts being hit by the progressive impact of the 1993 and 2003 reforms. For the type 3 individual, on the other hand, immediately the individual has an incentive not to stop work at 55 or later, since additional years of work are systematically productive in terms of access to the full rate at 60. This incentive paradoxically disappears at the end of the period, but this is due to the fact that, at this point, the level

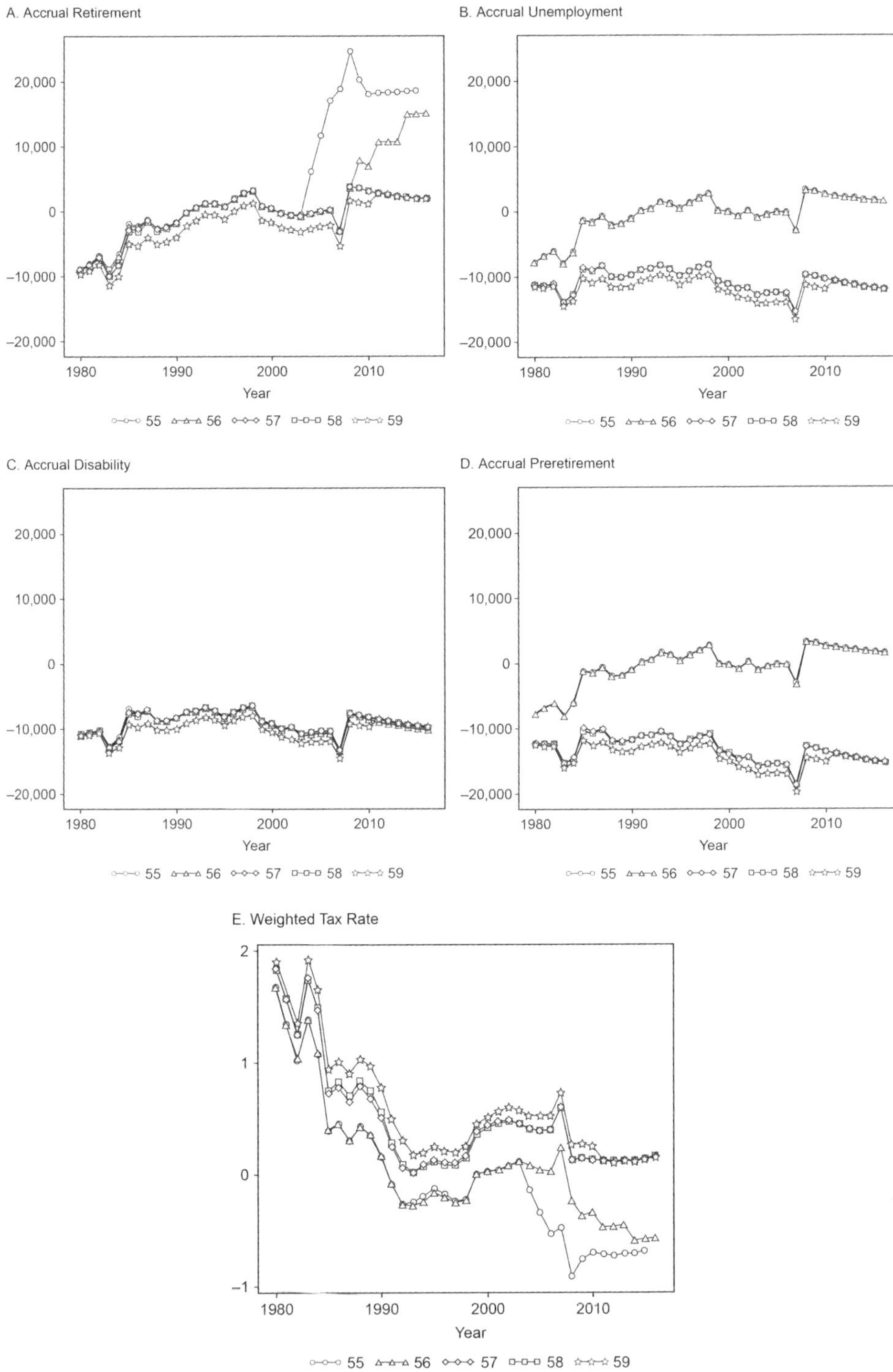

Fig. 4.5 Accruals 55–59 by pathway and aggregate tax rate (men, education level 1)

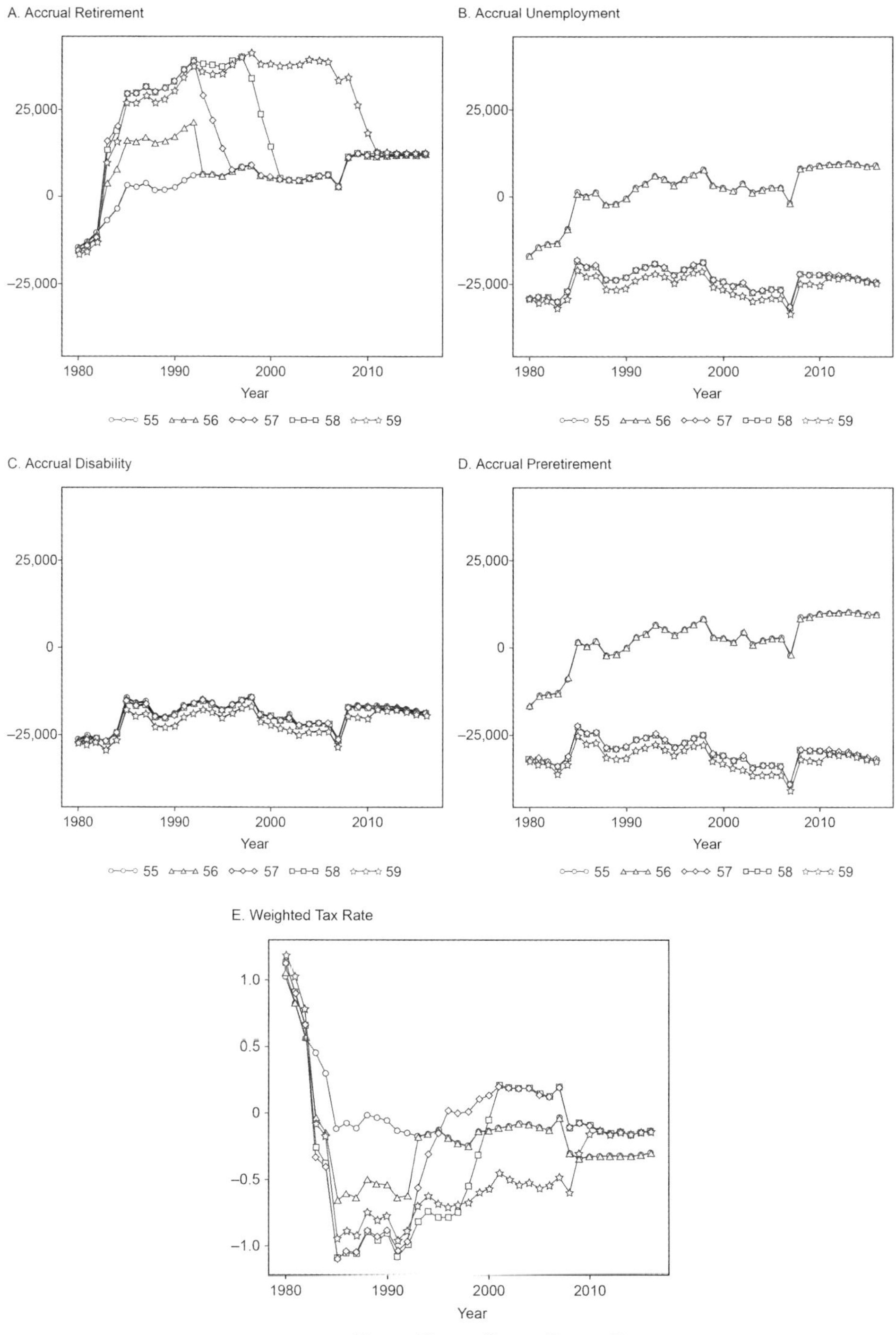

Fig. 4.6 Accruals 55–59 by pathway and aggregate tax rate (men, education level 3)

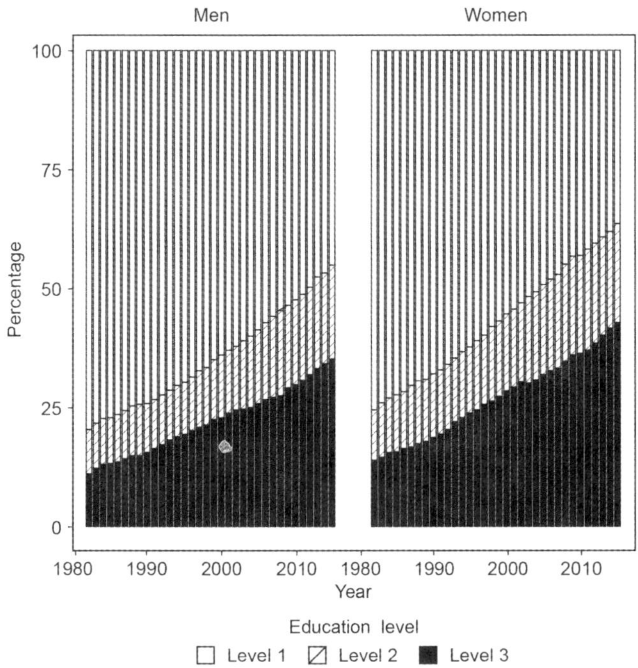

Fig. 4.7 Share of education level by year and gender
Source: French Labor Force Survey

of the pension at the minimum age is no longer determined by the length of career condition but is only determined by the distance from the statutory eligibility age: this individual will suffer the same penalty irrespective of how much he worked between 55 and 59.

Due to both the dominance of the normal route and the fact that it is this route that displays variable characteristics over time, the features of this route basically determine the profile of the aggregate tax rate displayed on the bottom of figures 4.5 and 4.6.

4.4.3 Synthesis

To summarize previous results, we then further aggregate tax rates over five-year age groups and education levels using the shares of each education level given in figure 4.7. We now reintroduce both men and women in the analysis and directly plot observed employment rates in the two aggregate age groups as functions of these tax rates. The expected correlation is negative: a higher average tax rate is expected to lead to lower employment levels.

Figures 4.8 and 4.9 confirm the presence of such a negative correlation, albeit with some irregularities, probably stemming from the fact that, as mentioned above, tax rates only capture one component of the incentive to

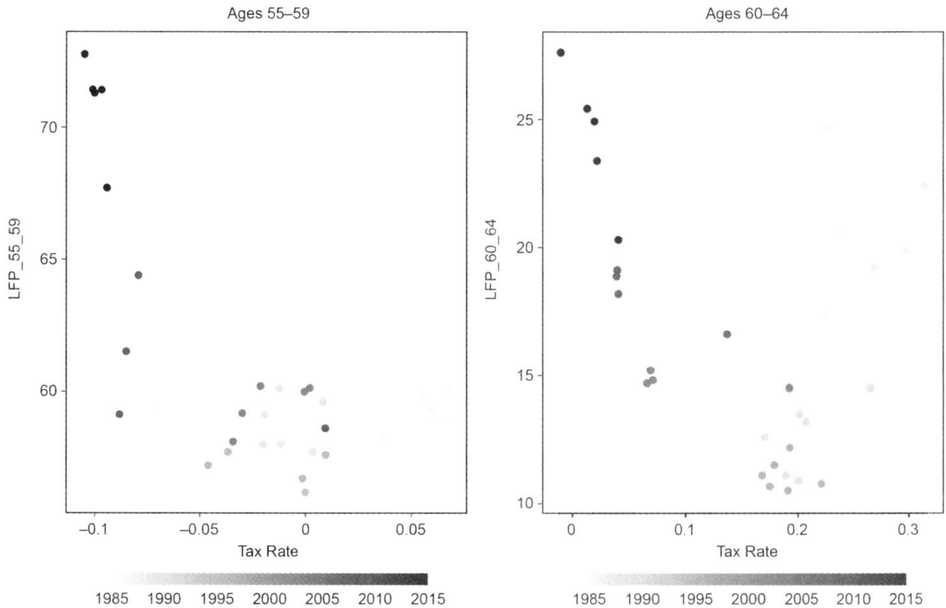

Fig. 4.8 Relationship between tax rate and labor force participation (men)

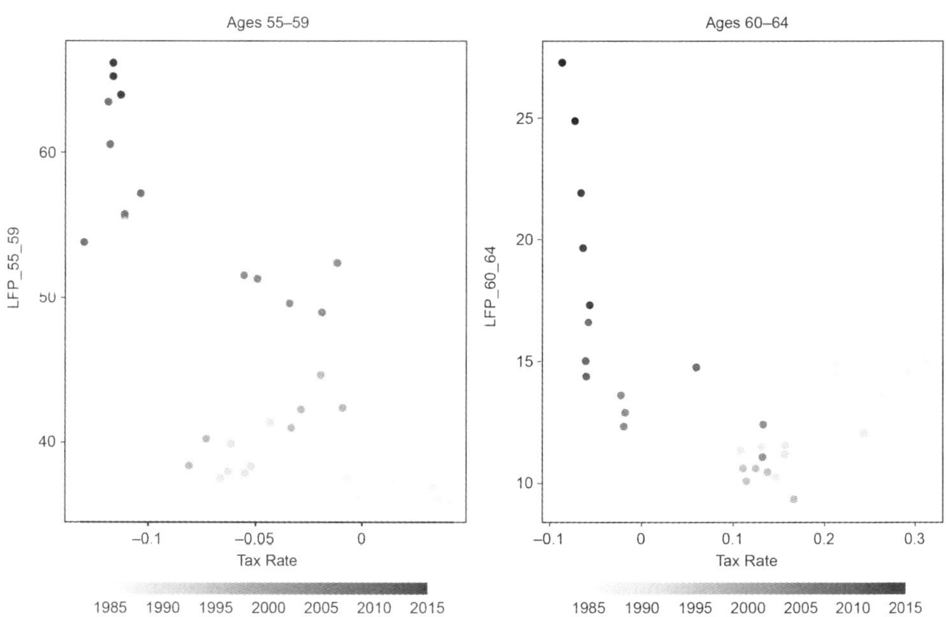

Fig. 4.9 Relationship between tax rate and labor force participation (women)

stay in the labor force: those resulting from deviations from marginal actuarial neutrality (i.e., the fact of having a social security wealth that varies with the age at exit from the labor force). This is not enough to characterize the way pension rules affect the retirement decision. Two distinct systems may be perfectly neutral, but with one offering low replacement rates and the other high ones, the former will clearly generate later departures than the second one.

The reform process in France also changed this parameter. The move closer to actuarial neutrality around the normal retirement age has been the distinctive feature of the 2003 reform, but in itself, it was not expected to be a major driving force for increasing retirement ages. Everything else equal, it even opened the possibility to leave earlier than before by reducing the penalty for departures before the full rate in the private sector, which, until 2003, was more penalized than that requested by actuarial neutrality. It is also and maybe mainly through shifts in FRA conditions that reforms have been the most effective in modifying retirement behavior.

4.5 Wage Earners in the Public Sector

This last section moves on with some results concerning retirement incentives for public-sector workers. Here the analysis will be limited to incentives in the 60–64 age group. Some specific categories of public-sector employees are entitled to retirement at much earlier ages—for instance, people in the armed forces, the police, or railway conductors. Such was also the case at the beginning of the period for primary school teachers. But these specific categories will be left aside. For other wage earners in the public sector, the minimum age has followed the same rules as in the private sector—that is, 60 until the 2010 reform and then moved up to 61 and 62. And for these people—except for the invalidity route, which will be neglected here—direct transition from employment to retirement is the general rule without the need for alternative transition routes, as these workers are not exposed to the risk of losing their jobs.

Other differences with private-sector employees have been presented above, and we briefly recall the main ones. Already before the 1983 reform, these public-sector employees only incurred a small penalty for retiring before the full-rate age, at 65. This remained true after this reform, with the new full-rate age determined by the alternative condition on age or number of years of contribution, and as for private-sector employees, no additional benefit was delivered in case of postponement beyond that age. The other difference with private-sector employees, until 2003, was that the length-of-career condition was kept equal to 37.5 years. It was only in 2003 that rules started to evolve for public-sector employees, with an almost complete convergence with the private sector: the condition on the number of years was raised to 40 and then, evolving in line for both sectors, the introduction of a

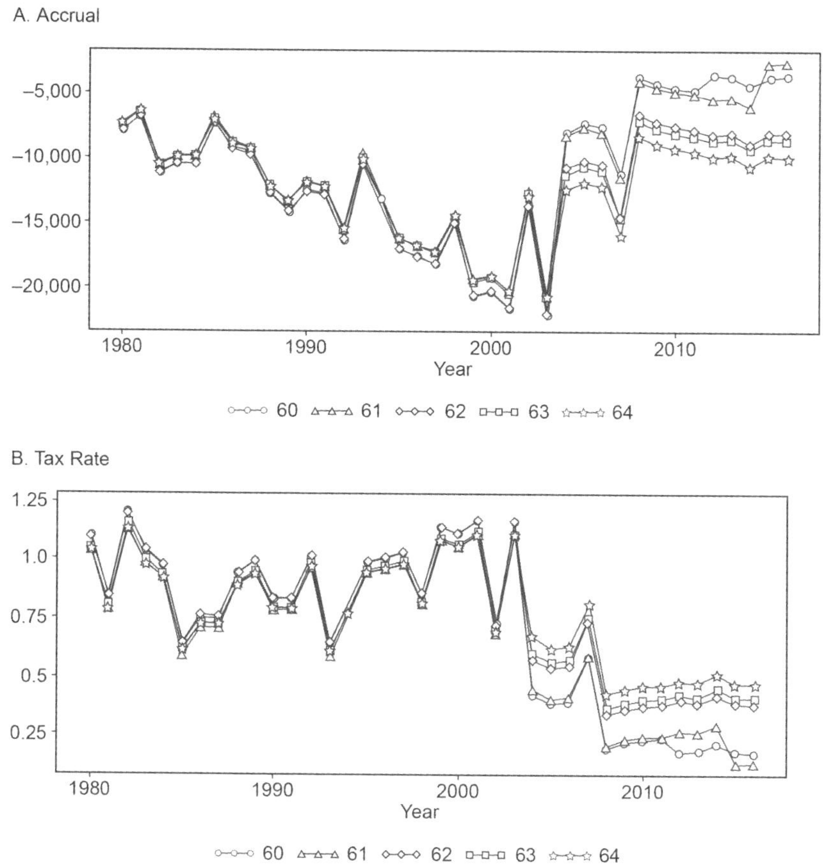

Fig. 4.10 Accruals 60–64, public sector (men, education level 1)

penalty for retiring before the full rate and the introduction of a bonification for retiring after. Lastly, the 2010 reform impacted the minimum age in the same terms in both sectors.

Figures 4.10 to 4.12 present the accruals for the same three "typical" workers. Results are presented for men only, being here again similar for both genders. For type 1 and type 2 workers, the tax rate is close to 100 percent at all ages until 2003. These people are entitled to the full rate as soon as 60 without any bonification if retiring later, so the "length of perception" effect dominates: foregoing one full year of benefits is equivalent to taxation at a rate roughly equivalent to the net replacement rate.

The situation is different for the type 3 individual. This person had to wait until 62.5 to get his or her full-rate pension. Despite the fact that no penalty existed on the "annuity rate," working at 60 and 61 is productive in terms of retirement benefits due to the simple proportionality between the level

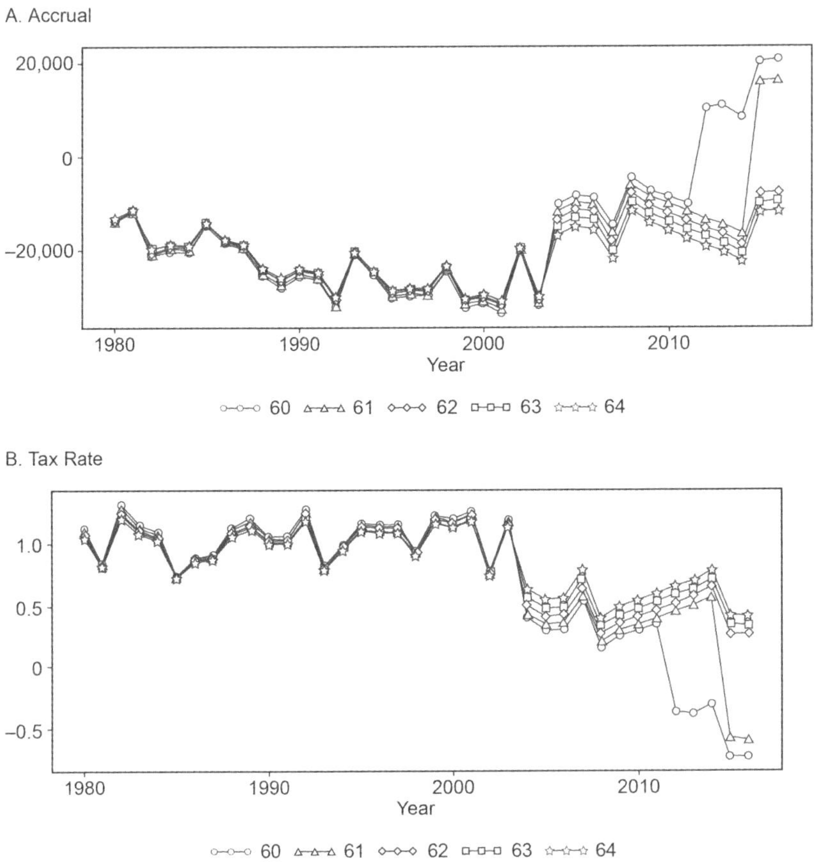

Fig. 4.11 Accruals 60–64, public sector (men, education level 2)

of the pension and the number of years of contribution, hence a lower tax rate at these two ages all over the period.

The 2003 reform affected incentives in relatively similar ways for the three levels, progressively bringing tax rates close to zero. The 2010 reform finally produced similar effects to those already commented on for workers in the private sector. It left the taxation rate close to zero at 60 and 61 for case 1: after the reform, additional years of work between 60 and 62 are not productive in terms of pension benefits, and working or not working between 60 and 62 is also neutral for the length of perception, which will start at 62 in all cases. For the type 2 worker, we have the same neutrality with respect to the length of the perception period, but now years worked between 60 and 62 do have an impact on the level of benefits: this person reaches age 60 with a number of years of contribution lower than the one needed to get

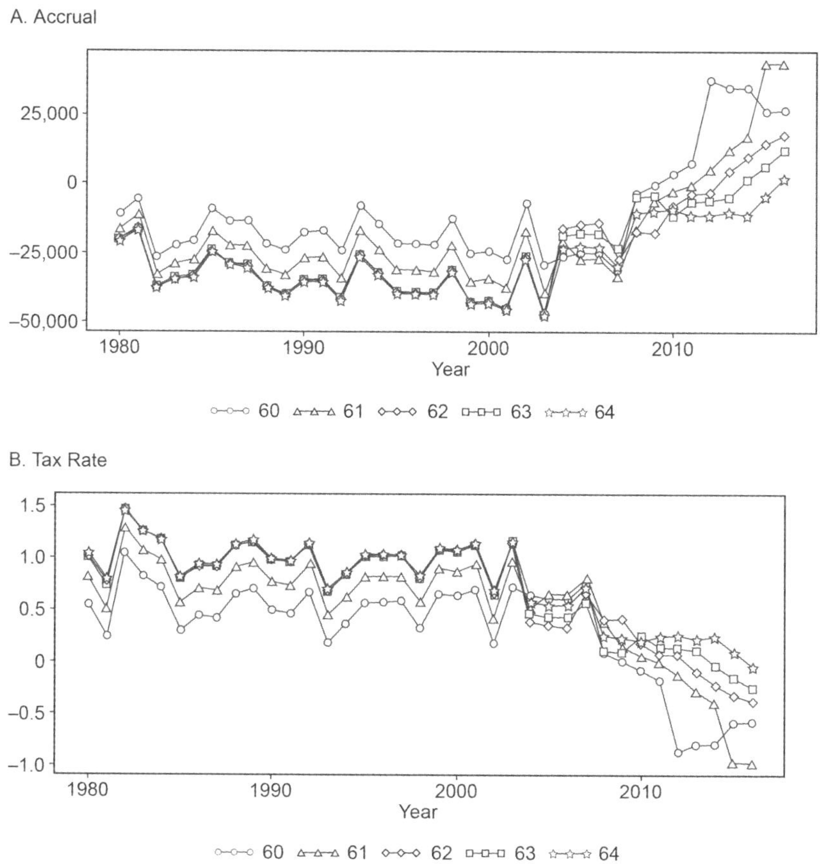

Fig. 4.12 Accruals 60–64, public sector (men, education level 3)

the full rate at 62, hence with a motivation to accumulate some more years of contribution.

The type 3 worker is not affected. Due to her very late entry to the labor market, the penalty when retiring at 62 will be based on the distance from the statutory eligibility age of 67 rather than on the distance from the number of years requested for the full rate. This penalty is therefore independent of labor market behavior at ages 60 and 61.

4.6 Conclusion

What is to be retained from this presentation? It has focused on monetary incentives to retire or not to retire and only on one of these monetary incentives—the so-called tax rate, which had already been the focus of the first volume of this project (Gruber and Wise 1999). This tax rate measures by how much the expected flow of benefits changes in case of working one more year as a result of two opposite effects: a negative "length of perception" effect, since postponing generally implies foregoing one full year of benefits, and a positive "benefit level" effect, since postponing generally leads to a higher benefit level. Actuarial neutrality is reached when both effects cancel out. Examination of this indicator in the 1990s had emphasized the high level of this tax rate for France, at least for workers reaching the full rate as soon as 60. The essential explanation for this high tax rate was the fact that under rules that existed at that time, postponement beyond the full rate did not lead to any increase in the pension level. This was an assumed consequence of the 1983 reform, according to which the full-rate age had to be considered as a social norm in terms of retirement, beyond which working did not have to be encouraged and even had to be discouraged, with the idea that this policy could improve access to the labor market for younger cohorts (Ben Salem et al. 2010).

Removing this implicit taxation has been one of the components of the reforms that have followed—more particularly the 2003 reform that has reintroduced bonuses for years worked beyond the full rate and simultaneously adjusted the penalty for retiring earlier than the full rate. This penalty has been reduced in the private sector, where it was higher than requested for actuarial neutrality, and reinforced in the public sector, where it was previously almost nonexistent. The main message of this chapter is that this 2003 reform was successful in removing a large part of this taxation effect yet with a lot of exceptions stemming from the complexity of the French pension rules, which include a lot of nonlinearities or threshold effects (Briard and Mahfouz 2011). In particular, additional years worked before the minimum age are not systematically productive in terms of additional entitlements, and once this minimum age is reached, the penalty does not systematically depend on the number of years of contribution: for people with very short careers, it is the distance from the maximum retirement age that is the determinant of the penalty. The subtlety of these interactions between the "length of career" and "age" effects remains an important feature of the French pension system.

Despite its still incomplete character, this move toward actuarial neutrality is one candidate to explain the fact that, as in most of the other countries, employment and labor force participation rates have started reincreasing for senior workers. Yet is it only one possible explanation among others. Several important points have to be made and discussed here.

First of all, a traditional criticism of the focus on actuarial neutrality is that it reduces retirement decisions to a financial arbitrage. Monetary considerations are considered to be the main determinants of retirement choices. This criticism has itself two subaspects. One may criticize the fact of describing exit from employment as a choice, and one may criticize the fact of considering that this choice is essentially governed by financial considerations.

On the latter point, some clarification is required. Economic models of retirement do not ignore at all that a lot of nonmonetary considerations are at play when deciding to retire (Blanchet and Debrand 2007). More elaborate models of retirement behavior used in ex-ante projections such as the option value model (Stock and Wise 1990) include parameters that capture these factors. The so-called preference for leisure parameter measures much more than what its standard denomination suggests; it implicitly captures work penibility—itself strongly dependent on health, but not on health alone—and/or the preference for nonmarket activities rather than for leisure *stricto sensu*. The preference for the present also includes some of these "nonmonetary" determinants of retirement behavior, such as subjective perceptions of life expectancy.

The point, therefore, is not to oppose an "enlarged" view of retirement behavior including all these determinants and a restrictive economic approach that would completely ignore them. The problem is rather to know what we gain in making "nonmonetary" determinants more explicit than has been done here, and the answer depends on what we intend to explain. Nonmonetary factors are definitely decisive in explaining behaviors at the microlevel: two people will not react in the same way to similar monetary incentives, and the explanation will necessarily stem from the nonmonetary side of the coin. The effects are less obvious when macro changes over time are of interest. Here, nonmonetary factors matter only if they change over time in a way that is likely to account for observed changes in labor force participation rates—more specifically here, the U-shaped pattern that was the topic of this chapter. On this point, most of the nonmonetary factors that one may have in mind do not appear to be natural candidates: health and life expectancy or education levels are rather trend variables; they can contribute to explaining the relative sizes of the descending and ascending branches of the U shape but not the fact that we have a U shape (Blanchet et al. 2019a). This gives sense to a focus on financial determinants, which are more likely to explain this U-shaped pattern.

The second subquestion of "choice" versus "no choice" is more difficult to set aside. For many people, the age at exit from the labor force is not the result of a free choice between working or not working: exit is a constraint and, when occurring before the minimum age, imposes a transition through an early retirement route independent from the relative financial "attractiveness" of these routes, which is captured by associated tax rates. The magnitude of this demand-side constraint may have changed over time and in a way that can potentially account for a significant part of the U shape. It may have changed both because labor market conditions have changed and also because of changes in regulations imposed on employers, with legislations or controls making it more or less easy to use senior employment as a regulation parameter. In France, variations of these facilities have certainly played a strong role in shaping labor force participation profiles in the 55–59 age group.

The last limit is that even in a world without demand-side constraints and where nonmonetary determinants of retirement behavior would be perfectly stable, tax rates are only one of the monetary factors that have to be considered. A zero tax rate can be attained in systems offering very high and very low replacement rates as soon as they offer the same progressivity rule in case of postponement. Yet two such systems will obviously have diverging impacts on the decision to retire.

It is indeed through direct changes of replacement rates offered at given ages or through shifts of the ages offering given replacement rates that French reforms have basically tried to change retirement behavior and are expected to go on doing so during the next decades. This has been done in three ways: by increasing the length or career condition for getting the full rate (in 1993, 2003, and 2014), by increasing the minimum age for getting this full rate (in 2010), and by lowering the level of expected benefits at this full rate through a computation of the pension on the basis of the 25 best years of one's career and through less favorable indexation rules, for both the reconstitution of past careers and the evolution of benefits during the retirement period. Changes in tax rates are only part of the general story explaining the U-shaped pattern of employment and labor force participation rates.

Appendix A

Pathways by Education Levels and Gender

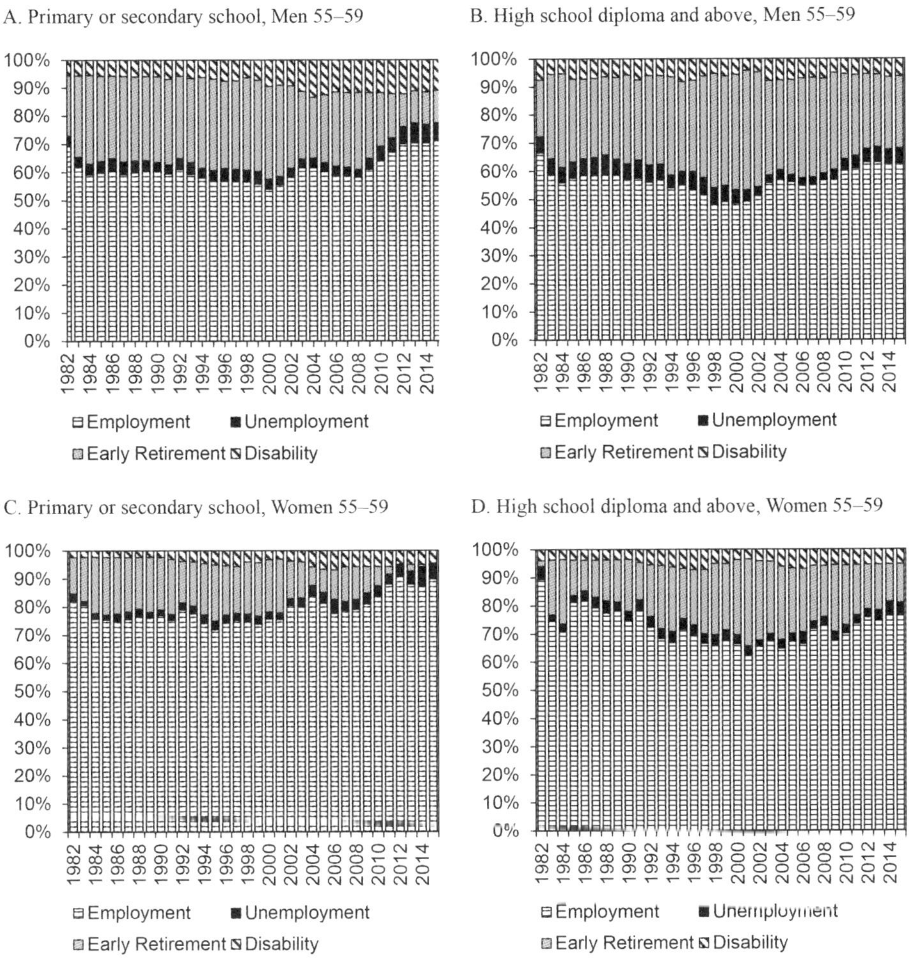

Fig. 4.A1 Pathways by education levels and gender

Sources: French Labor Force Survey and SIP survey

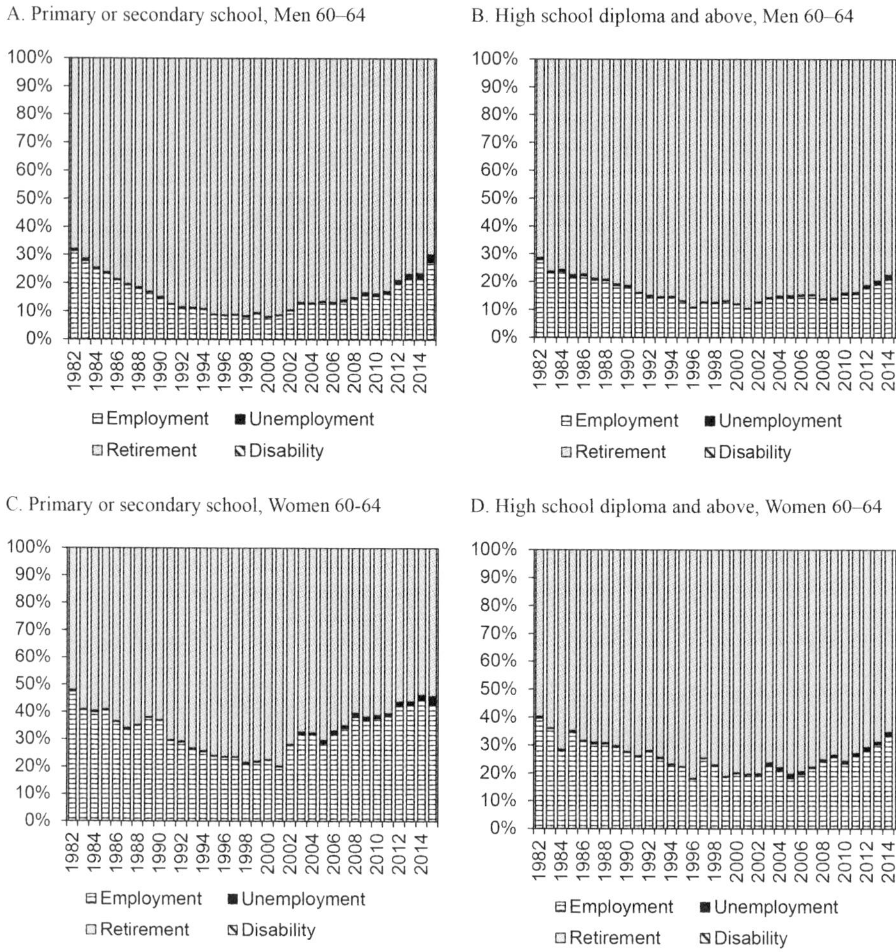

Fig. 4.A2 Pathways by education levels and gender

Sources: French Labor Force Survey and SIP survey

Appendix B

Accruals 55–59, Women

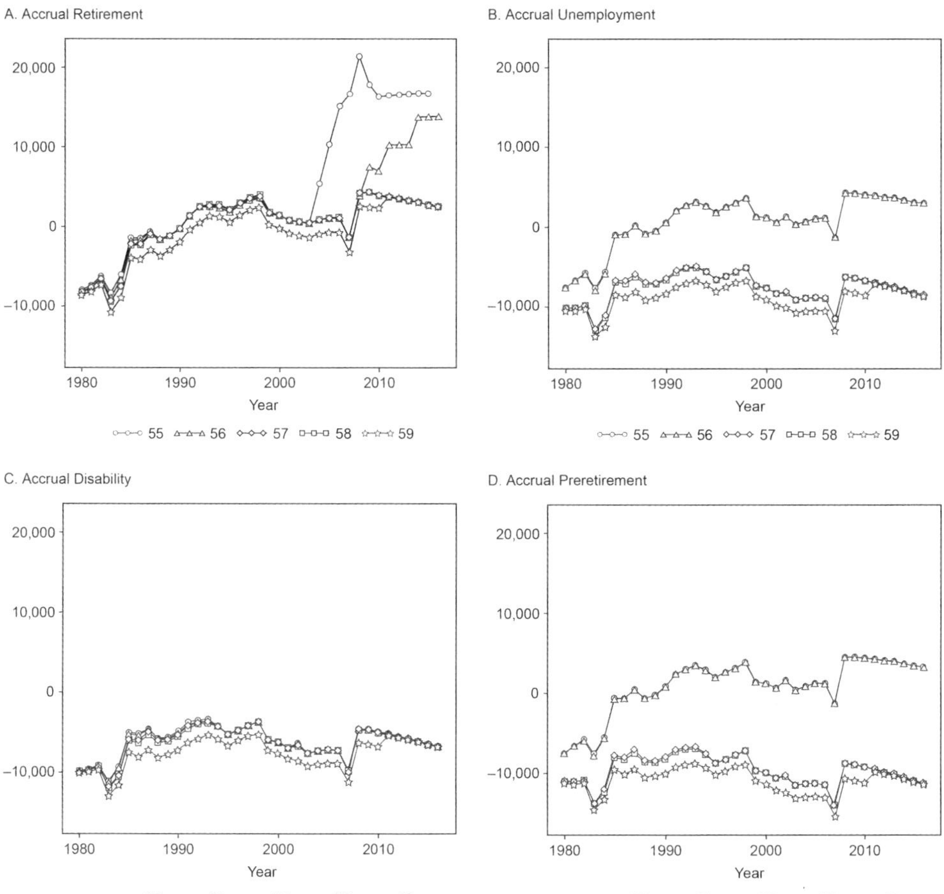

Fig. 4.B1 Accrual by year, age, and pathway (women, level 1)

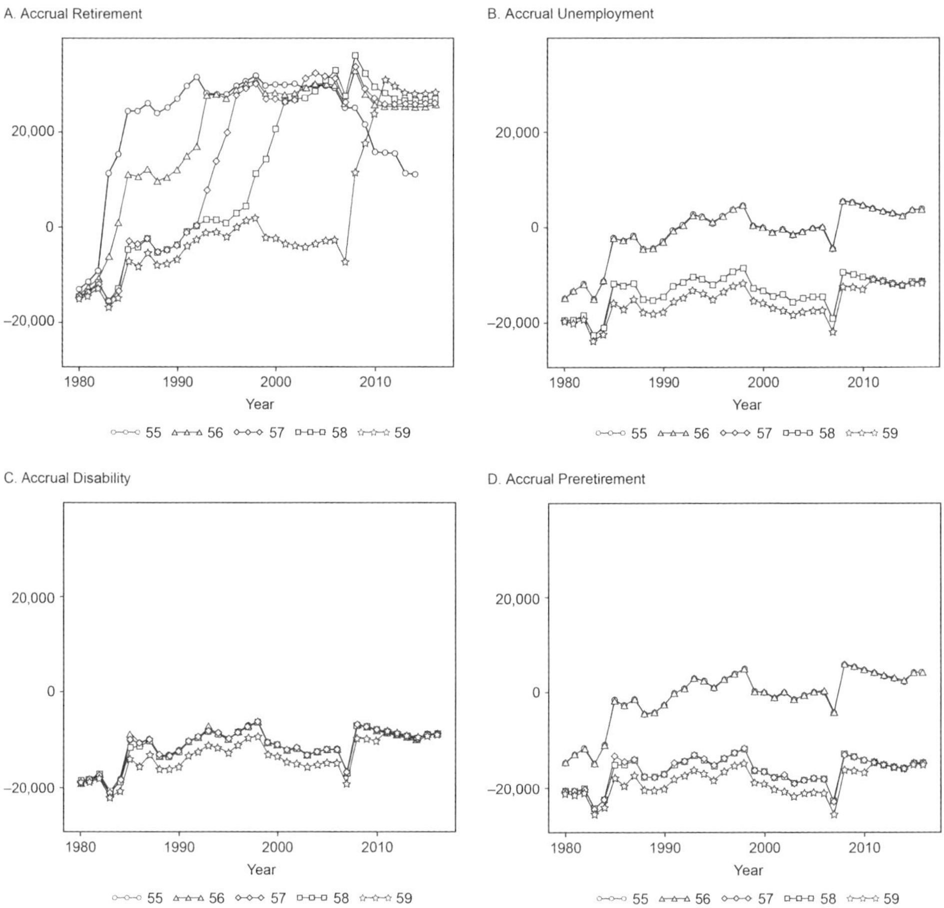

Fig. 4.B2 Accrual by year, age, and pathway (women, level 2)

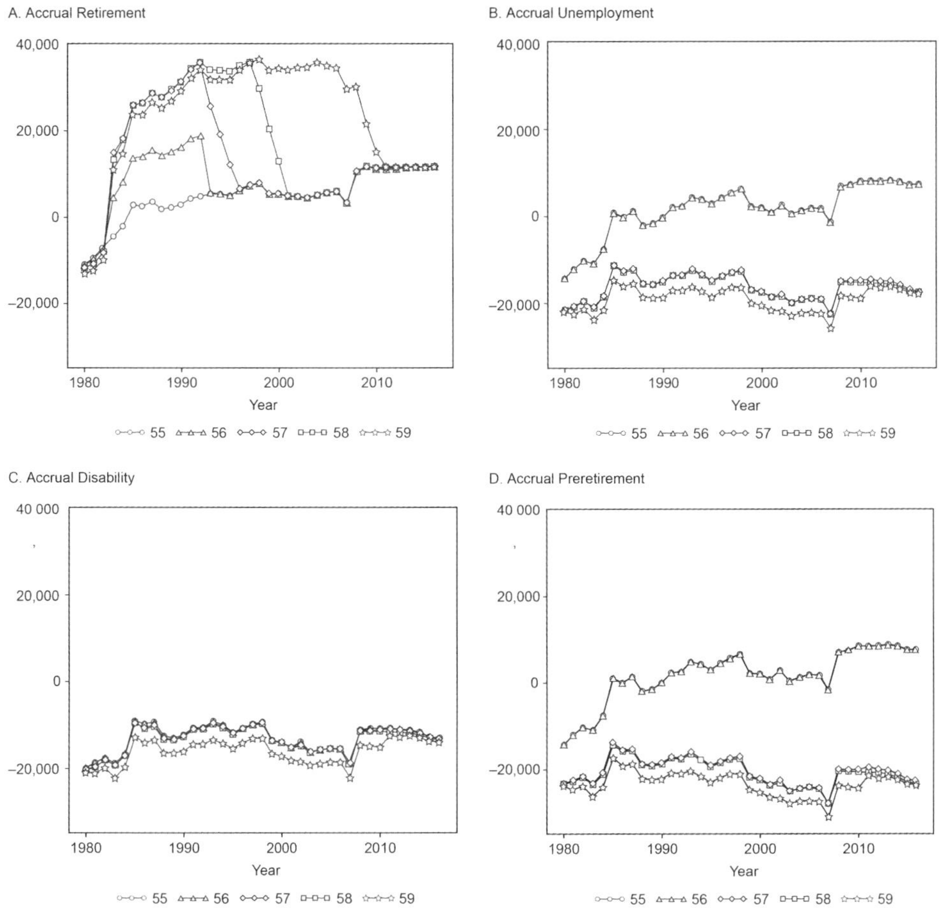

Fig. 4.B3 Accrual by year, age, and pathway (women, level 3)

References

Bachelet, M., M. Beffy, and D. Blanchet. 2011. "Projeter l'impact des réformes des retraites sur l'activité des 55 ans et plus: Une comparaison de trois modèles." *Economie et Statistique* 441–42:123–43.

Baraton, M., M. Beffy, and D. Fougère. 2011. "Une évaluation de l'effet de la réforme de 2003 sur les départs en retraite: Le cas des enseignants du second degré public." *Economie et Statistique* 441–42:55–78.

Benallah, S. 2011. "Comportements de départ en retraite et reforme de 2003: Les effets de la surcote." *Economie et Statistique* 441:79–99.

Ben Salem, M., D. Blanchet, A. Bozio, and M. Roger. 2010. "Labor Force Participation by the Elderly and Employment of the Young." In *Social Security Programs and Retirement around the World: The Relationship to Youth Employment*, edited by J. Gruber and D. A. Wise, 119–46. Chicago: University of Chicago Press.

Blanchet, D., A. Bozio, C. Prost, and M. Roger. 2019a. "Explaining the Reversal in the Trend of Older Workers' Employment Rates." In *Social Security Programs and Retirement around the World: Working Longer*, edited by C. Coile, K. Milligan, and D. A. Wise, 87–115. Chicago: University of Chicago Press.

Blanchet, D., A. Bozio, S. Rabaté, and M. Roger. 2019b. "Workers' Employment Rates and Pension Reforms in France." NBER Working Paper No. 25733. Cambridge, MA: National Bureau of Economic Research.

Blanchet, D., and L. P. Pelé. 1999. "Social Security and Retirement in France." In *Social Security and Retirement around the World*, edited by J. Gruber and D. A. Wise, 101–33. Chicago: University of Chicago Press.

Blanchet, D., and T. Debrand. 2007. "Souhaiter prendre sa retraite le plus tôt possible; santé, satisfaction au travail, facteurs monétaires." *Economie et Statistique* 403–4:39–62.

Bozio, A. 2011. "La réforme des retraites de 1993: L'impact de l'augmentation de la durée d'assurance." *Economie et Statistique* 441–42:39–53.

Briard K., and S. Mahfouz. 2011. "Modulations de la retraite selon l'âge de départ: Principes directeurs et évolutions depuis les années 1980." *Economie et Statistique* 441–42:15–38.

Burricand, C., and N. Roth. 2000. "Les parcours de fin de carrière des générations 1912–1941: L'impact du cadre institutionnel." *Economie et Statistique* 335:63–79.

Dubois Y., and M. Koubi. 2017. "La réforme des retraites de 2010: Quel impact sur l'activité des seniors?" *Economie et prévision* 211–12:61–90.

Govillot, S. 2013. "Le passage de l'emploi à la retraite: Travailler pendant la retraite une situation qui se développe." *Insee Première*, no. 1449.

Gruber, Jonathan, and David A. Wise, eds. 1999. *Social Security Programs and Retirement around the World*. Chicago: University of Chicago Press.

Hairault, J. O., F. Langot, and T. Sopraseuth. 2006. "Les effets à rebours de l'âge de la retraite sur le taux d'emploi des seniors." *Economie et Statistique* 397:51–63.

Mahieu, R., and B. Sédillot. 2000. "Microsimulation of the Retirement Decision: A Supply-Side Approach." Document de Travail Insee/Dese, G2000/07.

Mahieu, R., and D. Blanchet. 2004. "Estimating Models of Retirement Behavior on French Data." In *Social Security Programs and Retirement around the World: Micro-estimation*, edited by J. Gruber and D. A. Wise, 235–84. Chicago: University of Chicago Press.

Rabaté, S. 2017. "Can I Stay or Should I Go? Mandatory Retirement and Labor Force Participation of Older Workers." PSE Working Papers No. 2017–19.

Rabaté, S., and J. Rochut. 2016. "Labor Supply Effects of Raising the Minimum Claiming Age: Evidence from French Reforms." Draft.

Stock, J., and D. Wise. 1990. "Pensions, the Option Value of Work, and Retirement." *Econometrica* 58 (5): 1151–80.

5 Social Security Reforms and the Changing Retirement Behavior in Germany

Axel Börsch-Supan, Johannes Rausch, and Nicolas Goll

5.1 Introduction

As in the other countries in this volume, the retirement age in Germany has declined for a long time. This has put enormous fiscal pressures on Germany's pension system. Since about 2000, however, working in later life has been making a stunning comeback. Among the 12 countries involved in the study, Germany has experienced the largest increase in the employment rate of the 55–69 age group (see figure 5.1). Figure 5.1 and the remainder of the chapter refer to West Germany in order to avoid confounding pension policy effects with the strong unification effects in East Germany after 1989. West Germany used to feature a relatively low level of old-age employment, with a rate of only 36.8/21.5 percent (men/women) in 2000 for the 55–69 age group. Sixteen years later, this rate has reached a stunning 59.5/48.6 percent (men/women; OECD, 2018a). The trend reversal is particularly pronounced among men (see figure 5.1), while the picture is a bit more complex for women, who experienced a rather constant increase for the 55–59 age

Axel Börsch-Supan is director of the Munich Center for the Economics of Aging (MEA) at the Max Planck Institute for Social Law and Social Policy (MPISOC), a professor of the economics of aging at the Technical University of Munich, and a research associate of the National Bureau of Economic Research.

Johannes Rausch is head of the Old-Age Provision and Social Policy unit at the Munich Center for the Economics of Aging (MEA) at the Max Planck Institute for Social Law and Social Policy (MPISOC).

Nicolas Goll is a researcher at the Munich Center for the Economics of Aging (MEA) at the Max Planck Institute for Social Law and Social Policy (MPISOC).

For acknowledgments, sources of research support, and disclosure of the authors' material financial relationships, if any, please see https://www.nber.org/chapters/c14195.ack.

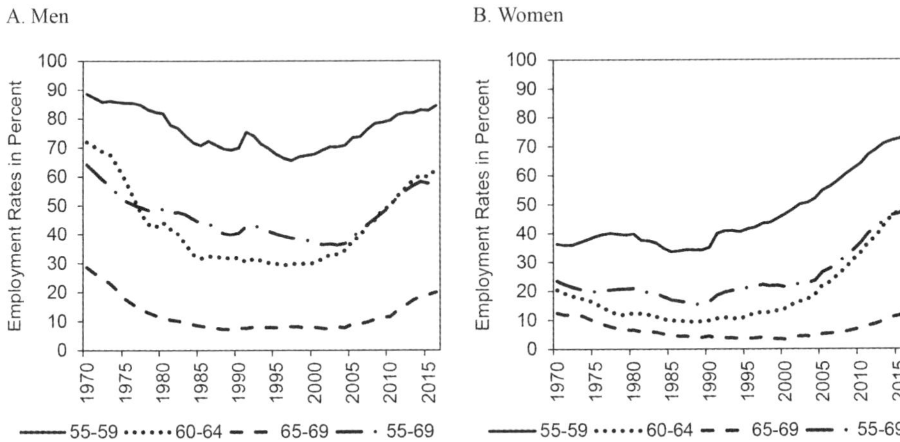

Fig. 5.1 West German employment rate by age group and gender

Source: Authors' own calculations based on OECD and German Federal Statistical Office

group and a mild reversal for the other age groups. The trends in labor force participation (LFP) are very similar (not shown).

Understanding the causes of this recent increase in employment and LFP is important if one wants to assess whether the current rising trend will continue, thus reducing the negative consequences of aging on fiscal sustainability. If the reversal is mainly caused by transitory or one-off events, old-age labor force participation may slow down again in the near future. However, if it is caused by a structural change, we may expect a lasting impact on fiscal sustainability.

One set of causes for the trend reversal in employment could be historical trends. Younger cohorts are healthier and have been better educated, permitting longer working lives. Moreover, the role of women in society has dramatically changed, affecting the LFP of both genders. The previous phase of the ISSP has shown that these secular developments have contributed astonishingly little to the trend reversal (Börsch-Supan and Coile 2018 for an overview; Börsch-Supan and Ferrari 2017 for Germany). In fact, even if many of the historical trends studied earlier may have contributed to the overall level of LFP, their trend does not show the U-shape pattern observed for LFP.

This chapter therefore investigates the role of structural policy changes since 1980. Our evidence presented suggests that much of the trend reversal of older men's labor force participation may be explained by changes in Germany's public pension rules—in particular, by the phasing in of actuarial adjustments for early retirement. Regarding women's LFP, it is less clear how much public pension rules play a role. Most probably, the secular change of women's role in society is the main driver of the steadily increasing LFP among the younger West German women, while we observe more of a trend reversal among older women.

The chapter is organized as follows. Section 5.2 describes the changes in the German LFP and pension-claiming behavior between 1980 and 2016. Section 5.3 provides a summary of the institutional changes and pension reforms in Germany that might be the causes for the stunning trend reversal. Section 5.4 is the main methodological part of the chapter and describes how we boil down the institutional changes into a few key statistics, especially the "implicit tax on working longer." Section 5.5 presents our results. We show how the implicit tax on working longer has changed between 1980 and 2016, using several alternative specifications and robustness checks. We then graphically relate the implicit tax on working longer to the prevailing employment rate. Section 5.6 concludes. We find a negative correlation between the employment rate and the incentives to claim benefits early. In other words, as the implicit tax on working longer decreased, employment at older ages increased.

This evidence is highly suggestive. However, such a bivariate correlation does not control for the many other potential explanatory factors and the heterogeneity in the population. This requires a much more elaborate multivariate analysis. The next step of the ISSP will be devoted to a causal analysis of the role of public pension policies in shaping LFP. This chapter is contributing to this effort by constructing the time series of the implicit tax for a small set of stylized household types. The next step will be to apply this machinery to real households in a population-representative survey and to embed our incentive variables, the macrovariables considered in Börsch-Supan and Coile (2018), and other determinants into an econometric analysis of retirement and LFP.

5.2 Employment Rate among Older Individuals and Pension-Claiming Behavior

In this section, we will take a closer look at the development of the employment rate of older workers and their actual pension claiming behavior. It is important to note that labor market exit and the beginning of pension benefit claiming may not take place at the same time. We therefore avoid the term *retirement* as much as we can, since in many languages it ambiguously refers to both decisions, which may be driven by different considerations and determinants. We also take care to distinguish between the group of older workers and the group of insured individuals. They do not precisely overlap. For instance, homemakers and emigrated workers do not belong to the German labor force but often have earned pension claims in Germany. We, therefore, first look at changes in employment and then at changes in claiming behavior.

Fig. 5.2 West Germany older women's employment rate with and without correction for general trend in younger women's employment rates

Source: Authors' own calculations based on OECD (2018a), Statistisches Bundesamt (2016)

5.2.1 Employment Rate

West Germany shares with other industrialized countries a U-shape pattern in the employment rate (LFP rate) of older workers over time. In its downward-phase from 1970 into the 1990s,[1] the employment rate of older men (55–69 age group) declined by 23.7 percentage points to 40.5 percent until 1990 (see figure 5.1). Even more pronounced was this decline for the 60 to 64 age group, with a decrease by 40 percentage points to 31.8 percent until 1990. The decline was much smaller for women with 7.1 (10.6) percentage points for the 55 to 69 age group (60 to 64). However, their employment rate was, at 23.5 percent, already rather small in 1970. Most studies (e.g., Börsch-Supan 1992; Siddiqui 1997; Börsch-Supan and Schnabel 1999; Hanel 2010) identified the introduction of early retirement opportunities as the main reason for the decline. The downward phase ended in the 1990s. A stagnation phase followed with more or less constant employment rates before the employment rates started to increase around the year 2000. The older men's employment rate then began to rise at a rather fast pace. Until now, the employment rate of older men has increased by 22.7 (32.5) percentage points for the 55 to 69 (60 to 64) age group. The women's employment rates started to increase earlier and more strongly. However, in the women's case,

1. The employment rate of the whole of Germany includes another drop in 1991. However, this drop results mainly from the unification of Germany and the small employment rates in East Germany. For younger age groups, we also observe an increase in the employment rate after 1990 due to the unification.

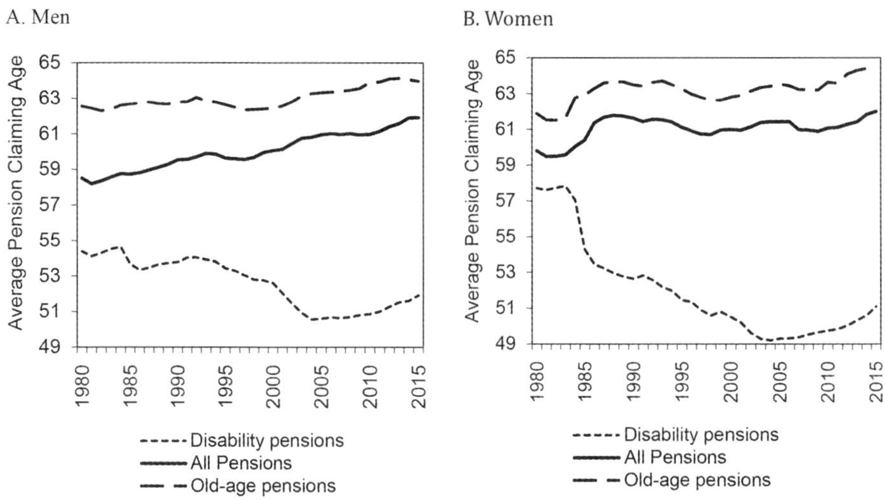

Fig. 5.3 Average pension-claiming age by gender (West Germany)
Source: Deutsche Rentenversicherung Bund, Rentenzugang (see DRV 2017)

the increase of LFP among younger women has to be taken into account. If we correct the development of the older women's employment rates for this general trend, we receive a similar pattern as that for men.[2] So adjusted, the employment rate for women increased between 2000 and 2016 by approximately 18.7 (31.4) percentage points for the 55 to 69 (60 to 64) age group (see figure 5.2).

5.2.2 Pension-Claiming Behavior

As already mentioned, the labor force is not identical to the insured population. Consequently, the development of the employment rate may vary from the actual pension-claiming behavior. Figure 5.3 depicts the average pension-claiming age of West German men and women separately for old-age pensions, disability pensions, and overall pensions. In the men's case, we observe that the general average claiming age steadily increased between 1980 and 2015 from 58.2 to 61.9. On the other hand, the average claiming age for old-age pension remained, similar to the employment rate, constant until 2000. The average pension-claiming age thereby stayed slightly below 63. Afterward it increased by 1.6 years to age 64. While the pension-claiming ages increase over all pensions, the claiming age of disability pensions dropped

2. We correct for the general trend by subtracting from the growth rate of the employment rate of the 60- to 64-year-old workers the growth rate of the employment rate of the 50- to 54-year-old workers. We thereby consider the growth rates of the same cohorts. The correction is consequently kept quite simple.

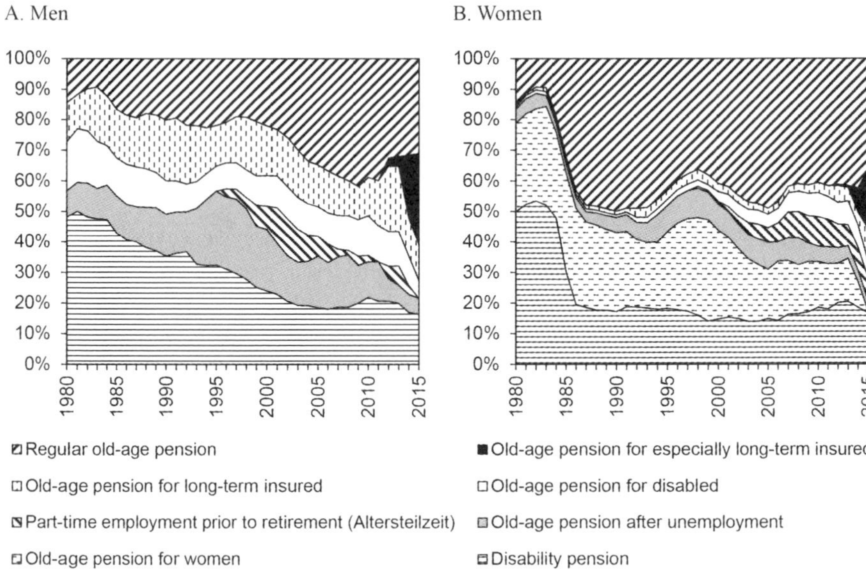

Fig. 5.4 Coverage of pathways to retirement on annual newly claimed pensions
Source: Deutsche Rentenversicherung Bund, Rentenzugang (see DRV 2017)

in 1984 by 1.3 years and decreased after 1992 with an accelerating pace by another 2.7 years. At first glance, the drop in the claiming ages of disability pension seems strange, since the requirements for disability pensions were tightened in 1984 and 2001 (see next chapter). However, due to the tighter requirements, the misuse of the disability pension as an early retirement pathway for healthy individuals had been blocked. Hence the average claiming age decreased, since fewer older but healthy workers misused the disability pension, and the share of younger but disabled workers increased in all variants of the German disability pension. The overall pension-claiming age increased, since the share of individuals who claimed a regular old-age pension among all new pension claims increased (see figure 5.4).

For women, the development of the average pension-claiming age for old-age pensions is nearly identical with the development of the average pension-claiming age over all pensions. We observe merely a one-year gap between both variables. At least after 1984, the average pension-claiming age of disability pensions seems to play a secondary role due to its being a small fraction of all pension claims (see figure 5.4). The pension-claiming age over all pensions (as well as all old-age pensions) rose after 1984 by 2.1 years, while the claiming age of disability pensions dropped by 4.5 years. As we will see in the following section, this pattern can be explained by the 1984 pension reform, which changed the requirements for disability pensions and for regular old-age pensions. It seems that many women older than 61 did not fulfill the old vesting period for a regular old-age pension of 15 years, while they did fulfill the shorter 5-year waiting time of a disability pension. Since at the same time the requirements for disability pension were tightened, older women switched from claiming disability pensions to claiming (regular) old-age pensions. As a consequence, the average claiming age for disability pension dropped, while the claiming age for regular old-age pension rose. After 1990, the claiming ages of old-age pensions remained first at an almost constant level before decreasing by one year until 2000. However, similar to the development of the employment rate, the women's claiming age also increased again since 2000. On the other hand, the women's average pension-claiming age of disability pensions decreased by another 4 years until 2004 before it rose again by 2 years.

All in all, the development of the men's average claiming age of old-age pensions is consistent with the observed development of their employment rate. Only the decline in the employment rate between 1980 and 1985 cannot be observed in the considered time period. For women, the comparison between the pension-claiming behavior and the employment rate is less straightforward, especially until 2000. One reason may be the differences in the considered groups. While the employment rate includes only the share of women working (in Germany), the average pension-claiming age takes the claiming ages of all insured women into account. The employment rate could, therefore, miss certain changes in the pension-claiming patterns of women.

In the last step, we study the distribution of the pension-claiming age by ages and its development over time (see figure 5.5). In the men's case, we observe three major pension-claiming ages. These are the ages of 60, 63, and 65, which are at the same time the earliest claiming ages for the most important pension pathways (see next chapter and table 5.1). Between 1980 and 2002, most individuals claimed a pension at age 60. However, the relevance of the age decreased rapidly with the introduction of actuarial deduction in 1999 and the abolishment of the old-age pension due to unemployment in 2012. At the same time, pension claiming at the regular eligibility age of 65 increased. The share of pension claimed at the eligibility age of 63 remained at first nearly constant. However, in the last years, it became more relevant for two reasons. First, the old-age pension with lower eligibility ages was abolished, and second, the actuarial deductions for claiming a pension at 63 were temporarily abolished for certain individuals ("pension with 63"). For the remaining ages, we can, moreover, observe a shifting process from early to later ages.

For women, two major pension-claiming ages can be observed. First, the eligibility age for the old-age pension for women at age 60 and, second, the statutory eligibility age at 65. Similar to the men's case, the share of pension claiming at age 60 declined after 1999 in two steps. The first drop after 1999 reduced the share on all pension claiming by almost 20 percentage points,

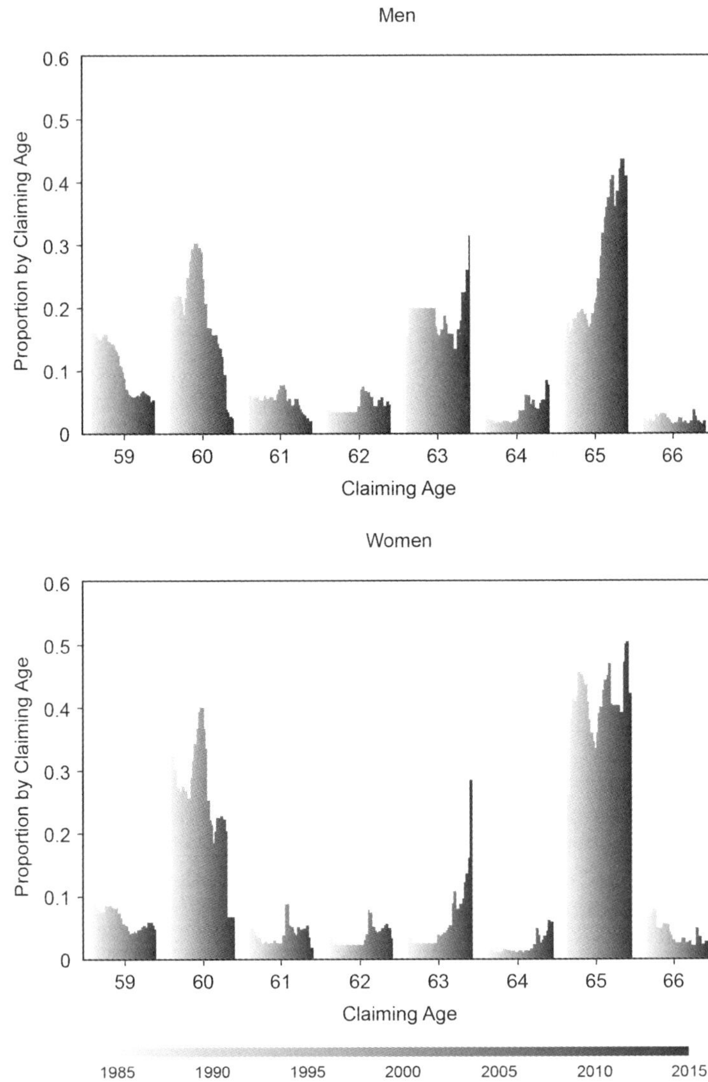

Fig. 5.5 Pension claiming by age and year (1985–2015) in West Germany
Source: Deutsche Rentenversicherung Bund, Rentenzugang (see DRV 2017)

while the second drop, which occurred in 2012 (abolishment of the old-age pension for women), covered a decline of 15 percentage points. At the same time, the earliest eligibility age for long-term insured (age 63) became more relevant. In total, the share of women claiming a pension at age 63 increased from 2.4 percent to 28.2 percent. Nonetheless, at over 40 percent, most women claimed their pension at the statutory eligibility age. Similar to the men's case between the ages of 60 and 63, a shifting process can be observed that moves the pension claiming from younger to older ages.

5.3 Institutional Changes: The German Pension Policy and Its Development

The main hypothesis of this chapter is that the reversals in labor supply and pension-claiming behavior around the year 2000 are to a large extent driven by changes in pension policies. To this end, this section presents the policy changes that occurred since 1980 and that are salient for changes in retirement behavior. We start with a brief summary of the structure of the German pension system in 1980 in order to assess the initial situation of the system at the beginning of the time span considered in this study.

5.3.1 The German Pension System until 1980

The German pension system originally began as a funded disability insurance scheme in 1889 but was quickly broadened into a general old-age security system with both disability pensions and old-age pensions. The statutory eligibility age was set to 65. After two world wars and a period of hyperinflation, about half of the capital stock was lost and the system was transformed into a pay-as-you-go (PAYG) system in 1957. Benefits from this public PAYG system were designed to maintain the living standard achieved during the working life into retirement. Therefore, individual pension benefits were set to be proportional to the individual labor income averaged over the entire working career such that the relative income position of an individual during the working life would be preserved during retirement. While the absolute level of pension benefits has been reduced in the subsequent reforms, the principle of maintaining the relative income position has been maintained until today. The German public pension system therefore features only a few redistributive properties, much less than, for example, the US Social Security system. The main redistribution instrument to prevent old-age poverty is a kind of minimum pension at the social assistance level that was introduced in 2001. The system is mandatory for all workers except for most self-employed, civil servants, and workers with earnings below the official minimum earnings threshold. In the case of the main earner's death, spouses and children are, moreover, protected through survivor benefits.

After anchoring the public pension benefits to gross wages in 1958, several pathways to claim a public pension before the statutory eligibility age were introduced in the 1960s and 1970s that enabled especially women, the unemployed, and disabled persons to claim a pension at age 60 and individuals with long service lives (i.e., at least 35 insurance years) to claim a pension at age 63 (see table 5.1). These early retirement pathways permitted an ear-

Table 5.1 **Pathways to retirement**

Pathway	Earliest eligibility age		Years of service		Actuarial deductions*	Earning tests	Other
Regular old-age pension	Until 2012	After 2029	Until 1984	Since 1984	None	None	
	65	67	15	5			
Long-term insured	63		35		Yes	Yes	
Especially long-term insured	Increase from 63 to 65 until 2029		45		None	Yes	
Old age for disabled	Until 2011	After 2025	35		Yes	(Yes)	50 percent disabled
	60	62					
Unemployed	Until 1996	After 2002					At least 52 weeks unemployed Born before 1952
	60	63	15 (8 in last 10 years)		Yes	Yes	
Part-time retirement	Until 1996	After 2002	15 (8 in last 10 years)		Yes	(Yes)	2 years part-time Born before 1952
	60	63					
Women	60		15 (10 after age 40)		Yes	Yes	Born before 1952
Disability pension	—		Until 1984	Since 1984	Yes	Yes	Medical exams
			5	5 (3 in last 5)			

Note: * Introduction of actuarial deductions between 1992 and 2004.
Source: Authors' own table

Table 5.2 **Standard net replacement rate and standard net replacement rate before taxes**

Year	Standard net replacement rate	Standard net replacement rate before taxes	Year	Standard net replacement rate	Standard net replacement rate before taxes
1980	70.3	57.6	1998	70.9	53.6
1981	69.9	57.4	1999	70.5	53.3
1982	71.5	58.4	2000	69.7	52.9
1983	71.3	57.9	2001	68.6	52.6
1984	72.0	58.1	2002	69.0	52.9
1985	71.8	57.4	2003	69.6	53.3
1986	70.2	56.4	2004	67.9	53.0
1987	70.6	56.2	2005		52.6
1988	70.3	56.3	2006		52.2
1989	70.7	56.1	2007		51.3
1990	67.6	55.0	2008		50.5
1991	67.4	53.9	2009		52.0
1992	67.1	53.1	2010		51.6
1993	67.0	53.4	2011		50.1
1994	69.5	54.8	2012		49.4
1995	70.1	53.9	2013		48.9
1996	70.2	53.4	2014		48.1
1997	71.5	54.0	2015		47.7

Notes: The standard net replacement rates based on the regular old-age pension of an individual with 45 earning points, the so-called Eckrentner. It is the official stated replacement rate. The standard net replacement rate before taxes considers the contributions to the social security system but no tax payments. It has been used in Germany since 2005 instead of the standard net replacement rate, as pension benefits are not taxed consistently anymore due to a stepwise introduction of a deferred taxation regulation (see reforms 2004).

Source: Deutsche Rentenversicherung Bund, Kenngrößen und Bemessungswerte (see DRV 2017)

lier claim of pension benefits but were based on the already earned pension claims with exactly the same benefit calculations as a regular old-age pension (see table 5.1; Börsch-Supan and Jürges 2012). Until 1992, there were no actuarial deductions for claiming a pension before the statutory eligibility age. However, actuarial supplements of 7.5 percent (15 percent) were granted for postponing the pension claiming by one (two) years.

The reforms in the 1960s and 1970s led to one of the world's most generous pension systems, with various opportunities to claim a pension at the age of 60 (table 5.1) and net replacement rates around 70 percent (table 5.2). The "standard net replacement rate" in table 5.2 refers to a German convention that relates the net pension income to the net earnings of a synthetic pensioner who constantly earned the average wage during the entire service life of 45 years. Replacement rates relating to the last earnings are presented in section 5.5.

5.3.2 Reform Process since 1980

The generous German public pension system proved to be financially unsustainable. This precipitated a sequence of reform steps starting around 1980 (see figure 5.6).

Elements of reform included the introduction of actuarial adjustments to the claiming age, a gradual increase of the eligibility ages, the closure of many early retirement pathways, a significant reduction of benefit generosity, the abolishment of earnings tests, and the introduction of partial ("flexible") retirement. The reform process can be divided into three phases. The first phase lasted until 1992 and can be described as a very cautious, limited, and at times contradictory departure from the previous era of increasing generosity. The second phase took place between 1992 and 2007 and consisted of several incisive reforms leading to a sustainable pension system. The third phase covers the time since 2007 and entailed some reform backlash, such as the introduction of a new early retirement pathway.

Phase 1 (1980 to 1992): Modest Retrenchment within the Pension System / Increasing Generosity outside the Pension System

With the 1984 reform, the requirements for disability pensions were tightened by making a minimum of three contribution years in the last five years a condition. Moreover, stricter medical examinations were introduced. As a kind of compensation, the vesting period for regular old-age pensions was reduced from 15 to 5 service years, which resamples the former nonmedical condition for disability pensions. Together, this seriously changed the balance between newly claimed old-age pension and disability pension in favor of old-age pensions. As figure 5.4 depicts, this was especially the case for women's pension-claiming behavior. The share of claimed disability pensions on all newly claimed pensions dropped for women by over 30 percentage points, while the share of regular old-age pensions increased by the same amount. This strong effect has two reasons. First, the number of women fulfilling the new requirements for disability pensions dropped, since many women stopped working after marriage or childbirth and therefore had paid no contributions in the last 5 years. Second, for similar reasons, maybe women were only able to claim disability pensions, as they did not fulfill the former vesting period of 15 service years for a regular old-age pension.

In a contradictory move, the opportunity to leave the labor market early was widened between 1984 and 1987 by extending the maximal duration time of unemployment benefits for older workers (age 56 and above) from 12 months to 32 months. In fact, since unemployment benefits are not means tested, nor do they require job-search attempts, they are often used to "build a bridge to retirement." The extension of the duration time widened this "bridge." Moreover, severance pay became a tax advantage for employers that facilitated the employee to find an agreement with the employer regard-

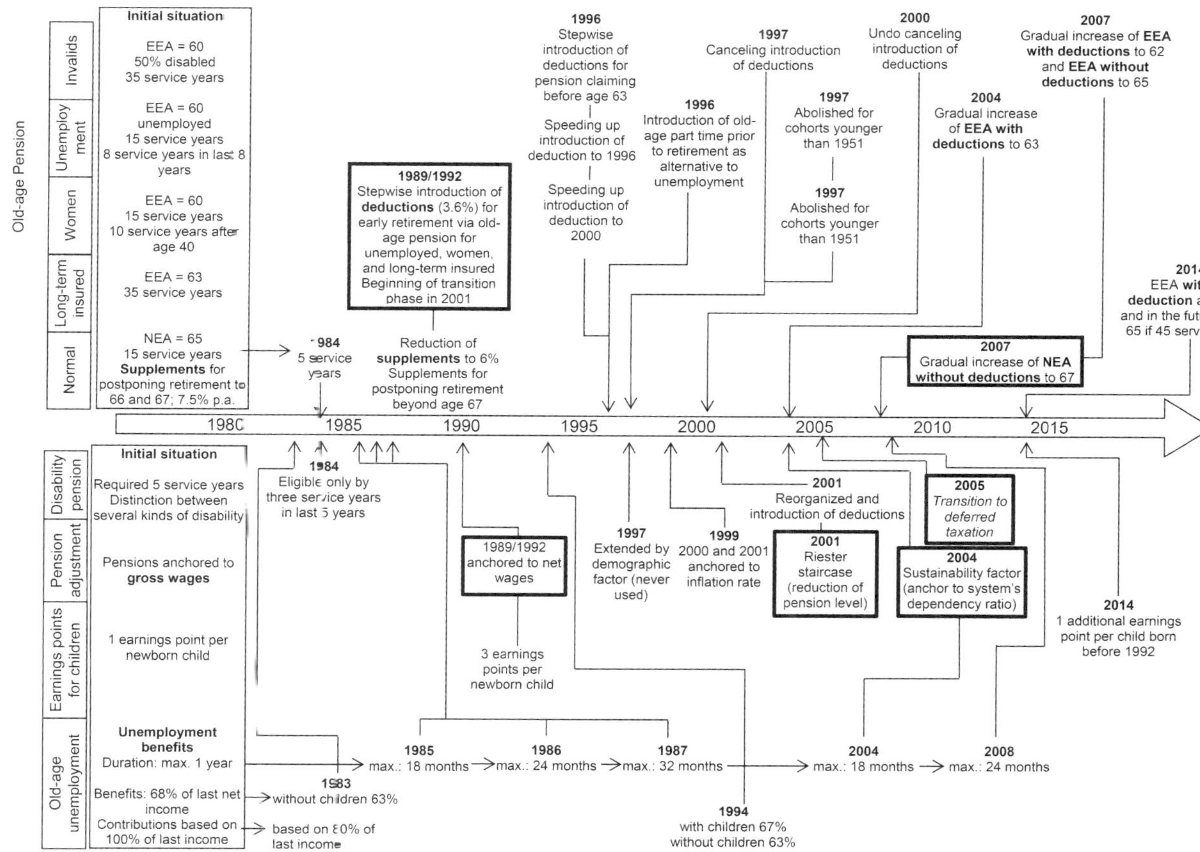

Fig. 5.6 Timeline of reforms to the social security system

Source: Authors' own diagram

ing ending the employment relationship with the right to claim unemployment benefits.

Phase 2 (1992 to 2007): Sustainability Reforms

Step 2.1 (1992): Toward Actuarial Adjustments and More Flexibility

The 1992 pension reform, which passed the parliament in 1989, represents a significant landmark in the German pension policy, as it marks the leap into an era of reforms striving to increase the system's sustainability. As a first step in this process, the 1992 pension reform introduced two significant changes to the pension system's framework. First, it switched the benefit adjustment from gross wage growth to net wage growth. This measure got rid of an odd situation where increasing social contribution rates would have led to a circle of rising net replacement rates. Second, starting in 2001, it provided a phased introduction (by cohorts) of actuarial adjustments for early pension claiming. This measure started a long sequence of changes in the system of pathways to retirement and their eligibility ages with and without actuarial adjustments. They are graphically displayed in figure 5.7 at the end of this section; each panel (a) through (h) presents an element in this sequence.

The stepwise introduction of actuarial adjustments dealt with the strong incentives to claim a pension early, as they reduce pension benefits by 3.6 percent per year of early pension claiming (counted from the statutory eligibility age or a respective earlier adjustment-free eligibility age; see table 5.6). However, these actuarial adjustments are not actuarial neutral, as several studies showed (see Werding 2012; Gasche 2012); hence an incentive to claim a pension early remains. Proper actuarial neutral adjustments would have to be at least twice as large as the current ones. Parallel to the introduction of actuarial deduction the actuarial supplements for postponing pension claiming beyond the statutory eligibility age were changed. From 1992 onward, actuarial supplements were granted for each year of later pension claiming (not only for the first two years). However, at the same time, the actuarial supplements were reduced to 6 percent per year of later retirement (an actuarial deduction of 20 percent).

Besides these sustainability-increasing measures, the 1992 pension reform contained two additional components. First, the number of earnings points parents receive for newborn children was increased from one to three. Second, a partial old-age pension was introduced, which enabled individuals to compensate for an income loss due to a reduction in working hours (part-time work) by drawing a partial pension. The partial pension could be drawn, however, only for certain proportions of the split between work and retirement: one-third, one-half, or two-thirds. The earning limits were calculated individually based on the labor income of the last three years before drawing the partial pension. In the end, this pension scheme was not successful, as only every few individuals used it.

In 1996, the timetable for the introduction of the actuarial adjustment was moved up to 1997 for the old-age pension due to unemployment and to 2000 for the old-age pension for women (see figure 5.7c). Moreover, it was decided to phase in actuarial adjustments for the old-age pension for disabled persons (see table 5.6).

In parallel, the old-age pension due to unemployment was expanded to also include part-time workers aged 55 and older.[3] This represented so far the most widely used model of preretirement work reduction. The scheme is based on a bilateral agreement between employee and employer and requires a reduction of working hours by half in the last five years before the public pension is claimed. The remaining "half" working time either can be distributed consistently over the whole period of five years or can be fulfilled entirely in the first two and a half years without a reduction in working (the so-called block model). In both cases, the employee gets an ongoing payment composed of his part-time work income and a supplementary income of 20 percent by the employer. Additionally, the employer pays pension contributions for 80 percent of the part-time work income. The scheme is subsidized in the sense that the supplementary compensation by the employer is tax exempted (see Börsch-Supan et al. 2015).

Step 2.2 (1997): Closing Early Retirement Schemes and the Demographic Factor

In December 1997, a reform package passed the German parliament that (would have) included three crucial components to further increase the sustainability of the German pension system. First, the old-age pension due to unemployment and for women was abolished for cohorts born after 1952 (see figure 5.7d); second, the pension adjustment indexation formula was amended by a demographic factor that would have adapted the benefit growth to the demographic development; and third, actuarial adjustments were introduced for disability pensions. Other than for old-age pensions, the actuarial adjustments were, however, limited to 10.8 percent and depended on the distance between the claiming of a disability pension and age 63. Moreover, the preadjusted disability pension benefits were enlarged if the disability happened before the age of 60, which compensated for a major part of the newly introduced actuarial adjustments. The reform package itself should have become effective in 1999. However, in 1998, the newly elected government of the Social Democrats and the Green Party suspended the second and third components of the reform package (demographic factor and changes to the disability pension) in order to find a more social regulation. For 2000 and 2001, the benefit adjustment was aligned to the inflation rate.

3. For readability, we will continue to call this pension scheme old-age pension due to unemployment.

Step 2.3 (2000 until 2001): Toward a Genuine Multipillar System

The new government presented the revised pension plan in 2000 and 2001. Regarding the disability pension, the new government adopted the plans of the former government. Hence the introduction of actuarial adjustments was combined with an improvement of the disability benefits (see table 5.6 and figure 5.7e). Additionally, the disability pension's original composition of pensions owing to vocational disability and "real" disability pensions (BU and EU-Rente) was abolished in favor of a two-step disability pension (partial/full earning incapacity) with strict health tests. Whether a disabled individual is eligible for a partial or full disability pension depends on his maximal working capacity (fewer than six hours per day for a partial disability pension or fewer than three hours per day for a full-rate disability pension). The new disability pension became effective in 2001.

In the same year, the so-called Riester reforms took place, which entailed a major reorganization of the German pension system by converting the formally monolithic pay-as-you-go pension scheme into a genuine multipillar system. Hereto, the pay-as-you-go financed system was partially substituted with a (nonmandatory) subsidized private funded system (Riester-Rente). The benefits of the original system were therefore gradually reduced in proportion to the maximal subsidized contribution rate of the newly created supplementary pension scheme (see decreasing replacement rates in table 5.2). This was done by adding an appropriate component to the pension benefit indexation formula.[4] The side effect of this rearrangement was that the pay-as-you-go system was relieved. This corresponded with the second aim of the Riester reform to stabilize the contribution rate by reducing the pension level. Actually, the Riester reform law stated that the contribution rate to the public retirement insurance must stay below 20 percent until 2020 and below 22 percent until 2030, while the standard net replacement rate must stay above 67 percent. Failure must precipitate further government actions.

Step 2.4 (2004): Toward Sustainability (Sustainability Factor)

It quickly became obvious that the contribution rate thresholds could not be fulfilled without further cost-cutting measures. As a consequence, the Commission for Sustainability in Financing the German Social Insurance Systems was established to develop appropriate reform plans at the end of 2002. In the following year, the commission proposed an entire reform package (Commission 2003) with two key components. First, the commission encouraged the government to anchor the statutory eligibility age to the

4. The components introduced in 1989 in the pension adjustment formula, which anchored benefits to the net wage growth, were thereby replaced by a sole consideration of the pension system's contribution rate's growth rate. Due to this, changes in the balance between the fiscal burden of pensions and wages no longer had an influence on the adjustment of the pensions.

Table 5.3 **Unemployment benefits as percentage of last net income**

	1975–83	1984–93	1994–2000	2005
ALG				
With children	68	68	67	
Without children	68	63	60	
ALH				
With children	58	58	57	ALH replaced by earning unrelated ALGII
Without children	58	56	53	

Note: ALG = unemployment benefits from the public unemployment insurance; ALH = unemployment assistance; ALGII = unemployment benefits II; since 1996, annual reduction of unemployment assistance by 3 percent.
Source: Authors' own table

expected change in the life length after retirement. To ensure a real increase in the actual retirement age, the reform plan suggested, furthermore, to raise the earliest eligibility ages of all retirement schemes and to introduce higher actuarially fair adjustments. Second, an additional factor for the pension benefit indexation formula was proposed that links the benefits to the systems dependency ratio, called the **"sustainability factor."**[5] Taking into account the lower bound for the replacement rates, this factor will further reduce the pension benefits so that the contribution rate's thresholds are fulfilled. Most of the commission's proposals—and, most significantly, the introduction of the sustainability factor—quickly passed the German parliament in 2004. An exception was the adaptation of the eligibility ages to life expectancy. It was argued that an increase in the retirement age would lead to higher unemployment, as it takes jobs away from the young.

Parallel to the pension reform, in 2004 the government passed the so-called Hartz reforms and reorganized the pension taxation. The Hartz reforms replaced, inter alia, the unemployment assistance by the lower "unemployment benefit II" (commonly called Hartz IV). Table 5.3 states the development of unemployment benefits. Moreover, the pension claims granted while receiving unemployment benefit II were stepwise reduced after 2004 from 16 percent to 0 percent of the last income (see table 5.4). Furthermore, the duration of normal unemployment benefits was reduced for older workers from a maximum of 32 months to 18 months. Both measures made unemployment less attractive as a substitute for early old-age and disability pension benefits.

5. The sustainability factor is to a certain degree similar to the demographic factor of 1997. However, the demographic factor only considers the increase of the life expectancy, while the sustainability factor considers the development of the ratio between beneficiaries and contributors.

Table 5.4 **Contribution to public pension system for unemployed as percentage of last gross income**

	Until 1978	1979–82	1983–99	2000–2004	2005–6	2007–10	Since 2011
ALG	80	100	80	80	80	80	80
ALH/ALGII	80	100	80	ca. 32	ca. 16	ca. 8	None

Note: ALG = unemployment benefits from the public unemployment insurance; ALH = unemployment assistance replaced by the unemployment benefits II (ALG II) in 2005; paid contributions indicate collected pension claims (earnings point) while unemployed.

Source: Authors' own table

Table 5.5 **Maximal duration time of unemployment benefits for older workers in months**

Age/year	Until 1985	1985	1986	1987–2003	2004–7	Since 2008
51–55	12	18	20	26		15
56					18	18
57			24	32		
58						24

Source: Authors' own table

The reorganization of the pension taxation was a consequence of a decision of the Federal Constitutional Court, which criticized the different taxation of public pension benefits and the pensions of civil servants (see Börsch-Supan and Quinn, 2015). Until 2004, public pensions were taxed only if they surpassed a quite large allowance. Actually, this applied only to relatively few cases. With the new regulations, a deferred taxation of pension was introduced. Hence the contributions to the pension insurance were tax exempt and the pension benefits taxable. To prevent double taxation, the reform included a generous transition period.[6]

Step 2.5 (2007): Toward Later Retirement Ages

In the end, population aging remained high on the political agenda along with the not-yet-implemented reform proposal of the commission—namely, the increase of eligibility ages. Finally in 2007, then labor secretary Franz Müntefering surprisingly unilaterally announced the increase of the statutory eligibility age, similar to the suggestion of the commission, by two years

6. The transition included, on the one hand, an implementation of the tax exemption between 2005 and 2025 and, on the other hand, constant tax allowances on pension claimed before 2040. The tax exemption increases stepwise from 60 percent to 100 percent. For pension claimed before 2005, the tax allowance was set to 50 percent of the gross pension benefits in 2005. For pensions claimed between 2005 and 2040, the allowance is a fraction of the first received gross pension, whereby the fraction itself depends on the pension-claiming year and decreases from 50 percent to 0 percent.

until 2029 (see figure 5.7g black and gray lines).[7] In parallel, the benchmarks for adjustment-free disability pensions would be raised from 63 to 65. Still unrealized remained the adoption of the early eligibility scheme (old-age pension for workers with a long service history) to the life expectancy (see figure 5.7g gray dotted line) as well as the introduction of actuarially fair adjustments (see table 5.6 for cohort-specific actuarial adjustments).

Phase 3 (2007 to 2016): Reform Backlash, the "Pension with 63"

With the 2007 pension reform, the process toward a sustainable pension system ended and a phase of moderate reform backlashes followed. This process actually started already within the 2007 pension reform as the decision to increase the statutory eligibility age was watered down by exemptions for those workers who have 45 years of active contribution payments (see figure 5.7g orange line). This new type of old-age pensions ("old-age pension for especially long careers") could be claimed at the age of 65 or older but not earlier, even with actuarial adjustments. The next backlash happened in 2008 as the duration of unemployment benefits was increased for older workers (older than 57) to 24 months (see table 5.5). The largest backlash so far took place in 2014, when, among other things, the Great Coalition enlarged the group of workers with 45 years of contributions by watering down the definition of "contribution year." Even more significantly, this group of individuals was now granted an adjustment-free retirement at the age of 63 (see figure 5.7h orange line), called "retirement at 63." The claiming age of 63 increased in parallel to the statutory eligibility age such that the claiming age for this type of pensions was set to two years before the statutory eligibility age. This type of early retirement became very popular and led to a standstill in the average retirement age, which had increased since the turn of the century. Finally, the rigid earning limits of the partial pension (see 1992 pension reform) were substituted by more flexible limits in 2016, coming into force in July 2017. Within the new system, each additional earned in excess of €6,300 per year is only counted as 40 percent toward the pension. The employee can retain 60 percent. With the new regulations, the German government tried to encourage partial pensioners to extend their labor supply. However, as actuarial adjustments are still not actuarially fair, it has to be shown whether this new regulation will meet their expectation.

Even though the most recent process clearly showed a backward movement in the pension policy, the backlashed reforms were still moderate. The main reform measures for the sustainable pension system remained untouched. However, the current political discussion is at least worrisome as the voices demanding a complete role back become louder.

7. Note that the statutory eligibility age was not automatically linked to the life expectancy.

Table 5.6 **Actuarial adjustment factor for early/late pension claiming in percentage by pathway to retirement, pension-claiming age, and cohort/pension-claiming year**

Pension-claiming age											
		60	61	62	63	64	65	66	67	68	69
	Cohort										
Long-term insured	<1937	—	—	—	100	100	100	107.2	114.4	114.4	114.4
	1937	—	—	—	96.4	100	100	106	112	118	124
	1938–48	—	—	—	92.8	96.4	100	106	112	118	124
	1948–64	**Stepwise increase of statutory eligibility age**									
	>1963	—	—	—	85.6	89.2	92.8	96.4	100	106	112
	Cohort										
	<1937	100	100	100	100	100	100	107.2	114.4	114.4	114.4
	1937–39	100	100	100	100	100	100	106	112	118	124
	1940	96.4	100	100	100	100	100	106	112	118	124
Women	1941	92.8	96.4	100	100	100	100	106	112	118	124
	1942	89.2	92.8	96.4	100	100	100	106	112	118	124
	1943	85.6	89.2	92.8	96.4	100	100	106	112	118	124
	1944–51	82	85.6	89.2	92.8	96.4	100	106	112	118	124
	Cohort										

Unemployed and part-time retirement	<1937	100	100	100	100	100	100	107.2	114.4	114.4	114.4
	1937	96.4	100	100	100	100	100	106	112	118	124
	1938	92.8	96.4	100	100	100	100	106	112	118	124
	1939	89.2	92.8	96.4	100	100	100	106	112	118	124
	1940	85.6	89.2	92.8	96.4	100	100	106	112	118	124
	1940–45	82	85.6	89.2	92.8	96.4	100	106	112	118	124
	1946	—	85.6	89.2	92.8	96.4	100	106	112	118	124
	1947	—	—	89.2	92.8	96.4	100	106	112	118	124
	1948–51	—	—	—	92.8	96.4	100	106	112	118	124
	Cohort										
	<1937	100	100	100	100	100	100	107.2	114.4	114.4	114.4
	1937–40	100	100	100	100	100	100	106	112	118	124
	1941	96.4	100	100	100	100	100	106	112	118	124
Disabled	1942	92.8	96.4	100	100	100	100	106	112	118	124
	1943–47	89.2	92.8	96.4	100	100	100	106	112	118	124
	1948–64	**Parallel increase of statutory eligibility age and disableds' eligibility age**									
	>1963	—	—	89.2	92.8	96.4	100	100	100	106	112
	Year										
	<1992	100	100	100	100	100	100	107.2	114.4	114.4	114.4
Disability pension	1992–2001	100	100	100	100	100	100	106	112	118	124
	2001–11	89.2	92.8	96.4	100	100	100	106	112	118	124
	2012–24	**Stepwise increase of disability pension's eligibility age and statutory eligibility age**									
	>1963	—	—	89.2	92.8	96.4	100	100	100	106	112

Source: Authors' own table

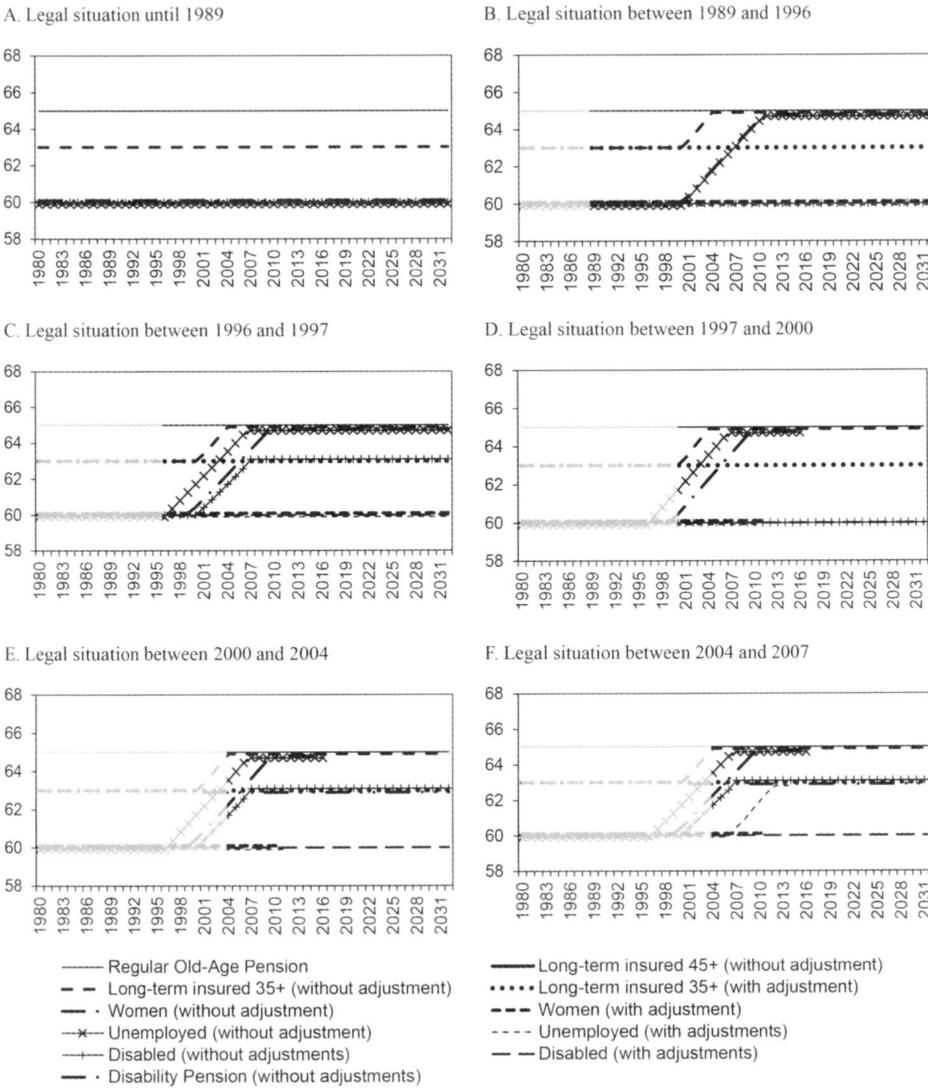

Fig. 5.7 Eligibility ages with and without actuarial deductions for each pathway to retirement with respect to legal situation

Note: The figures summarize three dimensions of policy changes regarding the eligibility age to claim pension benefits: the introduction of actuarial adjustments, the introduction and closure of entire pathways, and finally the gradual increase of the eligibility ages. Each panel (a) through (h) represents the legal status as seen from a specific year. The horizontal axis displays the time horizon of a worker making a decision about claiming her pension. The vertical axis displays the eligibility age pertaining to the year on the horizontal axis, and the graphs represent the pathways with and without actuarial deductions. Each panel thus presents the announced future development of the future legal situation. We assume that they correspond to the expectations of workers pondering a claiming decision. Past years are shown as faded lines.

Source: Authors' own diagram

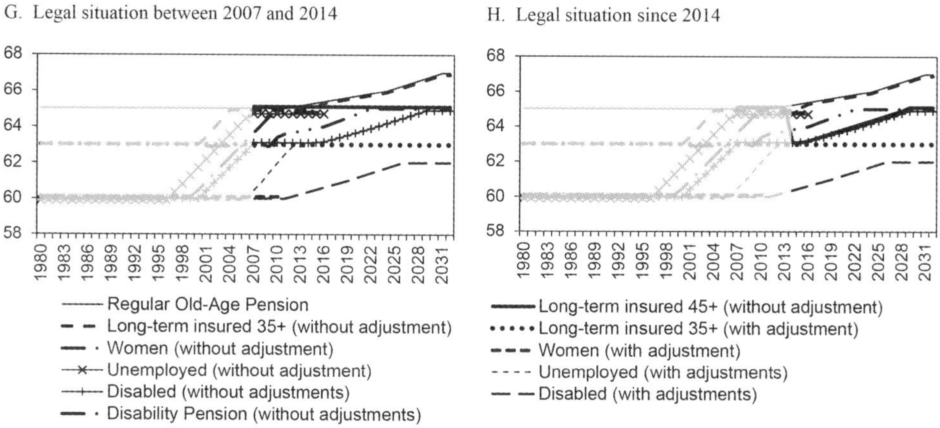

Fig. 5.7 (cont.)

5.4 The Implicit Tax on Working Longer

5.4.1 Definition

As described in the previous sections, German retirement insurance creates strong incentives to claim a pension and exit the labor force relatively early in life through a variety of mechanisms. These mechanisms can be summarized compactly in terms of a loss in social security wealth when postponing claiming and retiring from the labor force. Since Germany applies a relatively strict earnings test for ages below the normal eligibility age, claiming a pension invariably implies leaving the labor force at those younger ages, and we simply refer to "retiring" for this joint decision.

Social security wealth is the expected net present value of social security benefits minus contributions to the public pension and unemployment insurance during the retirement window, here defined as the age range from 55 to 69. Contributions before age 55 are sunk. Future contributions and benefits depend on the legal situation l at the planning age S and the used pathway to retirement k (e.g., via unemployment or disability pension). Seen from the perspective of a worker who is S years old and plans to retire at age R, *social security wealth* is given by

$$SSW_{S,k,l}(R,i) = \sum_{t=R}^{T} B_{t,k,l}(R,i) \cdot \sigma(i)_{S,t} \cdot \beta^{t-S} - \sum_{t=S}^{R-1} c_{t,l} \cdot Y_t(i) \cdot \sigma(i)_{S,t} \cdot \beta^{t-S}$$

with

SSW: net present discounted value of retirement/unemployment benefits

S: planning age

R: benefit-claiming age

i: gender and skill type
k: pathway to retirement
l: legal situation at planning age S
$Y_t(i)$: gross labor income at age t
$B_{t,k,l}(R,i)$: net benefits from pathway k at age t for benefit-claiming age R and legal situation l
$c_{t,l}$: contribution rate to pension and unemployment system at age t for legal situation l
$\sigma(i)_{S,t}$: probability to survive at least until age t given survival until age S
β: discount factor $\delta = 1/(1 + r)$. We choose the usual discount rate r of 3 percent.

Postponing retirement by one year has two negative effects on social security wealth: the worker must give up one year of (net) pensions, and he must continue to pay contributions to the pension system of about 10 percent of his gross earnings. On the other hand, postponing retirement raises pension benefits due to these additional contributions by roughly one-fortieth and due to the actuarial adjustments by 3.6 percent per year of postponement (after the 1992 reform has been fully phased in).

The incentives to leave the labor market and claim a pension can be expressed conveniently by the *implicit taxes*, which are based on the *accrual of social security wealth*. In this study, *accrual* is defined as the expected gain in social security wealth by postponing labor market exit by one year. The implicit tax is the negative accrual of social security wealth (ACC) divided by after-tax earnings (Y^{Net}) during the additional year of work:

$$ITAX = -\frac{ACC}{Y^{Net}}.$$

As long as the implicit tax is negative, it is rational to postpone withdrawal from the labor market unless labor/leisure preferences or similar considerations dominate the expected gain in social security wealth. Negative implicit taxes from a certain age onward are sufficient (although not necessary) for leaving the labor market and claiming a pension at that age.

5.4.1.2 *Empirical Implementation*

We compute the accrual of social security wealth and the implicit taxes for each year between 1980 and 2016. Individuals are assumed to anticipate the future development of the contribution rates and pension benefits based on the legal situation of the planning year S according to figure 5.7. We do not expect that individuals anticipate future reforms. For the past, the pension system's contribution rates and replacement rates are estimated for each relevant legal situation on the basis of historical data. For the future, we predict the development of the German public pension system's key parameters for each reform stage separately with the simulation model MEA-PENSIM (see

Holthausen et al. 2012). The (future) pension benefits depend on the earning history of the individual, the chosen pension-claiming age/pathway to retirement (actuarial adjustments, unemployment benefits), and the future replacement rate (pension value). The last two components may change with pension reforms.

We compute social security wealth, its accrual, and the implicit tax on working longer for 18 idealized constellations. We distinguish 3 gender groups (single female, single male, couple), 3 skill groups (low, medium, and high education/skill), and 2 macroenvironments (common environment across all 12 countries involved in the ISSP, German environment). For each of these 18 idealized constellations, we construct a matrix of 38 × 15 values (i.e., social security wealth, its accrual, and the implicit tax), where the 38 rows refer to the years of the time series (1980 to 2016) and the 15 columns refer to the claiming ages S (55 to 69). Moreover, each value is based on separate computations for each of the 6 pathways, which are then aggregated using as weights the frequency for each pathway.

In more detail, we calculate social security wealth for gender-specific synthetic income profiles of low, medium, and high education/skilled single households. The low skilled are expected to enter the labor market with 16, the medium skilled with 20, and the high educated with 25. For couples, we assume a rather simple case: a male (female) who is married to a partner 3 years younger (older) of the same skill/education type. We assume furthermore that the spouse's retirement behavior is fixed—that is, it will not react to the partner's retirement decision.

The macroenvironment is represented by assumptions on (a) the age-earnings profile; (b) the payroll taxation, including social security contributions; and (c) age- and gender-specific survival probabilities. We specify a common synthetic environment in order to avoid confounding cross-national differences in pension policy with other determinants of social security wealth, such as different age-earnings profiles, different taxation, and different survival probabilities. See the following more specifically.

A. Common Macroenvironment

Common synthetic earnings profiles for the three skill/education groups are calculated with data from the US, Germany, and Italy.[8] They are depicted in figure 5.8.

Common survival rates for 2010 were provided by Eurostat (average of EU-28 countries). The underlying life expectancy at age 15 is 67.8 years for women and 64.7 years for men. For men, the life tables are adjusted to generate life expectancies that are 2 to 4 years higher or lower to reflect the higher or lower life expectancy of high or low educated men. Similarly,

8. The data sources are the US Current Population Survey (CPS) and administrative data from the German and Italian pension system (SUF-VSKT 2011, see DRV 2011 and INPS).

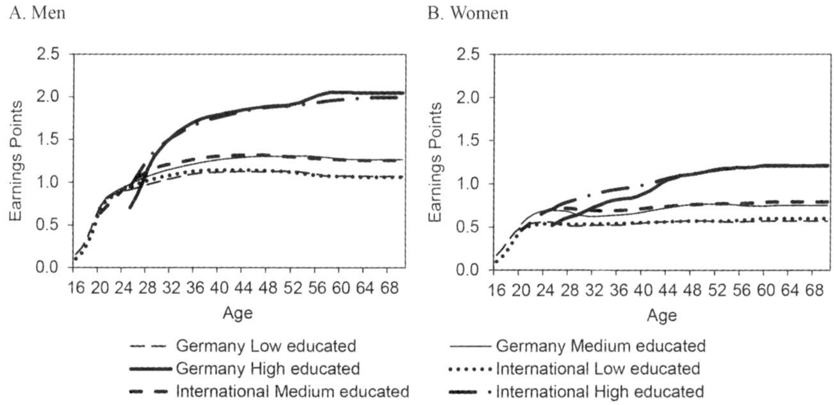

Fig. 5.8 (Synthetic) earnings profiles by gender and education

Source: Authors' own calculations based on US Current Population Survey (CPS), German SUF-VSKT 2011 (DRV 2011), and Italian INPS

the life tables for women are adjusted; however, here it is assumed that low educated women have a 4.5 year lower life expectancy.

Common payroll taxes are taken from the Organisation for Economic Co-operation and Development (OECD) tax database (see OECD 2018b) and refer to all income taxes and employee and employer social security contributions.

B. National Macroenvironment

In order to compare actual German retirement behavior with prevailing implicit taxes, we calculate implicit taxes for German earning profiles, life tables, and payroll taxes. The earnings profiles are calculated with administrative data from the German pension insurance (SUF-VSKT 2011; see DRV 2011). For women, we find only a small difference between the income profiles of younger and older cohorts. As a consequence, we consider cohort-specific income profiles only for men. The average income profiles are depicted in figure 5.8.

The cohort-specific life tables are provided by the German Federal Statistical Office in Statistisches Bundesamt (2015). Similar to the common cases, we adjusted the life tables for high/low educated individuals in order to control for the differences in life expectancy.

In terms of taxes, we use our own tax calculator, which calculates the tax rate according to the prevailing legal situation. To illustrate the influence of the stepwise introduced deferred taxation, we show additional results, which exclude this reform.

The matrices of outcome values are aggregated over six pathways:

- regular old-age pension (at the statutory eligibility age),
- early pension claiming via old-age pension for long-term insured or for women,
- leaving the labor market via unemployment,
- part-time employment prior to retirement,
- early pension claiming via old-age pension for the disabled, and
- disability pension.

It is important to notice that all of these pathways pay the same benefit once a person is eligible. They differ, however, by their eligibility criteria (see table 5.1). Among those, "strict" and "soft" eligibility rules can be distinguished. The first are tied to objective variables, such as age, gender, and previous contribution history, while the second are subject to discretionary decisions, notably the determination of a worker's disability status.

The conditions for the various retirement programs are, in our case, however, only relevant to a certain degree, since the social security wealth is computed for synthetic individuals. As a consequence, we calculate the social security wealth for each pathway separately and aggregate the resulting implicit taxes afterward by weighting them with the observed frequency of the corresponding pathway among all pension claims. We assume, accordingly, that the actual distribution of the various pathways reflects the probability to fulfill the eligibility requirements of the respective pathways. These probabilities vary between the group of insured individuals and the subgroup of insured individuals who did not drop out of the labor market at younger ages. We therefore consider two different weighting approaches. The first approach uses the distribution of the pathways on all public pension claims as depicted in figure 5.4. The second approach considers the distribution of the pension claims of those individuals only who paid contributions in the year before they claimed their pension (see figure 5.9). This second approach excludes "passively insured" individuals (e.g., homemakers).

This alternative frequency is used if the implicit taxes should be compared with the employment rate. Essentially, we aim to exclude those effects on the frequency that derived from insured individuals who did not belong to the labor market before claiming the public pension (e.g., homemakers). Actually, the 1985 shift in the balance between regular old-age pensions and disability pensions is much smaller under this approach (compare figure 5.9 with figure 5.4). The annual frequencies are used to combine the implicit taxes with the same labor exit ages. By definition, these are the implicit taxes with the same planning age S. In the following, this approach represents our basic weighing procedure.

The frequencies displayed in figure 5.4 are used only when the implicit taxes are compared with the development in the overall pension-claiming behavior. Under this approach the implicit taxes with the same underlying

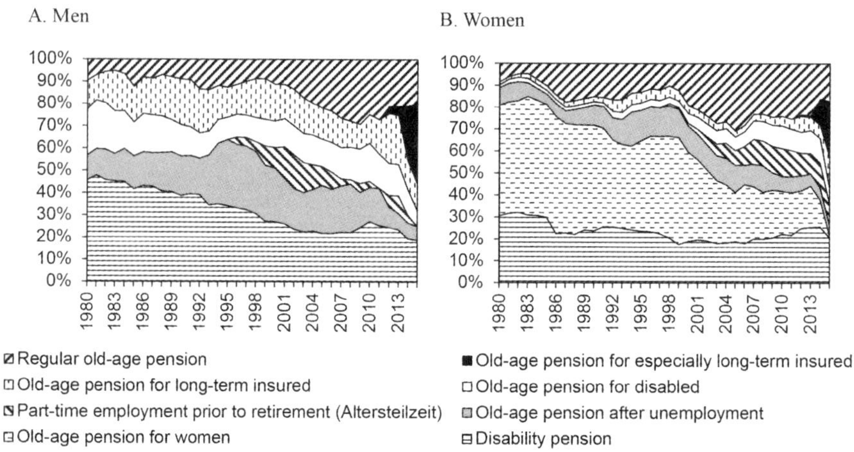

Fig. 5.9 Coverage of pathways to retirement on annual newly claimed pensions without passively insured individuals

Source: Authors' own calculations based on Deutsche Rentenversicherung Bund (DRV 2017), Rentenzugangsstatistik

pension-claiming age have to be combined. In most cases, these are again the implicit taxes with the same planning age S. Exceptions are the pathways via unemployment and part-time work. Here, the pension-claiming age is later than the labor exit age: one or two years (depending on the maximal duration of unemployment benefits) for the unemployment pathways and up to five years for the preretirement pathway via part-time work (by assumption).

5.5 Results

In the following, we will present the results of our calculations in a stepwise fashion. Subsection 5.5.1 presents individualized replacement rates and social security wealth—that is, the elements from which the implicit tax will be computed—on a scale more often used in the economics literature than the German-specific "standardized replacement rates" in section 5.3 (table 5.2). For comparability, we apply the German payroll taxes.

In subsection 5.5.2, we introduce the common macroenvironment. We first present general outcome variables, such as replacement rate and social security wealth and its accrual. Subsection 5.5.3 follows with the implicit tax on working longer for median-educated men, women, and couples. Subsection 5.5.4 shows how these implicit taxes vary between different skill groups.

Subsection 5.5.5 uses the differences between the common environment and the national case for a discussion of how the implicit taxes depend on specific national taxation, income profiles, and life tables.

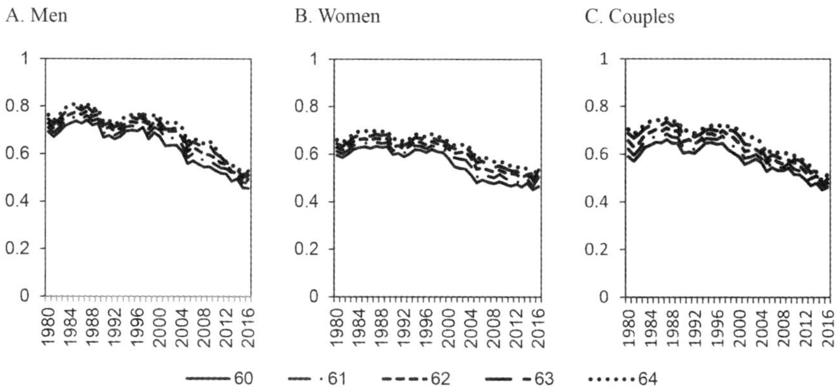

Fig. 5.10 Replacement rate for median-educated men, women, and couples by age
Source: Authors' own calculations

Finally, subsections 5.5.6 and 5.5.7 are devoted to a graphical juxtaposition of our computed implicit taxes with the actual development of employment and the changes in the distribution of the pension-claiming age. A formal multivariate regression analysis is the aim of a subsequent phase of the ISSP.

5.5.1 Replacement Rates and Social Security Wealth, Scaled for Germany

5.5.1.1 Replacement Rate

The standardized replacement rates shown in table 5.2 of a pensioner with constant average earnings over the entire work life do not reflect actual earnings profiles, which typically increase with age. Moreover, these standardized replacement rates do not take the introduction of the deferred taxation on pension benefits into account. As a consequence, we analyze the following individualized net replacement rates (pension benefits as a share of last earnings by the types of individuals and households defined in the previous section), which were computed in the calculation process of the implicit taxes.

In order to maintain some comparability to the official German figures, the calculations in this subsection are based on the tax rate calculations of the German macroenvironment (see section 5.4) but use the income profiles and survival probabilities of the common macroenvironment. The most critical difference is the fact that the common taxation does not only tax labor income but also taxes pension income, although German public pension benefits were not taxed until 2005. The common taxation therefore leads to much smaller net replacement rates than were actually the case. The net replacement rates are depicted in figure 5.10 for median-educated men,

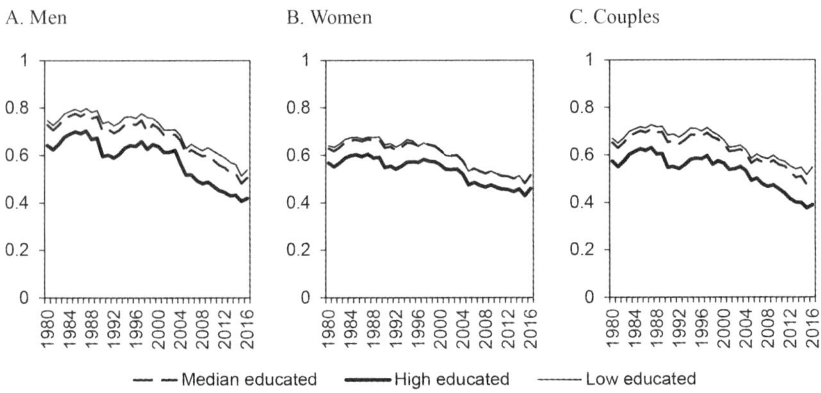

Fig. 5.11 Average replacement rate of 60–64 age group by education
Source: Authors' own calculations

women, and couples at the planning age 60 to 64 between 1980 and 2016. In the couples' case, the replacement rate is shown from the men's perspective, while the women's claiming age is three years younger.

First of all, we observe in all cases nearly constant replacement rates until 2004. The smaller fluctuations result from changes in the tax rates on the last labor income. As shown in subsection 5.5.2, these fluctuations do not appear in the case of common tax rates. After 2004, both the standardized replacement rates (table 5.2) and the individualized net replacement rates decrease. This is due to the introduction of the sustainability factor. The decrease, however, is more moderate for the standardized replacement rates, especially for men. This steeper decrease is due to the stepwise introduction of the deferred taxation, since the increasing taxation reduces the net pension benefits in addition to the sustainability factor.

The individualized replacement rates increase with age, since individuals earn additional pension claims while their labor income remains constant at older ages. Moreover, we observe in the past higher replacement rates for men than for women. This is due to lower taxation of women's last labor income, hence due to the progressivity of the tax system, and the now past tax exemption for public pension benefits. As a consequence, the gap disappeared in recent years due to the abolishment of the tax exemption for public pension benefits (i.e., the introduction of deferred taxation). Moreover, the progressivity of the tax system has led to a larger reduction of high pensions benefits (typically for men) than for small pension benefits (typically for women). As the replacement rates of couples are a product of the spouses' replacement rates, they lie somewhere between the replacement rates of single men and women and have a similar development.

Higher-skilled individuals have smaller replacement rates than less/median-educated individuals (see figure 5.11). The replacement rates of

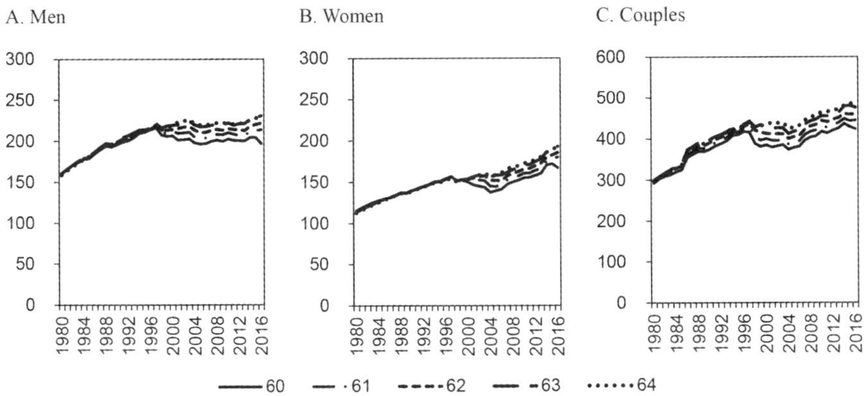

Fig. 5.12 Median-educated men's, women's and couple's social security wealth of leaving the labor market immediately in €1,000 by age
Source: Authors' own calculations

higher-educated individuals are lower due the higher share of their last income on their lifetime income. This is mainly a result of the shorter labor history of higher-educated individuals. Lower- and median-educated individuals accumulated, on the other hand, their pension claims over a longer time period such that their pension benefits are less strongly linked to their last income. There is a similar but smaller divergence between low and median-educated individuals.

5.5.1.2 Social Security Wealth

Figure 5.12 depicts the social security wealth that would be attained if the worker were to leave the labor market and claim a pension immediately. As before, it is based on common earnings profiles, common survival probabilities, and German tax rates, and the figures show median-educated single men, single women, and couples at claiming ages between 60 to 64 years. The level of social security wealth depends on lifetime income; hence men's social security wealth is larger than women's. Social security wealth increased for all groups between 1980 and 1996. The growth rate reflects the annual pension increase, which was first anchored to the average gross wage and after 1989 to the average net wage. After 1996, the increasing trend was reduced by the implementation of different reforms. The strongest effect was generated by the introduction of actuarial deductions for early retirement. Before their introduction, social security wealth increased only marginally with the claiming age.[9] This changed afterward, since the actuarial deduction

9. It is important not to mix this up with the incentive to postpone the labor market exit. For instance, remember that previous contributions to the social security system are sunk at a given plaining age, but not further contributiond.

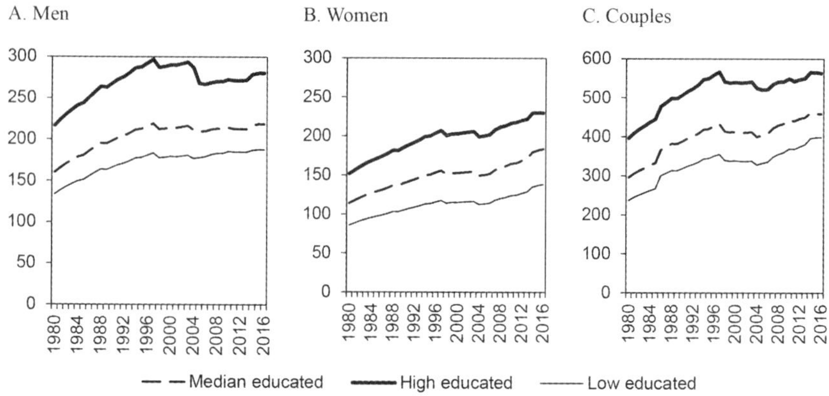

Fig. 5.13 Average social security wealth of 60–64 age group in €1,000 by education
Source: Authors' own calculations

reduced the social security wealth (pension benefits) of younger claiming ages/pension-claiming ages. This led to gaps between the social security wealth of different claiming ages.

Moreover, there were two reforms that reduced the social security wealth in general: first, the introduction of the demographic factor in 1998, which was later replaced by the sustainability factor, and second, the introduction of the deferred taxation. The influence of the deferred taxation depended, however, on the amount of the pension income. The social security wealth of pensioners with higher benefits (e.g., highly educated men; see figure 5.13) dropped more strongly than for those with low benefits. Lastly, the growth rate of the social security wealth decreased or even disappeared after 2005 for those groups with higher pension benefits, again due to the stepwise introduction of deferred taxation.

Couples' social security wealth results from the spouse's social security wealth and the possibility of receiving a survivor's pension. As a consequence, couples' social security wealth is larger than the sum of the social security wealth of single men and women.

Social security wealth increases with skill level (see figure 5.13), since higher-educated individuals have both larger pension claims and a higher life expectancy and thus a longer expected duration of pension benefits.

5.5.2 Common Macroenvironment: Replacement Rates and Social Security Wealth and Its Accrual

5.5.2.1 Replacement Rate

As a next step, we apply common taxation in order to maintain comparability across all countries involved in the project.

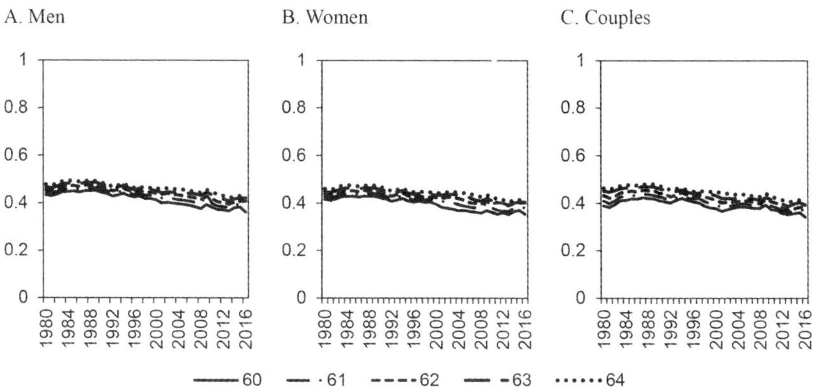

Fig. 5.14 Replacement rate for median-educated men, women, and couples by age (common case)
Source: Authors' own calculations

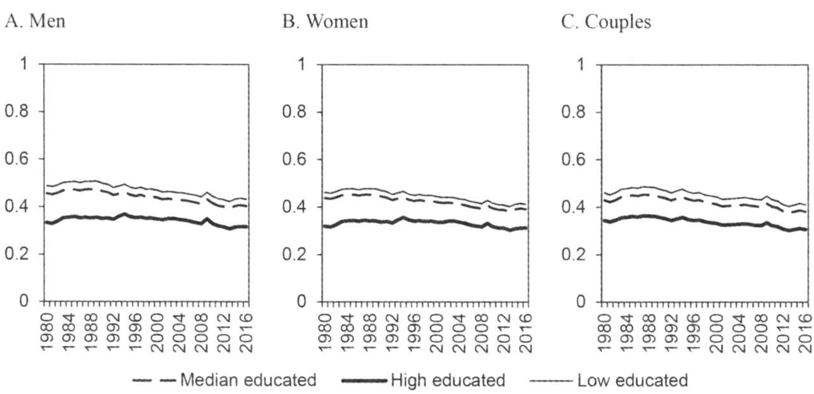

Fig. 5.15 Average replacement rate of 60–64 age group by education group (common case)
Source: Authors' own calculations

The respective net replacement rates are depicted in figure 5.14. Due to the taxation of the pension benefits, the replacement rates are much smaller than the replacement rates in figure 5.10. Moreover, the development of the replacement rates under the common case assumptions is less volatile, since the fluctuations caused by the changes in the time-specific German tax rates are smoothened. The decrease in the replacement rates is, moreover, less pronounced, since the taxation of the pension benefits has led to a smaller influence of marginal changes in the pension level on the replacement rate.

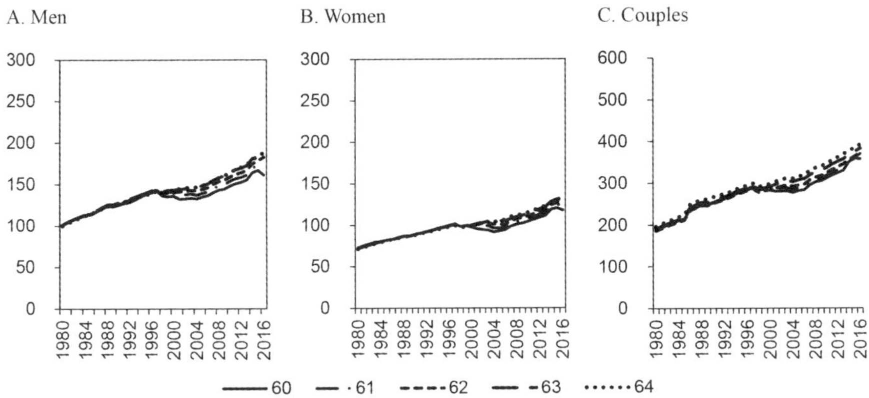

Fig. 5.16 Median-educated men's, women's, and couple's social security wealth of leaving the labor market immediately in €1,000 by age (common case)

Source: Authors' own calculations

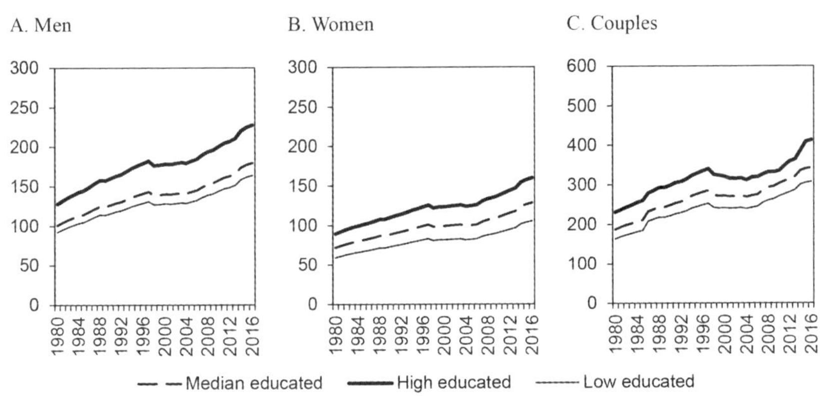

Fig. 5.17 Average social security wealth of 60–64 age group in €1,000 by education (common case)

Source: Authors' own calculations

5.5.2.2 Social Security Wealth

Figure 5.16 depicts the social security wealth of leaving the labor market immediately, now for the common case. Social security wealth is smaller in the common case, since the OECD tax rates are considerably larger. Also, the dynamics change: social security wealth increases after 2004 for both men and couples. This shows that the more or less constant social security wealth under German taxation is mainly a result of the introduction of deferred taxation.

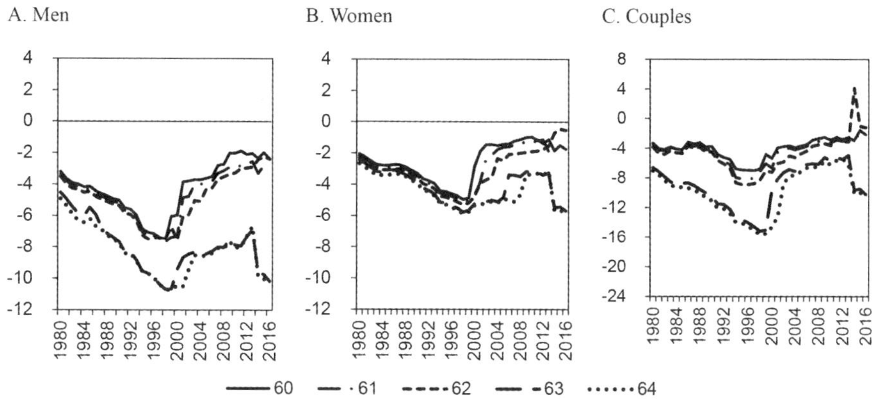

Fig. 5.18 Median-educated men's, women's, and couple's accrual of social security wealth of leaving the labor market immediately in €1,000 by age (common case)
Source: Authors' own calculations

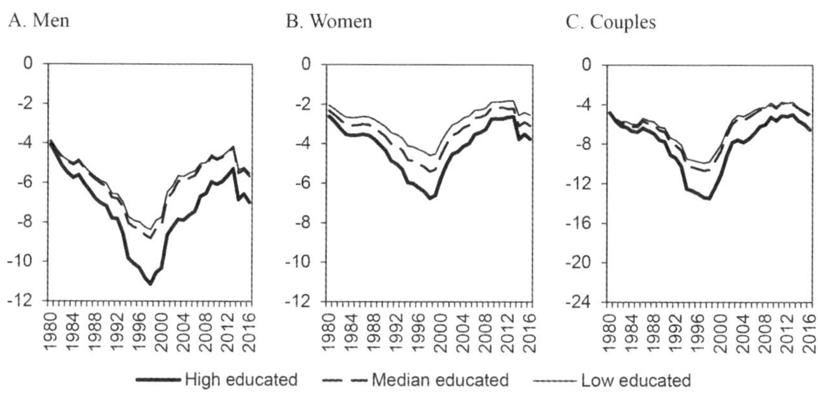

Fig. 5.19 Average accrual of social security wealth of 60–64 age group in €1,000 by education (common case)
Source: Authors' own calculations

5.5.2.3 Accrual Rates

We define the accrual of social security wealth as the change in social security wealth that workers expect when they postpone claiming benefits by one year. It is the numerator of the implicit tax on working longer as defined in section 5.4.

Figure 5.18 shows the accrual for median-educated single men, single women, and couples, while figure 5.19 studies the variation by education/ skill group. It is reported here for completeness and comparability to the other country chapters. Since the accrual is qualitatively very similar to the implicit taxes, we relegate a detailed description to the following subsection.

5.5.3 Common Macroenvironment: Implicit Taxes on Working Longer

Implicit taxes are defined as the accrual as shown in the preceding subsection divided by the most recent earnings. This subsection analyzes the median-educated single men's case and proceeds with the median-educated single women's and the median-educated couple's cases. Subsection 5.5.4 discusses the differences between the three skill groups.

Figures 5.20 and 5.21 display the median-educated men's implicit taxes in the common macroenvironment. Figure 5.20 shows for all considered claiming ages the development of the implicit taxes over time. For readability reasons, we divide figure 5.20 into three subgraphs. The first one shows the implicit taxes for the early labor market exit ages between 55 and 59, the second graph contains the implicit taxes of the main early retirement window between 60 and 64, and the third graph depicts the implicit taxes at and after the statutory eligibility age. Figure 5.21 depicts the same data for a selection of four planning years (1985, 1995, 2005, and 2015) by age.[10]

We observe for almost every case positive implicit tax and hence incentives to leave the labor market immediately. A general exception is ages 65 and 66, with negative implicit taxes until 1992. The implicit taxes at ages 55 to 57 lie over the whole observation time constantly around 19 percent. Hence there exists already at those early ages an incentive to leave the labor market immediately. Until 1985, the implicit tax at the age of 58 had a similar level. However, this implicit tax rose by more than 5 percentage points when the extension of the duration period of unemployment benefits in 1985 (see table 5.5) enabled individuals to build a bridge to retirement from this age onward. Moreover, the implicit tax grew further in the early 1990s due to the general increase in unemployment. This process ended in 1996, when the first cohort who had to accept actuarial deductions for claiming an old-age pension due to unemployment at the age of 60 reached the age of 58.[11] In fact, the implicit tax even decreased, as individuals can now avoid annual actuarial deductions of 3.6 percent by postponing claiming unemployment benefits and thereafter a pension to the following year. The overall deduction effect thereby increased over the introduction period of the actuarial deductions, since the total deduction for claiming a pension at the age of 60 increased stepwise from 3.6 percent to 18 percent (5 times 3.6 percent; see table 5.6). Since all actuarial deductions are introduced in an analogous pattern, we observe a similar qualitative development for other ages. In the further pro-

10. Note that in both cases, the same results are depicted. Only the considered dimension varies.

11. Note that the 58-year-old individuals draw unemployment benefits for age 58 and 59 and afterward claim their pension at the age of 60.

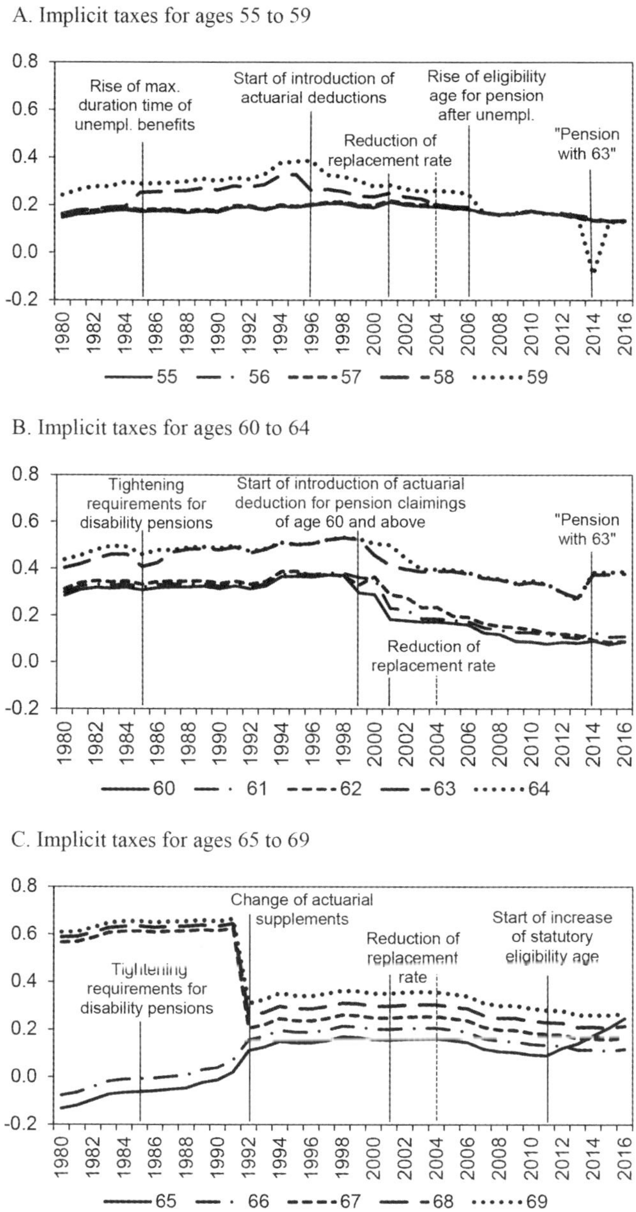

Fig. 5.20 Median-educated men's implicit taxes over time by age

Source: Authors' own calculations

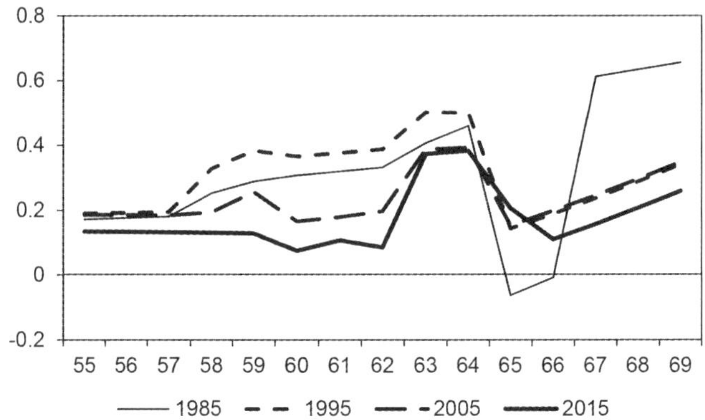

Fig. 5.21 Median-educated men's implicit taxes by age
Source: Authors' own calculations

cess, the implicit tax of age 58 went back to the level of the implicit taxes at ages 55 to 57. The main reason for this further decline is the abolishment of the old-age pension pathway due to unemployment (see table 5.1). The pattern is similar for age 59. However, the implicit tax was from the beginning larger than that for younger claiming ages, since one year of unemployment benefits was sufficient to build a bridge to retirement. Moreover, the drop in the implicit taxes appeared two years later, in 1998. This time lag results from the fact that the first cohort who had to accept actuarial deductions for claiming an old-age pension due to unemployment at age 61 reached the age of 59 two years later. In general, we observe the same two-year time lag for all subsequent ages and cases (introduction of actuarial adjustment for other pension pathways, like the old-age pension for women).

Between 1980 and 2000, the implicit taxes during the early retirement window (ages 60 to 65) were larger than the implicit taxes of the preceding claiming ages. Implicit taxes are around 35 percent for the claiming ages 60 to 62 and around 47 percent for the claiming ages 63 and 64. These rather large implicit taxes declined with the introduction of the actuarial deductions between 2000 and 2004. For ages 60 to 62, the implicit taxes dropped by more than 25 percentage points to the level of the implicit taxes of the 55 to 59 age group. This reduction occurs in two steps. The first drop results from the introduction of the actuarial deduction for the old-age pension for the disabled; the second one is due to the introduction of the actuarial deduction for the old-age pension due to unemployment. For ages 63 and 64, the implicit taxes dropped by 11 percentage points to 40 percent. After the introduction of the actuarial adjustments, we observe a further decrease of the implicit taxes, which can be explained by the reduction of the replacement rates caused by the introduction of the sustainability factor. Contrary to this general trend, the implicit taxes for claiming ages 63 and 64 increased in 2014. The reason is the introduction of a new early retirement pathway called "pension with 63," which enabled individuals to claim a pension at ages 63 and 64 without deductions (see section 5.3). In fact, the increase of the implicit taxes matches the now-abolished effect of the actuarial deductions.

As already mentioned, the implicit taxes for ages 65 and 66 were negative until 1992. Hence until 1992, there was an incentive to postpone pension claiming beyond the ages of 65 and 66. On the other hand, the implicit tax rates for ages 67 to 69 were extremely large, with values above 60 percent. This apparent contradiction results from the actuarial supplements for postponing pension claiming beyond the statutory eligibility age as they were organized until 1992. While actuarial supplements of 7.2 percent for postponing pension claiming to the age of 66 and 14.4 percent for postponing pension claiming to the age of 67 prevented positive implicit taxes (actuarially fair adjustments), there were no actuarial supplements for postponing pension claiming beyond age 67. As the general actuarial supplements of 6 percent were introduced in 1992, consequently the implicit taxes dropped considerably for claiming ages 67 to 69. All in all, we observe a reduction of more than 30 percentage points. The reduction was thereby larger for later claiming ages. However, since the actuarial supplements for postponing pension claiming at the ages of 65 and 66 were reduced at the same time, the implicit taxes of those claiming ages started to increase by approximately 20 percentage points, which corresponds to the reduction of the former actuarial supplements. Similar to the claiming ages of 60 to 64, the implicit taxes of the claiming ages of 65 to 69 started to decrease in 2004 due to the introduction of the sustainability factor. For most claiming ages, this decrease has continued until today. An exception is the claiming age of 65, for which the implicit tax started to increase in 2012. The explanation for this opposite development lies in the increase of the statutory eligibility age from 65 to 67. The incentive to leave the labor market increases due to the fact that an individual no longer receives higher actuarial supplements for postponing pension claiming beyond the statutory eligibility age but prevents only the smaller actuarial deduction for claiming a pension before the statutory eligibility age. Once the transition to the higher statutory eligibility age is completed, the implicit tax of the claiming age of 65 should have risen to a similar level as that of the implicit taxes of the claiming ages of 63 and 64.

The women's implicit taxes developed in a similar manner to the men's implicit taxes (see figures 5.22 and 5.23). However, women's implicit taxes are smaller due to their higher life expectancy, lower tax rates, and smaller replacement rates. Moreover, there are some additional differences from the men's case. First, we observe smaller differences between the implicit taxes of the claiming ages of 58 and 59 and the implicit taxes of the claiming ages of 55 to 57. The main reason is that the distribution of the women's pension claims includes only a small fraction of old-age pensions due to unemploy-

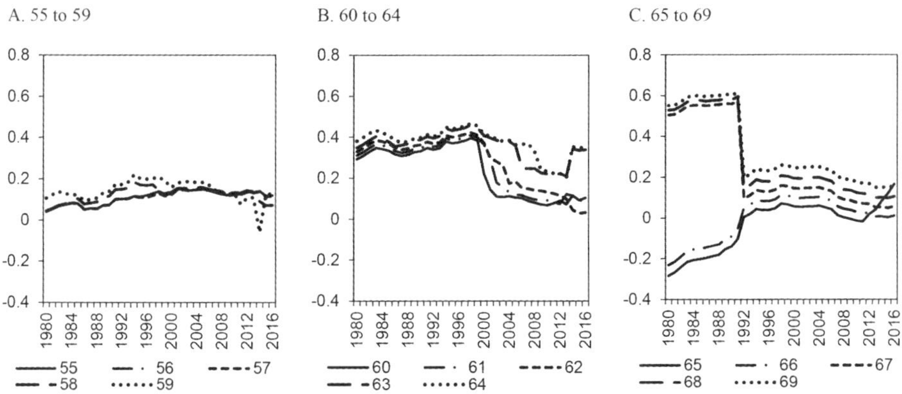

Fig. 5.22 Median-educated women's implicit taxes over time by age
Source: Authors' own calculations

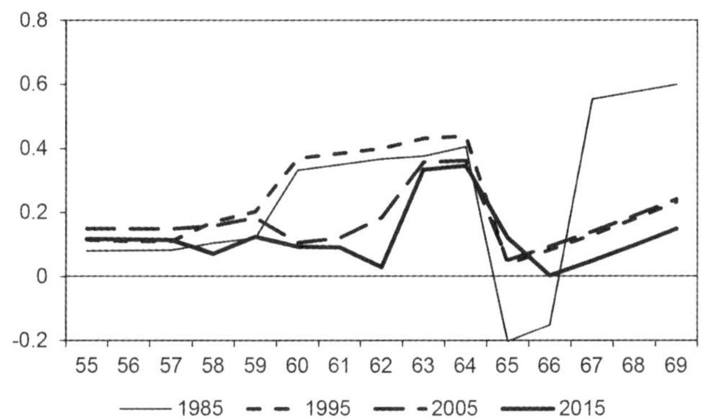

Fig. 5.23 Median-educated women's implicit taxes by age
Source: Authors' own calculations

ment. Hence the pathway via unemployment is less relevant in the women's case as compared to the men's case. Second, the implicit taxes at ages 60 to 62 are similarly as large as the implicit taxes at ages 63 and 64. This can be explained by the old-age pension for women, which enabled more or less all women to claim a pension at age 60 without eligibility requirements such as unemployment or disability. As shown in figure 5.9, most women used this retirement pathway. As a consequence, the introduction of the actuarial deductions for the old-age pension for women had a very large effect on the implicit tax.

Finally, figures 5.24 and 5.25 depict implicit taxes for median-educated couples. The claiming ages refer to the age of the husband; women are assumed to be three years younger. The general development is similar to

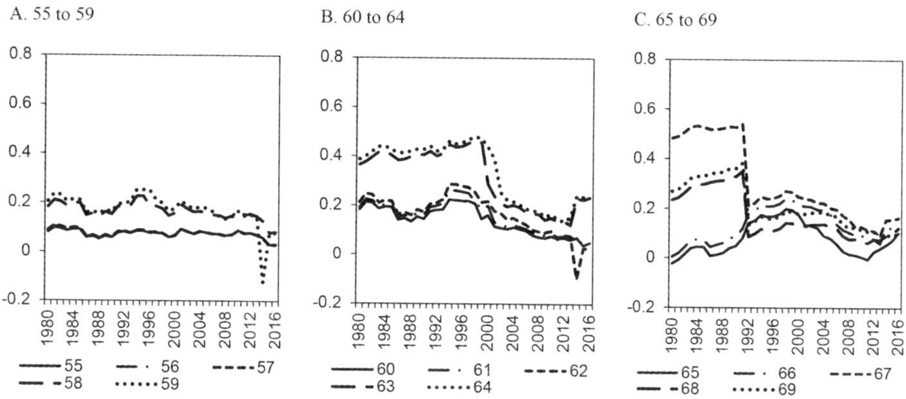

Fig. 5.24 Median-educated couple's implicit taxes over time
Source: Authors' own calculations

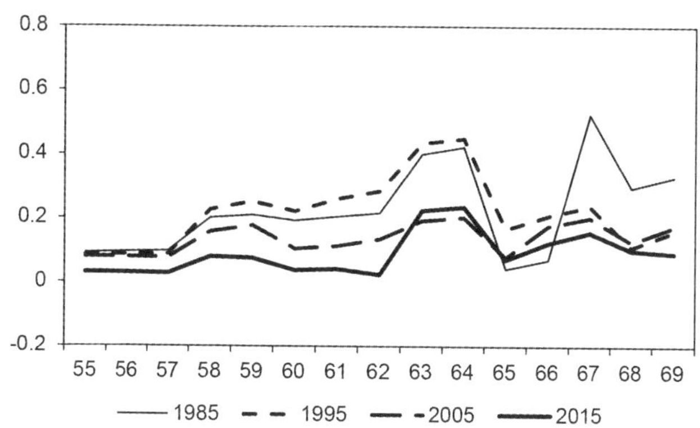

Fig. 5.25 Median-educated couple's implicit taxes by age
Source: Authors' own calculations

the single household case. However, there are some distinctions due to the age differences of the spouses. For example, the implicit tax at the husband's claiming age of 69 is smaller than in the single household case. The reason is that the wife is only 66 at this time. Hence if the couples postpone claiming by one year, the women could gain the actuarial supplement for postponing pension claiming beyond the statutory eligibility age. This had a large effect, especially before 1992. Similar observations can be made for other claiming ages.

5.5.4 Implicit Taxes on Working Longer by Education/Skill

So far, we have studied the implicit taxes for median-educated individuals. This subsection looks at the differences across the three skill groups. We con-

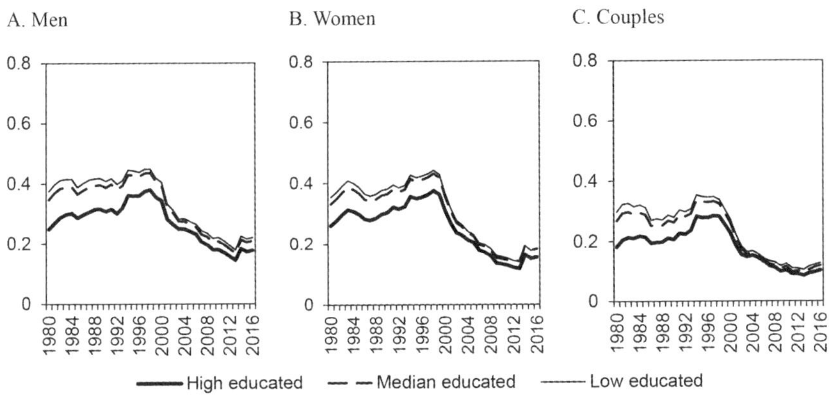

Fig. 5.26 Implicit taxes aggregated over ages 60 to 64 by education group
Source: Authors' own calculations

sider the average implicit taxes of the 60 to 64 age groups only. Our findings are similar for other age groups. Figure 5.26 depicts the implicit taxes over time separately for single men, single women, and couples by skill group. We can make two observations. First, implicit taxes decrease with education. The gap is especially large between high and median-educated individuals. Second, we observe that the gap between the implicit taxes decreases over time. This results from the introduction of the actuarial deductions, since they have a greater effect on individuals with a lower life expectancy. Hence the implicit taxes for low and median-educated individuals decrease more strongly due to the introduction of the actuarial deductions than the implicit taxes for the highly educated.

More generally, there are three reasons for the difference among the skill groups: first, there are differences in the assumed life expectancy; second, there are different tax rates on the last labor income; and third, there are differences in the replacement rates. A higher life expectancy reduces the implicit tax, since the additional pension claims for a postponement of claiming are received over a longer time horizon and offset a larger part of the pension benefits and contributions lost due to the additional working year. The relevance of the income tax rates and the replacement rates results from the division of the strictly gross income–related additional benefits and contributions by the last net income.

5.5.5 German Macroenvironment: The Influence of Changes in Taxation, Cohort-Specific Income Profiles, and Survival Probabilities

We now switch from the common macroenvironment to the German macroenvironment. We discuss ways in which taxation, cohort-specific income profiles, and survival probabilities influence the implicit taxes. We start with

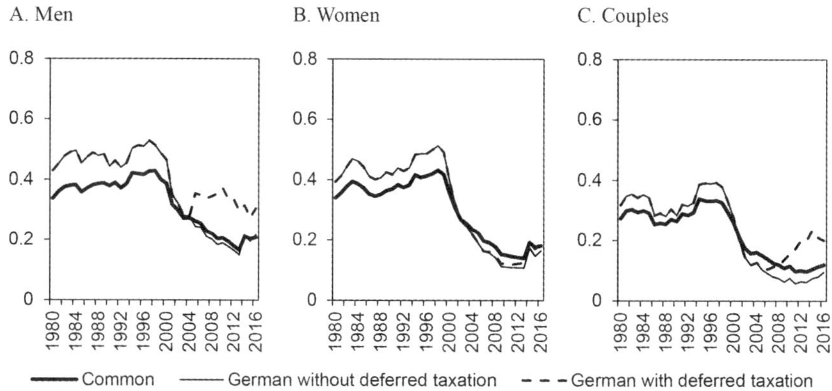

Fig. 5.27 Average implicit taxes (ages 60 to 64) for common and German taxation
Source: Authors' own calculations

taxation, then proceed with analyzing the income profiles, and close with the survival probabilities.

Figure 5.27 depicts the average implicit taxes of single men, single women, and couples at the claiming ages of 60 to 64 for different taxations of the gross pension and labor income. All figures are aggregated over the three education groups. We consider three cases: first, the common taxation used in the common macroenvironment; second, the German taxation according to our tax calculator but without the introduction of the deferred taxation; and finally, German taxation with deferred taxation. The income profiles and survival probabilities remain as before and are taken from the common macroenvironment.[12]

Until 2000, we observe for each case smaller implicit taxes under the common taxation than under the time-specific German taxation. The gap is larger for men than for women. It results from the fact that under common taxation, both the labor income and public pension benefits are taxed. At the end of the 1990s, the gap becomes smaller, and since 2000 the implicit taxes are larger under the common taxation than under the German time-specific taxation (at least if we do not consider the deferred taxation). This reversal is due to the introduction of the actuarial deductions, which reduce the gain of claiming a pension immediately.

We have already shown that deferred taxation has had a large influence on the determinants of the implicit taxes such as the replacement rate. Consequently, we also see a large reaction of the implicit taxes to the introduction of deferred taxation (see figure 5.27). The deferred taxation led to an increase in the implicit taxes for single men and couples. This effect

12. Note that the last case corresponds to the case for which we had presented the replacement rates and social security wealth shown in subsection 5.5.1.

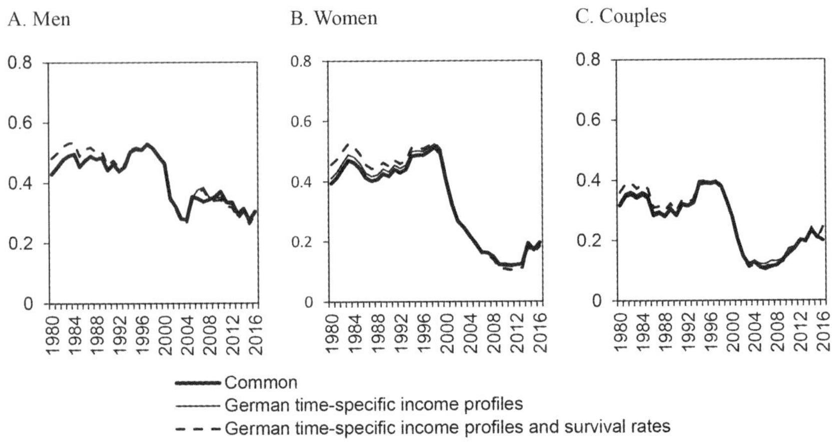

Fig. 5.28 Average implicit taxes (ages 60 to 64) for common and German cohort-specific income profiles and survival probabilities
Source: Authors' own calculations

is larger for higher claiming ages and conceals most of the effects that we have observed in the previous section—for example, the effect of the "pension with 63" or the effect due to the increase of the statutory eligibility age. That we do not observe an effect on the women's implicit taxes results from their rather small pension benefits and the large tax allowances that were granted at the beginning of the introduction of the deferred taxation. With the decrease of these tax allowances, the women's implicit taxes will be similarly influenced by the deferred taxation.

Figure 5.28 depicts implicit taxes for different income profiles and survival probabilities. The panel labeled "common" depicts the implicit taxes for the common macroenvironment but with German taxation. The other two lines replace, consecutively, the common earnings profiles with German cohort-specific earnings profiles and the common survival probabilities with the German cohort-specific survival rates.

We do not observe relevant changes in the implicit taxes if we change the underlying earnings profiles. A somewhat larger effect can be observed when we change the underlying survival probabilities. Implicit taxes of earlier ages increase due to much lower life expectancies of older cohorts. However, this effect is also rather small.

5.5.6 Relation between Implicit Taxes and Employment Rates

This subsection graphically links the development of the implicit tax with the development of the employment rate.[13] We plot the average employment

13. In the women's case, we will use the corrected employment rates.

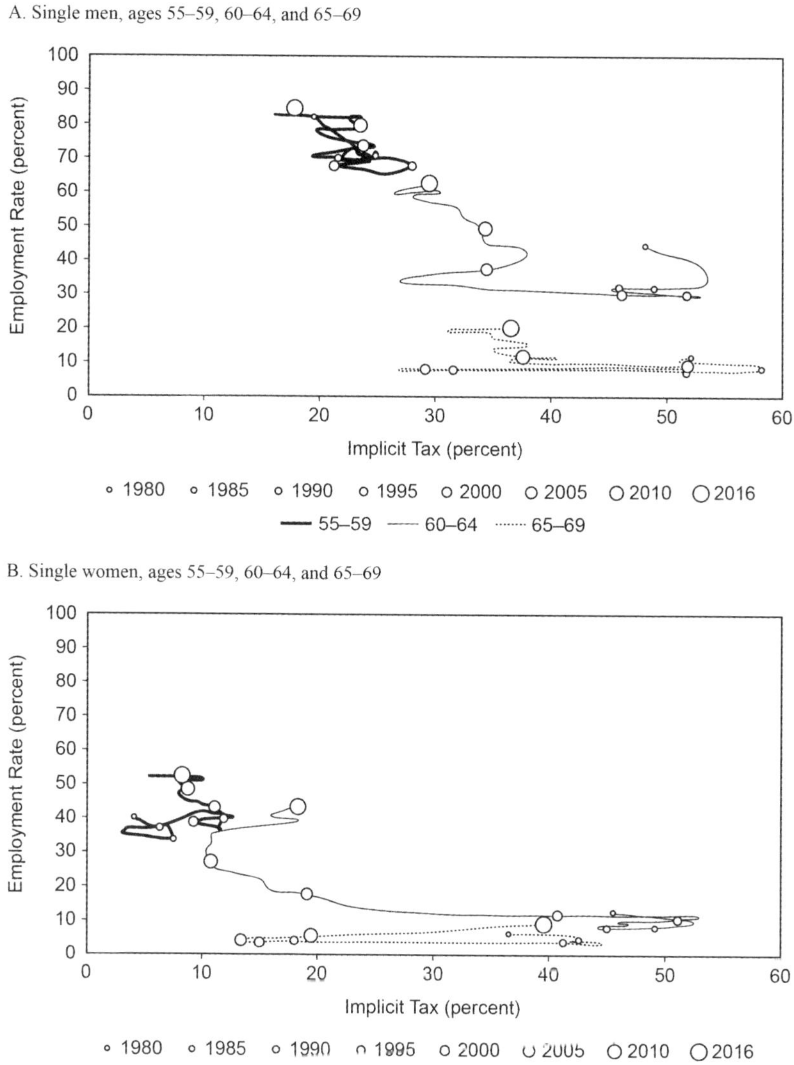

Fig. 5.29 Employment rate versus implicit tax
Source: Authors' own calculations

rates of older workers by age groups 55–59, 60–64, 65–69, and 55–69 (see figure 5.1) against the average implicit taxes of the same age groups (for the 60–64 age group; see figure 5.28). The result is shown in figure 5.29. We first discuss the differences among age groups. For both men and women, we see that younger age groups have large employment rates and smaller implicit taxes, while the older age groups have smaller employment rates and higher

C. Single men, ages 55–69

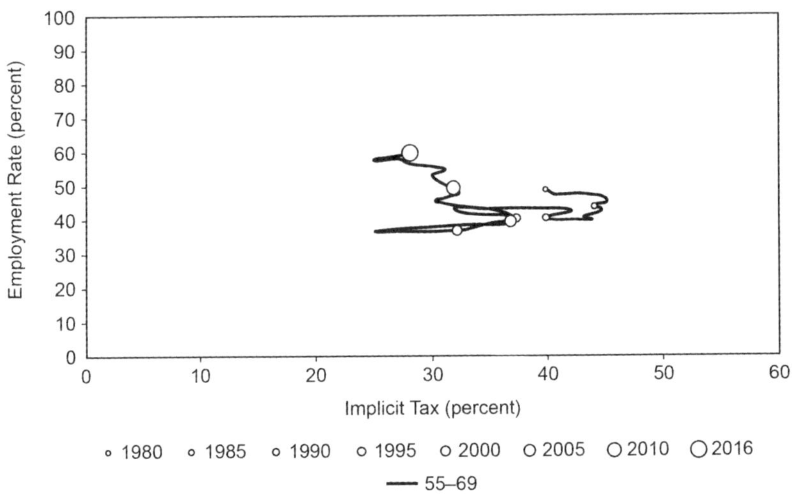

D. Single women, ages 55–69

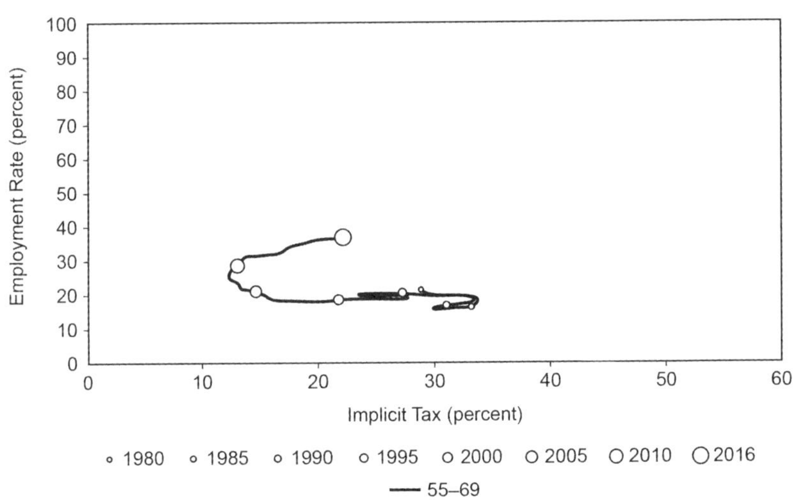

Fig. 5.29 (cont.)

implicit taxes. Hence we observe a negative correlation between employment rates and implicit taxes.

Within each age group, the picture is less clear. This is especially the case for the 55 to 59 age group, since their implicit taxes did not change much for both single men and single women. For the 65 to 69 age group, we observe for single men that the employment rate increased after the implicit taxes decreased. However, there seems to be a time lag between both events. In the women's case, the increase in the employment rate for the oldest age group is rather small. Moreover, the implicit taxes increased again after 2000, which yields a positive correlation. However, the increase of the implicit taxes results from the deferred taxation, which may not yet be anticipated in the pension plans of older individuals. The picture is clearer for the 60 to 64 age group. For instance, the men's picture resembles a U shape. First, the employment rate decreased while the implicit tax remained at a high level of around 50 percent. The implicit tax then decreased very rapidly. At the same time, the employment rate started to increase. This growth process accelerated and even continued after the implicit tax reached a new steady state of around 25 percent. The plot is quite similar in the women's case, although the initial decrease in the employment rate is missing. Another relevant difference is that the major part of the fast drop in the implicit tax happened in one year in the women's case, while this process needed three years in the men's case. On the other hand, the decrease of the implicit tax lasted longer in the women's case so that the implicit tax decreased from 45 percent to a value below 10 percent. However, in this case, the increase of the employment rate again started together with the decrease of the implicit tax. All observations taken together, we observe a negative correlation between employment rates and implicit taxes. The picture for the 55 to 69 age group is similar to the 60 to 64 age group. However, the quantitative changes are smaller.

5.5.7 Relation between Implicit Taxes and Pension-Claiming Ages

Finally, we compare the development of the implicit tax with the distribution of pension-claiming ages during the retirement window from 60 to 65. As mentioned before, we will consider hereby an alternative weighting procedure such that the implicit taxes may differ slightly from those just presented. However, the general development and the differences between the skill and age groups do not change.

For the pension-claiming behavior at a certain age a, two implicit taxes are relevant. First, there is the implicit tax of the previous age $(a - 1)$. If it becomes negative, it would indicate an incentive to postpone pension claiming by one year. Hence one year later the number of individuals claiming their pension at age a should increase. Actually, even only a decrease of the implicit tax at age $a - 1$ could lead to an increase of pension claiming as the monetary incentive to claim their pension immediately declines. The other relevant implicit tax is the implicit tax of the current age. If the implicit tax becomes smaller or even negative, postponing pension entry becomes less disadvantageous and can lead to a smaller share of pension claims at this age. Of course, there are other factors, like the abolishment of early retirement pathways, that may counteract the implicit tax's effect on pension-claiming behavior.

Figure 5.30 shows in separate graphs for each pension-claiming age between 60 and 65 the development of its share on all pension claims of the respective year (left side men; right side women). Moreover, each graph includes the development of the implicit tax at the observed pension-claiming

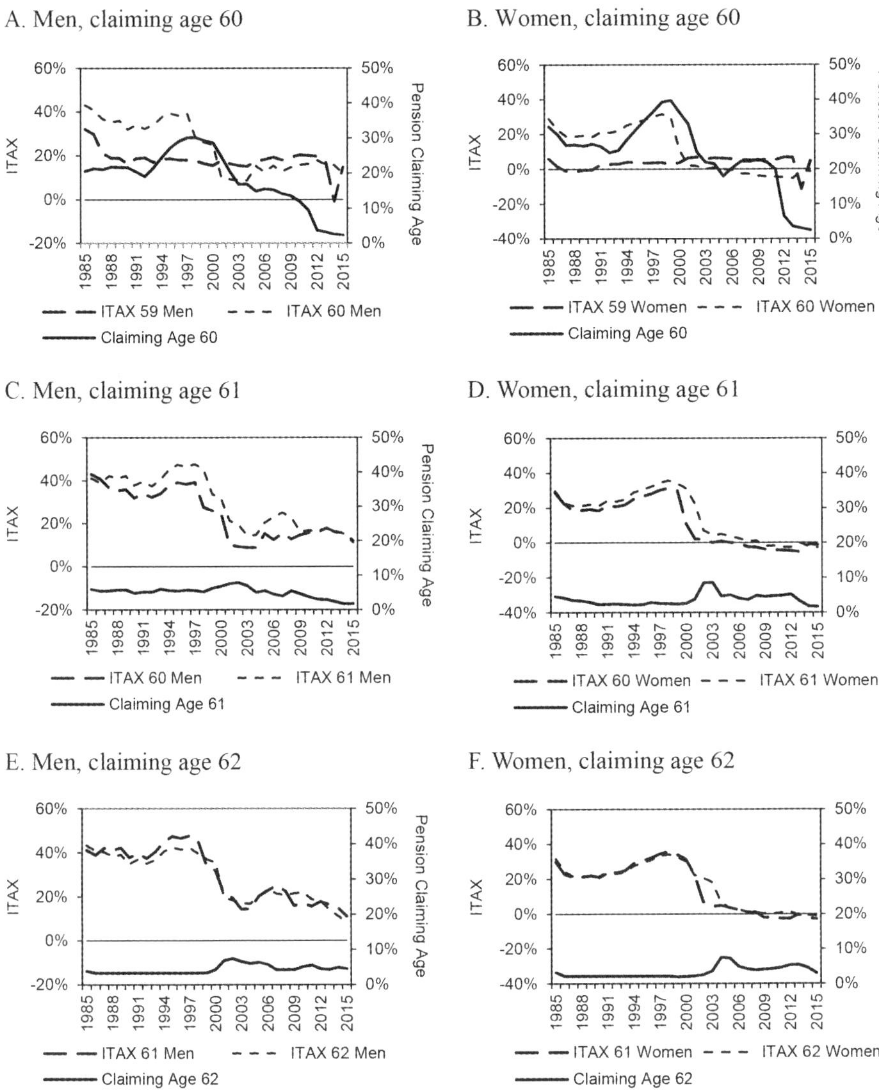

Fig. 5.30 Development of single person's implicit tax and pension claiming at different ages

Source: Authors' own calculations

age and the previous year. In general, our observations are in line with the previous discussions. We start with the pension-claiming age of 60. For both men and women, the implicit tax of the previous age (59) does not change in a relevant way. Hence there are no changes in the incentive to leave the labor market at the age of 59. On the other hand, there are quite large changes in the implicit tax at the age of 60, as we have seen in the previous subsection. In

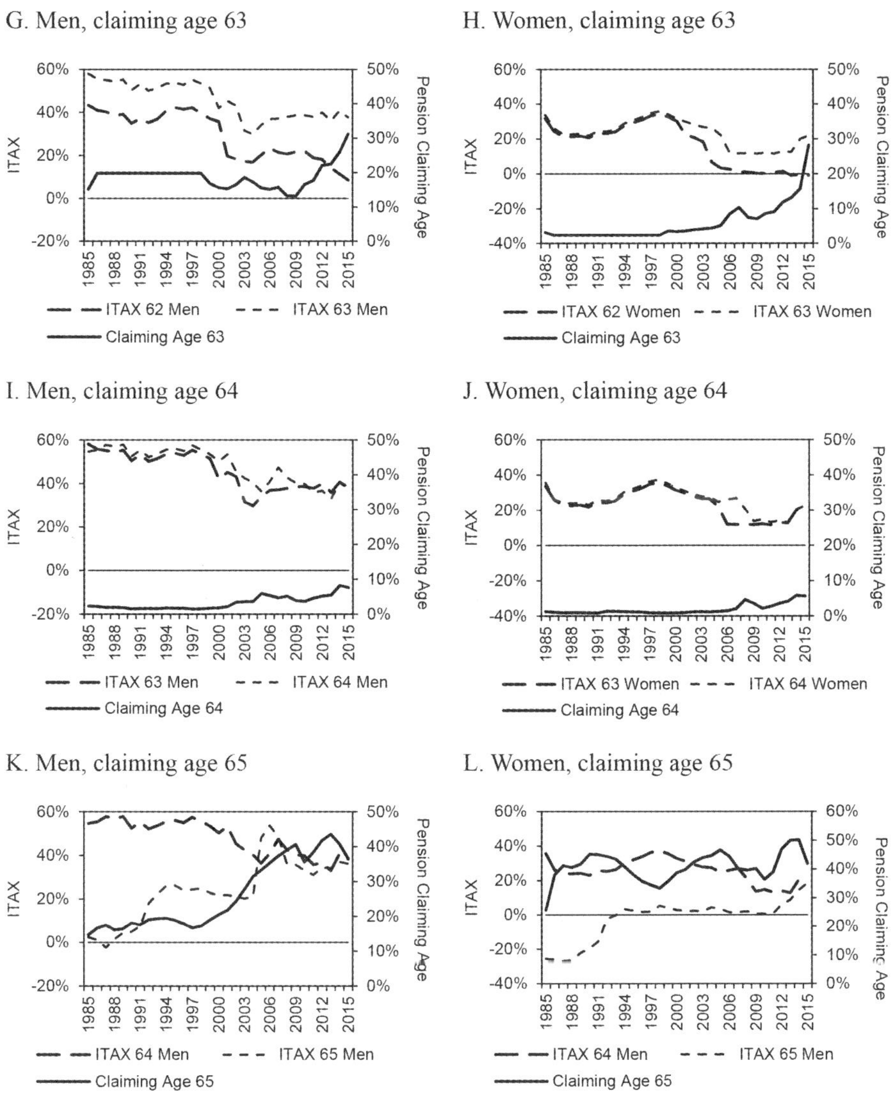

Fig. 5.30 (cont.)

line with our previous argument, these changes coincide with increases and decreases in the pension claims (higher [lower] implicit taxes lead to more [fewer] pension claims). The decrease in pension claims after the introduction of the actuarial deduction and their impact on the implicit taxes is remarkable. Only the decrease in pension claims after 2012 cannot be linked to a change in the implicit tax. In fact, the reason for the drop is the abolishment of the old-age pension for women and due to unemployment. Apparently, the abolishment of those pension pathways did not affect the implicit taxes of those age 60, since the social security wealth with both an immediate and a postponed labor market exit is affected equally. For the pension-claiming ages of 61 and 62, the opposite happens. First, pension claims increase after the implicit tax of the previous age declines. Afterward, the pension claims decrease several years later together with the decline in the implicit tax of the considered age. Hence pension claiming rose only for a limited time together with the shift of pension claiming from age 60 to age 63 or 65.

For the pension claiming age of 63, we find differences between the men's and the women's cases. In the men's case, the pension claims are rather constant until 2010. Smaller changes are again in line with the respective development in the implicit taxes. However, after 2009, the share of individuals who claim their pension at 63 increases rapidly. The main reason is that in 2009, the age of 63 became for nondisabled individuals the earliest eligibility age for an old-age pension. Moreover, the implicit tax still indicates a strong incentive to claim the pension immediately.

For women, most of the observations are the same. However, due to the actuarial deductions and their higher life expectancy, there remain no monetary incentives to leave the labor market before the age of 63 since 2003. In fact, the age of 63 is the first age with positive implicit taxes. In line with our argument, pension claims at this age have increased since 2000—that is, as soon as the actuarial deductions were introduced. The most recent and very strong increase in pension claims can be explained by the abolishment of the old-age pension for women. The pension claims at age 64 increase one year after the implicit tax of the previous age declined.

For the former statutory eligibility age of 65, we again need to differentiate between men and women. In the men's case, we again observe the assumed development. Hence the pension claims increase after the implicit tax at age 64 declines. At the same time, the implicit tax at age 65 is positive and even increased such that there is no incentive to further postpone pension claiming. For women, we observe an up and down pattern in the frequency of pension claiming that corresponds to the observed development of the implicit tax at age 64. However, since the implicit tax at age 65 is approximately zero, there is no incentive to retire immediately, which contradicts the observed high share of pension claims at age 65. The high share of initial pension claims at the historical statutory eligibility age 65, which is found in so many studies of retirement, may be due more to habit formation than to current monetary incentives.

5.6 Conclusions

Employment of older individuals in Germany experienced a remarkable reversal around the late 1990s. After a long declining trend that began in the early 1970s, the employment rate for older men has strongly increased again. This increase has lasted until today. In contrast, the employment of older women in Germany has experienced a less pronounced U-shaped pattern in particular because employment of younger women has steadily increased since the 1970s. This chapter has linked these trends to changes in public pension policies. The key instrument of our analysis was the concept of "implicit taxes on working longer," which represents the monetary incentives that individuals face in their labor supply and pension-claiming decisions. In this chapter, we compute implicit taxes for a set of synthetic individuals differing by household demographics and education/skill, once based on a common macroenvironment across all 12 countries in this project and once based on German age-earnings profiles, payroll taxes, and survival probabilities.

We find that for both men and women, the increase in the employment rate coincides with a reduction in the early retirement incentive expressed by the implicit taxes on working longer (figure 5.29). The reduction of incentives mainly stems from the introduction of actuarial deductions for claiming a pension before the statutory eligibility age. In recent years, the employment rate additionally increased due to the abolishment of early retirement pathways for the unemployed and women. We find similar correlations between the development of the implicit tax and actual pension-claiming behavior (figure 5.30).

The evidence in figures 5.29 and 5.30 is highly suggestive. However, these bivariate correlations of a relatively small set of synthetic individuals do not control for the many other potential explanatory factors and the heterogeneity in the population. This requires a much more elaborate multivariate analysis of actual individuals in panel data. The next step of the International Social Security project will therefore be devoted to a causal analysis of the role of public pension policies in shaping old-age employment. We are doing this by constructing, for each individual and separately for each country, the time series of the implicit tax. We will then use these incentive variables, the macrovariables considered so far, and other determinants on the individual level as explanatory variables in an econometric analysis of retirement and labor force participation.

References

Börsch-Supan, A. 1992. "Population Aging, Social Security Design, and Early Retirement." *Journal of Institutional and Theoretical Economics* 148:533–57.

Börsch-Supan, A., and C. Quinn. 2015. "Taxing Pensions and Retirement Benefits in Germany." MEA Discussion Paper 10-2015.

Börsch-Supan, A., and H. Jürges. 2012. "Disability, Pension Reform, and Early Retirement in Germany." In *Social Security Programs and Retirement around the World: Historical Trends in Mortality and Health, Employment, and Disability Insurance Participation and Reforms*, edited by D. A. Wise, 277–300. Chicago: University of Chicago Press.

Börsch-Supan, A., and I. Ferrari. 2017. "Old-Age Labor Force Participation in Germany: What Explains the Trend Reversal among Older Men? And What the Steady Increase among Women?" NBER Working Paper No. 24044. Cambridge, MA: National Bureau of Economic Research.

Börsch-Supan, A., and R. Schnabel. 1999. "Social Security and Retirement in Germany." In *Social Security and Retirement around the World*, edited by J. Gruber and D. A. Wise, 135–80. Chicago: University of Chicago Press.

Börsch-Supan, A., T. Bucher-Koenen, S. Kluth, M. Haupt, and N. Goll. 2015. "Vor- und Nachteile höherer Flexibilität als Instrument zur Erhöhung der Beschäftigung Älterer." MEA Discussion Paper 06-2015.

Börsch-Supan, A., and C. Coile. 2018. "Social Security Programs and Retirement around the World: Reforms and Retirement Incentives—Introduction and Summary." NBER Working Paper No. 25280. Cambridge, MA: National Bureau of Economic Research.

Commission for Sustainability in Financing the Social Security Systems (Kommission für die Nachhaltigkeit in der Finanzierung der Sozialen Sicherungssysteme). 2003. *Final Report (Abschlußbericht)*. Berlin: Bundesministerium für Gesundheit und Soziale Sicherheit. http://www.bmgs.bund.de/deu/gra/themen/sicherheit/kommission/index.cfm.

Deutsche Rentenversicherung Bund (DRV). 2011. FDZ-Biografiedatensatz für die Biografiedaten der Versicherten (VSKT) 2011.

Deutsche Rentenversicherung Bund (DRV). 2017. Rentenversicherung in Zahlreihen, DRV-Schriften, Band 22, Berlin.

Gasche, M. 2012. "Was sind die richtigen Rentenabschläge?—Neue Perspektiven." *Jahrbuch für Wirtschaftswissenschaften* 63 (2): 187–235.

Hanel, B. 2010. "Financial Incentives to Postpone Retirement and Further Effects on Employment Evidence from a Natural Experiment." *Labour Economics* 17 (3): 474–86.

Holthausen, A., J. Rausch, and C. B. Wilke. 2012. "MEA-PENSIM 2.0: Weiterentwicklung eines Rentensimulationsmodells, Konzeption und ausgewählte Anwendungen." MEA Discussion Paper 3-2012.

OECD. 2018a. "LFS by Sex and Age—Indicators." http://stats.oecd.org/Index.aspx?DataSetCode=LFS_SEXAGE_I_R.

OECD. 2018b. "Table I.5. Average Personal Income Tax and Social Security Contribution Rates on Gross Labour Income." http://stats.oecd.org/Index.aspx?DataSetCode=TABLE_I5.

Siddiqui, S. 1997. "The Pension Incentive to Retire: Empirical Evidence for West Germany." *Population Economics* 10:463–86.

Statistisches Bundesamt. 2015. *Generationensterbetafeln für Deutschland, Modellrechnungen für die Geburtsjahrgänge 1896–2009*. Wiesbaden: Statistisches Bundesamt.

Statistisches Bundesamt. 2016. *Mikrozensus, Bevölkerung und Erwerbstätigkeit Stand und Entwicklung der Erwerbstätigkeit in Deutschland.* Wiesbaden: Statistisches Bundesamt.

Werding, M. 2012. "Rentenbemessung und Renteneintrittsalter: Korrekte Abschläge bei vorzeitigem Rentenzugang." Mimeo, Lehrstuhl für Sozialpolitik und öffentliche Finanzen, Ruhr-Universität Bochum.

6

The Evolution of Incentives for Retirement in Italy, 1980–2015

Agar Brugiavini, Raluca Elena Buia, Giacomo Pasini, and Guglielmo Weber

6.1 Introduction and Motivation

The aim of this chapter is to explore and try to explain the increases in older Italian men and women's labor force participation (LFP) and employment over the past 20 years. This is a general pattern, common to most developed countries around the world, and many factors may have contributed to the recent increases in LFP and employment. These include changes in social security and disability insurance (DI) incentives, improving health and longevity, increasing education, a shift toward less physically demanding jobs, and rising female LFP (combined with the desire for joint retirement among couples).

The combination of high public debt and remarkably fast population aging prompted important changes in the Italian social security system. In fact, population aging in Italy poses important challenges to the public pension system for three reasons. First, Italian public debt is particularly high (over 130 percent of GDP), coupled with a particularly low GDP growth experienced in recent years; second, Italy has a low fertility rate, around 1.4 (its population is aging from below); third, Italians' life expectancy is among the highest in the world and rising (its population is aging from above). Given that the public pension system is basically a pay-as-you-go

Agar Brugiavini is a professor of economics at Ca' Foscari University of Venice and an international research fellow of the Institute for Fiscal Studies.

Raluca Elena Buia is a research associate in the Department of Economics at Ca' Foscari University of Venice.

Giacomo Pasini is a professor of econometrics at Ca' Foscari University of Venice and a research affiliate of Netspar.

Guglielmo Weber is a professor of econometrics at the University of Padua and an international research fellow of the Institute for Fiscal Studies.

For acknowledgments, sources of research support, and disclosure of the authors' material financial relationships, if any, please see https://www.nber.org/chapters/c14196.ack.

(PAYG) system, this combination calls for a substantial increase in LFP at all ages (see Brugiavini and Peracchi 2003 and 2007; Brugiavini, Pasini and Weber, 2017). Part of this increase may be obtained by encouraging female LFP (which is still relatively low in Italy compared to the US, the UK, or northern Europe), and part may be achieved by drawing in foreign workers (who compensate for aging from below). But there is no doubt that "aging from above" calls for longer working lives—and the very low average effective retirement ages experienced in Italy until two decades ago suggest there are major gains to be achieved by moving in this direction.

In light of these challenges, it is not surprising that the public debate has focused on how to increase the labor supply of workers in the 50 to 65 age group both by changing the incentives to retire and by introducing tighter conditions to be eligible for a public pension. Pension reforms have been implemented over the last three decades (starting in 1992), including a radical reform that was introduced in 2011 to ensure the sustainability of public debt and postponed retirement age—by a wide margin for several workers—without offering an easy transition out of the labor force. In particular, a relatively large number of workers who had agreed on a separation from the firm expecting to shortly retire on a public pension faced the prospect of long-term unemployment.

This chapter is organized as follows: we first provide some brief background on the trends in labor force participation in Italy; we then present the Italian pension system and main reforms in the last 30 years. Section 6.3 describes and analyses the financial incentives to retirement, while section 6.4 draws the main conclusions.

6.2 Employment Rates, Pathways to Retirement, and the Reforms Process

In order to provide a comprehensive view of the labor force trends prevailing in Italy, it is important to consider a sufficiently long time span: it is well known that many important changes took place during the 1970s and 1980s regarding the educational system, the welfare system, and the industrial structure of the country. As the underlying motivation of this chapter is to explain the patterns in labor supply and the role played by financial incentives, it is useful to first illustrate some facts about the Italian labor market. For comparability with the other chapters of this book, for later years, we take the data on labor force participation and employment rates from Organisation for Economic Co-operation and Development (OECD) statistics. However, the OECD database does not go back far enough in time—for earlier years, we gather the relevant information from the MARSS database provided by ISTAT (the Italian National Statistics Office).[1] As both datasets

1. The data sources are described in the appendix. We look at the years 1980–83 for the 55–59 age group and the years 1980–92 for the 65–69 age group.

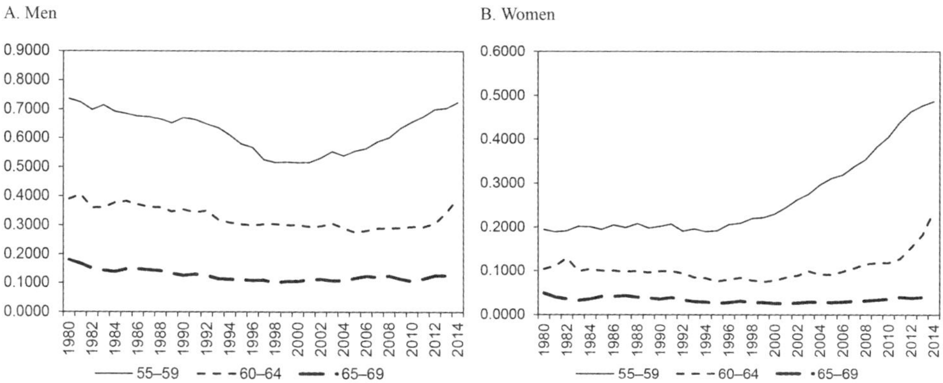

Fig. 6.1 LFP by age group, men (left panel) and women (right panel)

are based on the Labor Force Survey, we can safely link the two series.[2] Labor force participation (LFP) for older workers (grouped in three distinct age bands: 55–59, 60–64, and 65–69) is documented in figure 6.1 (left panel for men and right panel for women). There are clear gender and age differences. For men in the 55 to 59 age group, we observe a U-shaped pattern: a steady decline from 1980 until 1997, a stable pattern around 55 percent until the beginning of 2000, and then a substantial rise. The LFP of men aged 60–64 displays a slower but steady decrease until 2004 and a rather constant trend up to 2011, followed by a sharp rise afterward. A similar pattern emerges for the older age group, 65–69: LFP was as low as 20 percent in 1980 and decreased further to reach 11 percent in 2011. A modest increase of 2 percentage points occurs thereafter.

The pattern of LFP for women is markedly different, and it reflects the spectacular increase in labor market participation experienced by women all over the world in the second half of the 20th century. Still, some turning points are similar to what is observed for males.

The LFP of women aged 55–59 was equal to 20 percent in 1980 and remained almost unchanged until the end of the 1990s. The pattern changed in 1996: from that moment on, LFP increased at a fast pace, reaching values above 45 percent in 2011. In the next three years, LFP continued to increase, but its growth rate declined. As regards the 60–64 age band, only a small minority of women were involved in working activities until 2011: LFP hovered around 10–12 percent from 1980 until 2011. As we saw for males, 2011 is also a crucial year for females: starting in 2012, LFP starts to increase dramatically, reaching 24 percent in 2014. As regards older women (aged 65 to 69), less than 5 percent of them participate in the labor force throughout the period, with no relevant upward or downward trends.

2. Comparing the series for the overlapping period, they are almost identical.

The steady increase in education levels for both men and women, and in the number of workers affected by the tighter public pension eligibility criteria of both the 1990s pension reforms and the more radical 2011 reform, all contribute to explaining these patterns.

6.2.1 The Italian Pension System and Reforms

In what follows, we review the basic rules of the Italian pension system, which are relevant for the observed trends in the employment rate and the LFP rate of men and women in the 55–69 age group, stressing the institutional changes that took place over the last three decades. The main changes are also summarized in figure 6.2 in the form of a timeline of reforms.

Since 1969, the Italian public social security system envisaged two distinct retirement paths: an old-age pension and an early retirement (seniority) pension. Given the ease of access to and generosity of the public pension system, disability benefits or unemployment benefits have not been a common pathway to retirement in Italy.[3] Until 2011, eligibility criteria for both types of pension were based on the number of years of contribution and an age requirement. Before 1993, old-age benefits could be collected as early as 60 for men (55 for women), while early retirement (ER) pensions were granted irrespective of age, provided that at least 35 years of contribution had been paid into the system.[4] Pension benefits were earnings related and were computed as the product of the so-called *pension base* (E) obtained as average gross earnings over a five-year window before retirement and an accrual factor of 2 percent for every year of contribution (up to a maximum of 40 years). Thus a worker with average gross annual earnings of €30,000 and 40 years of contributions would retire with a gross pension of €24,000 (i.e., a replacement rate of 80 percent): quite a generous benefit. Given that earnings paid both income tax and pension contributions, while pensions paid only income tax, net replacement rates were even higher. Also, the ER benefits would not attract any actuarial penalty, even for very young retirees in their 50s, and pension benefits were indexed to nominal wage growth (this is referred to as "double indexation," as nominal wage growth is the sum of price inflation and average productivity growth).

In 1992, the Italian parliament approved an important reform of the public pension system that gradually increased the statutory retirement age from 60 to 65 for men and from 55 to 60 for women. It also changed the way benefits were indexed, by price inflation only, and changed the benefit computation pro-rata. In particular, the contributions paid by workers over their entire work history would be split into two parts: contributions paid before

3. Disability benefits have been of some relevance during the 1970s, but important changes to the award process took place in 1984, which made disability insurance basically negligible.

4. Some groups of workers could collect a pension at any age, having completed as little as 15 years of contributions.

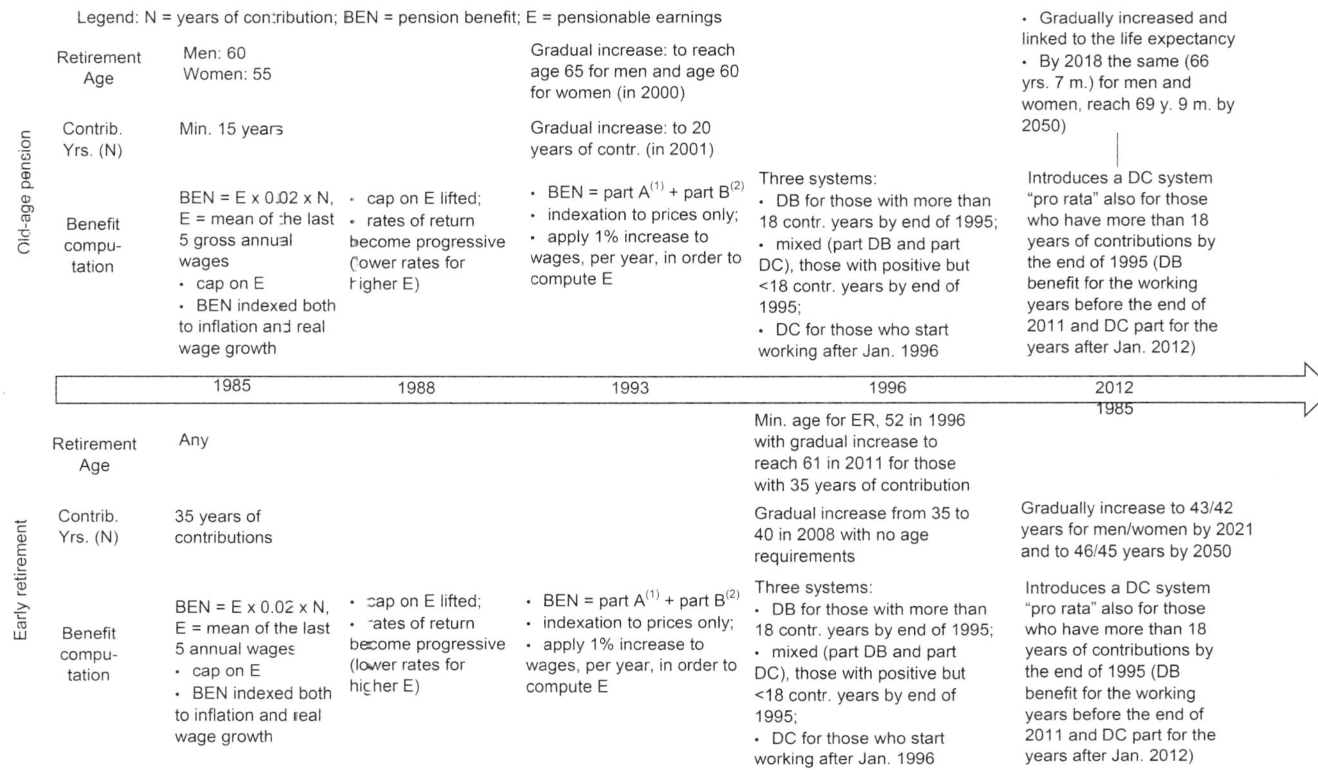

Fig. 6.2 Timeline of pension system reforms in Italy

1993 would be included in part A of the pension base; contributions paid since 1993 would be included in part B of the pension base. Part A of the pension base would produce benefits according to the pre-1993 rules. Part B of the pension base would produce benefits according to a different formula: benefits were computed as the product of a weighted average over a ten-year window before retirement and an accrual factor of 2 percent for every year of contribution after 1992. To compensate for the longer time period over which nominal earnings were averaged, past earnings were revalued at a 1 percent rate per year. Under the new system, the eligibility age for an old-age pension was increased gradually by one year of age every two years starting from 1994 until reaching age 65 for men and age 60 for women in the year 2000. The number of years of contribution required for an old-age pension was also increased gradually by one every two years starting from 1993 until reaching 20 years of contributions in 2001.

In 1995, a more radical reform was legislated that changed both the eligibility rules for early retirement and the calculation of old-age and early retirement pension benefits based on a notional defined contribution (NDC) system. These changes were characterized by a long transitional phase and a "grandfathering" approach, protecting the older cohorts of workers, which made them effective with a considerable delay. The transitional phase would be completed in 2032: by then, all retirees should receive a pension under the NDC system. In the interim phase, benefits are computed as a weighted average of the pension benefit resulting from the old regimes (parts A and B) and the new regime (part C) on a pro-rata basis. Early retirement pension eligibility ages were also gradually raised according to a formula that accounted for both age and years of contribution: thus a worker could take early retirement in the year 1996 if he was 52 years old and had accumulated 35 years of contribution. The age limit increased in such a way that in 2002 a worker would qualify at 57 years of age and with 35 years of contribution (for both men and women). It is worth pointing out that access to ER was also possible, independently of age, under the requirement that in 1995 a minimum contributive period of 35 years was satisfied. This requirement for ER increased over the sample period, reaching 40 years of contributions in 2008.

In 2011, the Italian government enacted an important reform that radically changed the calculation of benefits by implementing a more rapid convergence to the NDC system. Furthermore, eligibility for old-age pension became much tighter so that in the year 2018 there would be no difference between men and women, and by 2050 the age requirement would become 69 years and 9 months for all types of workers. Under the new regime, which is currently in place, retirees can still access the ER option, but a marked increase in the number of years of contributions needed for eligibility occurs: 42 (41) years for men (women) in 2012, which will increase up to 46 years for men and 45 for women by the year 2050.

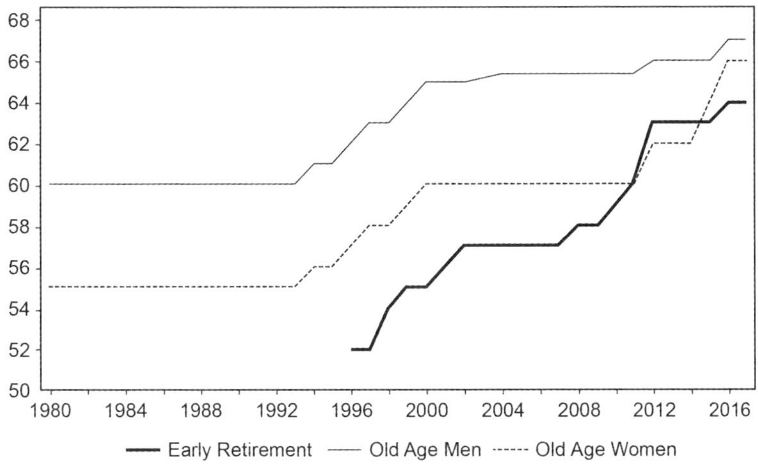

Fig. 6.3 Statutory and early pension eligibility ages in Italy by gender

Figure 6.2 presents the timeline of the main reforms of the pension system in Italy, while figure 6.3 shows the evolution of the statutory and early retirement ages over the last 30 years in Italy by gender.

An alternative source of information comes from the stock of social security benefits provided by the Italian social security administration INPS (Istituto Nazionale per la Previdenza Sociale). In terms of pathways, figure 6.4 shows the number of benefits by age group of the recipient using administrative data. Benefits can be old-age pensions, early retirement pensions, and disability pensions. The steady drop of benefits paid to the 55–59 age group (quite marked for men) largely reflects the coming into force of the 1990s reforms. The more dramatic fall in the number of recipients for the 60–64 age group starts immediately after the 2011 reform that curtailed the early retirement pension opportunities for both men and women in this age group and dramatically increased the statutory retirement age (especially for women). The number of benefits paid to the 65–69 age group is instead relatively stable over time, with a trough in 2011 and a peak in 2015. As we shall see, this apparent stability masks an important change in composition.

Figure 6.4 informs us about the stock of pensions paid out in any given year. Thus the benefit paid to someone aged 55 who retired and drew an early retirement pension in 2005 appears in 2014 for the 60–64 age group. In the next figure instead, we show how the stock is split among old-age pensions and early retirement pensions, which are the relevant ones in Italy.

Figure 6.5 covers the 1985–2016 period and is based on the data on the stock of beneficiaries aged 60–64 from INPS (up to 2004 the data refer to a representative sample of individuals, while from 2004 onward we have information on the entire stock of recipients).

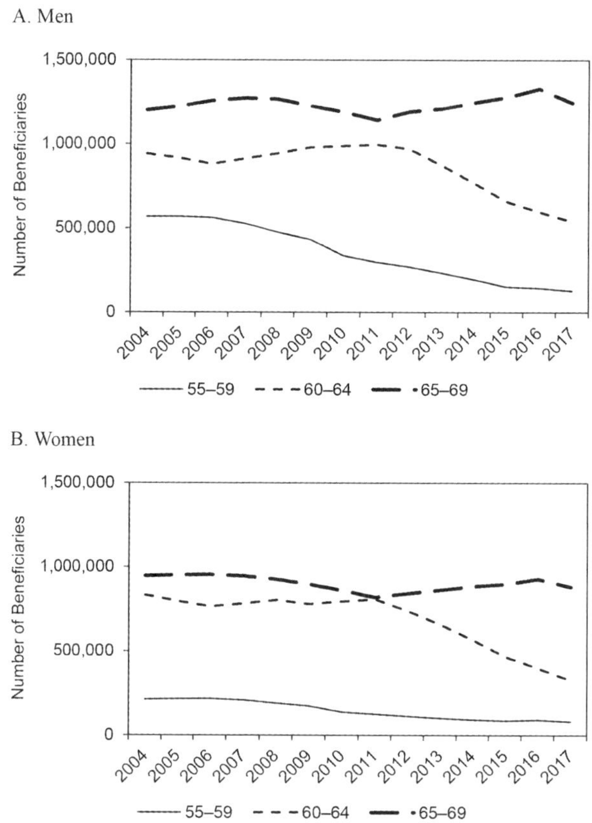

Fig. 6.4 Number of pensions by age group of the recipient
Source: INPS pension archive

The left panel shows that very few men could retire on an old-age pension at this age throughout the period. For women, instead, old-age benefits were the modal type until the late 1990s (as shown in the right panel). The early 2000s saw a major shift to early retirement pensions for women.

The sudden fall in the fraction of old-age pensions paid to women after the year 2000 calls for an explanation: pension eligibility ages varied a lot over the years, but statutory eligibility age for women reached age 60 in 2000 and was then stable until 2011.

This chapter will look at the financial incentives that kept changing over the years and may be partly responsible for the shift away from the old-age pension. One should also keep in mind that access to early retirement pension schemes may have increased as a result of the upward trend in female labor market participation, which implied that a growing fraction of women had enough years of contributions to qualify for an early retirement scheme.

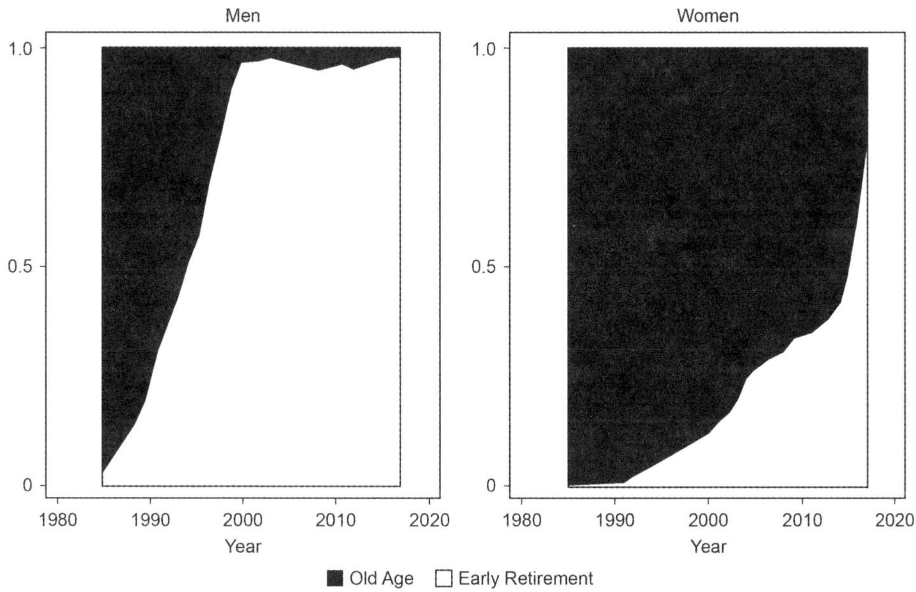

Fig. 6.5 Pathways to retirement by gender for the 60–64 age group
Source: Stock data from INPS pension archive

6.3 Financial Incentives

A first attempt at measuring the implicit tax for Italy was carried out in Brugiavini (1999); however, the changes following in the subsequent years and in particular the major reform in 2011 have heavily affected the dynamics of the relevant variables, hence making it necessary to provide a new set of estimates of the financial incentives. In this chapter, financial incentives for Italian workers and retirees are computed on the basis of the specific features of the Italian pension system each year and for each group and the relevant age-earnings profiles. A first set of results is based on gross values for the "common" European age-earnings profile of medium earners used throughout this book with the idea that this group of workers should correspond to the "median education" group in Italy. The calculations are then carried out for net values. This first round of calculations allows us to neglect any difference that may arise due to the peculiarities, if any, of Italian workers' earnings while focusing solely on the social security rules. In a second set of results, we make use of specific Italian data drawn from the Bank of Italy Survey of Income and Wealth (SHIW, several years). In this latter case, the results are closer to the actual experience of Italian workers, but they reflect a mixture of the social security rules and the patterns in earnings (figure 6.6).

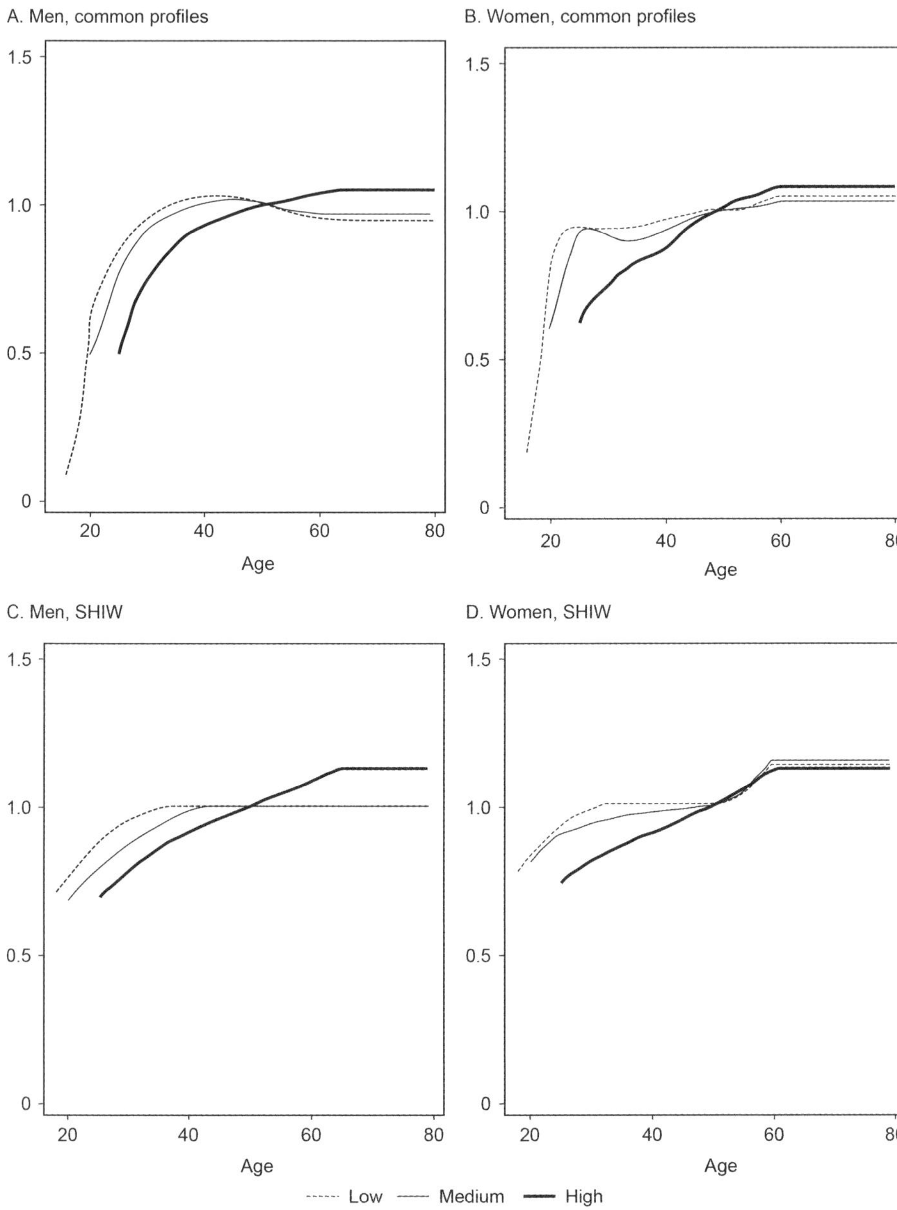

Fig. 6.6 Panels A and B, common profiles; panels C and D, SHIW

Source: Left panel, Italian profiles; right panel, SHIW

6.3.1 Middle-Income Men: Common Earnings Age Profile

The middle-income common earnings profile is characterized by continuous working careers starting at age 20. Earnings rise until age 47 and gently fall past age 50. This pattern is relevant in the Italian case, as the defined benefit rule adopted for much of the sample period largely reflects the last years of the working career.

Note that earnings profiles are in real terms. Hence, in our benefit computations, we do not take into account the prevailing inflation for each year. This is of some relevance, as a particular revaluation rule was introduced in 1993 to compensate for past price changes, inflating by 1 percent a year past earnings entering the benefit computation on top of the standard price indexation. Given that the earnings we use are already in real terms (i.e., they are already 100 percent compensated for inflation), the revaluation "artificially" increases benefits as it overcompensates for inflation. As a result, the replacement rates we compute increase in the later years because a growing share of the pension benefit is affected by this rule (the share of part B increases).

Another preliminary point is that the "gross to net" calculation and the "net to gross" grossing up of earnings (both common earnings profiles and earnings based on SHIW data) have been carried out consistently with the Italian pension rules. First, social security benefits are based on the average of past gross earnings (the pension base), where earnings are gross of income taxes and social security contributions paid by the employee, albeit net of the employer's contribution. Similarly, net earnings are obtained starting from the above gross earnings by subtracting employee's contributions and then income taxes. Finally, social security benefits only attract income taxes.[5] In our analysis, we used the same income tax rates both for earnings and for pension benefits, differentiated by three levels of income (67 percent, 100 percent, and 167 percent of the average income).

In figure 6.7a we show the financial incentive indicators for middle-income men aged 55–59. Given that the statutory retirement age was 60 or more throughout, we only show the incentives for early retirement. The gradual increase in early retirement pension eligibility age over the years is apparent in all graphs: all "55 years old" lines disappear after 2000, the "56 years old" lines disappear in 2006, and so forth. In fact, as of 2011 no man aged less than 60, characterized by the common medium age-earnings profile, could retire and claim a pension in Italy. Note that a person who retires from work at age 59 receives his first benefit when he is 60 years old. It is also important

5. The tax rates were computed as the mean of the values in the years 2000, 2005, 2010, and 2015 based on the data on average personal income tax from OECD. Note that following the assumption of this book, the tax rates are drawn from OECD and refer to incomes as percentages of average wages: we apply the same tax rates to all income values. In the Italian case, we make use of the relevant income tax rate and, separately, the corresponding employee's contribution rate.

A. Replacement rate

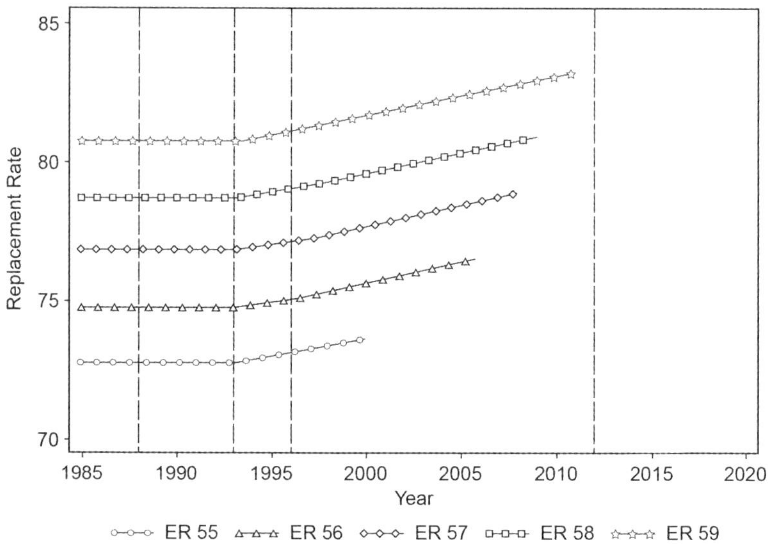

B. Social Security wealth

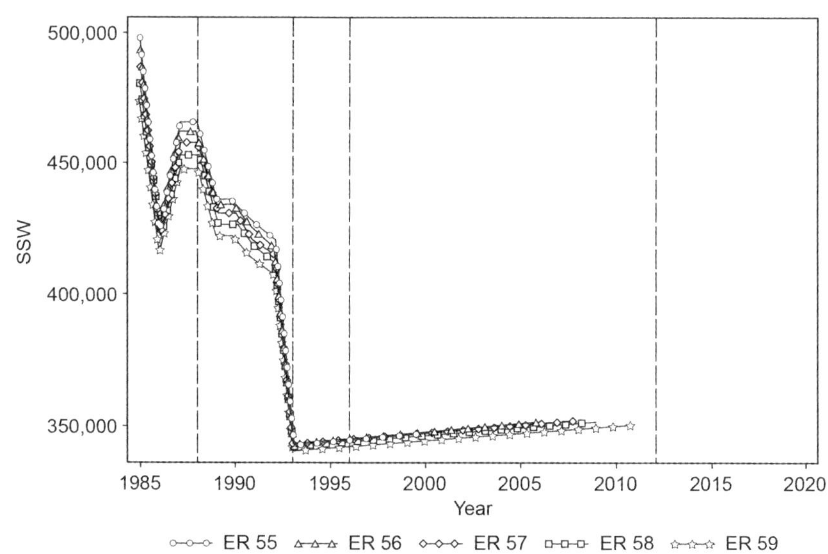

Fig. 6.7a Financial incentives for men aged 55–59, medium income, common earnings profile (gross values)

Note: Vertical lines mark (major) pension reform years.

C. Accrual

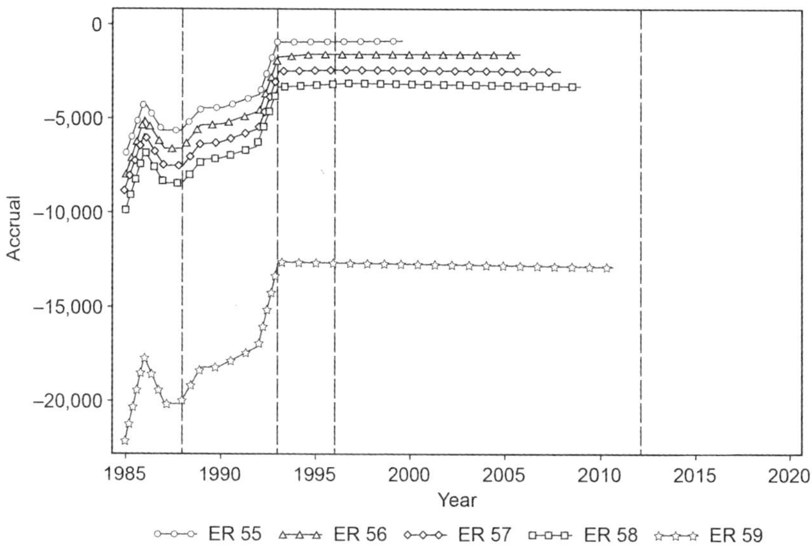

D. Implicit tax rate

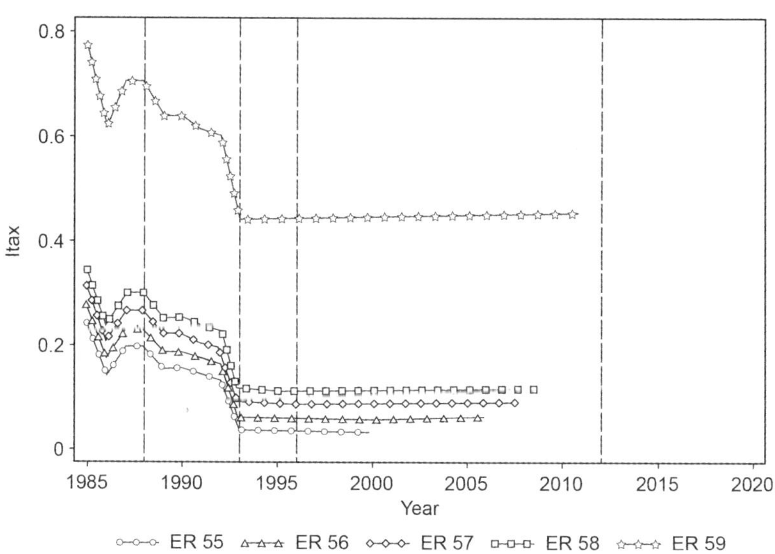

Fig. 6.7a (cont.)

to recall that while the benefit obtained through early retirement would be lower than a full benefit because the length of the working career (up to a maximum of 40 years) is part of the computation rules, no actuarial penalty was applied for early claiming. Hence early retirement benefits were typically lower than old-age benefits only because of the computation rules. It was also possible to observe early retirement benefits, which were "full benefits" if the worker contributed for 40 years or more toward his or her social security.

Panel A of figure 6.7a shows how replacement rates changed over the years for middle-income men aged 55 to 59. Replacement rates were stable before the 1993 reform, ranging between 73 percent for men aged 55 (who contributed for 36 years) and 81 percent for men aged 59 (as the latter had contributed four more years to the pension system). After 1993, replacement rates actually increased (albeit slightly) as a result of the way the first benefit was computed, as explained in section 6.1. In particular, the increase over time is due to the revaluation of past earnings at a 1 percent annual rate in the computation of the 10-year average of earnings that defines the pension base (part B). As we discussed above, this revaluation was meant to partly compensate retiring workers for inflation—as the pension base E now included 10 years of past nominal earnings. Given that the age-earnings profiles we use are in real terms, this revaluation mechanism appears to be beneficial to the newly awarded pensions, but this would not be the case over periods when inflation was high (as it was historically in Italy until the mid-2010s).

The social security wealth (SSW) panel shows social security wealth for men. SSW is computed on the basis of the prevailing legislation at the time the benefits are paid out: the basic assumption is that individuals do not have perfect foresight and cannot predict future reforms or future growth rates or tax rates. There are two distinct periods: pre-1993 and post-1993. During the pre-1993 legislation, benefits were indexed by using both a price index and real wage growth, which explains why SSW is much higher in the first half of the graph for all ages. The observed pre-1993 pattern is totally determined by the real-wage growth rate prevailing at each year of retirement, as this applies to all future benefits entering social security wealth. For example, the growth rate in 1985 was 3.0 percent, while the same rate in 1991 was 1.8 percent. Not surprisingly, in 1992 social security wealth steeply declines as a result of the change in the indexation rules. There is a second effect that should be considered: the earlier an individual retired, the longer the period in which pension benefits enjoyed full wage indexation, which explains why the 55-year-old line is above the 56-year-old line and so on before the year 1993, but the difference is negligible. The graph shows a slow increase for each retirement age after 1993 as a result of the rising benefit (and replacement rate) discussed above. Note that the replacement rates of retirees of the former group are lower than the corresponding replacement rates observed after 1993 due to the higher level of the pension base E and to the "1 percent indexation" rule (part B); however, the pre-1993 SSW is higher because all future benefits were indexed through a compounded wage growth rate.

The ACC panel shows the accrual of pension benefits for this group of individuals. The accrual was negative for all individuals before 1993 but got close to zero after that date for individuals aged 55 to 58. The accrual rose but remained heavily negative for 59-year-olds. It is worth stressing that for this latter age group, we are comparing the choice of retiring with 40 versus 41 years of contributions. Given that the benefit was roughly the same, there was no gain from working one more year (unless that was an exceptionally high earnings year—that is not the case with the common average earnings profile).

The IT panel shows the corresponding implicit tax rates: these are always positive and high for all ages before 1993 and become (almost) zero after 1993 for all ages but the oldest age considered here (age 59). Since the implicit tax represents a summary relative measure of the incentive to work an extra year, our results suggest that for a representative "average" worker, it was optimal to retire as soon as possible before the 1993 reform. The 1993 reform made the pension system more "age neutral," at least for ages 55 to 58 (but notice that a man could no longer retire at age 55 with 36 years of contributions past year 2000). A man who was 59 years old between 1985 and 1993 had a huge tax on working an extra year, as discussed above. The 1993 reform reduced the implicit tax to roughly 40 percent, but the incentive to retire, having collected 40 years of contributions, remained extremely strong.

Figure 6.7b presents the same calculations based on net values. In particular, earnings are net of income taxes and employee's contributions; benefits are net of income taxes.[6] The only difference with respect to figure 6.7a is that replacement rates are higher, ranging from 83 percent to 93 percent. For a man with 40 years of contributions, the first net pension benefit was a larger fraction of the last net salary because earnings pay contributions, while pensions do not. The remaining figures show an identical pattern to the gross earnings case; only the levels differ because of the different values of benefits and earnings.

In figure 6.8 we show similar graphs for men aged 60 to 66. We extend the calculation to 66-year-old men because their benefits exhibit an important variation due to the reforms, which in this time frame is not applicable for workers older than 66. For the 60–66 age band, a distinction must be made between early retirement and old age benefits because, depending on the eligibility conditions, some workers could claim one or the other form of pension.

6. We do not account for employers' contributions throughout this chapter, as they do not enter gross earnings used for the benefit computation. The tax rates and contribution rates (drawn from OECD) we use throughout are consistent with the definition of net earnings and net benefits adopted.

A. Replacement rate

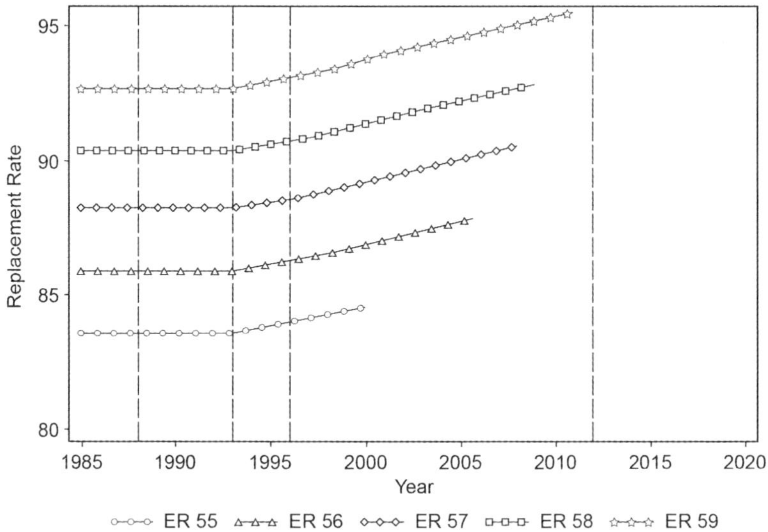

B. Social Security wealth

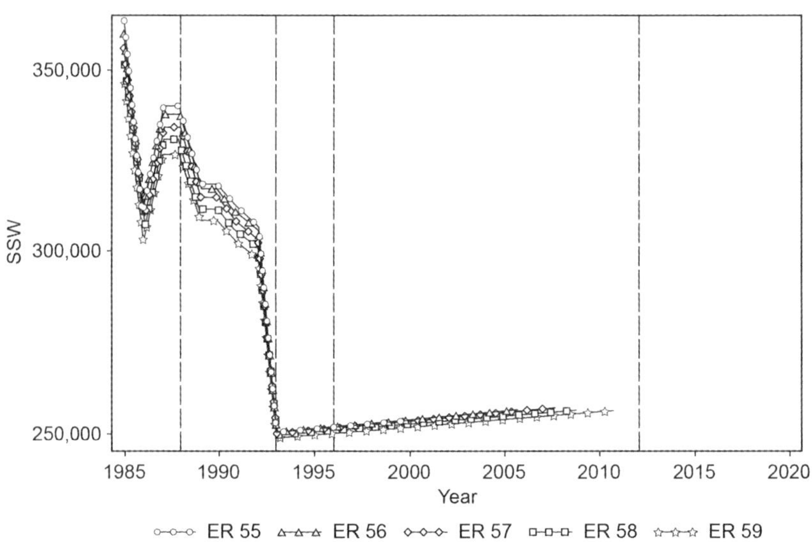

Fig. 6.7b Financial incentives for men aged 55–59, medium income, common earnings profile (net values)

Note: Vertical lines mark (major) pension reform years.

C. Accrual

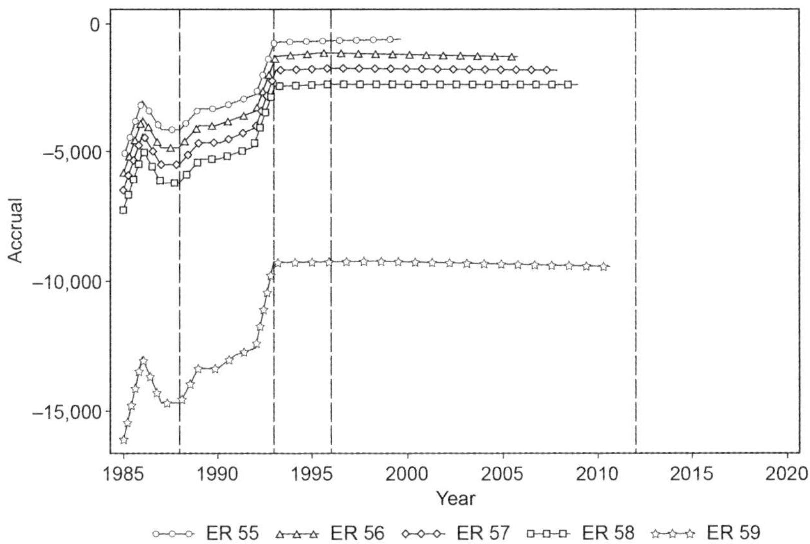

D. Implicit tax rate

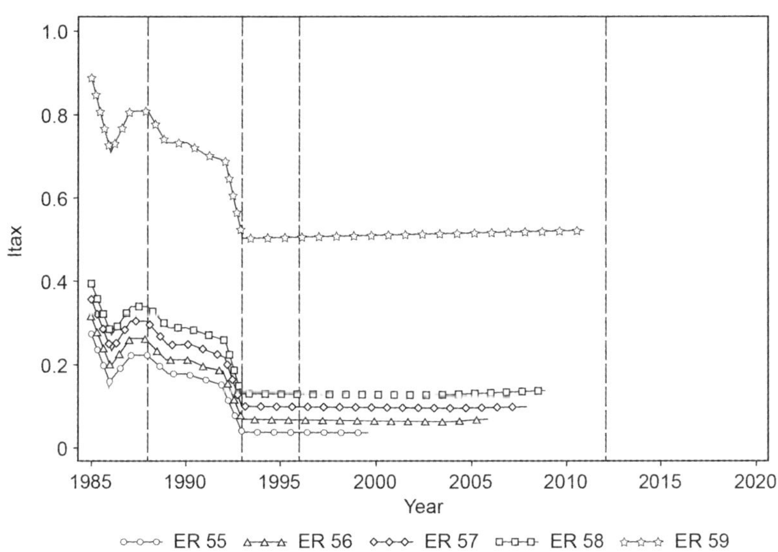

Fig. 6.7b (cont.)

A. Replacement rate

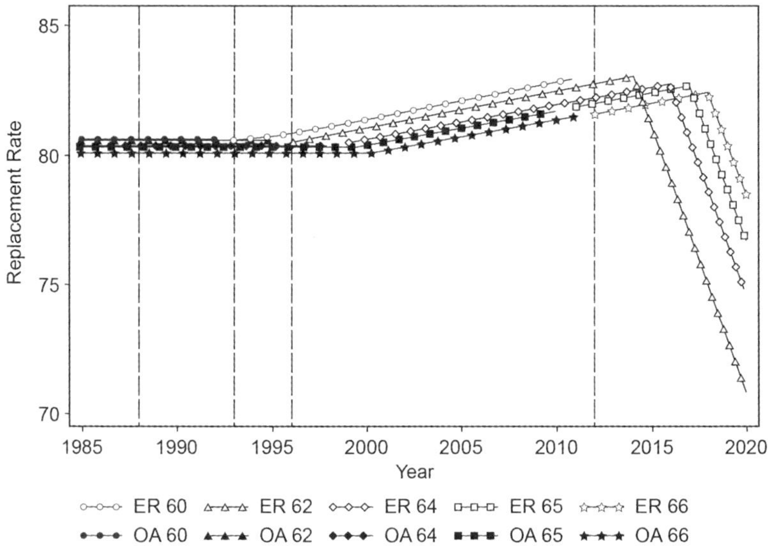

B. Social Security Wealth

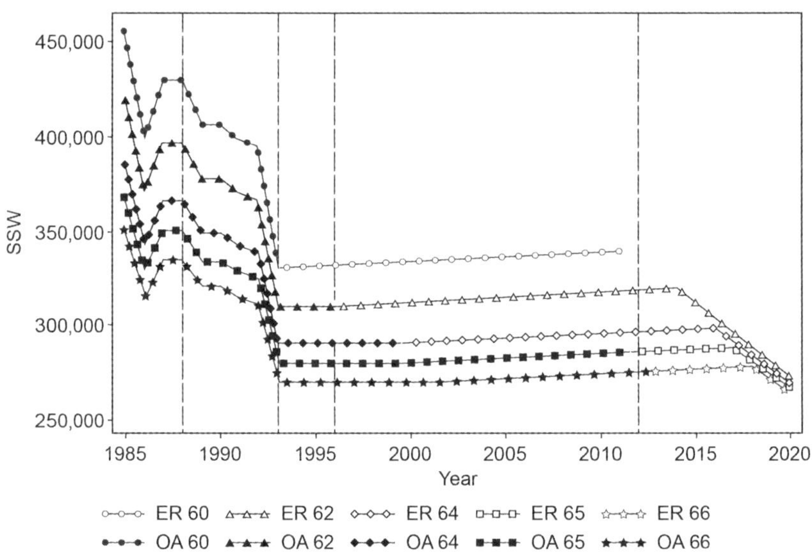

Fig. 6.8 Financial incentives for men aged 60–66, medium income, common earnings profile (gross values)

Note: Vertical lines mark (major) pension reform years.

C. Accrual

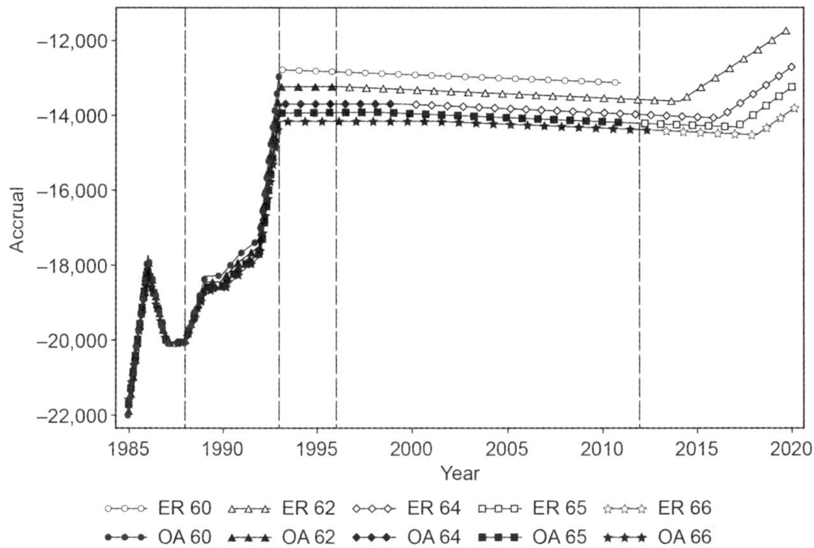

D. Implicit tax rate

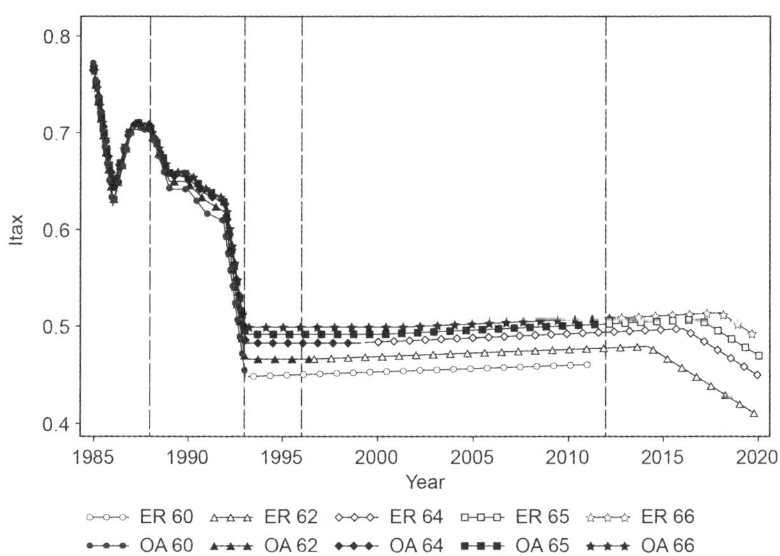

Fig. 6.8 (cont.)

Panel A of figure 6.8 shows, once again, the replacement rate for gross earnings and gross pension benefits over the years for middle-income men. Replacement rates were essentially flat in the first part, around 80 percent, and gradually increased to 83 percent in more recent years. The flat RR lines are explained by the simple defined benefit rule based on the last five years of contributions of the pre-1993 period (part A), affecting workers who had completed 40 years of contributions before 1993.[7] The increasing pattern is once again due to the "part B" component applied after the 1993 reform (in particular to the 1 percent annual revaluation rate): the line becomes steeper for 60-year-olds starting in 1994 but only in 1996 for 62-year-olds and so on. Younger individuals have higher replacement rates because of the compounding effect. Interestingly enough, this panel also shows the first effects of the 2011 reform. For a 62-year-old retiree, the effect becomes visible as of 2015, when his replacement rate takes a sharp downward turn. In fact, the 2011 reform introduced a "part C" defined contribution component on a pro-rata basis—given our assumptions about the starting working age—and such an individual would have fewer than 40 years of contributions in 2011, which makes him eligible for the part C share. A similar drop affects a 64-year-old individual in 2017 and so on.

The SSW panel reports social security. The first point to stress is that individuals of a given age (60, say) could enjoy old-age retirement in the early years (1993 for age 60) but only had access to early retirement in later years (1994 onward for age 60) because eligibility rules became more stringent. In fact, from 2011, a 60-year-old man could no longer exit the labor force and draw a pension benefit. The pattern of the SSW profiles is affected by the indexation rules, as explained in figure 6.7 above. On top of this, a 60-year-old would enjoy a higher SSW than a 62-year-old because the benefit was largely the same, but it was collected for two more years on average. Past 2015, one can observe drops in SSW for the men aged 62 and 64 and so on as a result of the 2011 reform.

The ACC panel shows the accrual of pension benefits for this group of individuals. The accrual was negative and large in absolute terms for all individuals, both before and after 1993, but grew (got closer to zero) after 1993. The fall of SSW for men aged 62 in 2015 is reflected in a rise of the accrual around that year—and similarly for 64-year-olds in 2017 and so on. These individuals increase their pension even when they exceed the 40 years of contributions threshold thanks to the 2011 reform because the contributory share of their pension (part C) is on top of the accrued defined benefit share of the pension.

Panel D of figure 6.8 shows the corresponding implicit tax rates: these are always positive and high for all ages before and after 1993, when they

7. The corresponding graphs for the "net values" are presented in the appendix. As in the previous case, the patterns of all the indicators are identical, while the levels differ.

all fall to 40 percent and hover around that number for the remaining years. The implicit tax is then stable but falls past 2015 in sequential order as the 2011 reform kicks in.

Overall, for the 60–66 age group, the pre-1993 social security system imposed an extremely high penalty on work. After 1993, the penalty is still high, inducing people to retire as soon as possible, but closer to what is also observed in other countries. Finally, the 2011 reform gradually reduces the implicit tax on work due both to the eligibility conditions and to the extra value accrued toward the pension benefit when working additional years.

It is useful to also show the role of financial incentives in terms of the same individuals over the life cycle. We present these results only for men, but we include two groups: medium earnings and high earnings. Figure 6.9 shows the implicit tax rates by age for different cohorts of medium- and high-income men, respectively. The implicit tax rate was highest for the oldest cohort and lowest for the youngest. But it remains above 40 percent for everybody in the medium-income group, past age 60. This is in line with what is observed in figure 6.7 above. The picture for high-income individuals is quite different: only the oldest cohort faced high implicit tax rates throughout, while for the other cohorts, the implicit tax was below 20 percent up to age 63 and passed the 40 percent mark as of age 64. This pattern reflects the assumption made that high-income individuals start working and therefore contributing later in life. The youngest cohort is effectively prevented from retiring until age 66.

In figure 6.10 we present a comparison of the level of SSW across levels of income (earnings) for men aged 62. This figure clearly portrays the relevance of the seniority rule. For a low-income retiree, SSW is the lowest in any year simply due to the lower earnings level, which directly enters the "pension base." However, low-income workers are assumed to experience an early entry into the labor market so that they can draw a pension at age 62 (an early retirement pension) even after 2011. On the other hand, the 2011 reform curtails their benefits by introducing a "part C" in the benefit formula on a pro-rata basis given that these workers had not completed 40 years of contributions in the relevant year (say, 2017). In a similar fashion, a medium-income worker could still retire through early retirement after 2011, but the impact of the 2011 reform would be more significant, as lower seniority is associated with a higher share of the part C component in the benefits. At the other extreme, a man of the same age characterized by a high-income profile has a higher SSW throughout, but he could no longer retire from 2011 because of the more stringent eligibility conditions.

6.3.2 Middle-Income Women: Common Earnings Age Profile

In this subsection we report and discuss financial incentive measures for middle-income women aged 55–59 and aged 60–66 based on common age-earnings profile, as we just did for men. The common profile (see figure 6.5)

A. Medium earnings

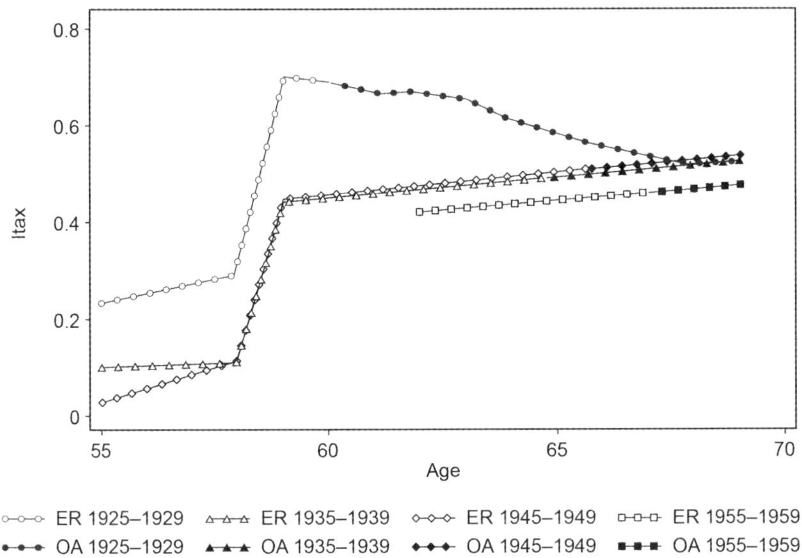

B. High earnings

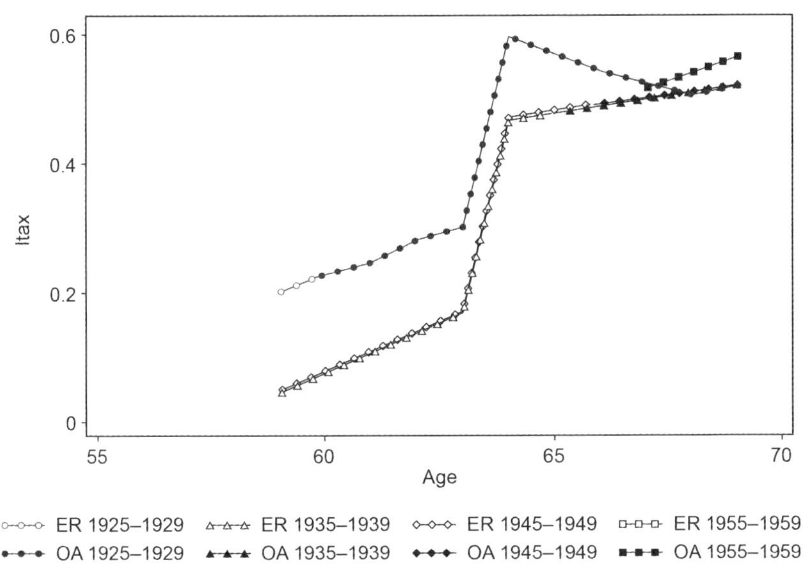

Fig. 6.9 Implicit tax rates by age and cohort, gross earnings, common earnings profile, men

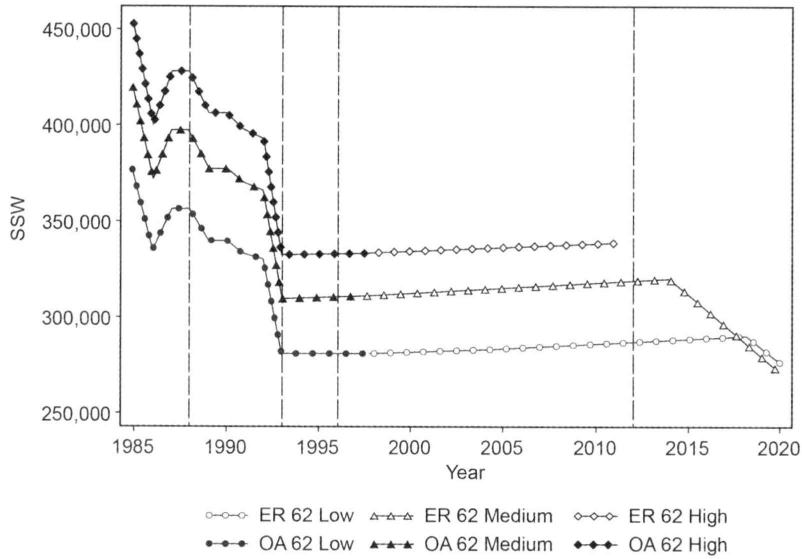

Fig. 6.10 Comparison of SSW for different income levels: Gross earnings, common earnings profile, men age 62

has the same starting age as for men but is characterized by a peak around age 25, followed by a gentle decline up to the mid-30s, and then a steady increase all the way until age 60. The presence of a hollow around childbearing and child-rearing ages is the way in which the profile accounts for the more limited labor market participation in midcareer for women.

Despite lower lifetime earnings and a different profile for women compared to men, the results do not look qualitatively different for the 55–59 age group because the early retirement ages were the same across genders over the years, and the common earnings profiles do not take into account the interrupted nature of female working careers that is an important issue in Italy. If one took into account that women typically have fewer years of contributions, one would be able to see the consequences of the gender-specific statutory retirement pension ages and their changes over time, which we discussed in section 6.1.

In figure 6.11 we show the financial incentive indicators for middle-income women aged 55–59. As was the case for men, the gradual increase in early retirement pension eligibility age over the years is apparent in all graphs: all "55 years old" lines disappear after 2002, the "56 years old" lines disappear in 2008, and so forth. In fact, as of 2011, no woman aged less than 60 characterized by the common medium-income profile could retire and claim a pension in Italy.

A. Replacement rate

B. Social Security wealth

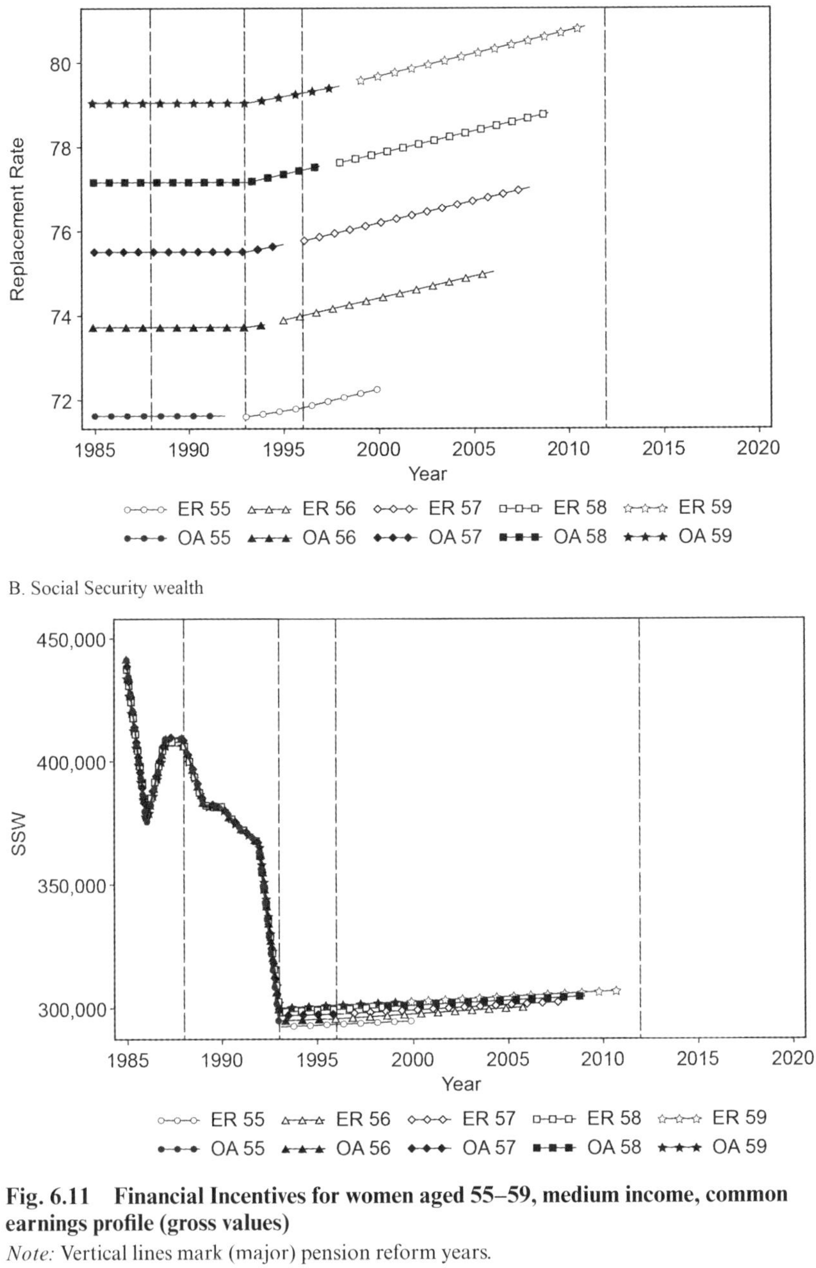

Fig. 6.11 Financial Incentives for women aged 55–59, medium income, common earnings profile (gross values)

Note: Vertical lines mark (major) pension reform years.

C. Accrual

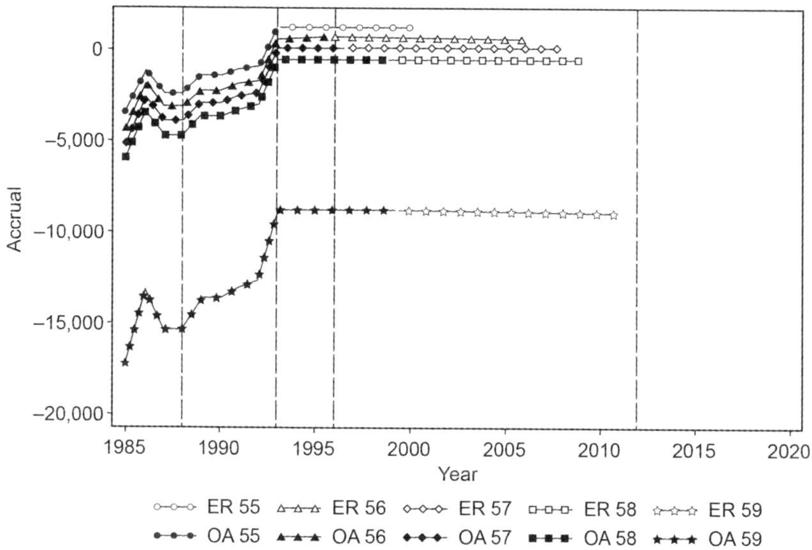

D. Implicit tax rate

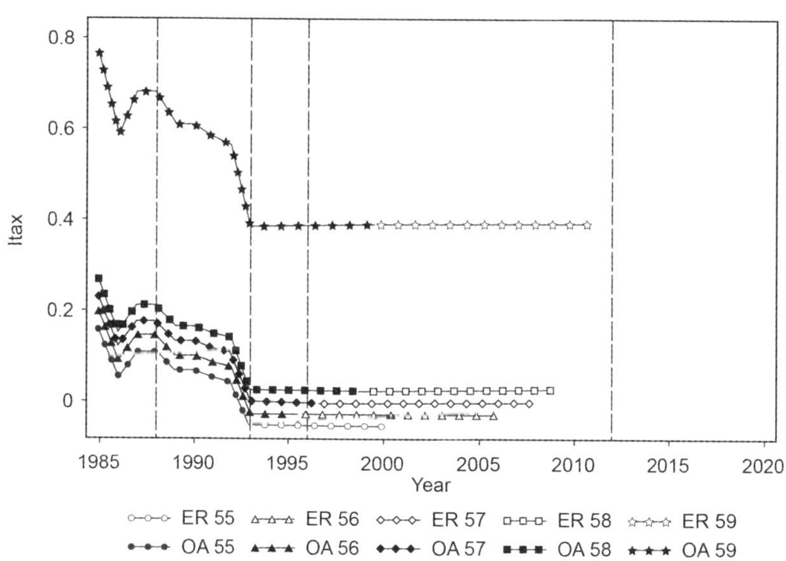

Fig. 6.11 (cont.)

Panel A of figure 6.11 shows how replacement rates changed over the years for middle-income women aged 55 to 59. Replacement rates were stable before the 1993 reform, ranging between 71 percent for women aged 55 and 79 percent for women aged 59, and then gently rose. These replacement rates are somewhat lower than the replacement rates for men, but the overall patterns are effectively the same. Panel B of figure 6.11 shows social security wealth for women: the patterns by age and over the years are similar to what we have already seen and discussed for men of the same age. However, we should stress that the actual values are 10 percent to 20 percent lower for women compared to otherwise identical men.

The ACC panel shows the accrual of pension benefits: it was negative for all women before 1993 but became positive after that date for individuals aged 55 to 58 (it remained heavily negative for 59-year-olds for reasons we already discussed: we are comparing the choice of retiring with 40 or 41 years of contributions). The IT panel shows the corresponding implicit tax rates: these are always positive for all ages before 1993 and become negative after 1993 for all ages but the oldest type, 59 years of age. Our results suggest that for a representative "average" female worker, it was optimal to retire as soon as possible before the 1993 reform. For women, the 1993 reform produced mild incentives to retire later, at least for ages 55 to 58 (but notice that a woman could no longer retire at age 55 with 36 years of contributions past year 2000). A woman who was 59 years old between 1985 and 1993 had a huge tax on working an extra year, as discussed above. The 1993 reform reduced the implicit tax to roughly 40 percent, but the incentive to retire with 40 years of contributions remained extremely strong.

In figure 6.12 we show similar graphs for women aged 60 to 66. Although the results are qualitatively similar to that observed for men, gender differences are more pronounced for these age groups.[8] Panel A of figure 6.11 shows replacement rates, which were essentially flat in the first part and gradually increased in more recent years, ranging between 80 percent and 83 percent. The flat lines are explained by the simply defined benefit called "part A," while the increasing part is once again due to the "part B" component applied after the 1993 reform. Younger women have lower replacement rates because the age profile is increasing until age 60 (in marked difference to what we saw for men), and therefore the later one retired, the higher the average of past earnings would be (whether it was 5 years until 1993 or 10 years after 1993). There are drops in the replacement rate for 60-year-old retirees as of 2011 and for 62-year-old retirees as of 2015 because of the 2011 reform for reasons we already discussed.

As for SSW, the first point to stress is that women aged 60 or more could continue drawing an old-age pension until at least the 2011 reform. As of 2011, a 60-year-old woman could no longer draw an old-age pension ben-

8. The corresponding graph for net values is presented in the appendix.

A. Replacement rate

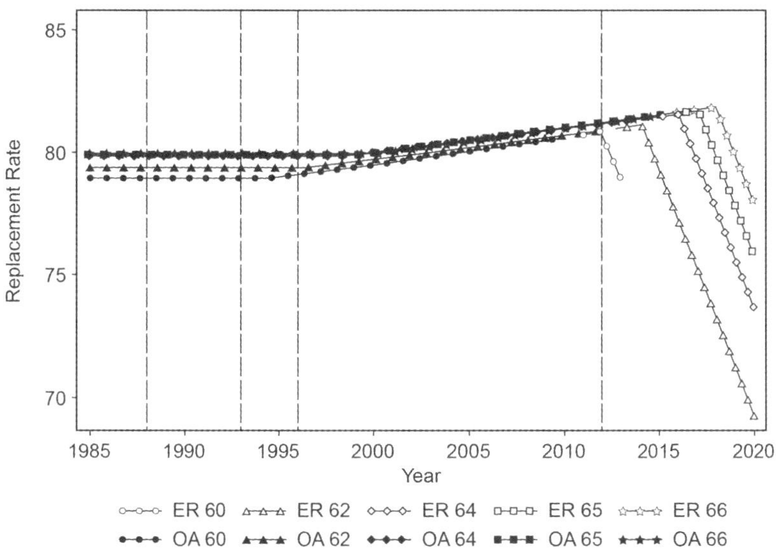

B. Social Security wealth

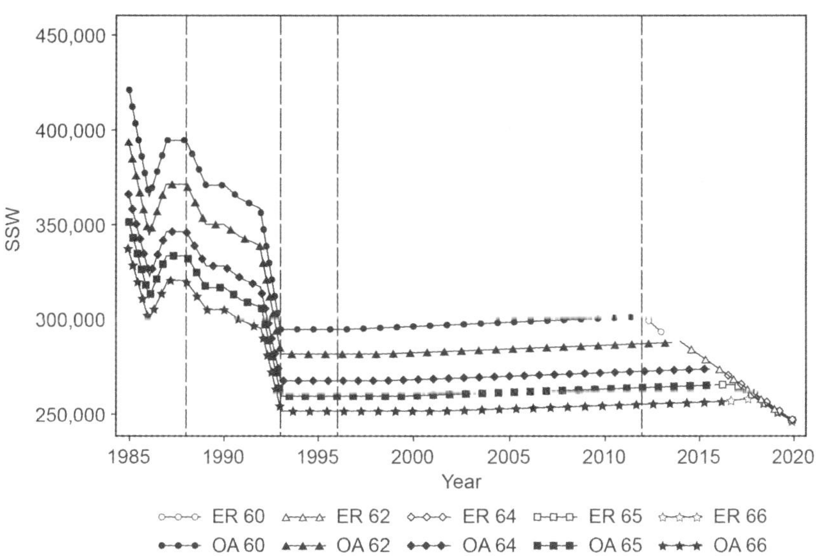

Fig. 6.12 Financial incentives for women aged 60–66, medium income, common earnings profile (gross values)

C. Accrual

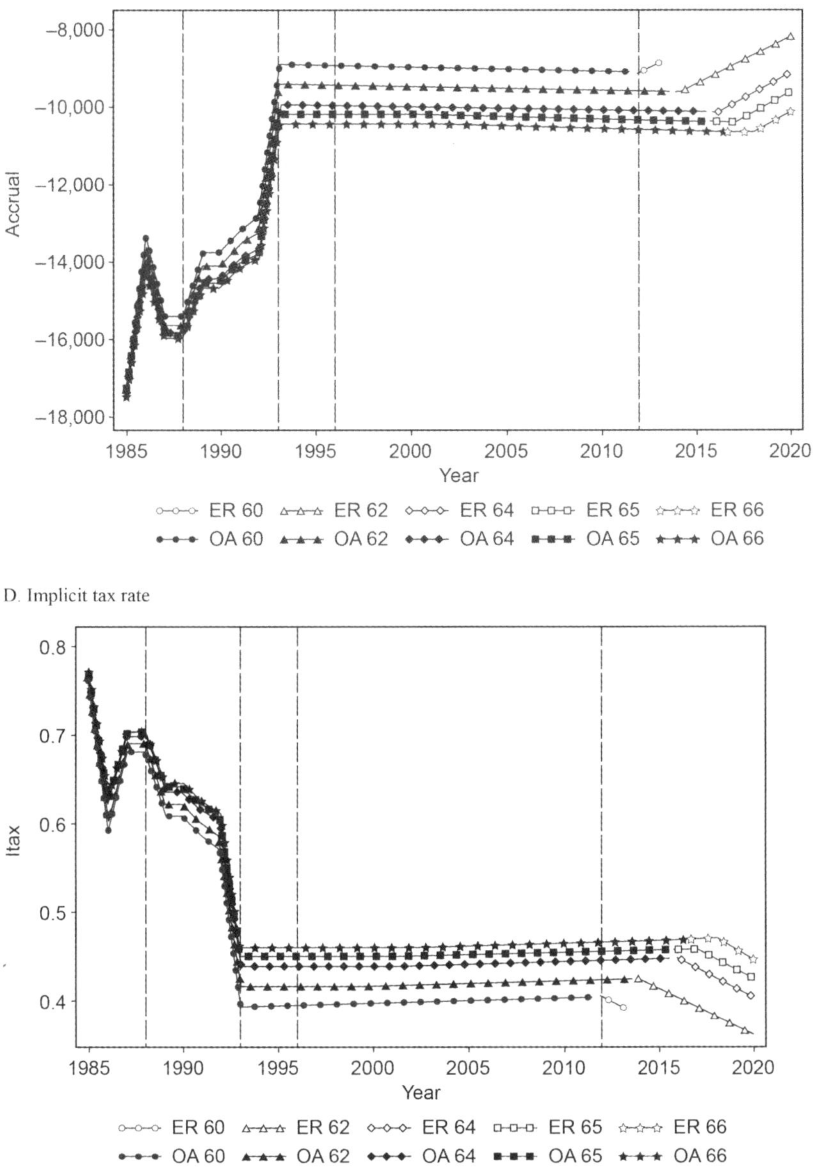

D. Implicit tax rate

Fig. 6.12 (cont.)

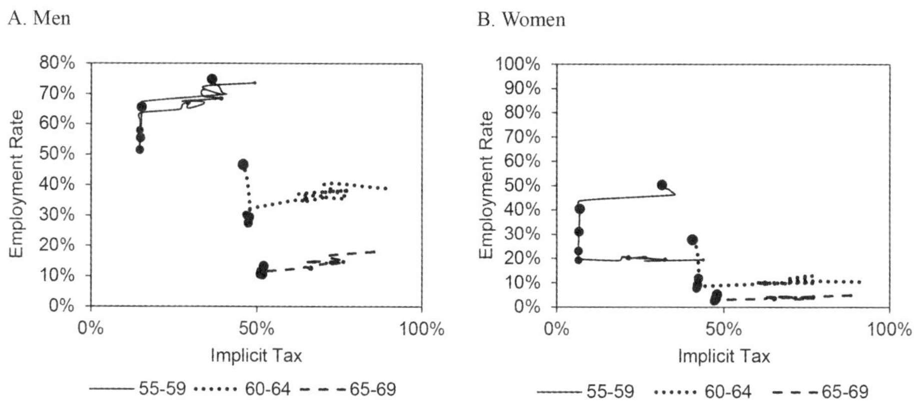

Fig. 6.13 Employment rate version, implicit tax

efit, but (unlike a man) she could still receive an early retirement pension if she had enough years of contributions. Only after the year 2013, she could no longer retire and draw a pension. As we have seen above, the pattern of the SSW profiles is affected by the indexation rules: prior to 1993, the earlier an individual retired, the longer the period in which pension benefits enjoyed full wage indexation, and the higher the SSW. On top of this, a 60-year-old woman would enjoy a higher SSW than a 62-year-old because the benefit was largely the same, but it was for two more years on average. This is enough to compensate for the lower replacement rate. Past 2015, one can observe drops in SSW for women aged 60, 62, and 64 as a result of the 2011 reform as explained above. The accrual of pension benefits for this group of individuals was negative for all individuals both before and after 1993 but grew after 1993 for all. The decreased SSW for women aged 60 in 2013 and 62 in 2015 is reflected in a rise of accrual around that year—and similarly for 64-year-olds in 2017. These individuals increase their pension even when they exceed the 40 years of contributions threshold thanks to the 2011 reform (part C). The IT rates are in line with these results.

Figure 6.13 describes the relationship between the implicit tax (ITAX) and the employment rate by age group, separately for men and women. We note that there is not a well-defined pattern for this relationship, and these graphs are not, on the whole, very supportive of the hypothesis that variations in ITAX are driving changes in employment at older ages. This may be due to several reasons. On the one hand, it may be that the changes introduced by the various reforms are not fully internalized by the variations in the ITAX. Indeed, we do not expect that the effects of the increase in the statutory eligibility ages are fully captured by the implicit tax. On the other hand, there is important heterogeneity among working careers and earning histories of the individuals, and the various policies affect them in a different way. Such heterogeneity is not perfectly captured by our calculations, which use some strong assumptions regarding the beginning of the working life and the continuity of the working career. We will address this drawback in the next phase of the project by using datasets that will allow us to exploit complete detailed information on real individuals' work profiles.

6.3.3 Implicit Tax: Comparisons

In this section, we focus on the key incentive variable, the implicit tax of postponing retirement by one year, and show how this differs when we change the earnings definition. In one case, we take the Italian earnings profile, which differs from the common earnings profile in ways that we shall discuss later; in another case, we consider a construct based on gross income and compare it to the corresponding net income measure.

We should stress that the Italian age-earnings profiles have been obtained with a methodology similar to the one adopted for the common earnings profiles. Even though they reflect some peculiarities of the Italian labor markets—particularly important for women—they are expressed in real terms. This implies that specific rules meant to partially compensate for inflation (such as the 1 percent revaluation of past earnings in the computation of the 10-year average that was introduced by the 1993 reform) appear generally beneficial to pension claimants even when in actual fact they were not.

As we can see from figure 6.14, the implicit tax rates are qualitatively similar across the two earnings profiles. They are slightly lower but otherwise similar when earnings and benefits are defined gross of tax and contributions rather than net. A very similar picture emerges for men in the 60–64 age group and is not reported here for brevity. In the sequel, we shall focus on net incomes for women and report only those cases where we observe nonnegligible differences between the common and the Italian age-earnings profiles.

As for women, the only relevant differences between the results deriving from the common earnings profile and the Italian earnings profile are due to the shape of the profile itself. As an example, we present the case of women 60–66 years old in figure 6.15.

Figure 6.15 shows the implicit tax rate for the 60- to 66-year-old women. Panel A has already been shown in the previous section and is computed using the common earnings profile; panel B corresponds instead to the Italian earnings profile. We see that the level of the implicit tax is some 20 percent lower when we use the Italian profile after 1993, even though in this case all implicit tax rates are positive throughout. This is because in the common profiles for women, there is a drop around ages 35–40 followed by a mild increase, while in the Italian profile, normalized wages are somewhat constant up to approximately age 58 and grow thereafter. Vertical distances across ages 60, 62, and 64 are much larger in the right-hand panel—they are very small instead across ages 64, 65, and 66 in both panels.

Finally, table 6.1 presents a summary of the implicit tax rates over time

A. Net income – common profile

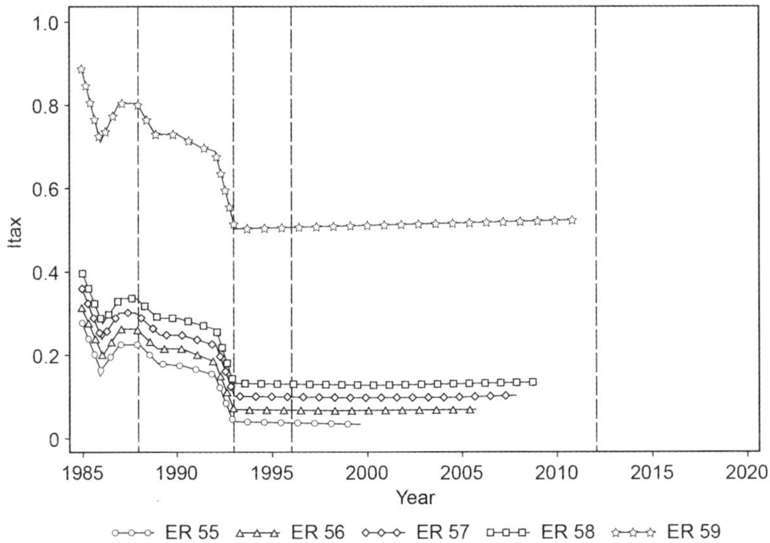

B. Net income – Italian profile

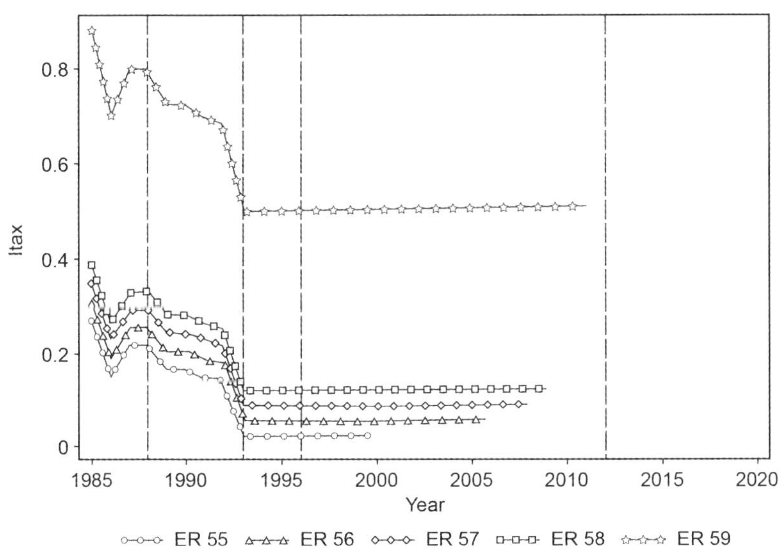

Fig. 6.14 Comparison of implicit tax rates for men aged 55–59

C. Gross income – common profile

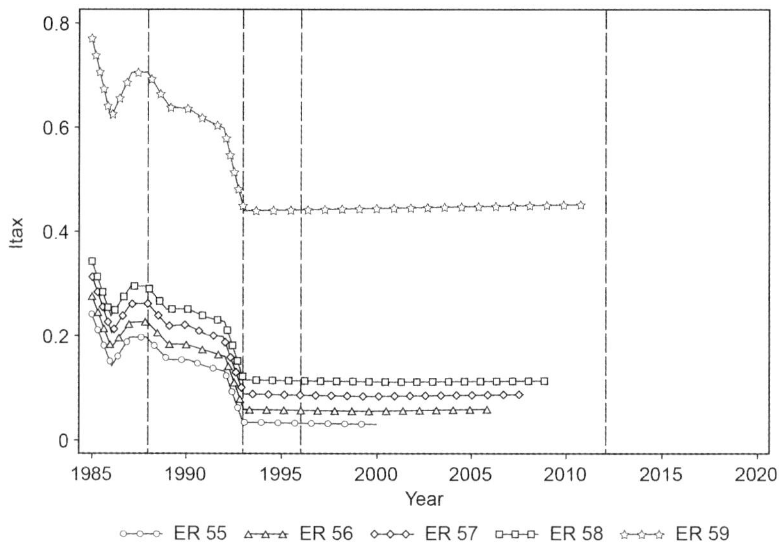

D. Gross income – Italian profile

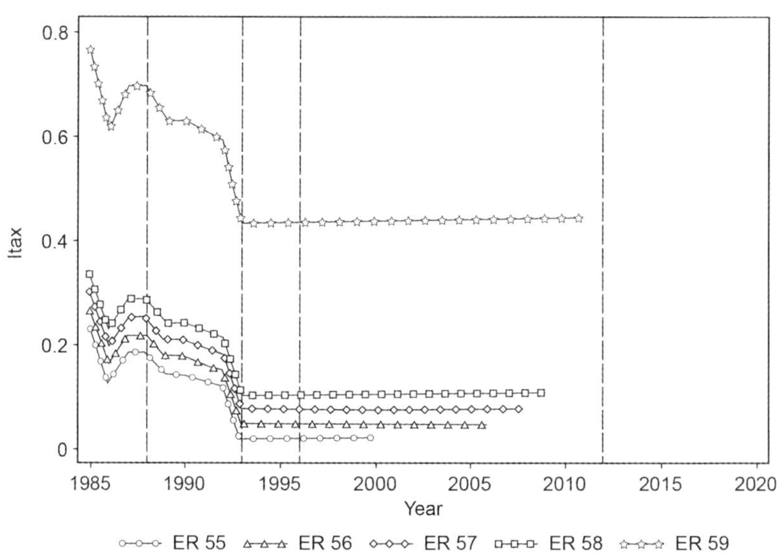

Fig. 6.14 (cont.)

A. Net income – common profile

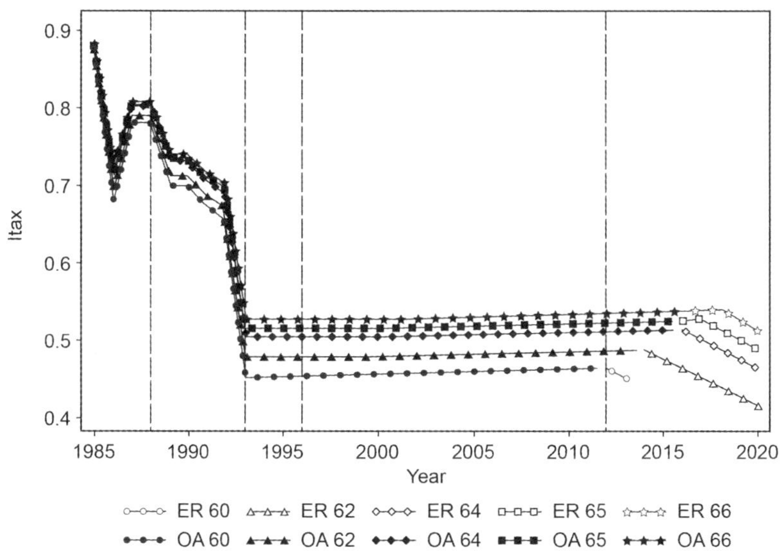

B. Net income – Italian profile

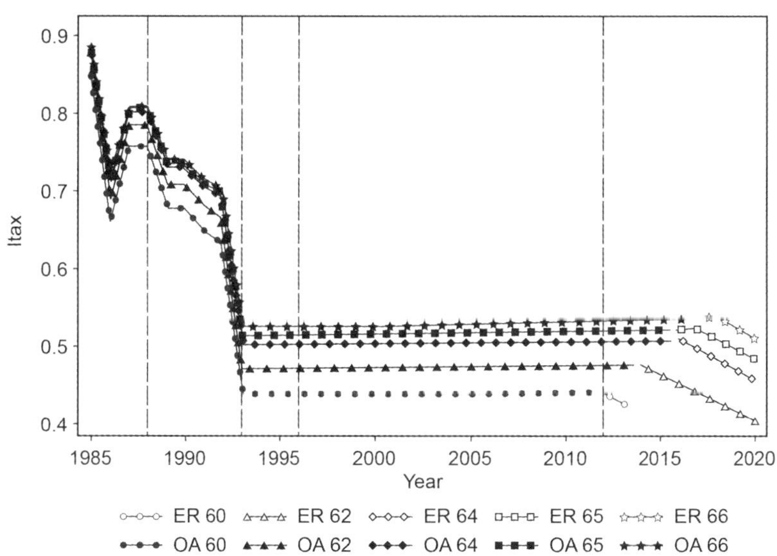

Fig. 6.15 Comparison of implicit tax rates for women aged 60–66 (net incomes)

Table 6.1 **Implicit tax rates for different years and ages (common earnings profile)**

Gender	Year	itax55	itax56	itax57	itax58	itax59	itax60	itax61	itax62	itax63	itax64	itax65	itax66	itax67	itax68	itax69
Men	1980	0.33	0.37	0.41	0.44	0.91	0.90	0.90	0.89	0.88	0.88	0.87	0.86	0.85	0.85	0.84
	1985	0.24	0.28	0.31	0.35	0.78	0.77	0.77	0.77	0.77	0.77	0.77	0.76	0.76	0.76	0.76
	1990	0.16	0.19	0.22	0.25	0.64	0.64	0.65	0.65	0.65	0.66	0.66	0.66	0.66	0.67	0.67
	1995	0.03	0.06	0.09	0.11	0.44	0.45	0.46	0.47	0.47	0.48	0.49	0.50	0.51	0.52	0.53
	2000	0.03	0.06	0.08	0.11	0.45	0.45	0.46	0.47	0.48	0.48	0.49	0.50	0.51	0.52	0.53
	2005		0.06	0.09	0.11	0.45	0.46	0.47	0.47	0.48	0.49	0.50	0.50	0.51	0.52	0.53
	2010					0.45	0.46	0.47	0.48	0.48	0.49	0.50	0.51	0.52	0.52	0.53
	2016								0.46	0.48	0.50	0.51	0.51	0.52	0.53	0.54
	2020								0.41	0.43	0.45	0.47	0.49	0.51	0.53	0.54
Women	1980	0.26	0.30	0.34	0.37	0.92	0.92	0.91	0.91	0.90	0.90	0.89	0.89	0.88	0.88	0.87
	1985	0.16	0.19	0.23	0.26	0.76	0.76	0.76	0.77	0.77	0.77	0.77	0.77	0.77	0.77	0.77
	1990	0.07	0.10	0.13	0.16	0.60	0.61	0.61	0.62	0.63	0.64	0.64	0.65	0.65	0.65	0.66
	1995	−0.05	−0.03	0.00	0.02	0.39	0.40	0.41	0.42	0.43	0.44	0.45	0.46	0.47	0.48	0.49
	2000	−0.05	−0.03	0.00	0.02	0.39	0.40	0.41	0.42	0.43	0.44	0.45	0.46	0.47	0.48	0.49
	2005		−0.03	0.00	0.02	0.39	0.40	0.41	0.42	0.43	0.44	0.45	0.46	0.47	0.48	0.49
	2010					0.39	0.40	0.41	0.42	0.43	0.44	0.46	0.47	0.48	0.49	0.50
	2016							0.38	0.40	0.43	0.45	0.46	0.47	0.48	0.49	0.50
	2020							0.34	0.36	0.38	0.40	0.43	0.45	0.47	0.49	0.50

and by age: the implicit tax is increasing with the age of retirement and decreasing over time.

6.4 Conclusions

This chapter has discussed the Italian evidence on labor force participation reversal at older ages over the recent decades in relation to pension reforms passed since the early 1990s. It has shown how eligibility for early retirement and old-age pension schemes has been restricted over the years, making it progressively more difficult for individuals in their 50s or early 60s to start drawing a pension. In this chapter we have computed retirement financial incentive measures in the public pension system and shown how these vary by age, year, and (lifelong) income. We have reported how the incentives system depends on the specific features of the earnings profiles of Italian workers by comparing them with those that would obtain if the earnings profiles were as in the common case considered in this volume.

The key message of this chapter is that pension reforms in Italy were most effective in raising the effective retirement age by restricting access to financially advantageous public pension schemes. The implicit tax rate of postponing retirement was in fact reduced for individuals in their 50s as a result of the 1993 and 1995 reforms but remained positive for most (with the notable exception of some middle-income women). The dramatic decrease in the flow of new pensioners below age 60 is mostly attributable to the operation of a combination of age and years of pension contributions restrictions that were phased in over the period.

An important cutoff in the public pension system can still be found at 40 years of pension contributions for the individuals who could retire and draw a pension during the 1990s and 2000s: under the old defined benefit rules, the replacement rate would effectively increase by 2 percent for each additional year of contributions up to a ceiling of 40, after which it would not rise any further. For middle-income individuals age 60 or more, who according to our earnings profile would have contributed 40 years or more to their public pension, the implicit tax remained high (roughly 40 percent), as postponing retirement by an additional year would simply imply foregoing one year of pension benefits.

The much more radical pension reform of 2011 further restricted the possibility to claim a pension at relatively young ages (less than 62), even for those individuals with 40 or more years of contributions, and introduced a pro-rata defined contribution component to the pension. This last change started having an effect on the implicit tax rate, but the financial incentive to draw a pension as soon as possible remains strong because pension benefits are still prevailingly computed according to the defined benefit formula.

Appendix

6.A1 Data Sources

The data on labor force participation (LFP) are drawn from two sources: (i) the MARSS database (the data on the LFP for the 55–59 age group [up to 1983] and for the 65–69 age group [up to 1993]) and (ii) the OECD database (the LFP series for the 60–64 band and for the remaining years of the 55–59 and 65–69 age bands). The MARSS dataset is provided by ISTAT (the Italian National Statistics Office) and is based on the Labour Force Survey. For the description of the pathways to retirement, we used data on the stock of beneficiaries from the Italian National Institute of Social Security (INPS). The data until 2004 are obtained from a representative sample of recipients while for the following years the information on the entire stock of beneficiaries was made available. In order to estimate the income profiles, we use data from the Survey on Italian Households Income and Wealth (SHIW, several years) conducted by the Bank of Italy. The survey takes place every two years and collects information both on households' wealth and assets and also on relevant individual characteristics and income of all family members. In order to estimate the income profiles, we use data from 1987 until 2014. We retain the employees in dependent employment (dropping the self-employed) so that the final sample contains 83,478 records (49,752 for men and 33,726 for women) for a total of 42,429 individuals. The income tax rates come from the OECD database (OECD.Stat).

6.A2 Additional Results

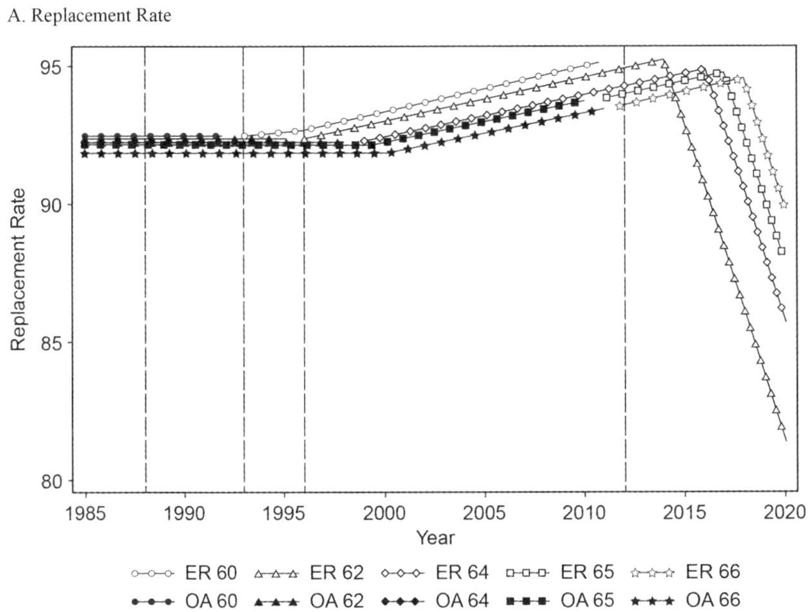

Fig. 6.A.1 Financial incentives for men aged 60–66, medium income, common earnings profile (net values)

Note: Vertical lines mark (major) pension reform years.

C. Accrual

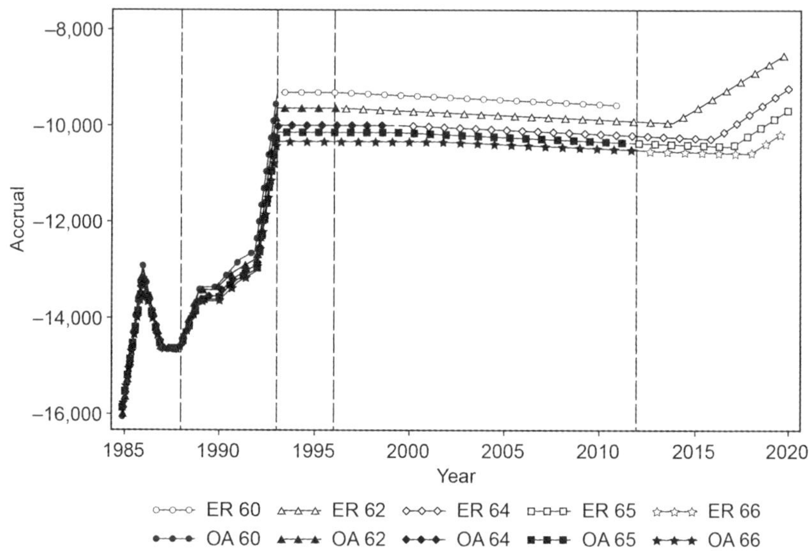

D. Implicit Tax Rate

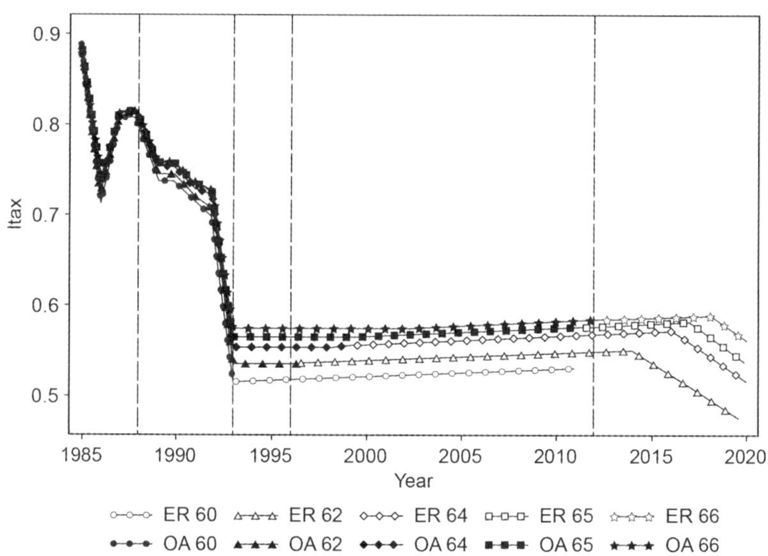

Fig. 6.A.1 (cont.)

A. Replacement rate

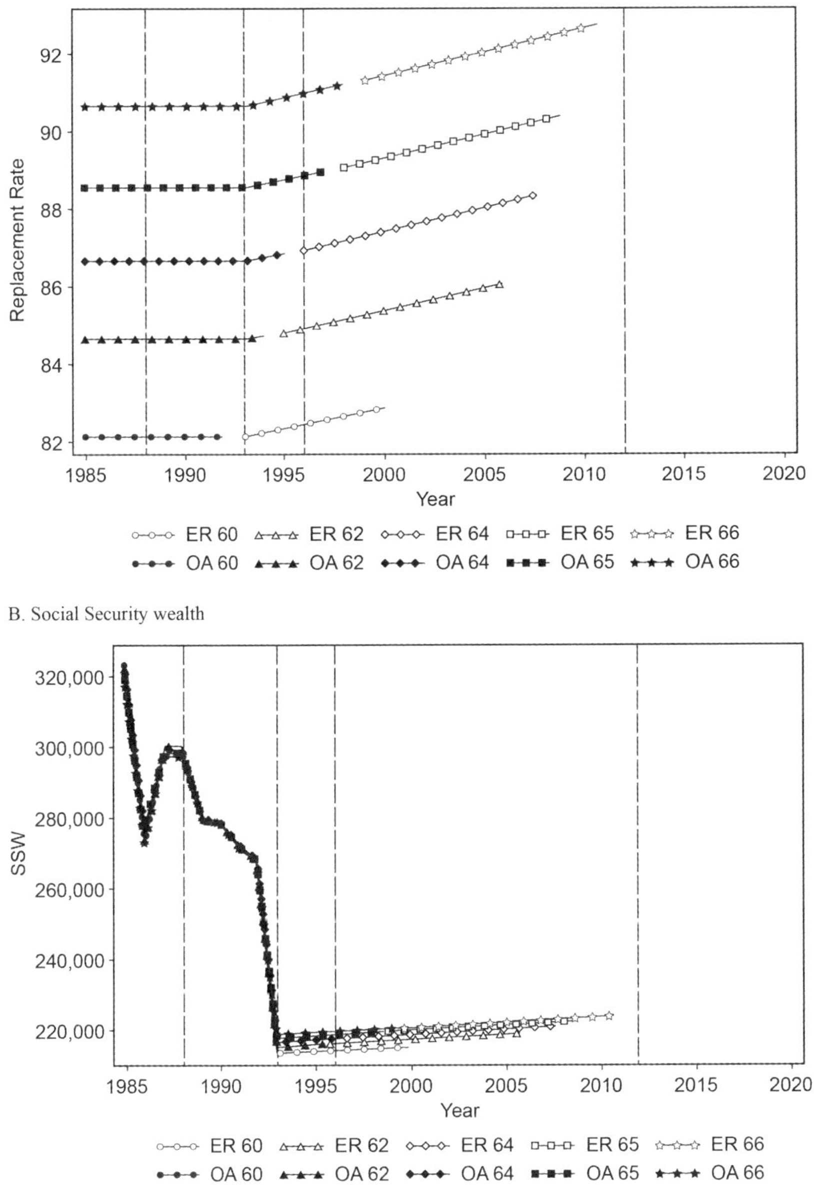

B. Social Security wealth

Fig. 6.A.2 Financial incentives for women aged 55–59, medium income, common earnings profile (net values)

Note: Vertical lines mark (major) pension reform years.

C. Accrual

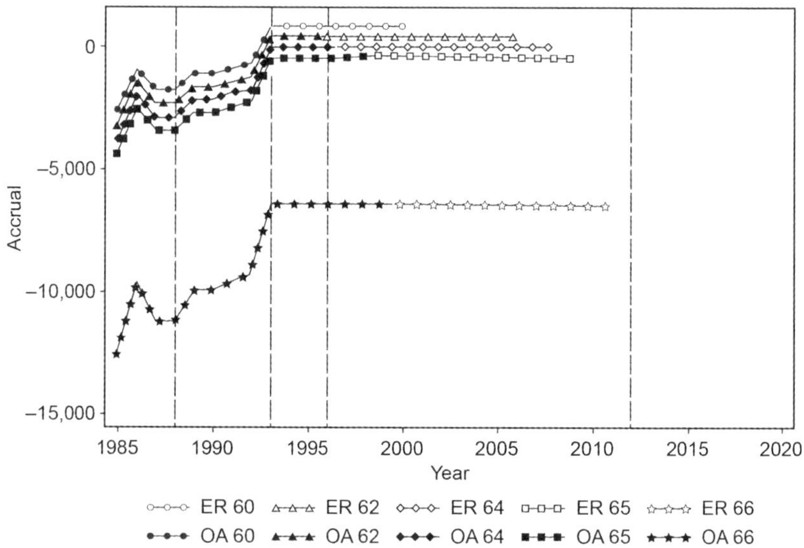

D. Implicit Tax Rate

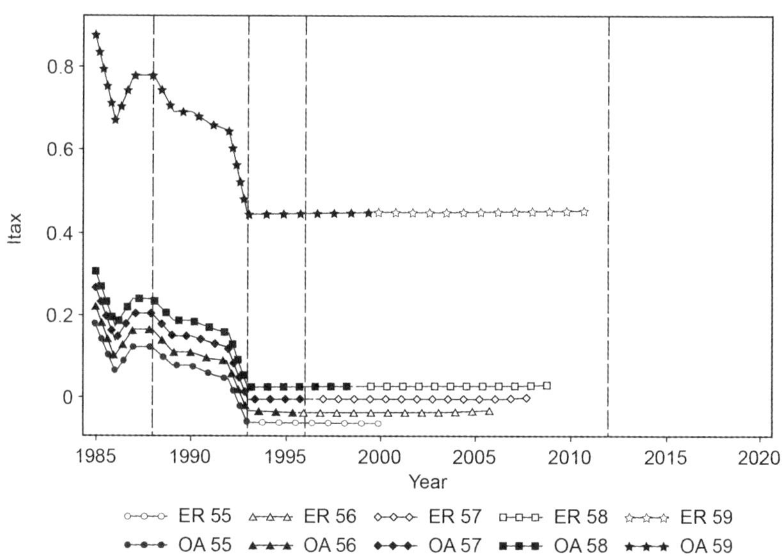

Fig. 6.A.2 (cont.)

A. Replacement rate

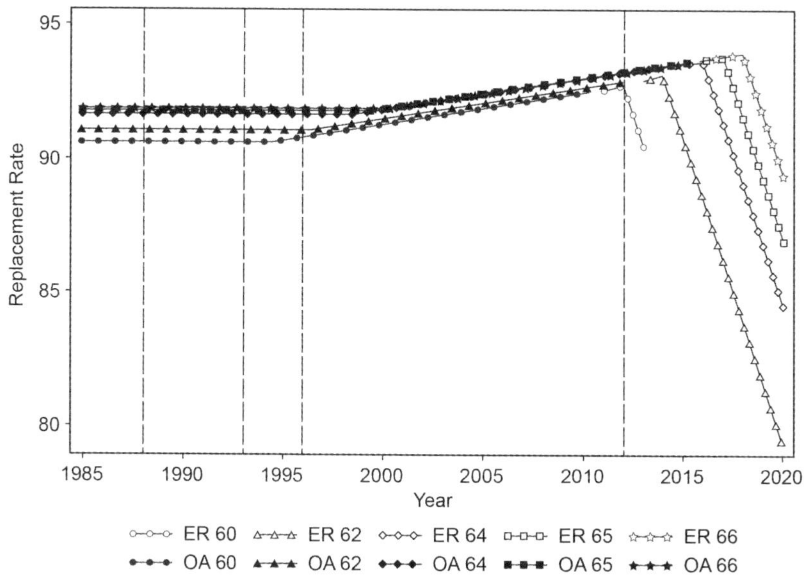

B. Social Security wealth

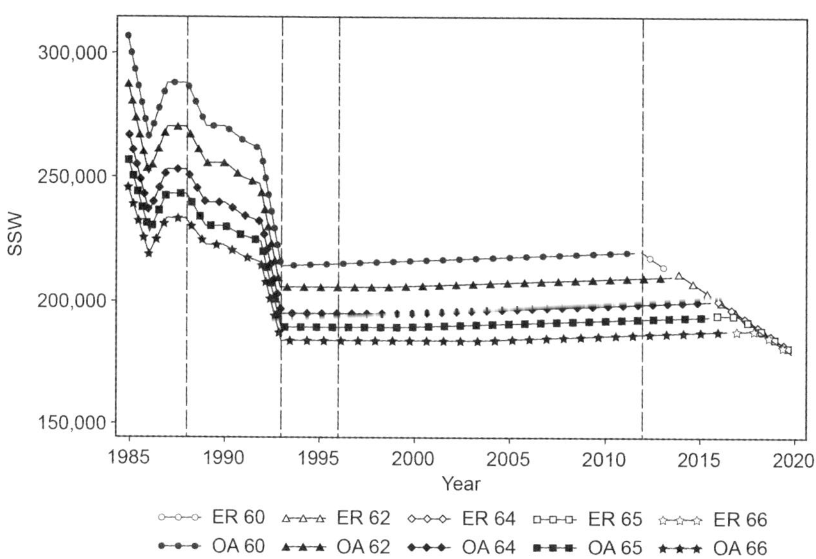

Fig. 6.A.3 Financial incentives for women aged 60–66, medium income, common earnings profile (net values)

C. Accrual

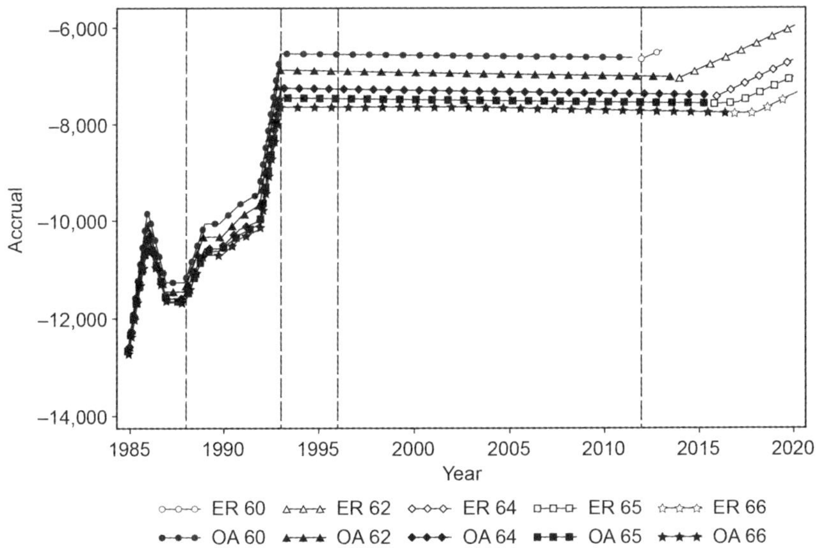

D. Implicit tax rate

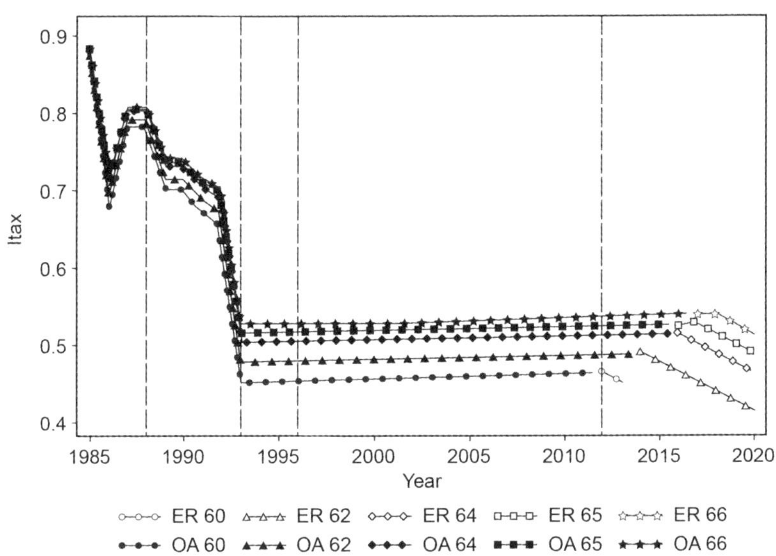

Fig. 6.A.3 (cont.)

References

Bank of Italy. Several years. *The SHIW Data Base* and *Historical Database of the Survey of Italian Household Budgets*. Rome: Bank of Italy. http://www.bancaditalia.it/statistiche/tematiche/indagini-famiglie-imprese/bilanci-famiglie/index.html.

Brugiavini, A. 1999. "Social Security and Retirement in Italy." In *Social Security and Retirement around the World*, edited by J. Gruber and D. A. Wise, 181–238. Chicago: University of Chicago Press.

Brugiavini, A., G. Pasini, and G. Weber. 2017. "Health Capacity to Work at Older Ages: Evidence from Italy." In *Social Security Programs and Retirement around the World: The Capacity to Work at Older Ages*, edited by D. A. Wise, 181–218. Chicago: University of Chicago Press.

Brugiavini, A., and F. Peracchi. 2003. "Social Security Wealth and Retirement Decisions in Italy." Special issue, *Labour* 17:79–114.

Brugiavini, A., and F. Peracchi. 2007. "Fiscal Implications of Pension Reforms in Italy." In *Social Security Programs and Retirement around the World: Fiscal Implications of Reform*, edited by J. Gruber and D. Wise, 253–94. Chicago: University of Chicago Press.

ISTAT Istituto Italiano di Statistica—INPS Istituto Nazionale Previdenza Sociale. Several years. *Trattamenti Pensionistici e Beneficiari*. http://www.istat.it/salastampa/comunicati/non_calendario/20100611_00/.

OECD Database. OECD.Stat. http://stats.oecd.org/.

7

Social Security Programs and Elderly Employment in Japan

Takashi Oshio, Akiko S. Oishi, and Satoshi Shimizutani

7.1 Introduction

The employment rates in Japan showed a modest recovery in the mid-2000s for men aged 60 and over (figure 7.1), although the business cycles made it ambiguous and the trend turned around a bit later compared to other advanced countries, which experienced this recovery in the late 1980s. Meanwhile, the employment rates for women aged 55–64 in Japan exceeded the pace of the recovery of labor participation of elderly men in the mid-2000s. At the same time, the Japanese government has been enacting a series of social security and labor market reforms since the mid-1980s, raising eligibility ages, reducing actuarial adjustment factors, and encouraging elderly workers to stay longer in the labor force.

In this study, we examine the extent to which the change in the trend of the employment rates for the elderly has been associated with the tax force to retire early, reflecting the social security programs and their related programs in Japan. We focus on the Employees' Pension Insurance (EPI; *Kosei Nenkin*) program, which we believe is a key driver of elderly employment rates. In addition to this EPI program, the public social security scheme in Japan has two core programs: National Pension Insurance (NPI; *Kokumin Nenkin*) and Mutual Aid Association Pension Insurance (MAAPI; *Kyosai Nenkin*). EPI, NPI, and MAAPI mainly cover private-sector employees, the self-employed, and public-sector employees, respectively. The benefits of EPI and MAAPI

Takashi Oshio is a professor at the Institute of Economic Research at Hitotsubashi University.

Akiko S. Oishi is a professor at the Graduate School of Social Sciences at Chiba University.

Satoshi Shimizutani is an executive senior research fellow at the JICA Research Institute.

For acknowledgments, sources of research support, and disclosure of the authors' material financial relationships, if any, please see https://www.nber.org/chapters/c14197.ack.

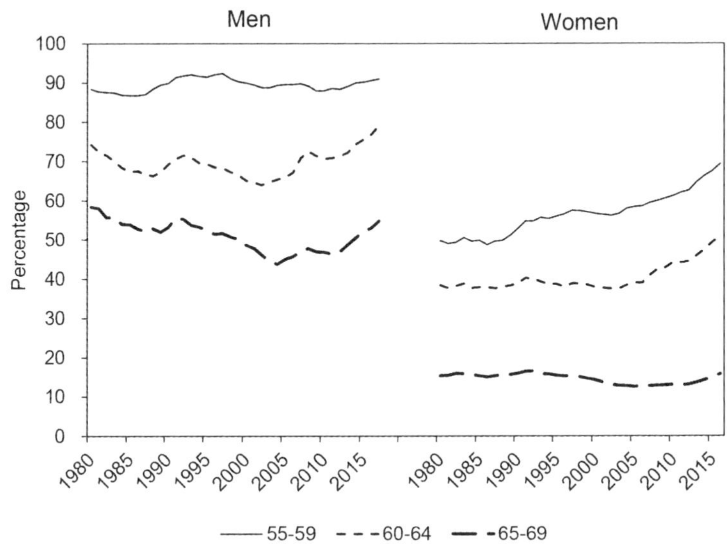

Fig. 7.1 Trends of the employment rates

include two components: flat-rate and wage-proportional benefits. MAAPI's structure is largely similar to that of EPI, and its reform has been following the same pattern as that of EPI. EPI and MAAPI members cover about 70 percent of all employees. Meanwhile, NPI only has a flat-rate benefit, and NPI members cover the remaining 30 percent. The eligibility age for availing the NPI has been fixed at 65 years since its introduction in 1961.

Based on the statistical analyses, our results suggest that a reduced disincentive to work due to a reduction in the overall generosity of the social security programs has been affecting the recent recovery of labor force participation of elderly men as well as the increasing upward trend of labor force participation of elderly women.

In what follows, we first present a brief overview of the social security reforms in section 7.2. In section 7.3, we construct the quantitative indicators of institutional changes and the tax forces to retire early. Using these variables, we examine the association between the tax force and the employment rates in section 7.4. Finally, we present the concluding remarks in section 7.5.

7.2 An Overview of Social Security Reforms in Japan

7.2.1 Increasing Eligibility Ages and Declining Generosity

Social security reforms, which have been enacted about every five years in response to their actuarial review, remarkably changed their direction in the mid-1980s in terms of the overall generosity of the programs (Oshio,

Oishi, and Shimizutani 2011). Before the 1985 reform, the government had continued to raise benefit levels to improve the standard of living of the elderly in line with a steady increase in per capita GDP. However, slower economic growth and a declining fertility trend raised concerns about the financial sustainability of social security programs. In addition, structural changes in the industry and labor force, such as a reduction in workers in the agricultural sector and self-employed workers, led to a larger disparity among the financial positions of the programs.

These concerns motivated the 1985 reform, which pushed for a reduction in the benefit multiplier and flat-rate benefit for the first time. At the same time, the basic pension benefit, which is commonly paid to all public pension members as a first-tier flat-rate benefit, was introduced, and the dependent spouses of the EPI beneficiaries became eligible to receive it without having to pay any premium. Overall, the EPI programs became less generous in terms of benefits. For example, a male EPI beneficiary who earned an average income of ¥254,000 per month in 1985, paid premiums for 40 years, and had a dependent wife was eligible to receive total benefits of around ¥176,000 per month under the 1985 scheme. This amount was less than the amount provided under the pre-1985 reform scheme—approximately ¥198,000, implying that the total benefit was reduced by more than 10 percent.

Subsequent reforms have consistently sought to improve the financial balance of the programs by raising the eligibility age, reducing the benefit multiplier, and scaling down benefit indexations. The eligibility age for receiving EPI benefits has been continuously raised. For male pensioners, the eligibility age for receiving both flat-rate and wage-proportional benefits was raised from 55 in 1957 to 60 years in 1973. In 2001, the eligibility age for the flat-rate component started to increase by one year every three years to reach 65 years in 2013; additionally, the eligibility age for the wage-proportional component has been scheduled to rise from 2013 by one year every three years to reach 65 years in 2025. The eligibility age for women until 1985 was 55 years, and it was gradually raised to 60 years in 2000. The eligibility age for women was set to be raised while keeping a five-year lag for men. The eligibility age for the flat-rate benefit was raised beginning in 2006, and the eligibility age for wage-proportional benefit was raised beginning in 2018.

In addition to an increase in the eligibility ages, the benefit multiplier[1] of the EPI wage-proportional benefit was reduced from 10/1,000 per year of contribution to 7.125/1,000 in 2001 and since then has remained at this level; this implies a 28.75 percent reduction in the benefit. During the same period,

1. The wage-proportional benefit per month is calculated in the following manner: average lifetime monthly wage * the number of months of contribution * the benefit multiplier. Since the current value of the multiplier is 7.125/1,000, the wage-proportional benefit per month is 21.4 percent of the average lifetime monthly wage earnings if one contributed the premiums for 30 years (7.125/1,000 * 30 = 21.4 percent).

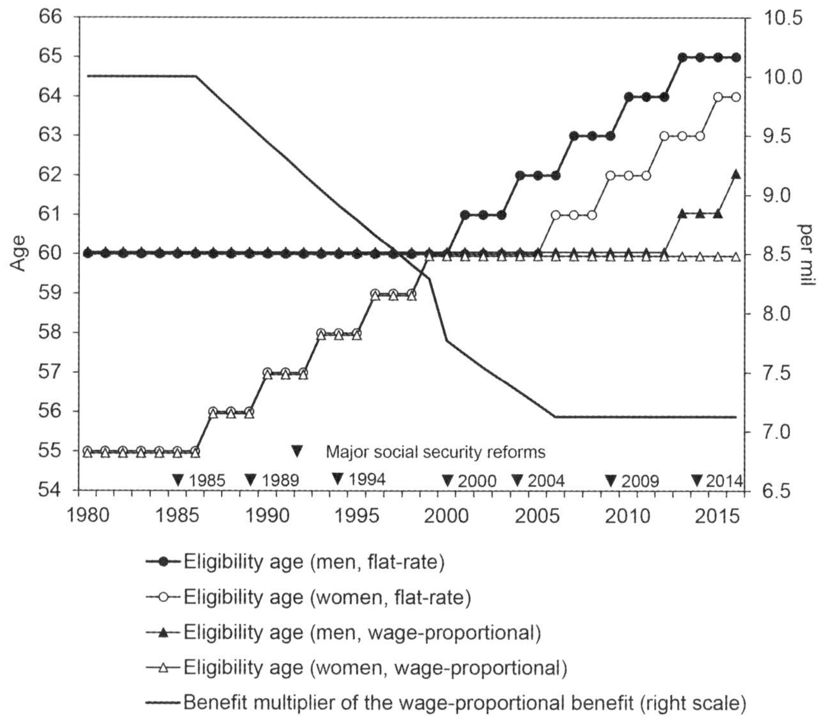

Fig. 7.2 Changes in the eligibility ages and benefit multiplier of the Employees' Pension Insurance program (EPI)

the fixed-rate benefit per month of contribution was reduced by 30.9 percent, from ¥2,424 to ¥1,675.

The wage and price indexations have also become less generous. The EPI benefits used to be price indexed every year and wage indexed during each reform almost every five years. In the 1994 reform, the base of the wage indexation was changed from gross wage to net wage (after the social security contribution) to subdue the degree of indexation. Additionally, the 2000 reform called for restricting the wage indexation only to the initially claimed benefits. Finally, the 2004 reform introduced automatic adjustments of benefit levels based on demographic and macroeconomic factors, with the upper limit set to the premium rate.[2]

To help understand the direction of the social security reforms, figure 7.2 presents how the eligibility ages of EPI benefits and the benefit multiplier of the wage-proportional benefit have been changing since the 1980s. As shown in this figure, the eligibility ages of EPI benefits and the benefit multiplier of the wage-proportional benefit have both contributed toward reducing the

2. Takayama (2005, ch. 6) discusses the key issues in the 2004 reform.

generosity of the programs; the eligibility ages have been gradually raised for both men and women, and the latter has been gradually reduced. Figure 7.3 summarizes major reforms in the social security and employment programs, which are closely relevant to the analysis in this study.

7.2.2 Earnings-Tested Benefits (*Zaishoku*), Actuarial Adjustments, and Wage Subsidy

In addition to reforming the core social security programs, the government has been making several revisions to the related programs, which are expected to affect incentives to work. First, the government has been reforming the *Zaishoku* pension program, which is an earnings-tested pension program applied to those who remain in the labor force past their eligibility age. Starting with a 20 percent reduction in the benefit given to the working beneficiaries in the 1950s, the effective tax rate on additional work has been revised several times. In 2015, 34.0 percent of the new EPI beneficiaries claimed the *Zaishoku* pension benefit.

Figure 7.4 illustrates the evolution of the *Zaishoku* pension program through major reforms. Each line represents the total amount of monthly wages and earnings-tested pension benefit that correspond to the monthly wages of those aged 60–64 years (upper panel) and 65 years or older (below) under the *Zaishoku* pension program in each respective year. As seen in the figure, the sum of the wage and pension benefit has become more smoothly adjusted to wage earnings, especially for those aged 60–64 years, resulting in reduced disincentives to work. Indeed, many empirical studies have estimated the impact of the *Zaishoku* pension program based on microlevel data.[3] Most found that the reforms of the program—especially the 2005 reform, which eliminated a 20 percent reduction in the benefit given to working beneficiaries—encouraged the elderly to remain in the labor force longer, although the magnitude of the estimated impact varies substantially.

Second, the government changed the actuarial adjustments of social security benefits, reducing the degrees of adjustments for both the early and delayed benefit claims for those born in 1941 or later. The actuarial reduction rate was reduced from 40 percent to 30 percent for the claim at 60 years of age for the full flat-rate benefit that was to be paid at 65 years of age, while the actuarial increase rate for the claim at 70 years of age was reduced from 88 percent to 42 percent (figure 7.5). These changes in the actuarial adjustments are expected to discourage workers from continuing work until they reach the eligibility age and delaying claims after that age. As discussed in section 7.3.5, however, the actuarial adjustments do not significantly influence the decision to retire.

In addition to these changes in the social security programs, the government introduced the wage subsidy program for the elderly in 1995. This

3. For example, see Abe (2001) and Shimizutani and Oshio (2013).

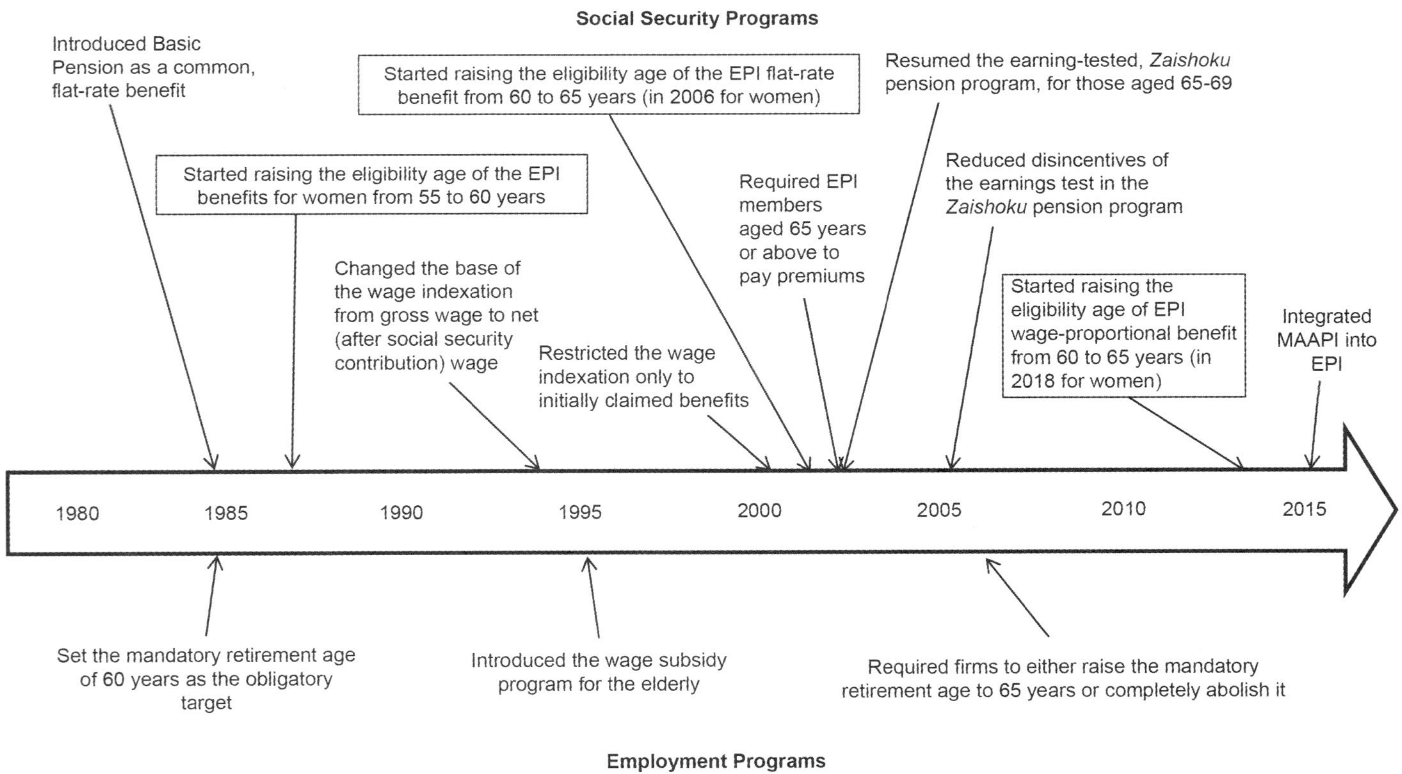

Fig. 7.3 Major reforms in social security and employment programs

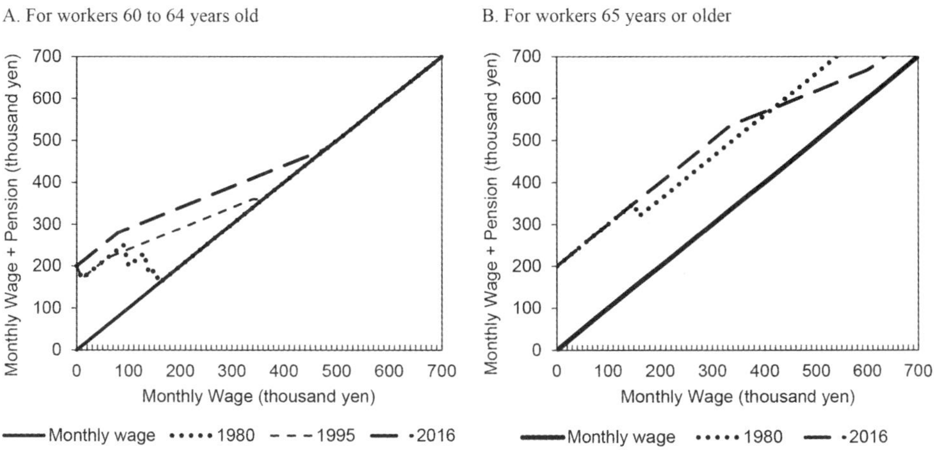

Fig. 7.4 Earnings-tested *Zaishoku* pension program

Note: Assuming a worker whose full amount of monthly pension is ¥200,000 (including the flat-part of ¥66,000).

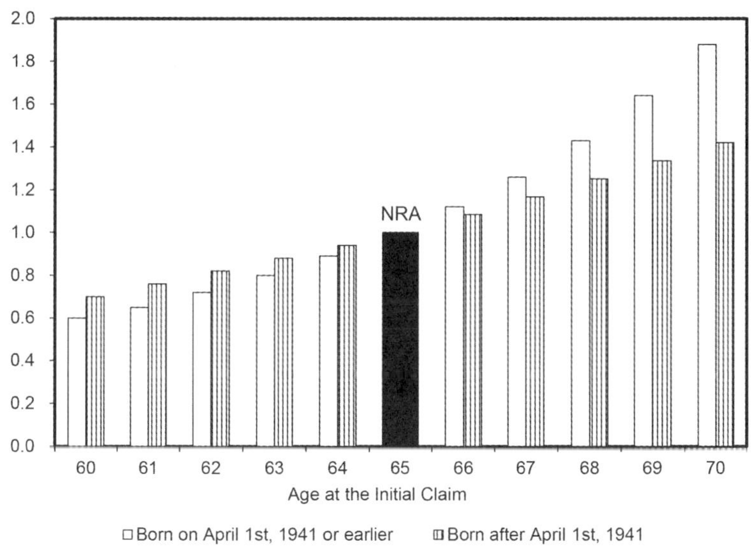

Fig. 7.5 Actuarial adjustment of the flat-rate benefit

program started by subsidizing 25 percent of the wages of individuals aged 60–64 years who continued to work for the same firm at a wage rate of less than 64 percent of the preretirement level. Since 1998, the *Zaishoku* pension benefit has been reduced for those who receive the wage subsidy, and the subsidy rate was reduced to 15 percent in 2003. Despite this reduced generosity, this wage subsidy is expected to encourage workers to continue working by offsetting an expected reduction in wage earnings after mandatory retirement. According to the Annual Survey of Employment Insurance provided by the Ministry of Health, Labour and Welfare (MHLW), about 178,000 individuals, equivalent to 15.9 percent of the EPI beneficiaries who initially claimed EPI benefits, obtained this wage subsidy in 2015.

7.2.3 Employment Policies

An increase in the eligibility age for claiming EPI benefits has prompted the government to consider policy measures to allow for a smooth transition from work life to retirement for those aged 65 years or above. In 1973, the government enforced the Elderly Employment Stabilization Law (EESL) to encourage firms to raise the mandatory retirement age to 60 years, which was set as the obligatory target in 1986. In 2004, the government revised this law to propose that firms either completely abolish the mandatory retirement age or raise it to 65 years. The revised EESL became effective in 2006. In 2013, the government further amended the law to compel the firms to continue hiring individuals who wished to work until 65 years of age, albeit on a part-time basis in most cases. Combined with an increase in the eligibility age for claiming EPI benefits to 65 years, these employment policies are expected to increase the chances of the elderly staying in the labor force, even if they are not likely to have a direct impact on the elderly's incentives to work.[4]

7.3 Calculating the Tax Force to Retire Early

7.3.1 Quantitative Indicators of Institutional Changes

We incorporated several quantitative indicators of institutional changes into the calculation of the changes in social security incentives. As pointed out in section 7.1, we mainly focused on the changes in the EPI program, which cover the private-sector employees and are most likely to be associated with the long-term trend of elderly employment rates.

We focused on the increase in the eligibility age for claiming benefits, a potential driver of change in the trends of the elderly employment rates, which is expected to encourage individuals aged 60–64 to stay longer in the labor force. Specifically, EPI beneficiaries receive only the wage-proportional benefit before 65 years since 2013, when the eligibility age for the flat-rate component reached 65 years; the eligibility age of this claim was first raised in 2013 from 60 years and is scheduled to increase to reach 65 years in 2025

4. By comparing cohorts that were affected and unaffected by the revision of EESL in 2006, Kondo and Shigeoka (2017) found that the revision increased the employment rate of males in their early 60s, although its effect was smaller when compared to the increase in the pension eligibility age.

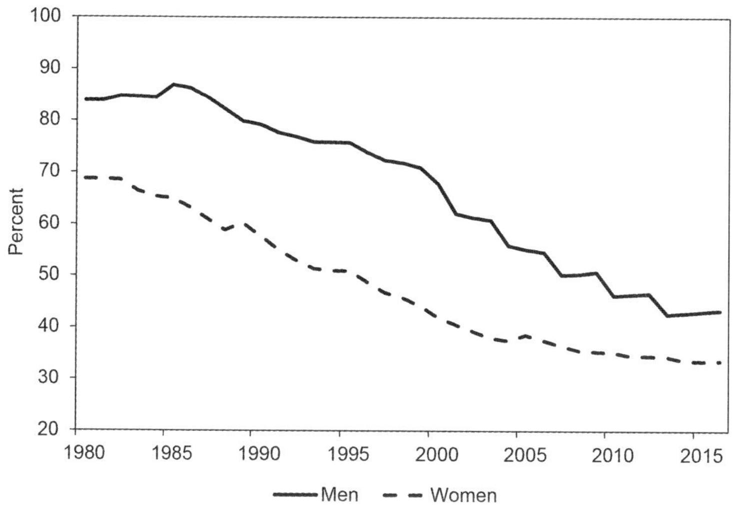

Fig. 7.6 Declining replacement rates
Note: Assuming median income.

(and five years later for women). At the same time, a gradual reduction in the benefit multipliers was expected to reduce the implicit tax rate for the postponed benefit claim.

Raised eligibility ages and reduced benefit generosity enhanced the importance of the earnings-tested *Zaishoku* pension program. The *Zaishoku* pension program for those aged 60–64 has been consistently revised to reduce its disincentive to work, along with the wage subsidy introduced in 1995. For those aged 65–69, the *Zaishoku* pension program was abolished in 1986 but reintroduced in 2002 (Shimizutani and Oshio 2013). The earnings-tested pension program tends to reduce the incentive to work in general, and this is remarkable for those considering to continue work, especially on a full-time basis, after the statutory eligibility age of 65 years.

To examine a long-term change in benefit generosity, we focused on the average replacement rate, which is defined as the ratio of the average net benefit to the average net wage. Using the institutional parameters, figure 7.6 shows the trends of average replacement rates for men and women aged 60–64 since 1980. As seen in this figure, the replacement rates have been gradually declining for both men and women over the past couple of decades, mainly reflecting the reduced generosity of benefits such as raised eligibility ages and reduced benefit multipliers.

7.3.2 Benefits Calculator

To examine the association between the social security incentives and elderly employment rates during 1980 and 2016, we constructed a benefits calculator to compute the after-tax benefit stream of each age group in the EPI program as a function of a synthetic earnings history for men and women as well as for the three educational levels. We programmed the benefits calculator for a time span from 1980 to 2016, reflecting on the reforms that might affect the trends of elderly employment rates. Although we focused entirely on the EPI program, we considered statutory changes in both flat-rate and wage-proportional benefits, which have been substantially different, especially in terms of the eligibility ages and benefit formulae.

For the benefits calculator, we carefully distinguished the two decisions: retiring and claiming benefits.[5] Individuals may retire and immediately claim benefits; if this would have been the case, then there would not have been a need to distinguish between the two decisions. In Japan, however, some individuals continue to work, especially on a part-time basis, after initially claiming benefits, even if their benefits are reduced to the earnings test under the *Zaishoku* pension program. Hence we distinguish these two decisions and their correspondingly different impacts on the social security incentives as discussed below. We also use an income tax calculator to make the wage earnings and benefit net of income taxes applicable in each year.

For earnings profiles, we based the calculation on the following three assumptions: (a) common synthetic earnings profiles in which the slopes are the same across all the countries, (b) Japanese earnings profiles that are constant over time (based on 2016), and (c) Japanese time-specific earnings profiles. The earnings profiles (a) are based on data from the US Current Population Survey (CPS) and the German Socio-economic Panel (GSOEP). Additionally, the administrative data from the Italian pension system (INPS) contain three skill/education groups (low, median, and high) for men and women, respectively. They are scaled in such a manner that the earnings at 50 years of age are one; we scale the groups by 50 years up to median income at the age of 50 in Japan.[6]

7.3.3 Social Security Wealth, Its Accrual, and the Implicit Tax Rate

Social security wealth (SSW) is the key concept employed for gauging the tax force to retire early; SSW is the discounted value of all future social security benefits.[7] The social security benefits are calculated using the benefit formulae applied to individuals of each age in each year and their assumed earnings profiles. Discounting has the following two components: the survival probability at each age in each year and the time discount rate, which is

5. Shimizutani and Oshio (2016) analyze the determinants of pension-claiming behavior.

6. The earnings of low and high groups of men with median income aged 60 years are 86.7 percent and 137.8 percent, respectively, and the earnings of women in the same age group are 60.0 percent and 160.0 percent, respectively.

7. Refer to Stock and Wise (1990a, 1990b) for the theoretical background of the study. Additionally, refer to Gruber and Wise (1999, 2004, 2007) and Oshio, Oishi, and Shimizutani (2011) for more details on the construction of these variables.

set at 3 percent. We first computed the accrual of SSW, which is the amount of SSW accrued when postponing the benefit claim by one year. As a benchmark, we calculated this accrual of SSW, denoted by ACC, assuming that individuals claim benefits upon retirement, although they sometimes receive benefits as well as earn wage income. Postponing benefit claiming has the following three effects on ACC: it raises future benefits due to additional contributions and actuarial adjustments, it leads to a one-year loss in benefits, and it entails additional contributions, which reduces ACC on a net basis.

In this definition of ACC, we assume that individuals will choose between (i) fully retiring and claiming benefits and (ii) continuing work without receiving benefits (even if they are eligible for claiming the benefits). This assumption is not fully realistic in Japan, where individuals sometimes continue working and receiving benefits, as discussed below. However, we applied this assumption for baseline calculations for cross-country comparisons. By dividing the negative value of ACC by after-tax earnings during the additional year of work, we computed the implicit tax rate (ITAX) for claiming benefits one year later. ITAX can have both positive and negative signs, which indicate the disincentive and incentive to work. We then created the matrix of ITAX for each age and calendar year.

7.3.4 Financial Loss Due to Postponement of Claim by One Year

ITAX, which is defined above, can precisely measure social security incentives only if social security or other rules enforce the equity of the age of retirement and that of the benefit claims. In Japan, however, there is a partial retirement scheme under which individuals are entitled to receive benefits when they continue working. Under this scheme, individuals will bear both ACC and the earnings lost due to the earnings test. In the Japanese context, the latter corresponds to a reduction in benefits due to the earnings-tested *Zaishoku* pension program. The sum of the negative value of ACC and the potential earnings lost due to the earnings test indicates the financial loss, denoted by LOSS, on account of working one year longer. Subsequently, we define the relative financial loss, denoted as RFL, by dividing LOSS by after-tax earnings during the additional year of work and construct the age-year matrix of RFL. As in the case of ITAX, RFL can be both positive and negative. If RFL is higher than ITAX, then we can argue that the earnings test adds to the disincentive to work.

7.3.5 Note on Actuarial Adjustments

EPI beneficiaries can claim actuarially reduced benefits even before the statutory eligibility age, and this adjustment is expected to allow individuals to freely choose when to claim the benefit. However, the MHLW's Annual Survey of EPI and NPI Programs (2015) suggests that only a limited proportion of EPI beneficiaries claim actuarially reduced benefits, presumably because they are entitled to claim the wage-proportional benefit at the age of 60 (for men and women born on or before 1952) or 61 (for men born on or after 1953).[8]

Meanwhile, the actuarially increased benefits are expected to encourage individuals to consider a delayed benefit claim beyond the statutory eligibility age of 65 years. However, this effect is partly attenuated for those who want to continue working on a full-time basis, especially if their pension benefits are high enough to be reduced by the *Zaishoku* pension program. The actuarial increase of the wage-proportional benefit will be applied only to the portion of the pension benefit that would have been obtained after the earnings test in the *Zaishoku* pension program. In addition, the male EPI members will lose the *Kakyu Nenkin* benefit, which is entitled to be given to their wives until they become 65 years old, if they claim the actuarial increase of the wage-proportional benefit. Probably owing to these institutional reasons, the proportion of delayed claimers was negligible—that is, only 0.2 percent of all the EPI new claimers in 2015 according to the MHLW's Annual Survey of EPI and NPI Programs (2015).

Considering these institutional backgrounds and statistical facts, we did not incorporate any actuarial adjustment in the benefit calculation. This means that we incorporated changes in (i) the eligibility ages, (ii) the benefit multipliers and other benefit parameters, (iii) the *Zaishoku* pension program, (iv) the wage subsidy, and (v) the social security premiums and income tax rates.

7.4 Results

7.4.1 Tax Force to Retire Early

First, we presented a set of replacement rates, SSW, ACC, and ITAX for median-educated men in the age group of 60–64 years, which is based on the common synthetic earnings profile in figure 7.7, to provide an overview of the calculated social security incentives. The replacement rate and SSW declined steadily at all ages, reflecting the declined generosity of benefits; the replacement rate dropped from about 90 percent in the early 1980s to about 60 percent in recent years. SSW also declined from the range of ¥45–50 million to about ¥30 million during the same period (in 2015 prices). Correspondingly, the negative values of ACC as well as ITAX showed downward trends, suggesting a reduction in the tax force to retire early. The ACC and ITAX curves dropped sharply for each age every three years starting in 2001, reflecting a stepwise increase in the eligibility age of the flat-rate benefit.

8. Early benefit claims are prevalent among the NPI beneficiaries, who only receive the flat-rate benefit. However, the proportion of early claimers out of the entire new NPI claimers had been steadily declining and reached 10.9 percent in 2015. The proportion of early claimers out of the entire new EPI claimers was much lower than that, although there are no official statistics to show it.

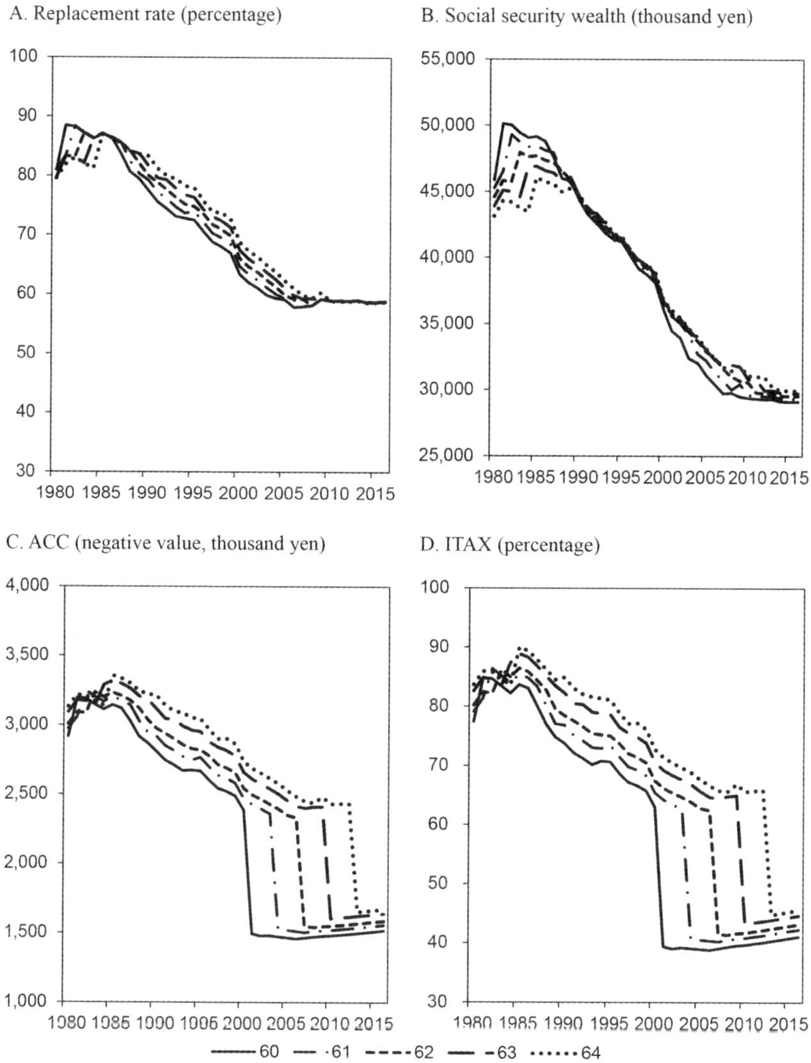

Fig. 7.7 Social security incentives at ages 60–64 for median-educated men

For example, the curve for individuals aged 61 dropped sharply in 2004. In the same year, individuals aged 61 did not lose the flat-rate benefit despite working one year longer; this is because of an increase in the eligibility age for the flat-rate benefit to age 62 in the same year. We obtained similar figures for men in the low- and high-educated groups (not presented due to space constraints). However, the replacement rates and ITAX were somewhat higher (lower) for high- (low-) educated men, reflecting the different levels of wage-proportional benefit.

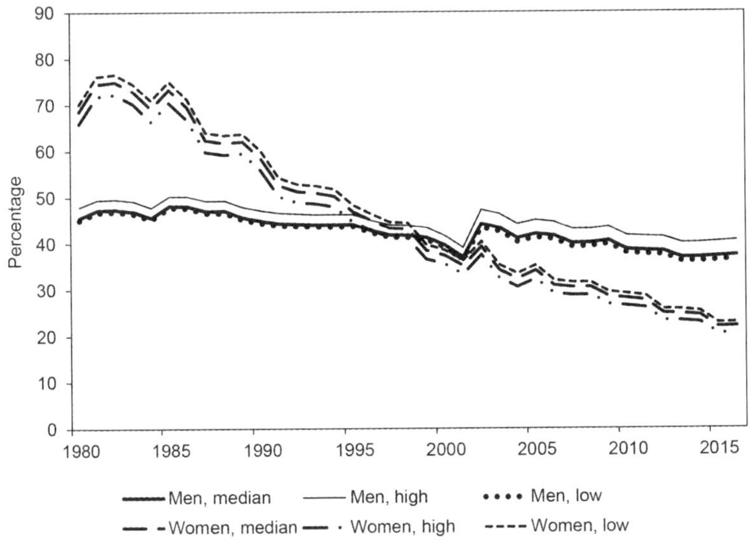

Fig. 7.8 Average ITAX over all ages for each combination of gender and educational level

The tax force to retire early can be computed at various levels of aggregation. First, we computed the average ITAX over all ages for each combination of gender and educational level, as shown in figure 7.8. For each subgroup, the ITAX curve has a downward trend, while its slope is somewhat steeper for women than for men largely due to delayed and continued increases in the eligibility ages of EPI benefits for women (from age 55 to age 60). An upward shift in 2002 reflects the resumption of the earning-tested *Zaishoku* pension program.

Second, we aggregated ITAX over the subgroups in figure 7.9. We observed different patterns of ITAX across age groups (55–59, 60–64, and 65–69 years). ITAX is the lowest for those aged 55–59, and it dropped below zero by the early 2000s, reflecting a stepwise increase in the eligibility age of the flat-rate and wage-proportional benefits for women. ITAX for this age group has been modestly negative for more than 10 years; it implies that social security programs currently encourage those below age 60 to stay in the labor force.

ITAX for those aged 60–64 has been on a downward trend since the mid-1980s, and it started dropping in 2001 in response to an increase in the eligibility age of the flat-rate benefit; each curve has two kinks reflecting a five-year interval in an increase in the eligibility age between men and women. ITAX for this age group dropped from about 70 percent in the 1980s to about 30 percent in recent years, pointing toward a substantial reduction

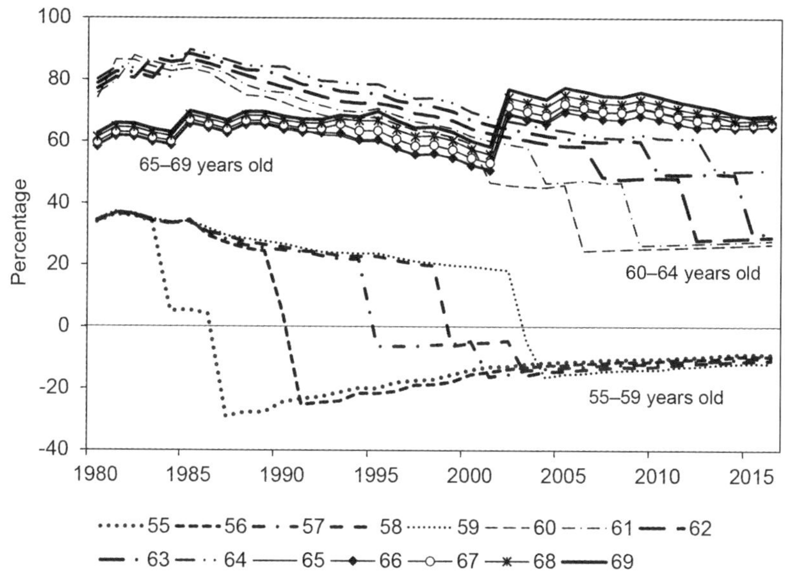

Fig. 7.9 Average ITAX over genders and educational levels

in the disincentive to work. Meanwhile, ITAX for those aged 65–69 rose modestly in 2002, reflecting the resumption of the earning-tested *Zaishoku* pension program. Thus we can argue that since the early 2000s, which is the period when the programs started raising the disincentive for those aged 65–69, social security programs have been reducing the disincentive to work for those aged 60–64.

Finally, we aggregated over genders, educational levels, and ages to observe the trend of a general measure of the tax force to retire early. The bold curve in figure 7.10 shows how ITAX aggregated for all subgroups and ages has been evolving since 1980, confirming its moderate downward trend. As already noted and confirmed in the figure, however, the trends of ITAX differs across age groups; ITAX has been declining for those aged 55–59 and 60–64 and rising for those aged 65–69.

We further compared the results between ITAX and RFL in figure 7.11, focusing on the case of median-educated men. There is no difference between the two with regards to those aged 55–59; this is because the *Zaishoku* pension program is not relevant to them. The RFL curve for those aged 60–64, deviating downward from the ITAX curve in 2005, reflects the change in the *Zaishoku* pension program that is aimed at a reduction in earnings-tested benefits. The most remarkable difference between ITAX and the RFL curve is observed for those aged 65–69. The *Zaishoku* pension program was not applied to them during 1986 and 2001, and this allowed the EPI beneficiaries

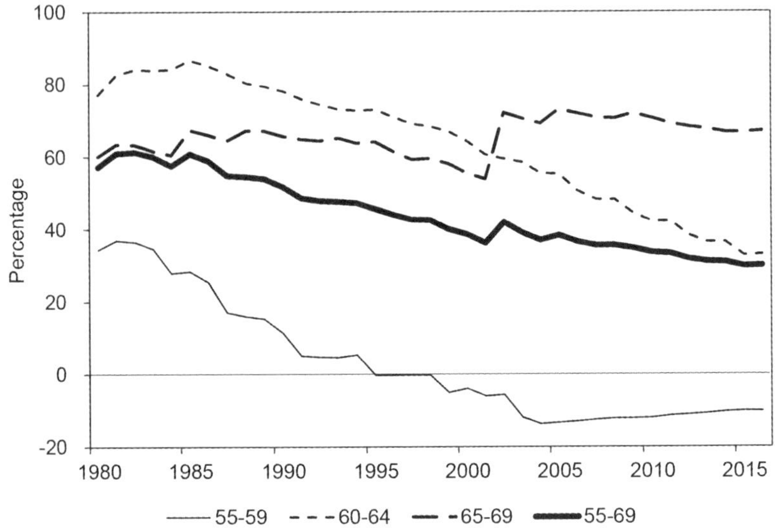

Fig. 7.10 Average ITAX over ages, genders, and educational levels

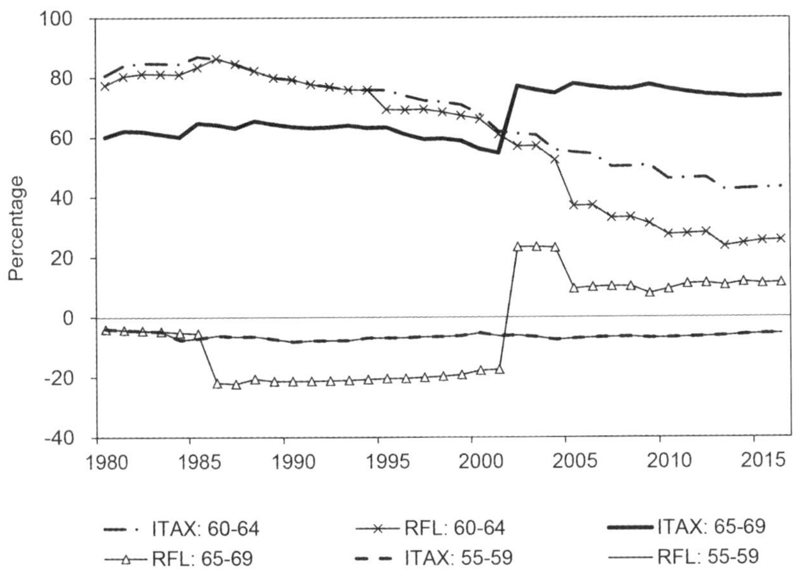

Fig. 7.11 Comparing ITAX and RFL for median-educated men

to obtain the full benefit while working. The *Zaishoku* pension program for those aged 65–69 was resumed in 2002, while the earnings test has been much limited when compared to those aged 60–64.

7.4.2 Relationship with Elderly Employment: Graphical Analysis

Based on the tax force measures obtained in the previous sections, we examined how elderly employment rates are related to social security incentives. We evaluated the tax force to retire early based on the Japanese earnings profiles, which have remained constant over time (based on 2016), to control for the cohort effect.

First, we plotted the tax force measures against the calendar year for men and women separately in figure 7.12. While the tax force has stayed somewhat below zero for men aged 55–59, it has been moving in the opposite direction between men aged 60–64 and those aged 65–69. For men aged 60–64, the tax force started dropping in 2001 and converged to around 40 percent, reflecting a stepwise increase in the flat-rate EPI benefit. Contrarily, the tax force for men aged 65–69 rose in 2002, reflecting the resumption of the earning-tested *Zaishoku* pension program."

For women aged 55–59, drops in the tax force first occurred during the late 1980s and early 2000s, and these drops started in 2006 for women aged 60–65. The former drops, which reflect increases in the eligibility ages for both flat-rate and wage-proportional benefits, are larger than the latter, which reflect stepwise increases in the eligibility age only for the flat-rate benefit. The rise in the tax force for women aged 65–69 is due to an extension of the period from which they were required to pay premiums, as in the case of men.

Subsequently, we transposed the presentation in figure 7.13 by showing the tax force against age, with different lines for the selected calendar year, for men and women. We observed that the tax force has been almost unchanged, falling, and rising for men aged 55–59, 60–64, and 65–69, respectively, in line with the results in figure 7.12. For women, the drop in ITAX was most remarkable for those aged 55–59, followed by those aged 60–64, while it was largely unchanged for those aged 65–69.

It is useful to have an overview of the trends of the employment rates separately for men and women in figure 7.1 before examining the association between the tax force to retire early and the employment rates. We observed that the employment rates for men aged 55–59 and 60–64 started recovering around 2005, while their recoveries were made obscure by the changes in the macroeconomic conditions during 1990 and 2000, when the economy experienced a long recession after the burst of the economic bubble. Contrarily, the employment rates for men aged 50–59 remained above 90 percent during the study period. For women, the employment rates show clearer upward trends for all three age groups, with the increase accelerating around 2005.

We plotted the dots connecting the employment rate and ITAX in each

A. Men

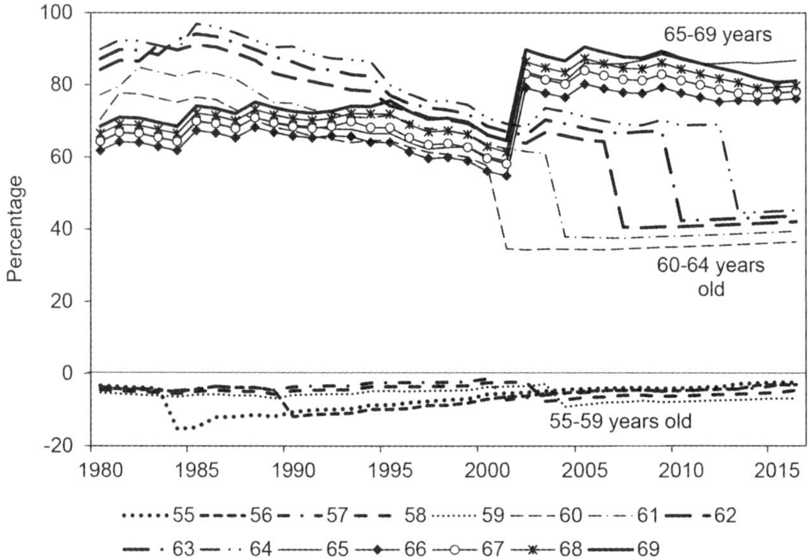

B. Women

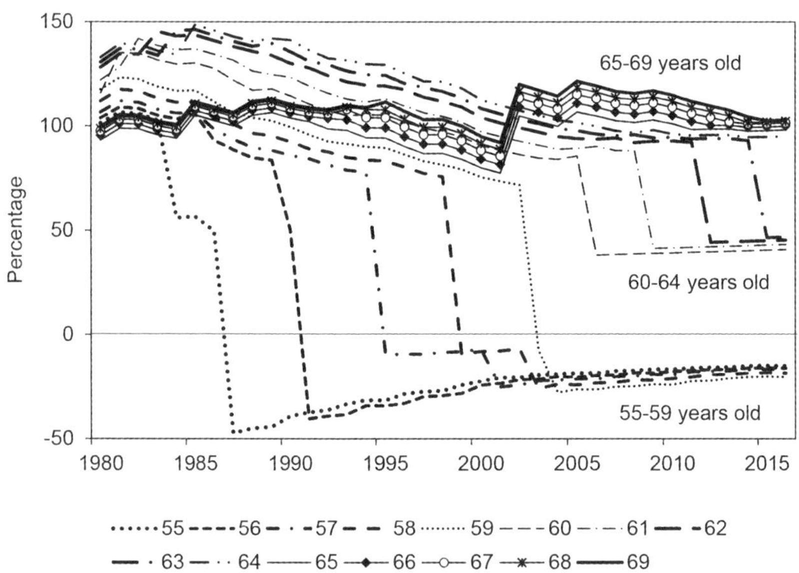

Fig. 7.12 Evolution of ITAX against year at different ages, using Japanese earnings profile in 2016

A. Men

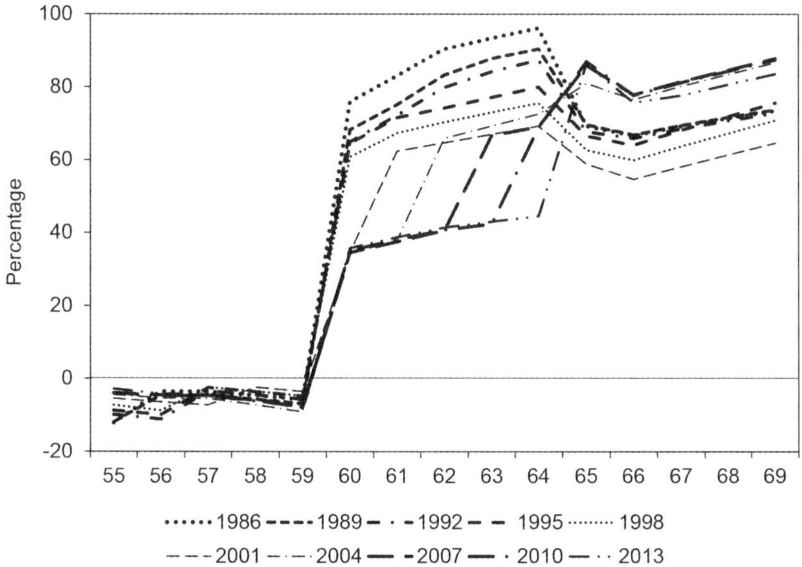

B. Women

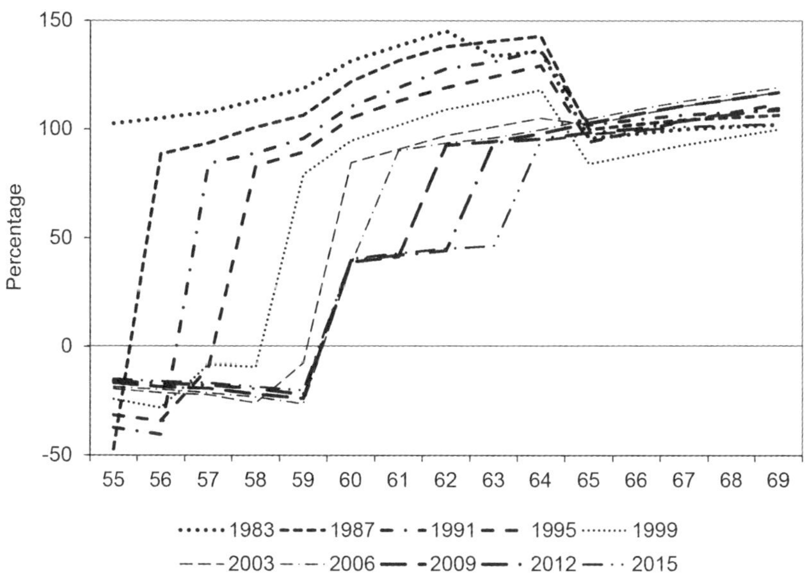

Fig. 7.13 Evolution of ITAX against age in different years, using Japanese earnings profile in 2016

A. Aged 60–64

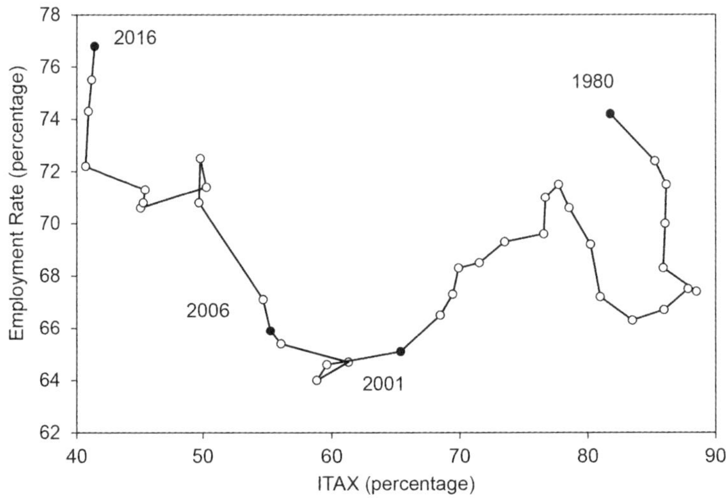

B. Aged 65–69

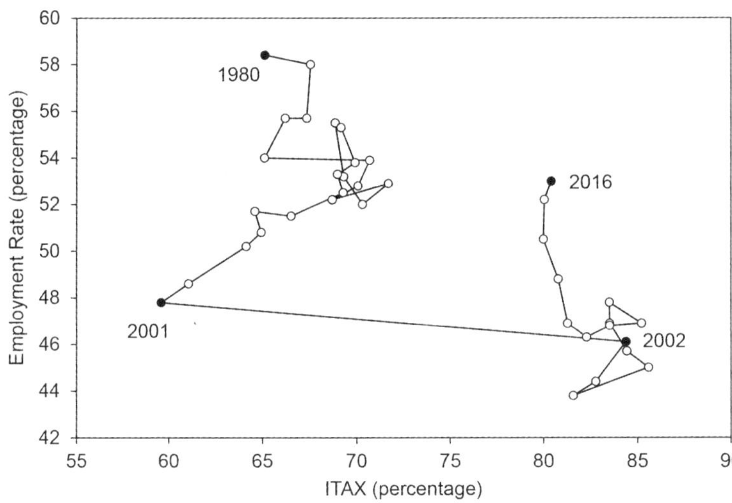

Fig. 7.14 The evolution of a combination of ITAX and the employment rate: men

year for selected age groups for men and women in figures 7.14 and 7.15, respectively. A cursory glance does not show a clear relationship between the employment rate and ITAX for men aged 60–64. While ITAX declined during most of the period between 1980 and 2016, the employment rate curve showed a positive association with the ITAX curve during the mid-1990s and the mid-2000s. However, the curve depicted a negative slope after the mid-2000s, prob-

A. Aged 55–59

B. Aged 60–64

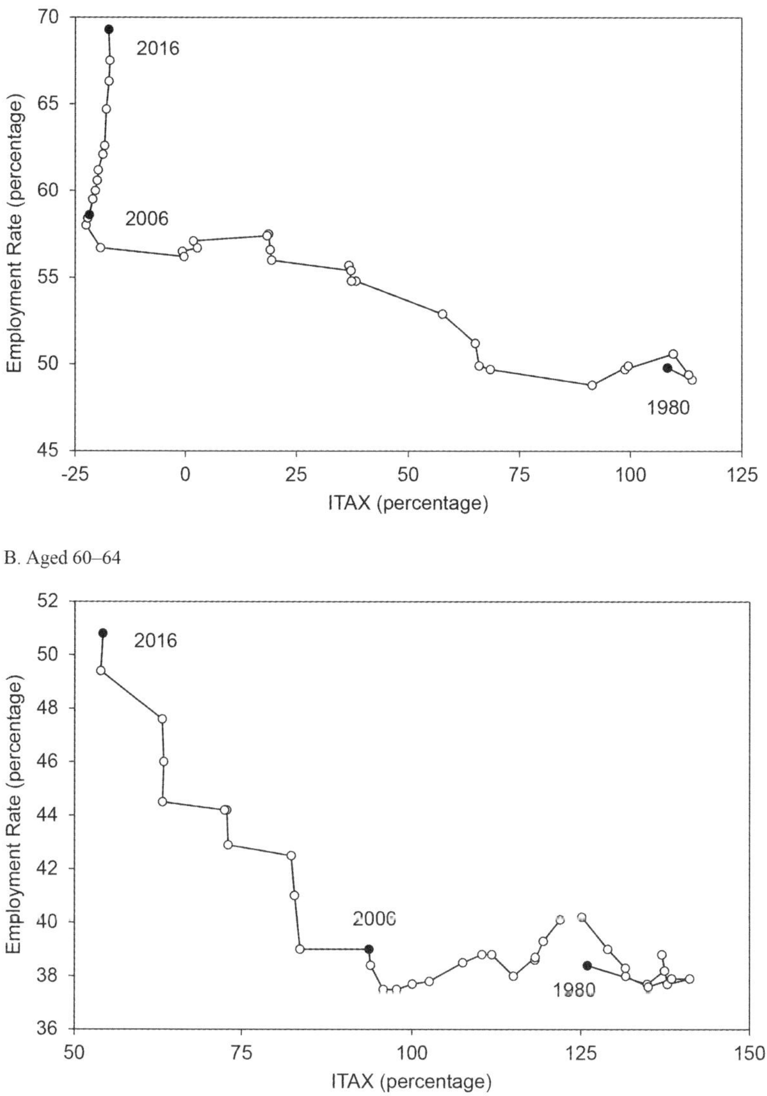

Fig. 7.15 The evolution of a combination of ITAX and the employment rate: women

ably reflecting a rise in the eligibility age for the flat-rate benefit and the enactment of the revised EESL, which required firms to completely abolish the mandatory retirement age or raise it to 65 years. For men aged 65–69, a sharp increase in ITAX in 2002, reflecting the resumption of the earning-tested *Zaishoku* pension program, shifted the combinations of ITAX and employment to the right. After this shift, a negative association between the two variables was observed.

In sharp contrast to men, women's employment rates indicated a clear negative association with ITAX for women in aged 55–59 and 60–64. Notably, in the mid-2000s, the employment rates for women aged 60–64 started rising, and they soared for women aged 55–59.[9]

7.4.3 Relationship with Elderly Employment: Simple Regression Analysis

To examine the association between ITAX and the employment rates for each of the four groups chosen in figure 7.14, we estimated simple regression models using the actual earnings profiles in Japan. Model 1 just regresses ITAX on the employment rate. Model 2 adds the industrial production index (2010 = 100) as a regressor to model 1 to control for the macroeconomic conditions. Model 3 further adds the employment rate, which was prevalent five years ago, of the age group in figure 7.13 as a regressor to control for its previous work/retirement decision.

Table 7.1 provides the estimation results. We observed a negative association between ITAX and employment rate only for men aged 65–69 in model 1. The addition of the industrial production index as a regressor in model 2 also showed a negative association for men aged 60–64, suggesting that the macroeconomic conditions make their association unclear. When the five-year lagged employment rate in model 3 was further added, the association remained negative and significant. A 1 percentage point increase in ITAX corresponds to a 0.21–0.26 percentage point decrease in the employment for men aged 60–64 and 65–69. For men aged 60–64, ITAX declined by around 40 percent during 1985 and 2016, implying that the change in the social security incentives raised the employment rate by about 8 percentage points during that period. This might have contributed to the recovery of the employment rate for this age group. For those aged 65–69, the ITAX jumped in 2002, and it might have had a negative impact on employment. A modest increase in the employment rate since mid-2005 seems to have been accounted for by other factors, including the cyclical recovery of the economy and the cohort effect, reflecting higher employment rates for those at younger ages.

For women, we observed a negative association between ITAX and the employment rate for those aged 55–59 and 60–64 even in model 1, and it is confirmed in Models 2 and 3. The impact of ITAX on the employment rate is 0.05–0.25 percentage points for those subgroups; notably, the magnitude of the association for those aged 60–64 is similar to those of men in the same age group.

By replacing ITAX with RFL, we obtained largely similar results, as presented in table 7.2. The employment rate is negatively associated with RFL

9. We do not depict the figures of men aged 55–59 years or women aged 65–69 years, whose employment rates do not bear any apparent relation to ITAX.

Table 7.1 **Regression results: Explaining employment rates by ITAX**

	Men						Women					
	Model 1		Model 2		Model 3		Model 1		Model 2		Model 3	
	Coeff.	(SE)	Coeff.	(SE)	Coeff.	(SE)	Coeff.	(SE)	Coeff.	(SE)	Coeff.	(SE)
55–59												
ITAX	−0.133	(0.288)	0.074	(0.232)	−0.151	(0.297)	−0.098***	(0.010)	−0.124***	(0.014)	−0.046***	(0.010)
Industrial production			0.092***	(0.020)	0.113**	(0.035)			−0.151*	(0.059)	0.003	(0.037)
Employment rate (5-year lag)					0.121	(0.402)					0.534***	(0.049)
Adj. R-squared	−0.022		0.360		0.223		0.738		0.774		0.941	
60–64												
ITAX	−0.058	(0.031)	−0.106**	(0.033)	−0.211***	(0.024)	−0.105***	(0.013)	−0.120***	(0.013)	−0.253***	(0.042)
Industrial production			−0.141**	(0.048)	0.013	(0.044)			−0.079*	(0.033)	−0.101*	(0.046)
Employment rate (5-year lag)					−2.114***	(0.275)					−0.843**	(0.256)
Adj. R-squared	0.063		0.230		0.734		0.653		0.695		0.763	
65–69												
ITAX	−0.320***	(0.060)	−0.253***	(0.055)	−0.256***	(0.062)	−0.066*	(0.030)	−0.052	(0.030)	−0.061	(0.033)
Industrial production			−0.147***	(0.040)	−0.110	(0.074)			−0.037*	(0.018)	−0.038	(0.032)
Employment rate (5-year lag)					−0.114	(0.269)					−0.115	(0.115)
Adj. R-squared	0.430		0.578		0.368		0.093		0.172		0.066	

Note: $n = 32$ for each subgroup; *** $p < 0.001$, ** $p < 0.01$, * $p < 0.05$.

Table 7.2 **Regression results: Explaining employment rates by RFL**

	Men						Women					
	Model 1		Model 2		Model 3		Model 1		Model 2		Model 3	
	Coeff.	(SE)	Coeff.	(SE)	Coeff.	(SE)	Coeff.	(SE)	Coeff.	(SE)	Coeff.	(SE)
55–59												
RFL	−0.133	(0.288)	0.074	(0.232)	−0.151	(0.297)	−0.098***	(0.010)	−0.124***	(0.014)	−0.046***	(0.010)
Industrial production			0.092***	(0.020)	0.113**	(0.035)			−0.151*	(0.059)	0.003	(0.037)
Employment rate (5-year lag)					0.121	(0.402)					0.534***	(0.049)
Adj. R-squared	−0.022		0.360		0.223		0.738		0.774		0.941	
60–64												
RFL	−0.041*	(0.020)	−0.068**	(0.020)	−0.130***	(0.015)	−0.064***	(0.009)	−0.079***	(0.009)	−0.124***	(0.029)
Industrial production			−0.135**	(0.047)	0.018	(0.044)			−0.106**	(0.036)	−0.139*	(0.055)
Employment rate (5-year lag)					−2.065***	(0.270)					−0.413	(0.257)
Adj. R-squared	0.084		0.244		0.736		0.587		0.660		0.674	
65–69												
RFL	−0.143***	(0.036)	−0.137***	(0.026)	−0.142***	(0.026)	−0.057***	(0.009)	−0.054***	(0.009)	−0.077***	(0.009)
Industrial production			−0.201***	(0.036)	−0.076	(0.066)			−0.035**	(0.013)	−0.013	(0.018)
Employment rate (5-year lag)					0.128	(0.229)					−0.317***	(0.076)
Adj. R-squared	0.295		0.622		0.507		0.498		0.580		0.714	

Note: $n = 32$ for each subgroup. *** $p < 0.001$, ** $p < 0.01$, * $p < 0.05$.

for men aged 60–64 and 65–69 and women aged 55–59 and 60–64, although the magnitudes of their associations and the goodness of fit are somewhat lower when compared to ITAX, and the associations become significant for women aged 65–69 as well.

7.5 Concluding Remarks

We examined how the change in the trend of elderly labor force participation has been associated with changes in incentives of social security and its related programs in Japan. Our results support the view that the recovery of labor force participation of the elderly has been at least partially accounted for by a reduction in the tax force to retire early due to a series of social security reforms, although the macroeconomic conditions tend to make their association obscure. Our results suggest that reducing the tax force to retire early would help alleviate pressures from the aging population and enhance the sustainability of the social security programs.

References

Abe, Y. 2001. "Employees' Pension Benefits and the Labor Supply of Older Japanese Workers, 1980s–1990s." In *Aging Issues in the United States and Japan*, edited by S. Ogura, T. Tachibanaki, and D. Wise, 273–305. Chicago: University of Chicago Press.

Gruber, J., and D. A. Wise, eds. 1999. *Social Security and Retirement around the World*. Chicago: University of Chicago Press.

Gruber, J., and D. A. Wise, eds. 2004. *Social Security Programs and Retirement around the World: Micro-estimation*. Chicago: University of Chicago Press.

Gruber, J., and D. A. Wise, eds. 2007. *Social Security Programs and Retirement around the World: Fiscal Implications of Reform*. Chicago: University of Chicago Press.

Kondo, A., and H. Shigeoka. 2017. "The Effectiveness of Demand-Side Government Intervention to Promote Elderly Employment: Evidence from Japan." *ILR Review* 70 (4): 1008–36.

Oshio, T., A. S. Oishi, and S. Shimizutani. 2011. "Social Security Reforms and Labour Force Participation of the Elderly in Japan." *Japanese Economic Review* 62 (2): 248–71.

Shimizutani, S., and T. Oshio. 2013. "Revisiting the Labor Supply Effect of Social Security Earnings Test: New Evidence from Its Elimination and Reinstatement in Japan." *Japan and the World Economy* 28:99–111.

Shimizutani, S., and T. Oshio. 2016. "Public Pension Benefits Claiming Behavior: New Evidence from the Japanese Study on Aging and Retirement." *Japanese Economic Review* 67 (3): 235–56.

Stock, J. H., and D. A. Wise. 1990a. "Pensions, the Option Value of Work, and Retirement." *Econometrica* 58 (5): 1151–80.

Stock, J. H., and D. A. Wise. 1990b. "The Pension Inducement to Retire." In *Issues in the Economics of Aging*, edited by D. A. Wise, 205–29. Chicago: University of Chicago Press.

Takayama, N., ed. 2005. *Pensions in Asia: Incentives, Compliance and Their Role in Retirement*. Tokyo: Maruzen.

8

Social Security Programs and Employment at Older Ages in the Netherlands

Klaas de Vos, Arie Kapteyn, and Adriaan Kalwij

8.1 Introduction

The rising labor force participation at older ages since the mid-1990s in the Netherlands has been attributed to, among other factors, older workers' improved health, increased levels of education and better-matched skills with labor demand, and changes in social security programs[1] such as disability insurance, unemployment insurance, and early retirement schemes (Kalwij, Kapteyn, and de Vos 2017). Kapteyn and de Vos (1999) have investigated the role of financial incentives induced by early retirement schemes in the decline in labor force participation during the 1980s and early 1990s in the Netherlands. This chapter expands on this study by examining the eligibility criteria and the generosity of the different social security programs from 1980 until 2016 and the changes during this period in the implicit tax rates on working longer at older ages induced by these programs. In addition, our chapter examines the importance of the state pension age (SPA) for working longer.

The outline of this chapter is as follows. Section 8.2 discusses institutional changes in social security over the last decades. Section 8.3 presents for each

Klaas de Vos is a researcher in the quantitative analysis department at CentERdata.

Arie Kapteyn is a professor of economics and director of the Center for Economic and Social Research at the University of Southern California and a research associate of the National Bureau of Economic Research.

Adriaan Kalwij is an associate professor at the Utrecht University School of Economics.

For acknowledgments, sources of research support, and disclosure of the authors' material financial relationships, if any, please see https://www.nber.org/chapters/c14198.ack.

1. Social security programs (SSPs) encompass state pension (SP), disability insurance (DI), unemployment insurance (UI), social assistance (SA), and other public transfer programs available at older ages, such as tax exemptions for early retirement (ER) pensions until 2006 and private pensions from the state pension age (SPA) onward.

of the most pertinent social security programs (SSPs) the implicit tax rates on working longer conditional on being eligible for them. Next, section 8.4 presents employment and SSPs' participation rates. Graphical evidence is provided using a cohort perspective on how labor force participation at older ages might have been affected by the introduction and reforms of SSPs. In addition, empirical evidence is presented on the effect of recent changes in the statutory state pension age (SPA) on working longer. Section 8.6 concludes.

8.2 Description of Institutional Changes

Table 8.1 provides an overview of the most important reforms over the last decades of the state pension (SP), unemployment insurance (UI), disability insurance (DI), early retirement (ER), and private/occupational pension (PP) schemes.

UI, DI, and ER are available for workers before the state pension age. After the state pension age (SPA), individuals can no longer receive benefits from these schemes and receive a flat-rate public pension benefit. Hence after the SPA, all individuals are covered by the SP scheme. The PP schemes often have two regimes: providing early retirement pensions before the SPA and providing private pensions after the SPA. The pensions to be received may vary depending on the PP/ER schemes in which the worker is enrolled. These PP/ER schemes can be occupation, firm, or sector specific.

8.2.1 State Pension (SP)

The flat-rate state pension (SP) is financed by pay-as-you-go social insurance contributions. By and large, since 1974, the flat-rate state pension is indexed by the after-tax minimum wage. Revisions have included the introduction of an independent pension entitlement for married women in 1985[2] and an entitlement to supplementary state pension benefits for persons with a spouse younger than 65 (1985; revised 1994; abolished in 2015). As of 2013, the state pension age, which had been 65 from the start, has been increasing gradually. The state pension age will reach 67 in 2021. After 2021, it will increase further, following the average increase in life expectancy.

8.2.2 Early Retirement (ER)

ER was introduced in most sectors of the economy during the 1970s. In most cases, it entailed an offer too good to refuse at least until the end of the 1990s. The ER benefit usually amounted to 80 percent of previous earnings without actuarial adjustment for later take-up. It lasted until the state pension age, when state pension and occupational/private pensions kicked in. The prospect of exploding costs once the large baby boom cohorts started

2. Before 1985, only the husband in a married couple was entitled to the state pension.

Table 8.1 **Timeline reforms to state pension (SP), disability insurance (DI), unemployment insurance (UI), and early retirement (ER) and occupational pension (PP)**

	SP (flat rate, age 65)	ER, PP	DI / (long-term) sickness insurance	UI
Until 1980	1957: State pension replaces earlier emergency benefit 1974: Benefit raised and linked to net minimum wage	1975–82: Gradual introduction of ER by sector/firm/department	1967: Introduction of DI (20,000 beneficiaries expected)	1949: Introduction of UI
1980		ER contribution tax deductible		
1985	Married women get independent claim Earnings tested supplement when partner is younger than 65		764,000 beneficiaries; replacement rate reduced from 80 to 70 percent	UI: Replacement rate reduced to 70 percent
1987	SP: Distinction between married and cohabiting couples abolished SP: Introduction single-parent allowance		No more (full) DI for (partially) unemployed	UI: Changes in eligibility and benefit period Earnings-related benefit followed by continuation benefit
1991				UI: Eligibility revised
1993			(i) Persons younger than 50 receive DI for a limited period (ii) Stricter disability criteria (iii) Retesting of younger DI recipients	
1994	SP: Earnings-tested partner supplement adapted		Introducing employer-paid periods of sickness (2–6 weeks)	
1995				UI: Eligibility revised; introduction short-term benefit
1996			(i) Sickness benefit privatized: employer pays 70 percent of earnings (1 year) (ii) Exemptions for earnings tested supplement abolished	
1998			(i) Introduction of (limited) experience rating DI contributions employer (ii) Public employees included in DI	

(continued)

Table 8.1 **(continued)**

	SP (flat rate, age 65)	ER, PP	DI / (long-term) sickness insurance	UI
2000–2005		ER/PP: Trend toward actuarially fairer flexible ER age including options for partial retirement Entitlement based on average wage instead of final wage		
2001				UI: Public employees included
2002			Stricter reintegration rules in case of sickness	
2003			Experience rating for small employers abolished	UI: Abolition of continuation benefit
2004			(i) Sickness benefit period extended to 2 years (ii) Strict reevaluation DI recipients younger than 50	UI: Persons aged 57.5+ have to apply for jobs
2006		ER: Fiscal-friendly treatment of ER contributions repealed	Introduction of new DI: strict distinction between partially and fully, permanently disabled	UI: benefit period shortened; higher benefit first two months
2008			Experience rating DI abolished	
2013				UI: Employment period calculation revised
2013–	SP: Gradual increase in SP age			
2015–	Partner <65 supplement abolished			
2016–				UI: Gradual shortening of benefit period

Source: Kroniek van de sociale verzekeringen 2008, http://www.uwv.nl

to reach the ER age led to reforms by the end of the 1990s. In most cases, a reduction of the ER benefit was combined with the introduction of more or less actuarially fair adjustments for the age at which one would take early retirement. As a result, the employee could still opt for retiring early, but with a reduced pension. By 2006, the government terminated the tax exemption for ER contributions that would enable a retirement age lower than 65. Only systems offering a replacement rate of at most 70 percent of previous earnings at the state pension age of 65 and actuarially fair reductions for early claiming could still collect tax-exempt contributions.

8.2.3 Occupational/Private Pensions (PP)

In addition to the state pension, most employees accumulate fully funded occupational pension rights and supplement their state pension to (ideally) 70 percent of previous earnings. Participation in PP schemes is mostly mandatory. Pension funds, operating by sector and, in a number of cases, by firm invest the pension contributions, which are usually shared by the employer and employee. Since the early 2000s, pension funds have started to reduce the generosity of occupational pensions by shifting from benefits based on final earnings to benefits based on average earnings. Moreover, in general, the indexation of benefits, which used to be based on the wage index, has become less generous following successive stock market downturns, affecting the investment returns of pension funds. Some pension funds had to reduce the pension benefits in nominal terms (Kalwij, Alessie, Gardner, and Ali 2018).

8.2.4 Disability Insurance (DI)

Introduced in 1967, the Dutch DI aimed to insure employees against loss of earnings as a result of long-term illness or incapacity. If after one year of illness the employee could not resume work, he or she would be entitled to an earnings-related DI benefit that could last until the state pension age.

Starting in the 1970s, the number of individuals on DI showed a steady increase until the 1990s, much more than expected when the DI legislation was introduced and much more than could be expected given the average health status of the population. In fact, with unemployment rising fast in the mid-1970s, the route to DI was generally used by employers and employees as an alternative to unemployment. As a result, expenditures on DI soared. Since the start of the 1980s, government policy has sought to reverse this trend by various reforms to limit access to DI, increase outflow out of DI, and lower the average DI benefit. In 1985, the replacement rate of DI was lowered from 80 percent to 70 percent. In 1987, access to the full DI was limited for partially disabled unemployed new entrants. In the early 1990s, the duration of the full DI benefit was limited for new entrants younger than 50, stricter disability criteria were introduced for entry into DI, and younger DI recipients were to be retested. Still, mainly because most employees took out private insurance to compensate for the shorter duration, DI remained an attractive option.

Next to limiting the access and the generosity of the benefit, policies were also introduced to shift the costs to firms with high numbers of employees exiting to DI. First, the costs of sickness benefits were charged directly to the employer for two to six weeks (1994) and later on for a full year preceding the exit to DI, and second, in 1998, experience rating was introduced for large firms. All these reforms did not succeed in substantially reducing the number of DI recipients, however. As a result, as of 2002, employers and employees were made jointly responsible for taking sufficient action for reintegration into the workforce during the year of sickness preceding exit to DI. Moreover, this sickness period could be extended if insufficient reintegration measures were taken. As of 2004, exit to DI only happened after two years of sickness, during which time the employer paid sickness benefits. As of 2006, a new DI law made a strict distinction between fully and permanently disabled and partially or temporarily disabled workers. The former group was to receive a generous 75 percent of their previous earnings until the state pension age. The latter group would receive a less generous benefit depending on previous earnings, the number of weeks worked before, and the current earnings (if any) and the percentage of previous earnings that the employee was deemed to be capable of earning. Furthermore, once again a retest operation was set up for existing DI beneficiaries younger than 50.

8.2.5 Unemployment Insurance (UI)

For workers approaching 60 who were not entitled to ER and who could not plausibly retire via DI, unemployment insurance (UI) offered a third pathway out of the labor force before the state pension age. In most cases, it offered a replacement rate of 70 percent, and furthermore, no obligation existed to search for employment after the age of 57.5. As of 2004, persons aged 57.5 or older receiving UI are no longer exempt from the requirement to seek work. In other words, they are no longer "automatically" receiving UI until the state pension age but have to try to find work and accept a job offer. Moreover, as of October 1, 2006, the maximum duration of UI is 38 months. After that period, all that is left is a means-tested entitlement to social assistance (SA) with a benefit equal to the after-tax minimum wage.

8.3 Stylized Implicit Tax Rates

For workers eligible for one or more retirement pathways, some of the reforms discussed in the previous section heavily affect the financial incentives to retire. Other reforms only affect eligibility while, given eligibility, financial incentives are hardly affected. One convenient incentive measure that adequately summarizes the monetary effect of retiring now compared to postponing it one more year is the implicit tax rate on work, defined as

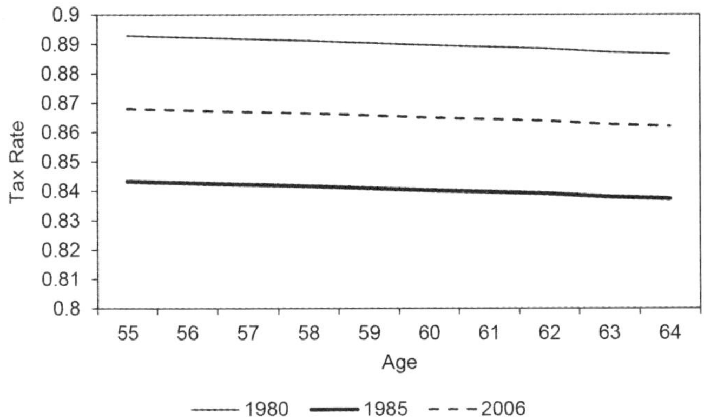

Fig. 8.1 Implicit tax rates for Disability Insurance (conditional on eligibility)
Note: We assume for the 2006 series that the shortening (in 1993) of the duration of income replacement benefits to three years at the ages under 58 and to six years from age 58 onward is fully insured away. That is, effectively DI recipients receive a 75 percent replacement of their income until SPA.

the difference between the discounted future benefits when retiring now or one year later divided by the yearly earnings.[3] A positive implicit tax rate is an incentive to retire now, and a negative implicit tax rate is an incentive to postpone retirement.

Figures 8.1 through 8.4 present stylized implicit tax rates for average-waged workers eligible for, respectively, DI, UI, ER/PP, and SP for selected years between 1980 and 2015. All tax rates are conditional on eligibility. As mentioned above, various reforms have been attempted to limit the number of workers eligible for DI, of which the most recent appears to have been the most successful. Figure 8.1 shows that for those eligible, the incentives have not changed very much between 1980 and 2006. With an implicit tax rate on continued work of 80 to 90 percent, the financial incentive to retire via the DI channel remains strong. In other words, once eligible, the implicit tax rate suggests that retiring via the DI pathway is a financially attractive proposition.

From figure 8.2 we can infer that from 1987 to 2004, the implicit tax rate on postponing retirement via the UI pathway was also positive, at least for persons aged 58 and over. However, the tax rates are clearly lower than for the DI pathway.

Figure 8.3 suggests that for workers eligible for ER at age 60, until recently, postponing retirement from age 59 until age 60 would have been a very smart

3. Notably, the stylized implicit tax rates presented in this chapter divide the difference between future discounted after-tax benefits (net Social Security Wealth) when retiring now and one year later by annual after-tax earnings. The payroll taxes on earnings incurred when retiring one year later are not deducted from the future benefits.

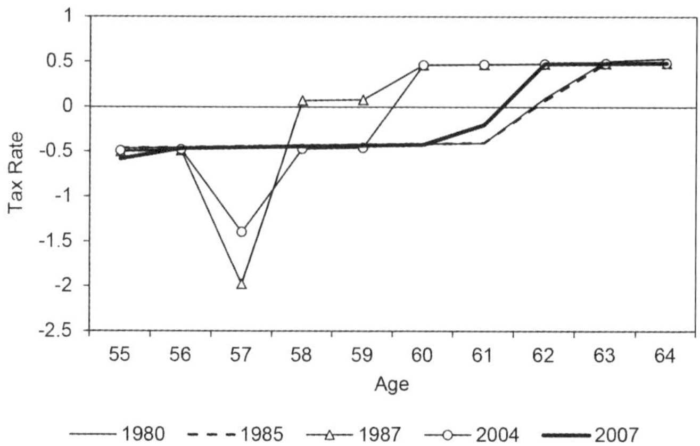

Fig. 8.2 Implicit tax rates for Unemployment Insurance (conditional on eligibility)

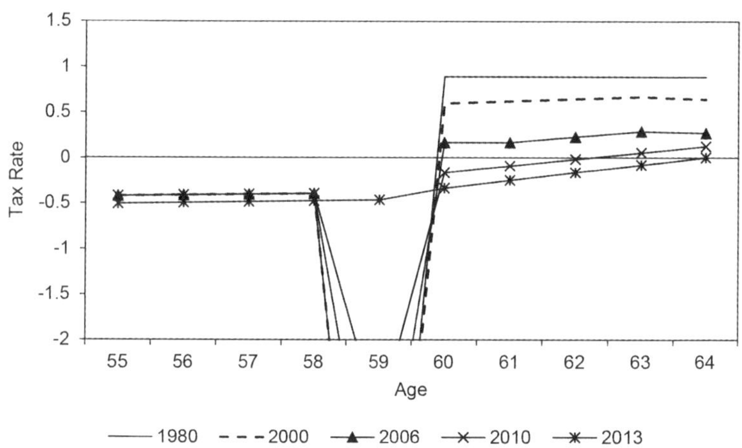

Fig. 8.3 Implicit tax rates for Early Retirement (conditional on eligibility)

Note: We assume eligibility at age 60. Eligibility age varies across pension funds and over time within about the age range 58-62.

decision from a financial standpoint because the potential retiree would lose all entitlements to ER benefits if he or she would retire earlier. On the other hand, postponing retirement after age 60 was not very attractive, because there used to be hardly any actuarial compensation for retiring later than the earliest possible retirement age. Only recently, an actuarially fair compensation is being offered for postponing retirement. As a result, this no longer has a negative impact on social security wealth (SSW). In addition, the negative tax rate on postponing retirement from age 59 to age 60 has also disappeared, since eligibility for early retirement no longer depends on being employed. Notably, while some large pension funds offered ER as of

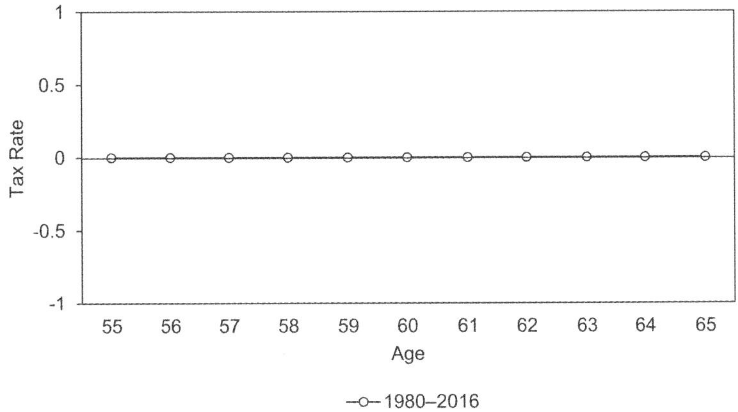

Fig. 8.4 Implicit tax rates for State Pension (SPA = 65 years)

age 60, others had an early retirement age (ERA) of 61 or 62, and figure 8.3 would shift accordingly.

Figure 8.4 shows that for persons who are only eligible for the state pension, SSW is not affected by the retirement date. These workers would receive the same state pension starting from the statutory state pension age, no matter at which age they would choose to retire.

It is clear that these incentives differ considerably depending on the pathways a potential retiree is eligible for. Unfortunately, data that allow us to obtain a reliable estimate of the effects of these incentives at the individual level, taking account of the possible eligibility for various pathways, are not available. For the DI pathway, the problem is that eligibility can only be inferred for persons taking up DI. However, not taking up DI does not necessarily imply not being eligible. For many retirees, the ER/SP pathway would be financially more attractive, and by taking this pathway, they would also avoid the possible stigma associated with retiring via DI. In addition, despite the fact that there is a positive tax on working associated with postponing retirement via DI, the net replacement rate is still below 100 percent.

The incentives associated with the ER/SP pathway depend on the specific program (pension fund) in which the potential retiree is enrolled. This determines the early retirement age, the replacement rate, the actuarial adjustment (if any), and/or the date at which actuarial adjustment was introduced. The exact conditions also depend on possible membership in other pension funds in earlier years as well as on previous earnings.

8.4 Labor Force Participation

The fall in men's employment rates at older ages from the mid-1970s until the mid-1990s in the Netherlands and the rise in employment rates there-

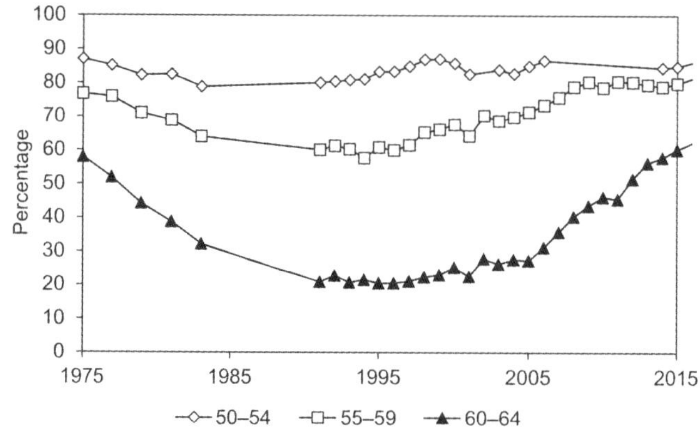

Fig. 8.5 Men's employment rate

Source: Statistics Netherlands, Labor Force Survey (Enquête Beroepsbevolking; EBB)

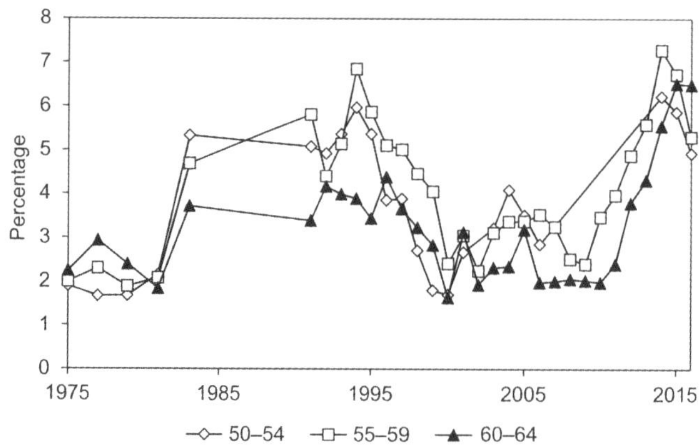

Fig. 8.6 Men's unemployment rate

Note: The unemployment rate includes individuals on unemployment insurance and social assistance.

Source: Statistics Netherlands, Labor Force Survey (Enquête Beroepsbevolking; EBB)

after (see figure 8.5) have, in part, been attributed to SSP reforms (Kalwij, Kapteyn, and de Vos 2017; and reference therein).

Figure 8.6 shows men's unemployment rates, including individuals who receive unemployment insurance benefits and social assistance, from 1975 onward. Figures 8.7 and 8.8 show men's participation in DI and ER programs from 1975 onward. DI participation decreased during the 1980s, possibly due to better health of older workers and increasing participation in early retirement schemes (figure 8.7) and perhaps due to some minor DI reforms, such as a reduction in the replacement rate from 80 percent to 70 percent (table 8.1). Until the mid-1990s, ER participation increased

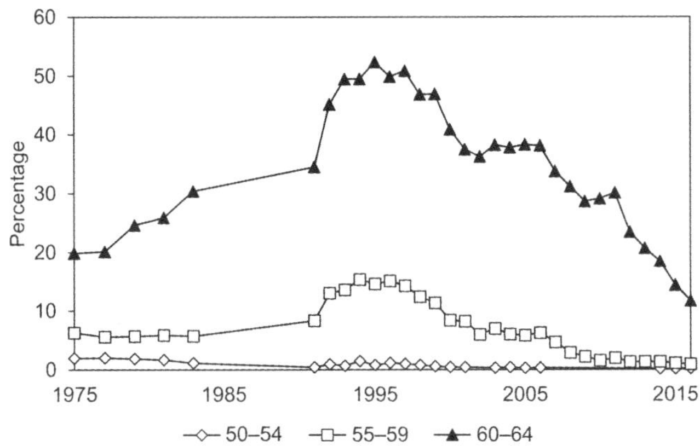

Fig. 8.7 Men's early retirement rate
Source: Statistics Netherlands, Labor Force Survey (Enquête Beroepsbevolking; EBB)

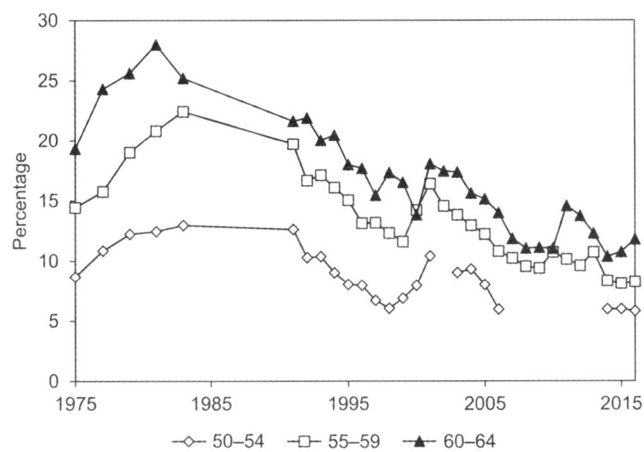

Fig. 8.8 Men's disability insurance rate
Source: Statistics Netherlands, Labor Force Survey (Enquête Beroepsbevolking; EBB)

(figure 8.7), most likely due to the implicit taxes on continuing work once eligible (figure 8.3). In addition, the sharp rise in ER participation during the first half of the 1990s may also be related to more stringent eligibility criteria for DI and UI (table 8.1). Together with rising unemployment rates, employment rates continued to decrease until the mid-1990s.

Since the mid-1990s, there have been a vast number of SSP reforms aimed at individuals working longer, which made it more difficult or less attractive for individuals to go on DI or UI or retire early (table 8.1). Figures 8.5–8.8 suggest that these reforms have been effective, but it is difficult to pinpoint which reforms have been most effective.

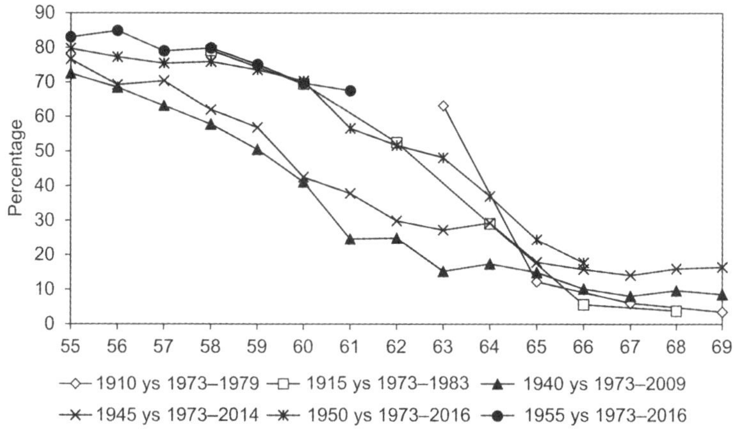

Fig. 8.9 Cohort specific age profiles (ages 55–69) of employment rates
Source: Statistics Netherlands, Labor Force Survey (Enquête Beroepsbevolking; EBB)

8.4.1 A Cohort Perspective

Different cohorts have faced different retirement incentives through the various pathways over their lifetimes. This may have resulted in different age profiles of employment rates across cohorts. Indeed, figure 8.9 shows this for the employment rates for men aged 55 to 69 for the cohorts born in 1910, 1915, 1940, 1945, 1950, and 1955. The three generations considered here were or are facing different social security programs over their life course (table 8.1). The old (1910 and 1915 cohorts) faced less-generous social security provisions, especially in the years when most SSPs were not yet in place; the young (1950 and 1955 cohorts) face stricter eligibility rules and less-generous benefits than the cohorts in between (the 1940 and 1945 cohorts). The employment rates in the figure mirror these lifetime differences in SSPs; compared to the young and old generation, the in-between generations who enjoyed a relatively more generous or accessible SSPs over their life course have the lowest employment rates at older ages. If we look at 60-year-old individuals, we see that in 1975, before the introduction of ER, their participation rate was 70 percent, while in 2000 and 2005 their participation rate was only 40 percent. In 2010 and 2015, the participation rate of 60-year-old individuals was back to 70 percent. The participation rates for 60- to 63-year-old individuals show a similar trajectory. These numbers suggest that the eligibility and generosity of SSPs are important for the decision whether or not to remain employed at older ages.

Figure 8.10 shows participation rates in the different SSPs for three groups of cohorts. Due to low numbers of observations, cohort years needed to be aggregated. We followed the same approach as above and only present it for selected cohort groups that we a priori believe to have faced rather

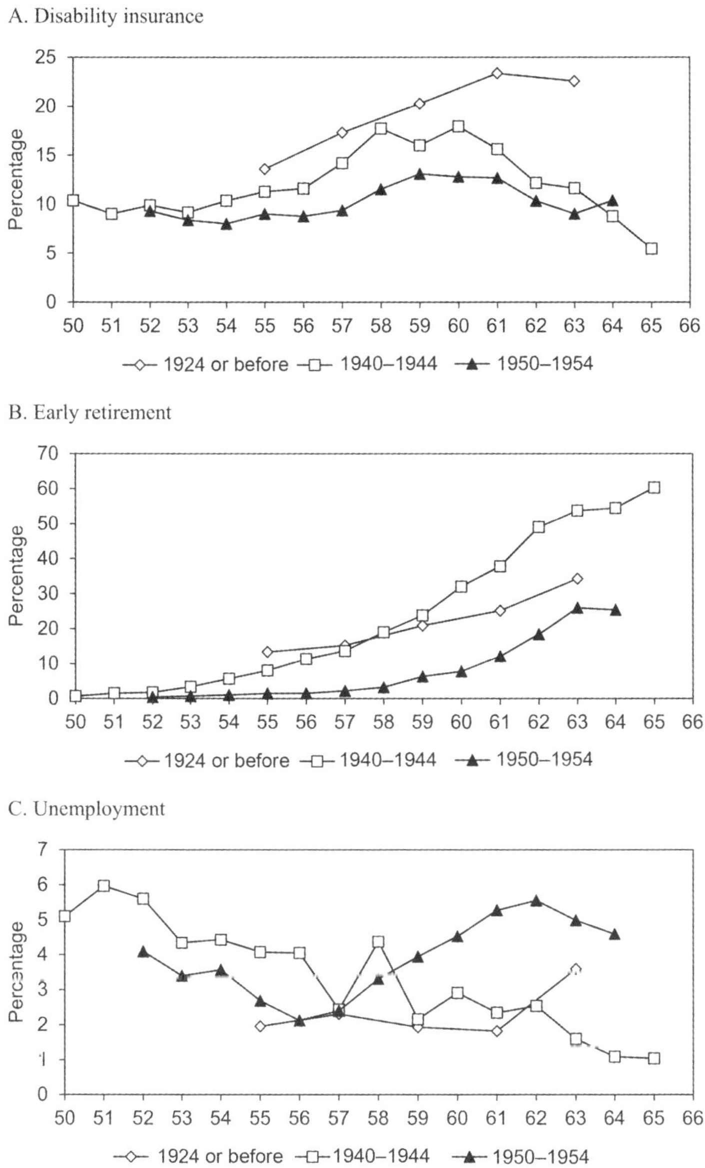

Fig. 8.10 Cohort differences in DI and ER participation and unemployment

Note: The unemployment rate includes individuals on unemployment insurance and social assistance

Source: Statistics Netherlands, Labor Force Survey (Enquête Beroepsbevolking; EBB)

Table 8.2 The state pension age by age and calendar year

	Receives a state pension (yes/no)				
Age in years and months	<=2012	2013	2014	2015	2016
64y + 11m	No	No	No	No	No
65y	Yes	No	No	No	No
65y + 1m	Yes	Yes	No	No	No
65y + 2m	Yes	Yes	Yes	No	No
65y + 3m	Yes	Yes	Yes	Yes	No
65y + 4m	Yes	Yes	Yes	Yes	No
65y + 5m	Yes	Yes	Yes	Yes	No
65y + 6m	Yes	Yes	Yes	Yes	Yes
65y + 7m	Yes	Yes	Yes	Yes	Yes

Source: http://wetten.overheid.nl/BWBR0002221/2017-01-01

Notes: Individuals receive a state pension from the day they reached SPA and from that day their labor contracts are terminated by law.

different SSPs over their life courses (in terms of eligibility and generosity). The 1940–44 generation shows higher rates of ER than the old and young generations (born before 1924 or between 1950 and 1954, respectively). This is the generation that faced generous ER incentives at the ages that mattered. Concerning DI participation, we see a higher DI rate for the older generations. This can be from a combination of better health and stricter DI eligibility rules for the younger compared to the older generations. Concerning generational differences in unemployment at older ages, figure 8.10 shows that the unemployment rate is higher for the 1950–54 generation than for the other generations.

8.4.2 The Effect of an Increase in the State Pension Age (SPA) on Employment

In the Netherlands, employment contracts are terminated by law when workers reach SPA and state pensions are automatically received. This does not prevent employees and employers from entering into a new employment contract, but it does mean that employment can be terminated without the need for severance pay. It may also be interpreted as a signal that this is the right age to stop working. Thus SPA may be a barrier for working longer. To obtain insights into this, we exploit recent increases in SPA and examine their impact on working longer. Table 8.2 and figure 8.11 present the SPA reforms: a gradual increase by one or three months depending on the year and month of birth and effective in the calendar year individuals reach their SPA age.

We analyze the impact of SPA on men's employment rates around the age of 65 using a difference-in-difference methodology (Angrist and Pischke 2009). Figures 8.12 and 8.13 are based on regression results and show predicted employment rates by age and year—that is, the years signify the

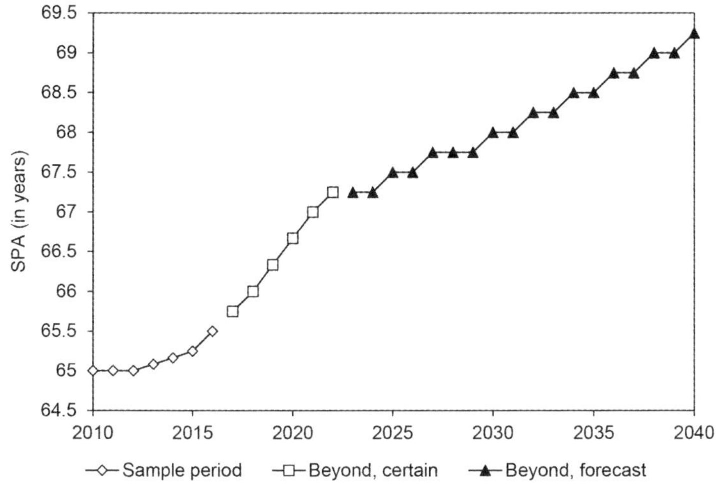

Fig. 8.11 State pension age (SPA) by calendar year

Note: From the introduction of SP in 1957 until and including 2012, SPA was equal to 65

Source: Overheid.nl, http://wetten.overheid.nl/BWBR0002221/2017-01-01

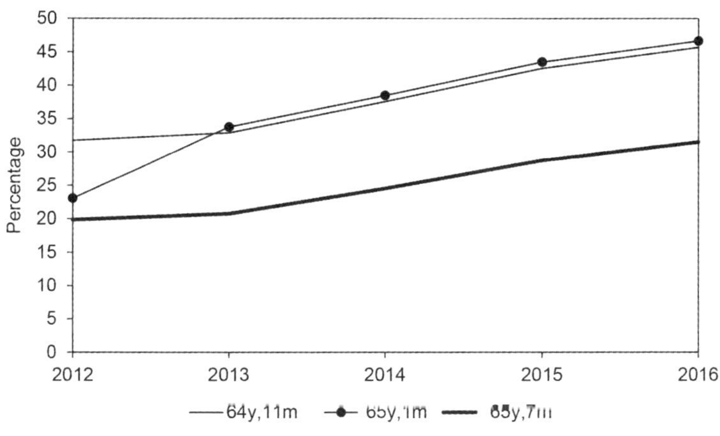

Fig. 8.12 Predicted men's employment rate at three selected ages by calendar year

Source: own calculations using the Labor Force Survey, Statistics Netherlands (Enquête Beroepsbevolking; EBB)

reforms listed in table 8.1. Figure 8.12 shows the impact of an SPA increase from age 65 to age 65 plus one month, an increase that occurred between 2012 and 2013. As this figure shows, the employment rate of individuals aged 65 plus one month who are affected by this reform increases to the level for individuals who are 64 years plus 11 months of age. This increase is statistically significant at the 1 percent level—that is, almost all of them remain

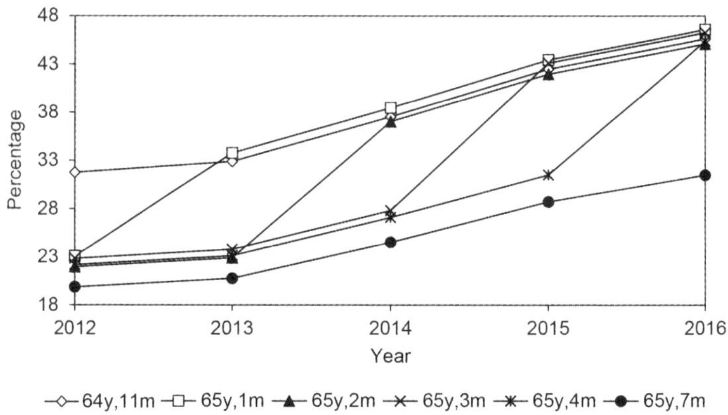

Fig. 8.13 Predicted men's employment rate at different ages by calendar year
Source: own calculations using the Labor Force Survey, Statistics Netherlands (Enquête Beroepsbevolking; EBB)

employed at the age of 65 plus one month. Individuals aged 65 plus 7 months are not affected by the SP reforms during these years—that is, during those years, employment rates at 64 plus 11 months and 65 plus 7 months serve as upper and lower bounds, respectively.

Next, figure 8.13 shows the employment rates related to all the stepwise increases in SPA until 2016. This figure shows that a one-month increase in SPA leads to workers, on average, working one month longer. This shows up in figures 8.12 and 8.13 as approximately 10 percentage point increases in the employment rate (the "jumps"). This increase is statistically significant at the 1 percent level.

8.5 Conclusions

The findings of this chapter show the importance of incentives provided by social security programs for the pathways to retirement and working longer. Implicit tax rates on working are a measure of the financial incentives to exit the labor force. The implicit tax rates show for the various pathways that (i) DI remains an attractive option (if eligible); (ii) UI has been an attractive option for older workers (if eligible) until 2004, after which the scheme became less generous; and (iii) early retirement remained an attractive option until 2006, after which ER pensions became close to being actuarially fair. Regarding state pensions, the SPA has since 2013 been increased stepwise, but the benefits remained unchanged.

Given eligibility for DI, UI, and/or ER/SP, retiring considerably earlier than the SPA (65 until 2013) used to be a financially attractive decision, at least between 1987 and 2004. UI and ER have become less attractive options, and nowadays the financial incentives for these schemes no longer encourage early retirement. For persons eligible for DI, the financial incentive to retire has hardly changed, but here eligibility appears to have been successfully reduced by the most recent reform in 2006. Generally, the Netherlands has seen a vast number of reforms, which makes empirically assessing the effect of each individual reform difficult. Nevertheless, the combined reforms of SSPs seem to have had large positive effects on employment at older ages.

We have shown, using the stepwise increase in SPA from 2013 onward, that an increase in SPA leads to working longer. While this effect is strong, we cannot identify the mechanisms that play a role in this relationship. As noted before, employment protection terminates at SPA, so at least one mechanism is that employers can initiate severance without facing severance costs. On the other hand, workers could still exit at age 65 if they wanted to. It appears, however, that generally this does not happen. This may indicate a preference for working longer or adoption of a shifting social norm whereby one is expected to keep working until SPA. Another factor is that state pensions are received from SPA onward. Liquidity-constrained workers may therefore prefer to keep working until their income is supplemented with SP. Identifying the relative roles of the various mechanisms is of importance for evaluating the welfare implications of an increase in SPA. Nevertheless, it is likely that the continuing increase in SPA will further increase employment at older ages.

Appendix

Table 8.A.1 Key parameters of retirement pathways for selected years

	EEA			
	DI	UI	SP (eea = nea)	ER
1980	—	—	65	60–62
1985	—	-; 57.5	65	60–62
1990	—	-; 57.5	65	60–62
1995	—	-; 57.5	65	60–62
2000	—	-; 57.5	65	60–62
2005	—	-; 57.5	65	60–62
2010	—	-; 61.83	65	60–62
2015	—	-; 62.08	65.25	

DI: No EEA, unlimited duration until 65
UI: No EEA, 1984–2006 unlimited duration from age 57.5 until age 65
ER: EEA depends on sector/firm

	Earnings tests			
	DI	UI	SP	ER
1980	*	*	None	0
1985	*	*	None	0
1990	*	*	**	0
1995	*	*	**	0
2000	*	*	**	0
2005	*	*	**	0
2010	*	*	**	None
2015	*	*	**	None

* Benefit depends on earnings
** Supplement depends on earnings spouse < 65
None: Benefit does not differ with earnings
0: Usually no benefit if earnings > 0 (working not allowed)

	Required service years			
	DI	UI	SP	ER
1980	> 0	*	**	Usually: 10
1985	> 0	*	**	Usually: 10
1990	> 0	*	**	Usually: 10
1995	> 0	*	**	Usually: 10
2000	> 0	*	**	Usually: 10
2005	> 0	*	**	Usually: 10
2010	> 0	*	**	***
2015	> 0	*	**	***

* Duration depends on service years
** Benefit depends on years of residence 15–65
*** Flexible ER/PP depends on years of service

	Other eligibility requirements			
	DI	UI	SP	ER
1980	*	**	None	None
1985	*	**	None	None
1990	*	**	None	None
1995	*	**	None	None
2000	*	**	None	None
2005	*	**	None	None
2010	*	**	None	None
2015	*	**	None	None

* Deemed disabled for work, criteria have shifted
** Unemployed and looking for work (1984–2006): from age 57.5 job no search needed)

Actuarial adjustments				
	DI	UI	SP	ER
1980	No	No	No	No
1985	No	No	No	No
1990	No	No	No	No
1995	No	No	No	No
2000	No	No	No	No
2005	No	No	No	Yes
2010	No	No	No	Yes
2015	No	No	No	Yes

Replacement rates				
	DI	UI	SP + PP	ER
1980	80	80/75	<=70	80
1985	70	70	<=70	80
1990	70	70	<=70	80
1995	70	70	<=70	80
2000	70	70	<=70	80
2005	70	70	<=70	80
2010	75	75/70	<=70	70
2015	75	75/70	<=70	70

Coverage				
	DI	UI	SP	ER
1980	All emp	All emp	All res	*
1985	All emp	All emp	All res	**
1990	All emp	All emp	All res	**
1995	All emp	All emp	All res	**
2000	All emp	All emp	All res	**
2005	All emp	All emp	All res	**
2010	All emp	All emp	All res	*
2015	All emp	All emp	All res	*

* Employees in many sectors/firms
** Employees in most sectors/firms

References

Angrist, Joshua D., and Jörn-Steffen Pischke. 2009. *Mostly Harmless Econometrics*. Princeton, NJ: Princeton University Press.

Kalwij, Adriaan, Rob Alessie, Jonathan Gardner, and Ashik Anwar Ali. 2018. "Inflation Experiences of Retirees." *Journal of Pension Economics and Finance* 17 (1): 85–109.

Kalwij, Adriaan, Arie Kapteyn, and Klaas de Vos. 2017. "Why Are People Working Longer in the Netherlands?" Mimeo.

Kapteyn, Arie, and Klaas de Vos. 1999. "Social Security and Retirement in the Netherlands." In *Social Security and Retirement around the World*, edited by Jonathan Gruber and David A. Wise, 269–304. Chicago: University of Chicago Press.

9

Trends in Employment and Social Security Incentives in the Spanish Pension System, 1980–2016

Pilar García-Gómez, Sílvia Garcia-Mandicó,
Sergi Jiménez-Martín, and Judit Vall-Castelló

9.1 Introduction

Labor force participation rates at older ages have been on the rise since the mid-1990s in many Organisation for Economic Co-operation and Development (OECD) countries. In Spain, participation rates of men aged 55 to 64 have increased by almost 10 percentage points over the last decades, while participation rates of women have more than doubled (see panels A and B of figure 9.1). Existing descriptive evidence points to the potential role of changes in the skill composition of workers, favorable economic conditions until the Great Recession, or the effect of wives' labor market participation on the probability that men will retire later (see Coile 2018; García-Gómez, Jiménez-Martín, and Castelló 2018).

Panels C and D in figure 9.1 show the employment rate over time for men and women aged 55 to 59, 60 to 64, and 65 to 69. For men, employment was decreasing for all age groups until the mid-1990s. At the end of the 1990s, the employment rate began to rise until the financial crisis hit in 2008. The result-

Pilar García-Gómez is an associate professor at the Erasmus School of Economics at Erasmus University Rotterdam.

Sílvia Garcia-Mandicó is a junior economist in the Directorate for Employment, Labour, and Social Affairs at the Organisation for Economic Co-operation and Development (OECD).

Sergi Jiménez-Martín is a professor of economics at Universitat Pompeu Fabra, an affiliated professor at Barcelona Graduate School of Economics, and an associate researcher at FEDEA.

Judit Vall-Castelló is an associate professor of economics of the University of Barcelona and a researcher at Centre de Recerca en Economia i Salut (CRES) at Universitat Pompeu Fabra.

We acknowledge financial support from the Spanish ministry of economy projects ECO2014-52238-R and ECO2017-83668-R and helpful comments from the International Social Security (ISS) group meeting participants and Alfonso Sánchez. For acknowledgments, sources of research support, and disclosure of the authors' material financial relationships, if any, please see https://www.nber.org/chapters/c14199.ack.

A. Labor force participation, Men

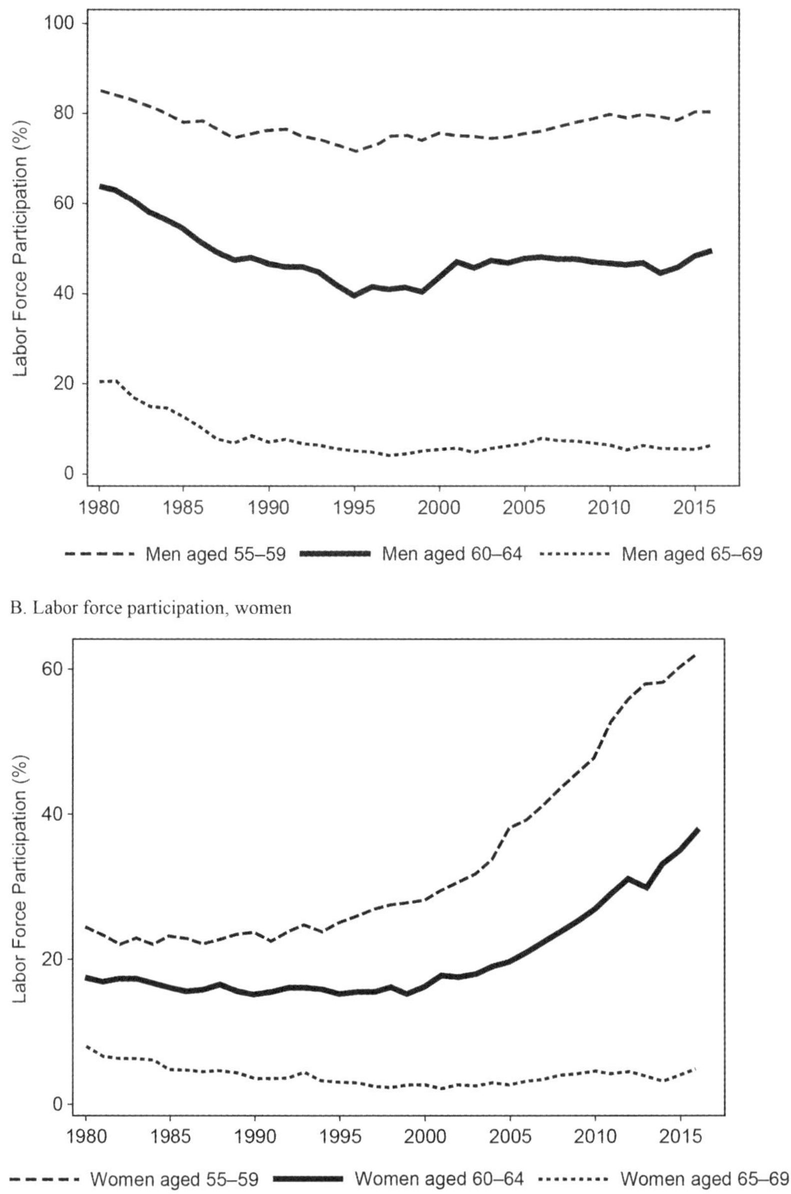

Fig. 9.1 Trends in employment rates and labor force participation of men and women from 1987 to 2017

C. Employment rates, Men

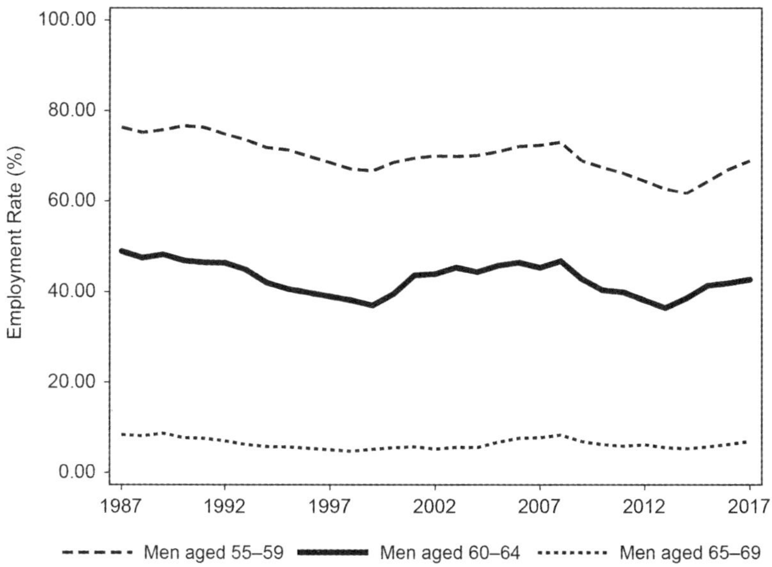

D. Employment rates, Women

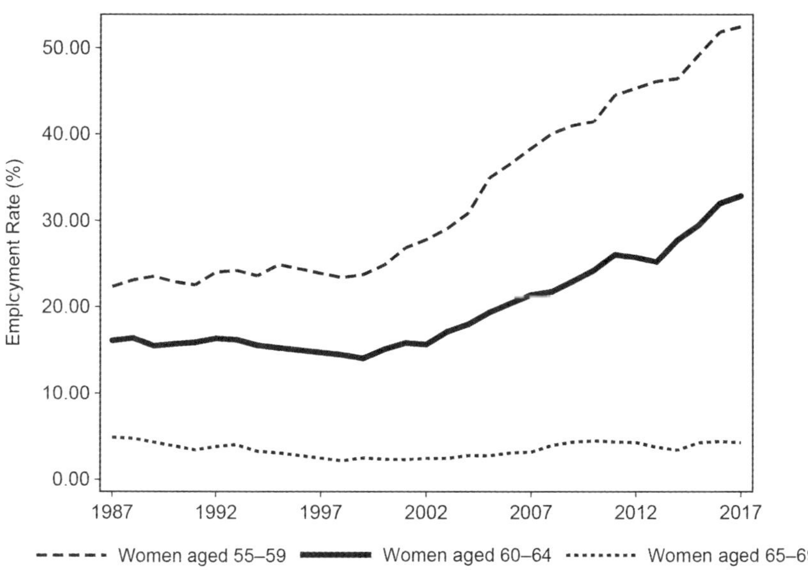

Fig. 9.1 (cont.)

ing drop in employment, however, did not translate into lower labor force participation (see panel A of figure 9.1). From 2015 onward, we observe again an increasing trend in employment coinciding with the recovery of the Spanish economy. Both employment and labor force participation of men aged 65 to 69 remained relatively constant at low levels over the entire period. The picture for women aged 55 to 64 is distinctively different. Women experienced flat employment and labor participation trends until the late 1990s, when their employment rate soared (see panels B and D in figure 9.1). These increasing trends continued even during the period of economic recession from 2008 to 2013. As for men, employment and participation rates of women aged 65 to 69 were rather constant at low levels throughout the entire period. In this chapter, we investigate to what extent changes in financial incentives from Social Security (SS) programs can explain these trends.

Changes in the Social Security system, defined as the old-age pension system (OA) as well as unemployment insurance (UI) and disability insurance (DI), have the potential to modify the incentives of workers to retire at a given age. The empirical literature exploring the effect of financial incentives on retirement behavior of employed workers is extensive (Samwick 1998; Gruber and Wise 1999, 2004; Börsch-Supan 2000; Belloni and Alessie 2009). The general finding of this literature is that financial incentives do affect retirement decisions—that is, more generous financial incentives significantly increase the probability of (early) retirement.

A more recent line of research also investigates the responses of unemployed workers to Social Security financial incentives. Coile and Levine (2007, 2011) use US data to investigate how the Social Security system affects the retirement responses of older unemployed workers. Using French data, Hairault, Sopraseuth, and Langot (2010) find that the distance from the statutory retirement age is a key predictor of retirement behavior. Although, in general, the authors find that financial incentives affect retirement behavior, eligibility conditions turn out to be the most important determinant of retirement behavior.

For the Spanish case, the seminal papers by Boldrin, Jiménez-Martín, and Peracchi (1999, 2004) and Jiménez-Martín and Sánchez-Martín (2004) find that financial incentives have a significant effect on retirement probabilities, although the magnitude is small. More recently, Cairó-Blanco (2010); García-Pérez, Jiménez-Martín, and Sánchez-Martín (2013); and Sánchez-Martín, García-Pérez, and Jiménez-Martín (2014), who explicitly consider the behavior of unemployed workers, also find a significant but weak influence of financial incentives on labor force exit. This chapter extends previous work for the Spanish case by analyzing a longer time series (1980–2015), which allows us to cover several reform periods.

We analyze the association between financial incentives and retirement decisions using aggregate data over four decades in Spain. We first compute expected social security benefits from each possible retirement pathway (OA, UI, and DI) at ages 55 to 69 for a representative worker for each cohort falling in this age range in our observational period. We allow representative workers to differ by marital status, gender, and earnings level. We then move on to calculating the *implicit tax rate on employment*, a measure that weights the gains and losses from working one additional year for each representative worker. Finally, we test the correlation between the implicit tax rate on employment and the employment rates for older workers using both graphical inspection and regression analysis with data aggregated at the regional level. Our results suggest that financial incentives play a role in explaining the retirement patterns of Spanish workers. However, they seem to play a less important role in consistently explaining changes in overall employment rates among older workers. In other words, while aggregate financial incentives are associated with the aggregate exit rate of older workers, other factors seem to play a more crucial role in explaining aggregate employment trends. This is consistent with the descriptive evidence in García-Gómez et al. (2018).

The rest of the chapter is organized as follows. Section 9.2 describes the reforms of the Spanish social security system over the last three decades. Section 9.3 explains the measurement of the Social Security incentives and the assumptions behind our calculations. Section 9.4 reports the resulting calculations, and section 9.5 analyzes the relationship between the Social Security incentives and employment rates since 1980. Section 9.6 concludes.

9.2 Reforms in the Spanish Social Security System

9.2.1 Changes in the Old-Age Pension System

The Spanish old-age pension system is a defined benefit pay-as-you-go system. There have been several reforms of the system over the last 30 years, which we briefly summarize here (see table 9.1 for a summary and Boldrin, García-Gómez, and Jiménez-Martín 2010 and García-Gómez, Jiménez-Martín, and Castelló 2012 for a detailed exposition of the changes in the old-age pension system in Spain). We start describing the system before the 1985 reform. Since this reform, there have been substantial parametric reforms in 1997, 2002, 2007, and 2011 and a nonparametric reform in 2013. Figure 9.2 depicts the timeline of the reforms of the Spanish social security system from 1980 until 2015 as well as the main parameters that were modified in each of the reforms.

9.2.1.1 The System before the 1985 Reform

As described in Boldrin et al. (1999), the transition from the old *Mutualidades* system to a system of Social Security contributions was completed in

Table 9.1 Main reforms of the old-age pension system in Spain since 1980

Year of the reform	Main changes
1985	Minimum mandatory annual contributions increase from 8 to 15 Number of contributive years used to compute the pension increases from 2 to 8 Several early retirement schemes introduced; partial retirement and special retirement at age 64
1997	Number of contributive years used to compute the pension increases from 8 to 15 (progressively by 2001) Formula for replacement rate made less generous. 8 percent penalty applied to early retirees between ages of 60 and 65 reduced to 7 percent for individuals with 40 or more contributory years
2002	Early retirement only from age 61 Impulse partial retirement; possible to combine it with work Unemployed aged 61 can retire if contributed for 30 years and the previous 6 months registered in employment offices Incentives to retire after age 65
2007	15 "effective" contributory years used to calculate the pension Reduction from 8 percent to 7.5 percent of the per-year penalty applied to early retirees between 60 and 65 for individuals with 30 contributory years Broaden incentives to stay employed after age 65 Increase contributions made by the social security administration for individuals receiving the special scheme of UA for 52+ (they will receive a higher old-age pension when retiring)
2011	Number of contributive years used to compute the pension increases from 15 to 20 Normal retirement age increases from 65 to 67 Eligibility conditions for early retirement modified
2013	Introduction of sustainability factor (SF) Intergenerational equity factor Pension revaluation index

1979 with the removal of *bases tarifadas* (fixed covered wages). The crucial ingredients of the system until 1985 were as follows:[1]

- The earliest eligibility age was 60, and the statutory eligibility age was 65 if the individual did not have any job that required affiliation with the social security system.

1. See Boldrin et al. (1999, 2004) for other details regarding disability and survivor pensions.

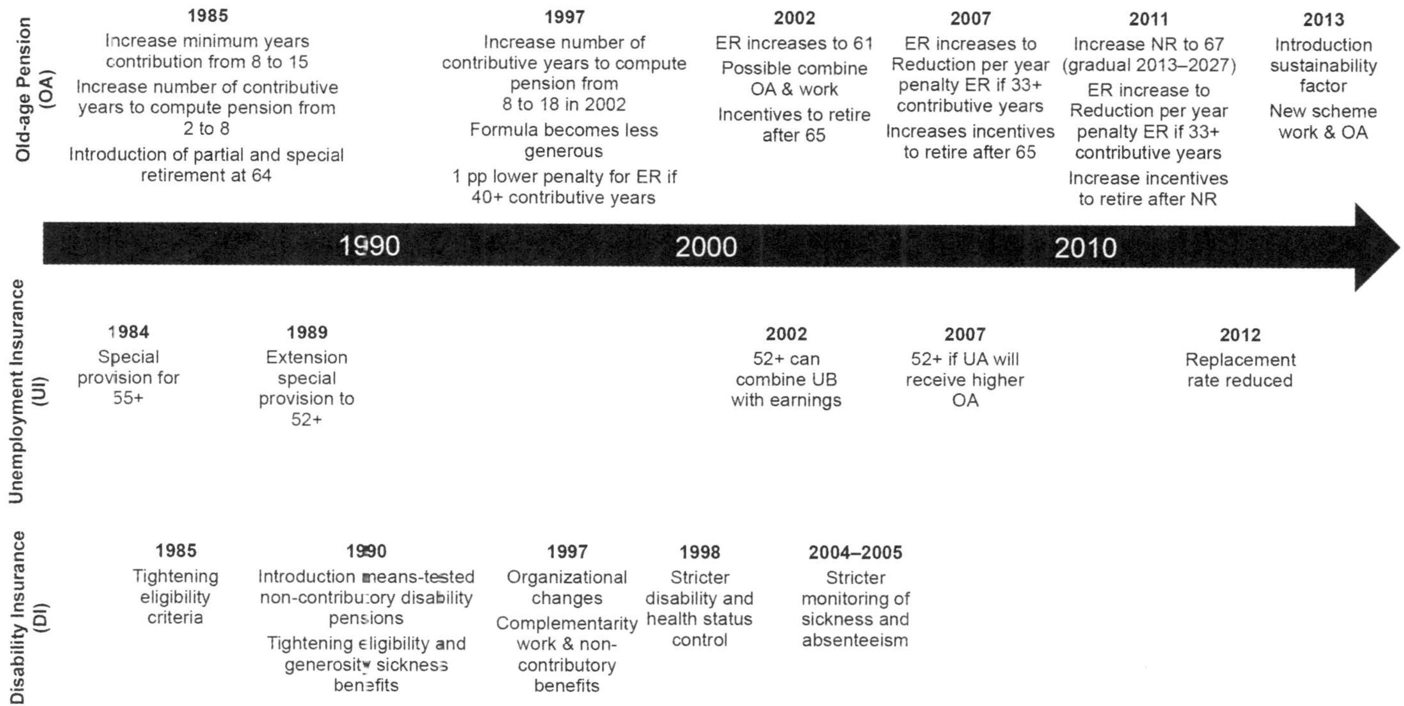

Fig. 9.2 Timeline of the reforms of the Spanish social security system

- A minimum of 10 years of contributions was required to gain access to a contributive pension.
- The pension was calculated on the basis of three elements: (1) the average of the contributions in the 24 months preceding retirement, (2) the penalty for early retirement (8 percent per year anticipated), and (3) the penalty for insufficient contributions (2 percent per year not contributed; full benefit reached with 35 contribution years).

9.2.1.2 *The Old-Age Pension System after the 1985 Reform*

The key elements of the Spanish pension system prevailing until 2011 were set in 1985. Eligibility for the old-age benefits increased from 10 to at least 15 years of contributions to the system. The pension amount was calculated by multiplying a regulatory base by a percentage, which depended on the age of the individual and the number of years contributed to the system. Under the 1985 regime, the regulatory base was obtained by dividing by 112 the wages of the last 96 months (8 years) before retiring, and the percentage applied to this regulatory base depended on the number of years of contributions (n) as follows:

$$\begin{cases} 0, \textit{ if } n < 15 \\ .5 + 0.03(n - 15), \textit{ if } 25 > n \geq 15 \\ .8 + 0.02(n - 25), \textit{ if } 35 > n \geq 25 \\ 1, \textit{ if } n \geq 35 \end{cases}.$$

The pension amount was capped from below by the minimum pension (see Jiménez-Martín 2014 for details) and from above by the maximum benefit (between four and five times the minimum wage).

9.2.1.3 *The 1997, 2002, and 2007 Reforms*

In 1997, the number of contributory years used to compute the benefit base was progressively increased from 8 to 15 years in 2002, and the formula to calculate the replacement rate was made less generous. On the other hand, the 8 percent penalty applied to early retirees between the ages of 60 and 65 was reduced to 7 percent for individuals with at least 40 years of contributions at the time of early retirement.

In 2002, further changes were introduced. Before 2002, only individuals who had contributed to the system earlier than 1967 could benefit from early retirement at 60, while the rest had to wait until the statutory eligibility age of 65. In 2002, early retirement at 61 was made available for the rest of the population. At the same time, there was an impulse toward partial and flexible retirement with the possibility of combining income from work with old-age benefits and the introduction of incentives for individuals to retire after the statutory eligibility age of 65.[2] At the same time, the possibility to access retirement was extended to individuals unemployed for reasons beyond their willingness at 61 and who had contributed for at least 30 years and had been registered in the employment office for the previous six months.

In 2007, the incentives to retire later than 65 were further increased by providing an additional 3 percent instead of the 2 percent agreed upon in 2002. The 8 percent penalty applied to early retirees between the ages of 60 and 65 was reduced to 6 to 7.5 percent, depending on the number of years contributed, for individuals with at least 30 years of contributions. In addition, the contributions for unemployed workers older than 52 were increased so that they would receive a higher old-age pension when retiring.

Although these reforms tried to increase the labor supply of older male workers, the existing evidence (see, e.g., Cairó-Blanco 2010; García-Pérez et al. 2013) does not show any clear link between these reforms and the increased labor supply of older male workers.

9.2.1.4 The 2011 Reform

The discouraging demographic and labor market scenarios prevailing during the first years of the great recession led the Spanish government (forced by EU pressure to reduce the future deficit) to deeply reform the pension system in 2011. Two main elements were targeted: (1) the number of contributive years in the pension calculation was increased from 15 to 25, and (2) the statutory eligibility age was raised from 65 to 67, gradually. The latter was particularly relevant for Spain, since the statutory eligibility age had not been modified since the year it was first established in 1979. These two changes severely cut the generosity of the pension system (see Sánchez 2017 for a recent evaluation). The reform also restricted the eligibility conditions for early retirement, although the effect of this change on the generosity of the system is less clear. In particular, because the reform barely changed the eligibility conditions to access the minimum pension, workers expecting to receive the minimum pension (i.e., workers with low income and short contributive careers) were less affected by the reform (Jiménez-Martín 2014).

The Spanish case is far from isolated, as most European countries have initiated or are about to initiate a process of pension reforms (EU 2012). Reforms mostly involve the following three elements: (1) a delay in the statutory eligibility age, together with relaxing the requirement to make compatible work and pension income; (2) a reduction of the system's generosity; and

2. An additional 2 percent per each year of contribution beyond the age of 65 for workers with at least 35 years of contributions on top of the 100 percent applied to the regulatory base.

(3) the introduction of a sustainability factor, which adds some uncertainty to the final benefit, thereby transitioning the system from a defined benefit to a defined contribution model. The 2011 Spanish reform (law 27/2011), which included elements (1) and (2) above, may have not been sufficient to alleviate the medium-term financial pressure on the pension system (Díaz-Giménez and Díaz-Saavedra 2017; Sánchez 2014).

9.2.1.5 The 2013 Reform and the Sustainability Factor

In an attempt to stabilize the short- and long-term financial sustainability of the Social Security system, the Spanish government amended the 2011 reform in 2013. In particular, this amendment introduced a sustainability factor (SF), which links the initial pension level to the evolution of life expectancy (Conde-Ruiz and González 2013). This mechanism can be seen as transforming defined benefit schemes into defined contribution schemes.

The SF has two key components: the intergenerational equity factor (IEF) and the pension revaluation index (PRI). The aim of the IEF is to provide equal treatment to those who retire at the same age and with the same employment history but with different life expectancies (which are specific to the cohort they belong to). The introduction of this factor didn't give rise to much controversy, since it was perceived as reasonable that if pensioners were to receive the same total pension throughout their retirement, an individual with a greater life expectancy should receive a little less each year. The second factor, the PRI, fixes a budgetary constraint on the economic cycle and, as such, is relatively flexible in the short term. However, the discretionary rule chosen by the government guarantees that even if Social Security revenues are insufficient to cover pension costs, pensions will rise each year by at least 0.25 percent and by no more than the annual change in the consumer price index (CPI) + 0.25 percent.

We expect the 2011/2013 pension reform to incentivize the labor supply of older workers in Spain by reducing benefit expectations and including incentives to work longer (partial benefit compatibility after the normal retirement age; Sánchez 2014).

9.2.1.6 Evolution of Key Parameters

To conclude this section, we show the temporal evolution of the key parameters of the old-age pension system. Panel A in figure 9.3 shows the increase in the years of contributions included in the benefit calculation. Reform years are marked with a vertical dashed line. We see that after the reforms in 1985, 1997, and 2011, the number of years included increased staggeringly. Panel B shows the earliest and statutory eligibility pension ages. The latter has only increased at the end of the period with the reform of the pension system in 2011. The earliest eligibility at age 60 was initially only available for those who started contributing before January 1967. In 2002,

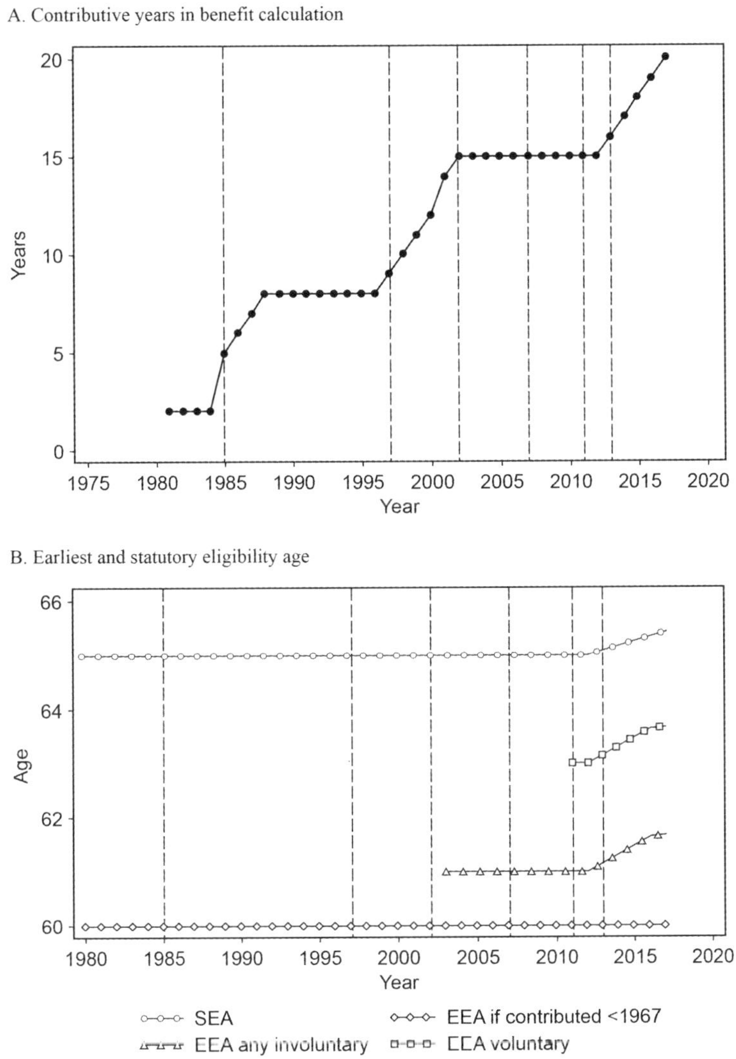

Fig. 9.3 Time trends of key parameters

early retirement at age 61 was introduced for all other workers. In 2011, this possibility became restricted to situations of involuntary retirement. At the same time, the earliest eligibility age for voluntary retirement was set at 63. Panel C shows the increasing trend in the ratio of minimum benefit to minimum wage, highlighting the generosity of the Spanish pension system. This trend was reverted with the 2013 reform and the introduction of the SF. Panel D shows the ratio of the minimum to the maximum benefit. Since the early

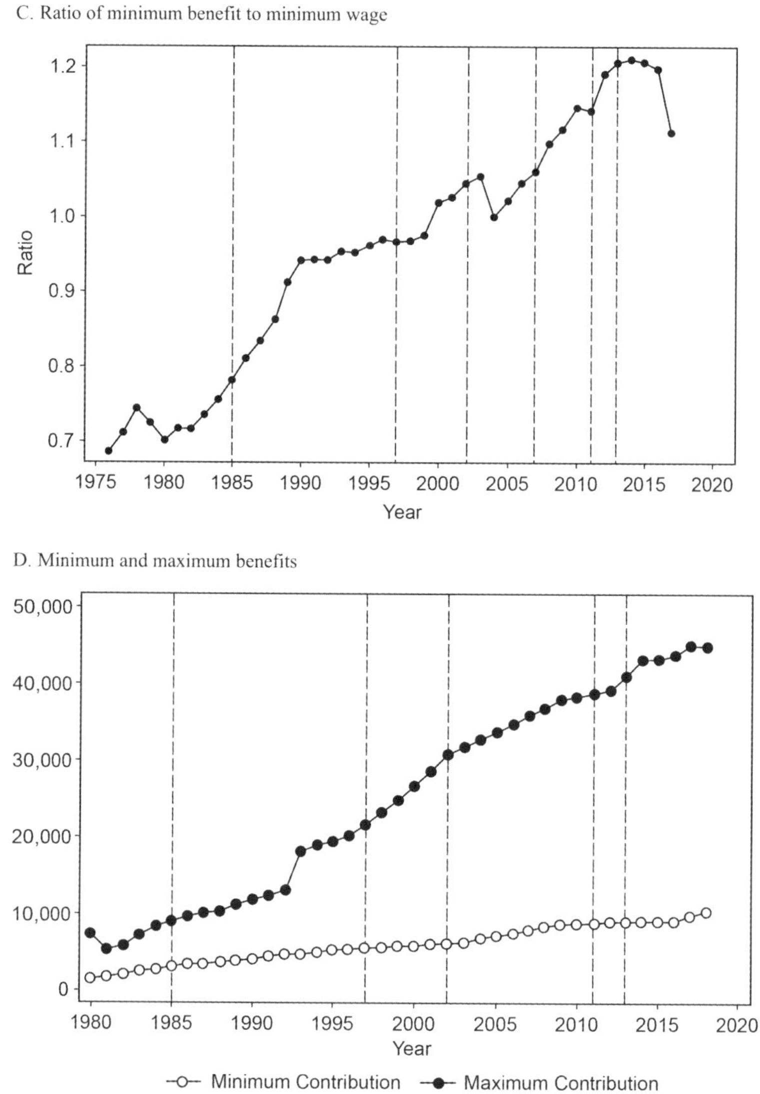

Fig. 9.3 (cont.)

1990s and, in particular, after the 1997 and 2002 reforms, the gap between minimum and maximum benefits widens over time. This tendency seems to have been curbed with the 2013 reform.

9.2.2 Reforms in the Disability and Unemployment System

Another factor that may affect the labor market behavior of older workers is disability and unemployment insurance policies (García-Gómez, Jiménez-

Martín, and Castelló 2012). In what follows, we summarize the main reforms of both the disability and unemployment systems in Spain.

9.2.2.1 *Disability Insurance*

Permanent disability benefits were used extensively as an early retirement mechanism for workers in restructuring industries (such as shipbuilding, steel, mining, etc.) or as a substitution for long-term unemployment subsidies in depressed regions during the late 1970s and 1980s (OECD 2001), which resulted in an increase in the inflows into the disability system and permanent disability benefits.

These events prompted a number of reforms introduced during the second half of the 1980s and the beginning of the 1990s (see table 9.2 for a summary). The main objective of these reforms was to abolish the incentive effects to permanently leave the labor market before reaching the statutory eligibility age for retirement through the disability system. Here we focus on some distinctive features of the main reforms since the creation of the National Institute of Social Security (NISS) in 1979, while we refer the reader to table 9.2 for a summary of all the reforms in the disability system in Spain during this period.

The first large disability insurance reform took place in 1997 and included four main points:

1. Sickness benefits: stricter control of the sickness status by Social Security physicians, a reduction of the level of long-term sickness benefits, and the replacement of the old job assessment with a more objective definition of the usual occupation of the individual.
2. Permanent disability pensions of individuals aged at least 65 were automatically transferred to the old-age pension system. This was just a change in the classification within the pensions system.
3. Organizational reform: all the issues related to disability insurance were transferred to the NISS. The permanent disability status was, in the past, assessed and granted by local GPs, and this reform created a group of experts (the disability assessment team inside the NISS) that was in charge of assessing applicants' ability to work on the basis of the available medical files and a medical assessment from an NISS physician.
4. The claimant no longer lost entitlement to noncontributory disability benefits if she started working. She would remain entitled to receive noncontributory disability benefits in case of job loss.

In addition to this major reform in 1997, the 1998 budget law introduced the possibility for NISS physicians and mutual insurance companies to review the health situation and status of beneficiaries. Effectively, very few claimants in the permanent disability system effectively exited the program.

In 2004 and 2005, monitoring of the use of sick leave was tightened with the creation of a new subdepartment at the NISS and a new monitoring tool

Table 9.2 Main reforms of the disability insurance and unemployment systems in Spain since 1980

Year of the reform	Main changes
1984	Introduction of temporary contracts and noncontributory unemployment benefits (also called unemployment assistance benefits) **Special provision** for **workers 55+** to receive unemployment assistance benefits until retirement age Eligible if satisfying the old-age pension entitlement requirement except for the age Paid 75 percent of the minimum wage Years spent under this scheme counted as contributive years toward an old-age pension
1985	Tightening of eligibility criteria for DI
1989	Extension of special provision for older workers to all **workers 52+**
1990	Introduction of **means-tested noncontributory disability pensions** for people aged 65+ and for disabled people aged 18+ who satisfy residency requirements
	Sickness benefits:
	Stricter control of the sickness status by doctors of the social security system
	Reduction of the level of long-term sickness benefits
	Replacement of the old own job assessment by a more objective definition of the usual occupation of the individual
1997	**Permanent disability pensions individuals 65+** automatically converted to old-age pensions
	Organizational change; creation of the National Institute of Social Security (NISS):
	Disability assessed by benefit administrators based on a medical assessment performed by the NISS's own doctors
	Complementarities between work and benefits:
	Entitlement to noncontributory benefits not lost if working and can be collected if losing the job
1998	Possibility for NISS doctors and mutual insurance companies to review health situation of beneficiaries
2002	Individuals aged 52+ receiving unemployment benefits could combine the receipt of these benefits with earnings (50 percent of the total benefits paid by the employer, and 50 percent paid by the Social Security)
	Extension of program that helps integrate people into the labor market to all individuals aged 45+ who have been unemployed for one month and to people with disabilities, among others.
2004–2005	Stricter monitoring of sickness and absenteeism through creation of a department at the NISS; general absence control put in place when duration of absence was greater than six months; possibility to combine noncontributory disability with some earnings
2007	Increase contributions made by the social security administration for individuals receiving the special scheme of UA for 52+ (they will receive a higher old-age pension when retiring)
2012	Replacement rate reduced from 60 percent to 50 percent after 180 days of unemployment spell—for first six months, kept constant at 70 percent—for all unemployment spells starting after July 15, 2012

to reduce absence rates. In 2005, a general absence control was put in place for cases of absenteeism longer than six months.

Finally, at the end of 2007, the minimum contributory period to access permanent disability pensions was reduced for young workers in order to adjust for the current later entrance into the job market. At the same time, the formula to calculate the regulatory base of the benefit was slightly modified: since then, the regulatory base of permanent disability due to a common illness decreased by 50 percent if the individual had not contributed at least 15 years, and it is lower the further the individual is from age 65.

All these reforms ensured the financial stability of the disability system in Spain, as inflow rates have remained stable compared to the dramatic increase experienced by other industrialized countries.[3]

9.2.2.2 Unemployment Insurance

In 1984, the government introduced unemployment benefits for workers employed in temporary contracts and noncontributory unemployment benefits (also called unemployment assistance benefits). In addition, it established a special provision for workers aged over 55 who were allowed to receive unemployment assistance benefits until the claiming age. To receive these benefits, individuals had to satisfy the entitlement requirements of the retirement pension, except for the age. The subsidy paid 75 percent of the minimum wage until reaching the age to be transferred to the old-age pension system. Furthermore, the years spent unemployed under this special scheme were counted as contributive years toward an old-age benefit.

In 1989, the special provision of unemployment assistance benefits until the statutory eligibility age of 65 for individuals aged at least 55 was extended to individuals aged 52, thus increasing the incentives for older workers to leave the labor market at younger ages.

The reform in 2002 opened up the possibility for individuals aged at least 52, receiving unemployment benefits, to combine the UI payments with earnings. They could receive 50 percent of their previous unemployment insurance entitlement, and the employer would pay the remaining amount in wages.

Finally, in 2012, the amount an individual receives from unemployment insurance after the first six months was reduced from 60 to 50 percent of previous earnings.

9.3 Measurement of Social Security System Incentives

The Spanish social security system provides different incentives to leave the labor market at different ages and over time, as detailed in the previous section. In this section, we explain the measures we use and the assumptions

3. See Jiménez-Martín, Mestres, and Castelló (2018).

we make to capture the impact of social security programs on retirement decisions.

9.3.1 Definitions and Methodology

The key concept used to assess the impact of social security programs on retirement decisions is the annual accrual of social security wealth (SSW), which is the present discounted value of lifetime social security benefits. For an individual of type *i*, where the type is defined by her gender, skill level, and marital status, starting to claim benefits from program *k* at age *R*, her social security wealth is defined as

$$SSW_{k,t}(R,i) = \sum_{a=R}^{T} B_{k,t,a}(R,i)\sigma_{t,a}\beta^{a-R}, \tag{1}$$

where $\sigma_{t,a}$ is the survival probability at age *a* in year *t*, *T* is the maximum length of life, and β^{a-R} is the discount factor set at a rate of 3 percent.

Postponing claiming by one year has two effects on SSW. On the one hand, annual benefits $B_{k,t,a}(R,i)$ increase with later claiming due to additional contributions and actuarial adjustments. On the other hand, however, benefits are received one year less. We thus define the accrual of SSW as

$$ACC_{k,t}(R,i) = SSW_{k,t+1}(R+1,i) - SSW_{k,t}(R,i). \tag{2}$$

The social security system provides incentives to retire when $ACC_{k,t}(R,i) \leq 0$ and to continue working otherwise—that is, when the accrual of SSW is negative, the social security system imposes an implicit tax on working longer and claiming later. We define the resulting implicit tax rate as the (negative) ACC divided by the after-tax earnings obtained during the additional year of work ($Y_{t+1,1}$):

$$ITAX_{k,t}(R,i) = -\frac{ACC_{k,t}(R,i)}{Y_{t+1,i}}. \tag{3}$$

Finally, we also consider the replacement rate, *rr*, defined as the ratio of the initial benefit to the last wage, for (planned) retirement at age *R*:

$$rr(R,i)_{k,t} = B_{k,t}(R,i)/Y_{t-1,i}. \tag{4}$$

9.3.2 Assumptions and Scenarios

In order to compute SSW and its corresponding accrual and implicit tax rate, we take the following steps.

We first calculate the previously defined measures for 12 different types of individuals: men, women of three different earnings levels, and two marital statuses (married and single). We thus evaluate the retirement incentives for low-earner males and females, median-earner males and females, and high-earner males and females. The earnings profiles are based on educational attainment. In particular, low earners are those workers having up to some secondary education, median earners are those having at most completed upper secondary education, and high earners are those having tertiary education. We consider three potential pathways to retirement: old age, unemployment, and disability insurance. Figure 9.4 shows the share of the population aged 55 to 69 that reports being, in any given year, in to unemployment or disability or receiving an old-age pension, obtained from the Spanish Labor Force Survey (Encuesta de la Poblacion Activa, EPA).[4] DI and UI represent about 20 percent of all transitions to retirement, with an increasing trend in recent years.

In order to construct the financial incentive measures, we first obtain age-earnings profiles for each of our six types of workers (married and single workers do not differ in their earnings profiles). We define low earners as workers with, at most, lower secondary education (low skilled); median earners as workers with upper and/or postsecondary education (medium skilled); and high earners as workers with tertiary educations (high skilled). We use two different age-earnings profiles. First, and given the comparative nature of the whole project, we use a synthetic earnings profile obtained from earnings of the US Current Population Survey (CPS), the German Socio-economic Panel (GSOEP), and administrative data from the Italian pension system (INPS) for 2016. Using these data, we compute a simple average of the median income separately for three earnings levels and by gender. We then rescale this synthetic profile so that earnings at age 50 are one and multiply them by the Spanish median annual earnings at age 50 reported in the Spanish working histories survey (Muestra Continua de Vidas Laborales, MCVL)[5] in 2014 for the respective sex and earnings groups. We refer to this earnings profile as the *common earnings profile* and use it in our main incentive calculations.

Second, we use a time-invariant Spanish earnings profile based on the Spanish median earnings by age, gender, and earning level in 2014, calculated from the MCVL. We take the median earnings of workers in each category to calculate the earning-specific wage profile. We refer to this earnings profile as the *Spanish earnings profile*.

For both earnings profiles—that is, common and Spanish—we deflate/inflate the cross-sectional earning profile obtained (for 2014) to construct the earnings profiles of workers in earlier years (from 1980 to 2013) and in 2015.

4. The EPA is a rotating quarterly survey carried out by the Spanish National Statistical Institute (Instituto Nacional de Estadística, INE). The planned sample size consists of approximately 150,000 adult individuals. Although the survey has been conducted since 1964, publicly released cross-sectional files are available only from 1977. The 1977 questionnaire was modified in 1987 (when a set of retrospective questions were introduced), in the first quarter of 1992, in 1999, and in 2004. The EPA provides fairly detailed information on labor force status, education, and family background variables, but it does not include information on earnings. The reference period for most questions is the week before the interview.

5. The MCVL is a random draw of the stock of Social Security affiliates (4 percent of the total) and provides information on employment and unemployment spells of the entire labor history.

Fig. 9.4 Pathways to retirement for men and women from 1975 to 2016

Notes: Data obtained from the shares of males and females in each pathway from the EPA. There was a major change in the survey in 1988, so we cannot obtain a consistent definition of the different pathways prior to 1988. We then normalize each share in this time interval to the level in 1988.

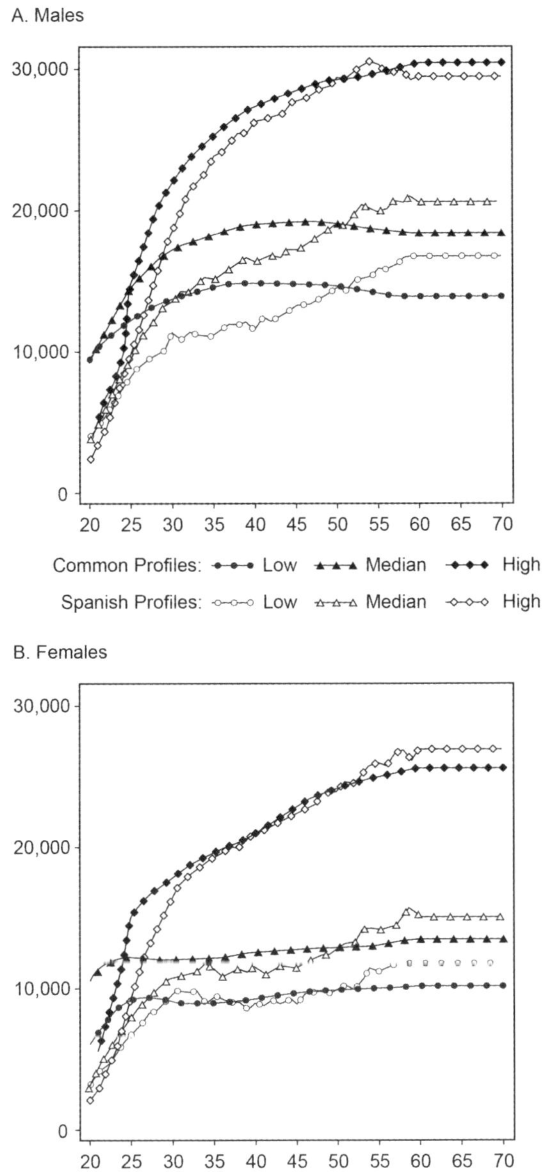

Fig. 9.5 Common and Spanish earning (real) profiles for a worker born in 1925

Figure 9.5 shows how the two earning profiles compare for male and female workers born in 1925, by different earning levels. We note that for high earners, the common earnings profile follows the Spanish time-invariant one quite closely. However, the common earnings profiles of median and low earners are much flatter than what we observe for the one based on Spanish workers.

We construct survival probability curves for each type of worker using average EU-28 survival rates (Eurostat 2016). The underlying life expectancy at age 15 is 67.8 years for women and 64.7 years for men. We adjust these survival curves for differences in life expectancy across skill levels. In particular, we generate a life expectancy that is three years higher (lower) to reflect the difference in life expectancy across the three earnings categories (Van Baal et al. 2016; Regidor et al. 2016).[6]

All calculated magnitudes are net of social security contributions and personal income taxes. Exact calculations of after-tax social security wealth and replacement rates are complicated by the fact that the number of bend points in the Spanish marginal tax schedule is high, although decreasing over time (34 in 1985, 17 in 1995, 7 in 2011, and 5 in 2016). As an approximation, we proceed as follows. We first use the 1995 tax schedule to trace out the relation between the average tax rate (net of standard deductions) and income (net of social security contributions paid by a worker). We then fit by least squares a fourth-order polynomial to this relation. Finally, the estimated coefficients are used to determine after-tax earnings for all previous and subsequent years.

The following sections present the results of the social security incentives calculations using the previous definitions and assumptions. We show measures of financial incentives by type of worker, age or cohort, and route into retirement. In addition, we also present some aggregate measures using the following weights. First, we aggregate the old-age, DI, and UI pathways to retirement using as weights the population share that moves in a given year from employment to retirement through each of the three programs, as presented in figure 9.4. As we have information on these shares over time and gender, we are able to attribute a particular weight to each gender-age time observation. The second step is to aggregate the retirement incentives over gender, earnings level, and age. We obtain population data by age, gender, and earnings level over time from Eurostat (Eurostat 2016) and construct sample averages by gender and earnings level for each age over time. We use these sample averages as the second weight to compute aggregate retirement incentives.

9.4 Social Security Incentives over Time

In order to ease the explanation of how the different components of the Spanish social security system shape financial incentives to retire over time and facilitate comparison with the evolution in other countries, most of our results are presented for a base-case worker. This worker is a male median earner born in 1925. In addition, we focus on the social security incentives

6. The measures of financial incentives remain practically unchanged using Spanish survival rates in 2014. Results are available upon request.

for workers retiring through the old-age pension pathway, but we present a comparison of the incentives for workers retiring through the disability or unemployment pathway in subsection 9.4.7.

9.4.1 The Base Case

Our base case is a male worker at the median earnings level born on January 1, 1925, who has been contributing to social security without interruption since he turned 20 on January 1, 1945. He reaches the earliest eligibility age of 60 in 1985 and the statutory eligibility age of 65 in 1990. He is married to a woman who is three years younger than he is and has never worked, and they have no dependent children.

Simulations start in 1980, when our base-case worker turns age 55 and completes 35 years of contributions, and run for each year until he turns 69 in the year 1994.

Our basic assumptions are the following. First, if the worker stops working before age 60, then he chooses to first claim his old-age pension benefits at age 60, the earliest eligibility age, whereas if he stops working past age 60, then he starts receiving his old-age pension immediately. Second, if he stops working before age 60, then he receives no benefits or unemployment compensation in the interim years until he starts drawing old-age benefits.

It may be worth summarizing the main qualitative effects of working one more year beyond age 60 in the simulations we are about to present: (1) It may increase social security benefits by increasing the benefit base or the replacement rate. The benefit base increases if earnings from the extra year of work exceed average earnings during the last eight years. The replacement rate increases if the worker has contributed for fewer than 35 years, in which case an extra year of work buys an extra 2 percent of the benefit base. If the worker has already contributed for 35 years, as in the base case, only the effect on the benefit base is relevant. (2) It reduces the penalty for early retirement by 8 percentage points. (3) It reduces by one year the expected period over which the worker will receive a pension. (4) It implies paying additional social security contributions. (5) The marginal tax rate on labor income may turn out to be higher than the marginal tax rate on pension income, owing to the high progressiveness of the Spanish income tax schedule.

Figure 9.6 depicts the computed replacement rate, social security wealth, accrual of social security wealth, and implicit tax rate at each age between 55 and 69 for our base case. Social security wealth and its accrual are net of income taxes and presented in €1,000 at 2015 prices.

The replacement rate is zero before reaching 60, the earliest eligibility age for retirement. It then increases gradually, converging to one and exceeding it slightly by age 65. SSW starts up at €92,982, remains flat until reaching 58, and increases steadily, peaking at 65 with a value of €260,958. This increase is due to a very progressive reduction of the penalty for early retirement (effect 2) and the reduction in one year in the expected period

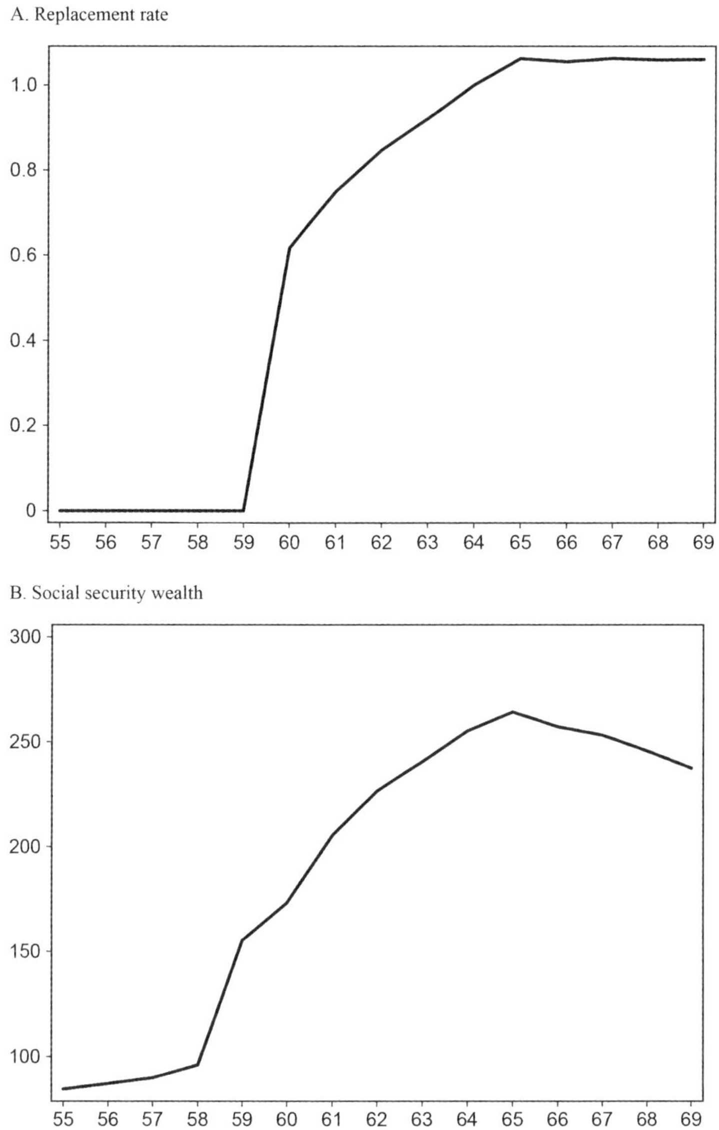

Fig. 9.6 Incentives calculation for a male median-earner worker born in 1925 (after-tax values in €1,000 at 2015 prices)

of pension receipt and increases in one year of social security contributions (effects 3 and 4). There are no further gains from claiming after age 65, as the base-case worker reaches the statutory retirement age in 1990, a year without incentives for late retirement. Thus from age 65 onward, when additional years of work add nothing to the expected pension amount, effects 3 and 4 dominate, and the social security wealth falls. The

C. Accrual of social security wealth

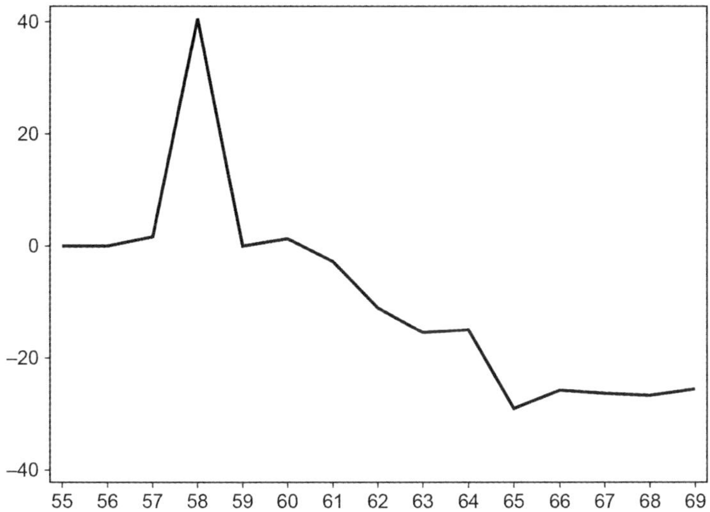

D. Implicit tax rate

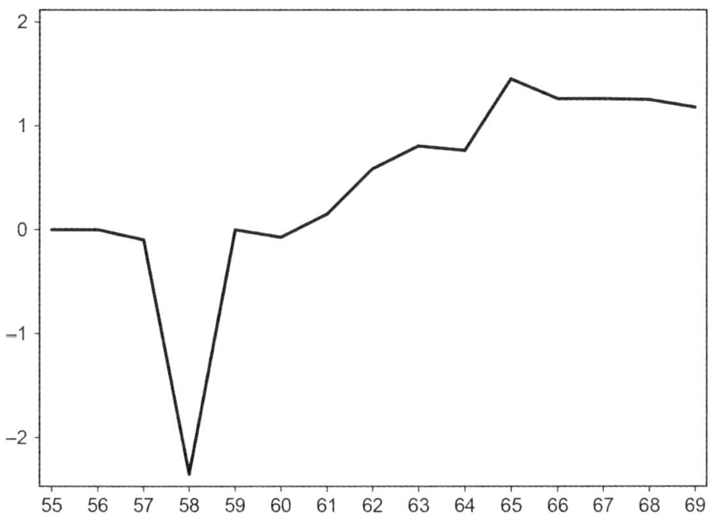

Fig. 9.6 (cont.)

implicit tax rate on continuing work is negative between ages 55 and 60, due to the earliest eligibility age for retirement, and becomes positive thereafter. From 60 to 65, the implicit tax rate increases, showing the disincentives generated by the program to work an additional year. From age 65 onward, the implicit tax rate falls slightly but remains large and positive.

We compare the previously specified base-case worker born in 1925 to an analogous worker (a male median earner) born in 1945. The latter will likely face different social security incentives, as he would retire under a different old-age pension system. For this worker, simulations start in year 2000, when he reaches 55 and completes 35 years of contributions, and run for each year until he turns 69 in 2014. Figure 9.7 shows the comparative incentives calculation for both cohorts of workers, with a solid line for workers born in 1925 and a dashed line for workers born in 1945. In panel A, we note that the replacement rate at the earliest eligibility age is higher for the younger worker than for the older one. It converges when reaching the statutory eligibility age and then becomes larger again for the younger worker. The social security wealth follows a similar pattern: workers born in 1945 started at age 55 with a social security wealth around €15,000 larger than workers born in 1925. Through the age period, their social security wealth remained larger until reaching 65, where they converged. The drop in social security wealth upon reaching the statutory eligibility age for retirement was smaller for workers born in 1945, possibly due to the late retirement incentives introduced by the 1997 reform. Panel D shows the implicit tax rate for both cohorts of workers. We note that the incentives to retire at different ages faced by workers born in 1945 were quite different than the ones of workers born in 1925. First, as with workers born in 1925, workers born in 1945 had a negative tax rate on working before age 60. However, they did not experience the subsidy peak at age 58 that workers born in 1925 did. This is clearly related to the diverging age trends in social security wealth prior to the earliest eligibility age for retirement. Second, younger cohorts experienced a peak tax rate at age 60, whereas the tax rate was close to zero for older cohorts. This results from the heightened generosity of the old-age pension system at age 60 for younger cohorts. Following this peak, the implicit tax rate fell to zero at age 62 before increasing steadily until age 69.

The comparison of these two cohorts of workers is informative of the significant changes in retirement incentives initiated by reforms to the old-age system. In particular, male workers becoming eligible for retirement under the 1980 system seem to have smaller incentives to retire at the earliest eligibility age than male workers eligible for retirement under the 2005 system. This could be due to two factors. The first one is that the penalization for early retirement became smaller, in particular for workers having already contributed 30 years at the time of first eligibility for retirement. The second one comes from the adjustment of the earning profiles for older cohorts, which are slightly disproportionate and intercept the maximum contribution base at several points in time, resulting in smaller incentives for the 1925 cohort to retire prior to the statutory eligibility age.

9.4.2 Differences in Social Security Incentives by Skill Level

In this section, we evaluate to what extent workers with different skill levels face different social security incentives. Figure 9.8 depicts our calculations for the base-case worker described in the previous section, a married

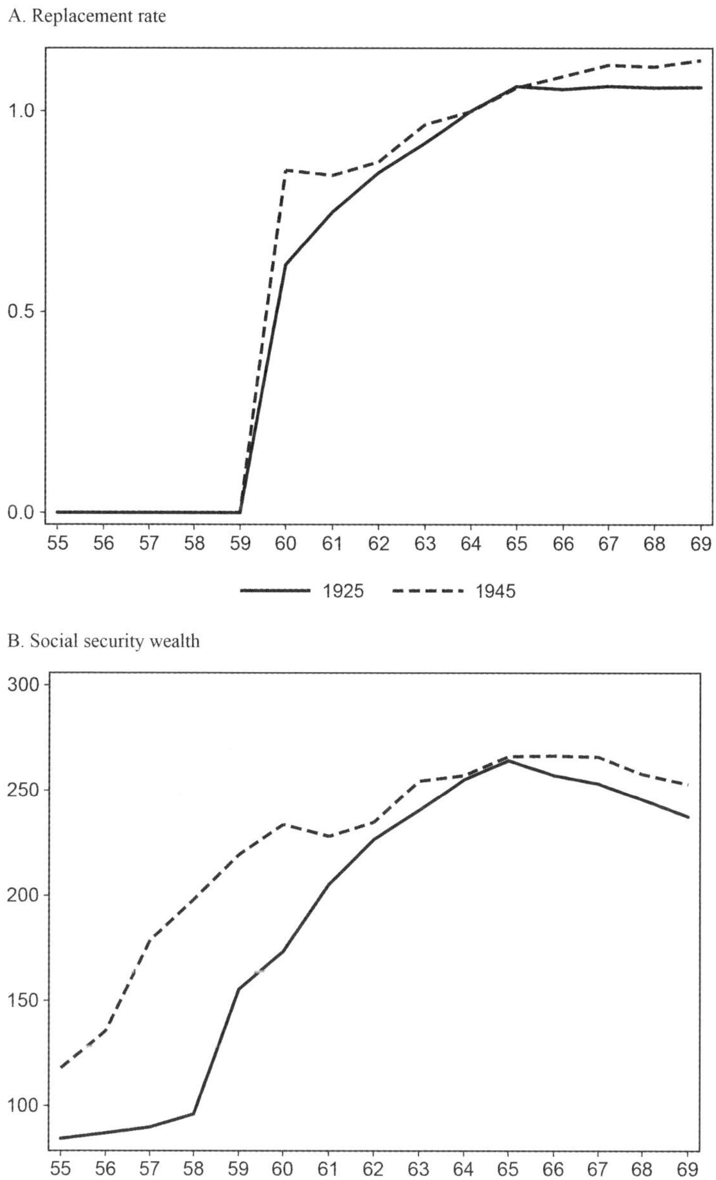

Fig. 9.7 Incentives calculation for a male median-earner worker born in 1925 and in 1945 (after-tax values in €1,000 at 2015 prices)

C. Accrual of social security wealth

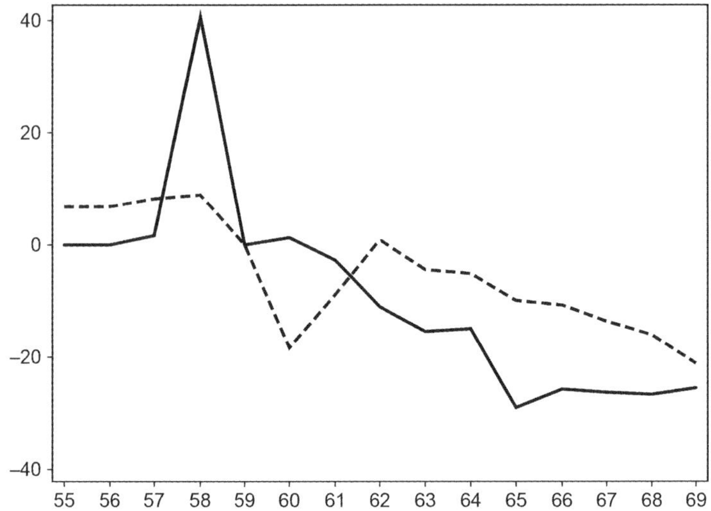

D. Implicit tax rate

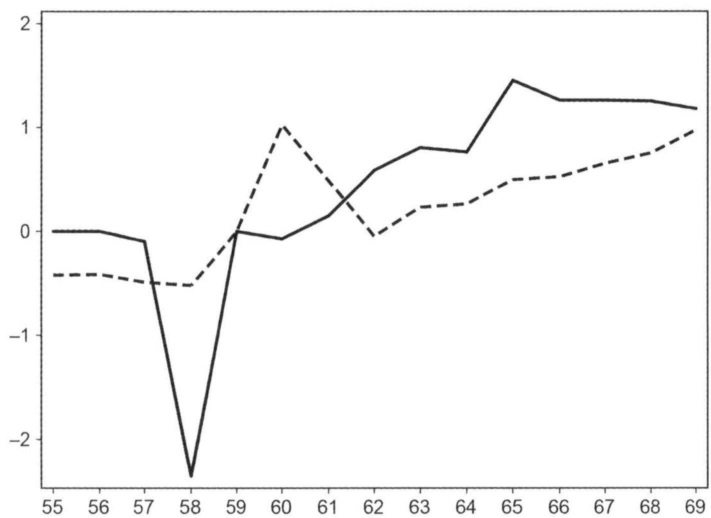

Fig. 9.7 (cont.)

male born in 1925, varying his skill level from medium to low and from medium to high. In each figure, the line with circles corresponds to low skills, the line with triangles to medium skills, and the line with diamonds to high skills. Panel A shows the replacement rate for each type of worker, and we note that low- and medium-skilled workers have identical replacement rates. The replacement rate of high-skilled workers follows the same pattern until

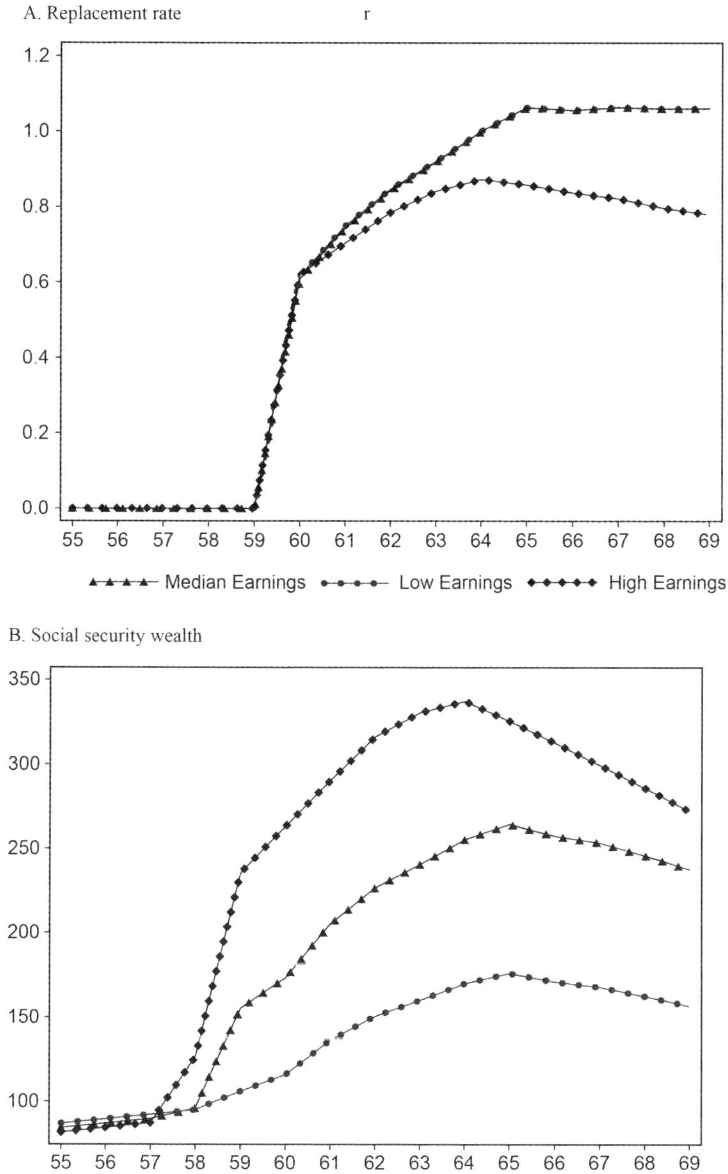

Fig. 9.8 Incentives calculation for a male married worker born in 1925 by skill level (after-tax values in €1,000 at 2015 prices)

C. Accrual of social security wealth

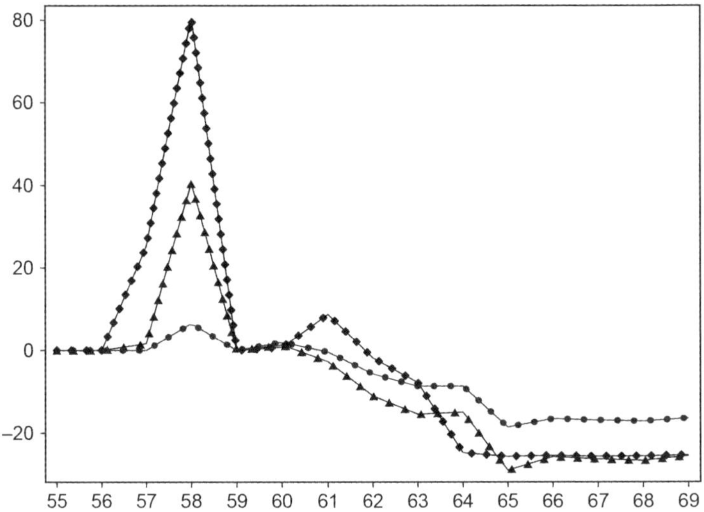

D. Implicit tax rate

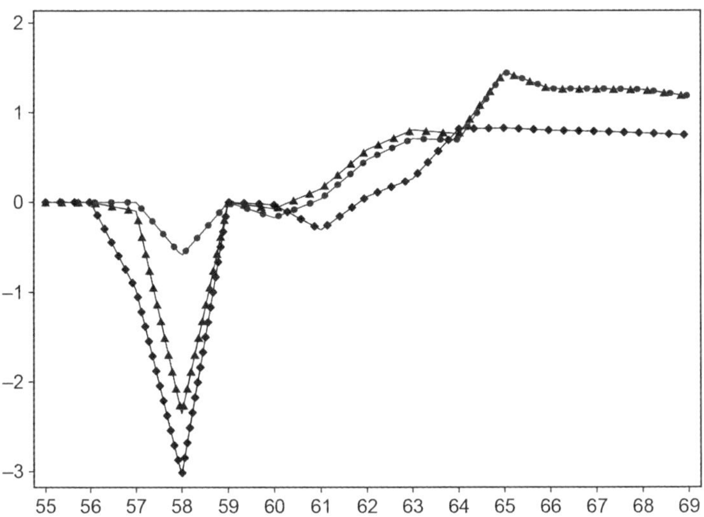

Fig. 9.8 (cont.)

age 60 and then remains at a significantly lower level for all subsequent ages. This is possibly due to the fact that earnings for high-skilled workers born in 1925 were significantly above the maximum contribution level, implying that they get a capped pension that only partially replaces their earnings. The social security wealth and resulting implicit tax rate follow a similar pattern across workers, but with different levels. High-skilled workers experience larger social security wealth at all ages, followed by medium-skilled workers (base case) and then low-skilled workers. The incentives to retire before the statutory eligibility age are lower for high earners through the ages analyzed.

9.4.3 The Effects of Varying the Earnings Profile

In this section, we assess to what extent the measures of social security incentives are sensitive to the earnings profile used. We thus reproduce our simulations using the Spanish time-invariant earning profile. Figure 9.9 compares the resulting incentives using the common earnings profiles (black) and the Spanish earnings profiles (white). The shape of all the measures across all ages is very close independent of the earnings profiles used. In addition, there are marginally no differences in the levels for any of the measures of incentives for low and median earners between the synthetic and Spanish-specific earnings profiles. The differences in the level of social security wealth become more notable the higher the earnings level: common earnings profiles seem to overestimate the social security wealth of median and, particularly, high earners before reaching the statutory eligibility age. This results in a slightly lower implicit tax rate when using the common earnings profiles. Overall, these differences are minimal and do not affect the trends of our measures. In what follows, we continue using the common earnings profiles.

9.4.4 Social Security Incentives by Gender and Marital Status

Figure 9.10 presents a comparison of the calculations for single (in white) and married (in black) male and female workers.[7] The main difference between a married and a single worker is the survivor benefit that can potentially be added at each age point. Across genders, the main difference in the incentives simulated comes from the differences in earnings profiles and survival probabilities. From panel A, we conclude that replacement rates are very close across gender. We note a small difference regarding the replacement rate of high-earning women, which is higher than that of men, most likely because the earnings of women are above the maximum contribution level to a lower extent than those of men. Social security wealth and implicit tax rates are very close across genders, in both shape and levels. The differences across single and married workers are also quite marginal consistently across gender. For males, married workers have a slightly higher social security wealth than single workers across all earning levels. For females, the difference between married and single workers is much smaller and only becomes noticeable from age 60 onward. There are virtually no differences across marital status in the resulting tax rates for males. For females, the resulting tax rate on working an additional year is slightly larger for married than single workers.

7. We assume that husbands are three years older than wives for all types.

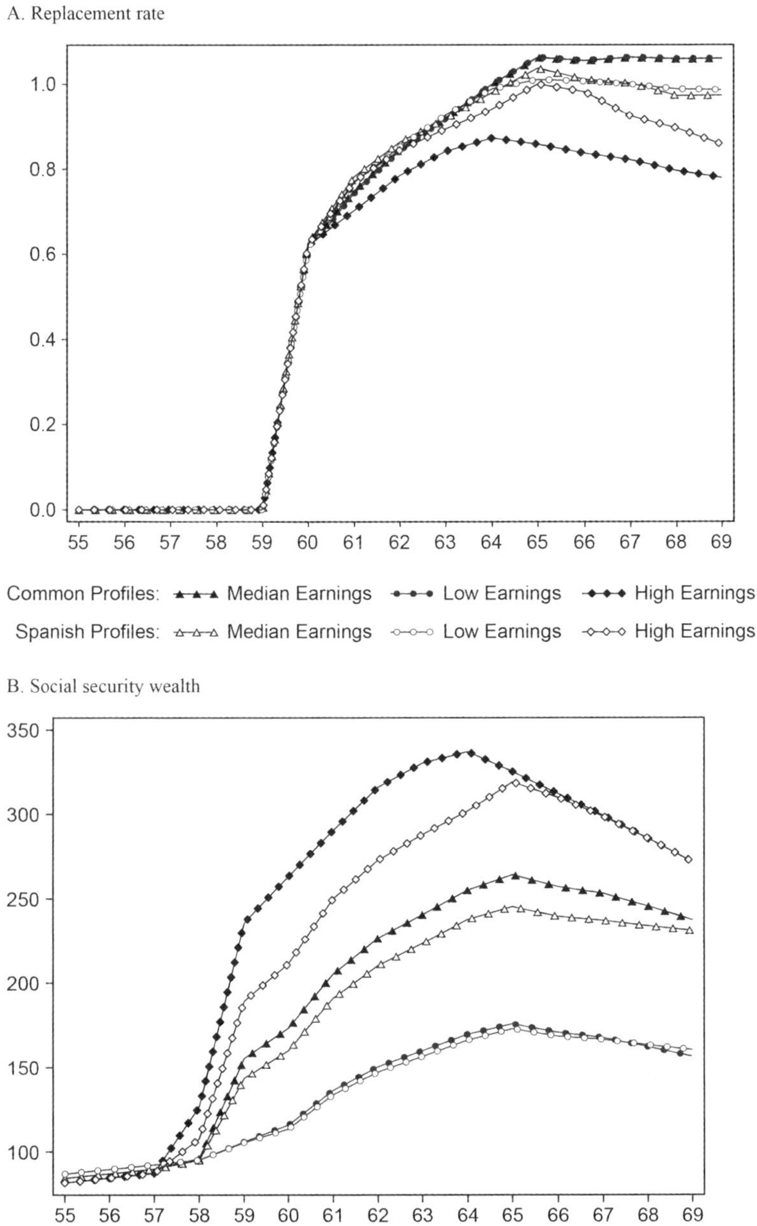

Fig. 9.9 Incentives calculation for a male married worker born in 1925 by level of earnings and earnings profile (after-tax values in €1,000 at 2015 prices)

C. Accrual of social security wealth

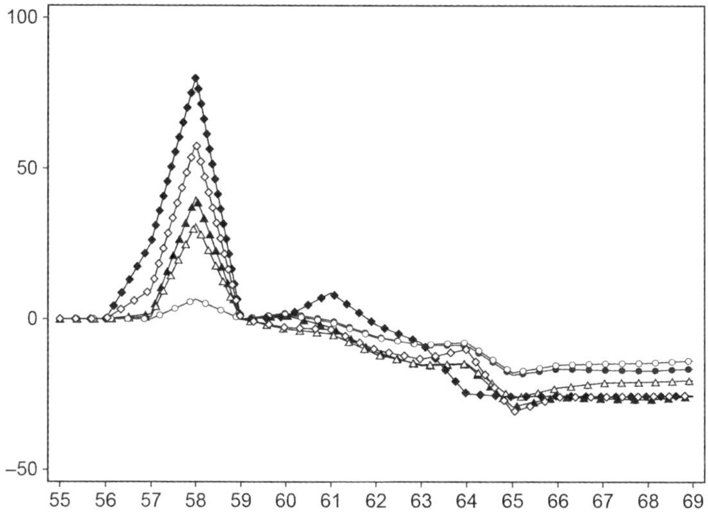

D. Implicit tax rate

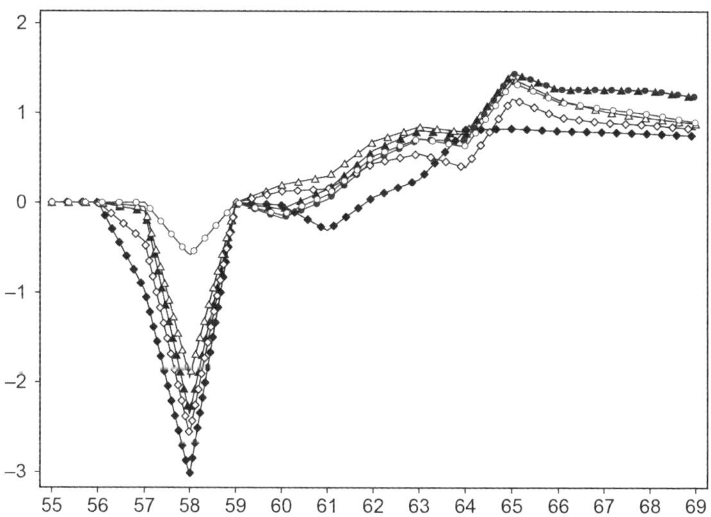

Fig. 9.9 (cont.)

9.4.5 Temporal Variation of Retirement Incentives

The evidence shown in the previous subsections provides an interesting snapshot of the incentives to retire for a worker born in 1925 from his 55th to his 69th birthday. However, it fails to encompass the role of the numerous reforms to the Spanish social security system over the last three decades in

A. Replacement rate, Males

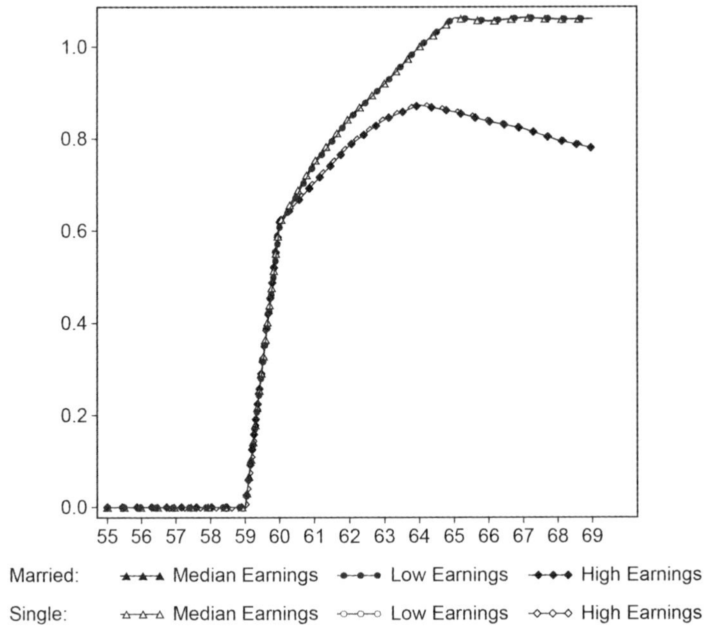

A. Replacement rate, Females

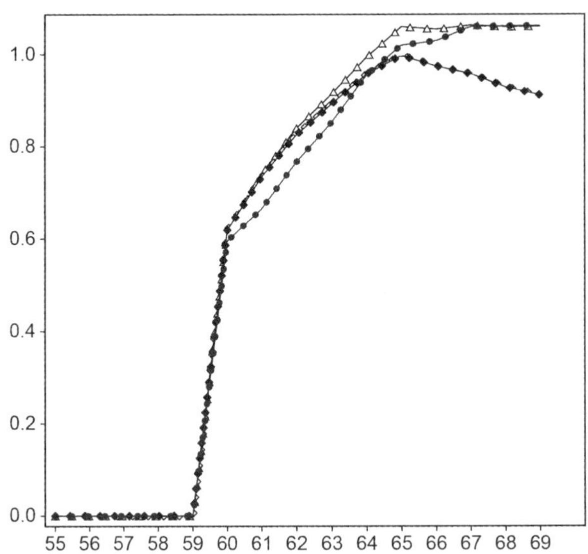

Fig. 9.10 Incentives calculation for a male and female worker born in 1925 by level of earnings and marital status (after-tax values in €1,000 at 2015 prices)

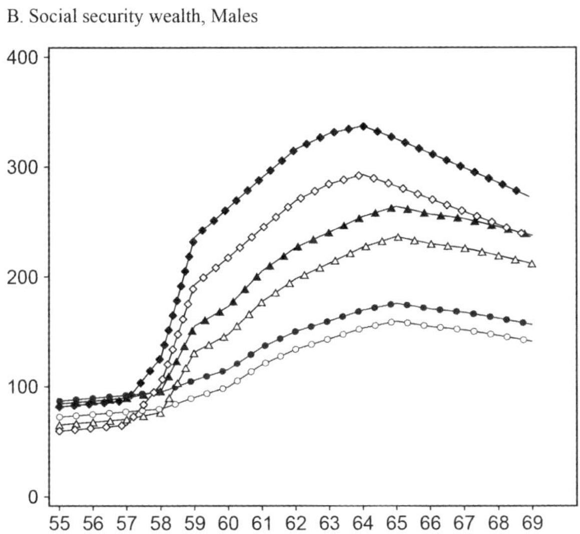

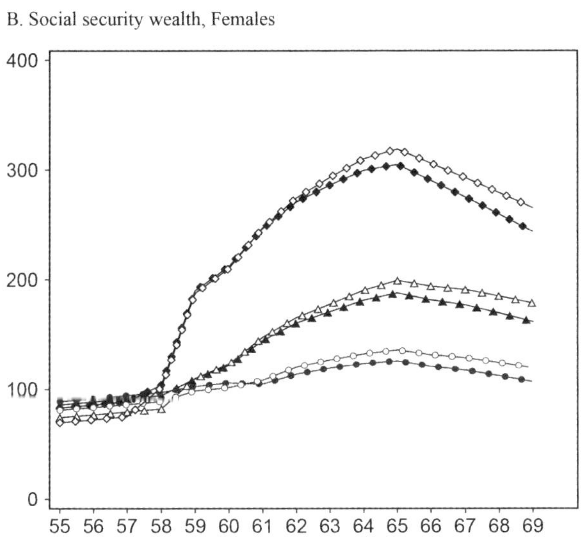

Fig. 9.10 (cont.)

shaping social security incentives. In this subsection, we show how the measures evolve over time and how they relate to policy reforms.

Figure 9.11 shows the evolution of the replacement rate, social security wealth and its accrual, and the implicit tax rate for different age groups. Panel A shows the calculated replacement rate from 1980 to 2015 for workers aged 56, 58, 60, 62, 64, and 65. The replacement rate is zero for workers not eligible for retirement. We note in the figure the change in the penalties for

C. Accrual of social security wealth, Males

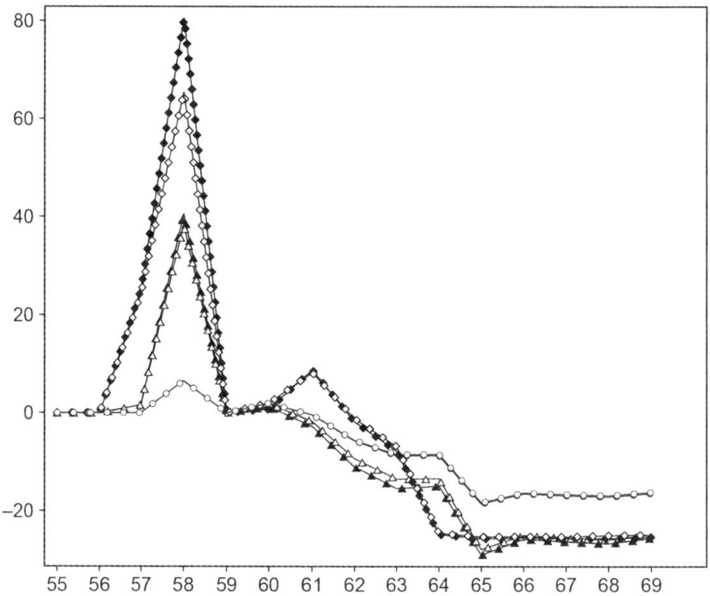

C. Accrual of social security wealth, Females

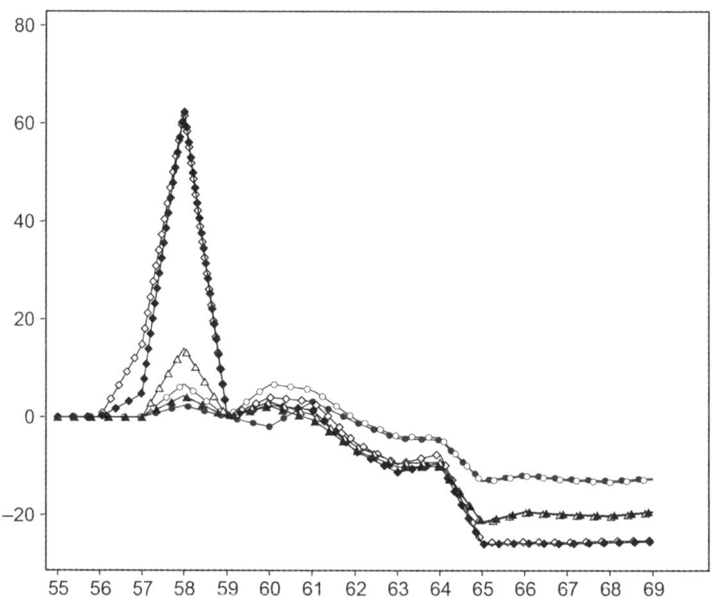

Fig. 9.10 (cont.)

D. Implicit tax rate, Males

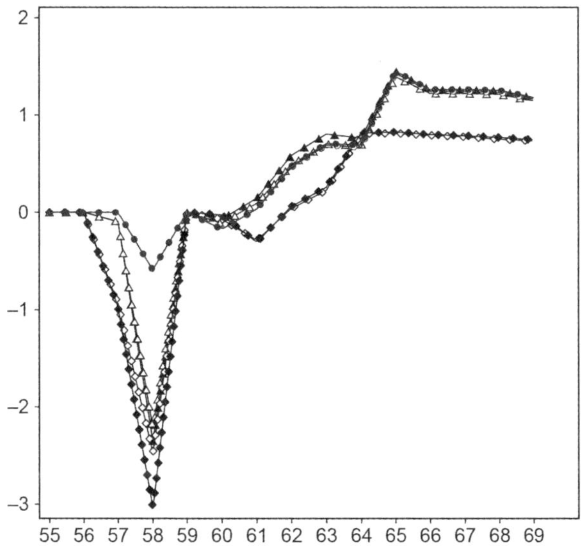

D. Implicit tax rate, Females

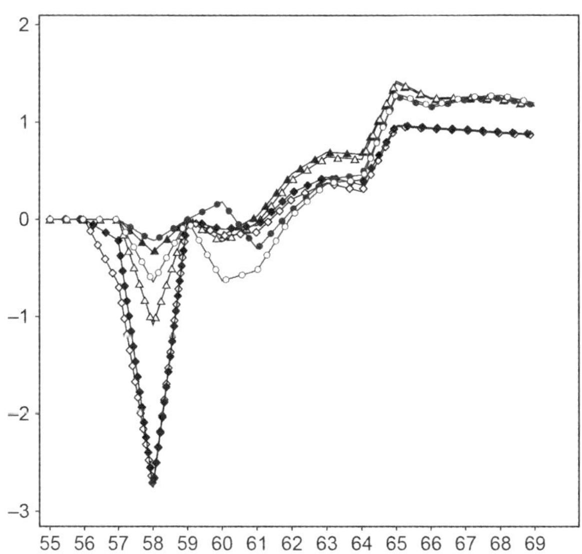

Fig. 9.10 (cont.)

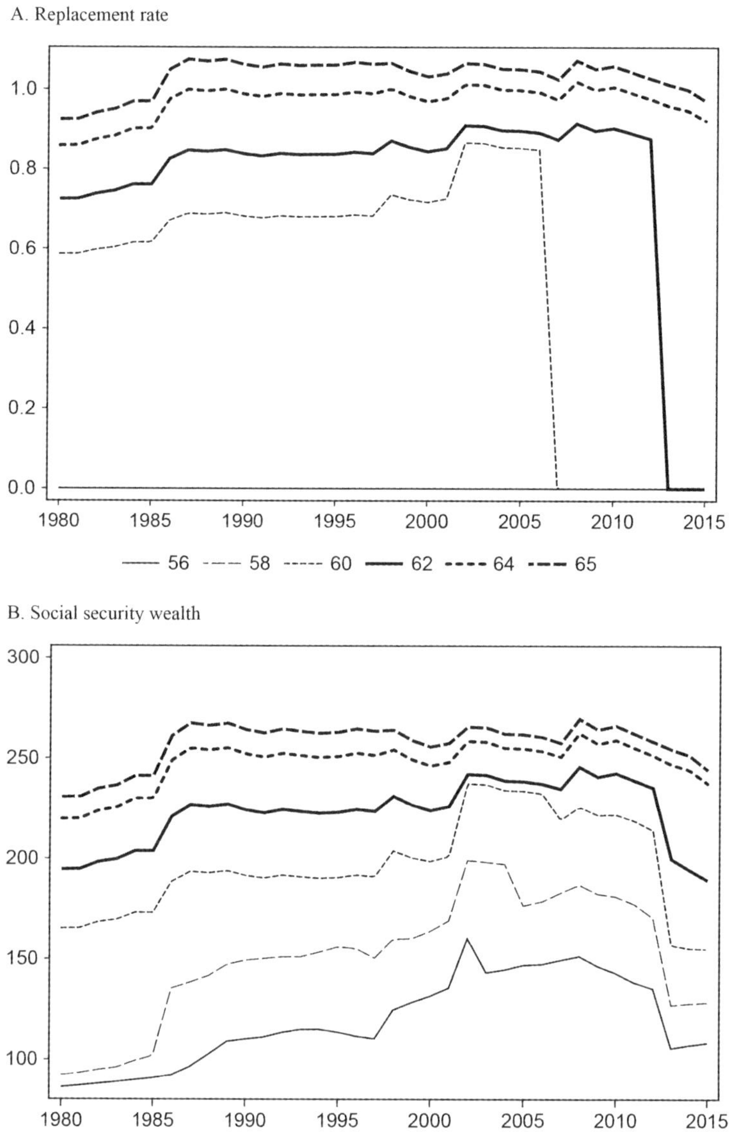

Fig. 9.11 Time-varying incentives calculation for a married male worker with median earnings (after-tax values in €1,000 at 2015 prices)

early retirement in 2002, the change in the earliest eligibility age from 60 to 61 in 2007 (year at which the first cohort unable to contribute before 1967 turned 60), and the change in the earliest eligibility age from 61 to 63 in 2013. Besides these changes, replacement rates are quite stable over time.

Panel B presents the social security wealth, which has been rather constant over time. We note some discontinuities in the trends that correspond

C. Accrual of social security wealth

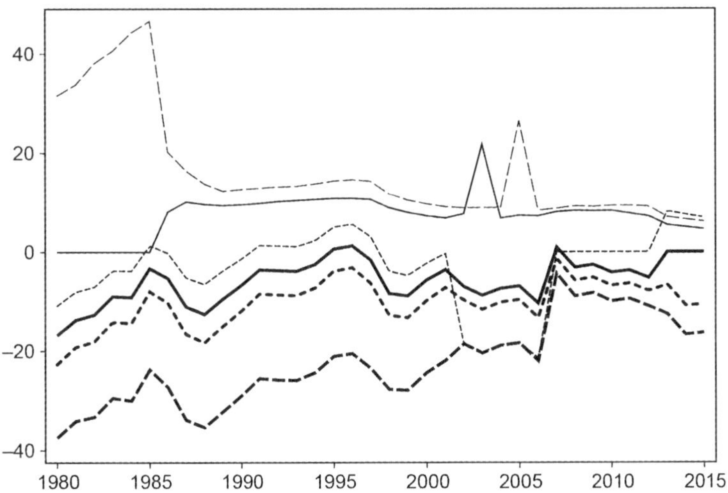

D. Implicit tax rate

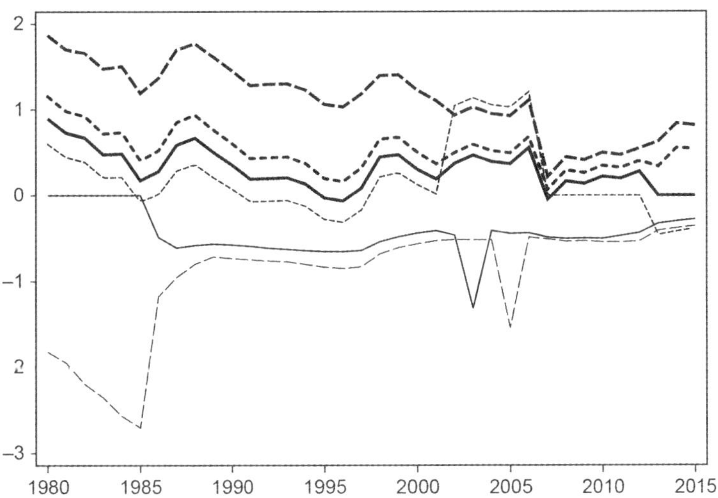

Fig. 9.11 (cont.)

to reform periods of the system. For instance, we note an increase in social security wealth in 1985 for ages 58 to 65 associated with the significant reform in 1985. The principal changes were an increase in the minimum number of years of contributions for pension eligibility (from 8 to 15) and an increase in the number of years entering the computation of the benefit base. Although this reform was implemented to tighten the generosity of the old-age pension system, we observe the opposite effect on the expected social security wealth of workers. This larger incentive to retire may actually have been generated by the increase in the number of working years entering the benefit base, together with decreasing earning profiles from ages 45 to 60.

In 2002, we observe a peak in the social security wealth for ages 56 to 60, coinciding with the introduction of the earliest eligibility age at 61 for workers who started contributing into the system after 1967. The increase in social security wealth seems to affect only a few cohorts. For instance, for those aged 56, the increase in social security wealth peaks in 2002 and entirely subsides in 2003. Those aged 58 experience this increase for three years, from 2002 to 2004, and those aged 60 for five years. This means that only workers born in 1942–46 experience an increase in social security wealth.

The latest reform of the pension system in 2011 (introduced in 2013) generated a drop in social security wealth for all claimants younger than 64. This is possibly due to an increase in the earliest eligibility age from 61 to 63 for workers (there are some exceptions for unemployed workers with long contributive careers).

The implicit tax rate moderately responds to the changes in social security wealth previously described. The trends first change in 1985 and then in 2002, coinciding with the introduction of the earliest eligibility age at 61 for claimants contributing after 1967. The observed changes in the implicit tax rate from 2002 to 2007 are due to different cohorts with different rules regarding the earliest eligibility age approaching the different key ages.

Regarding the level of the implicit tax rate, we note that workers 64 or above are incentivized to retire through the observed period. Similarly, workers aged 62 faced a positive implicit tax rate until 2012; the incentive became zero in 2013 with the increase of the earliest eligibility age from 61 to 63. The incentives to retire faced by workers aged 60 change over time. They were incentivized to retire under the 1980 system and part of the 1985 system. In the mid-1990s, the system seemed to subsidize employment, but by the late 1990s, it was incentivizing retirement. Lastly, from 2007 onward, claimants aged 60 have been incentivized to work, mostly due to the increase in the earliest eligibility age. As expected, workers aged below 60 have always been incentivized to remain employed.

9.4.6 Average Old-Age Pension System Incentives

Figure 9.12 summarizes the previous results on the implicit tax rate by aggregating it over workers aged 55 to 69.[8] The vertical dashed lines signal the reform years, and the notes indicate the main change in the parameters of the old-age pension system in each reform. In 1985, following the increase in the minimum required service years for eligibility, we see a large spike in the implicit tax rate. As previously described, this is due to using decreasing income profiles from age 45 onward. The reduction in the generosity of benefits in 1997 decreased the implicit tax rate, albeit with some delay.

8. We use time-varying population weights on the fraction of individuals in each age category (55 to 59, 60 to 64, and 65 to 69) to compute these averages.

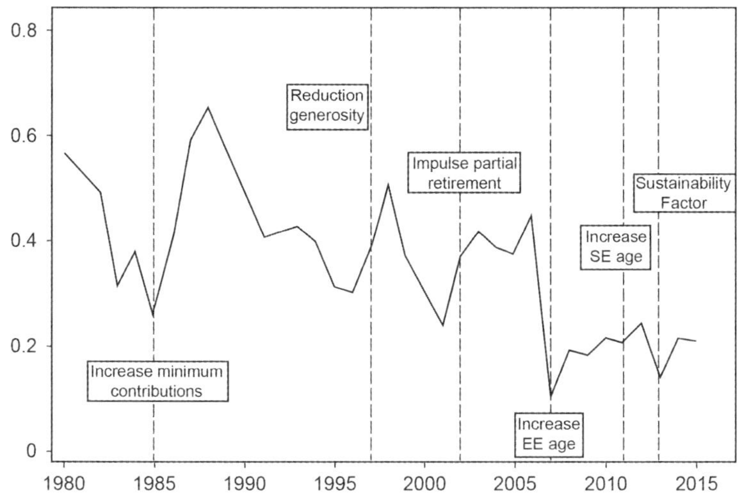

Fig. 9.12 Implicit tax rate

The impulse toward partial retirement in 2002 had mild effects in curbing the implicit tax rate on work. A bigger drop in the retirement incentives was induced by the increase in the earliest eligibility age in 2007. The latest reform in 2011 and the increase in the statutory eligibility age and the introduction of the sustainability factor in 2013 have surprisingly mild effects on the aggregated measure of retirement incentives.

9.4.7 Other Pathways to Retirement

In this subsection, we explore two additional pathways to retirement in the Spanish social security system—namely, disability and unemployment insurance programs. Figure 9.13 shows the incentives for our base-case worker for each retirement pathway. Panel A shows the replacement rate for the three different pathways over ages 55 to 69 for a married male worker with median earnings. First, we notice that the replacement rate is not zero for UI and DI pathways before 60. For DI, the replacement rate is the fraction of benefits to the wage at the onset of disability, and it is linked to the severity of the disability but not to age. For the unemployed, the system contemplates the possibility to enter in an early retirement route if losing their job at age 52 or later, where a positive replacement rate is ensured. From the age of the early eligibility onward, the workers in this pathway are automatically moved to the old-age pathway. It is thus not surprising that the old-age and UI pathways are very close in the social security wealth they provide (panel B). The DI pathway ensures a rather constant social security wealth to disabled workers. From age 60 onward, there is a small decline in wealth. Correspondingly, the implicit tax rate for the DI pathway is flatter and always positive.

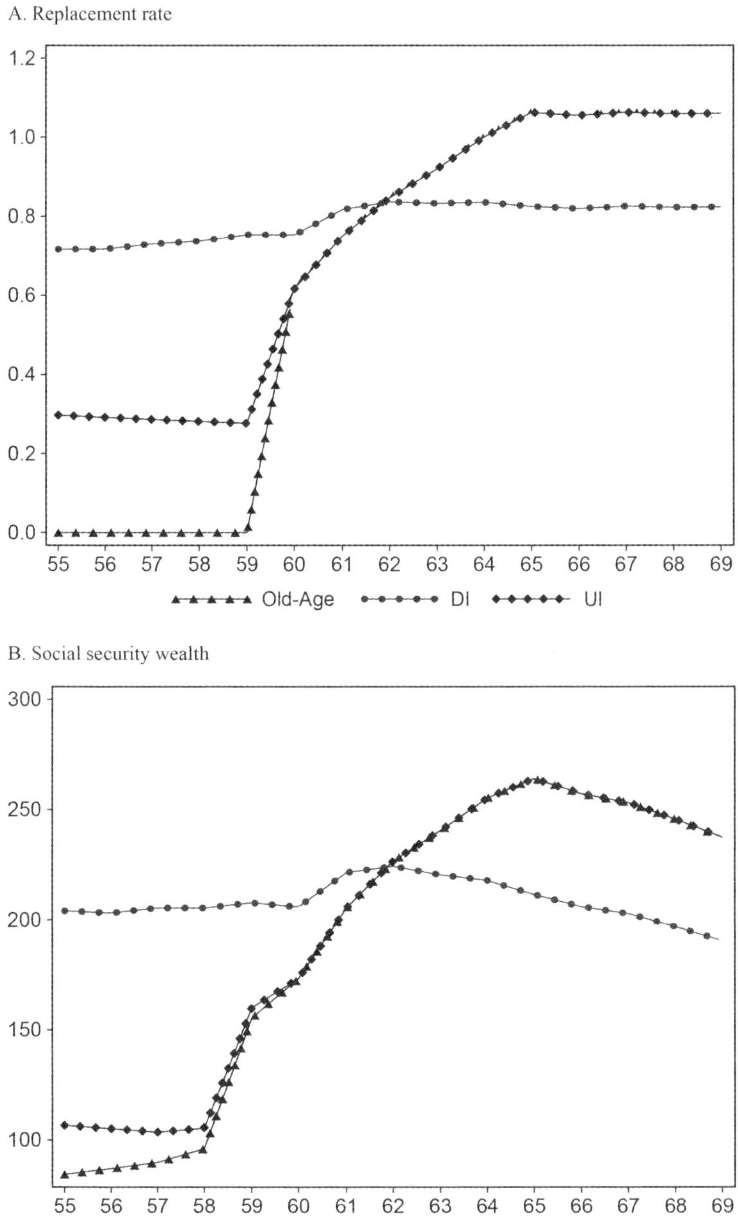

Fig. 9.13 Incentives calculation for a base-case worker born in 1925 by retirement pathway (after-tax values in €1,000 at 2015 prices)

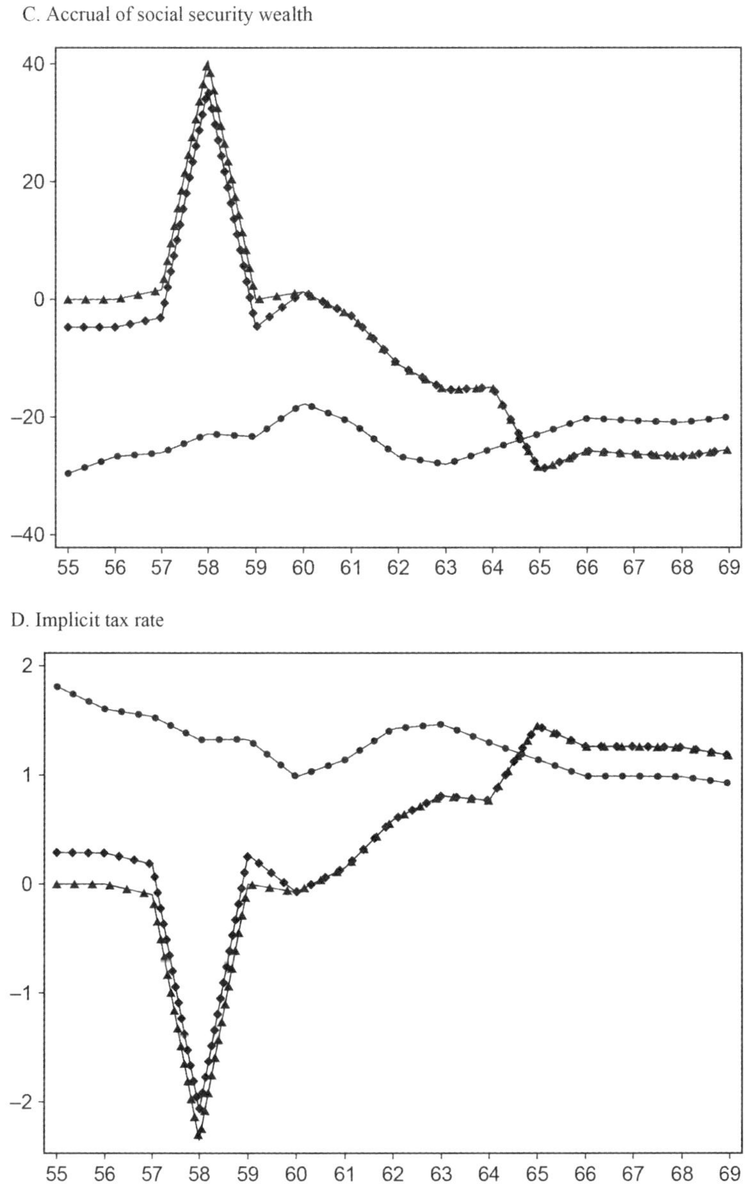
C. Accrual of social security wealth
40
20
0
−20
−40
55 56 57 58 59 60 61 62 63 64 65 66 67 68 69
D. Implicit tax rate
2
1
0
−1
−2
55 56 57 58 59 60 61 62 63 64 65 66 67 68 69

Fig. 9.13 (cont.)

9.4.8 Weighted Temporal Variation of Retirement Incentives

We reproduce the figures showing the temporal variation of the retirement incentives in Spain, aggregated over gender, level of earnings, and pathway to retirement. As explained in subsection 9.3.2, we weight the previously presented results by gender, earnings level, and pathway using the time-varying share of the population in each pathway and from each gender and earning level. Figure 9.14 depicts these aggregated financial incentives to retire. In panel A, we notice that the replacement rate is no longer zero for workers younger than the earliest eligibility age at any point in time given that UI and DI programs offer a positive replacement rate before reaching this threshold. Panel B shows the trends in the aggregated weighted social security wealth. We see that weighted social security wealth has been increasing over time for all ages. This is the result of the aggregation of the different routes into retirement, as social security wealth in each of the pathways either has been constant or has depicted a small increase over time.

9.5 Social Security Incentives and Employment

In this section, we analyze the correlations between the employment rate and the retirement incentives from the social security program. We first examine these correlations graphically by plotting the employment rate against the weighted implicit tax rate of working an additional year. We present the results in subsection 9.5.1. In subsection 9.5.2, we use out-of-labor-force transitions from the Labor Force Survey (EPA) to provide estimates of the association between the implicit tax/subsidy rate and transitions from employment to retirement.

9.5.1 Graphical Representations

Figure 9.15 plots the employment rate of men and women over the implicit tax rate from the old-age pension scheme weighted over earnings level for age groups 55 to 59 and 60 to 64. The graphs also show a linear fitted line over the scatter plot as well as the correlations between the employment rate and the implicit tax rate.

We find that both the significance and the sign of these correlations vary across age groups and gender. For men aged 60 to 64, we find a significant positive correlation between their employment rate and the implicit tax rate. This suggests that the higher the implicit tax (i.e., the incentives to retire), the higher the employment rates of this population group. We find a similar counterintuitive result, albeit statistically insignificant, among women aged 54 to 59. The sign of the correlation is as expected for men aged 54 to 59, albeit statistically insignificant, and among women aged 60 to 64. Only among this group, we find that a higher implicit tax rate is statistically significantly associated with lower employment rates.

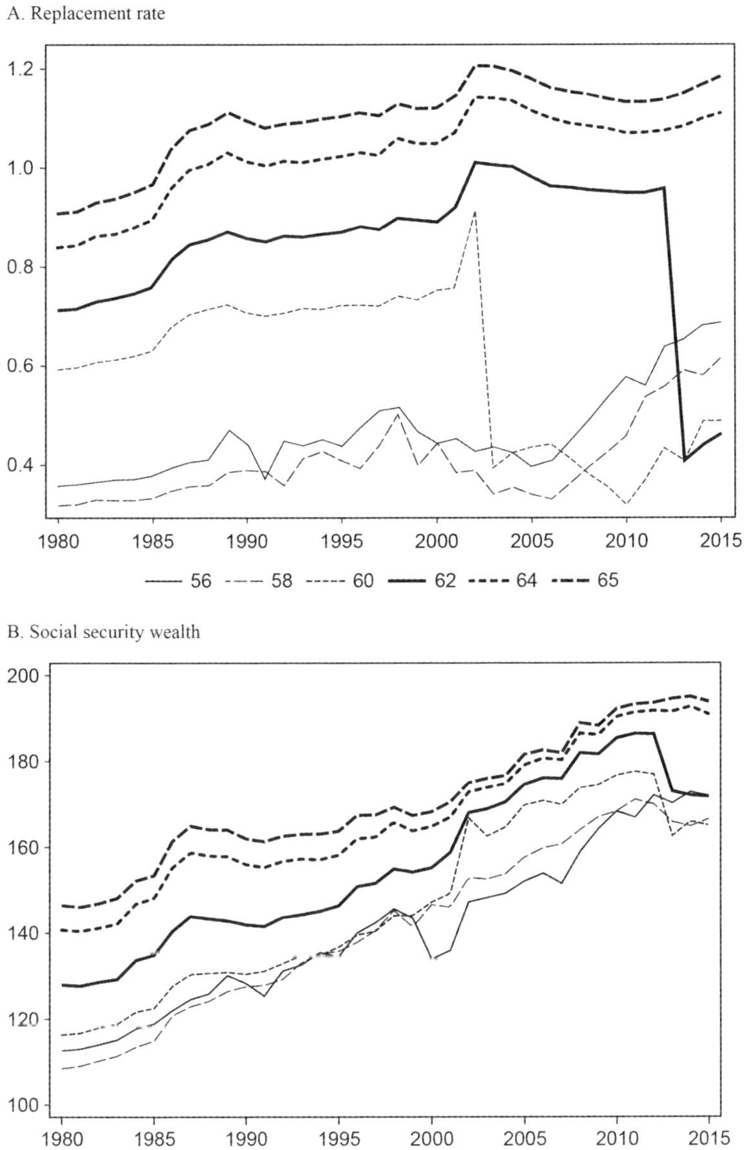

Fig. 9.14 Time-varying weighted incentives calculation (after-tax values in €1,000 at 2015 prices)

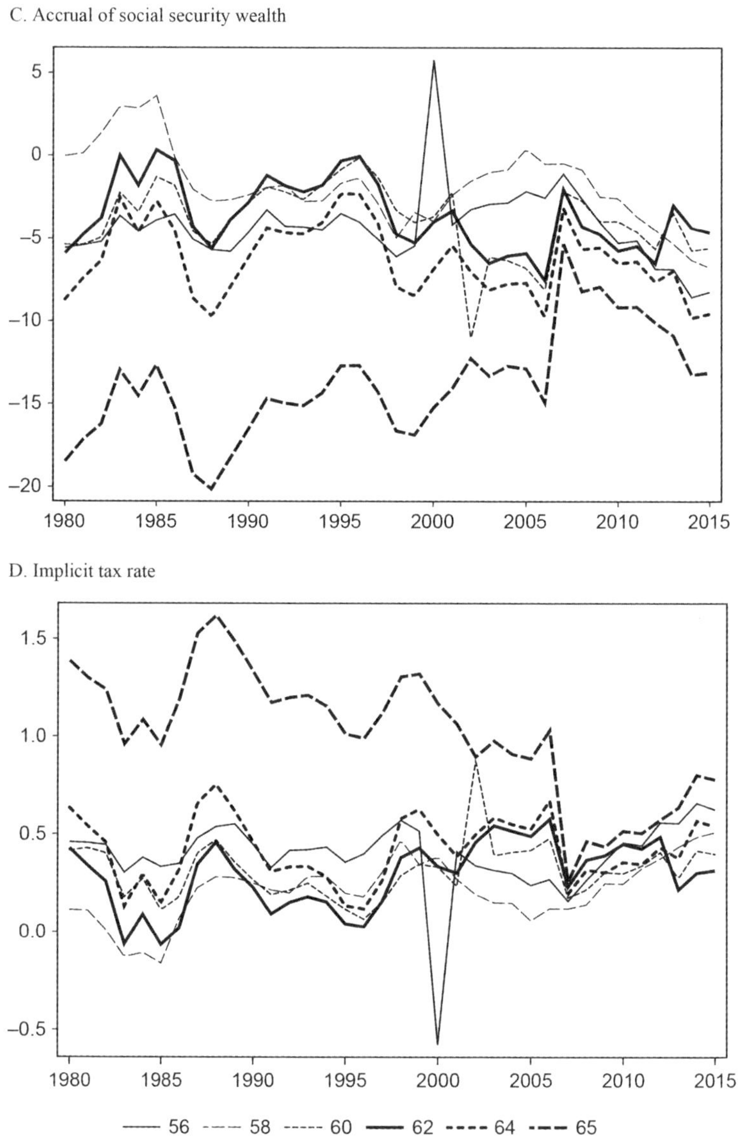

Fig. 9.14 (cont.)

Because part of their implicit tax rate had negative values, this could indicate that higher retirement incentives were correlated with lower employment rates. However, it could also indicate a counterintuitive correlation, where higher retirement incentives were correlated with higher employment rates. As expected, for men aged 54 to 59, we find a positive association,

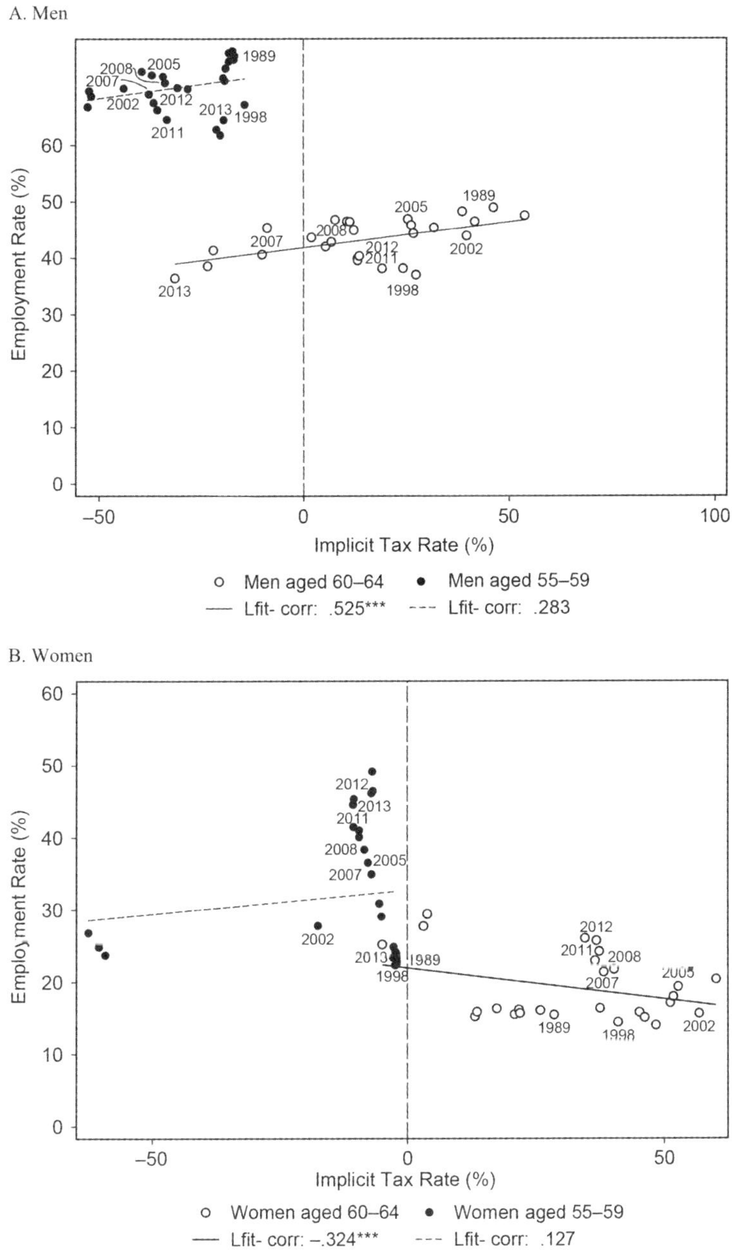

Fig. 9.15 Employment rates over weighted implicit tax rates of men and women

albeit statistically insignificant. Women aged 60 to 64 experienced a negative association between the implicit tax rate and the employment rate. The correlation is statistically significant, but of lower value than for males (–0.324 and 0.525, respectively). For women aged 54 to 59, we find a positive nonsignificant correlation between the retirement incentives and the employment rate, in line with the fact that the implicit tax rate is negative for this group.

9.5.2 Correlation Estimates

The previous graphs showed that the incentives stemming from social security systems could be impacting the national employment rates. However, we were not able to explain all the results. For instance, we found a positive correlation between the incentives and employment rate for males aged 60 to 64 and were not able to explain whether this result was due to the sign of the incentives or was counterintuitive.

The previous figures suggest that trends in financial incentives are not associated with changes in the employment rate. However, the lack of a simple relationship between overall employment rates and aggregate financial incentives measures can be driven by the importance of other factors. García-Gómez et al. (2018) show that other factors, such as changes in the skill composition of workers, cohort effects in female labor force participation, or economic conditions, have probably played a larger role in explaining trends in employment rates among older Spanish workers over the past decades. However, this does not rule out that financial incentives are still important determinants of transitions out of the labor force among Spanish workers.

To get a better idea of the potential effect of social security incentives, we assess their association with the probability of transitioning out of the labor force. In this section, we provide such estimates. We focus in particular on transitions out of the labor force for employed workers and contrast them with the incentives provided by the old-age pension system. For each individual, we obtain information on her current employment status and the situation in the previous year from the EPA for years 1978–2004 and 2006–16. We then construct an indicator for transition out of the labor force using the information from the employment situation in the previous year compared to the current employment situation. As we only consider the incentives from the old-age pathway, we focus on claimants who were employed at time $t - 1$. We aggregate the data at the regional level for the analysis. We estimate the following linear model:

$$Tr_{art}^{emp} = \alpha + \beta INC_{at} + X_{at} + \mu_t + \varepsilon_{art}, \tag{5}$$

where Tr_{art}^{emp} is the share of the employed population of age a in region r in year $t - 1$ transitioning out of the labor force, INC_{at} are the incentive measures aggregated at the region level (implicit tax rate and social security wealth), X_{at} are the covariates (age in all models and dummy variables for the

Table 9.3 Exit from the labor force of employed individuals

	Model 1	Model 2	Model 3	Model 4
Implicit tax rate	0.129***		0.134***	0.137***
	(4.342)		(4.133)	(4.034)
Social security wealth (log)		0.163***	0.180***	0.186***
		(1.958)	(2.805)	(1.563)
Earliest eligibility age				0.015***
				(0.002)
Statutory eligibility age				0.007***
				(0.001)
N	420	420	420	420
Adj. R-squared	0.380	0.339	0.409	0.409

Notes: Estimates of the association between aggregate social security incentives and the share of the employed population aged 55 to 69 that exits the labor force. We aggregate these shares over gender and earnings for each region. All models control for age and year fixed effects and have their standard errors clustered by region and year. Model 1 includes the implicit tax rate as an explanatory variable, whereas model 2 includes the logarithm of the social security wealth. Model 3 includes both variables. Model 4 also includes a dummy variable for the earliest eligibility age and a dummy variable for the statutory eligibility age.

earliest and statutory eligibility age in model 4), and μ_t are year fixed effects. Standard errors are clustered at the region and year levels.

Table 9.3 shows the results. Model 1 shows a statistically significant positive impact of the implicit tax rate on the share of the population that exits the labor force. In particular, a 0.1 increase in the implicit tax rate increases the share of the population that exits the labor force by 1.3 percentage points. This effect is quite similar to that obtained in model 3, where we also include the logarithm of the social security wealth. The magnitude of the association with the aggregate social security wealth is smaller: a 1 percent higher social security wealth increases the share of the population that exits the labor force by 0.163 percentage points. And the estimated effect of social security wealth is similar when we also control for the implicit tax rate. Lastly, we include two dummy variables for the earliest and statutory eligibility ages in model 4. We estimate statistically significant positive effects from both the earliest and statutory eligibility ages, although the effects are small compared to the estimated effect of the implicit tax rate. Importantly, the inclusion of these controls does not change the magnitude of the estimates for the implicit tax rate or the social security wealth, and it does not affect their significance either. Our results suggest there is a strong association between the social security incentives and the exit from the labor force.

9.6 Concluding Remarks

Employment and labor force participation trends of older male workers in Spain and elsewhere reverted and started to increase around the mid-

1990s after two decades of continually falling. In this work, we analyze to what extent the incentives from the social security system can play a role in explaining this evolution. In this respect, we extend existing evidence on the impact of financial incentives on labor force participation in Spain (Boldrin et al. 1999) by computing the financial incentives to leave the labor market that Spanish workers aged 55 to 69 have faced during the past four decades through three different pathways: the old-age pension system, disability insurance, and unemployment insurance. Our primary measure is the implicit tax rate, which compares the change in social security wealth from working an additional year with the earnings obtained during the additional year of work. We compute the implicit tax rate for different types of workers based on their gender and skill level using both a common earnings profile based on data from Germany, the US, and Italy and a Spanish-specific earnings profile.

Our results show that in general, and excluding those having very low wages or discontinued careers, which lead to minimum pensions at all ages (Jiménez-Martín 2014), incentive profiles for the different cohorts are very similar, except for some specific cases in which changes in eligibility ages play a crucial role. Regarding the variation of incentives over time, we find that apart from the substantial real growth of pension rights (social security wealth) observed in the last 35 years and the effect of changes in eligibility conditions, the results seem to be remarkably stable.

As a summary exercise, we compute bivariate correlations between the implicit tax rate and the employment rate of the different types of workers over time and estimate simple regression models exploiting the regional and temporal variations of the data. We find that both the implicit tax rate and social security wealth are important determinants of transitions out of the labor force even after controlling for the earliest and the statutory eligibility ages. Therefore, our results contrast with the previous evidence (see Boldrin et al. 2004; García-Pérez et al. 2013; or Sánchez-Martín et al. 2014), probably due to the availability of long time series in our analysis. Our results provide suggestive evidence that financial incentives and later reforms may be able to explain part of the initial decrease and later increase in labor force participation at older ages in Spain.

Our analysis and conclusions are based on estimates for workers without interrupted working careers or very low wages leading to minimum pensions at all ages (which generally disincentivize work; see Jiménez-Martín 2014 for a discussion). This limitation is more important among women, who are more likely to experience interrupted labor market trajectories due to maternity episodes. This is particularly relevant for the oldest cohorts of women in our analysis. In this sense, further research should exploit individual variation to investigate the role of financial incentives among a more representative sample of the Spanish working population.

Appendix

9.A1 Key Parameters of the Spanish Social Security System from 1980 Onward

Table 9.A1 Key parameters of old-age pensions from 1980 onward

	Before 1985	From 1985 to 1997	From 1997 to 2001	From 2002 to 2007
		A. Eligibility conditions		
A1. Normal retirement age [ā]	65 years	Id.	Id.	Id.
A2. Minimum contribution years [n]	10 years	15 years	Id.	Id.
		B. Pension computation		
B1. Contributions entering in benefit base [BB]	2 years	8 years	15 years[a]	15 years
B2. Replacement rate	0, if $n < 10$ $\begin{cases} .5 + 0.02(n-10), \text{ if } 35 > n \geq 10 \\ 1, \text{ if } n \geq 35 \end{cases}$	0, if $n < 15$ $\begin{cases} .6 + 0.02(n-15), \text{ if } 35 > n \geq 15 \\ 1, \text{ if } n \geq 35 \end{cases}$	0, if $n < 15$ $\begin{cases} .5 + 0.03(n-15), \text{ if } 25 > n \geq 15 \\ .8 + 0.02(n-25), \text{ if } 35 > n \geq 25 \\ 1, \text{ if } n \geq 35 \end{cases}$	Id.

(continued)

Table 9.A1 **(continued)**

	Before 1985	From 1985 to 1997	From 1997 to 2001	From 2002 to 2007
C. Early retirement				
C1. Early retirement age	60, if first contribution prior to 1967	Id.	Id.	60, if first contribution prior to 1967; 61 if after 1967
C2. Penalization [κ] where benefit = 1 − κ(ā − a)	κ = .08	κ = .08	$\kappa \begin{cases} .08 \text{ if } n < 40 \\ .07 \text{ if } 40 \geq n \end{cases}$	$\kappa \begin{cases} .08 \text{ if } n = 30 \\ .075 \text{ if } 31 \leq n \leq 30 \\ .07 \text{ if } 35 \leq n \leq 37 \\ .065 \text{ if } 38 \leq n \leq 39 \\ .06 \text{ if } 40 \geq n \end{cases}$
C2. Minimum pension				27 percent average income
C3. Partial retirement	No	No	No	Yes; working hours reduced from 25 percent–85 percent; replacement of working hours mandatory
D. Late retirement				
D1. Incentives for late retirement	No	No	$0.8 + .02(a - 65)$ if $35 \geq n > 25$ and $a \geq 65$	$1 + .02(a - 65)$ if $n \geq 35$ and $a \geq 65$
D2. Partial retirement	No		No	Yes

[a] In 1997, the last 108 months are included, the last 120 months in 1998, the last 132 months in 1999, the last 144 months in 2000, the last 156 months in 2001, the last 180 months from 2002 onward.

Table 9.A2 Key parameters of old-age pensions from 1980 onward (cont.)

	From 2007 to 2010	From 2011 onward	2013 amendment
		A. Eligibility conditions	
A1. Normal retirement age	65 years	67 years,[a] or 65 years old if 38.5 years of contributions	
A2. Minimum contribution years [c]	15 years	Id.	
		B. Pension computation	
			Introduction of new adjustment index (IRP)
B1. Contributions entering in benefit base [BB]	15 years	17 years. 25 years from 2022 onward.	$IPR_{t+1} = \overline{g}_{I,t+1} + \overline{g}_{P,t+1} + \overline{g}_{s,t+1} + a\left(\frac{I^*_{t+1} - G^*_{t+1}}{G^*_{t+1}}\right)$
B2. Replacement rate	0, if $n < 15$ $\begin{cases} .5 + 0.03(n - 15), \text{ if } 25 > n \geq 15 \\ .8 + 0.02(n - 25), \text{ if } 35 > n \geq 25 \\ 1, \text{ if } n \geq 35 \end{cases}$ 1, if $n < 35$	$\begin{cases} 0, \text{ if } a < 15 \\ 0.5 + 0.023(n - 15), \text{ if } 37 > n \geq 15 \\ 1, \text{ if } n \geq 35 \end{cases}$	where $\overline{g}_{I,t+1}$ is growth rate of contributions, $\overline{g}_{P,t+1}$ is the growth rate of the number of pensions, $\overline{g}_{s,t+1}$ is the growth of the median pension due to substitution effects
B3. Minimum pension	32 percent average earnings w/o dependent spouse. 39.9 percent w/ dependent spouse	34 percent average earnings w/o dependent spouse. 42 percent w dependent spouse	Minimum: .25 percent.
Maximum: CPI + .50 percent			
B4. Maximum pension	159 percent average earnings	153 percent average earnings	

(continued)

Table 9.A2 (continued)

	From 2007 to 2010	From 2011 onward	2013 amendment
		C. Early retirement	
C1. Early retirement age	61 (involuntary retirement) or 63 (voluntary retirement), with 33 years of contr.	63 (involuntary retirement) or 65 (voluntary retirement), with 33 or 35 years of contr. resp.	Introduction of sustainability factor (SF)
C2. Actuarial reduction of benefits	$1 - \kappa(a - 61)$, if $65 > a \geq 61$ where $\kappa \begin{cases} 0.75 \text{ if } 30 \leq n \leq 34 \\ .07 \text{ if } 35 \leq n \leq 39 \\ .06 \text{ if } 40 \leq n \end{cases}$	$1 - \kappa(a - 63)$, if $67 > a \geq 63$ where $\kappa \in$ [0.08; 0.085]	Intergenerational equity factor (IEF) $IEF_{j,t+s} = \frac{e_{j,t}}{e_{j,t=s}}$ $e_{j,t}$ life expectancy of pensioner retiring at age j and period t $e_{j,t+s}$ life expectancy of pensioner retiring at age j and period $t + s$
C2. Minimum pension	30 percent average earnings w/o dependent spouse; 37 percent w/ dependent spouse	32 percent average earnings w/o dependent spouse; 39 percent w/ dependent spouse	C2. Minimum pension
C3. Partial retirement	Yes; working hours reduced from 25 percent–75 percent, replacement of working hours mandatory, proportional contribution to the pension system	Yes, full contribution to the pension system	
		D. Late retirement	
D1. Incentives for late retirement	If $a \geq 65$, then $\begin{cases} 1 + .02(a - 65) \text{ if } n \geq 35 \\ 1 + .03(a - 65) \text{ if } n \geq 40 \end{cases}$	If $a \geq 67$, then $\begin{cases} 1 + .02(a - 65) \text{ if } 15 \leq n < 25 \\ 1 + .0275(a - 65) \text{ if } 25 \leq n < 37 \\ 1 + .04(a - 65) \text{ if } n \geq 37 \end{cases}$	
D2. Partial retirement	Yes; no replacement of working hours	Yes; no replacement of working hours	

[a] The retirement age of 67 will be reached in 2027. From 2013 to 2018, retirement age will ncrease in one month per year. From 2019 to 2026, retirement age will increase in two months per year. CPI = consumer price index

Table 9.A3 **Summary of key parameters of DI**

	Ordinary illness	Work-related accident	Work-unrelated accident	Noncontributory
		A. Eligibility conditions		
	Incapacity to perform current job (IPT), workers older than 55 (IPTC)			
	Age >26: Contributed 1/4 time between 20 years old and disabling condition, >5 years	No contributive requirement	No contributive requirement	Not eligible for contributory disability insurance
	Age ≤26: Contributed 1/2 time between 16 years old and disabling condition			Means-tested
	Full incapacity (IPA) and Severe incapacity (GI)			
	15 years of contribution			
		B. Benefit calculation		
B1. Regulatory base	0.86*wage of last 8 years of work	Last year of work	0.86*highest wage of 24 months within last 7 years	
B2. Replacement rate	**IPT:** 55 percent; **IPTC:** Up to 75 percent, **IPA:** 100 percent; **GI:** 150 percent	Id.	Id.	55 percent of minimum wage
B3. Income tax rules	**IPT** and **IPCT:** General income tax reg. [a] **IPA** and **GI:** Tax exempted	Id	Id.	

[a] There are tax deductions for IPT beneficiaries who are employed at the same time than receiving benefits. Precisely, there is a reduction in the earnings used to calculate the income tax of €2,800/year if their degree of disability is low (between 33 percent and 65 percent) or €6,200 if the disability level is higher (more than 65 percent) or if the disabled have reduced mobility.

Classification of degrees of disability:

Incapacity to perform current job (IPT and IPTC): The individual is impaired to develop all of the fundamental tasks of his or her usual job or professional activity, but he or she is still capable of developing a different job or professional activity.

Full incapacity (IPA): The individual is impaired for the development of any kind of job or professional activity.

Severe incapacity (GI): Individuals who, as a result of anatomic or functional losses, need the assistance of a third person to develop essential activities of daily living.

References

Belloni, M., and R. Alessie. 2009. "The Importance of Financial Incentives on Retirement Choices: New Evidence for Italy." *Labour Economics* 16 (5): 578–88.

Boldrin, M., P. García-Gómez, and S. Jiménez-Martín. 2010. "Social Security Incentives, Exit from the Workforce and Entry of the Young." In *Social Security Programs and Retirement around the World: The Relationship to Youth Employment*, edited by Jonathan Gruber and David A. Wise, 261–94. Chicago: University of Chicago Press.

Boldrin, M., S. Jiménez-Martín, and F. Peracchi. 1999. "Social Security and Retirement in Spain." In *Social Security and Retirement around the World*, edited by Jonathan Gruber and David A. Wise, 305–53. Chicago: University of Chicago Press.

Boldrin, M., S. Jiménez-Martín, and F. Peracchi. 2004. "Micro-modeling of Retirement Behavior in Spain." In *Social Security Programs and Retirement around the World: Micro-estimation*, edited by Jonathan Gruber and David A. Wise, 499–578. Chicago: University of Chicago Press.

Börsch-Supan, A. 2000. "Incentive Effects of Social Security on Labor Force Participation: Evidence in Germany and across Europe." *Journal of Public Economics* 78 (1–2): 25–49.

Cairó-Blanco, I. 2010. "An Empirical Analysis of Retirement Behaviour in Spain: Partial versus Full Retirement." *SERIEs* 1 (3): 325–56.

Coile, C. C. 2018. "Working Longer in the U.S.: Trends and Explanations." In *Social Security Programs and Retirement around the World: Working Longer*, edited by Courtney Coile, Kevin Milligan, and David A. Wise, 299–324. Chicago: University of Chicago Press.

Coile, C. C., and P. B. Levine. 2007. "Labor Market Shocks and Retirement: Do Government Programs Matter?" *Journal of Public Economics* 91 (10): 1902–19.

Coile, C. C., and P. B. Levine. 2011. "The Market Crash and Mass Layoffs: How the Current Economic Crisis May Affect Retirement." *BE Journal of Economic Analysis and Policy* 11 (1): 22.

Conde-Ruiz, J. I., and C. I. González. 2013. "Reforma de pensiones 2011 en España." *Hacienda Pública Española/Review of Public Economics* 204 (1): 9–44.

Díaz-Giménez, Javier, and Julián Díaz-Saavedra. 2017. "The Future of Spanish Pensions." *Journal of Pension Economics and Finance* 16 (2): 233–65.

European Union. 2012. *The 2012 Aging Report: Economic and Budgetary Projections for the 27 EU Member States (2010–2060)*. European Commission.

Eurostat. 2016. "Life Table." https://appsso.eurostat.ec.europa.eu/nui/show.do?dataset=demo_mlifetable&lang=en.

García-Gómez, P., S. Jiménez-Martín, and J. V. Castelló. 2012. "Health, Disability, and Pathways into Retirement in Spain." In *Social Security Programs and Retirement around the World: Historical Trends in Mortality and Health, Employment, and Disability Insurance Participation and Reforms*, edited by David A. Wise, 127–74. Chicago: University of Chicago Press.

García-Gómez, P., S. Jiménez-Martín, and J. V. Castelló. 2018. "Trends in Labor Force Participation of Older Workers in Spain." In *Social Security Programs and Retirement around the World: Working Longer*, edited by Courtney Coile, Kevin Milligan, and David A. Wise, 205–30. Chicago: University of Chicago Press.

García-Pérez, J. I., S. Jiménez-Martín, and A. R. Sánchez-Martín. 2013. "Retirement Incentives, Individual Heterogeneity and Labor Transitions of Employed and Unemployed Workers." *Labour Economics* 20:106–20.

Gruber, J., and D. A. Wise, eds. 1999. *Social Security and Retirement around the World*. Chicago: University of Chicago Press.

Gruber, J., and D. A. Wise, eds. 2004. *Social Security Programs and Retirement around the World: Micro-estimation*. Chicago: University of Chicago Press.

Hairault, J.-O., T. Sopraseuth, and F. Langot. 2010. "Distance to Retirement and Older Workers' Employment: The Case for Delaying the Retirement Age." *Journal of the European Economic Association* 8 (5): 1034–76.

Jiménez-Martín, S. 2014. "The Incentive Effects of Minimum Pensions." *IZA World of Labor* 84.

Jiménez-Martín, S., A. J. Mestres, and J. V. Castelló. 2018. "Great Recession and Disability Insurance in Spain." *Empirical Economics* 56 (5): 1623–45.

Jiménez-Martín, S., and A. R. Sánchez-Martín. 2004. "The Effect of Pension Rules on Retirement Monetary Incentives with an Application to Pension Reforms in Spain." *Hacienda Pública Española, IEF* 169 (2): 35–66.

OECD. 2001. *Economic Survey—Spain*. Paris: OECD.

Regidor, E., L. Reques, M. J. Belza, A. E. Kunst, J. P. Mackenbach, and L. de la Fuente. 2016. "Education and Mortality in Spain: A National Study Supports Local Findings." *International Journal of Public Health* 61 (1): 139–45.

Samwick, A. A. 1998. "New Evidence on Pensions, Social Security, and the Timing of Retirement." *Journal of Public Economics* 70 (2): 207–36.

Sánchez, A. R. 2014. "The Automatic Adjustment of Pension Expenditures in Spain: An Evaluation of the 2013 Pension Reform." Technical report, Banco de España.

Sánchez, A. R. 2017. "Proyecciones Financieras y de Bienestar del Sistema Español de Pensiones: Modelizacióon en Equilibrio General." Technical report, FEDEA.

Sánchez-Martín, A. R., J. I. García-Pérez, and S. Jiménez-Martín. 2014. "Delaying the Normal and Early Retirement Ages in Spain: Behavioural and Welfare Consequences for Employed and Unemployed Workers." *De Economist* 162 (4): 341–75.

Van Baal, P., F. Peters, J. Mackenbach, and W. Nusselder. 2016. "Forecasting Differences in Life Expectancy by Education." *Population Studies* 70 (2): 201–16.

10

Social Security Reforms and the Changing Retirement Behavior in Sweden

Mårten Palme and Lisa Laun

10.1 Introduction

The labor force participation of men in the 60 to 64 age group has changed dramatically over the most recent decades in Sweden. In the early 1980s, more than 70 percent of this age group participated in the labor market. By the end of the 1990s, this decreased to around 55 percent. Since then, however, there has been a steady increase in the participation rate, and in 2016, the labor force participation of this group exceeded 75 percent. For females, there is partially another story. In the 1980s and 1990s, there was still an increase in labor force participation following the large overall trend toward increased female labor force participation. The recent increase in labor force participation has, however, been very similar to the development among males.

Over the same period, there has been a steady improvement in health for both males and females, and there have also been improvements in the work environment. The population has become more educated (see, e.g., Laun and Palme 2019). Guided by the correlation between all these characteristics in the population and old-age labor force participation, we would expect a steady increase in employment among the elderly during the past decades, but as described above, this prediction only concurs with the development since the late 1990s.

Mårten Palme is a professor of economics at Stockholm University.

Lisa Laun is a researcher at the Institute for Evaluation of Labour Market and Education Policy (IFAU).

This chapter is a part of the National Bureau of Economic Research International Social Security project, headed by Axel Börsch-Supan and Courtney Coile. For acknowledgments, sources of research support, and disclosure of the author's or authors' material financial relationships, if any, please see https://www.nber.org/chapters/c14200.ack.

During the 35-year period covered in this study, there have also been several changes in income taxes and public income security programs that have affected the economic incentives for workers to stay in the labor force. The most important changes are the major reform of the income tax system in 1991; the introduction of earned income tax credits in a series of reforms starting in 2007; a large reform of the old-age pension system, replacing the old defined benefit scheme with a notional defined contribution (NDC) scheme; introduction of gradually more stringent eligibility rules for the disability insurance (DI) program; and, finally, a change in the rules for mandatory retirement in 2001.

In this chapter, we focus on the effect of the reform of the old-age pension system and the stricter eligibility rules in DI and use earnings histories of different hypothetical workers to calculate changes in the economic incentives to stay in the labor force between 1980 and 2015. This means that we leave out several changes in incentives that may have played a role, such as changes in income taxes, negotiated occupational pension programs, or private pensions. We calculate three sets of measures for economic incentives. First, we calculate the replacement rate (RR)—the ratio between post- and preretirement earnings—and the social security wealth (SSW). These two measures reflect the income level after retirement. Second, we calculate the accrual in SSW of staying one additional year in the labor force, which measures the marginal gain in benefits of remaining employed. Finally, we calculate the implicit tax of remaining employed (ITAX), which includes both income levels and changes in income as a result of staying one additional year in one statistic.

The results show very large effects on economic incentives of the transition rules for the implementation of the prereform old-age pension scheme in the 1980s. It is likely that these incentives contributed to the fact that very few claimed old-age pension before age 65 under the prereform system. The dominant pathway for those who left the labor force earlier was the DI pathway.

The results also show surprisingly small effects of the implementation of the new pension scheme starting in 1999. This means that our results do not lend support to the claim that the pension reform was the main reason behind the marked increase in labor force participation rates among older workers since the late 1990s that coincided with the implementation of the new pension system.

The chapter is organized as follows. Section 10.2 gives an overview of changes in labor force participation and employment rates between 1980 and 2015. Section 10.3 presents changes in Sweden's income security programs, income taxes, and mandatory retirement rules over the past 35 years. Section 10.4 explains the methodology behind the empirical analysis. Section 10.5 presents the results, and finally, section 10.6 concludes.

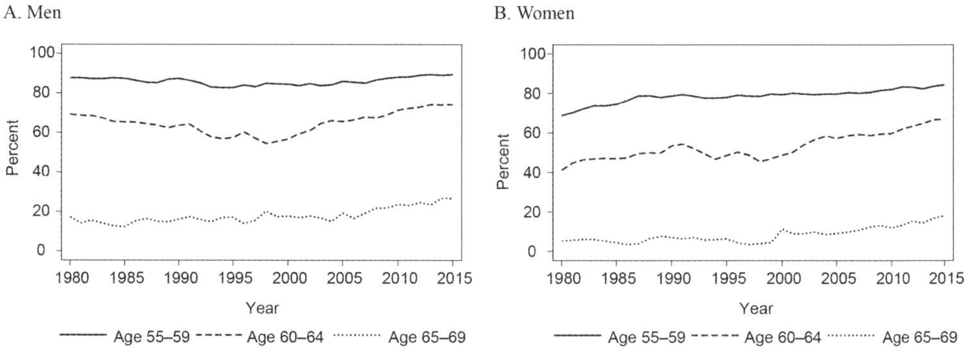

Fig. 10.1 Labor force participation rates by the age groups 55–59, 60–64, and 65–69

Source: Swedish Labor Force Survey. Statistics Sweden

10.2 Labor Force Participation of Older Workers in Sweden

Figure 10.1 shows the evolution of labor force participation in Sweden between 1980 and 2015 for the age groups 55–59, 60–64, and 65–69, respectively. The left panel shows the development for men and the right one for women. For men, the most dramatic changes are in the 60–64 age group. For this group, there is a U-shaped pattern over time, starting above 70 percent in 1980, then decreasing to around 55 percent by the end of the 1990s, and then finally recovering to around 75 percent by the end of the period. In the 55–59 age group, there are very small changes over the period included in the diagram, although the changes follow the same pattern as in the 60–64 age group. Finally, in the 65–69 age group, there is a steady increase in labor force participation (LFP) toward the end of the period, although it is at a very low level.

For females, figure 10.1 shows a partially different development. Seen over the entire period, there is an increase in the labor force participation rates of all three age groups. The main background of this pattern is the overall trend toward higher labor force participation seen in all industrialized countries. However, interestingly, one can see a slight decrease in the labor force participation of the 60–64 age group during the 1990s, parallel to the development for men, and a recovery, again parallel to the development for men.

Figure 10.2 shows the development of the employment rate between 1980 and 2015 for the same age groups as in figure 10.1, again for males and females separately. Compared to figure 10.1, it is evident that the general patterns of the developments are very similar—that is, the changes are not driven by changes in the unemployment rate. However, one can see that the decrease in the employment rate following the economic crisis in the 1990s

Fig. 10.2 Employment rates by the age groups 55–59, 60–64, and 65–69
Source: Swedish Labor Force Survey. Statistics Sweden

was more sizeable compared to the corresponding decrease in labor force participation rates shown in figure 10.1.

10.3 Institutional Changes

Figure 10.3 summarizes the main institutional changes affecting incentives to exit the labor market. The figure differentiates between four different fields of impact: old-age pensions, mandatory retirement rules and early eligibility ages (EEAs), the disability insurance (DI) program, and finally, income taxes. In this section, we will summarize the main changes. We follow the same division of fields in our subsections as in figure 10.3.

10.3.1 Old-Age Pension Systems

The most important change in the old-age pension system between 1980 and 2015 was the major pension reform decided in the Swedish parliament in 1998. In this reform, the old defined benefit (DB) plan was gradually replaced by a scheme consisting of a pay-as-you-go (PAYG) notional defined contribution (NDC) scheme and a fully funded scheme where people can choose between a large number of privately managed funds or stay in a default fund managed by the pension authorities.

Those born in 1938 were the first ones to be assigned to the postreform public pension system. Twenty percent of this cohort was in the postreform system, and 80 percent were in the prereform system. After the 1938 cohort, the share in the postreform system was increased by 5 percent per cohort, implying that those born in 1954 are fully covered by the postreform pension system.

10.3.1.1 The Prereform Public Old-Age Pension System

The prereform public old-age pension system consisted of two main parts. The first part, the *basic pension* (*Folkpension*), was unrelated to the insured

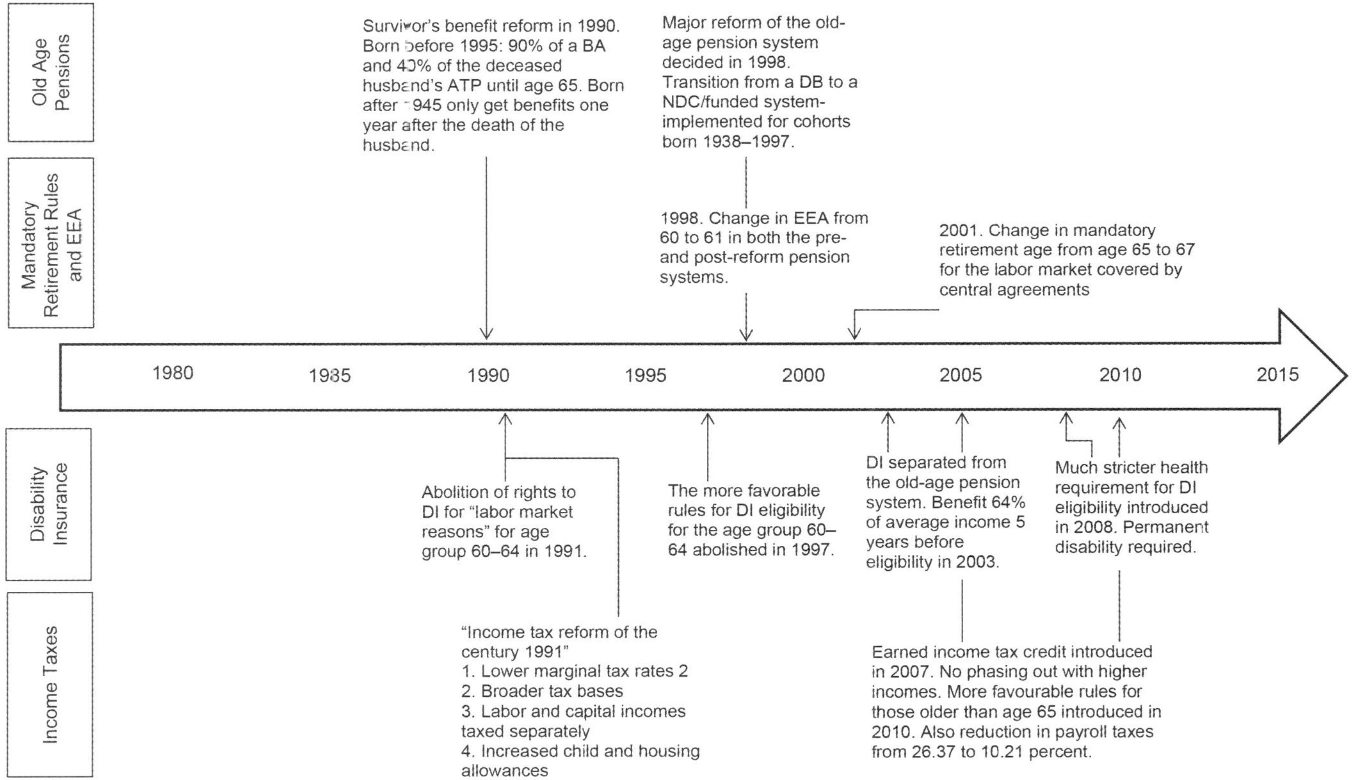

Fig. 10.3 Major institutional changes affecting incentives to exit from the labor market between 1980 and 2015

individuals' previous earnings. For a single pensioner, this pension amounted to 96 percent of a *basic amount* (BA)[1] and was reduced to 78.5 percent of a BA for a married pensioner. The BA indexed a large part of the Swedish income security system. The BA was politically decided but followed the consumer price index (CPI) very closely. It deviated from the CPI on a few notable occasions.[2] In 2018, the level of the BA was 45,500 SEK.[3]

The second main part of the prereform public pension system was a supplementary pension (*Allmän tilläggspension* [ATP]). This part is related to the retirees' previous earnings. The size of the benefit was determined by equation (1):

$$Y_i = 0.6 \cdot AP_i \cdot min\left(\frac{N_i}{30},1\right) \cdot BA, \tag{1}$$

where AP is the average pension points obtained by averaging the pension points of the 15 best years of the insured individual's earnings history. The pension points were obtained by dividing the individual's annual earnings by the BA below the social security ceiling of 7.5 BAs. Earnings below 1 BA were not counted. N is the number of years the individual has positive pension points—that is, the number of years he or she had contributed to financing the pension scheme. The expression $min[(N_i/30), 1]$ implies that the benefit was linearly reduced if the individual contributed less than 30 years to the system.

In addition to these two main parts, the prereform public pension system also included a *special supplement* (*Pensionstillskott*). The special supplement was introduced in 1969 and given to those with no or very low supplementary pension. It was decreased on a 1:1 basis with the supplementary pension (ATP).

Until 1997, all benefits from the prereform public old-age pension system could be claimed from the month the insured individual turned age 60, with a lifelong actuarial adjustment on 0.5 percent for each month of early withdrawal relative to age 65. After age 65, there was an actuarial addition of 0.7 percent for each month of delayed withdrawal.[4] In 1998, the age of early withdrawal was changed to age 61.

An important feature of the prereform old-age pension system was the special rules during the phasing-in of the program. Labor earnings for the income-related part of the system were recorded for the first time in 1960.

1. *Prisbasbeloppet* in Swedish.

2. The first time was between November 1980 and November 1982, when the BA was linked to a price index that reflected changes in oil and electricity prices to a lesser extent than the CPI. The second time was when price changes due to the 16 percent devaluation of the Swedish currency in 1982 was not fully accounted for in the BA (see Palme and Svensson, 1999).

3. About 4,000 € or 5,000 US$ in 2018.

4. Until 1988, the actuarial addition beyond age 65 was 0.5 percent.

Those born in 1914 or earlier only required 20 years of contributions to receive full benefits, and the benefits were linearly reduced by the factor $N/20$, where N is the number of years of contribution if the worker contributed less than 20 years. For each birth cohort between those born in 1914 and 1924, one year of contributions were added to this requirement. This means that for the 1915 birth cohort, 21 years of contributions were needed. The 1924 cohort was the first to meet the requirement of 30 years of contributions.[5]

10.3.1.2 The Postreform Public Old-Age Pension System

The postreform public pension system consists of three main parts. The first part is a guaranteed benefit level (*Garantipension*) for those with no or low income-related benefit that is financed through the general state budget and indexed by the CPI. The benefit level is independent of the insured individual's previous contribution to the pension scheme. In 2018, the level of the benefit was set to 8,076 SEK (about €800 or US$880) for single pensioners and to 7,204 SEK for married pensioners.

The second and third parts of the postreform system are financed through employers' and employees' contributions. The part of these contributions devoted to the pension system is set to 18.5 percent of annual earnings. Of these, 16.0 percentage points, or 86.5 percent, are devoted to a PAYG NDC scheme, and 2.5 percentage points, or 13.5 percent, are devoted to a fully funded scheme.

The NDC system is based on individual notional accounts. The benefits are proportional to the contributions made below the social security ceiling. Since 2003 the social security ceiling is indexed by *the income basic amount*, which is indexed by the income index. The income index measures the percentage change in the average income from labor for all those permanently living in Sweden between ages 16 and 64.[6] The transition from indexing the social security index with a wage rather than a price index is important, since it prevents the income-related part of the PAYG pension from "fading out" with economic growth.

The income basic amount is also used for indexing previous earnings. All individual contributions recorded since 1960 are included in the individual accounts. Inheritance gains from deceased individuals are allocated proportionally to still active persons in the same age cohort proportionally to

5. Since labor earnings were recorded from age 16 and the first year this was done was in 1960, one could claim the system was not fully matured until the cohort born in 1944 reached the normal retirement age at age 65 in 2009. This means that the ATP system was abolished before it was fully implemented.

6. Formally, the income index is based on the sum of labor income qualifying for old-age pension—that is, labor income above 42.3 percent of a *BA*—divided by the number of individuals with a positive pension-qualifying income from labor.

the size of their account balance (see Swedish Pension Agency 2017). The accounts are also reduced by a factor corresponding to the administrative cost of the pension system.

When the individual decides to retire, the account balance is divided by the so-called *annuity divisor* to get the size of the annual pension benefit at the date of retirement. The annuity divisor is a function of an interest rate, which is set to 1.6 percent, and the life expectancy of the individual's age cohort at 65. If the individual retires before age 65, the annuity divisor is recalculated when he or she turns 65. For each year during retirement, the benefit is changed following the *adjustment indexation*. At the turn of the year, the benefits are adjusted with the factor $(I_t/I_{t-1})/1.016$, where I_t is the income index of the coming year and I_{t-1} corresponds to the past year. If there is a growth rate of exactly 1.6 percent, there is no adjustment. If the real wage sum grows faster than 1.6 percent, there is a real growth rate in the benefit levels. However, if the growth rate is smaller, there will be a real decrease in the benefit levels.

Since the employers' contribution to the NDC scheme is fixed to 16.0 percent of the annual earnings, there is an uninsurable risk of the system to encounter financial problems, primarily related to unexpected changes in life expectancies or a smaller labor force. To handle these risks, the pension scheme includes a special "balancing mechanism" that lowers the benefits proportionally in order to reach a balance in expected incomes and liabilities of the NDC system.[7]

In the third part of the postreform public pension system, the fully funded premium pension (PPM), the insured individual is able to choose between almost 850 different funds (see Palme, Sundén, and Söderlind 2007 for a more detailed overview of the PPM). When the system was introduced in 2000, all fund managers with active businesses in Sweden were allowed to participate in the system. However, since then, somewhat stricter rules for participation have been implemented.

The system contains a default fund for those who do not make an "active choice" of fund manager. When the system was introduced, about 68 percent avoided the default alternative by choosing a different fund manager. However, since then, the share of those who make an active choice has decreased, and today almost 50 percent of the insured individuals have their savings in the default fund managed by the pension authorities.

The annual benefits from the fully funded part of the public pension are calculated using an annuity divisor. The advance rate is currently set to 1.75 percent, where 0.1 percent is reserved to cover administrative costs for the Swedish Pension Agency. The premium pension can be drawn as traditional insurance, where the fund shares are sold at the date of retirement

7. See the *Orange Report* 2016 for a description.

and managed by the Swedish Pension Agency, or as fund insurance, where the pension benefits remain in the fund chosen by the insured individual.

10.3.2 Mandatory Retirement and Early Eligibility Rules

Most of Sweden's labor market is covered by central agreements between trade unions and employers' confederations. These include agreements on retirement ages, and in most cases, the mandatory retirement age was 65. This was also supported in the labor market legislation. Workers older than age 65 were not covered by employment security legislation and were exempted from seniority rules. In addition, they were not covered by the unemployment insurance (UI), disability insurance (DI), or compulsory sick pay insurance. Central and local government employees automatically lost their jobs at age 65. Exceptions to this rule were permitted for one year only.

New legislation implemented in 2001 postponed the mandatory retirement age to 67, meaning that those aged between 65 and 67 were now covered by the employment security legislation. The special rules for central and local government employees were also adjusted to age 67. However, the rules for the income security programs remained at age 65 after the reform. Depending on ongoing collective agreements in some sectors of the labor market, the reform was not fully implemented until 2003.

10.3.3 The Disability Insurance Program

The disability insurance program replaces forgone earnings due to permanent health problems. Since 1980, there have been several changes to the program. A series of reforms that gradually made the eligibility rules more generous were implemented in the 1970s. The most important changes were the introduction of special eligibility rules for older workers (initially older than age 63) and rights for older workers to receive DI for labor market reasons. These reforms were reversed in the 1990s. The eligibility for DI for long-term unemployed workers older than age 60 was abolished in 1991. Six years later, in 1997, the special eligibility rules were completely abolished. This meant that workers older than age 60 no longer had lower medical eligibility rules, had to participate in rehabilitation programs, and were covered by the same requirements for taking suitable jobs and accepting geographical mobility as younger workers (see Karlström, Palme, and Svensson 2008 for a detailed description of the reform and its effects on employment).

Before 2003, the DI program was a part of the public old-age pension system. Like the old-age pension, it consisted of a basic and an income-related supplementary part. In 2003, following the reform of the Swedish pension system, the DI program became independent of the public old-age pension system. The benefits were calculated as 64 percent of the "assumed income" below the social security ceiling. The assumed income is the average of the five to eight best years of annual income from labor before the worker became eligible for DI.

The reform in 2003 also included changes in eligibility rules for DI. The most important change was that the DI benefit was no longer permanent; eligibility would be reconsidered every fifth year. The disability insurance program for those younger than age 30 changed its name to "activity support" (*Aktivitetsersättning*), and the recipients were automatically required to reapply for benefits when they turned 30. In addition, rehabilitation programs in collaboration with unemployment offices were initiated.

In 2008, the government implemented a new reform of the DI system. The most important element of the new eligibility rules was that the person applying for DI had to show that his or her ability to work was permanently lost. For obvious reasons, this change implied that the threshold for receiving DI increased significantly. Simultaneously, the rules for the sick pay insurance program, which replaces foregone earnings from temporary health problems, was changed so that the maximum spell length was limited to one year. The reform also implied a much more structured rehabilitation program (*Rehabiliteringskedjan*) that was imposed very early on in a sickness spell.

Figure 10.4 shows the development of DI prevalence and incidence between 1980 and 2015 for males and females, respectively. The most striking result in figure 10.4 is the sharp drop in DI entry from the late 1980s to today. The analysis in Jönsson, Palme, and Svensson (2012) indicates that changes in eligibility criteria during the 1980s and 1990s clearly affected program caseloads and may also have had an impact on labor force participation. However, for our purposes, the most interesting change is the decline in DI entry since 2005. It is apparent that the background to the decline is the more stringent eligibility rules following the reforms of the DI system in 2003 and 2008.

10.3.4 Income Taxes

10.3.4.1 The 1991 Income Tax Reform

In 1991, Sweden implemented a major reform of the income tax system—"the tax reform of the century" (see Agell, Englund, and Södersten 1996; or Björklund, Palme, and Svensson 1995 for an overview). There were four main elements to the reform:

1. *Substantially lowered marginal tax rates*. The highest marginal tax rate in the prereform system was 75 percent. This rate was decreased to 50 percent, and a majority of the income earners only paid municipality tax at around 30 percent after the reform.
2. *Broadened tax base*. Several "fringe benefits" from employment, such as free meals and cars, were included in the tax base after the reform.
3. *Separate taxation of labor and capital income*. In the prereform tax system, income from labor and capital were added together and taxed at the

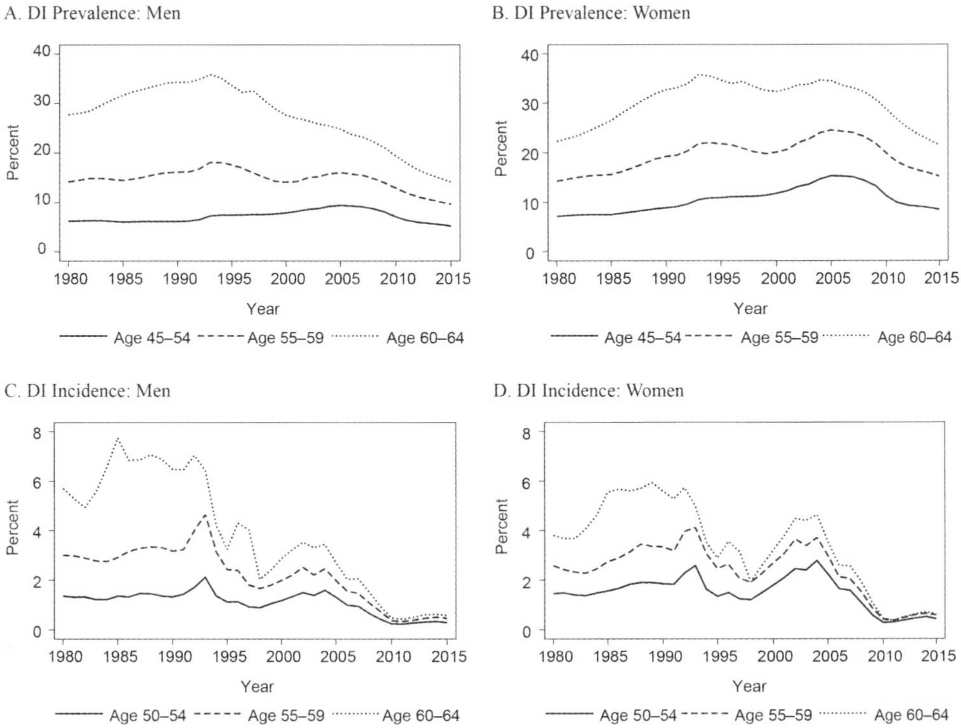

Fig. 10.4 Upper panels: Share of the population receiving DI in different age groups. Lower panels: Share of DI entry in different age groups
Source: Swedish Social Insurance Agency

same rate. After the reform, the tax base was divided, and all income from capital was taxed at a flat rate of 30 percent.

4. *Increased child and housing allowances*. To offset undesired effects on income inequality, the child allowance, which is unrelated to parental income, and the housing allowance, which is related to income and housing costs, were substantially increased.

10.3.4.2 Introduction of Earned Income Tax Credit Schemes, 2007–14

In recent years, the most important change in income taxes is the introduction of the earned income tax credit (EITC). The EITC was implemented in a series of reforms between 2007 and 2014. Unlike in most other countries, the Swedish EITC was not phased out at higher earnings.[8] Importantly, the size of the tax credit was larger for workers who were above age 65 at the beginning of the tax year. The EITC applies to earnings, but not to income

8. A phase-out range in the earned income tax credit was introduced in 2016.

from public pension or public transfers. The tax credit is a function of earned income, the basic deduction, and the municipality income tax rate.

An additional element of the 2007 reform was that the payroll tax rate was reduced from 26.37 percent to 10.21 percent for workers above age 65 at the beginning of the tax year.[9] The purpose was to stimulate the demand for older workers. The reforms in 2007 substantially increased the net-of-participation tax rate of workers above age 65. The introduction of the EITC also slightly increased the net gain from working for those below age 65, although not to the same extent. Laun (2017) analyzes the combined effects of the EITC and the payroll tax reduction for workers above age 65 and finds that the tax credits increased employment at the extensive margin among workers just above age 65 by about 5 percent.

Overall, the changes in taxation for older workers are potentially important for encouraging a delayed labor force exit above age 65, and there is evidence of a response to the tax credits introduced in 2007. For workers below age 65, it is unclear if the smaller change in the tax burden due to the introduction of the EITC in 2007 impacts retirement decisions in these ages.

10.4 The Implicit Tax on Working Longer

Our measures of economic incentives to remain in the labor force are all based on social security wealth. The individual's social security wealth at a particular age S is defined as the net present value of all future social security benefits. It will depend on individual retirement age R and which pathway k of the income security system the individual chooses to exit from the labor market—that is,

$$(3) \qquad SSW_{k,t}(R,i) = \sum_{t=R}^{T} B_{k,t,a}(R,i)\sigma_{t,a}\beta^{a-R},$$

where t is an index for time and a for age, $\sigma_{t,a}$ is the survival probability in time t at age a, and finally, β is the discount factor.

Postponing retirement has two counteracting effects on social security wealth. Delaying retirement increases, through the actuarial adjustment in the pension system, the size of the pension benefits. However, the individual will also receive fewer benefit payments, which will decrease social security wealth. The net value of these effects is measured in the benefit accrual measure,

$$(4) \qquad ACC_{k,t}(R,i) = SSW_{k,t+1} - SSW_{k,t},$$

for a particular exit path k out of the labor force. This measure could also be constructed as a weighted average for all exit routes combined—that is,

9. The payroll tax rate above age 65 was raised to 16.36 percent in 2016.

$$ACC_t(R,i) = \sum_{k=1}^{K} p_{k,i} ACC_{t,k}(R,i), \tag{5}$$

where $p_{k,i}$ is the individual's specific probability to exit the labor market through path k.

From this measure we can obtain the following expression for the *implicit tax rate* on remaining in the labor market:

$$ITAX_t(R,i) = -[ACC_t(R,i) - W_{t+1}(i)PT_{t+1}] / \{W_{t+1}(i)[1 - TAX_t(i)]\}. \tag{6}$$

This implies that the tax on continued work is calculated as the gain in social security wealth for working one additional year minus what the individual would have contributed to the pension system through the payroll tax on labor earnings as a share of net labor earnings during that additional year. The reversed sign is due to the fact that a tax by definition is a reduction in wealth, meaning that a negative change in wealth is a positive tax. All contributions to the pension system through the payroll tax made before the hypothetical last year are regarded as sunk costs to the individual.

A negative tax rate tells us that the income security system works as a subsidy for continued work given the assumed discount rate. This implies that it is rational for the individual to remain in the labor force if he or she values work and leisure time equally. If the tax rate is positive, the individual will remain in the labor force if he or she values the increase in social security wealth more than he or she values leisure.

10.4.1 Empirical Implementation

We calculate four different measures of the incentives to stay in the labor force for older workers in Sweden between 1980 and 2015 for a number of representative (hypothetical) individuals:

- replacement rate (RR)
- social security wealth (SSW)
- benefit accrual (ACC)
- implicit tax rate (ITAX)

The first two (RR and the SSW) measure the income or the consumption possibilities of the individuals, and the second two (ACC and ITAX) measure the change in income of staying one additional year in the labor market.

The hypothetical individuals are obtained from three different education groups: (1) low education, with compulsory schooling only; (2) medium education, with vocational schooling or secondary education; and (3) high education, with college or university education. We do the calculations for single men and women separately. We assume that the low educated are employed since age 16, the medium educated since age 20, and the high educated since age 25.

To facilitate comparisons of how the social security system affects retire-

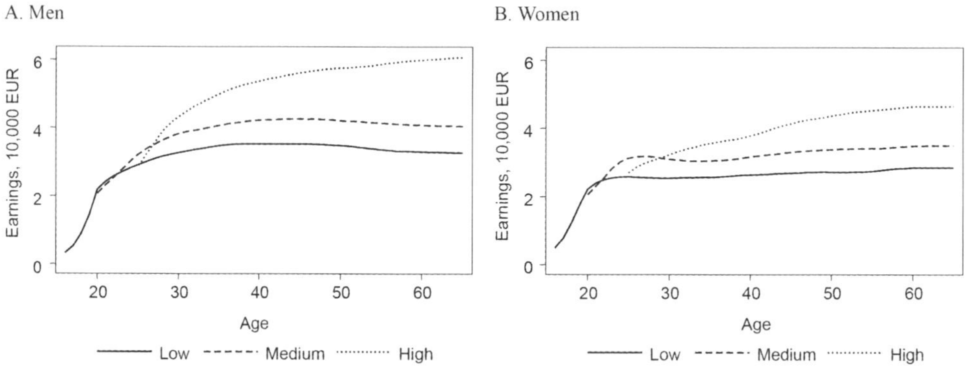

Fig. 10.5 Earnings histories obtained from combining data from the US
Source: US Current Population Survey (CPS), Germany (SUF-VSKT 2011) and Italy (INPS)

ment in comparable countries represented in the other chapters of this volume, we use earnings profiles combining data from the US (US Current Population Survey [CPS]), Germany (SUF-VSKT 2011), and Italy (INPS). These are shown in figure 10.5. Common survival rates were provided by Eurostat (average of EU-28 countries). According to these survival probabilities, life expectancies at age 15 were 67.8 years for women and 64.7 years for men.

We consider two different pathways out of the labor force. First is the old-age pension pathway—that is, that the individual chooses to leave the labor force through the public old-age pension. Second is the disability pension pathway. For this pathway, we assume that the individual uses the DI program to finance his or her exit from the labor force before reaching age 65, when he or she is automatically transferred to the old-age pension system. To measure the overall incentives, we calculate the weighted average based on age-specific probabilities for each pathway from observed exit patterns. Figure 10.6 shows these probabilities between 1980 and 2015 for males and females, respectively.

10.5 Results

10.5.1 Replacement Rates and Social Security Wealth and Its Accrual

Figure 10.7 shows the replacement rates of the public old-age pension system between 1980 and 2015 for the representative individuals with median education by age of labor market exit. We consider ages between 60 and 64—which is the age span when most Swedish workers leave the labor force. The left panel shows the results for the hypothetical male worker and the right panel for the female one. The most apparent change revealed in the figures

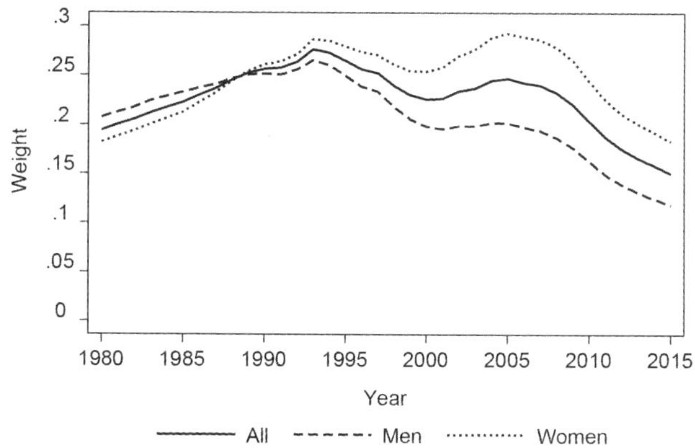

Fig. 10.6 Share of workers leaving the labor force through the disability insurance program in Sweden between 1980 and 2015; males and females
Source: Authors' own calculations

Fig. 10.7 Replacement rates 1980–2015 for median-educated men, women, and couples by age of retirement 60–64.
Source: Authors' own calculations

is the 1998 change in the early eligibility age (EEA). This change implied that the worker could only get benefits if eligible for the DI program. The result—that the replacement level deviates from zero after 1998—is attributed to the fact that we weight the two different exit paths by the observed shares of workers using each of them.

It may appear surprising that the replacement rate increased after the implementation of the new pension system. This result is different from previous research based on actual outcomes.[10] Our simulations are, how-

10. Granbom (2017) studies the pension outcomes of those born between 1938 and 1945 and finds that these cohorts, who are in both the pre- and postreform systems, would have had higher benefits on average if they would have been in the prereform system only.

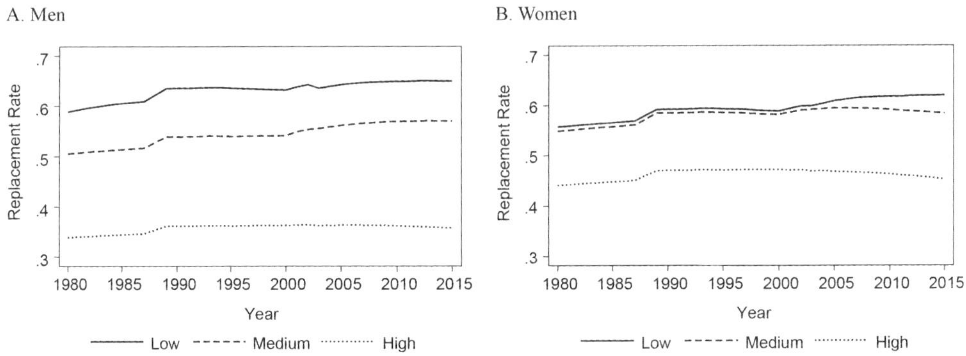

Fig. 10.8 Average replacement rates 1980–2015 for those retiring at age 63 by education group.

Source: Authors' own calculations

ever, based on two strong assumptions. First is the assumption that the worker contributes to the system every year from a very young age. This is particularly important for the workers in the low educated group, who are assumed to enter the labor force at age 16. Second, we assume that the system works without activating the balancing mechanism, as we described in section 10.3.1.2.

Figure 10.8 shows the replacement rate for the hypothetical individuals retiring at age 63 representing the three different education groups. The replacement level is, as expected, highest for the hypothetical man and woman representing the lowest education group because of the social security ceiling. For low educated men as well as low- and medium-educated women, the ceiling is not at all binding, while it is for high educated from both gender groups and for medium-educated men.

Figure 10.8 also shows that the replacement level increases for the low and medium educated when the postreform old-age pension scheme is gradually implemented, while it decreases slightly for the high educated. The background to this result is that income earned relatively early in the worker's career is weighted more heavily in the benefit calculation in the postreform system than later earnings, while it was not included at all when determining the benefits in the prereform system.

Figure 10.9 shows the social security wealth (SSW) calculated at the age of retirement for the median-educated hypothetical worker retiring at ages between 60 and 64. The lower SSW for those who retire early shows that the increase in the size of the benefits, following the actuarial adjustments in both the pre- and postreform schemes, exceeds the loss from fewer benefit payments following delayed retirement. The figure also shows, confirming the results from our analysis of the replacement level, that SSW increases slightly after the implementation of the postreform pension system.

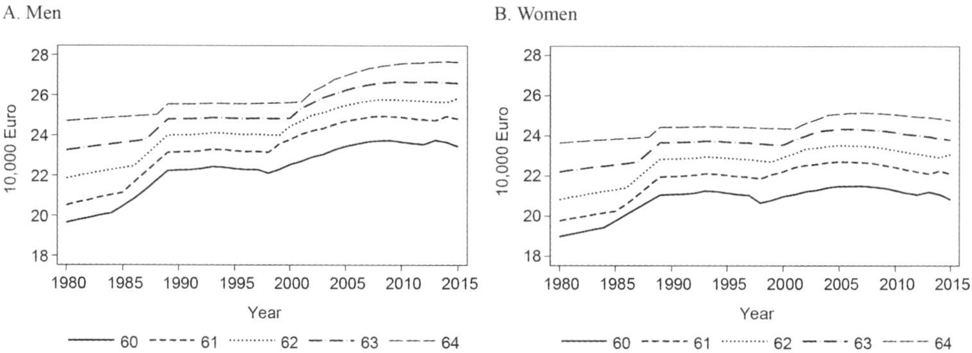

Fig. 10.9 Median-educated men's and women's social security wealth 1980–2015 if leaving the labor market at ages 60–64
Source: Authors' own calculations

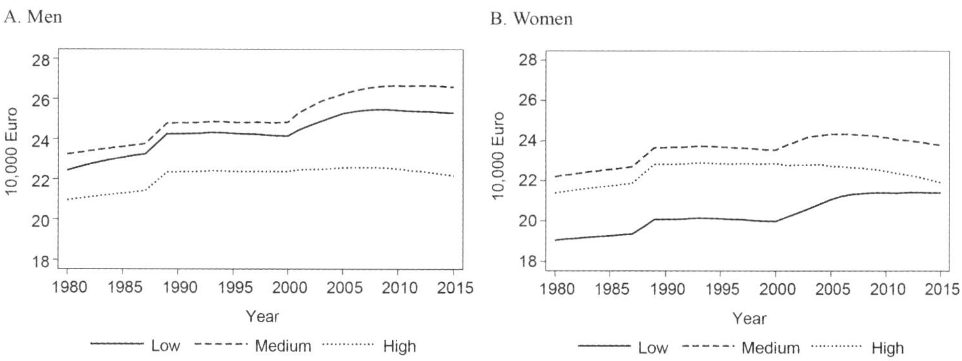

Fig. 10.10 Social security wealth 1980–2015 if leaving the labor market at age 63 by education group.
Source: Authors' own calculations

Figure 10.10 shows heterogeneity in SSW among the three different education groups. As for the replacement level, it may appear confusing that for both men and women, the high-educated hypothetical worker has a lower SSW than the medium-educated worker. However, the result can be attributed to the fact that the high educated pay higher taxes based on the tax bases for which incomes from occupational pensions are also included.

Figure 10.11 shows the changes between 1980 and 2015 in the accrual in SSW from staying an additional year in the labor force for the hypothetical worker from the medium education group by age of retirement between ages 60 and 64. The left panel shows the results for the male worker and the right for a female worker. The most striking results in figure 10.11 are the sharp drop in the accrual in the late 1980s and the sharp increase in accrual

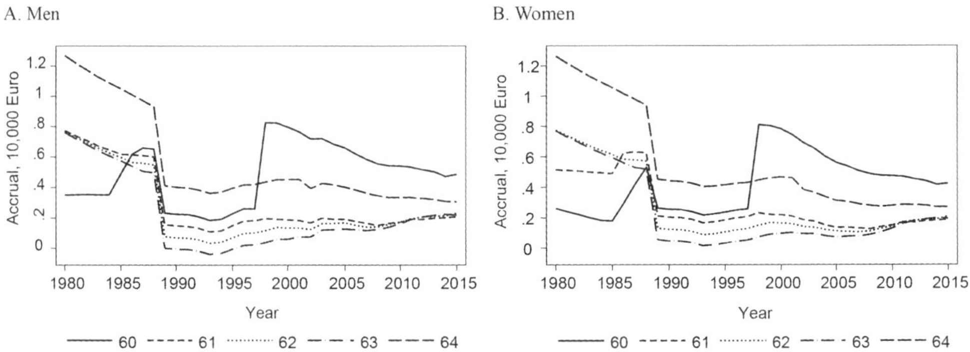

Fig. 10.11 Median-educated men's and women's change in social security wealth from staying one additional year in the labor force 1980–2015 by age of leaving the labor force 60–64

Source: Authors' own calculations

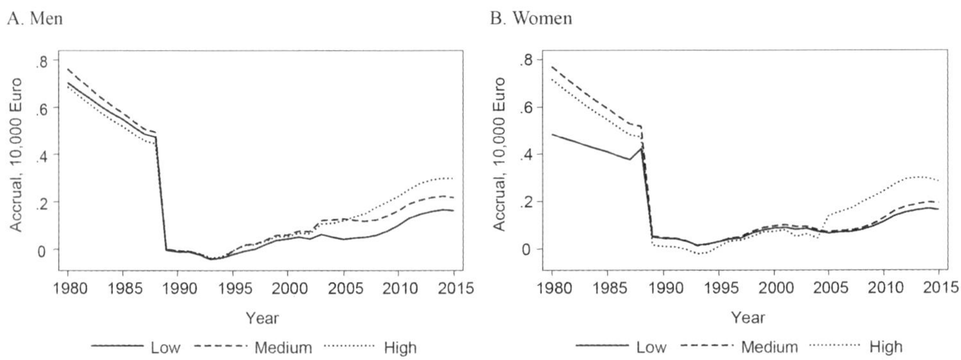

Fig. 10.12 Changes in the accrual in social security wealth 1980–2015 from staying one additional year in the labor force at age 63 by education group

Source: Authors' own calculations

in 1998 for those retiring at age 60. As we pointed out in section 10.3.1.1, the late 1980s drop has to do with the transition rules in the implementation of the ATP system (the prereform supplementary public pension system). Since contributions to the scheme were first recorded in 1960, the cohorts retiring in the late 1980s got an additional actuarial adjustment for each year they remained in the labor force. The 1998 increase for those retiring at age 60 is fully attributed to the change in the early retirement age from 60 to 61.

The most important result revealed in figure 10.11 is the quite stable development in the age groups retiring between 61 and 64. This means that the reform of the old-age pension system did not imply any drastic changes in the incentives to stay in the labor force. For those retiring at age 63, there is a slight increase in SSW accrual toward the end of the period. Figure 10.12

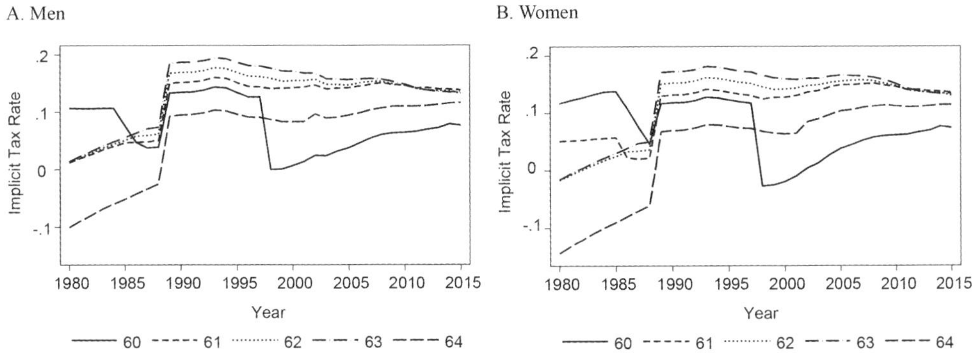

Fig. 10.13 The development of the implicit tax rate (ITAX) 1980–2015 by age of retirement of the hypothetical worker between age 60 and 64
Source: Authors' own calculations

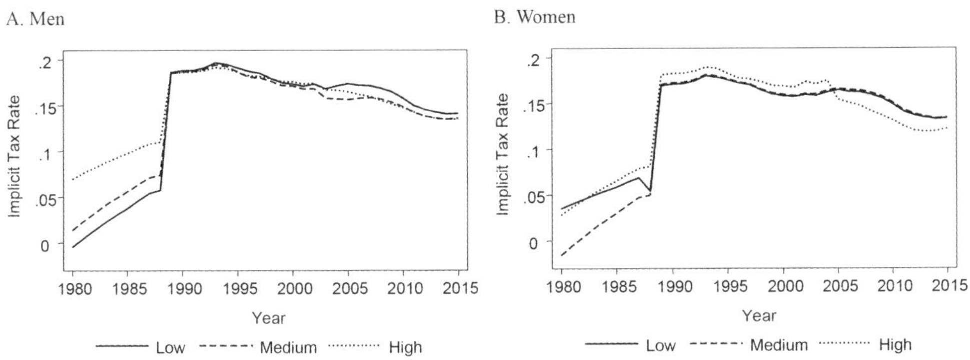

Fig. 10.14 The development of the implicit tax rate (ITAX) 1980–2015 by education level of the hypothetical worker retiring at age 63
Source: Authors' own calculations

shows that this also applies to the other education groups considered in this study. In fact, the increase is slightly stronger for the high education hypothetical worker.

10.5.2 The Implicit Tax Rate on Working Longer

The implicit tax rate from the weighted average of the public old-age pension system and the DI program summarizes the economic incentives to exit from the labor force induced by the income security program. Apart from the tax increase in the late 1980s and the sharp drop in 1998 for those retiring at age 60, figure 10.13 reveals a steady decrease in the tax rate at ages 60–63 and a stable tax rate for those retiring at 64. This pattern applies to both men and women. Figure 10.14 further reveals that for the hypothetical worker retiring at age 63, this pattern applies for each education level.

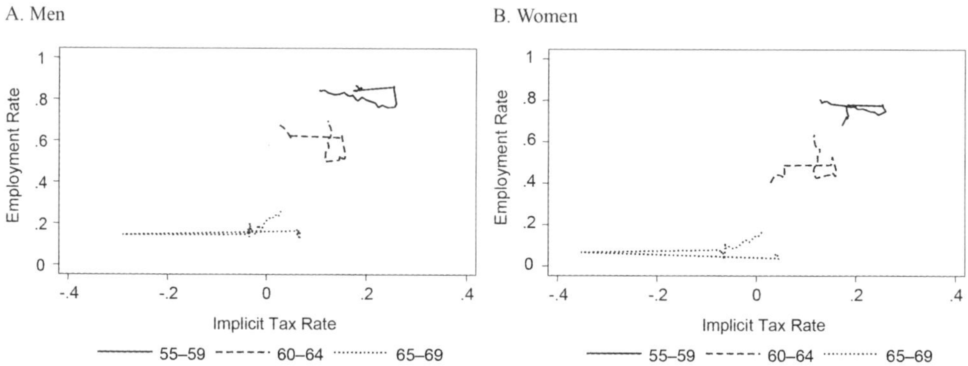

Fig. 10.15 The association between the implicit tax rate on remaining employed (ITAX) and the employment rate in different age groups
Source: Authors' own calculations

10.5.3 Relation between Implicit Tax Rates and Employment Rates

Can changes in economic incentives induced by the public old-age pension program and the DI program explain the pattern of decreased labor force participation between 1980 and the late 1990s and the subsequent increase between years 2000 and 2015 among older workers in Sweden? One way to approach this important issue is to investigate to what extent the changes in our measures of economic incentives to stay in the labor market concur with the development in labor force participation of the relevant age groups.

An obvious weakness of this research strategy is that a similar development very well could be attributed to some underlying trend in society, such as improved health or work environment, that could have driven the increase in labor force participation of the elderly and may also have coincided with changes in economic incentives. An advantage of the time period that we cover from this perspective is, however, that it includes both a downturn and an increase in labor force participation.

Figure 10.15 plots the development of the implicit tax rate (ITAX) on staying in the labor force and the employment rate in three different age groups: 55–59, 60–64, and 65–69. The upper panel shows the development for men and the lower one for women. To the extent that there is a role for economic incentives in explaining the development of the employment rate of older workers in Sweden, we would see a negative association in these graphs. It is, however, important to stress that the development in the different age groups should be viewed independently. The fact that both labor force participation and the implicit tax rate are higher among younger workers is not a part of our analysis.

The within-age-group development in figure 10.15 reveals no obvious negative relation in any of the age and gender groups included in our analysis.

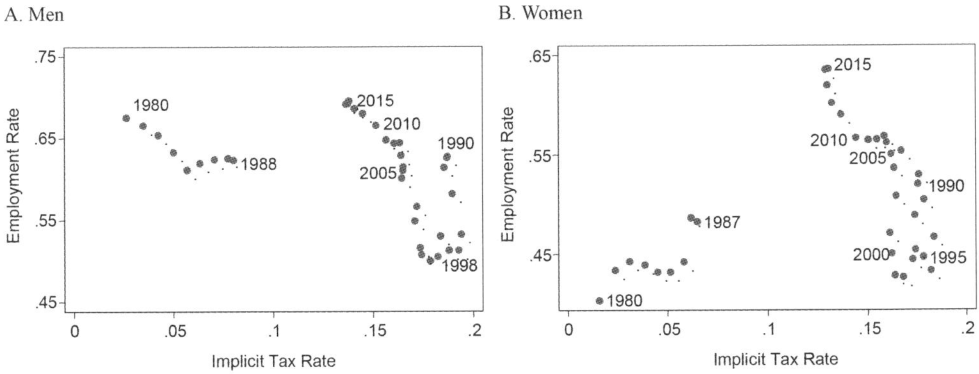

Fig. 10.16 The association between the implicit tax rate on remaining employed (ITAX) at age 63 and the employment rate in the 60–64 age group, 1995–2015
Source: Authors' own calculations

It is therefore not possible for us to conclude that the economic incentives that we measure in this study are driving the development toward later exit from the labor market among older workers in Sweden since the late 1990s.

If we instead use the ITAX measures for the medium-education worker from figure 10.14—that is, the ITAX measure for a worker retiring at age 63—figure 10.16 shows a different picture. For men, the figure shows a clear negative relation between the implicit tax to remain in the labor force in two different eras: the first one including the 1980s and the second 1990–2015. For women, the negative relation emerges for the second era only.

Taken together, our results suggest that the changes in economic incentives, primarily driven by stricter eligibility rules in the DI program, may have contributed to increased labor force participation among older workers since the late 1990s. For men, this is true also for the development in the 1980s. For women, it is obvious that the general trend across cohorts toward higher labor force participation among females dominates the development in this era.

10.6 Conclusions

In this chapter, we measure how the economic incentives induced by the public pension system and the disability insurance program have changed between 1980 and 2015. We find a large change in the late 1980s, when the cohorts affected by the transition rules for the prereform supplementary pension (ATP) reached the retirement age. For this generation, the linear reduction in the scheme for workers who did not contribute the required number of years for full benefit was binding and worked as an additional actuarial adjustment. It is conceivable that these transition rules contributed to the fact that very few, less than 9 percent (see, e.g., Palme and Svensson 1999), retired before age 65 through the old-age pension pathway during these years.

For the main focus of our study—how the major reform of Sweden's old-age pension system affected incentives to remain in the labor force—we found surprisingly small changes. We could therefore conclude that our results do not support the claim that the major increase in labor force participation seen for both men and women in the 60–64 age group was driven by the pension reform. However, as pointed out in Laun and Palme (2019), in the prereform public old-age pension system, as opposed to the postreform system, there was an incentive for some workers to delay claiming of their benefits to some years after actual retirement. Since we in this study assume that the hypothetical workers claim their benefit immediately after retirement, a limitation of our study is that the overall incentive effect of this aspect of the pension reform was not assessed.

Our results show that the eligibility rules of the disability insurance program were the main background to the development toward stronger incentives to stay in the labor force since the 1990s. This change coincided with the increased labor force participation rate among older workers. This result supports the conclusions in Laun and Palme (2019) that the more stringent eligibility rules contributed to the increased labor force participation rates. In Palme and Laun (2018), we also concluded that improved health—in particular among men in the 60–64 age group—is likely to have reinforced the development. In future research, we plan to come back to the important question of how changes in the population have interacted with policy changes in prolonging the work lives of Swedish workers in recent decades.

References

Agell, J., P. Englund, and J. Södersten. 1996. "Tax Reform of the Century—the Swedish Experiment." *National Tax Journal* 49 (4): 643–64.

Björklund, A., M. Palme, and I. Svensson. 1995. "Tax Reforms and Income Distribution: An Assessment Using Different Income Concepts." *Swedish Economic Policy Review* 2:229–66.

Granbom, S. 2017. "Jämförelse I utfall av inkomstgrundad allmän pension i det nya och gamla pensionssystemet för födda 1938–1945." Swedish Pension Agency, Study PID156047.

Jönsson, L., M. Palme, and I. Svensson. 2012. "Disability Insurance, Population Health, and Employment in Sweden." In *Social Security Programs and Retirement around the World: Historical Trends in Mortality and Health, Employment, and Disability Insurance Participation and Reforms*, edited by David A. Wise, 79–126. Chicago: University of Chicago Press.

Karlström, A., M. Palme, and I. Svensson. 2008. "The Employment Effect of Stricter

Rules for Eligibility for DI: Evidence from a Natural Experiment in Sweden." *Journal of Public Economics* 92 (10–11): 2071–82.

Laun, L. 2017. "The Effect of Age-Targeted Tax Credits on Labor Force Participation of Older Workers." *Journal of Public Economics* 152:102–18.

Laun, L., and M. Palme. 2019. "The Recent Rise of Labor Force Participation of Older Workers in Sweden." In *Social Security Programs and Retirement around the World: Working Longer*, edited by Courtney C. Coile, Kevin Milligan, and David A. Wise, 231–65. Chicago: University of Chicago Press.

Palme, M., A. Sundén, and P. Söderlind, 2007."How Do Individual Accounts Work in the Swedish Pension System?" *Journal of the European Economic Association*, 5 (2–3): 636–46.

Palme, M., and I. Svensson. 1999. "Social Security, Occupational Pensions, and Retirement in Sweden." In *Social Security and Retirement around the World*, edited by Jonathan Gruber and David Wise, 355–402. Chicago: University of Chicago Press.

Swedish Pension Agency. 2017. Orange Rapport: Pensionssystemets årsredovisning 2017. https://www.pensionsmyndigheten.se/statistik-och-rapporter/Rapporter/arsredovisningar.

11 A Lifetime of Changes
State Pensions and Work Incentives at Older Ages in the UK, 1948–2018

James Banks and Carl Emmerson

11.1 Introduction

Over recent decades, older individuals in advanced economies have enjoyed substantial increases in longevity. This is undoubtedly good news, but without adjustments to retirement ages, it does have the consequence of placing a greater strain on all types of pension arrangements. Pay-as-you-go schemes require higher tax rates on the (relatively smaller) working population to finance a given level of retirement benefits, while funded schemes require greater contributions from either government, individuals, or employers or the resulting annual retirement income they are able to deliver will be lower. Given this, it is unsurprising that increased retirement ages are considered, alongside greater pension contributions and reduced pension incomes, as a potential part of the appropriate adjustment to rising longevity at older ages.

This chapter sets out how pension reforms have evolved in the United

James Banks is a professor of economics at the University of Manchester and senior research fellow of the Institute for Fiscal Studies (IFS).

Carl Emmerson is the deputy director of the Institute for Fiscal Studies (IFS).

This chapter forms part of the National Bureau of Economic Research's International Social Security (ISS) project. The authors are grateful to Richard Blundell and David Sturrock and to the other participants of the ISS project for useful comments and advice. We are grateful to the ESRC-funded Centre for the Microeconomic Analysis of Public Policy at IFS (grant number RES-544-28-001) and the "Policies for Longer Working Lives: Understanding Interactions with Health and Care Responsibilities" project (grant ES/P001688/1) that is part of the Joint Programme Initiative "More Years, Better Lives" for providing funding for this project. Data from the Family Expenditure Survey (FES) and the Labour Force Survey (LFS) were made available by the UK Data Archive. Responsibility for interpretation of the data, as well as for any errors, is the authors' alone. For acknowledgments, sources of research support, and disclosure of the authors' material financial relationships, if any, please see https://www.nber.org/chapters/c14201.ack.

Kingdom and puts this information alongside trends in labor-market participation at older ages. We build on and update analyses that have previously been carried out prior to the most recent policy developments in the last 15 years, such as that contained in the studies of Blundell and Johnson (1999) or Disney and Emmerson (2005). As set out in Wise (2017), male employment rates at older ages have risen markedly across many advanced economies since the mid-1990s, and the UK is no exception, so it is tempting to ask whether such recent trends could be at least partially caused by recent trends in the pension system, and hence we consider our study, along with the other chapters in this volume, to be timely.

In one sense, the UK is a good country for such a study, since, as we show, there has been a sequence of rather major pension reforms—much more so than in most other Organisation for Economic Co-operation and Development (OECD) countries. Some, like the rise in the female state pension age, have reduced the generosity of the system, while others, such as the introduction of the State Earnings-Related Pension Scheme (SERPS) in the mid-1970s or triple-lock indexation in the early 2010s, have made the system more generous. Some have changed the way in which the pension system implicitly taxes or subsidizes an extra year of work at older ages; some have not. But overall, as we will also show, while there have been some quite large changes to the pension wealth of cohorts, in recent years (since the mid-1990s) the public pension system has been largely neutral when it comes to work incentives or disincentives, so in this sense, the UK may be a less satisfactory laboratory for such analysis than some of the other European countries in this volume.

Rather than immediately setting about building a full individual-based option value type of analysis of the effects of pensions on work incentives and employment (as in, e.g., Meghir and Whitehouse 1997; Blundell, Meghir, and Smith 2004) or developing a fully structural dynamic model of public and private pension choices, savings, labor supply, and retirement (as in O'Dea 2018), our goals in this chapter are considerably more modest. We simply set out to characterize the effects of the long history of UK pension reform on a number of different (crude) types of individuals and then relate these reform effects to employment outcomes for the same types. Despite this rather aggregate methodology, we show that the sequence of reforms generates variations over time by sex, education, and single year of age/cohort that allow us to estimate the effects of pension wealth and accrual on employment while controlling flexibly for potentially confounding effects using a full set of dummies for age, education, and time. As well as documenting the effects of the pension reforms on pension wealth and work incentives of each type, we also show that changes in pension wealth and the implicit tax rates on work implied by the pension system have both been statistically significantly associated with changes in employment.

Of course, a range of other factors will be changing over time and also will potentially impact the labor supply decisions of older individuals. For a recent discussion, see Banks, Emmerson, and Tetlow (2019). These include successive cohorts of individuals approaching retirement ages with higher levels of education, differences in health over time, the changing state of the economy (in particular, the labor demand in industries that different cohorts of older individuals work in), the generosity of other parts of the tax and benefit system, and changes to compulsory retirement ages. Some of these will be controlled for by our empirical methodology, but to the extent that these are correlated with the cohort- and type-specific experiences of pension reform, then their presence would be a limitation on the degree to which any part of our analysis could be interpreted as indicating causal evidence in favor of the hypothesis that the employment outcomes of older adults respond to the financial incentives in state pensions as would be predicted by a standard economic model.

One final aspect, however, that directly relates to financial incentives to retire will be the incentives coming from private pension arrangements, which may well be changing over time and across types in a way that is correlated with state pension changes. We attempt to provide some very simple approximations for such arrangements in our final simulations and empirical estimations and show that, if anything, this strengthens our conclusions.

The remainder of this chapter is structured as follows. Section 11.2 begins by describing historical trends in employment rates by age and sex and then goes on to outline the reforms to the UK state pension system in some detail. Section 11.3 explains how we approach the simulation of state pension entitlements and the implied work disincentives for men and women born in different years and with different earnings profiles and documents the resulting variation seen over time as successive reforms take effect. The results from assessing the effect of changing financial incentives from the state pension system on employment rates are presented in section 11.4. Section 11.5 concludes.

11.2 Historical Background and Context

11.2.1 Labor Market Trends

The UK is no exception to the broad international picture, shown in Wise (2017), of rising male labor market participation at older ages since 1995. Having fallen sharply during the late 1970s and the first half of the 1980s, employment rates of men aged 55 to 69 have risen since the mid-1990s. Figure 11.1, which uses data from the UK *Labour Force Survey* (LFS), shows that the increase has been common across each five-year age group within the male 55 to 69 population (the employment rate for each group in 2017 was 12 to 14 percentage points higher than its low in the mid-1990s). Since the earlier decline in employment among men aged 65 to 69 was smaller, this

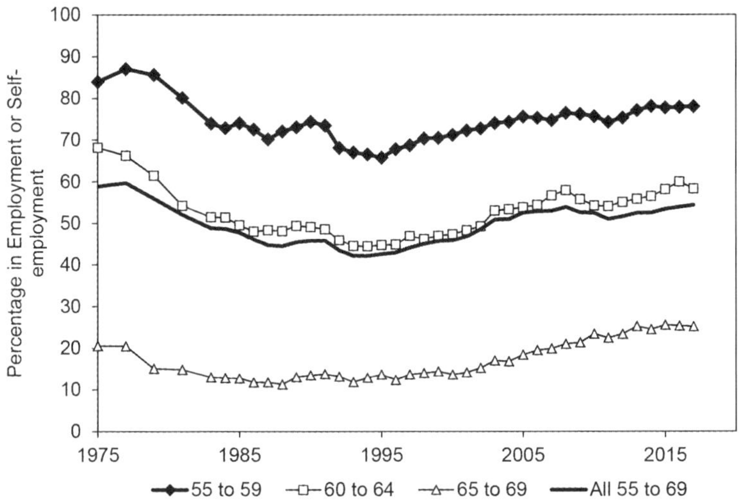

Fig. 11.1 Employment rates of men, by age band, 1975–2017
Source: Labour Force Survey.

means that the employment rate of this group of older men—which now stands at 25 percent—is at its highest level for at least 40 years. In contrast, the employment rates of men aged 55 to 59 and men aged 60 to 64, while at levels not seen since the start of the 1980s, remain quite some way below their level in the mid-1970s.

As is also seen in other advanced economies, the trends in employment rates among older women have been markedly different from those seen among older men. These were relatively flat during the late 1970s and most of the 1980s, rose gradually through the second half of the 1990s, and have risen particularly sharply since then. As a result, the employment rate of women aged 55 to 69, which in 2017 had reached 44 percent, is well above its rate in the mid-1970s and is probably at its highest level ever.

Looking more closely at the employment rates of each five-year age group shown in figure 11.2, a particularly sharp increase can be seen among women aged 60 to 64 since 2010. This coincides with the rise in the female state pension age, described in more detail in the next subsection, with this being the earliest age at which a state pension can be received in the UK (and is the only focal age in the UK state pension system). The female state pension age was 60 in 2010 and has risen gradually since such that by the end of 2018, it aligns with the state pension age for men age 65 (before both the male and female state pension ages rise further so that they reach age 66 in October 2020). Separating out the effect of this reform from other labor market trends, Cribb, Emmerson, and Tetlow (2016) show that the rise in the female state pension age for women aged 60 to 62, which occurred between

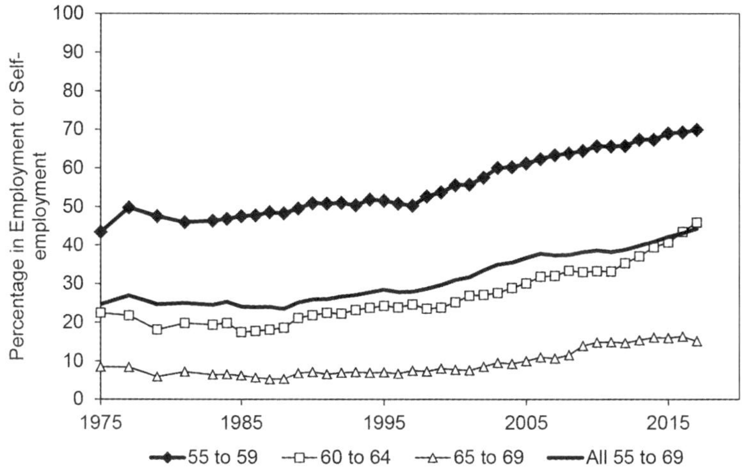

Fig. 11.2 Employment rates of women, by age band, 1975–2017
Source: Labour Force Survey.

April 2010 and March 2014, caused a sizeable 6.3 percentage point increase in the employment rate of women aged 60 and 61. Despite these increases in employment—and those seen among the other age groups presented in figure 11.2—the employment rates of older women still remain some way below those seen among older men.[1]

11.2.2 Institutional Changes and Pension Reforms

The modern UK state pension system came into being in 1948, when the basic state pension was introduced as a result of the National Insurance Act of 1946, which was the then Labour government's response to the Beveridge Report. Consistent with trying to tackle the five "giant evils" of want, disease, ignorance, squalor, and idleness, the intention was not that this pension would provide individuals with a standard of living related to that which they enjoyed during their working life but instead that it would provide insurance against income poverty in old age. Therefore, while the pension did depend on the *number* of contributions that had been made during working life, it did not depend on the *level* of those contributions. So those who paid national insurance contributions (NICs) for 90 percent (or more) of their working lives (post-1948) received the same flat-rate state pension from the state. This was payable from age 60 for women and from age 65 for men. And

1. While it is not the topic of this chapter, recent years of data from the English Longitudinal Study of Ageing or Labour Force Study reveal that all of this difference between male and female employment rates can be accounted for by different probabilities of self-employment. If one looks at employees only, then participation rates for older men and women aged 50–60 are now equal.

unlike in many other countries, individuals did not (and still do not) have to withdraw from the labor market to receive their state pension.

The next important reform was the Social Security Act of 1975, which had three major elements. First, the value of the state pension—which until then had been indexed on an ad hoc basis—was to increase each year by the greater of growth in prices or earnings (a "double lock"). Second, since married women with children would be particularly likely not to qualify for a full basic state pension (due to being in paid work for less than 90 percent of a full working life), the Home Responsibilities Protection (HRP) was introduced, which reduced the length of what was deemed to be a full working life due to periods spent with certain formal caring responsibilities (such as being in receipt of child benefit), though at least 20 years of paid contributions were still required to receive a full basic state pension. Third, from April 1978, it introduced SERPS, the UK's first significant earnings-related state pension arrangement. This was in response to a concern with the roughly 50 percent of the workforce that did not have access to any occupational pension, as their employer did not offer one.

In terms of significance, the second element of the 1975 act is the one that has best stood the test of time—with subsequent reforms consistently reinforcing this and moving in the direction of further increasing the generosity of how the basic state pension treats periods out of the labor market. But it was the third element, the introduction of SERPS, that was structurally and financially the most significant, and it was one that was gradually unpicked by successive reforms over the following 40 years.

The 1975 act had made the UK state pension system much more generous. But as the implications of this for the UK taxpayer became apparent (Hemming and Kay 1982), reforms in the 1980s and 1990s moved in the opposite direction: they reduced the generosity of the offer from the state and therefore the cost to the public purse. There were three major reforms over this period:

- The 1980 Social Security Act removed the earnings link. The value of the basic state pension was instead formally indexed in line with growth in prices (as measured by the Retail Prices Index). While SERPS accrual would still depend on average earnings growth during an individual's working life, once in payment it would also be formally indexed to growth in prices rather than to the greater growth in prices or earnings.
- For those reaching state pension age after 2000, the 1986 Social Security Act reduced the generosity of SERPS considerably through two changes. First, the accrual rate was gradually reduced from 25 percent of band earnings for years in work after 1988 down to 20 percent of band earnings, thereby at a stroke reducing its long-run generosity by a fifth. Second, entitlements became based on earnings over a full working life (from age 16 to state pension age, with years not in paid work

counted as having earnings of zero) rather than being based on the highest-earning 20 years of paid work (but years of working life prior to 1978 were still not included, so this did not affect those reaching the state pension age within 20 years of 1978). A further change was, from 1989, the abolition of the state pension earnings test. Prior to this, individuals who remained in paid work in the first five years of reaching the state pension age would, if their earnings were sufficiently high, see their state pension clawed back. Further details—and an assessment of its impact on labor supply—can be found in Disney and Smith (2002).
- The 1995 Pensions Act further reduced the generosity of SERPS. A technical change was made to the formula that had the effect of reducing band earnings. In addition, in response to a European Court of Justice ruling that pensionable ages that vary by gender should be phased out, this act legislated for a rise in the female state pension age from 60 to 65 over the 10 years from 2010 so that by 2020 it would be aligned with the male state pension age.

Concern with the UK pension system subsequently switched from being primarily about whether the implied cost of the state pension system would be one that the taxpayer was willing to bear, given projections of the aging population, to being about concerns regarding the overall adequacy of retirement provision (i.e., whether individuals were going to provide enough retirement support for themselves in order to offset the reducing state earnings–related benefits). The Child Support, Pensions, and Social Security Act of 2000, which came into force in April 2002, replaced SERPS with the State Second Pension (S2P). This provided a more generous second-tier state pension than SERPS to low and middle earners. In addition, for the first time, it provided a second-tier pension accrual to those with certain formal caring responsibilities (primarily those receiving child benefit in regard to a child under age five).

This was followed by the 2007 Pensions Act, which legislated for the restoration of the earnings link for the basic state pension (but not SERPS or S2P in payment), reduced the number of years of contributions required for a full basic state pension to 30 (for those reaching the state pension age after April 2010), removed the requirement to have to contribute for at least 25 percent of a full working life to receive any state pension, and going forward replaced HRP with a more generous system of credits for those with formal caring responsibilities. It accelerated the differential indexation of parameters in the system—which would, in the long run, return the UK to having a flat-rate state pension—and acknowledged that S2P was evolving to be, eventually, a flat-rate top-up to the (still flat rate) basic state pension. The cost of these reforms was partially offset by increases in the state pension age for men and women to 66, 67, and then 68 that were legislated to take place in the mid-2020s, mid-2030s, and mid-2040s.

Two further changes followed in 2011. First, the government announced that rather than index the basic state pension to earnings, it would instead move to a system of "triple lock" indexation, where it would be uprated each year by the greater of growth in prices (as measured by the consumer price index), growth in earnings, or 2.5 percent. Second, the increase in the female state pension age to 65 was accelerated so that it would be complete by the end of 2018, and the increase in the male and female state pension age from 65 to 66 was brought forward so that it would now be complete by October 2020.

Finally—at least for now—2014 saw a further very radical reform. For those reaching the state pension age from April 2016, the basic state pension, SERPS, and S2P are abolished and replaced with a new single-tier pension. This is a flat-rate pension for which 10 years of contributions (either paying NICs or receiving credits) are required to receive any pension (mainly removing state pension entitlements to some who work in the UK only for a relatively short time) and 35 years are required to receive the full amount. This is more than the 30 years required for a full basic state pension but fewer than that required for a full entitlement to S2P (which was 50 years for someone with a state pension age of 66). This will eventually make the UK state pension system much simpler: the only parameters will be the state pension age, the weekly amount of flat-rate pension per year of contributions (currently £164.35/35) and how it is indexed (currently triple-lock indexation), the contributions required to receive any pension (currently 10 years), and the number required to get the full pension (currently 35 years). This simplicity may—though this is as yet unproven—have the added benefit of being more stable over time.

The single-tier pension reform is backdated, so someone reaching the state pension age in April 2016 with 35 years of contributions up to that point could receive a full single-tier pension. But in addition, rights accrued up to April 2014 (when the legislation was passed) are protected: if, on reaching the state pension age, the amount of state pension already accrued up to April 2014 is greater than the amount of single-tier pension that person can qualify for, then he or she will receive the greater amount. The value of the full single-tier pension has been set such that it is more generous than the full basic state pension but less generous than the full basic state pension plus the maximum entitlement to S2P. Therefore, the new system is more generous to those who would not accrue any or much S2P (e.g., the lifetime self-employed who did not qualify for any SERPS or S2P and, in the near term, those who had long periods contracted out of the second-tier state system prior to this option being removed[2]) and less generous to those with

2. Contracting out was abolished for defined contribution arrangements from April 2011 and for defined benefit arrangements from April 2016. As a result, employees—and, where those employees had been contracted out into occupational pension arrangements, their employers—pay more NICs, but in return are not opting out of part of the state pension.

long working lives on higher levels of earnings. On average, over the longer term (once the protection for already-accrued rights has worked through), the reform makes the system less generous overall, with most individuals receiving a lower state pension than they would have done under the system it replaced—with the noticeable exception of the lifetime self-employed (Crawford, Keynes, and Tetlow 2016).

The 2014 Pensions Act also sped up the increase in the male and female state pension age to age 67, bringing it forward by eight years so that it will now occur between 2026 and 2028. This does not affect the generosity of the system in the long run but does make it less generous—and therefore less expensive—in the eight-year window, where the state pension age is now going to be higher than it would otherwise have been. The key features of these reforms are summarized in the timeline presented in figure 11.3.

One way of showing how these reforms have affected the generosity of the UK state pension system is to calculate the state pension entitlements of example individuals who are alike in many aspects but who differ in terms of their year of birth and who therefore at a given age face different state pension rules. Updating the calculations of Disney and Emmerson (2005), we take data on individuals born in the five years centered around 1952 (i.e., 1950 to 1954 inclusive) from the Family Expenditure Survey (FES) from 1968 to 2014, adjust for inflation, and calculate the median earnings among men and women who are in paid employment at each age. This provides us with a "midearning" profile for men and women from age 18 to age 62. We then assume that the earnings of earlier and later birth cohorts at the same ages are 2 percent per year higher or lower in real terms due to economy-wide real earnings growth. Adjusting back for inflation to each year's price level gets us nominal earnings at each age for each year of birth.

With an earnings profile for each cohort (defined by the year in which the cohort reaches age 65), we are then able to estimate the resulting state pension entitlements for our "midearning" men and our "midearning" women for different years of birth, with an additional assumption of their being in continuous employment from age 18 to age 62 (and not being in paid work outside those years). Since the reforms described above happen to each cohort at different ages in their lifecycle, there is considerable variation in the value of the resulting state pension by year reaching retirement age. The results for men, for those reaching age 65 between 1950 and 2050 (i.e., born between 1885 and 1985), are shown in figure 11.4. The equivalent results for women, for those reaching age 60 between 1950 and 2050 (i.e., born between 1890 and 1990), are shown in figure 11.5.

For those reaching the state pension age between 1950 and 1978, the generosity of the system is entirely governed by the value of the basic state pension. Over this period, it was indexed sporadically, increasing overall relative to both prices and earnings but with some years in which its value fell with respect to both. Since our midearning female earns less than our

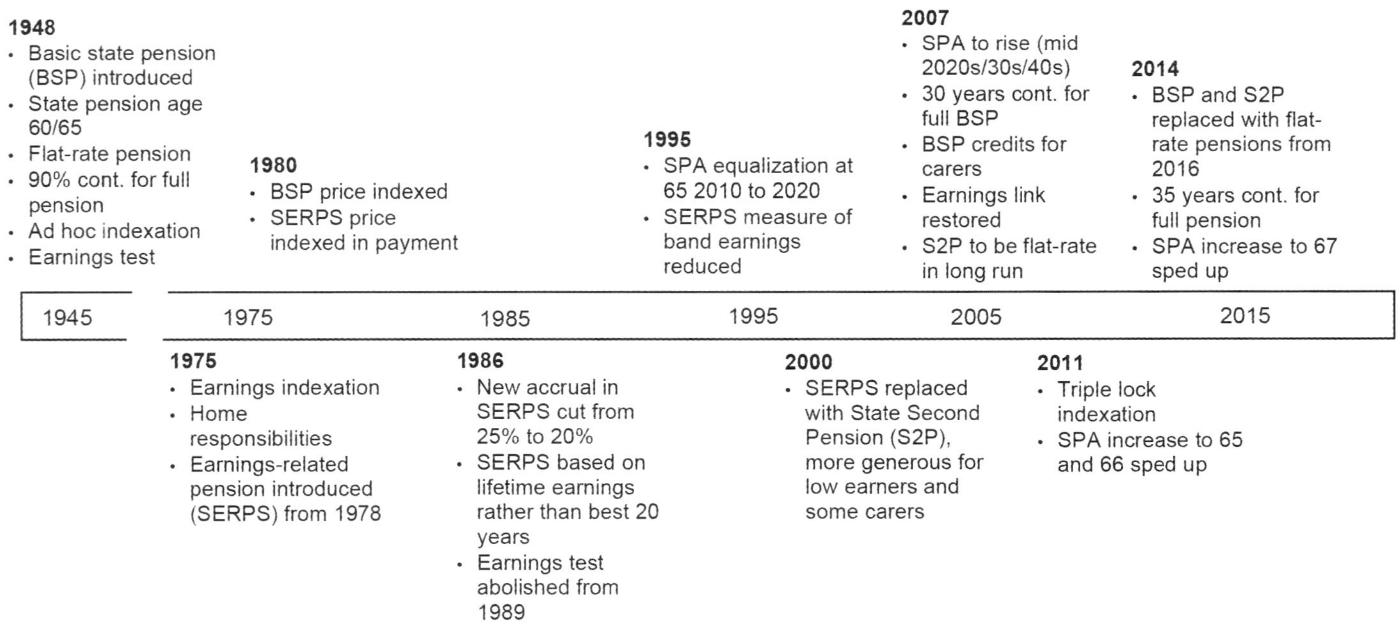

Fig. 11.3 Timeline of UK state pension reforms: Beveridge to 2017

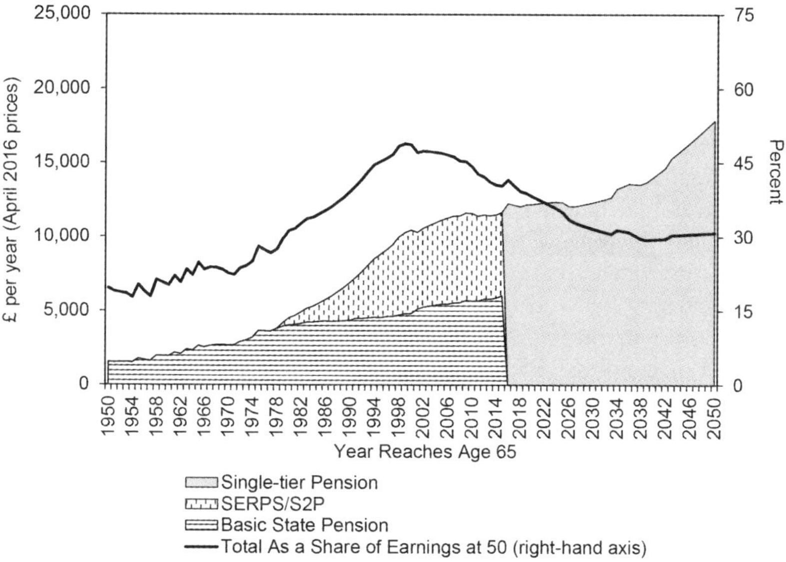

Fig. 11.4 Simulated value of state pension at state pension age over time, "midearning" male

Source: Authors' calculations using earnings profiles estimated from the Family Expenditure Survey, 1968–2014.

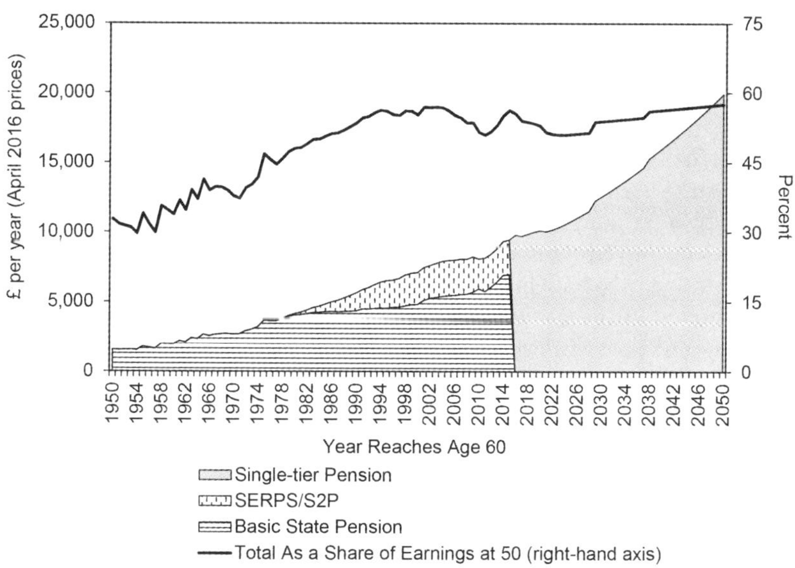

Fig. 11.5 Simulated value of state pension at state pension age over time, "midearning" female

Source: Authors' calculations using earnings profiles estimated from the Family Expenditure Survey, 1968–2014.

midearning male, the basic state pension is worth a greater share of her earnings at age 50 than his.

For those reaching the state pension age between 1978 and 2000, the system is more generous the later the individual's year of birth. This is because entitlement to SERPS depends on earnings in years beyond April 1978 (but before the state pension age), so those born later have more years of working-age life post-1978 in which to accrue entitlement. This is more than sufficient to outweigh the reduction in the basic state pension, relative to earnings, arising from it being indexed to growth in prices. This is especially true of our midearning male, as his greater earnings accrue him a larger SERPS entitlement than our midearning female.

As the original SERPS was based on the highest-earning 20 years and the subsequent cuts to SERPS only applied to those reaching the state pension age after 1998, the generosity of the UK state pension peaks for men reaching the state pension age around the turn of the century. But even then, for our midearning male, the UK state pension system does not provide a replacement rate above 50 percent of their earnings at age 50. Thereafter the generosity of the system is calculated to rise slightly in real terms but to fall relative to earnings at 50. This continues until the impact of triple-lock indexation, which causes the generosity of the state pension to ratchet up relative to earnings over time, starts to outweigh the impact of other cuts to the state pension.

For our midearning female, the cuts to SERPS are less important, since her lower earnings meant that she would have had a lower entitlement anyway. More important is the indexation of the basic state pension, with the triple lock boosting the value of the state pension after 2011, and the introduction of the single-tier pension, which is more generous to lower earners reaching the state pension age from 2016 onward.

The figures above focus on the annual state pension income that would be received by our example men and women in the first year after they reach the state pension age, with our example individuals being in paid work continuously from age 18 to 62. This means that the impact of two important aspects of the reforms of the last 40 years is not shown here. First, the treatment of periods out of paid work due to having certain formal caring arrangements has been made more generous. This will mean that, in particular, the system has become more generous for women with children in a way that is not captured in the figures. This will be particularly the case for married women who had children after 1977.[3] Second, the increase in the state pension age represents a significant cut to the total amount of state pension that some individuals can expect to receive but not a significant change to the amount

3. HRP was introduced from 1978. Note that women born after 1932—who therefore reached age 16 after the introduction of the state pension in 1948—are the ones who would have otherwise needed the most years in paid work to receive a full state pension.

per year received once the state pension age has been reached. Under current legislation between 2010 and 2050, the male state pension age will have increased by three years from 65 to 68, while the female state pension age will have increased by eight years from 60 to 68.

The remaining sections of this chapter simulate the pension wealth and work incentive consequences of these reforms in more detail and use the resulting information to quantify the extent to which the changes in financial incentives arising from these reforms have affected employment outcomes at older ages.

11.3 Simulations

11.3.1 Lifetime Earnings Profiles

For the main simulations in what follows, we not only take men and women with different years of birth but also construct our measures for low-, mid-, and high-earning individuals in each group in order to examine the differential effects of the pension reforms across the lifetime earnings distribution. The construction of the earnings profiles that crucially underlie the simulations is done in two different ways. First, as in other chapters in this volume, we utilize the common earnings profiles constructed for use across all countries, as described in the introduction to this volume. These provide us with a prototype "shape" of a lifetime earnings profile for men and women with low, mid, and high earnings (i.e., six person types in total), with each profile normalized to one at age 50. To apply these to the UK context, we pool data on 49- to 51-year-olds from the 2015 and 2016 waves of the LFS (with the 2015 data uprated to 2016 prices) and use these data to estimate median earnings at age 50 for those with low, middle, and high levels of education, split separately by sex.[4] These six earnings levels are then applied to the relevant common profile, which gives us the lifetime profile for each type of group within the cohort that reaches age 50 in 2016. We then assume that economy-wide productivity growth will be (and always has been) 2 percent per year—so that successive birth cohorts are assumed to earn 2 percent more than their predecessors at each age, giving us real earnings profiles for earlier and later cohorts. And to get nominal earnings in different years (since this will often matter for the rules governing the pension system), we reflate or deflate these profiles by the retail price index (RPI).

In order to consider the sensitivity of our calculations to the use of these common earnings profiles, we also compute a set of UK-specific earnings profiles. If we were running a full microsimulation or dynamic programming

4. Despite the large sample size of the LFS, we need to pool years in order to boost the sample size, since we are dealing with a very small age window and six types of people within that window.

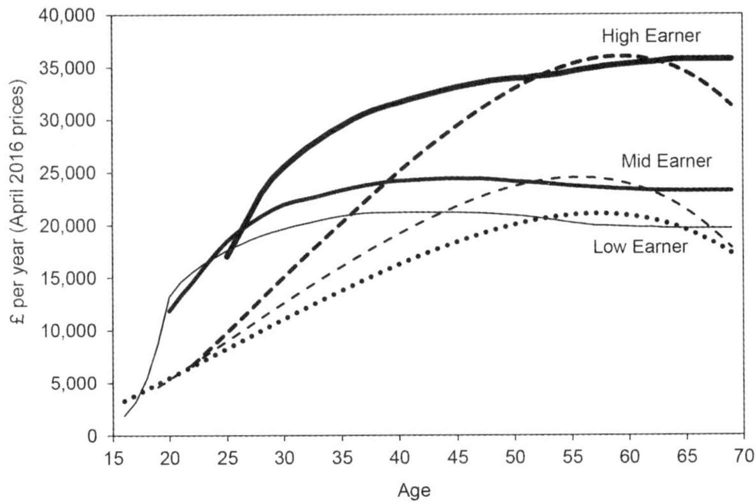

Fig. 11.6 Common earnings profiles and cross section profile against actual cohort profile, men born in 1952, by earnings

model of the effects of the pension reforms, we would want to pay particular attention to the estimation of earnings dynamics and ideally use a sophisticated econometric model of earnings processes estimated from the long time series of panel data available in the UK from the British Household Panel Survey and Understanding Society studies. But our goals in this chapter are different, and we want a UK-specific earnings process that is not too dissimilar to the common profiles in spirit, so we instead construct a simple shape for lifetime income based on the LFS data. We once again take the most recent two years of LFS data and, using data on all individuals aged 18–65, estimate a quantile (median) regression of earnings on age and age squared, with estimations carried out separately for each of the six groups (men and women interacted by three education groups). As with the common earnings profile, we then assume economy-wide productivity growth of 2 percent per year to get the shape of the real earnings profile for different birth cohorts and reflate/deflate by household inflation to get nominal earnings in earlier and later years.[5]

5. Ideally, we would use a long time series of repeat cross-sectional data to plot an actual earnings profile for a cohort, as was done for the construction of figure 11.4 in the previous section. Unfortunately, the FES only contains information on education from 1978 onward and therefore cannot yet provide an earnings profile for a full working life if we are to split by education level. In order to investigate this issue, we can, however, compare the earnings profile not split by education from the times series of FES cross-sections to an equivalent one estimated on the basis of the 2015–16 LFS cross section, for the same cohort born in 1952. This is presented in appendix figure 11.A.1 (men) and 11.A.2 (women).

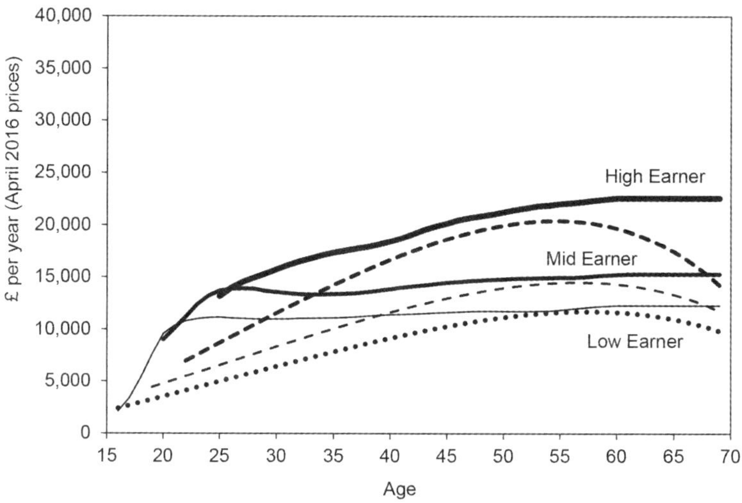

Fig. 11.7 Common earnings profiles v cross section, women born in 1952, by earnings

Sources: Solid lines from the common profiles combined with data from the Labour Force Survey (2015 and 2016). Dotted lines estimated using data from the Labour Force Survey (2015 and 2016).

A comparison of the profiles is shown for men (in figure 11.6) and for women (in figure 11.7). These are shown for the case of our example individuals born in 1952. The solid lines are the "common" profile, while the dotted lines are the profiles estimated from the UK cross-sectional data. The lines are shaded from lightest to darkest in ascending order of education level from low to high. For women, and especially for men, the profiles estimated from UK data show earnings at a lower level earlier in working life and then increasing more quickly with age than the common profile. The profiles estimated from UK data also exhibit more evidence of declining earnings at the oldest working ages. The former will have obvious effects on simulated pension wealth levels, and the latter will have effects on pension accrual at older ages and hence implicit work disincentives.

11.3.2 Social Security Wealth

Using the six common earnings profiles, we then calculate accumulated state pension entitlements at every age from 55 to 69 for men and women from each year of birth from 1881 through to 1995 given the particular set of pension contribution and benefit "rules" each cohort will have lived through by the time they reach retirement. Having done this, we then compute the present discounted value of the resulting future stream of state pension income. To do this, we need to make an assumption about when individuals will die: for this, we take the common life expectancy tables used throughout

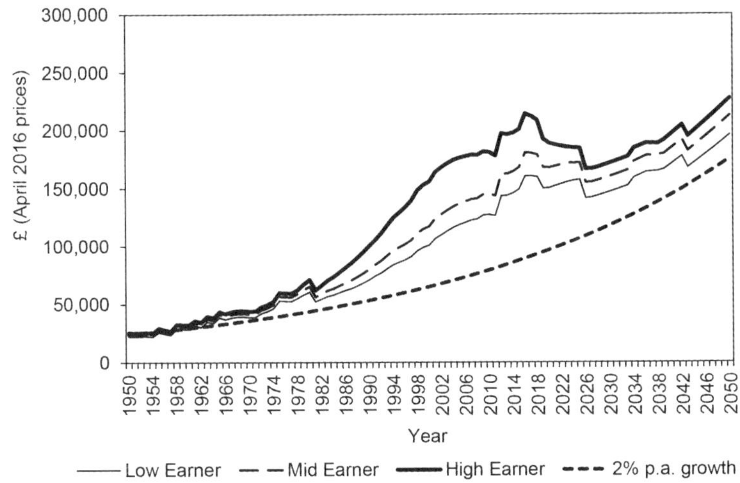

Fig. 11.8 Estimated social security wealth: Man at age 65, by year and earnings level

this volume, as described in the introduction. These give the chance of survival at each age, with a larger chance for women than men and for higher earners than for lower earners, but they do not allow for any improvement in longevity among later birth cohorts. In order to take the present discounted values, we assume a real annual discount rate of 3 percent.

The estimated accumulated level of social security wealth for 65-year-old men, in each year from 1950 to 2050 (under current policy), is shown by the three solid lines in figure 11.8. As before, the lines are shaded from lightest to darkest in ascending order of education level from low to high. The graph reveals that reforms have often changed the level of wealth quite markedly. In particular, the introduction of more generous indexation in 1975 (the double lock), less generous indexation in 1980 (the move to price indexation), and more generous indexation from 2011 (the triple lock) can all be seen. The gradual introduction—and subsequent move away from—an earnings-related state pension can be seen with the difference in entitlements between the lowest and highest education groups increasing over the period from 1978 to the turn of the century (as earnings-related pensions are worth more in cash terms to higher earners) before falling again. The introduction of the single-tier pension in 2016 also boosts average entitlements. Finally, the impact of increases in the state pension age (to 66 in the late 2010s, to 67 in the mid-2020s, and to 68 in the mid-2040s) on reducing accumulated social security wealth can also be clearly seen.

Despite the increases in the state pension age from 65 to 68 over the century from 1950, the generosity of the state pension system for our example

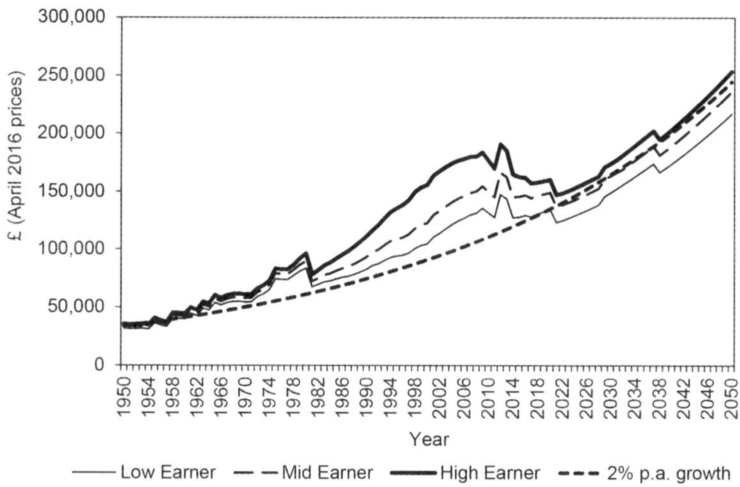

Fig. 11.9 Estimated social security wealth: Woman at age 60, by year and earnings level

men will, at least under current policies, still have grown by more than 2 percent per year in real terms on average.

The equivalent estimates for the accumulated social security wealth of women (instead looking at accumulated wealth at age 60 rather than age 65 given that the former is the most common state pension age for women over this period) are shown in figure 11.9. In many cases, the reforms highlighted above can also be seen to affect the accumulated state pension wealth of women. One notable difference is that the phasing in of SERPS over the 20 years from 1978 boosts the accumulated state pension wealth of women by less than it does for men. This is explained by women having, on average, a lower level of weekly earnings (despite the fact that women are able to receive SERPS for longer as a result of their greater life expectancy and, at least for the period up to the end of 2018, the fact that the female state pension age is lower than the male state pension age). Conversely, women receive a larger boost from the introduction of the single-tier pension (affecting women reaching the state pension age after April 2016), though this only partly offsets a decline in accumulated wealth for successive cohorts reaching age 60 through the 2010s, who have progressively higher state pension ages (the state pension age for women rising from 60 in March 2010 to 66 in October 2020).

In terms of the average increase in the generosity of the state pension system over the entire century from 1950, it is striking that, unlike for men, it will grow (at least under current policies) by less than 2 percent per year in real terms. This is due to the fact that there has been a larger increase in the female state pension age than in the male state pension age over this period (eight years versus three years). It is, however, worth noting that women with children will have particularly benefited from the increasing generosity of the treatment of the state pension system to periods out of the labor market due to formal caring responsibilities (introduced from 1978), and these benefits are not valued in the example profiles shown here, since these calculations are for women who have been in the labor market for most of their adult lives.

11.3.3 Pension Wealth and Work Incentives

In order to characterize the effects of these pension reforms more fully and begin to document the variation that will be used in our empirical analysis that follows, we construct four different measures of the generosity of the UK state pension system and the financial incentive it provides to remain in paid work. We focus just on the period 1978 to 2017, which is the period where we have employment rates split by education and sex. And we also look at how these measures have been evolving for older adults at different ages in the run-up to the state pension age—that is, from 60 to 64 for males and from 55 to 59 for females.[6]

The evolution of these measures by age and year/cohort is shown in the four panels of figure 11.10 (for midearning men) and figure 11.11 (for midearning women), respectively. The top left panel shows the replacement rate, defined here as the present discounted value of state pension wealth divided by earnings at age 50. The top right panel shows accumulated social security wealth (corresponding to figures 11.8 and 11.9). Social security wealth and replacement rates are both typically rising over successive years from the mid-1970s to 2000 as SERPS matures. Older men and women have typically accrued slightly more wealth and therefore have a slightly higher replacement rate than younger men and women. The phasing in of the cuts to SERPS across birth cohorts for those reaching the state pension age after 2000 results in greater differences in accrued wealth, and therefore replacement rates, in the later years. Finally, among women, the impact of the rise in the female state pension age from 60 in 2010 to 65 in 2018 can be seen among successive cohorts of women starting with those aged 55 in 2005 (who are the first cohort to be affected).

The bottom left panel shows state pension accrual. This is defined as the (discounted) increase in social security wealth that individuals would expect to accrue if they were to remain in paid work for one more year and if there were no further reforms to the state pension system implemented net of any employee and employer NICs that would be paid on the earnings. So this is the value, in pounds, of the boost to state pension wealth that one

6. Of course, we have computed corresponding series for all ages between 55 and 69 for both men and women of each earnings/education type, and the full sets of series are used in the estimation that follows, but just these particular age ranges are selected for the purposes of the illustrative figures.

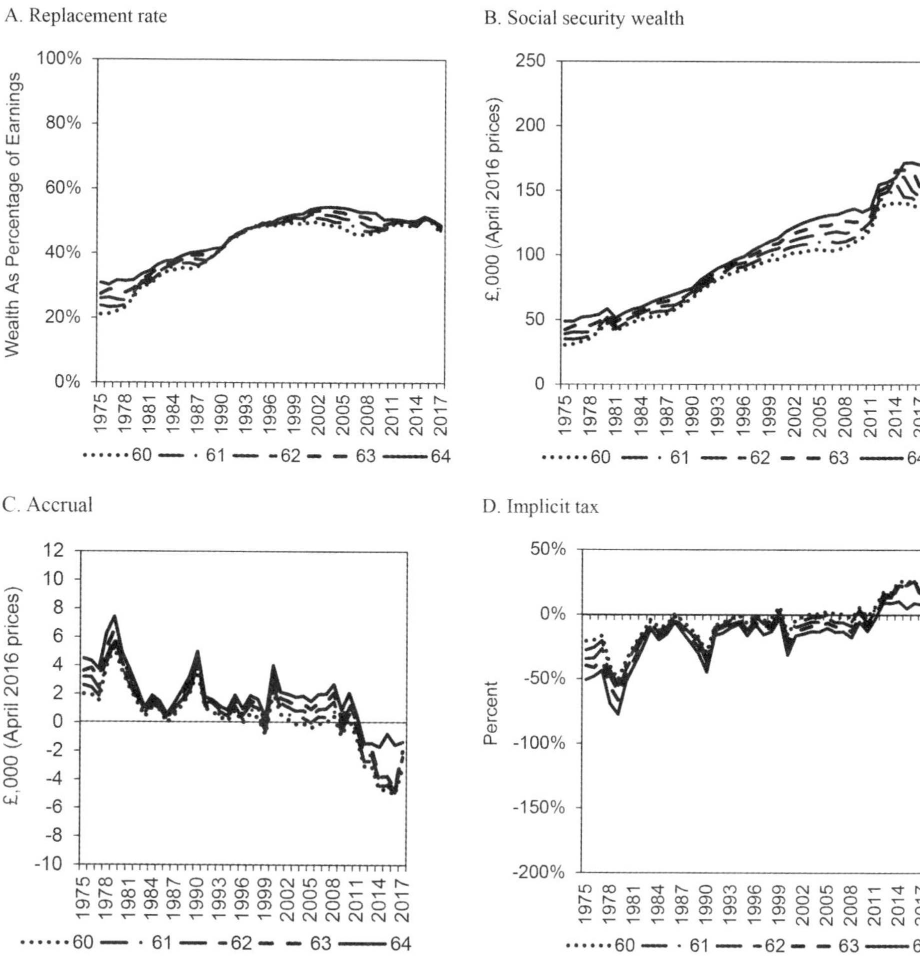

Fig. 11.10 Estimated social security replacement rate, wealth, accrual and implicit tax: midearning men aged 60 to 64, by single year of age; common earnings profile

might expect from remaining in paid work net of the payroll taxes required to finance this. Therefore, positive accrual shows that by remaining in paid work, state pension entitlement would rise by more than the amount of NICs paid, while negative accrual shows that state pension entitlements would rise by less than the additional NICs paid. An oddity for the UK analysis is that NICs payments are not exclusively used for, nor are they the sole funder of, the state pension. Rather, the revenues are pooled with those of other taxes and used as the government sees fit. Increases in the rates of NICs—for example, in 1993, 2002, and 2011—were motivated by other demands on public finances (such as a desire to reduce the deficit or to

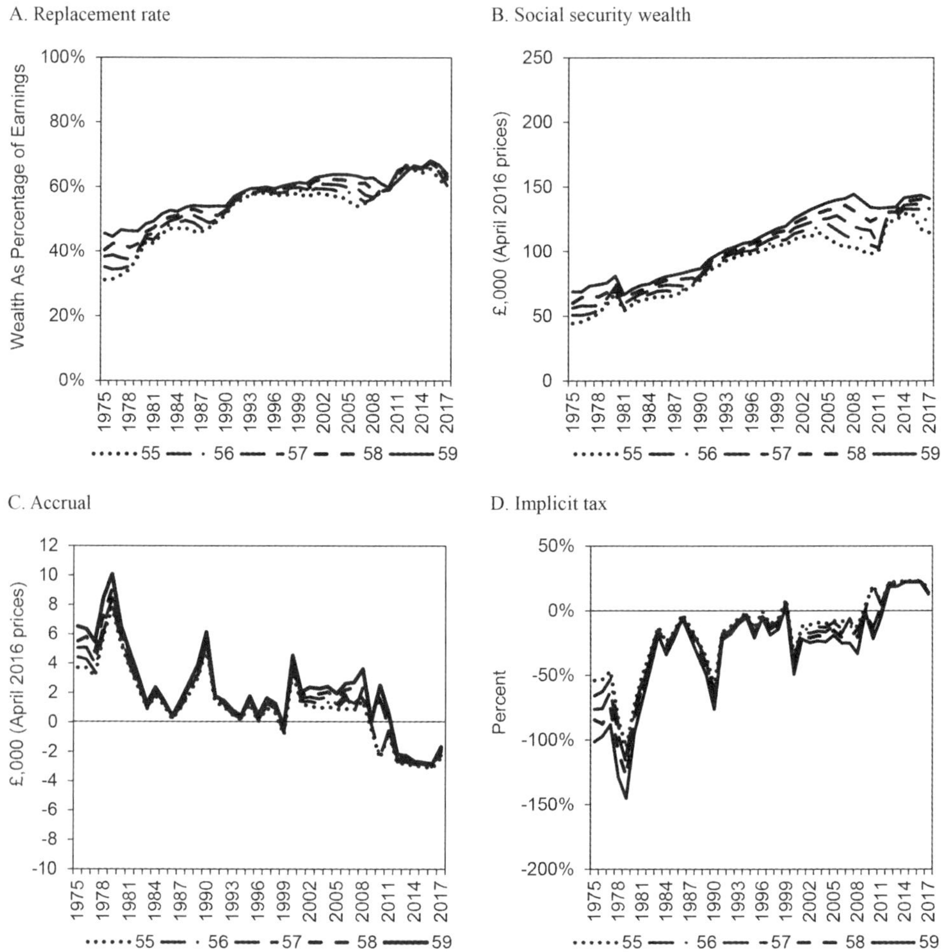

Fig. 11.11 Estimated social security replacement rate, wealth, accrual and implicit tax: midearning women aged 55 to 59, by single year of age; common earnings profile

increase spending on, for example, the National Health Service) rather than a need to finance an increase in spending on the state pension. Conversely, cuts to the state pension have not directly led to cuts in the rates of NICs.

Finally, implicit tax is defined as negative accrual less the impact of any earnings tests, all divided through by the earnings that the individual would expect to receive net of direct taxes.[7] Therefore, a positive implicit tax rate

7. These are computed using OECD statistics on direct taxes on earnings, which do not vary over time but do vary by earnings level. Total cost to the employer of employment is calculated using an employer social security contribution of 9.4 percent, 10.5 percent, or 11.3 percent for low, mid, and high earners, respectively. A direct tax wedge of 28.8 percent, 32.5 percent, and 35.5 percent—again for low, mid, or high earners—is then applied.

shows that the state pension system (combined with the NICs paid on earnings) is imposing, implicitly, a tax on remaining in paid work, whereas a negative rate implies that there is an implicit subsidy. It is worth remembering that, given the age groups presented in these particular figures, these are implicit taxes or subsidies on work in the five years before the state pension age rather than at or after it. At older ages, the key variation comes from the fact that prior to 1989, an earnings test applied to earnings in the first five years after the state pension age, which particularly affected higher earners, whereas from 1989 onward, individuals are free to draw their state pension and continue in paid work.

The evolution of accrual and the implicit tax rates over time can be affected in complicated ways depending on the type of reforms being implemented and when they are announced. Reforms only affect these measures after they have been announced, but even then, certain reforms may not affect these profiles and hence have no effect on marginal work incentives. Some reforms may announce effects that will be implemented sufficiently in the future so that certain cohorts are unaffected. Other potentially quite significant reforms may not affect the measures (much) if they have a similar impact on both current social security wealth and the level of wealth expected to be accrued if one were to remain in paid work for a further year. For example, changing the indexation of state pension rights or the state pension age, which can have a substantial impact on social security wealth, will have a more muted impact on accrual and implicit tax, as they will affect both wealth already accrued and that which can be attained from remaining in paid work for one more year.

In general, over the period from the late 1970s to the mid-2010s, once the early effects of the 1978 reform are out of the way, we do not see huge taxes or subsidies on work prior to the state pension age (SPA; i.e., on early retirement) that are often observed in other countries. Nor do we see huge differences in the evolution of these incentive variables by males or females (and by different levels of earnings, presented in appendix figures 11.A.3–11.A.6); the broad shapes of the changes over time are similar. There are small but noticeable differences among the patterns over time for different age, education, and gender groups, however, and these will be important in the identification of potential effects on employment rates in the analysis that follows.

With more specific reference to the broader time trends resulting from the reforms, rates of accrual have been falling and therefore the implicit tax rate has been rising for all groups. The introduction of SERPS in the late 1970s increases accrual and reduces implicit tax, with the reverse being true of the move to price indexation of the state pension from 1980. Spikes in accrual in the early 1990s and the early 2000s were due to the basic state pension rising by more than inflation. In the most recent years, accrual, on average, turns negative and implicit tax, again on average, turns positive. This is because fewer years of contributions are required to qualify for a full flat-rate pension (30 years under the basic state pension and 35 years under the single-tier pension), meaning that our example individuals will have all qualified for a full amount before these older ages. A further contribution to falling accrual and rising implicit tax over this period has been successive increases in rates of NICs over this period: for example, with increases in April 2003 and April 2011 (which were not related to changes to the state pension system).

The appendix contains equivalent figures to figures 11.10 and 11.11 for low- and high-earning men (appendix figures 11.A.3 and 11.A.4) and for low- and high-earning women (appendix figures 11.A.5 and 11.A.6). In addition, the equivalent figures have also been constructed using the UK-specific earnings profile (described earlier in this subsection). These are presented for midearning men and midearning women in appendix figures 11.A.7 and 11.A.8.

11.4 Results

In this section, we analyze the degree to which the sequences of pension wealth and implicit tax rates for each of our six types of agents, at every age between 55 and 69, are associated with the employment rates for that group at that age. To describe and motivate the analysis and to compare with other chapters in this volume, we begin by carrying out a naïve analysis looking at the association between average employment rates and the time series for average implicit tax rates (i.e., averaged across individuals' type and across all ages in the 55–69 window). We go on to carry out a more detailed empirical analysis that allows us to exploit differences by individuals' type and the age at which their cohort is observed. These models are both carried out for our baseline case using the common earnings profiles as described above. Following that, we carry out two different variants of our analysis, with the former making some attempt to control for the possible confounding effects of private (occupational) pensions and the latter looking at how our conclusions would be affected if we use UK-specific as opposed to common earnings profiles.

11.4.1 Employment Rates and State Pension Accrual: Baseline Model

The first correlation we document is the time series of average employment against the time series of average implicit tax. For this, we take the average employment rate of those aged 55 to 69, by sex, from the Labour Force Survey. By interpolating the employment rate for a few early years (1976, 1978, 1980, and 1982) in which LFS data were not collected, this allows us to look at the period from 1975 to 2017 (inclusive, as shown in the left-hand panel of figure 11.12). The implicit tax rate is calculated as set out in the previous section and is constructed using the common earnings profile. To get the average implicit tax rate, we take the simple average of the low-,

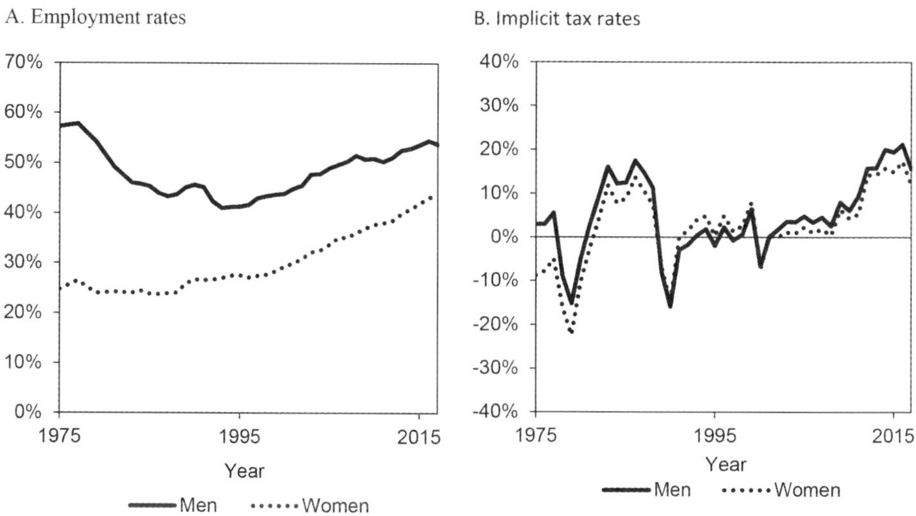

Fig. 11.12 Employment rates and implicit tax rates, by sex, 1975 to 2017

mid-, and high-earning groups for each sex/age in each year. These are plotted in the right-hand panel of figure 11.12. Among men, the employment rate falls from 1975 to the mid-1990s and rises again. But in most years, the implicit tax rate rises over this period, though there are years in which the implicit tax rate falls and the employment rate does rise (such as 1990). Among women, the employment rate is fairly stable from 1975 to the early to mid-1990s and then rises more quickly. But again, the average tax rate is typically rising through this period.

If anything, this suggests a positive correlation between implicit taxes and employment probabilities, counter to the predictions of the most elementary labor supply model. Simple time-series regressions of the tax rate on the employment rate for each sex yield the following estimates (with standard errors in parentheses):

$$\text{Male: Employment rate} = \underset{(0.008)}{0.478} + \underset{(0.084)}{0.090} * \text{Implicit Tax}$$

$$\text{Female: Employment rate} = \underset{(0.009)}{0.293} + \underset{(0.094)}{0.347} * \text{Implicit Tax}$$

These show that it is indeed the case that, on average, in years in which the estimated average tax rate faced by men and women is higher, the employment rate of men and women is also higher. This is particularly true for women, where the coefficient is large and statistically significant.

One final alternative way to see this correlation, presented for comparabil-

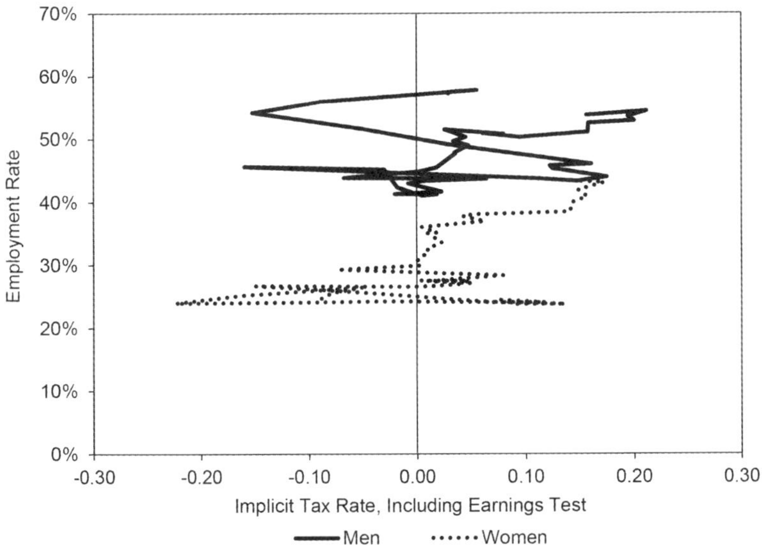

Fig. 11.13 Evolution of Employment rate and Average Implicit Tax Rate, 1975–2017

ity with other chapters in this volume, is by plotting the evolving relationship between the two variables over time, as in figure 11.13.

The rest of the analysis in this subsection uses the profiles estimated separately by education group and the time-series variation for each cohort-education group as they age. As a result, we focus on the period from 1978 to 2014, since that is the period in which we can construct the employment rate by education (and sex) from the FES. There are 15 ages (55 to 69) and three education groups covering the 37 years (from 1978 to 2014 inclusive). This would imply a total of 1,665 observations (15*37*3) for each sex, although there are a handful of missing cells in the earlier years of data due to the FES not containing any individuals of high education at older ages. Again we run regressions with the employment rate as the dependent variable. Given that we have variation in our pension wealth and incentive effects by age, cohort, and time, we are now able to control for a full set of age dummies, a full set of year dummies, and dummies for each education group, thus taking out the potentially confounding effects of other macroeconomic trends or any other age- or education-specific variables that may be simultaneously affecting pension wealth, earnings, or employment rates. Separate regressions are run for men and women. We also use weighted regression, using the number of observations in each cell that are observed in the FES as weights, so that our distribution of example types has the same average composition as the aggregate employment rate.

The results from these two regressions are shown in figure 11.13. For men, both of the financial incentives have the "right" sign and are statistically significant at the 1 percent level. The coefficient on implicit tax is, however, economically small. It implies that a 10 percentage point increase in the tax rate would only reduce the employment rate by 0.91 percentage points.[8] The coefficient on social security wealth is more substantial, suggesting that a 10 percent increase in wealth would lead to a 1.5 percentage point fall in the employment rate.

For women, the coefficient on implicit tax has the opposite sign—and again is statistically significant—implying that an increase in implicit tax would *increase* the female employment rate, albeit by a modest amount. Social security wealth has the same sign as, and is of a similar magnitude to, that of men, implying that a 10 percent increase in wealth would reduce the female employment rate by about 1.5 percentage points.

11.4.2 Accounting for Private Pension Wealth

The analysis so far has focused on what the assumed earnings profiles mean for the level and accrual of state pension wealth and the extent to which changes in these are associated with changes in employment rates. But private pensions can—and do—also provide financial incentives to retire at particular ages. In particular, final salary pension schemes often provide a strong incentive to remain in paid work—or at least not to draw that pension—until the normal pension age (NPA) is reached. Prior to 2006 in the UK, it was also not possible to work for an employer and to draw a private pension from that employer at the same time. This meant that to draw a pension from an employer, individuals had to move to another employer or move out of the labor market altogether. From 2006 onward, that requirement has been removed, and individuals can now draw a private pension from an employer while continuing to work for that same employer.[9]

To attempt to control for any confounding effects of the final incentives from defined benefit arrangements, we modify our framework in a very crude way in order to include two different types of schemes. One has an NPA of 60 (such as many public service pension arrangements did for most of the period included in this study) and the other has a NPA of 65 (as was more

8. This would correspond to an elasticity that is almost certainly smaller than we might expect in a microeconometric analysis of labor supply at older ages but is perhaps explained by the fact that within each type, we have an employment rate that is in reality an average over a distribution of individuals of many different subtypes, each with different circumstances and earnings histories, whereas our pension measures for this type assume there is no such heterogeneity. Put differently, one might say the pension wealth variables are measured with considerable error. Hence we would not want to make serious quantitative microeconometric inferences about the overall magnitude of effects from such a model, but the sign of the resulting coefficients and qualitative conclusions would seem to us to be meaningful.

9. Note that the analysis in this chapter does not consider job-to-job moves. Instead, it is assumed that remaining in paid work means remaining in the same job or at least in the same pension arrangement.

common among private-sector employers who provided a defined benefit arrangement). Both schemes are assumed to offer accrual of 1/60th of the final salary scheme for each year of service, with this capped at 40 years. This implies a pension worth two-thirds of a final salary after a 40-year career. And both are assumed to reduce benefits by 4 percent for each year that they are drawn before the NPA is reached and no "bonus" for not drawing the pension until after the NPA.

Based on a crude characterization of the participation in private defined benefit pensions in the UK, we assume that 50 percent of both men and women have some kind of private defined benefit. Given the increased propensity of women to work in the public sector, we also assume that 25 percent of women are in each type of scheme, while 15 percent of men are in the first (NPA = 60) scheme and 35 percent of men are in the second (NPA = 65) scheme. Those without defined benefit arrangements may have no private pension coverage, or they might be members of defined contribution (DC) arrangements, but that should not matter for the focus of our analysis, as DC schemes do not provide strong financial incentives to retire at any particular age. More fundamentally, these assumed proportions do not vary over time/cohort (whereas in reality membership of defined benefit schemes among private-sector employees has been falling sharply) or over education levels (despite the fact that higher earners will be more likely to be members of a generous pension arrangement). While including weights with such variation would be advantageous, constructing them for the whole period of our analysis would not be straightforward. And if we were to move in such a direction, we would be moving increasingly further to a full individual-level microeconometric analysis of reforms and incentives, which is our goal for future work in this project as opposed to this particular chapter.

With our private-sector scheme rules characterized and assumptions on the fraction of each group in each type of scheme, we can calculate private pension wealth and private pension accrual following a similar methodology as state pension wealth and accrual. These are then added to state pension wealth and state pension accrual to obtain measures of total pension wealth and total pension accrual. Our task is made simpler because there are no interaction effects in the state pension whereby which an individual's private pension wealth would affect their state pension wealth or accrual (or vice versa).

Figure 11.14 (right-hand panel) shows the average implicit tax rates over time equivalent to those presented in figure 11.12 but now includes the estimated incentive from private defined benefit pension arrangements. This has the effect of increasing the tax rate, and by a roughly similar amount (around 12 to 14 percentage points for men and around 14 to 16 percentage points for women), in each year for the period from 1975 to 2005 (inclusive). This is because in those years, individuals who have already built up the maximum 40 years of pension tenure in a final salary scheme and reached their NPA

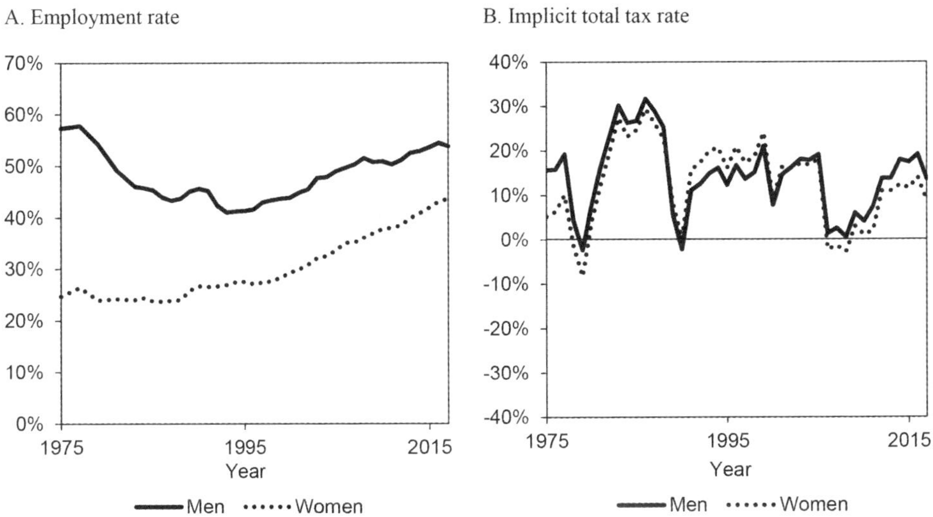

Fig. 11.14 Employment rate and implicit total tax rate, including private pensions, by sex, 1975 to 2017

will be disincentivized to remain in paid work. For years beyond 2005, the inclusion of these schemes makes no difference to the average tax rate, since individuals are now able to draw their defined benefit pension and continue to work for the same employer if they wish. Rather than falling over the period, once these defined benefit pension arrangements are included, the implicit tax rates are more stable—and are possibly on a downward trend.

The inclusion of defined benefit pension incentives in the implicit tax calculations therefore has a significant impact on the time-series correlation between employment rates and average tax rates. Whereas before the regression, the coefficient on the implicit tax rate was positive for both men and women (and statistically significant for women), once defined benefit pensions are included, the coefficient on implicit tax becomes negative for both men and women:

$$\text{Male: Employment rate} = \underset{(0.014)}{0.504} - \underset{(0.087)}{0.152} * \text{Implicit Tax}$$

$$\text{Female: Employment rate} = \underset{(0.015)}{0.329} - \underset{(0.098)}{0.219} * \text{Implicit Tax}$$

As before, we now switch to the FES employment data from 1978 to 2004, which allow us to exploit variation by age cohort and education levels. Equivalent regressions to those presented in table 11.1 are run, but this time controlling for the implicit tax rate, including defined benefit pension

Table 11.1 **Main regression results, employment and state pension wealth and implicit tax**

	Men	Women
Implicit tax	–0.091***	+0.052***
	(0.016)	(0.012)
Log social security wealth	–0.153***	–0.146***
	(0.039)	(0.026)
Other controls:		
Age dummies	Included	Included
Year dummies	Included	Included
Education dummies	Included	Included
R-squared	0.902	0.882
Sample size	1,660	1,660

Note: *** denotes that the coefficient is significantly different from zero at the 1 percent level, ** at the 5 percent level, and * at the 10 percent level.

Table 11.2 **Main regression results, including defined benefit pensions**

	Men	Women
Implicit tax	–0.079***	+0.053***
	(0.013)	(0.010)
Log pension wealth	–0.381***	–0.228***
	(0.070)	(0.038)
Other controls:		
Age dummies	Included	Included
Year dummies	Included	Included
Education dummies	Included	Included
R-squared	0.902	0.883
Sample size	1,660	1,660

Note: *** denotes that the coefficient is significantly different from zero at the 1 percent level, ** at the 5 percent level, and * at the 10 percent level.

arrangements, and for the log of total pension wealth (i.e., the sum of state pension wealth and private defined benefit wealth). Here we find that the estimated coefficients on implicit tax are changed remarkably little. The coefficients continue to be negative and significant for men and positive and significant for women (and both economically quite small). The coefficients on wealth both become more negative, now implying that a 10 percent increase in wealth would reduce the employment rate of men aged 55 to 69 by 3.8 percentage points and of women aged 55 to 69 by 2.3 percentage points.

11.4.4 UK-Specific Earnings Profiles

Finally, we move from using the common earnings profiles to using those constructed from UK data (as shown in figures 11.6 and 11.7 and described in the surrounding text), and the resulting incentive measures for mid-earning men and women are shown in the appendix in figures 11.A.7 and 11.A.8. The

Table 11.3 Employment, implicit tax, and wealth, with and without private pension wealth included, UK-specific earnings profiles

	Social security wealth only		Private pension wealth included	
	Men	Women	Men	Women
Implicit tax	–0.116***	+0.054***	–0.079***	+0.053***
	(0.017)	(0.011)	(0.012)	(0.009)
Log wealth	–0.1520***	–0.170***	–0.381***	–0.216***
	(0.037)	(0.026)	(0.064)	(0.038)
Other controls:				
Age dummies	Included	Included	Included	Included
Year dummies	Included	Included	Included	Included
Education dummies	Included	Included	Included	Included
R-squared	0.902	0.883	0.902	0.884
Sample size	1,660	1,660	1,660	1,660

Note: *** denotes that the coefficient is significantly different from zero at the 1 percent level, ** at the 5 percent level, and * at the 10 percent level.

results from this analysis are presented in table 11.3 (and can be compared to those in tables 11.1 and 11.2). Qualitatively, they are remarkably similar to those estimated using the common earnings profile. For men, we continue to find a statistically significant but economically small negative impact of implicit tax on employment. And this effect continues to be little changed by the inclusion of private defined benefit pension wealth. For women, the coefficients on implicit tax are also little changed by the inclusion of private wealth, and in both cases, they remain statistically significant. For all cases, we find that higher wealth is associated with lower employment, with this relationship being statistically significant. And—again as before—we find that the effect is stronger once private-sector defined benefit pension wealth is included.

11.5 Conclusions

The UK has implemented substantial pension reform over the last 50 years, having first supplemented the basic (flat-rate) state pension with an earnings-related scheme and then made successive reforms to its generosity and design, before effectively abolishing it and going back to a flat pension. And while the disincentives to work implied by the UK pension system have perhaps never been as large as those observed in some countries, we have, for a few years now, been in a situation where the pension system is largely neutral with regard to work incentives both before and after the state pension age. These headlines are well known, at least within the UK economics and policy communities. In this chapter, we have gone beyond such a headline description and used a set of illustrative example types of individuals to model the effects of the sequence of reforms for different birth cohorts who will have been "hit" by the various pension reforms at differing points in their working lives.

To a certain extent, we have been repeating and updating analyses that have previously been carried out prior to the most recent policy developments in the last 10 years, such as those contained in the studies of Blundell and Johnson (1999) or Disney and Emmerson (2005). But in addition to updating the evidence base with regard to the effects of recent pension reforms on the public pension wealth of cohorts and on their implicit incentives to work at older ages, however, we have also used a long and detailed series of information on employment rates by various types of individuals and age groups to examine the extent to which the sequence of pension reforms might be correlated with, and even a potential explanation for, trends in labor market participation at older ages. And the recent (post-1995) trends in labor market participation for all older adults in the UK, which have occurred over the period in which there have been a number of pension reforms, make it tempting for commentators to attribute trends in the labor market with trends in pension arrangements, particularly changes in the state pension age, so it is important to identify any such effects in a concrete manner.

We have deliberately limited our analysis to a crude "example individual" type of analysis, distinguishing six types of people within each date-of-birth cohort (three education levels for each sex) and simulating the effects of pension reforms for each type using a very crude approximation to a lifetime earnings profile and assuming each "type" is in paid work at all ages over the lifecycle. Even this simple exercise is fairly laborious, however, given the extensive and rather complex history of pension reform in the UK. And despite our crude and somewhat aggregate method, we are able to show that the reforms have generated variation in pension wealth and implicit tax rates by age, cohort, education, and sex, which, as well as being important to document in their own right as indicators of the effects of the reform, can be used to show that the pension variables and hence the pension reforms have had statistically significant effects on employment probabilities even when controlling very flexibly for any potential age and time effects that might be thought to confound such an analysis. Increased pension wealth is shown to reduce the likelihood of work at older ages and, if the work disincentive (as measured by the implicit tax) is higher than this, will also tend to lead to lower levels of labor market participation.

It is clear that a more detailed fully microdata-driven individual-level analysis should be carried out, and we leave this as a direction for future research and a natural continuation of the research agenda in this chapter. The pension wealth and accrual calculations we carry out in this chapter can be applied to all individuals in a microdata survey sample and can also be based on a more sophisticated model of past and future earnings dynamics. Long panel data, such as that in the British Household Panel Study, Understanding Society, or the English Longitudinal Study of Ageing, can also be used to look better at the effects of reforms for those with spells in an out of the labor market or to account for more individual-specific heterogeneity in earnings processes. Such an analysis, which might also control much more concretely for the precise incentive effects of any private pension arrangements each individual might have, would be a major exercise but also a useful step forward from what we have done here.

Appendix

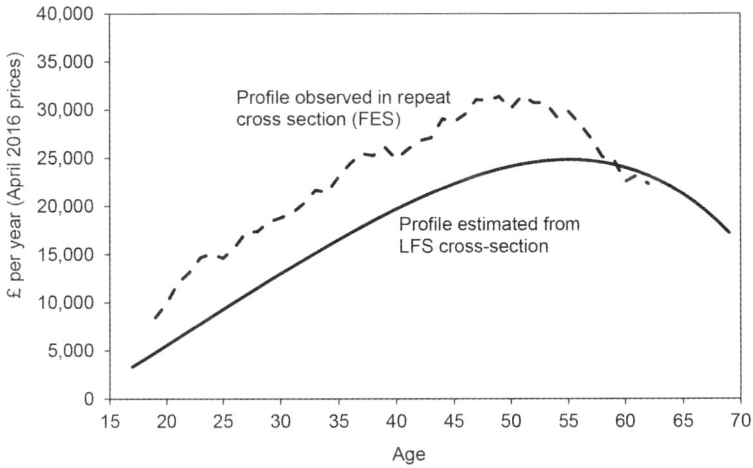

Fig. 11.A.1 Men born in 1952: comparison of actual cohort profile (from repeat cross section) with cohort profile estimated from cross-sectional data

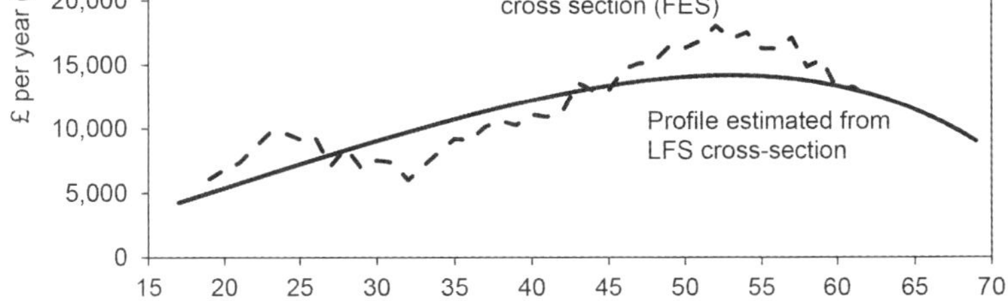

Fig. 11.A.2 Women born in 1952: comparison of actual cohort profile (from repeat cross section) with cohort profile estimated from cross-sectional data

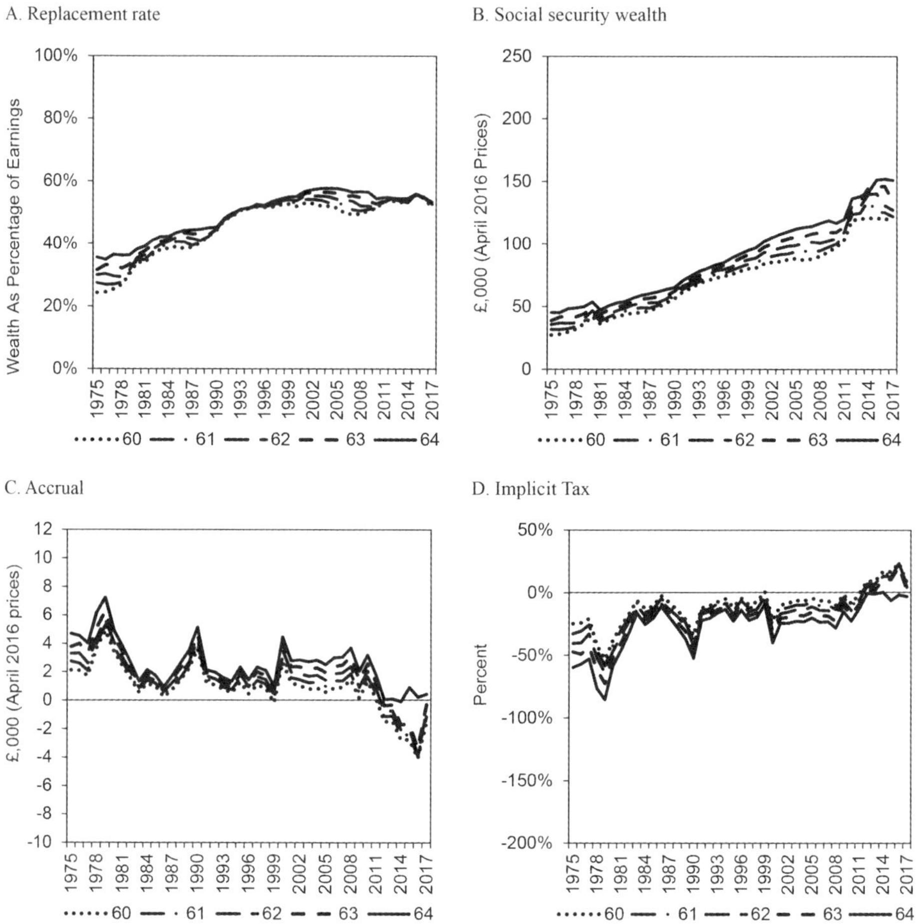

Fig. 11.A.3 Estimated social security replacement rate, wealth, accrual and implicit tax: low-earning men aged 60 to 64, by single year of age; common earnings profile

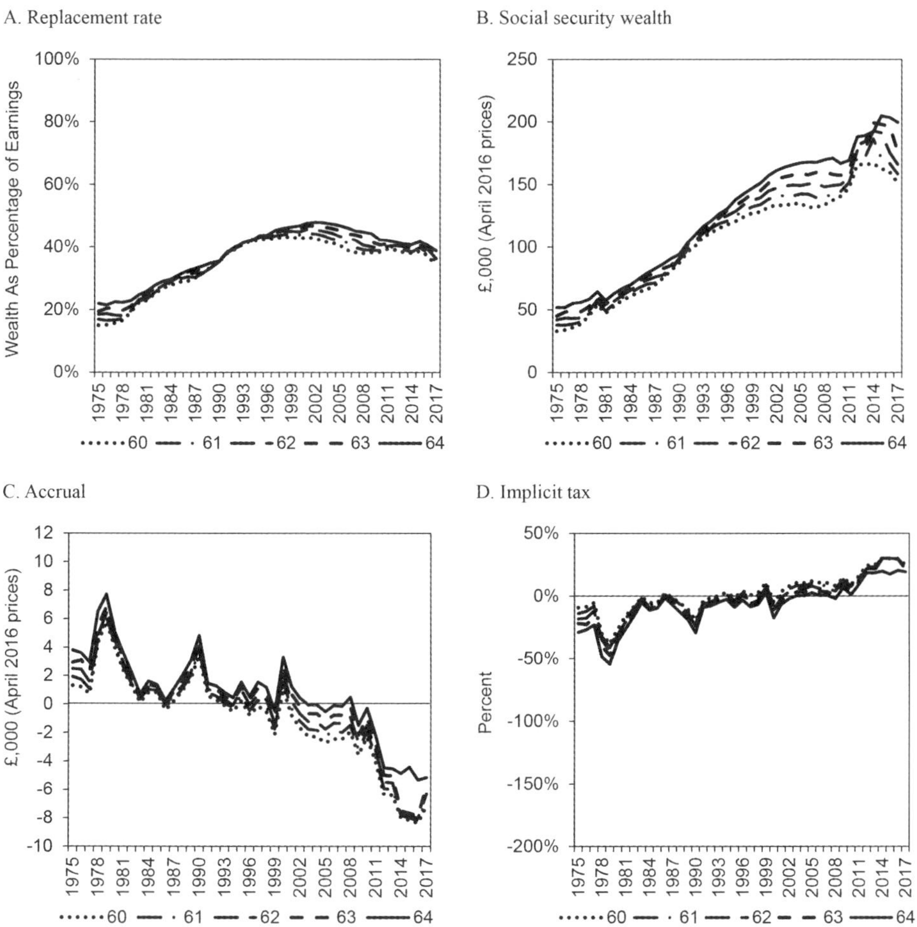

Fig. 11.A.4 Estimated social security replacement rate, wealth, accrual and implicit tax: high-earning men aged 60 to 64, by single year of age; common earnings profile

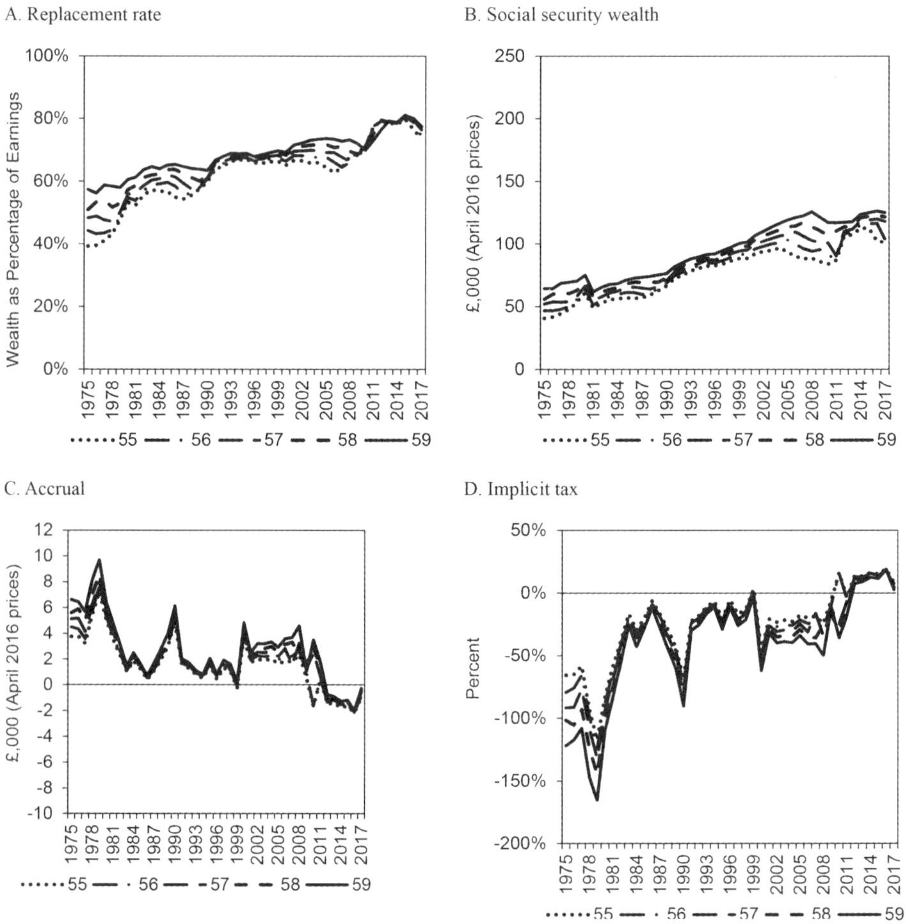

Fig. 11.A.5 Estimated social security replacement rate, wealth, accrual and implicit tax: low-earning women aged 55 to 59, by single year of age; common earnings profile

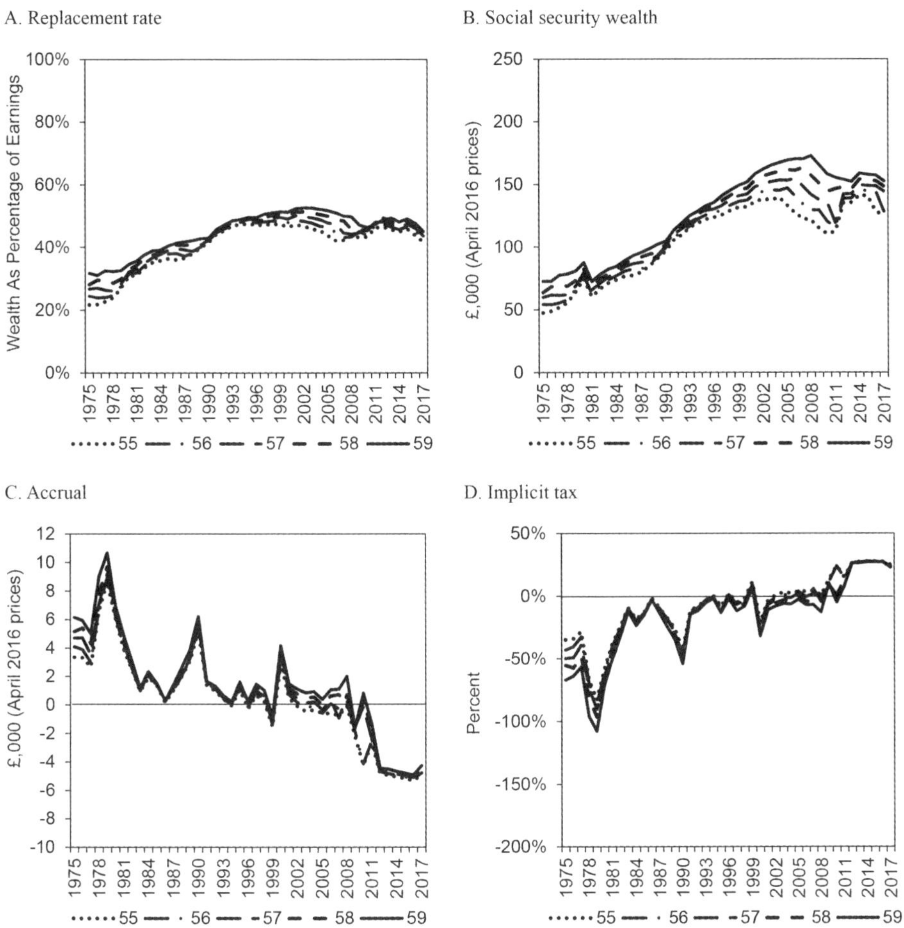

Fig. 11.A.6 Estimated social security replacement rate, wealth, accrual and implicit tax: high-earning women aged 55 to 59, by single year of age; common earnings profile

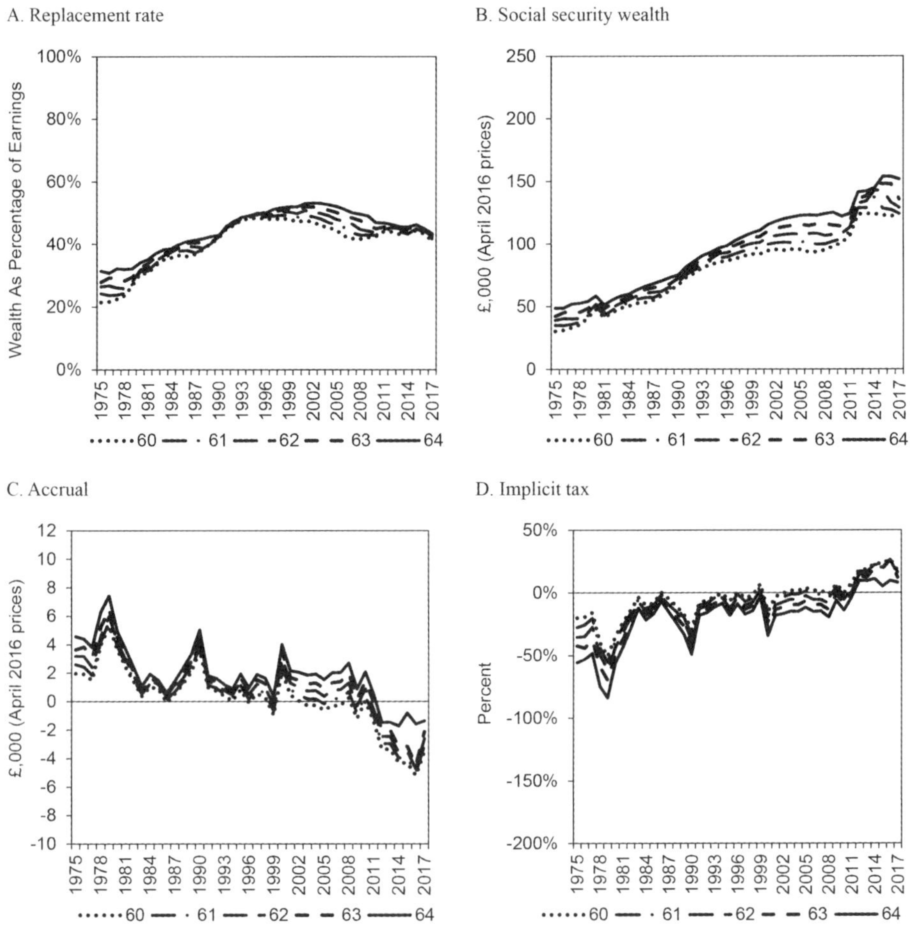

Fig. 11.A.7 Estimated social security replacement rate, wealth, accrual and implicit tax: mid-earning men aged 60 to 64, by single year of age; UK cross-sectional earnings profile

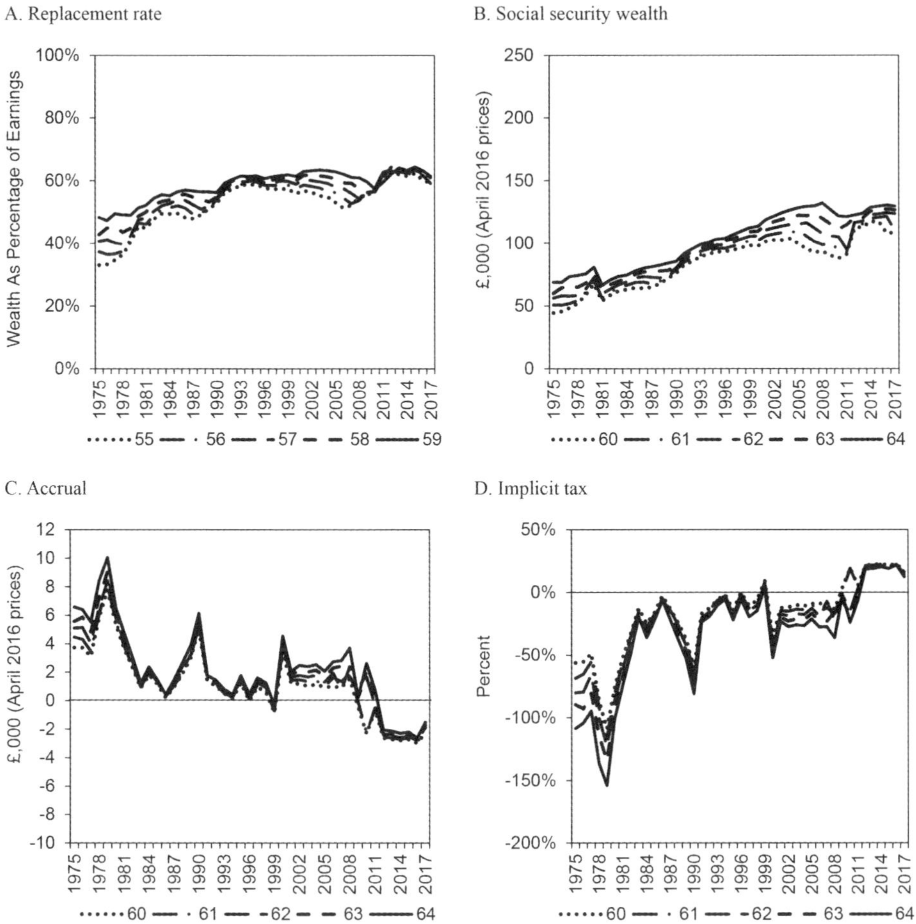

Fig. 11.A.8 Estimated social security replacement rate, wealth, accrual and implicit tax: mid-earning women aged 55 to 59, by single year of age; UK cross-sectional earnings profile

References

Banks, J., C. Emmerson, and G. Tetlow. 2019. "Long-Run Trends in the Economic Activity of Older People in the United Kingdom." In *Social Security Programs and Retirement around the World: Working Longer*, edited by Courtney C. Coile, Kevin Milligan, and David A. Wise, 267–97. Chicago: University of Chicago Press.

Blundell, R., and P. Johnson. 1999. "Pensions and Retirement in the UK." In *Social Security Programs and Retirement around the World*, edited by J. Gruber and D. Wise, 403–35. Chicago: University of Chicago Press.

Blundell, R., C. Meghir, and S. Smith. 2004. "Pension Incentives and the Pattern of Retirement in the United Kingdom." In *Social Security Programs and Retirement around the World: Micro-estimation*, edited by J. Gruber and D. Wise, 643–89. Chicago: University of Chicago Press.

Crawford, R., S. Keynes, and G. Tetlow. 2016. *A Single-Tier Pension: What Does It Really Mean?* IFS Report No. 82. https://www.ifs.org.uk/comms/r82.pdf.

Cribb, J., C. Emmerson, and G. Tetlow. 2016. "Signals Matter? Large Retirement Responses to Limited Financial Incentives." *Labour Economics* 42:203–12. https://doi.org/10.1016/j.labeco.2016.09.005.

Disney, R., and C. Emmerson. 2005. "Public Pension Reform in the United Kingdom: What Effect on the Financial Well-Being of Current and Future Pensioners?" *Fiscal Studies* 26:55–81. https://doi.org/10.1111/j.1475-5890.2005.00004.x.

Disney, R., and S. Smith. 2002. "The Labour Supply Effect of the Abolition of the Earnings Rule for Older Workers in the United Kingdom." *Economic Journal* 112 (478): C136–C152.

Meghir, C., and E. Whitehouse. 1997. "Labour Market Transitions and Retirement of Men in the UK." *Journal of Econometrics* 79 (2): 327–54.

Hemming, R., and J. Kay. 1982. "The Costs of the State Earnings Related Pension Scheme." *Economic Journal* 92:300–319.

O'Dea, C. 2018. "Insurance, Efficiency and the Design of Public Pensions." Mimeo, Yale University.

Wise, D., ed. 2017. *Social Security Programs and Retirement around the World: The Capacity to Work at Older Ages*. Chicago: University of Chicago Press.

12

The Evolution of Retirement Incentives in the US

Courtney C. Coile

When the Social Security Act was last amended in 1983, the labor force participation rate of older men in the US was at a historic low, having fallen throughout the preceding century (Costa 1998). Primarily intended to put the Social Security system on firmer financial footing, the 1983 amendments included several provisions that altered the financial incentives to work and delay Social Security benefit claiming at older ages. A subsequent law, the Senior Citizens' Freedom to Work Act of 2000, made changes to the Social Security retirement earnings test, also affecting these incentives.

A second striking change to the retirement landscape since 1980 has been the shift in employer-provided pensions from defined benefit (DB) to defined contribution (DC) plans. By one estimate, the share of workers with a DB plan fell from 83 percent in 1980 to 39 percent in 2004 (Munnell and Perun 2006). The incentives for continued work at older ages are quite different in the two types of plans, as DB plans typically grow in value—sometimes quite significantly—until the worker reaches the plan's early or normal retirement age and decline thereafter, while DC balances continue to grow with additional work at any age.

In the three and a half decades since the passage of the 1983 amendments, employment rates for men and women in their 60s have risen dramatically, as seen in figures 12.1 and 12.2. While the changes in Social Security and

Courtney C. Coile is a professor of economics at Wellesley College and a research associate of the National Bureau of Economic Research.

This chapter is part of the National Bureau of Economic Research's International Social Security (ISS) project. The author thanks other members of the ISS team for helpful suggestions that benefitted this analysis and the project as a whole. For acknowledgments, sources of research support, and disclosure of the author's material financial relationships, if any, please see https://www.nber.org/chapters/c14202.ack.

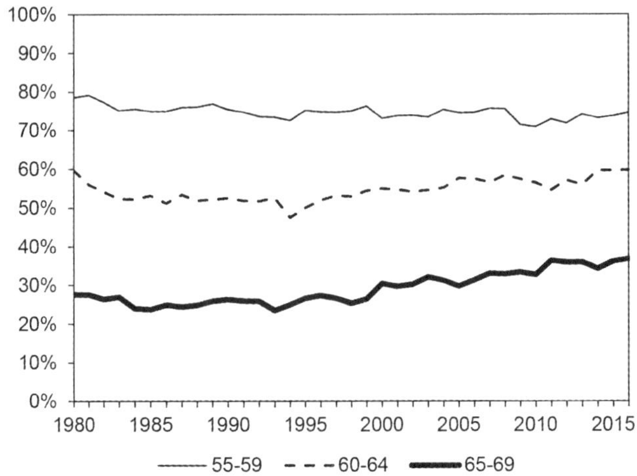

Fig. 12.1 Male employment rate by age, 1980–2016
Source: author's calculation from March Current Population Survey.

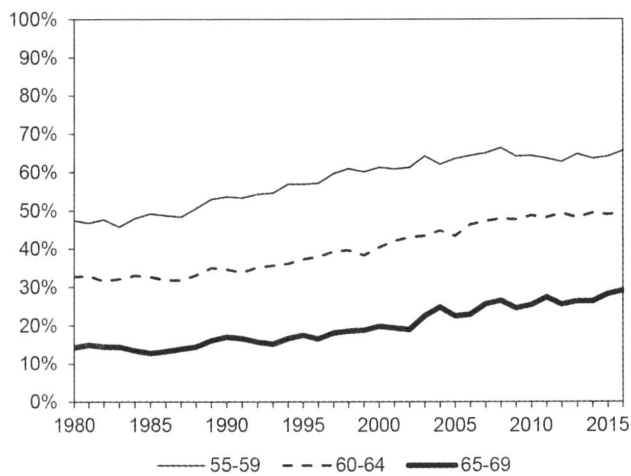

Fig. 12.2 Female employment rate by age, 1980–2016
Source: author's calculation from March Current Population Survey.

private pensions since the early 1980s present one potential explanation for this trend toward longer work lives, there are alternative hypotheses as well. As mortality rates decline, people may be healthier and more able to work at older ages or see a need to retire later in order to finance a longer expected retirement. As the education level of the population rises, increases in work at older ages may follow, as those with more education tend to retire later (Rutledge 2018). As women's engagement in the labor force grows, husbands may choose to work longer due to the complementarity of leisure between spouses (Schirle 2008). Identifying the contribution of each of these factors to the trend of longer work lives presents a significant challenge (Coile 2018).

In order to assess how changes to Social Security and private pensions have contributed to the rising employment of older men and women over the past several decades, it is useful to document how the financial incentive to work at older ages has been affected by these changes. The goal of this study is to examine the evolution of retirement incentives from 1980 to the present and to begin to explore the possible connection between changes in incentives and employment trends over this period.

To isolate the effect of Social Security reforms on the return to work at older ages, we focus first on a median-earner male and female worker, holding their earnings histories fixed over time but incorporating changing Social Security rules in order to create a time series of retirement incentives. We examine how incentives differ for high or low earners and by marital status and also show how the addition of private pensions alters retirement incentives. The key incentive measure is the implicit tax rate on work (ITAX), which measures the change in the net present discounted value of social security wealth (SSW) associated with working an additional year relative to earnings.

We have several findings. First, at a given point in time, the implicit tax on work varies by age in ways that correspond to Social Security program provisions. Second, Social Security reforms have reduced the implicit tax on work after age 65 by about 15 percentage points since 1980, while leaving the tax rate at other ages relatively unchanged. Results are fairly similar across earnings type and marital status. Third, incorporating DB pensions can result in significantly higher implicit tax rates after age 65. Therefore, the shift from DB to DC pensions has also served to reduce the implicit tax on work after age 65. Finally, there is suggestive evidence that changes in retirement incentives may be associated with changes in employment, although further research is needed to more definitively establish this relationship.

12.1 Background

12.1.1 Social Security and Private Pension Provisions

When President Reagan signed the Social Security Amendments of 1983 into law, the Old-Age, Survivors, and Disability Insurance (OASDI) program was three months away from not being able to pay full cash benefits on time and faced an estimated deficit of 1.8 percent of taxable payroll over the next 75 years (Svahn and Ross 1983). The urgent need to shore up the system's finances motivated the 98th Congress to pass the amendments just three months after receiving recommendations from a national reform commission.

While financial concerns were of primary importance, a desire to increase the incentive to work at older ages was a secondary motivation for at least some players. In announcing the administration's reform proposals in 1981, Secretary of Health and Human Services Richard Schweiker declared that the reforms would "keep the system from going broke, protect the basic benefit structure, and reduce the tax burden of American workers" (Svahn and Ross 1983). Although the final law differed from the administration's proposal in numerous ways, it included multiple provisions that affected the incentive to work at older ages.

A brief (and necessarily incomplete) overview of Social Security rules as of 1983 is useful before explaining the changes brought about by the 1983 amendments. Individuals who have 10 years (or more precisely, 40 quarters) of earnings in covered employment are eligible for Social Security retired worker benefits. The benefit amount is based on the worker's highest 35 years of earnings, where past earnings are adjusted by a wage index; average earnings are translated into a basic monthly benefit, the Primary Insurance Amount (PIA), by applying a progressive, nonlinear formula. Workers who claim at the full retirement age (FRA), traditionally age 65, receive a monthly benefit equal to the PIA. The benefit may be claimed starting at age 62 but is reduced by 6.67 percent for each year of receipt prior to the FRA. Claiming after the FRA raises the benefit through the delayed retirement credit (DRC), traditionally by 3 percent per year of delay. A dependent or surviving spouse of a retired worker receives a benefit of 50 and 100 percent, respectively, of the worker's PIA, subject to actuarial adjustment for early claiming. An individual who is dually entitled to retired worker and spouse or survivor benefits receives her or his own benefit plus a top-up to the amount of the other benefit (if larger), not the sum of the two. For consistency with other chapters in this volume, we note that FRA is equivalent to the term *statutory eligibility age* (SEA) used elsewhere.

One important change brought about by the 1983 amendments was an increase in the DRC. As shown in table 12.1, the increase was phased in over time in increments of 0.5 percent every two years, rising from 3 percent per year of delay (for those born by 1924) to 8 percent (for those born in or after 1943). This change significantly increases the return to delaying claiming past the FRA (Shoven and Slavov 2014). While an individual could obtain the benefit of delayed claiming without changing his or her retirement behavior, in practice most people claim at or shortly after retirement (Coile et al. 2002), even if they have financial resources that would allow them to delay claiming (Goda et al. 2018).

A second change was an increase in the FRA from 65 to 67. This change is being phased in over a longer period of time, rising in increments of two months per year from 65 (for those born by 1937) to 66 (for those born by 1943) and later from 66 to 67. As the FRA rose, the actuarial adjustment was tweaked such that the benefit would be reduced by 6.67 percent per year for

Table 12.1 Social Security provisions by cohort

Birth cohort	Delayed retirement credit (%)	Full retirement age
Up to 1924	3.0	65
1925	3.5	65
1926	3.5	65
1927	4.0	65
1928	4.0	65
1929	4.5	65
1930	4.5	65
1931	5.0	65
1932	5.0	65
1933	5.5	65
1934	5.5	65
1935	6.0	65
1936	6.0	65
1937	6.5	65
1938	6.5	65 + 2 months
1939	7.0	65 + 4 months
1940	7.0	65 + 6 months
1941	7.5	65 + 8 months
1942	7.5	65 + 10 months
1943	8.0	66
1944–54	8.0	66
1955	8.0	66 + 2 months
1956	8.0	66 + 4 months
1957	8.0	66 + 6 months
1958	8.0	66 + 8 months
1959	8.0	66 + 10 months
1960 onward	8.0	67

the first three years of early claiming and by 5 percent per year beyond this (e.g., for a total reduction of 30 percent, not 33.3 percent, for claiming at 62 with an FRA of 67). The effects of this change on the incentive to continue working are discussed below. Finally, the 1983 amendments accelerated a scheduled increase in the payroll tax; it rose from 6.7 percent of earnings (up to a taxable maximum) on both employer and employee in 1983 to 7.65 percent each (or 15.3 percent total) by 1990.

Social Security benefits are subject to an earnings test. Traditionally, benefits have been reduced by $1 for each $2 of earnings above a threshold amount, with a higher threshold above the FRA than below it. Starting in 1990, the reduction of benefits was changed to $1 for each $3 of earnings above the FRA, and then in 2000, the earnings test above the FRA was eliminated by the Senior Citizens' Freedom to Work Act of 2000. Although benefits lost to the earnings test are treated as additional months of claiming delay, and the monthly benefit amount is subsequently recalculated to reflect this, this provision appears to be poorly understood (Liebman and

Luttmer 2012). The changes in the earnings test thus reduced the perceived (if not actual) tax on work after the FRA.

While Social Security is the dominant retirement income program in the US, with 84 percent of households with members aged 65 and above receiving benefits, employer-provided pensions are also quite important, with 44 percent of older households receiving non–Social Security retirement benefits (Social Security Administration 2016). Workers who participate in a pension plan must consider how continued work at older ages affects their entitlement to future pension as well as Social Security benefits.

Pension plans are established by firms operating within government guidelines, and thus plan provisions vary by employer. In a DB plan, key features include the vesting period (years of service required for future benefit eligibility), retirement eligibility provisions (age and/or years of service required to initiate benefit receipt), and benefit formula (often a function of average earnings over the final or highest few earnings years; Mitchell 1999). Plans may include an early and/or normal retirement age and often feature higher pension accruals in the years before attaining these ages and lower accruals thereafter. This pattern can create strong financial incentives to stay with the firm until attaining these ages and to leave the firm thereafter (Stock and Wise 1990). In a DC plan, key provisions include the employer contributions to the retirement account and whether they are made automatically or only as a match to employee contributions, as well as the withdrawal options when the employee leaves the job. Critically, DC plans lack strong incentives to work to or retire at particular ages that are present in many DB plans.

Over the past 35 years, there has been a dramatic shift in private pension plan coverage, as shown in figures 12.3 and 12.4.[1] While the share of private-sector workers participating in any employer-sponsored pension plan (DB only, DC only, or DB and DC) has remained roughly constant at 45 to 50 percent, the share with only a DB plan plummeted from 28 percent in 1980 to 2 percent in 2014. Meanwhile, the share with only a DC plan rose from 9 percent to 34 percent, and the share with both a DB and a DC plan remained roughly constant. Thus the share with any DB plan (DB only or DB and DC) fell from 39 percent of private-sector workers in 1980 to 13 percent in 2014.[2] Due to DC plans' lack of strong age-based incentives, the shift over time from DB to DC plans in the private-sector workforce has the potential to significantly affect the incentive to work at older ages (Coile and Stewart 2020).

Figures 12.3 and 12.4 also illustrate what programs workers turn to for retirement income when they exit the labor force, which we term *pathways*

1. Data on private pensions is from the Employee Benefit Research Institute (https://www.ebri.org/publications/benfaq/index.cfm?fa=retfaqt14fig1). The data they report is for all private-sector workers and is not age or sex specific, so the same pension data are used for figures 12.3 and 12.4.

2. The public sector has not experienced a similar change, as the vast majority of its employees continue to have a DB plan (Munnell et al. 2014).

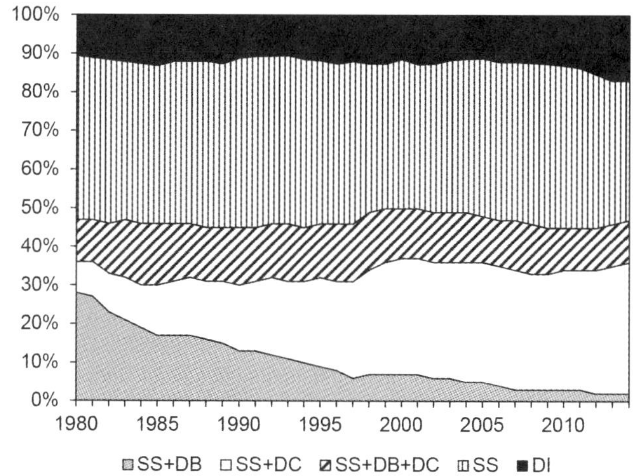

Fig. 12.3 Pathways to retirement, men, 1980–2014
See chapter notes for sources.

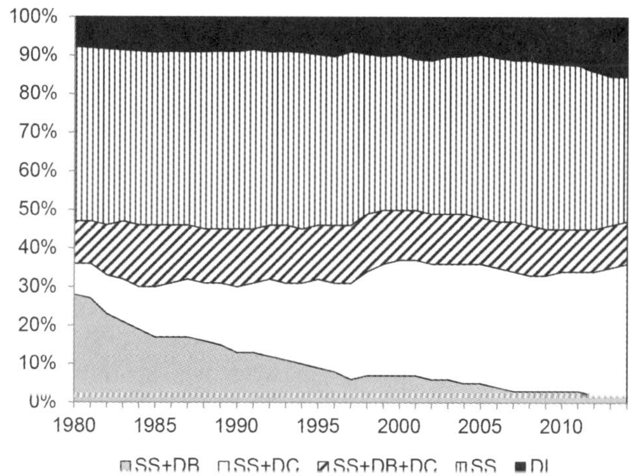

Fig. 12.4 Pathways to retirement, women, 1980–2014
See chapter notes for sources.

to retirement.[3] The share of workers who exit via the disability insurance (DI) pathway has risen over time, from 8 to 16 percent for men and from

3. Data on disability insurance (DI) is from the Social Security *Annual Statistical Supplement, 2017* (table 6.B.5, disability conversions). Figures 12.3 and 12.4 assume that all workers receive Social Security (SS), although a small percentage of individuals (an estimated 4 percent in 2010) will never receive SS, usually because they are late-arriving immigrants or infrequent workers (Whitman, Reznik, and Shoffmer 2011). For simplicity, figures 12.3 and 12.4 also assume that DI recipients do not receive pensions.

11 to 17 percent for women. As already noted, nearly half of private-sector workers have a pension of some kind, typically in addition to Social Security. Thus the share of male and female workers who exit the labor force and receive Social Security but do not have access to pension income or assets is estimated to be 36 and 38 percent, respectively. This share has declined over time due to the increased use of DI.

12.1.2 Employment Trends

Before exploring how the changes in Social Security and pension provisions have affected the financial incentive to work at older ages, it is useful to take a closer look at trends in employment for older men and women, as illustrated in figures 12.1 and 12.2. For older men, employment at ages 60 to 64 and 65 to 69 exhibits a distinct U shape over time, with declining employment initially but rising employment beginning in the mid-1990s for the younger group and in the mid-1980s for the older group.[4] Employment has risen by 10 or more percentage points in both of these groups between the trough and 2016, from 50 to 60 percent in the case of men aged 60 to 64, and from 24 to 36 percent in the case of men aged 65 to 69. Any effects of the recent Great Recession are not apparent in these two series. For men aged 55 to 69, the trend is quite different, as employment declined during the first half of this period and has been more or less steady since, with a noticeable impact of the Recession and gradual recovery. The divergent pattern for this group is most likely related to other factors that are affecting the labor market for prime-age men in the US (Council of Economic Advisers 2016) rather than a reflection of the effect of changing retirement incentives.

The trend over time for women does not exhibit a U shape. Rather, women's employment rates have risen more or less continuously, with an increase among women aged 55 to 59 evident beginning in the early 1980s and an increase among women 60 to 64 and 65 to 69 evident beginning in the late 1980s. The magnitude of the increase for women is substantially larger than that for men, with employment rising by 20 points for women ages 55 to 59 and by 18 and 16 points, respectively, in the 60 to 64 and 65 to 69 age groups. The trend appears to have slowed or stalled since the Great Recession for the two younger groups, perhaps reflecting the impact of that event. Some of the steady rise over time in employment at older ages reflects cohort effects, as successive cohorts of younger women increased their labor force participation for various reasons, and women who work more when they are young also work more when they are older (Goldin and Katz 2018).

In sum, over the past 35 years, there have been numerous changes to Social Security and private pensions that have affected the return to work at older

4. While sampling variation makes it difficult to be certain from figure 12.1 that the increase for the older group began in the mid-1980s, labor force participation rates from the Bureau of Labor Statistics (series LNU01300190) confirm that the trough occurred in 1985.

ages. The employment rates of older men and women have climbed steadily over much of the same period. Ascertaining how much of the latter trend can be explained by the former is the ultimate objective of this chapter and the larger research agenda of which it is a part.

12.2 Methodology

To begin to explore the connection between these trends, we aim to calculate a time series of retirement incentives from 1980 to the present. We make these calculations for a small number of sample worker types—first for a married male worker with median earnings and a married female worker with median earnings and then for high and low earners and for single individuals to show how incentives vary with earnings history and marital status. As explained more below, the three earner types correspond to high, medium, and low education individuals.

As our goal is to show how changes in Social Security policy and employer-provided pensions have affected retirement incentives, we initially make these calculations holding the earnings history fixed over time. In so doing, we distinguish the effect of policy and pension changes on incentives as separate from any changes in incentives that may arise from other trends, such as rising income inequality or changing mortality. This shows, in the case of Social Security, the direct effect of reforms, which may be undone or magnified by future reforms.

For comparability with the other studies in this volume, we first make the calculations using a common synthetic earnings profile. More specifically, we use a common age-earnings profile that is scaled to one at age 50 and apply it to US median earnings at age 50 to generate the US version of the common earnings profile.[5] This is done so that the level of earnings is appropriate for each country, but differences across countries in retirement incentives will otherwise reflect differences in public pension provisions rather than in age-earnings profiles. This process is repeated for the three earner types and two sex groups; positive earnings begin at ages 16, 20, and 25 for the low, median, and high earner types, respectively, corresponding to the ages at which they are assumed to have completed their education and entered the labor force. Appendix figures 12.A.1 and 12.A.2 show the earnings profiles for the low-, median-, and high-earning male and female worker types, contrasting the common earnings profile with one based only on US data.

5. As explained in more detail in the appendix to the introductory chapter in this volume, the synthetic earnings profile is calculated using data for the US, Germany, and Italy. As the age-earnings profiles in the three countries are fairly similar by age, we use the simple average of these profiles, smoothed to prevent artificial spikes at older ages. Earnings are kept flat at higher ages when selection effects dominate the data. The median US earnings at age 50 used to create the US version of the common synthetic earnings profile are $48,200 for men and $39,400 for women.

The central incentive measure for this chapter is the implicit tax rate, denoted by ITAX. Calculating this measure is methodologically straightforward but involves several steps. The first step is to calculate the Social Security benefit that the individual is entitled to at each possible retirement age from age 55 to age 69 using the Social Security benefit formula. As the basic benefit entitlement (PIA) is based on the best 35 years of indexed earnings, additional work may increase the benefit by replacing a zero or low earnings year in the calculation.

The second step is to calculate the net present discounted value of social security wealth (SSW) associated with each possible retirement age. The individual is assumed to claim Social Security benefits when he or she retires, or at age 62 if retiring before that age. We use a discount rate of 3 percent. We use common (rather than US) survival probabilities to purge the cross-country comparisons that are made elsewhere in this volume of the effect of mortality differences across countries.[6] For a married individual type, we assume that he or she is married to another individual of the same education level (or earner type), where the wife is three years younger. For the purpose of calculating the individual's own incentives, we treat the spouse's retirement behavior as fixed and assume that the spouse retires at age 62 in order to ensure that calculations reflect the effect of the change in the worker's own retirement behavior and not that of the spouse (as could be the case if we assumed joint retirement, for example). SSW is net of Social Security payroll tax contributions, and we assume full incidence of payroll taxes (employer and employee share) on the worker.

Working another year has multiple effects on SSW. First, the individual pays an additional year of payroll taxes. Second, the Social Security monthly benefit amount may increase, as discussed above. Third, the individual forgoes one year of benefit receipt for an additional year of work beyond age 62. Fourth, the monthly benefit amount increases due to the actuarial adjustment (pre-FRA) or to the DRC (post-FRA). The net effect of additional work on SSW thus may be positive or negative, depending on the relative importance of these different factors. The accrual refers to the change in SSW that results from working one additional year. It is computed for each age, 55 to 69.

Finally, the ITAX is calculated as the negative of the accrual, scaled by earnings. A positive ITAX indicates that Social Security taxes work at older ages—any increase in the benefit amount that results from additional work is not enough to compensate for extra payroll taxes and the loss of a year

6. The survival probabilities are provided by Eurostat and refer to the EU29 countries. The rates are adjusted to generate a life expectancy that is three years higher (or lower) to reflect differences in life expectancy across the three education groups. This adjustment is a mixture of a proportional increase (or decrease) of survival rates and a shift of the survival curve to the right (or left). These values are used to calculate the conditional probability that a 55-year-old will be alive at every future age from age 56 to age 100.

of benefits, so the system effectively penalizes work at older ages. A negative ITAX indicates the reverse, that SSW is rising with additional work. The scaling by earnings is done so that ITAX is a tax rate, comparable, for example, to the marginal income tax rate. ITAX is also calculated for each age, 55 to 69.

This calculation is done under a given set of Social Security rules—say, those in effect in 1980. We then repeat the calculation using the rules in effect in 1981, 1982, and so on through 2016 to generate a time series of retirement incentives, where the variation in ITAX comes only from changes in the Social Security rules. This calculation is repeated for the 12 sample worker types: male/female, low/median/high earner, and single/married.

The first set of calculations is done without pensions so that they reflect the retirement incentives for an individual who either does not have a pension or has a DC pension.[7] However, it is also important to calculate incentives for workers with a DB pension, since as noted above, the decline in DB pensions is an important change in the retirement landscape since 1980.

To do so, we calculate incentives using a sample DB pension plan. Naturally, a calculation using a single sample plan will not be able to capture the diversity of retirement incentives facing the population of workers given that DB plan provisions vary by employer. Indeed, calculating incentive measures using workers' heterogeneous earning histories and heterogeneous DB plan provisions and then examining the effect of the actual (not simulated) incentives on behavior in a large sample is an important task left for future research. However, by calculating incentives using a sample plan with features that are common to many DB plans, this exercise will capture the essence of the incentives facing many (if not all) workers.

The assumptions for our sample DB pension plan are as follows, informed by typical plan parameters of this era. The basic benefit amount is based on the average earnings during the last five years of service (YOS)—more specifically, it is equal to 2 percent times YOS times average earnings. This plan has an early retirement age of 55 (meaning benefits are first available then) and a normal retirement age of 65, with an actuarial reduction of 4.8 percent per year of receipt before the normal retirement age; delay beyond 65 does not result in an actuarial adjustment, although the benefit amount may still rise if wages are rising. A worker with 30 YOS, then, would have a benefit equal to 60 percent of her average earnings in the final five years of work if she retires at (or after) age 65 but only 36 percent of average earnings if she retires at age 60. While the ITAX calculation is needed to see the exact tax or subsidy at different ages, it is evident from this overview of

7. In excluding DC pensions from the retirement incentive calculation, we are effectively treating employer contributions (whether automatic or matching) to a DC plan as similar to receiving a higher wage. While DC pension contributions from employers clearly affect the employee's welfare, they do not change the dynamic incentives to retire at particular ages, which are the focus of this chapter.

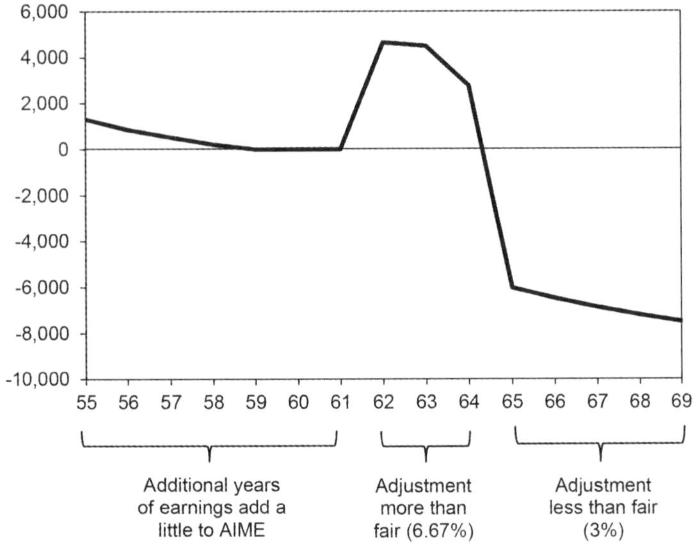

Fig. 12.5 SS accrual (without SS taxes) by age, male median earner, common earnings, 1980

the plan rules that the incentive (or disincentive) for work in a plan such as this will vary substantially by age.

12.3 Results

12.3.1 Retirement Incentives by Age, Worker Type, and Pension Status

We now turn to the results, beginning with a married male median earner who is subject to the Social Security rules in place in 1980 and does not have a DB pension. In figure 12.5, we report the benefit accrual by age for this worker prior to incorporating payroll tax contributions. This figure shows the effect of having another year of earnings incorporated in the calculation of the PIA (relevant at all ages) as well as the effect of delayed claiming (relevant starting at age 62). As noted above, delayed claiming has an ambiguous effect on SSW, since the worker forgoes one year of benefits now but receives a higher benefit for the rest of his or her life through the actuarial adjustment or DRC.

For a worker of this type, working at age 55 results in an increase in SSW of approximately $2,000 (ignoring additional payroll taxes). This is the total effect of the higher PIA in present discounted value terms—that is, by retiring at age 56 instead of at age 55, this worker will have a slight benefit when he or she claims at age 62 and will continue to receive this higher amount for the rest of his or her life. This positive accrual declines with age, since as the

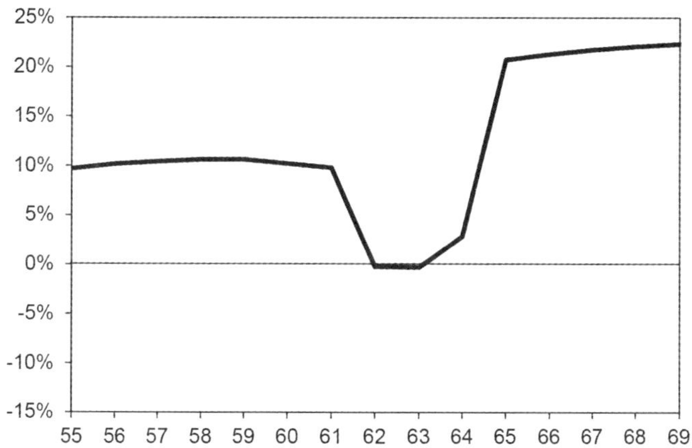

Fig. 12.6 Implicit tax rate (with SS taxes) by age, male median earner, common earnings, 1980

worker's earnings history gets longer, there are fewer zeroes or low earnings years left to replace with a current earnings year. In fact, for this median earner, the value of replacing a low earnings year quickly approaches zero.

At age 62, the benefit accrual rises to about $4,500, reflecting the value of delayed claiming. The benefit accrual declines just a bit at ages 63 and 64, since the adjustment factor is constant, but mortality increases slightly at each age. However, the benefit accrual turns sharply negative at age 65, as the DRC of 3 percent per year in place in 1980 is insufficient to compensate the worker for the certain loss of a year of benefits at age 65 (unlike the more generous adjustment of 6.67 percent at ages 62 to 64). By working at ages 65 to 69, the median male worker is losing $6,000 to $7,500 of SSW per year of work.

In figure 12.6, we incorporate payroll tax contributions and report the ITAX rather than the benefit accrual. With a payroll tax rate being (roughly) 10 percent in 1980, the implicit tax on work reaches 10 percent by age 57, drops to 0 percent at age 62, and then jumps to 20 percent at age 65 and rises slowly thereafter. In short, the Social Security system in place in 1980 is roughly actuarially fair at age 62 for a typical male worker (using our mortality and discount rate assumptions) but imposes a tax rate of over 20 percent on work by that individual beyond the FRA.

Figure 12.7 reports the results for low-, median-, and high-earner married males, reflecting sample workers with different levels of education. For the median- and high-earner types, the tax rate prior to age 62 is very slightly lower than that for low earners, as median and high earners began their careers later and have steeper age-earnings profiles and thus have more to gain from replacing a zero or low earnings year in the benefit calculation; however, the magnitude of the difference in ITAX is quite small. Starting at

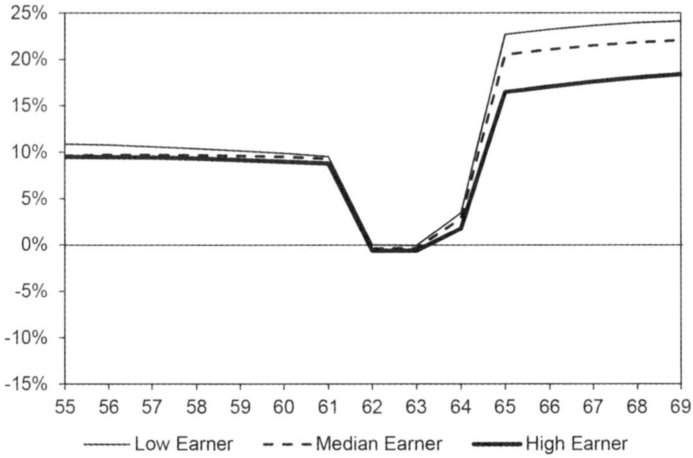

Fig. 12.7 Implicit tax rate (with SS taxes) by age, all male earners, common earnings, 1980

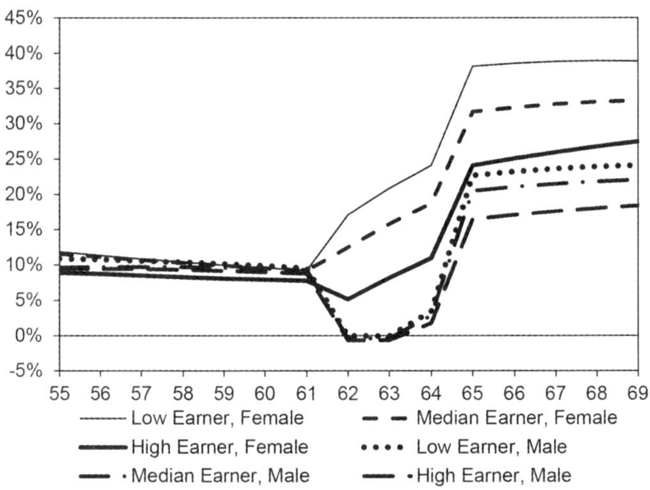

Fig. 12.8 Implicit tax rate (with SS taxes) by age, all married earners, female versus male, common earnings, 1980

age 65, however, the implicit tax on work is about 6 percentage points lower for the high earner as compared to the low earner. This difference arises primarily because of their different survival probabilities, which makes the DRC of 3 percent somewhat less unfair for the high-earner type, though it remains less than actuarially fair for all three types.

Figure 12.8 augments the previous figure by adding the results for married women of all earner types to those for married men. Up through age 61, tax

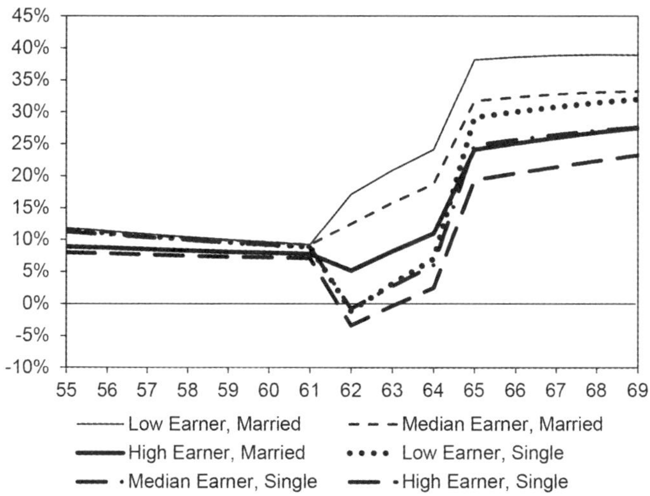

Fig. 12.9 Implicit tax rate (with SS taxes) by age, all female earners, married versus single, common earnings, 1980

rates are similar across both sex groups. At ages 62 to 64, however, the tax rates for married women are higher than those for married men—at age 62, for example, the tax rate is about 12 percent for a married female median earner versus near 0 percent for a married male median earner.

To understand why this is the case, it is useful to turn to figure 12.9, which displays results for the six female types, who vary by marital status and earner type. The tax rates for single women are very similar to those of married men (seen in figures 12.6, 12.7, and 12.8). However, switching women from single to married raises the implicit tax rate. By construction, the single and married women of a given earner type differ only in their marital status—that is, only in their access to dependent spouse and survivor benefits through their husbands. In fact, it is precisely because married women have access to these benefits that they have less to gain from delaying claiming beyond 62, and thus they face higher tax rates. Returning to figure 12.8, the women also face higher implicit tax rates at ages 65 and above as compared to the men.

Figure 12.10 shows the implicit tax rate calculated using the US earnings histories versus the common earnings profile for married men of all earner types. As the results are extremely similar across the two earnings history calculations, we focus on the common earnings results for the remainder of the chapter.

The results presented thus far reflect Social Security incentives only. In figure 12.11, we show the incentives inherent in a typical DB pension plan, focusing on a married male median earner. We first examine the incentives of the pension plan on its own before combining the pension incentives with

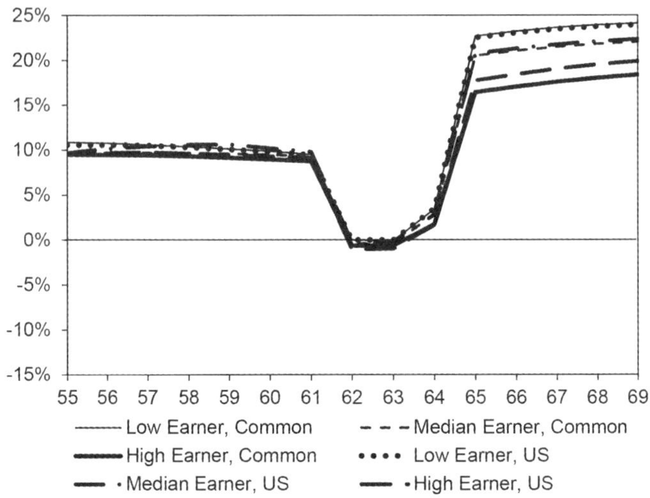

Fig. 12.10 Implicit tax rate (with SS taxes) by age, all male earners, common versus US earnings, 1980

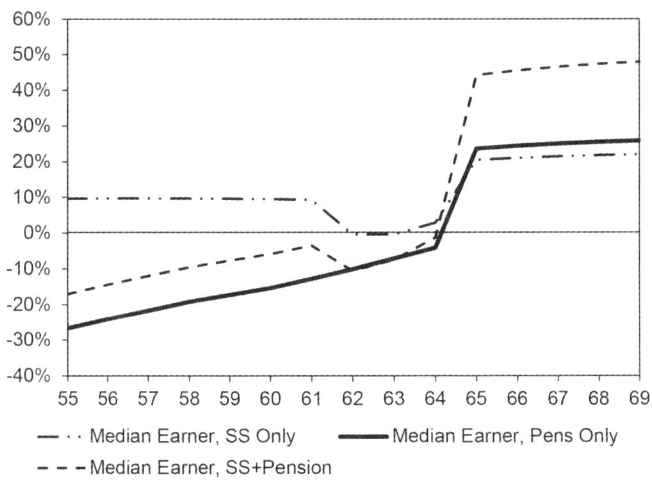

Fig. 12.11 Implicit tax rate with SS taxes and pensions by age, male median earner, common earnings, 1980

those from Social Security. At ages prior to age 65, the pension plan's normal retirement age (NRA), there is a large subsidy for continued work. At age 55, for example, the increase in pension wealth resulting from an additional year of work is equivalent to a subsidy of over 25 percent of earnings. The large subsidy arises because the actuarial adjustment for delaying retire-

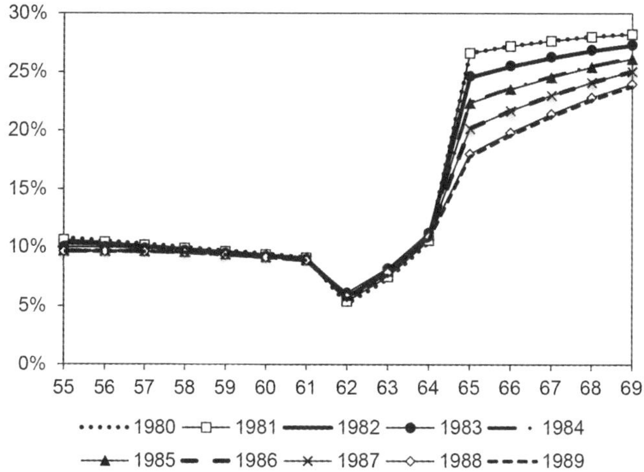

Fig. 12.12 weighted implicit tax rate (SS only) by age, 1980–89

ment and claiming before the NRA is more than sufficient to compensate for the loss of a year of benefits. The subsidy falls slowly with age, since the actuarial adjustment factor is age invariant, but the worker has less to gain from receiving a higher future benefit for the rest of his life when he is older, and his remaining life expectancy is shorter. Even so, for our sample plan and worker, the subsidy remains positive through age 64.

At age 65, the plan's NRA, the small implicit subsidy is replaced by a large implicit tax of about 25 percent. The reason for the jump in ITAX is that there is no further actuarial adjustment for delayed claiming beyond age 65. While the worker may benefit slightly from a higher average wage in the benefit formula if his wages are still rising with age, this is far from sufficient to compensate for the certain loss of a year of benefits. Incorporating the incentives from both Social Security and pensions, this worker faces a subsidy that declines from about 17 percent to near 0 over ages 55 to 64 and then jumps to a tax of 45 to 50 percent at ages 65 and above. When one considers that this worker is also subject to federal and state income taxes, the total marginal tax rate on work past age 65 is extremely high.

12.3.2 Changes in Retirement Incentives over Time

While the preceding discussion helps clarify how Social Security and private pension provisions translate into implicit taxes or subsidies for workers of various types at a given moment in time, they do not shed any light on how incentives are changing over time. It is this question we turn to next. In figures 12.12–12.15, we show how the implicit tax rate by age has varied over time. These figures reflect Social Security incentives only. Rather than

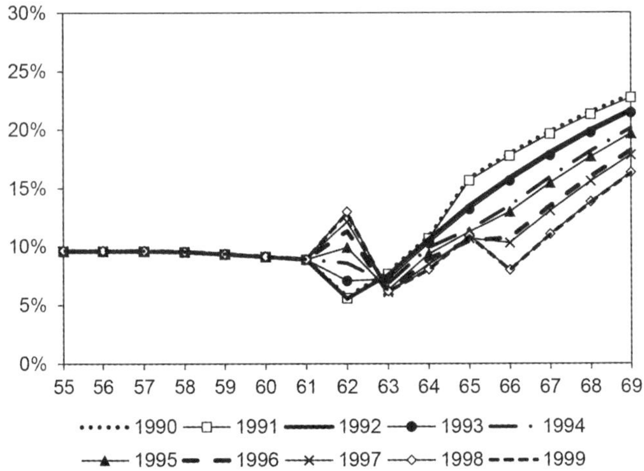

Fig. 12.13 Weighted implicit tax rate (SS only) by age, 1990–99

focus on one worker type, we show the implicit tax rate weighted across the 12 sample worker types using population weights.[8]

Figure 12.12 shows the weighted implicit tax rate for the years 1980 through 1989. This is the time period during which the increases in the DRC began to be phased in. The various ITAX series are visible for only 5 of the 10 years, since the DRC was increased by 0.5 percentage points every other year; by construction, the ITAX is unchanged unless Social Security program provisions are changing, so the values for adjacent years (e.g., two years with the same DRC value) are the same. The first four DRC increases (from 3 to 5 percent) lowered the implicit tax on work at age 65 by 9 percentage points, from 27 to 18 percent, and reduced the tax on work at age 66 to 69 as well.

Figure 12.13 shows the change in the weighted implicit tax rate during the 1990s. The additional increases in the DRC are again clearly reflected in the reduction in tax rates after age 65. The unusual pattern around age 62 is driven by the increase in the FRA from 65 to 66. Due to the decrease in the actuarial adjustment from 6.67 percent per year to 5 percent per year for early claiming beyond 36 months (see discussion above), there is a rising tax on work at age 62, as each two-month increase in the FRA results in more of the age 62 delay being credited at only 5 percent instead of the previous 6.67 percent. Over the decade, the implicit tax on work at age 62 rises by 7 percentage points. Figure 12.14 shows the weighted ITAX for the 2000s. There are modest additional changes as the FRA increase continues to be

8. Population weights are time invariant, so changes over time in ITAX are driven only by changes in Social Security provisions.

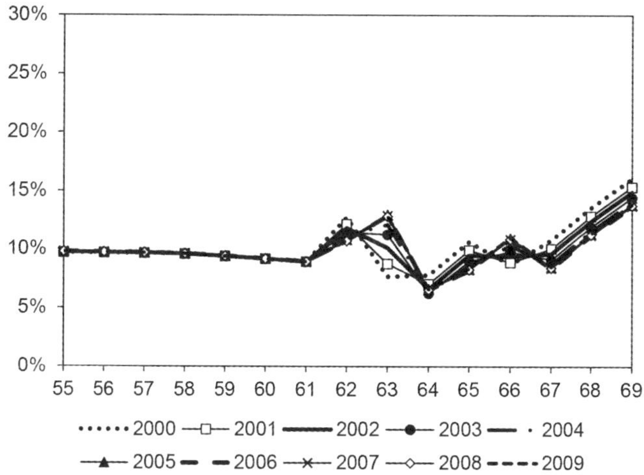

Fig. 12.14 Weighted implicit tax rate (SS only) by age, 2000–2009

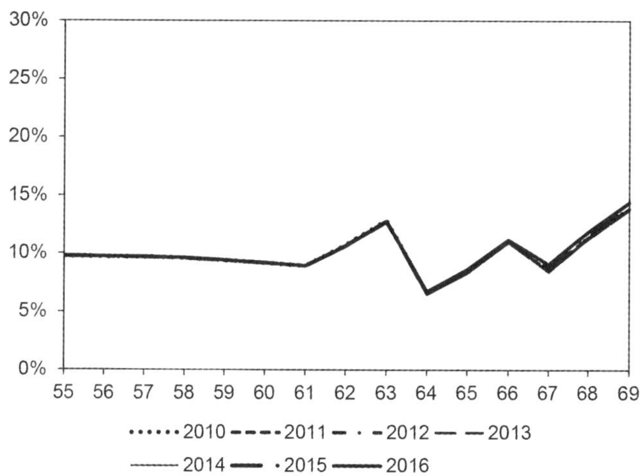

Fig. 12.15 Weighted implicit tax rate (SS only) by age, 2010–16

phased in. Finally, figure 12.15 shows the weighted ITAX for the years 2010 through 2016. As there were no further Social Security program changes, the incentives are the same every year.

Figure 12.16 presents this information in a different format, reporting the implicit tax rate at ages 62 through 69 by year. Between 1980 and 2016, the implicit tax on work fell by nearly 20 percentage points at age 65 and by 14 to 16 points at ages 66 to 69. This represents a substantial decline in the tax on work after age 65, and it is due to the increase in the DRC from 3 to 8 percent. By contrast, there was essentially no change in the tax on work

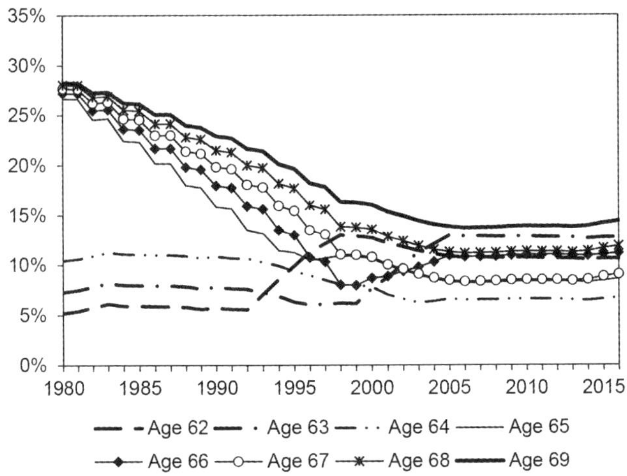

Fig. 12.16 Weighted implicit tax rate (SS only), 1980–2016, ages 62–69

at ages 55 to 61 (not shown on graph) and a modest increase in the tax on work at ages 62 and 63 due to the increase in the FRA. While the changes in the retirement earnings test are not incorporated in these incentive measures due to our assumption that people retire and claim simultaneously (making the test irrelevant), to the extent that people consider this a tax, the actual decline in the (perceived) tax on work beyond the FRA may be even greater than that measured here.

Figure 12.17 shows the change in incentives over time when we incorporate pensions, again weighting across the 12 sample worker types. The results appear similar to those in figure 12.16, although the decreases in the implicit tax rate after age 65 are somewhat larger. The relatively small difference between the results with and without pensions is expected. The share of the population with a DB pension has declined by about 25 percentage points since 1980. As seen in figure 12.11, DB pensions add an extra tax of 22 percent (for the male median-earner type) at age 65. Thus having one-quarter of the population lose access to a DB pension would be expected to reduce the weighted implicit tax rate at age 65 for the population as a whole by 4 to 5 percentage points (one-quarter of 22 points). Naturally, for any individual, the difference between having a DB pension and not is still the 22-point difference in the ITAX.

12.3.3 Incentives versus Employment

Finally, we turn to the question of whether changes in the implicit tax rate on work resulting from Social Security reforms and the shift from DB to DC pensions have contributed to the rise in older men and women's employment over the past several decades. It seems highly unlikely that changes in incen-

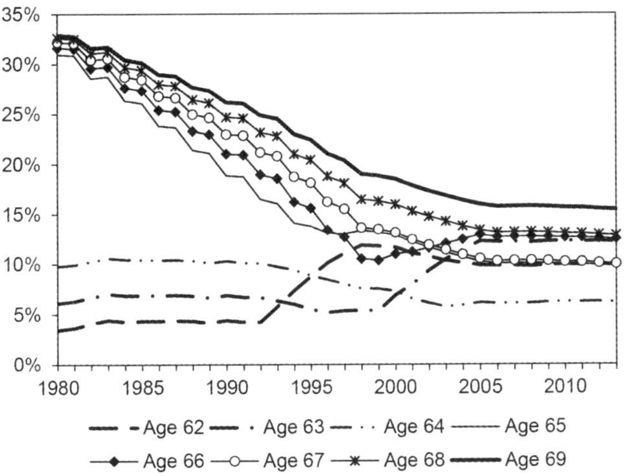

Fig. 12.17 Weighted implicit tax rate with pensions, 1980–2013, ages 62–69
Note: Figure ends in 2013 due to lack of data on share of workers with pensions in most recent years.

tives explain changes in employment at ages 55 to 59. In the case of men, employment has declined during this period, likely due to economy-wide factors that have little to do with retirement income programs. For women, employment has risen dramatically at ages 55 to 59 since 1980. Incentives, however, are essentially unchanged in this age range, suggesting that they are not a factor in the increase.

At ages 60 to 64, employment has risen for both men and women. However, the implicit tax on work has not fallen but rather has risen modestly at ages 62 and 63 as a result of changes to the actuarial adjustment around the FRA increase. Changing Social Security incentives—as captured by the ITAX measure—thus do not seem to have affected work at these ages, except insofar as a reduction in the tax on work after age 65 could potentially encourage an individual to keep working during his or her early 60s as well. On the pension side, a decline in DB pensions has, for some workers, eliminated the subsidy to work until the pension plan's NRA (age 65 in our sample plan). This might be expected to reduce, not increase, work at older ages under standard assumptions about labor supply behavior. On the other hand, the loss of a pension creates a negative wealth effect that could lead the individual to work longer. We need to look beyond the ITAX measure to the changes in retirement wealth in order to explore this possibility.

So what of the possibility that the reduction in the implicit tax on work after age 65 may have contributed to the increase in work after age 65? We provide a preliminary means of assessing this in figures 12.18 and 12.19, which plot data on employment rates at ages 65 to 69 against the sum of the weighted ITAX at ages 65 to 69 for each year 1980 to 2016, separately for men

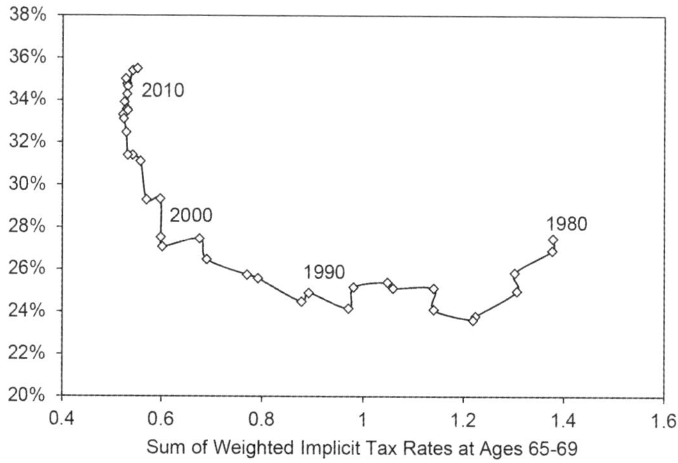

Fig. 12.18 Employment of men aged 65–69 versus weighted implicit tax, 1980–2016

Note: Employment data are from http://stats.oecd.org/ (data from US Bureau of Labor Statistics).

and women.[9] The ITAX summary measure reflects the loss in SSW relative to earnings that would occur from working between ages 65 and 69. For men, this value falls from about 140 percent (1.4 years of earnings) in 1980 to less than 60 percent in 2010. Whether changes in ITAX are driving changes in employment is somewhat difficult to discern from this graph, as the ITAX is falling both during periods when employment is declining or relatively flat and during periods when employment is rising rapidly. For women, there is a clearer negative association between falling ITAX values and rising employment rates, though it is not clear if this is due to a stronger causal effect of ITAX for women or is simply due to the fact that women's employment rates are rising more continuously over this period.

12.4 Discussion

Over the past several decades, older men's and women's employment rates have risen substantially during the same period when numerous changes to Social Security and private pensions were implemented. This naturally raises the question, how much of the increase in employment at older ages can be explained by changing retirement incentives?

A first step in answering this question is to provide a careful examination of how retirement incentives have changed over the past several decades due to Social Security reforms and changes in employer-provided pensions. This

9. The weighted ITAX measure in this case is weighted across the six sample worker types for each sex.

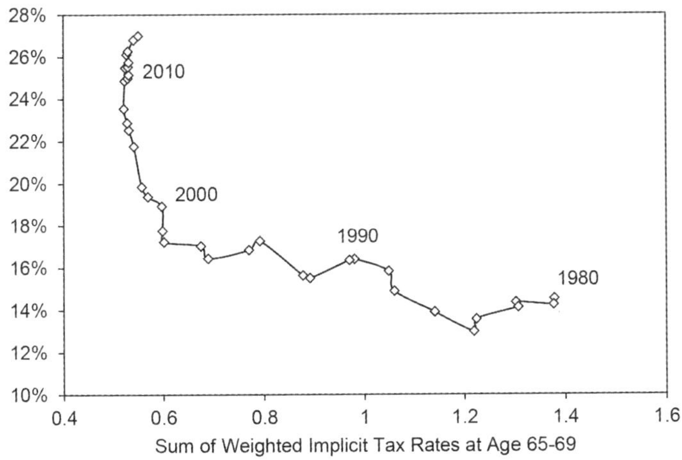

Fig. 12.19 Employment of women aged 65–69 versus weighted implicit tax, 1980–2016

Note: Employment data are from http://stats.oecd.org/ (data from US Bureau of Labor Statistics).

chapter finds that changes to Social Security have reduced the implicit tax on work at ages 65 to 69 by about 15 percentage points, while the tax rate on work at younger ages was either less affected or unaffected by these reforms. We also find that DB pensions add an additional 20 to 25 percent to the implicit tax after age 65 for the sample pension plan we explore. Given that the share of workers with DB pensions has fallen by about one-quarter since 1980, the effect of the shift from DB to DC plans on the average retirement incentive is to reduce the implicit tax on work by an additional 5 or so percentage points for a total decrease in the tax rate on work at these ages of about 20 percentage points once Social Security and pension incentives are incorporated.

One must proceed cautiously when exploring the possible link between changing incentives and changing employment using the highly aggregated data analyzed here. There is little apparent connection between changes in employment and changes in the ITAX measure at ages 55 to 59 or 60 to 64, though a large enough change in ITAX after age 65 could theoretically affect work at these younger ages also. The DB to DC shift could affect work at these ages through a wealth effect, a possibility we raise but do not explore here. The effect of the earnings test changes is also not explored here. There is suggestive evidence that declines in ITAX at ages 65 to 69 that are driven by the DRC increase and the DB to DC shift line up with employment increases, particularly for women, but this is far from conclusive. Future research that employs microdata to capture the heterogeneity in retirement incentives and controls for retirement wealth, as well as other factors that have changed over time, is needed in order to draw a stronger conclusion about the link between Social Security reforms and retirement.

Appendix

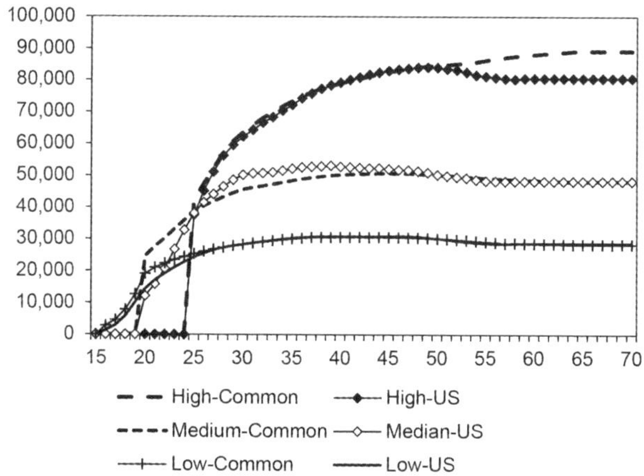

Fig. 12.A1 Common versus US age-earnings profile for men, by education

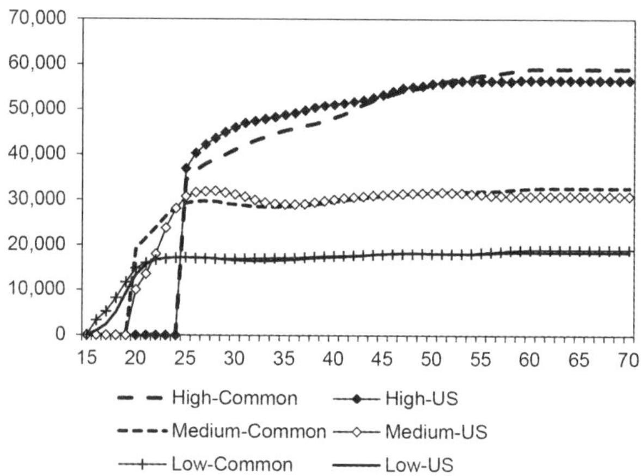

Fig. 12.A2 Common versus US age-earnings profile for women, by education

References

Coile, Courtney. 2018. "Working Longer in the U.S.: Trends and Explanations." NBER Working Paper No. 24576. Cambridge, MA: National Bureau of Economic Research.

Coile, Courtney, Peter Diamond, Jonathan Gruber, and Alain Jousten. 2002. "Delays in Claiming Social Security Benefits." *Journal of Public Economics* 84 (3): 357–85.

Coile, Courtney, and Stewart, Susan. 2020. "Retirement Incentives and Behavior of Private and Public Sector Workers." *Journal of Pension Economics and Finance*, 1–17. doi:10.1017/S1474747219000416.

Council of Economic Advisers. 2016. *The Long-Term Decline in Prime-Age Male Labor Force Participation.* https://obamawhitehouse.archives.gov/sites/default/files/page/files/20160620_cea_primeage_male_lfp.pdf.

Costa, Dora. 1998. *The Evolution of Retirement: An American Economic History, 1880–1990.* Chicago: University of Chicago Press.

Goda, Gopi Shah, Shanthi Ramnath, John B. Shoven, and Sita Nataraj Slavov. 2018. "The Financial Feasibility of Delaying Social Security: Evidence from Administrative Tax Data." *Journal of Pension Economics and Finance* 17 (4): 419–36.

Goldin, Claudia, and Lawrence F. Katz. 2018. "Women Working Longer: Facts and Some Explanations." In *Women Working Longer: Increased Employment at Older Ages*, edited by Claudia Goldin and Lawrence F. Katz, 11–53. Chicago: University of Chicago Press.

Liebman, Jeffrey B., and Erzo F. P. Luttmer. 2012. "The Perception of Social Security Incentives for Labor Supply and Retirement: The Median Voter Knows More Than You'd Think." In *Tax Policy and the Economy*, volume 26, edited by Jeffrey Brown, 1–42. Chicago: University of Chicago Press.

Mitchell, Olivia. 1999. "New Trends in Pension Benefit and Retirement Provisions." NBER Working Paper No. 7381. Cambridge, MA: National Bureau of Economic Research.

Munnell, Alicia H., Jean-Pierre Aubry, and Mark Cafarelli. 2014. "Defined Contribution Plans in the Public Sector: An Update." Center for Retirement Research, State and Local Pension Plans Brief 27.

Munnell, Alicia H., and Pamela Perun. 2006. "An Update on Private Pensions." Center for Retirement Research, Issue Brief 50.

Rutledge, Matthew S. 2018. "What Explains the Widening Gap in Retirement Ages by Education?" Center for Retirement Research, Issue Brief 18-10.

Schirle, Tammy. 2008. "Why Have the Labor Force Participation Rates of Older Men Increased since the Mid-1990s?" *Journal of Labor Economics* 26 (4): 549–94.

Shoven, John B., and Sita Nataraj Slavov. 2014. "Recent Changes in the Gains from Delaying Social Security." *Journal of Financial Planning* 27 (3): 32–41.

Social Security Administration. 2016. *Income of the Aged Chartbook, 2014.* SSA Publication No. 13–11727.

Stock, James H., and David A. Wise. 1990. "Pensions, the Option Value of Work, and Retirement." *Econometrica* 58 (5): 1151–80.

Svahn, John A., and Mary Ross. 1983. "Social Security Amendments of 1983: Legislative History and Summary of provisions." *Social Security Bulletin* 46 (7): 3–48.

Whitman, Kevin, Gayle L. Reznik, and Dave Shoffmer. 2011. "Who Never Receives Social Security Benefits?" *Social Security Bulletin* 71 (2): 17–24.

Contributors

James Banks
Department of Economics
University of Manchester
Oxford Road
Manchester M13 9PL, United Kingdom

Paul Bingley
VIVE—The Danish Center for Social Science Research
Herluf Trolles Gade 11
1052 Copenhagen K, Denmark

Didier Blanchet
INSEE
88 Avenue Verdier
92541 Montrouge CEDEX, France

Axel Börsch-Supan
Munich Center for the Economics of Aging (MEA)
Max Planck Institute for Social Law and Social Policy
Amalienstraße 33
80799 Munich, Germany

Antoine Bozio
Paris School of Economics
48 boulevard Jourdan
75014 Paris, France

Agar Brugiavini
Department of Economics
Ca' Foscari University of Venice
Sestriere Cannaregglo, 873
30121 Venezia, Italy

Raluca Elena Buia
Department of Economics
Ca' Foscari University of Venice
Sestriere Cannareggio, 873
30121 Venezia, Italy

Courtney C. Coile
Department of Economics
Wellesley College
106 Central Street
Wellesley, MA 02481

Klaas de Vos
CentERdata
Tilburg University
Warandelaan 2
5037 AB Tilburg, The Netherlands

Carl Emmerson
Institute for Fiscal Studies
7 Ridgmount Street
London WC1E 7AE, United Kingdom

Anne-Lore Fraikin
UNU-MERIT
Boschstraat 24
6211 AX Maastricht, The Netherlands

Pilar García-Gómez
Erasmus School of Economics
P.O. Box 1738
3000 DR Rotterdam, The Netherlands

Sílvia Garcia-Mandicó
OECD
2, rue André Pascal
75016 Paris, France

Nicolas Goll
Munich Center for the Economics of Aging (MEA)
Max Planck Institute for Social Law and Social Policy
Amalienstraße 33
80799 Munich, Germany

Nabanita Datta Gupta
Department of Economics and Business Economics
Aarhus University
Fuglesangs Allé 4
8210 Aarhus V, Denmark

Sergi Jiménez-Martín
Universitat Pompeu Fabra
Ramon Trias Fargas 25–27
08005 Barcelona, Spain

Alain Jousten
Law Faculty, HEC—ULg and Tax Institute
University of Liège
Place des Orateurs 3
4000 Liège 1, Belgium

Malene Kallestrup-Lamb
Department of Economics and Business Economics
Aarhus University
Fuglesangs Allé 4
8210 Aarhus V, Denmark

Adriaan Kalwij
Utrecht University School of Economics
Adam Smith Hall
Kriekenpitplein 21–22
3584 EC Utrecht, The Netherlands

Arie Kapteyn
Center for Economic and Social Research
University of Southern California
635 Downey Way
Los Angeles, CA 90089-3332

Lisa Laun
Institute for Evaluation of Labour Market and Education Policy (IFAU)
Box 513
SE-751 20 Uppsala, Sweden

Mathieu Lefebvre
BETA, University of Strasbourg
61, avenue de la Forêt Noire
67085 Strasbourg Cedex, France

Kevin Milligan
Vancouver School of Economics
University of British Columbia
6000 Iona Drive
Vancouver, BC V6T 1L4, Canada

Akiko S. Oishi
Graduate School of Social Sciences
Chiba University
Yayoi-cho 1-33, Inage-ku
Chiba 263-8522, Japan

Takashi Oshio
Institute of Economic Research
Hitotsubashi University
2-1 Naka, Kunitachi
Tokyo 186-8603, Japan

Mårten Palme
Department of Economics
Stockholm University
SE-106 91 Stockholm, Sweden

Giacomo Pasini
Department of Economics
Ca' Foscari University of Venice
Cannaregio 873
30121 Venice, Italy

Peder J. Pedersen
Department of Economics and Business Economics
Aarhus University
Fuglesangs Allé 4
8210 Aarhus V, Denmark

Simon Rabaté
Institut des Politiques Publiques
48 boulevard Jourdan
75014 Paris, France

Johannes Rausch
Munich Center for the Economics of Aging (MEA)
Max Planck Institute for Social Law and Social Policy
Amalienstraße 33
80799 Munich, Germany

Muriel Roger
CES Université Paris 1 Panthéon-Sorbonne
106–112 boulevard de l'Hôpital
75013 Paris, France

Tammy Schirle
Department of Economics
Wilfrid Laurier University
75 University Avenue West
Waterloo, ON N2L 3C5, Canada

Satoshi Shimizutani
JICA Research Institute
10-5 Ichigaya Honmuracho, Shinjuku-ku
Tokyo 162-8433, Japan

Judit Vall-Castelló
Department of Economics & IEB
Universitat de Barcelona
John M. Keynes, 1–11
08034 Barcelona, Spain

Guglielmo Weber
Department of Economics and Management
University of Padua
Via del Santo 33
35123 Padua, Italy

Author Index

Subject Index

Note: Page numbers followed by "f" or "t" refer to figures or tables, respectively.